ISSUES IN BUSINESS

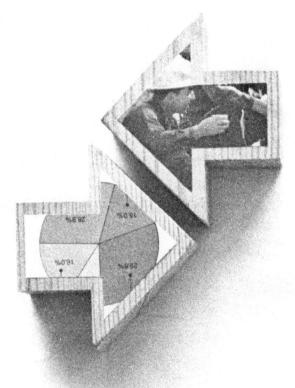

Karl F. Price
Temple University

James W. Walker
Towers, Perrin, Forster, & Crosby

JOHN WILEY & SONS
SANTA BARBARA · NEW YORK · LONDON · SYDNEY · TORONTO

A WILEY/HAMILTON PUBLICATION

Chapter opening photos courtesy of
United Press International and Graphics Two.

Design and production by Graphics Two, Los Angeles.

Library of Congress Cataloging in Publication Data:

Price, Karl F
 Issues in business.

 Includes index.
 1. United States — Commerce.   2. Business.
I. Walker, James W., 1941–   joint author.
II. Title.

HF3031.P7   1977   658   76-30750
ISBN 0-471-69734-6

Printed in the United States of America

10 9 8 7 6 5 4 3 2

Before We Begin . . .

You can tell this is an unusual book just by looking through it. It's up to date, with current ideas and issues from the real world of business. Issues are interesting — because they are relevant. ISSUES is an interesting book because it is easy to read, easy to understand, and easy to relate to the business world we read about in the newspapers each day.

In fact, one reason this book is unusual is its many articles from newspapers and magazines that businesspeople read. It has pictures, articles, cartoons, and other things besides text.

As you read the book, you'll discover that business has changed in many ways in recent years. There are new technologies, new products, international issues, large and more complex organizations — and government, economic crises, social and environmental challenges, and new career options.

The book will help you examine what has been happening, what business is all about these days, and what it is likely to become in the future.

And a side of business is presented that you may not have seen before:
— tough problems being solved by businesses today
— people doing things they feel are important to our society
— business looking after the interests of consumers, investors, the public, and you
— companies making profits and at the same time contributing in important ways to our society, our economy, and our environment
— career opportunities open to you in business.

ISSUES

The book is titled ISSUES IN BUSINESS because you'll discover concerns that face people in business, labor unions, employees, government, consumers, and the public. You may have given a lot of thought to issues such as inflation, pollution, careers, minority employment, or unemployment.

Other issues may not have been on your mind: advertising, investments, accounting practices, the goals of business, or the impact of profit and loss.

If you gain a better understanding of these aspects of business and develop your own opinions about issues in business, you will have achieved the purposes intended.

We have an enterprise system in America, a system of business competition in which there are at least two different viewpoints about every issue. Business is changing, as our society, our environment, and you are changing. In this book you'll find different viewpoints as well as basic facts and concepts, and you'll be challenged to take your own stand on important issues.

You'll find a multitude of topics covered, one in each chapter. Real business case situations help bring the topics to life. You'll get to know Sears, Ford, Con Ed, Playboy, Hershey, IBM, McDonald's, and many other businesses, large and small.

By the way, don't be put off by the use of the masculine pronoun or the word businessman. More and more women are finding careers in business, and job opportunities are available both to women and to men.

FEATURES

Each chapter starts out with a list of the articles, cases, and text on the subjects covered.

Each chapter ends with a recap — a concise restatement of the key points in the chapter.

Tear-out worksheets provide a "think-about-it, fill-it-out, and turn-it-in" page to help you wrap up what you got out of your reading and thinking.

Also each chapter has WHAZZITS, CHALLENGES, and CONSIDERS.

WHAZZITS are sensible definitions of the business terms used in the text. At the back of the book is a SUPERWHAZZIT, a complete listing of all the terms defined. If you don't like our definitions, try a dictionary.

CHALLENGES are suggested action projects you may conduct to discover more about business.

CONSIDERS are questions to provoke your thinking and to kick off some discussion (and maybe even some lively arguments) on controversial issues. These don't always have right or wrong answers, so don't get uptight — just give them some good thinking.

SUGGESTIONS

This Third Edition of Issues has a lot of meat for you to chew on. So take it easy — read through each chapter once, think about the considers, and then read through everything once again. By then the worksheet should come easily, and only the challenges lie ahead of you.

Think, too, about your career. There's a career planning worksheet at the back of the text, but lots of information on career possibilities before you get there. Ask yourself what turns you on in business; what you think you can do well, and what you would like your career plan to include.

By spanning centuries of business issues — from the nineteenth century to the twenty-first, you'll have a pretty good idea of what business has to offer you.

K.F.P.
J.W.W.

About the Authors

Karl F. Price is an Associate Professor of Management and Chairman of the Department of Industrial Relations and Organizational Behavior at Temple University. Prior to joining Temple University in 1972, Dr. Price was on the faculty of Management at San Diego State University and was a member of the Computer Science faculty at Drexel University.

Dr. Price earned his B.A. in Business Administration from Drexel University in 1961 and received his Ph.D. in Business and Applied Economics from the University of Pennsylvania in 1970. He is the co-author of two books, Management Today and Issues in Business, as well as many articles and papers on various aspects of Management.

James W. Walker is a principal in the management consulting firm of Towers, Perrin, Forster & Crosby. Based in the headquarters office in New York his work takes him to all parts of the United States and Canada where he helps client organizations improve the effectiveness of their management policies, systems, and practices. His consulting experience includes individual, business, and public organizations.

A 1963 graduate of Millikin University, Dr. Walker earned an M.A. in Labor and Management and a Ph.D. in Industrial Relations and Organizational Behavior from the University of Iowa. He has held faculty posts at Indiana University and the United States International University, San Diego and was on the faculty and held the position of Director of the Bureau of Business and Economic Research at San Diego State University. He is the author of Manpower Planning and Programming and co-author of Issues in Business, and numerous articles on human resource management.

CONTENTS

PART I

OUR BUSINESS SYSTEM

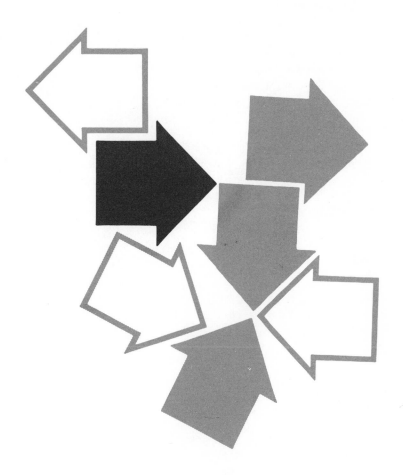

CHAPTER 1

The Enterprise System

Business enterprises exist to allow people to produce and distribute effectively goods and services that are needed in our society. Very simply, these enterprises will satisfy our society's needs, create employment, and yield profits for their owners. Business enterprises that fail to do this will disappear in the long run.

An enterprise system depends on a free market economy. This means that certain conditions are necessary:

1. Individuals may make their own choices (freedom of choice).

2. Individuals may seek to earn profits (the profit motive).

3. A competitive market system (competition for goods and services in the marketplace).

4. The right to own and use property (private property).

All of these conditions are necessary for the successful operation of a "free" enterprise system.

In order to survive in this system, a business must accurately appraise the needs of people that can be served by resources that are available.

Business activities so designed will result in profits -- incentives for people to continue to operate a business and a means to expand and improve the services provided to society.

In the process of earning profits, a business earns revenues which support the activities of other needed business functions: providing livelihood for individuals, producing economic goods and services and providing revenues to sustain other firms --

suppliers, transporters, insurers, and distributors, for example -- through the links of the enterprise system.

A portion of profits is paid in taxes, thus supporting governmental activities. As our population grows, our economy expands, and technology develops, problems emerge that cannot be solved by any one business enterprise alone. Acting in the public interest, the government plays an increasingly important role in our economic system directly and by guiding and regulating business activities.

But while profits are important to business enterprises, other factors must be considered and balanced with the making of profits. All enterprises operate in a social setting in which demands are made upon the enterprise. Businesses are called upon to make profits, hire minorities, produce safe and useful products, stop pollution, and in general be "good corporate citizens."

This concept of balancing profits with the needs of society is becoming more and more important for business enterprises. They are required to be "socially responsible" in their activities. The business enterprise must be flexible enough to respond to the changing needs of society and at the same time meet the basic requirement for survival, being profitable.

There is every reason to expect that our economic system will continue to respond effectively to man's changing needs and his changing environment.

In this Chapter

The Profit Motive

The idea of business enterprise is that people will pay a price for products or services they want to have. Why should an enterprise supply these products or services?

Because the price not only pays for the cost of the materials and labor that went into the product, but also provides a return to the owner for his investment of time and money. This return is called PROFIT.

The owner of a business enterprise may, of course, be an individual or a number of individuals, depending on the type of enterprise. We'll discuss these types of businesses later in this chapter.

The difference between cost and price is the PROFIT MARGIN. A business needs to keep a reasonable profit margin if it is to survive. If costs of production rise, then the prices charged must rise in order to maintain the profit margin. When costs rise above prices, a business is losing money.

One of the critical issues in business today is the task of maintaining profits in the face of rising costs. Yet, as we shall discuss, the need to maintain profits must be balanced by broader social needs -- such as pollution control, employment, and satisfying consumer needs.

Profits are an incentive for owners to invest in a business enterprise and to provide for efficient management. In a sense, profits are a critical factor in the operation of our enterprise system.

What if there are no profits? In our system, if there are no profits, a firm goes out of business or requires subsidy to operate at a loss. Such subsidies may be provided by government, by the owners or by using up available assets.

Profits With Honor: Some Thoughts Thereon

The word "profit" comes to us from the Latin *profectus,* meaning "advance" or "progress." It is related to "proficient," which in turn derives from the Latin *proficere,* meaning "to go forward."

The idea behind the word has traveled a long, downhill route from its early origins. It once implied reward for effort. Now it is looked upon by many as indecent, unconscionable and probably excessive.

From time to time, certain takers of polls go out among the people and ask them to estimate corporate profits. Invariably, speculation outruns fact. A recent survey places the popular guess at an average of 33 cents for every dollar of sales.

The fact is that, for industry as a whole, the actual figure was slightly over 5 cents in 1974, and was undoubtedly lower in 1975. Maybe those higher figures reported by the pollsters represent what the people surveyed would demand if they faced the burdens and risks of enterprise.

What happens to all that money gushing in at one end of the pipeline when so little drips out at the other end? We can't speak for others, but we do have a firm grip on where our own flow went.

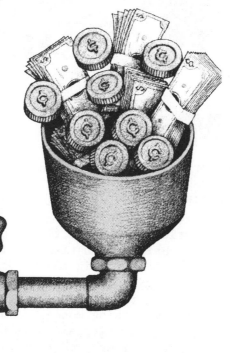

Those unfamiliar with the market system may look at the relatively minor amount that trickles back each year and wonder why we could not arrange things to provide a plumper cushion against risk. The answer, of course, is that others in the industry cope with the same factors that confront us. Any cutting of corners or raising of prices beyond logical bounds would quickly find us losing business to our competitors. That's the way the system works, and we accept it gladly as a constant challenge to our ingenuity.

We have often said that profits are to a corporation what breathing is to a human being. Profits are not the sole purpose of business activity, any more than breathing is the sole purpose of life. But choking off a company's profits will result in extinction just as surely as choking off a person's oxygen will terminate his prospects here on earth.

What, then, *is* the purpose of the corporation?

It should be remembered that the mechanism we call a corporation did not spring fully formed from the soil of enterprise. It is not specified or even mentioned in the Bible or the Constitution. Neither, on the other hand, has it been imposed upon us by ruthless manipulators.

Rather, the corporation is an institutional form that our society has evolved, naturally, in response to changing need, in order to accomplish certain ends—to make products, to provide services, to channel human effort and material and financial resources into useful structures.

Above all, it is the means by which we have organized our individual efforts to create material abundance out of raw resources. The history of man's progress has been one of upgrading the materials he has found lying around the planet

in order to improve their worth, and thereby to produce the surplus beyond simple sustenance that gives us what we used to call the good life. (Remember?)

Other forms might have accomplished the same thing. Might have. It is not inevitable. Given a quarry, one man will create nothing but a pile of stones. Another will build a castle.

A surplus beyond simple sustenance. That is the key to the civilized amenities we enjoy today. We cannot support poets unless we first have machine tool operators. We cannot subsidize symphony orchestras unless we first establish finely tuned marketing mechanisms. We cannot build schools or hospitals or museums or libraries unless we first build factories.

These are some of the elements we think of as surplus. In a way, they represent the true "profits" of society. They exist in any society only because certain instrumentalities—whether government ministries or agricultural co-operatives, private corporations or village guilds—have directed the contributions of many to create more out of much.

What they wind up with may or may not be identified as profit, but the idea is the same, and basic to human advancement.

Time for some definitions.

Let's start by explaining what corporate profits are *not.*

They are not funds pocketed by a select few at the expense of the unfortunate many.

They are not "mad money" to be spent on unproductive frills.

They are not a tax imposed upon helpless consumers by greedy producers.

They are not a stockpile of funds to be taken out of circulation and set aside as a cushion against hard times.

What, then, *are* profits?

One simple—and simplistic—answer is that profits are what is left after you have subtracted all of your costs from everything you take in.

That sum, small as it may be in terms of the whole, does not sit around idly while we try to decide what to do with it. It has already been committed to programs that will permit us to keep the Company on an upward course as it fulfills the many missions assigned to it by society, not the least of which require us to improve job opportunities and issue reasonable returns to the

shareholders who have entrusted their savings to us.

Profit is often expressed as a percentage of sales. Not an entirely meaningful indicator, we think. If we understand anything about numbers, a larger fraction of a declining whole does not necessarily denote progress.

More valid, we believe, is a look at profits in terms of their relationship to the amount of money invested in the business. This, after all, is what people think of when they place their money in savings accounts, certificates of deposit, commercial paper, bonds and other instruments. It is what eventually determines—or should determine—the true value of a company's shares.

That is why we strive for better profits, which, in the final analysis, make it possible for us to assure our shareholders that their funds have not left home only to support a holding action.

Shareholders are not the only concern. Any responsible corporation has a further duty to the people on its payroll, now and in the future, whose commitment in time and service commands as much respect as investments of money.

Now and in the future. It is projected that our economy will have to provide from 15 to 20 million new jobs for the American work force between now and 1985. These openings cannot be created overnight. Unless the jobs are there, this country will face a worsening of the economic and social ills already manifest in rising levels of unemployment. It takes approximately $60,000 in capital investments to create a single job. Most of the money must

come from retained earnings. No earnings, no jobs. It is that simple. And, potentially, that tragic.

We all know the story of the laborer who offered to work for a penny a day, with the sum to be doubled each day of the month. His employer snapped at the deal—only to learn that, by the end of the 30th day, he was in hock for more than $5 million.

We don't expect to duplicate the fortunes of that clever laborer. We do know that much of our success must be measured in the fourth dimension known as time. In a world of rising population and exploding expectations, with vast numbers of people unemployed and even vaster numbers unfulfilled, this acceleration of growth may be the only way to avoid disaster.

Some final thoughts on what may be described as the line below the bottom line:

As we said above, profits are not what the popular mind imagines them to be, in terms of either size or application.

Some have suggested that we should find a new word to replace one that has come into disrepute. Others have opted for no word at all, arguing that, upon close inspection, it turns out that there is no such thing as profits.

It hardly matters.

What matters is that we recognize our national needs—to provide high levels of employment, to safeguard the savings of individuals, to improve the general welfare by an upgrading of social and material resources.

The private enterprise system may not be the only way to reach these goals, but most of the other systems that have

been tried are suspect, and some have been rejected. What *has* worked over the two centuries of our existence as a Republic is the incentive to greater productivity guaranteed by the knowledge that effort will be rewarded, however modestly.

This is true for the athlete in competition, for the laborer in the plant, for the teacher at her desk, for the government official in the seat of power—and for the corporation dedicated to ensuring the future, its own and that of those it serves.

Only in the case of the corporation is it called profit. Perhaps the word should be applied to everyone who justifies his existence by leaving the world better than he found it.

THE COMPETITIVE
We believe in it...

The <u>Modern</u> Little Red Hen.

Once upon a time, there was a little red hen who scratched about the barnyard until she uncovered some grains of wheat. She called her neighbors and said, "If we plant this wheat, we shall have bread to eat. Who will help me plant it?"

"Not I," said the cow.

"Not I," said the duck.

"Not I," said the pig.

"Not I," said the goose.

"Then I will," said the little red hen. And she did. The wheat grew tall and ripened into golden grain. "Who will help me reap my wheat?" asked the little red hen.

"Not I," said the duck.

"Out of my classification," said the pig.

"I'd lose my seniority," said the cow.

"I'd lose my unemployment compensation," said the goose.

"Then I will," said the little red hen, and she did.

At last it came time to bake the bread. "Who will help me bake the bread?" asked the little red hen.

"That would be overtime for me," said the cow.

"I'd lose my welfare benefits," said the duck.

"I'm a dropout and never learned how," said the pig.

"If I'm to be the only helper, that's discrimination," said the goose.

"Then I will," said the little red hen.

She baked five loaves and held them up for her neighbors to see.

They all wanted some and, in fact, demanded a share. But the little red hen said, "No, I can eat the five loaves myself."

"Excess profits!" cried the cow.

"Capitalist leech!" screamed the duck.

"I demand equal rights!" yelled the goose.

And the pig just grunted. And they painted "unfair" picket signs and marched round and round the little red hen, shouting obscenities.

When the government agent came, he said to the little red hen, "You must not be greedy."

"But I earned the bread," said the little red hen.

"Exactly," said the agent. "That is the wonderful free enterprise system. Anyone in the barnyard can earn as much as he wants. But under our modern government regulations, the productive workers must divide their product with the idle."

And they lived happily ever after, including the little red hen, who smiled and clucked, "I am grateful. I am grateful."

But her neighbors wondered why she never again baked any more bread.

At the conclusion of the required business of the 1975 Pennwalt Annual Meeting, Chairman and President William P. Drake, commenting on the state of the company in today's economy, read this, his own adaptation of a modern version of the well-known fable of The Little Red Hen.

For 125 years we've been making things people need – including profits.

ENTERPRISE SYSTEM

...here's why:

Dedication to the simple truths implied in the story of "The Modern Little Red Hen" built this company, and has guided its successful growth.

Today, Pennwalt supplies socially useful products, including chemicals, dental products, pharmaceuticals and equipment. 80 percent of our sales are concentrated in these five major markets:

- Agriculture and food processing
- Chemical process industries
- Environmental cleanup
- Health
- Plastics

But unlike the unfortunate Modern Little Red Hen, we have been able to share our "bread" with the many who have helped produce it, while at the same time fulfilling the other obligations to society expected of a responsible, profitable corporate citizen. This sharing is in the form of equitable wages and fringe benefits, quality products fairly priced, substantial purchases, taxes, the support of charitable and cultural organizations and, from what's left, dividends to our shareholders.

That we have been successful is evidenced by the fact that we started paying a regular dividend on our common stock 114 years ago and have not missed a payment since.

We think our performance bears this out:

Operating record (000):	1971	1972	1973	1974	1975
Net Sales	$405,507	$441,010	$504,034	$641,002	**$713,736**
Net Earnings	$ 13,050	$ 16,072	$ 20,113	$ 26,983	**$ 31,633***
Per Share of Common Stock	$ 1.22	$ 1.58	$ 2.13	$ 2.81	**$ 3.25***

*Before special credit of $1,813,000 or $.19 per share.

For 125 years we've been making things people need—including profits.

PENNWALT
CORPORATION
Three Parkway, Philadelphia, Pa. 19102
Chemicals • Dental Products • Pharmaceuticals • Specialized Equipment

Corporate Responsiveness and Profitability

by Richard Gerstenberg, Chairman of General Motors

If the public has come to believe what it has so often been told about profits—that they are unconscionable, swollen, filthy, and earned at the expense of the workingman and the helpless consumer—business has only itself to blame. For some reason or other we have never gotten across the truth about profits. The public needs to know more than it does about business—about, among other things, its performance and its profits.

Public misunderstanding about profit extends, of course, to the need of a business to earn a profit. This unawareness provides a ready climate for the introduction of limitations on corporate profits, a situation—we hope only a temporary one—which we have with us today.

When I say earn a profit, I mean just exactly that. A business must earn a profit by making products people want to buy and which in some way contribute to their lives. It must earn a profit by the proper control of costs, by making these products as efficiently as it can. It must earn a profit through its willingness to invest and take risks. It must earn a profit through innovation and product development. It is only after all of these things are done, and done well, that there is any profit to report.

In the last few years the traditional critics of business and profits have been joined by new voices, young voices, and most often sincere voices. They ask fundamental questions about the proper role of the corporation in our society. They ask not only is this or that particular corporation fulfilling its responsibilities to society, but they question whether the entire corporate structure in America—the system we call free enterprise, the profit system—is not in need of a major overhaul.

These critics of free enterprise neither understand nor accept the necessity of profits as a means to progress, and the essential dependence of one upon the other.

Many of the new breed of business critics have rallied around the phrase "corporate responsibility." The phrase deserves a close examination. Every business has certain traditional obligations to the society which supports it and which it serves. For its customers it must make products of quality and value, selling goods and services at attractive prices; for its employees it must provide good jobs with good working conditions at good wages; for the owners of the business—those who take the risks—it must earn a profit; and in addition to all of this, the business must be a good citizen of the community in which it operates.

However, many of the so-called corporate responsibilities which people today expect business to fulfill go far beyond. They enter the well-established domains of government or nonprofit organizations. These are areas where business—its best intentions notwithstanding—may not be most effective, nor best-equipped to handle basic decision-making responsibilities. I have to doubt if the advocates of corporate responsibility would really want our educational system, our environment, or minority opportunity to be wholly "corporate responsibilities."

I have always questioned whether "responsibility" is the right word. In the acceptance and performance of societal responsibilities, business should not dominate American society, no more than government should, or labor should, or the military should, or the universities. What I do believe is called for—and should be expected—from American business is not responsibility but rather a responsiveness to the manifest expectations of society. In fact, this response is a clear necessity of our times.

Business and society are bound together and are vitally affected by each other. Business success, in fact, often depends upon keeping in very close touch with, and informed about, basic social trends. The successful business responds resourcefully to these trends, and when it responds rightly it profits both the business and society.

This implies more rather than less business involvement and participation in social change. The individual businessman, today more than ever, must have an ability to stay close to trends and a willingness to use the resources of the business in new directions where they can be usefully applied. The successful business will be one that succeeds in matching its resources to society's changing demands, that gives the most creative response to new opportunities and challenges. The business that fails will be one that fails to understand how it is related to the society around it, and will therefore overlook opportunities for service, for growth, and for profit.

Doing Business

A business enterprise that is owned by one person who receives all of the profits earned and who assumes all of the risks of doing business is called a PROPRIETORSHIP.

In this type of enterprise, the owner is usually the manager of the business and does a lot of the work himself. As suggested in the chart below, most sole proprietorships are small businesses. The advantages of doing business as a proprietorship are flexibility, freedom of action and a sense of being on your own, simplicity, and ease of getting started in business. Disadvantages include an unlimited personal liability for debts of the business, lack of capital, and the problems associated with being small.

A business that is owned by two or more individuals as co-partners who agree to divide profits and losses is called a PARTNERSHIP.

In a partnership, as in a proprietorship, the owners still have unlimited personal liability for the debts of the business. That's still a disadvantage, and perhaps is more critical because all partners are liable for the actions of each. If one partner blows it, they all pay. There is such a thing as a LIMITED partnership, in which a partner may be liable only to the extent of his investment, but this isn't very common.

A partnership may provide added financial strength to a business, more talent and managerial strength by bringing a number of people together as co-owners. Their success really depends on the nature of the business, the attitudes and abilities and resources of the partners, and the circumstances.

A business that is owned by a number of people through shares of stock is a CORPORATION.

Unlike the other two basic forms of enterprise, a corporation is an entity created by law -- a "person" established by law. Owners, or stockholders, are liable for the debts of the business only to the extent of their investment. Managers are employees of the corporation and so have a different interest than proprietors or partners.

BUSINESS ENTERPRISES IN THE UNITED STATES

CORPORATIONS

PARTNERSHIPS

PROPRIETORSHIPS

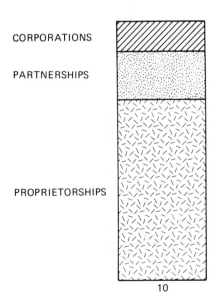 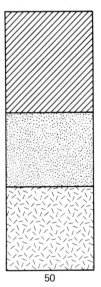 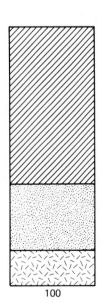 

10   50   100   1000 or more

SIZE OF FIRM - NUMBER OF EMPLOYEES

Source: SURVEY OF CURRENT BUSINESS, United States Department of Commerce.

The Company —
A Which or a Who?

A business is an organization, a complex of jobs, relationships, and technology, all combined for the purpose of producing goods and services. It is an impersonal "IT" that lives longer than any of its managers or employees.

But a company is more than an "IT". A company is an association of real, live people. Only through the efforts of different people -- managers, employees, stockholders, customers, and others -- can the organization achieve its objectives.

People who work for WAGES AND SALARIES are obviously important to a business organization. They provide the LABOR that is essential in performing tasks that lead toward the accomplishment of the organization's objectives.

People who own land, buildings, and equipment used by a business organization contribute directly to the life of the enterprise through this PROPERTY. These people receive RENT in payment for their contributions.

A business may use money to purchase land, equipment, supplies, raw materials, and to pay business expenses. When this money is borrowed, INTEREST is the payment made for this contribution to the firm's survival. We call such money financial resources or CAPITAL.

Another source of capital is the OWNERSHIP of the business. The money the owners put into the company is a major resource that is used to finance business activities. Owners assume the risk that the business will succeed or fail. Their rewards are DIVIDENDS when the business succeeds and is profitable.

In most business organizations, not all of the profits are paid out to the owners in the form of dividends. Some of the money is kept in the firm to buy new equipment, land, supplies, and anything else that is needed to help the firm grow. These profits that are held in the firm are called RETAINED EARNINGS, and they represent a growth in the owner's contribution to the business.

Finally, all the rest of us get into the action, because virtually every business in the nation pays TAXES. Through these tax payments, businesses support social programs and other governmental functions. Public taxes are also used to support the efforts of other business enterprises through government contracts for purchase of goods and services, subsidies, and the support of research.

WHERE REVENUES GO

WAGES AND SALARIES are paid for *LABOR*

RENT is paid for the use of property, such as *LAND*

INTEREST is paid for the use of financial *CAPITAL*

DIVIDENDS are paid for the risk of *OWNERSHIP*

RETAINED EARNINGS are kept in the firm to finance *GROWTH*

TAXES are paid for the *PUBLIC GOOD*

Building a Business

If you were to start a business enterprise, you would probably begin on a small scale, on your own, as a sole proprietor. You would be the owner and the active manager of the business; you would be "self-employed." As such, you might have the advantage of low taxes, freedom of action, and a high incentive for success. Sears, Roebuck and Co., America's largest retailer started as a sole proprietorship when Richard Sears founded the R. W. Sears Watch Company. You might find, as Sears did, however, that growing pains soon set in. Sears reacted by bringing in other talent.

On the other hand, you might start out with partners. When two or more persons work together as co-owners, the business may have greater financial strength, more management talent, and more specialized skill, while retaining the advantages of a proprietorship. In a later chapter you'll read about the partnership formed in 1837 by Charles Tiffany and John Young, today the prominent jeweler, Tiffany & Co.

As your business grows and more capital (money) is needed, you may incorporate your enterprise, giving it the legal rights and obligations of a person. This allows you to raise money by issuing and selling stock, and borrowing money in the name of the corporation. It's often easier to obtain business capital as a corporate enterprise.

An advantage of a corporation is that it doesn't die -- as a proprietorship or partnership does if the principals die. When a proprietor or partner dies, a new organization must be formed, if the business is to continue.

There is another type of business that you may run into -- a cooperative. A cooperative is an association of people with the primary aim of providing a service to its members. It does not aim for profit for itself; any gains are distributed among the membership, usually as a rebate on their purchases. You may have a campus bookstore operated by the student body that is oriented this way.

TYPES OF BUSINESSES: HOW MANY, HOW BIG, HOW PROFITABLE?

	Number	Revenues	Profits
Proprietorships	10,173,000	$276 Billion	$39 Billion
Partnerships	992,000	104 Billion	10 Billion
Corporations	1,813,000	2,117 Billion	96 Billion
500 Largest Industrials		833 Billion	44 Billion

Sources: Fortune, May 1976; U.S. Department of Commerce (1974 data)

An Entrepreneur? Who, Me?

It used to be that a person started a business in order to earn a living -- as a craftsman, a merchant, or in a trade. His decisions and actions were governed by the rule of profit, for his survival depended on his business. In small businesses today this is still largely true.

Large business enterprises must also have "enterprising men and women" -- whom we call ENTREPRENEURS -- to seek opportunities for new profitable activities, identifying and meeting the needs of customers. As an employee or a manager, you may assume risks by standing up for an idea you believe in and then undertaking to see it implemented. Such entrepreneurs in large organizations often make the difference between a "just so-so" business and one that is alive and moving ahead.

It's not impossible to start a new enterprise, even today. (Although nearly 200,000 business enterprises, many of them new, go belly up each year.) There are always opportunities for true entrepreneurs.

en·tre·pre·neur \ˌäⁿ·trəp(r)ə¦nər, +V -nər·, ¦äⁿ·t-, -nȝ(r, -n(y)u̇(ə)r, -u̇ə\ n -s [F, fr. OF, fr. *entreprendre* to undertake + -*cur* -or — more at ENTERPRISE] **1** : the organizer of an economic venture; *esp* : one who organizes, owns, manages, and assumes the risks of a business ⟨he aimed at . . . increased opportunities for the small ∼ —A.M.Schlesinger b. 1917⟩ **2** : one that organizes, promotes, or manages an enterprise or activity of any kind : PRACTITIONER, PROMOTER ⟨a doctor or lawyer, who, as an independent ∼, provides service to a client —Bernard Goldstein⟩ ⟨an ∼ of the theater⟩ ⟨alert historical ∼s —J.D.Hicks⟩ ⟨the Yankee ∼ . . . who descended on the desolate South to make his fortune —*Holiday*⟩ **3** : one who serves as an intermediary : MIDDLEMAN, GO-BETWEEN ⟨New York is . . . becoming world-city and ∼ between Europe and the American hinterland —Donald Davidson⟩ ⟨they are . . . the ∼s, the links between the businessmen . . . and the fanatics —Eric Ambler⟩

WEBSTER'S THIRD NEW INTERNATIONAL DICTIONARY

en·tre·pre·neur·i·al \-nər·ēal, -n(y)u̇r- *also* -nȝr-\ *adj* : of or relating to an entrepreneur ⟨∼ history⟩ ⟨∼ risks and rewards⟩ en·tre·pre·neur·ship \-nər,ship, -nȝ,sh-, -n(y)u̇(ə)r,sh-, -u̇ə ,sh-\ *n* -s : the condition of being an entrepreneur : the role or function of the entrepreneur : entrepreneurial ability or activity ⟨recent American experiences have proved how imaginative private ∼ can continue to be —L.M.Hacker⟩ ⟨voices a plea for the study of ∼ in history —W.C.Scoville⟩ ⟨it is now generally accepted that ∼ consists in the meeting of uncertainty —Donald Dewey⟩ en·tre·pre·neuse \-¦nə(r)z, -¦nȝz, -¦nəiz, -¦n(y)u̇z\ *n* -s [F, fem. of *entrepreneur*] : a woman entrepreneur

Bich The Ballpoint King

In seventy-five countries, people ask for a Bic when they want a ballpoint pen. Over the past fifteen years Baron Marcel Bich, a sardonic and eccentric Frenchman in his early fifties, has turned the first three letters of his name into a household word, and cornered about a quarter of the world market for ballpoint pens. In 1967, Bich sold about one billion pens for some $60 million. Global profits are estimated at $10 million before taxes.

Bich runs his operations from a small office in Paris. He has no stockholders, and no time for fashionable theories of participative management. As sole owner of his companies, he makes decisions without consulting anybody. "It's all mine, I can do what I want with it," he said during one of his rare interviews. "What matters is to dare and to attack. In sport the reward is a gold medal. In business it is profit." Bich says he will bet on a 70 percent chance in business: "Winning seven races out of ten is not bad. It means a step forward even if the other three are rotten losers."

Bich went to school in France, and worked in an office-equipment firm while he studied law. After World War II he bought a small company that made fountain pens. Soon thereafter, like the American promoter, Milton Reynolds, Bich saw the potential of ballpoints. They were then relatively expensive, unreliable, and hard to get in Europe. Bich redesigned the ballpoint to improve its writing quality, put the ink cartridge into a transparent plastic body, and made some models cheap enough to be disposable. By 1955, Bich had sales of more than $5 million, and was ready to expand out of Europe.

In 1958 he heard that the ailing U.S. Waterman pen company was for sale. Typically, he plunked down $1 million in cash for 60 percent of the stock, accepting the balance sheet at face value. This turned out to be so misleading a document that Bich's lawyers later picked up the remaining 40 percent of the company for nothing. It took seven years, and $10 million more, to make Waterman profitable.

In that period, Bich commuted across the Atlantic almost monthly. He applied to Waterman the formula that had brought him success elsewhere: massive advertising of an improved, cheap product. (Bic pens cost as little as 19 cents.) As Bich recalled later, his U.S. managers advised him then to concentrate instead on making a more expensive pen, with a metal clip and an opaque body. But he snapped back: "Waterman is 100 percent mine. You are going to do what you are told."

In 1967, Waterman-Bic Pen Corp. produced some 480 million pens in the U.S. But in 1968, according to its president, Robert P. Adler, the company's production dropped by nearly one-third, to 325 million units. Bich is not a communicative man under any circumstances, and neither he nor Adler has publicly commented on the reasons for the drop.

But it may be the result of competition from soft-tipped pens—the new writing instruments which Bich, despite his penchant for innovation, is not yet making in the U.S. That refusal may yet turn out to be one of the "rotten losers" in Bich's career.

The Business of Business is People

Business today is concerned not just with profits, but also with a wide range of social, human, technological, and economic problems and their solution.

There seems to be a popular myth that businessmen are different from normal people, that they don't have personal motives and human emotions, that they devote their lives to maximizing the almighty dollar at the cost of society and our physical environment.

No. Businessmen are people. They have very human emotions, values, personal wants and needs, and the same concerns that everyone feels from day to day.

Because businessmen bring companies to life, the policies and goals that guide manufacturing, marketing, finance, and other activities all reflect the personal qualities of the key managers. This human factor may run a company amuck, but generally it is a very positive quality of business enterprise.

Further, the sensitivity and capability of key executives will determine whether companies effectively respond to the demands of changing social, economic, and environmental conditions. The qualities of executives discussed in the following article may or may not be the qualities that will prove to be necessary to effectively manage business or-

"Now, Simpkins, this project will require skill, know-how, ingenuity! . . . send in Hooper."

ganizations in the seventies and future decades. Higher education, for example, is becoming increasingly important as technology in business and industry advances and sophisticated decision techniques using computers become necessary to manage world-wide business organizations.

We often think of major corporations as large lifeless creatures. Yet I.B.M., for example, is wholly owned by some 580,000 stockholders. The corporation employs more than 265,000 persons. Sears is owned by 252,000 stockholders and by many of its employees through a special stock plan.

Further, no business can operate in an environmental vacuum. To survive and prosper a company must meet the needs of its customers: customers like us and other business organizations -- that represent other consumers like us.

Even the federal, state,

and local governments represent basically HUMAN interests -- of the public at large. Governmental organizations must also continue to be responsive to human needs if they are to be effective and survive.

By satisfying the needs of PEOPLE as consumers, business also generates work. This work provides direct employment to people, hopefully meaningful, challenging jobs. The companies that provide more satisfying work tend to be more profitable. Where people are encouraged to express themselves -- through their work and through their personal behavior -- they tend to do better work. This has a positive impact on our entire society.

Employees, managers, consumers, owners, and the public -- PEOPLE are what business is all about. There's really nothing impersonal that really matters.

A Self-portrait of the Chief Executive

Despite their prominence on the public scene, the top executives of very large U.S. corporations remain something of an enigma. Sociologists, novelists, and political scientists have tried to isolate the characteristics that distinguish this elite managerial class. To Sinclair Lewis in the Twenties, the fatuous Babbitt embodied the successful businessman, to Marxists in the Forties he was a conspiratorial instigator of the cold war, to sociologist C. Wright Mills in the Fifties he was a calculating politician who masked his intelligence on his way to the top. Caricatures aside, who runs big business? More than half of the chief executives whose companies are listed in this year's FORTUNE directory supplied personal data about themselves for this survey, which was conducted in association with Daniel Yankelovich, Inc.

There is no way neatly to categorize these chief executives, and the evidence is rather clear that there is no sure path to the top. Possibly the most unifying characteristic is that most are conservative politically and grew up in middle- and upper-middle-class families. Four out of five were born in the period either before, during, or just following World War I; about half of them are now between fifty and sixty, while another fourth are over sixty. Though the vast majority (79 percent) didn't assume the post of chief executive until the 1960's, most of them helped steer their companies through the postwar industrial boom. Sixty-four percent joined their present companies before 1950, and another 9 percent came aboard before 1956. Among executives in the largest industrial and retail outlets with more than $1 billion of annual sales, three out of four have been with their companies for more than twenty years.

If one is to judge from the background of these men, the promise of an open society that rewards achievement has been fulfilled. Twenty-two percent of the chief executives started out in such mundane jobs as stockboy, trainee, junior clerk, or hourly shift worker. Another third had special skills as chemists, engineers, lawyers, accountants, or marketing men. But a striking number (14 percent) of the executives started out in their present company at, or very near, the top—as president, chairman, or founder. Among this group are men who headed family businesses that have grown with the economy and become large public corporations.

The much-publicized belief that chief executives work long hours turns out to be true—58 percent work in the office a minimum of nine hours a day, and among the younger executives, those fifty-five and under, some 70 percent work more than a nine-hour day. But the patterns of that workday appear to be much influenced by the demand put on the executives' time by business and social lunches and dinners, plus the interminable intracompany meetings. Some 60 percent prefer working during the morning hours and, contrary to lore, they rarely work late at night.

Their long hours extend well beyond the office, however, since most of the executives command corporations that have expanded not only throughout the U.S. but around the world. Face-to-face meetings with the heads of operating divisions require these chief executives to travel frequently, and 13 percent spent more than *half* their time away last year at corporate outposts. Among the heads of the largest industrials and retailers, the number who spent more than half their time away was even higher (21 percent).

Within a decade most of these successful professional managers, who have weathered three wars and a depression and are now grappling with the youth revolution and demands for a more sensitive corporate conscience, must hand on power to younger men. From the sum total of his experience, the chief executive must try to measure as best he can the kind of leadership needed for an uncertain future. The key traits sought in a successor are, in a sense, an idealization of what the present chief executive hopes he, too, possesses—the ability to inspire loyalty, a strong, decisive manner, exceptional intelligence. Surprisingly, the incumbent chiefs do not give high priority to such attributes as youth or the ability to get along well with people of different races and classes.

Beyond traits of character, the chief executives are looking for successors who, like themselves, have years of experience in the company (40 percent), or at least in the industry (26 percent). They look with particular favor upon men with marketing (32 percent), financial (31 percent), or technical and engineering (17 percent) experience. But they are only marginally interested in successors whose backgrounds include legal experience.

Some fun and games as well

Compensation for the men at the top is handsome indeed; nine out of ten have income before taxes ranging from $100,000 to over $1 million. But most are not wealthy men. More than half count on their salaries for at least 80 percent of their annual income, and despite stock options, more than half have a net worth of less than $1 million.

Though certainly not rich by the standards of Texas oilmen, they live and spend in a handsome way. Almost all of them own their homes, and 60 percent rent or own additional "getaway" places, too. A surprisingly large number (48 percent) collect original works of art. The most popular leisure-time activity is golfing (56 percent), followed by fishing, boating, hunting, tennis, and swimming. They don't especially like watching TV, nor are they ardent theatre or movie goers. Their choice of reading matter for relaxation is eclectic, ranging all the way from novels and mysteries to books on sociology and philosophy. It is a sign of these uneasy times that only a small number (18 percent) still read newspapers mainly for pleasure.

If the chief executive doesn't travel outside the U.S. on business, most likely he'll go abroad for pleasure. Last year more than four out of five made at least one foreign trip. For business, the U.K. was the leading destination (56 percent), followed by Germany, Belgium, Austria, the Netherlands, and then France. Some 20 percent had occasion to travel to South America, while 39 percent visited Asia. To unwind, the chief executive headed first for the sandy beaches of the Caribbean islands (15 percent), the U.K. (12 percent), Mexico (8 percent), and France (7 percent).

For obvious reasons, chief executives are forced to lead a distinctive kind of social life. Three out of five say they prefer to fraternize with other executives. But only 12 percent prefer the company of doctors, lawyers, and other professionals, and only 6 percent have academicians as social companions.

This generation of corporate leaders is well aware of the toll exacted by social and business demands, and to a remarkable degree they are taking precautions to safeguard their health. A very significant majority—55 percent—say they do not smoke at all, and only slightly more than one in five smoke cigarettes. Another 17 percent smoke cigars and 11 percent prefer pipes. Concern about acquiring the middle-age paunch and attendant cardiac problems has spurred almost half of them to adopt diets to avoid weight gains, and about the same number are also exercising frequently.

Bearers of cultural baggage

The incumbent executives were born at a time when the U.S. population was less than half today's 204 million. The Far West was barely settled, and statehood had just come to the last two of the forty-eight contiguous states. Mostly, they come from the medium and small-sized towns that dotted the East and the Middle West. Virtually half were born in eight key states that compose the industrial heartland—New York, New Jersey, Pennsylvania, Ohio, Michigan, Indiana, Illinois, and Wisconsin. And only 5 percent were born in the Pacific region, including what is now the nation's most populous state, California. Even though more executives were born in New York City, Chicago, Philadelphia, or Minneapolis than in any other city or town in America, the big-city boys are definitely a minority among the chief executives. Less than a third were born in urban centers with a population of more than a half million.

From their birthplaces they took with them the prevailing Protestantism. Over all, 80 percent of chief executives are Protestant, with a surprisingly high 93 percent holding the top jobs in banking and insurance. The barriers to Jews, however, seem to be disappearing; some 7 percent of chief executives are Jewish, more than double the total representation in the national population. The real mystery is the failure of Catholics to penetrate the top ranks of business. The election of President Kennedy in 1960 had symbolized for many Catholics the final proof, if indeed it was needed, of their total assimilation in the national life. But although Catholics represent about 23 percent of the population today, they account for only 9 percent of chief executives nationwide.

The path of upward mobility

American lore is filled with tales of the up-from-nowhere achiever, but the reality is that most chief executives grew up in comfortable middle- and upper-middle-class surroundings. Only 16 percent are the sons of blue-collar workers or farmers. All the rest got a firsthand view of the executive world from fathers with an entrepreneurial frame of mind or who closely served those who did. Forty-five percent of their fathers stood at the very top of the business hierarchy either as founder, chairman of the board, or president of a company, or as a self-employed businessman.

Unlike their fathers, however, today's corporate leaders became the first truly college-educated generation of executives. The Thirties and Forties clearly marked the beginning of an era in which young Americans were college-educated on a scale unparalleled anywhere in the world. This was partly due to the recognition that industry, in growing more complex, required able men with special skills or expertise. To that end the chief executives departed sharply from family tradition. Most chief executives attended a different school than their fathers. And the sum total of their majors and degrees certainly gave no early evidence of a consuming interest in business. Only a third majored in business administration, 40 percent majored in science and engineering, and 35 percent specialized in the humanities and the social sciences. Their graduate degrees are just as varied. About a third studied for an M.B.A. and an equal number took a law degree. There's a smattering of other degrees, too, including 3 percent who have Ph. D.'s.

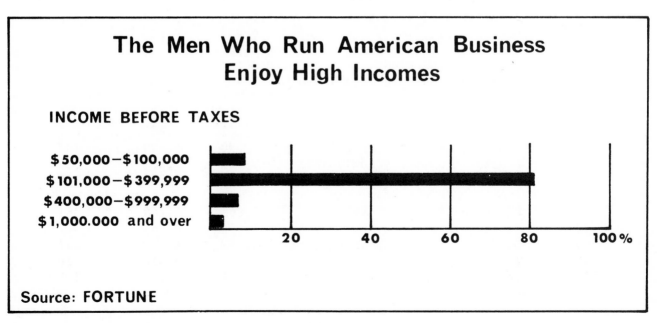

The Men Who Run American Business Enjoy High Incomes

INCOME BEFORE TAXES

$50,000–$100,000	
$101,000–$399,999	
$400,000–$999,999	
$1,000.000 and over	

20   40   60   80   100%

Source: FORTUNE

Giants of Yesterday and Today

Listed below are the twenty-five largest industrial corporations in the United States. They are listed in order of total revenues (sales).

Ten of the companies listed are oil companies. Six are manufacturers of electrical or electronic equipment. Three are automobile manufacturers. The remaining companies represent chemical, consumer goods, and other industries.

The importance of the automobile is reflected by the number of automobile and oil companies. Oil companies sell more than just oil and gas for automobiles, but this remains a big share of their business activity. Auto companies have also moved into electronics, aerospace, household appliances, and other goods. But they, too, are primarily keyed to automobile and truck transportation.

Electronics, chemicals, and aerospace represent advanced technologies in today's industrial world. Companies such as IBM have grown rapidly as the technology and market for their goods have matured.

Why do companies grow to be so large? Certain types of businesses require large amounts of capital equipment in order to produce goods effectively and efficiently. Oil refining and automobile production are large-scale

25 LARGEST INDUSTRIAL CORPORATIONS

(All figures in millions of dollars)

Rank	Corporation	Sales	Assets	Profits
1	Exxon (New York)	44,864	32,839	2,503
2	General Motors (Detroit)	35,724	21,664	1,253
3	Texaco (New York)	24,507	17,262	850
4	Ford Motor (Dearborn)	24,009	14,020	322
5	Mobil Oil (New York)	20,620	15,050	810
6	Standard Oil of California	16,822	12,898	772
7	International Bus. Machines	14,436	15,530	1,989
8	Gulf Oil (Pittsburgh)	14,268	12,425	700
9	General Electric (Fairfield)	13,399	9,763	581
10	Chrysler (Highland Park)	11,699	6,267	(260)
11	International Tel. & Tel.	11,367	10,407	398
12	Standard Oil (Ind.) (Chicago)	9,955	9,854	787
13	U.S. Steel (Pittsburgh)	8,167	8,148	559
14	Shell Oil (Houston)	8,143	7,010	514
15	Atlantic Richfield (L.A.)	7,307	7,364	350
16	Continental Oil (Stamford)	7,253	5,184	330
17	E.I. duPont de Nemours	7,221	6,425	271
18	Western Electric	6,590	4,999	107
19	Procter & Gamble (Cincinnati)	6,081	3,652	334
20	Westinghouse Electric	5,862	4,866	165
21	Union Carbide (New York)	5,665	5,740	381
22	Tenneco (Houston)	5,599	6,584	342
23	Goodyear Tire & Rubber (Akron)	5,452	4,173	161
24	International Harvester	5,335	3,510	79
25	Occidental Petroleum (L.A.)	5,334	3,503	171

Source: Fortune, May 1976

manufacturing operations, requiring lots of capital.

Companies grow as their markets grow, as technology changes, and as they compete successfully with other companies in the industry. Business enterprises usually fall by the wayside if their goods and services are not in demand or if they slip in keeping up with the changing technology.

THE OLDEST COMPANIES

Of the largest 500 industrial companies, 80 claim to be more than a century old. In addition, 12 of the largest transportation companies, 26 banks, 25 life-insurance companies, 5 retailers, and 5 utilities claim similar vintage.

Some of these companies were large companies in the 1800's. Others had not even been thought about yet. Pullman was a big business; Simmons Co. was a small one.

Merck & Co., a pharmaceutical company, claims the title as oldest of the 500 industrials. Merck's origins go back to 1668, when the German company began. It was set up as an American branch with the same name in the late nineteenth century.

Caterpillar Tractor Co. traces its origins to the founding of the Holt Co., a predecessor firm. But 1925 was the year Caterpillar was actually formed, through a merger of Holt and the C.L. Best Tractor Co. (which was founded in 1910).

Other venerable firms are Phelps Dodge (1799), Revere Copper & Brass (1801), Scovill Manufacturing (1802), and E.I. duPont de Nemours (also 1802).

1929 Rank	COMPANY	1929 assets ($000,000)	1969 assets ($000,000)	1969 Rank	Percent increase
1.	U.S. Steel	2,286	6,560	9	187
2.	Standard Oil (N.J.)	1,767	17,538	1	893
3.	General Motors	1,131	14,820	2	1,210
4.	Standard Oil (Ind.)	850	5,151	13	506
5.	Bethlehem Steel	802	3,224	20	302
6.	Ford Motor	761	9,199	4	1,109
7.	Mobil Oil	708	7,163	7	912
8.	Anaconda	681	1,764	45	159
9.	Texaco	610	9,282	3	1,422
10.	Standard Oil (Calif.)	605	6,146	10	916
11.	General Electric	516	6,007	11	1,064
12.	Du Pont	497	3,453	18	595
13.	Shell Oil	486	4,356	15	796
14.	Armour	452	607	150	34
15.	Gulf Oil	431	8,105	5	1,781
16.	Sinclair Oil	401			
17.	International Harvester	384	2,026	37	428
18.	General Theatres Equipment	360			
19.	Swift	351	744	128	112
20.	Kennecott Copper	338	1,652	52	389
21.	Republic Steel	332	1,782	44	437
22.	Pullman	316	461	198	46
23.	Western Electric	309	3,172	21	927
24.	Uniroyal	308	1,259	79	309
25.	Union Carbide	307	3,356	19	993

Some firms change names as fortunes wax and wane. Colt Industries dates to 1830, as Fairbanks, Morse. The business came under control of Penn-Texas in 1958, and the name was changed. But a year later, in hard times, the name was changed to Fairbanks, Whitney. In 1964 the name of a 1955 acquisition, Colt's Manufacturing Co., was taken as the corporate name. The Colt firm had been founded in 1836.

CHANGES IN THE BIGGEST

In 1929, Hoover was in the White House and pot was something to have chicken in every one of. At that time U.S. Steel was our nation's largest industrial corporation.

In the decades to follow, some companies have fallen back relative to others. New firms have swelled in assets and revenues. The accompanying chart shows the largest companies in 1929. These are ranked by assets rather than by sales, but you can easily see that the fate of major corporations is tough to predict. Big companies are not invincible -- they have to work hard to keep healthy and ahead of the pack.

Who would have thought that Pullman, a giant in 1929, would slip so far? Or that the rich General Theatres Equipment would be in bankruptcy within three years?

With inflation considered, Armour and Swift fell far behind. U.S. Steel barely kept even pace. Standard Oil (N.J.), now Exxon, grew rapidly, as did General Motors.

Companies that were among the top ones in 1929 that have slippped on the scale of the biggest include: Sinclair (but now a part of Atlantic Richfield), Anaconda, International Harvester, Republic Steel, Uniroyal (U.S. Rubber).

Merchants to Millions

You go to the store to buy an item you want or need. You find what you want... the price is right...you pay for it, take it home. Or you order something by mail or telephone from a catalog or from a newspaper ad. What exactly are you paying for?

You pay, of course, for the cost of producing what you buy, for turning raw materials into finished products. You also pay the cost of getting the item from producer to you; the cost of distribution, which in some cases takes as much as fifty-three cents of your dollar.

These figures -- fifty-three cents out of every dollar -- help to highlight the importance of distribution in the American economy. If Sears and other specialists in distribution do a good job, keep distribution costs low, you pay less, have more to spend and save. If Sears and the others do a poor job, you pay more, and have less to spend or save. Only through efficient distribution can our standard of living remain high and go still higher.

> This article is the first in a series examining the organization and management of our nation's largest retailer. Future articles will discuss its structure, management policies, its advertising and marketing policies, its product policies, employee and public relations, and its relationships with our society and economy.

THE SEARS OF YESTERDAY

At age sixteen, Richard W. Sears faced a problem. His father, James Warren Sears, a blacksmith and a Civil War veteran of English descent, died virtually penniless, leaving his widow to raise two small daughters and Richard in the little town of Spring Valley, Minnesota.

Dick Sears' response was to learn telegraphy. After he became a qualified telegrapher he began a series of railroad jobs and eventually became agent of the Minnesota and St. Louis Railway Station in North Redwood, Minnesota, near Redwood Falls.

Sears' job as station agent left him plenty of spare time. So he sold lumber and coal to local residents on the side to make extra money. A few years later, when the Chicago Jewelry Company shipped a package of watches, Sears was ready. The watches, unwanted by the neighboring Redwood Falls jeweler who received them, were purchased by Sears, who sold them at a handsome profit to other station agents up and down the line. So he ordered more watches for resale.

In 1886, Sears was in business for himself in Minneapolis as the head of the R. W. Sears Watch Company. Thus started an enterprise which was destined to become one of the most dramatic stories in American business.

Sears' watch business grew and grew, and so did his problems. When some watches didn't work, customers wanted them repaired. In 1887 Sears had moved his business to Chicago and there he inserted a classified ad in the Chicago Daily News:

> WANTED: Watchmaker with references who can furnish tools. State age, experience, and salary required. ADDRESS T39, Daily News.

An Indiana-born lad of English parentage, Alvah C. Roebuck, answered the ad. He told Sears he knew watches and brought a sample of his work to prove it. At the time he read the ad, in fact, Roebuck was employed as a watchmaker in Hammond, Indiana -- for $3.50 a week plus room and board.

Sears hired him. Thus began the association of two young men, both still in their twenties, that led to events that were to make their names famous. It was in 1893 that the corporate name of the organization became Sears, Roebuck and Co.

SEARS SETTLES IN CHICAGO

Chicago in the 1890's was the rail hub of the Middle West, a bustling, brawling young city soon to become the mail-order capital of the world. With most of the new company's business coming from Pennsylvania, Georgia, Texas, and Iowa, Chicago seemed a far better site for Sears than did Minneapolis.

Richard W. Sears   Alvah C. Roebuck

While the earliest catalogs featured only watches, the new firm by 1895 was producing a 507-page catalog with many other items. This book offered shoes, women's garments and millinery, wagons, fishing tackle, stoves, furniture, china, musical instruments, saddles, firearms, buggies, bicycles, glassware, and baby carriages in addition to watches and jewelry.

Richard Sears was the guiding genius of the new mail order firm. He knew farmers, understood their needs and desires. Better yet, he could write advertising copy that made farmers send in money and orders. Under his leadership, sales in 1893 topped $400,000. They exceeded $750,000 in 1895.

SEARS REORGANIZED

Selling . . . advertising . . . merchandising -- these were Dick Sears' talents contributed to the firm; not organizing

the company so it could handle orders on an economical and efficient basis. That was left to a Chicago clothing manufacturer, Julius Rosenwald, who, with his brother-in-law bought into the company in 1895.

Sears was reorganized. Rosenwald became Vice President. His brother-in-law, Aaron Nusbaum, became Treasurer and General Manager. Sears retained the presidency. Suffering from ill health, Roebuck resigned, although he still lent his name to the firm and eventually served as head of the watch and jewelry department. In 1903, Sears and Rosenwald bought out Nusbaum, and Rosenwald became Treasurer as well as Vice President. Three years later, needing additional capital, Sears and Rosenwald for the first time sold common and preferred stock on the open market. The company has been publicly owned ever since.

MAIL ORDER EXPANDS

Sears' business expanded fast . . . so fast, in fact, that the company soon outgrew its rented five-story building. In 1896 Sears moved to a new six-story building -- with a basement.

In early times, daily help was hired on the basis of order volume indicated by weight of day's mail

MEN WANTED

U.S. MAIL

But even the new building wasn't enough. By the turn of the century, Sears built or leased additional buildings in various sections of Chicago. Meanwhile, construction was started on a new forty-acre, $5 million mail order plant and office building on Chicago's West Side. When opened in

1906, the mail-order plant was -- at the time -- the largest business building in the world. Today, it is still one of the largest, with more than 3,000,000 square feet of floor space.

About the time the mortar was drying in the new plant, Sears made the first move to establish the company in a branch location. In 1906, a branch office was opened in Dallas, Texas.

Six years later, in 1912, the branch office blossomed into the Dallas mail order plant, offering the Southwest complete mail order facilities, lower freight rates, faster delivery, and reduced damage to merchandise.

Richard Sears came amazingly close to guessing the eventual total of Sears' mail order plants. Eleven operate today. The Seattle plant opened in 1910, the Philadelphia plant in 1920, the Kansas City plant in 1925. Other plants are located in Boston, Atlanta, Minneapolis, Memphis, Los Angeles, and Greensboro.

The change in the catalog -- from the flamboyant to the factual -- appears to have started by the turn of the century although Richard Sears' influence continued for some time after. Julius Rosenwald blue-penciled some of Sears' advertising claims.

MAIL ORDER SCHEDULING

Building mail order plants was one thing. Making them operate efficiently was something else. Around the turn of the century, a customer complained:

> "For heaven's sake, quit sending me sewing machines. Every time I go to the station I find another one there. You have shipped me five already."

Sears mail order executives knew of these problems and were as unhappy as the customers about them. Gradually, after much experimenting, they introduced a time schedule system. Under it, each order was given a time to be shipped.

Then, no matter what happened, the order had to be in the appropriate bin in the merchandise-assembly room at the assigned time. It traveled to the room by an intricate system of belts and chutes. This system, working by 1910, enabled the Chicago plant to handle ten times the business it handled before the system was introduced. It is said that Henry Ford was one of the men who visited the plant to study the assembly line technique used in the system.

SEARS ENTERS RETAIL

In 1906 Richard Sears wrote:
> "We do comparatively very little business in cities, and we... assume the cities are not at all our field -- maybe they are not -- but I think it is our duty to prove that they are not...."

Nineteen years later, the time came for Sears, Roebuck and Co. to prove that cities were its field. The man who proved it was Robert E. Wood, then a Sears Vice President, later to become President and Chairman.

Wood entered Sears with excellent credentials. He was a West Point graduate. During the building of the Panama Canal, he had served as chief quartermaster. Later, as a brigadier general in World War I, he had been the Army's acting quartermaster general. He rose to the vice presidency of a rival mail order company after the war. And now, at Sears, he was to garner additional fame as the father of Sears' retail expansion.

As soon as he was on the job, Wood began to move. Early in 1925 he experimented with one store -- located in the Chicago mail order plant. It was an immediate success. Before the year was over he opened seven more retail stores, four of them in mail order plants. By the end of 1927 he had twenty-seven stores in operation.
Why retail stores? By 1925, retail chain stores were beginning to blanket the country, cutting into Sears'

mail order business. In 1914 there were about 24,000 chain stores. Fifteen years later there were 150,000.

Further, the whole face of the country was changing. Modern roads and cars made it no longer necessary for rural customers to shop by catalog. They could hop in the "tin lizzie" and chug off to town. And American cities were growing up. Customers were abandoning the farm for the factory.

In 1900 rural population exceeded urban population. By 1920 this was reversed.

City dwellers, Wood reasoned, weren't good catalog customers. They shopped in city stores which offered more and better merchandise. Unless Sears opened stores of its own, the company would end up serving only a small fraction of the American buying public.

WHAZZIT?

PROPRIETORSHIP

A business owned by one individual who gets all the profits (if there are any after taxes) and assumes all of the liabilities as personal debts. (If his business goes broke, he may lose his shirt.)

You can start a proprietorship simply by hanging out your sign (your "shingle") saying you are in business and registering your business name with the County recorder's office so the public will know that your company name is really you. The sole proprietorship may use the name "Company" but "Inc." means the business is a corporation.

PARTNERSHIP

A business owned and operated by two or more individuals, but not necessarily equally is a partnership. As in a sole proprietorship, all partners are personally liable for the firm's debts, including the actions of the other partners. This provides more managerial talent and often more financial resources, but requires a good working relationship. Law firms and other professional firms are often partnerships.

In addition to registering the name, a partnership requires a formal agreement between the partners. If the composition of the partnership changes (one of the partners dies or a new partner is added to the firm) the old partnership is dissolved and a new one must be formed.

CORPORATION

"...an artificial being, invisible, intangible, and existing in the contemplation of the law. Being the mere creature of law, it possesses only those properties which the charter of its creation confers upon it, either expressly or as incidental to its existence." -- Chief Justice John Marshall, 1819.

As an "it" a corporation outlives its owners because the stock, representing the ownership interest, may be transferred or sold. Unlike the other forms of businesses, the liability of the owners (stockholders) is limited to their investment in the stock of the corporation.

Pollution and Profits

For decades we have successfully pushed to expand our nation's economy. Rapid economic growth has been a primary objective in our economic system -- to keep people working and to raise our standard of living.

But now we are having second thoughts -- as our environmental quality becomes one of our top concerns. As Harvard Economist John Galbraith's "Affluent Society" turns into an "Effluent Society" we are recognizing that the pursuit of material wealth pollutes our rivers, our air, and creates an urban atmosphere that contains dangerous social tensions and misery.

Rising public concerns make us ask whether there is a trade-off between economic growth and the quality of life. "In a consumer-oriented society everything we produce leads to waste," says Senator Edmund Muskie. "Maybe we ought to set some limits on the standard of living."

One of the basic premises of the "free" enterprise system is often thought to be that the output of goods and services and material welfare are prime aims. Society is presumed better off if it produces more, regardless of the quality, the need, or the adverse impact. The use of natural resources, the environmental impact, or the social good are not always key.

What the consumers want and will buy is not necessarily what should be produced. It may be that the problems created by more production outweigh the value of "more cars, radios, prepared foods, plastic objects of art, and containers."

PRICES AND POLLUTION

A former president proposed that "the prices of goods should be made to include the cost of producing and disposing of them without damage to the environment." It has been estimated that about $20 billion must be spent each year during the years ahead to combat pollution. The tab must be paid by someone -- if not the consumers, then the taxpayers or the stockholders.

Let's remember, though, that pollution control expenditures aren't money down the drain. They create new value for the consumer -- general improvement of the environment which we enjoy. Such satisfactions can be just as real as from the goods themselves.

In the case of automobiles, pollution controls have been developed and built right in each year's new models, and the price jacked up to cover the cost involved. We can call it "quality improvement of products" and are willing to pay the higher price.

Electricity costs have gone up rapidly due to the cost of fuels, but also in part to the cost of building pollution free (or at least a lot better) generating facilities.

From another point of view we could see that the costs of pollution control are far less costly than the hidden costs that we bear with pollution. Water pollution damages fishing industries and

recreation. Air pollution, in addition to causing respiratory diseases, forces people to clean their clothes more often and paint their houses more frequently. "An ounce of pollution prevention is worth a pound of cure," since most studies show these costs tend to outweigh abatement costs by a ratio of 16:1.

Society would be better off, even materially, if pollution were brought to an end.

QUALITY OF LIFE

It would be nice, and quite appropriate today for us to use a measure of the quality of life along with our measures of economic growth and profits. To some economists this idea is as absurd as the attempt by British economist Jeremy Bentham more than 150 years ago to develop an index of human happiness.

Many companies today are reporting their steps in combatting pollution

25 THE ENTERPRISE SYSTEM

generated by their own production. In many speeches, reports, and in advertising, businessmen are talking about product quality and environmental impact. We may not have an overall measure or index of the quality of life, but we certainly have a lot of information we can carefully weigh to reach our conclusions about how we're doing.

Advertising is particularly important because it influences consumer decisions. Instead of urging more and more consumption, and the disposing of goods that are still usable, we can emphasize quality and durability. We can educate consumers and shift buying patterns to become more environmentally responsible. One example is the successful promotion of pollution free detergent.

We simply can't go on living in a "cowboy" economy, where consumption is rampant. Our social values are changing and business values will reflect this change.

WHAZZIT?

ASSETS

Anything of value that is owned, including cash, securities, inventories, prepaid charges, property, receivables, land, equipment, buildings, and patents.

REVENUES

Total cash or other property (such as securities or goods taken in trade) received as a result of business activities; including investments and the sales of goods and services.

PROFITS

The income of a firm after all costs and expenses are paid, but before taxes or the payment of dividends. If profits are "after tax", they are so indicated.

A View From the Top

One of the largest of our nation's companies is U.S. Steel. It's a massive old company in one of the oldest and most essential of our industries -- steel production.

At a time when attention is often drawn to the newer, more dynamic companies, with newer technologies and services, it is helpful to consider the long experience of a company such as U.S. Steel, and of its chief executive. In the article that follows, Edwin H. Gott, retired chairman and chief executive officer, provides some personal observations on the key issues that face the corporation, and on his own career with the firm.

The steel industry is a basic user and processor of natural resources: iron ore, coal, oil, and water. The basic technology and many of the plants in the industry are old and, frankly, are polluters. It is very costly for steel companies to do their part in cleaning up the environment.

As chief executive, Mr. Gott had major responsibilities for finding the solutions to these problems.

A Steel Boss Looks at his Industry

PITTSBURGH — Edwin H. Gott retires today after 36 years with U.S. Steel Corp., the last four as its chairman and chief executive. Few of the company's 180,000 employes are likely to pause in their labor to reflect on the event and certainly no town will be named Gott City in his honor, as the company did for former chief executives such as Elbert Gary and more recently Benjamin Fairless. Barons of business don't command that kind of public respect any more.

Nevertheless, it's worthwhile to pause for a moment and reflect with Ed Gott on the close of his career. It spanned one of the most difficult periods in industrial history.

He joined U.S. Steel during the depths of the Depression, and presided over it when earnings again plunged to depression levels in 1970 and 1971. His first year with the company, 1937, saw the organization of the mills by the forerunner of the United Steelworkers of America and the institution of the $5-a-day wage. Today, with steel labor costs averaging $7.30 an hour, even the union is considering surrendering its right to strike in order to save jobs and protect industry profits. And while the streets of Pittsburgh were once so clogged with soot and smoke that street lights burned at noon, Mr. Gott is able to survey a 20-mile horizon from his 61st floor office in the new U.S. Steel Building and discuss the quarter-billion dollars his company has spent on pollution control in the past five years.

As the $300,000-a-year head of the nation's largest steel company and as leader of the American Iron and Steel Institute, the industry's trade group, Mr. Gott, to paraphrase his company's advertising, has been "involved." He has been jawboned by Presidents over steel prices. He's been picketed by environmentalists who, he says, mistake steam for smoke. And he's watched as the growth of domestic markets has been washed away by a flood of imports while critics in Washington seek to plug alleged tax "loopholes" instead of trade ones.

Mr. Gott's thoughts on these subjects aren't likely to win over his critics, and in fact may stir new criticism. But they are important, not only because of the role he's played, but because he articulates a viewpoint shared by many in our society, including many in positions of corporate power and others who've just begun to climb the corporate ladder.

Big Business Booster

Mr. Gott, first and foremost, is a believer in his company and his country. "I don't know what this country would do without big business," he says. "When I look at how far this country we all love has come—in food, in communication, in transportation—it's all due entirely to big business."

Thus it bothers him, he says, when Congress listens to ecologists who press for "zero pollution" on the basis of a "small group profile" which doesn't consider "the whole picture. It's foolish to let these people dictate the whole future of our country."

With the exception of cleaning up its coke batteries, which Mr. Gott maintains is still beyond the bounds of modern technology, the executive believes steel has "done a fantastic job" cleaning up the environment. "We spent a quarter of our profit (of $157 million, or $2.90 a share) on pollution control last year and it netted us absolutely nothing but criticism."

To what extent should the mills be forced to clean up? "We shouldn't have to do more than what is right for health," he says.

The gray-haired, blue-eyed executive isn't a harsh man. He's a national vice president of the Boy Scouts of America. And on a recent weekend he flew medical supplies (via one of U.S. Steel's corporate jets) to families in earthquake-ravished Nicaragua. "I felt so damn sorry for them," he says, speaking with deep emotion of the horror he saw.

Whether hunting pheasants or making corporate policy, Ed Gott is a competitor—and he likes to win. Domestic markets lost to imported steel and soaring national trade deficits are abhorrent to him since they signal a surrender to foreign competition. "We can't have the U.S.A. as anything but Number One in the world," he stresses. "At one time we were primarily a producing country; that's when you have a healthy, viable economy. Now two-thirds of our workers are on the service side and the further that trend swings the tougher it will be to be competitive in the world market."

And why isn't steel, which accounted for a third of the total U.S. trade deficit last year, competitive on the world market? For one reason, Mr. Gott declares, foreign mills "are subsidized by their governments. In many cases you have private companies here competing against government-owned steel com-

panies in Britain, France, Spain and Italy."

Mr. Gott continues: "Mexico subsidizes its steel at the rate of $25 a ton because it pays the freight to ship it to this country. In Japan, where mills have a 20-to-1 debt-to-equity ratio, the mills are subsidized with low interest government loans."

To equalize the picture and make competition "fair," the U.S. should offset such subsidies with higher tariffs, the outgoing executive believes. "Big business brought everything there is in the country and the government should do everything it can for big business."

Aren't U.S. companies already assisted through the investment tax credit and foreign tax allowances, so-called "loopholes," which critics contend allowed U.S. Steel to escape paying any U.S. income tax in 1971? Mr. Gott's answer is an emphatic No. "With all the taxes we pay it's a wonder we have any profit at all," he contends.

"Look at our plant in Gary. Our tax bill there is $30 million a year in property taxes alone. And then (Ralph) Nader and his crowd says we're not paying sufficient taxes there. It's ridiculous."

Steel profits have been severely hurt in the past by the boom-bust nature of its labor negotiations. Every three years, as a strike deadline approaches, buyers hoard the metal and then after a settlement is reached, they work off their inventories while steel mills bank their furnaces and steelworkers are placed on lengthy layoffs. Because the problem is so damaging to both labor and management, the two sides have launched a joint campaign to supplant the strike threat with something else, perhaps binding arbitration.

Mr. Gott is hopeful that the campaign will succeed. "I think labor is more aware of steel's problems today than ever before."

Security analysts and others often contended that U.S. Steel's profits were low because managerial bureaucracy was so cumbersome. Mr. Gott clearly doesn't agree. "We have an amazing organizational structure here. We sell our products in every country of the world, produce in 30 countries, explore in 80 and have plants and offices in every state in the union, and all of these report to just a handful of executive vice presidents here."

He continues: "When I joined the company I was with the old Carnegie Steel division (in Ohio). We had other divisions in Birmingham and Gary. In my opinion it was a very inefficient setup. Since then we've pulled it all together into one operating structure and finally (two years ago) into this new building." The consolidation of offices into a single headquarters building, a resulting sizeable reduction in middle level managers and leadership in diversifying U.S. Steel away from basic steel to chemicals and raw materials are widely regarded as Ed Gott's finest accomplishments.

"I've never had a more fascinating experience in my life," he says of his 36 years with U.S. Steel. Then with a grin, he adds, "I guess it's been my life." Despite retirement, it will continue to be his life for a while, too. He'll remain a director of the company and a member of both its executive committee and finance committee. He also intends to remain in Pittsburgh, where he's on the board of Mellon National Corp., the bank holding company, and several civic organizations.

CONSIDER

1. Is it necessary for us to have to work at all?

2. Do business objectives have to conflict with personal, human objectives and values?

3. To what extent is it in the public interest for companies to earn bigger profits?

4. Who should bear the financial risk in developing a new product such as toothpaste? a jet plane? a nuclear power plant?

5. Why do companies provide liberal employee benefits such as paid vacations and medical benefits? Do these practices conflict with the objectives of the companies? With profits?

6. What do you imagine top executives will be like in the year 2000? The year 2050?

7. Do you believe that the profitability of a company depends on what its executives do?

8. When the survival of a business is on the line, how do you reconcile the need for profits and the need for social action, both of which draw upon the limited resources of the enterprise?

9. How important were the key men (Wood, Sears, Roebuck, and Rosenthal) in the growth of Sears?

10. What resources are necessary to build a business organization that can prosper?

CHALLENGES

Pick one of the companies listed in this chapter and find out what has happened to its revenues and profits since 1975. Look up the company name in The Wall Street Journal Index, the Business Periodicals Index, or one of the business financial services such as Moody's or Standard and Poor.

Look for an article in a current issue of The Wall Street Journal that reports a company action affecting environmental or social conditions. Assess what the company is doing and the effect on the firm's profits. If you disagree with the company or if you support the company's action, write a letter stating your view to the executive mentioned in the article or to the president of the company.

Write the Public Affairs Office at U.S. Steel in Pittsburgh for information on the company's efforts to reduce pollution. Analyze the current views of the company and compare them with thoughts outlined by Mr. Gott.

RECAP

Our business enterprise system is a copmpetitive system based on profits. Individuals (proprietors), partnerships, corporations, and cooperatives are the enterprises that comprise our system. Each type of business can buy, own, and sell property, and use it as it wishes (within the limits of social needs and law) to achieve profits in competition with other enterprises.

Business enterprise is human enterprise. The activities of business organizations are aimed at serving human needs. Businesses are governed and brought to life by people who work in them. The activities of the people in a business enterprise reflect individual interests and personal abilities and aspirations.

Even in major industrial corporations we find that the nature of the business reflects the personality and management style of the executives.

We have examined the historical development of a major retailer, Sears, Roebuck & Co. We see that this company was in large part shaped by the personal qualities of its founders and early executives. We have also examined the historical patterns and personal qualities of other executives, finding that backgrounds, habits, and personalities are quite diverse.

In this chapter we have examined some of the concerns that businessmen face in their companies: Profits, competition, environmental protection, and other responsibilities. Two chief executives, Richard Gerstenberg (General Motors) and Edwin Gott (Retired from U.S. Steel) presented their views of the role business organizations serve in our society. They held that profits are important not only to the survival and growth of business, but to our economic system itself.

Along with profit, however, are other objectives to be satisfied. Pollution control, product quality, providing jobs, safe working conditions, and providing needed goods and services at reasonable prices are all important to business.

A business can try to make a fast buck -- and successfully profit in the short-run. In a few years or less, however, most firms find that long-term survival depends on competing fairly and acting responsibly.

It is really fun to be in business. There's nothing quite like having an idea and making it come alive as a living, growing enterprise. That's entrepreneurship.

WORKSHEET NO. 1

NAME_____

INSTRUCTOR'S NAME_____

DATE_____

1. Do the biggest companies necessarily make the biggest profits?
    Explain.

2. Exxon's 1975 profits (after taxes) were $2,503,013,000. Do you
    feel these profits were excessive? Explain your answer.

3. Compare Mr. Gott's views about profits and the environment with those of Mr. Gerstenberg. With whom do you agree? Why?

4. If Mr. Gott's successor retires after 36 years of service (in 2009), do you think his observations will be much different at that time? What changes in industry, corporations, and society do you think will occur?

CHAPTER 2

Business and Society

A business enterprise must be a responsible member of society if it is to survive, be profitable, and grow. A business can take from society for the short-term, but for the long-term, it must be a good citizen.

There are some who argue that the "business of business is business" and that businesses and businessmen should stay out of social problems. They argue that we pay taxes to government so that government can take care of social issues leaving business alone to its real task, that of making profits.

Others, and they seem to be in the majority, believe that the business enterprise must attempt to balance the profit motive with a real concern for the society in which it operates. There is the assumption that business does have a "social responsibility" beyond simply making as much profit as possible.

In the development of new products, in manufacturing, in marketing, in building new facilities, and in virtually every other aspect of management, the needs of consumers and the public are of prime importance. The capacity of an enterprise to identify these critical needs and to meet them effectively is the most important factor in business.

We shall examine the various environments that the business must operate within: economic, social, political and physical. For most business enterprises the economic environment is of primary importance because the firm must be profitable in order to survive. But we shall also see that the other areas of the enterprise's environment are also quite important.

The need for greater consideration of envrionmental issues is clear. Society has made it plain that it will not tolerate uncontrolled pollution or wasteful use of scarce natural resources. A business enterprise must carefully consider the impact of its activities and operations upon environmental quality.

This is particularly true for a company such as Con Edison because its basic operation, the production of energy, creates pollution. Her the company faces the challenge of controlling the amount of pollution while also controlling the costs of operations and facilities for providing electrical power to meet the needs of the people.

Business must weigh the tradeoffs of profits for a better environment. Even small businesses, which have a relatively small impact by comparison with large corporations, must act responsibly.

A tool that is often used by companies today in assessing the trade-offs of profit versus pollution is an Impact Report. In building a new factory, for example, management would carefully study the effects of that construction on the surrounding environment -- the social, physical, economic, biological, and geological conditions.

A broader type of assessment, covering the full range of a company's activities including its positive contributions to society is the Social Audit. Companies provide this type of report to tell how they are acting as responsible members of society.

In this Chapter

Business and its Environment

You may have heard people say that:

"Businesssmen are money-grabbers."

"Industry and pollution go hand in hand."

"All business cares about is profit."

"The most profitable businesses exploit the workers and ruin the environment."

There may be some truth in these statements. Some businesses have acted irresponsibly in our society yet have survived and made profits for a time.

Today, however, most businessmen recognize that long-term success depends on how well they respond to social needs and changes in the environment.

The physical environment includes all of the resources available to the firm. These may include natural resources such as air, water, minerals, and lumber, or man-made resources such as roads, airports, buildings, and communications systems.

The economic environment is the market system by which these resources are made available and by which the firm sells its goods and services.

The political environment is the governmental system under which the firm operates. It may be a free democratic system or a controlled system. A few executives in a small number of companies have been found trying a little bit

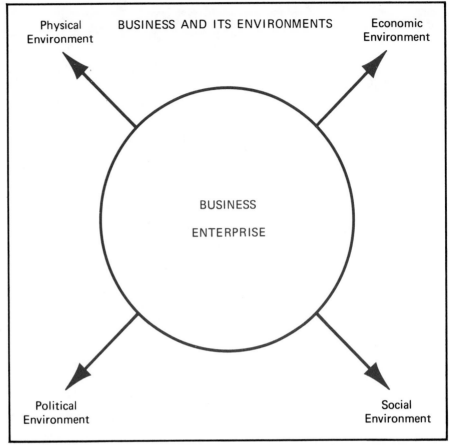

Physical Environment — BUSINESS AND ITS ENVIRONMENTS — Economic Environment

BUSINESS ENTERPRISE

Political Environment — Social Environment

too hard to influence the political environment. Bribes, kickbacks, and secret relationships are not the best way to relate to the political environment. Most companies have public affairs activities which seek to influence openly the course of events.

The social environment includes the prevailing attitudes, needs, and demands of the people in society. As long as business depends on choices by consumers, it must be sensitive to social change.

ISSUES

Businessmen today are facing a bunch of questions, all of them loaded.

Con Edison's chairman, Charles Luce, asks, "Should a utility spend $140 million to put 25 miles of power lines underground when they can be placed overhead for $12 million? If so, who should pay the added cost?"

Should a company pay for child care while a mother works? Should companies help pay for housing? transportation? political campaigns?

Should nuclear power plants be built even when a risk (however small) is known to exist regarding safety for residents nearby?

Stockholders recognize that they share the benefits of the company's operations: with consumers, employees, and the public at large. A corporation is not just a private organization, it is a social institution serving society's needs.

The Role of the Corporation in a Changing Era

At a recent meeting of senior management, discussion focused on TRW's responsibility to the constituents it serves: shareholders, customers, employees, government, plant communities and the general public. In answer to the question, "How do you define the social impact of a corporation?" Dr. Ruben F. Mettler, president of TRW, expressed the corporate policy:

"A meaningful definition requires looking at the three levels at which TRW should have a positive impact on society.

"The first level concerns the basic performance of the company as an economic unit. How many jobs does it provide? Is its productivity increasing? Is it profitable enough to pay employees and shareholders fairly? What is the quality of its goods and services? Does it provide stability and growth in employment? What is its contribution to the economy of the countries in which it operates? Clearly, TRW's primary social impact lies in our success as an economic institution efficiently producing quality products to fill society's needs.

"The next level concerns the quality of the conduct of our internal affairs. For example, are we ensuring equal employment and advancement opportunity for all? Is there job satisfaction? Do we provide proper health protection and safety devices and adequate pollution control? Is our advertising truthful?

"The third level concerns the additional things we do in relating to our external environment. This includes charitable and cultural contribution programs, youth projects, urban action programs, assistance to educational institutions, employees' participation in community affairs and our good government program. TRW focuses its activities in these areas in communities where we have plants because we can have the most meaningful impact there.

"It would be a mistake to think that any one, or two, of these levels fully defines our corporate impact, and hence our responsibility. We must meet our responsibilities at all three levels. The corporate constituents that we're concerned about—shareholder, employee, customer, government, community, general public—have a particular interest at each level.

"For example, shareholders are not just interested in their return on investment—a part of the first level. They want to be sure that our activities at the second level and third level will not adversely affect that investment. Employees are interested in more than their paycheck. They want to be treated fairly and to enjoy equal rights and opportunities. They want to be proud of their company's outside activities and to participate in them.

"We are determined to meet the needs and expectations of each of our constituents at each of these three levels. That's how I believe TRW will be measured and judged on its impact and its responsibilities to society."

Trade-offs for a Better Environment

Clean air, clean water, preserved wilderness, less noise, livable cites: These are the new national priorities long urged by ecologists and conservationists and now supported in growing numbers by the man in the street.

Until a decade ago, a few groups—the Sierra Club, the National Audubon Society, the Wilderness Society—and a few lone voices were pretty much talking to themselves in decrying our deteriorating habitat. But now, after years of choking smog, Torrey Canyons, Santa Barbaras, and the threat of silent springs, an aroused public is challenging the despoilers. With President Nixon's endorsement of environment as a major concern, it promises to become the issue of the '70s.

It is an issue that quickly raises other issues: What are we willing to give up to achieve a clean world? How committed are we to these high-priority demands? What are the trade-offs? And who will pay the bills? These are hard questions, social as well as economic.

To the growing band of environmentalists, however, healing the battered planet is of first importance—no less than a matter of survival. These crusaders cut across all economic and social lines; they come from the ghetto and the suburb, the factory and the campus. And the most militant among them view "quality of life" as the sum total of environment, embracing poverty, crime, and even war.

Industry's stake in this is obvious. But its view is a skeptical one. Businessmen simply do not believe that, in a showdown, consumers would accept a "lower standard of living." They believe that given a choice between having autos with pollution and banning autos to rid pollution, the American consumer will stick with his wheels. Partly because of this credibility gap, industry has not gone all out to end pollution.

The attitude may be summed up by Joseph S. Whitaker, coordinator of environmental health at Union Carbide Corp.: "Industry will do whatever people ask us to do and

whatever they will pay us for doing."

But companies, like consumers, must struggle to assess their own and their customers' commitments. A lot of executive brainpower is dealing with industry's special problem: How does a profit system accommodate to a demand that may yield no profit at all?

"Business has no choice. We will have to accept responsibility for caring for our world," says William F. May, chairman and president, of American Can Co. "We have to consider the social cost of a research development. We have to evaluate what we do by a new criterion, by non-market values."

May is not junking market values or profit criteria. But he has joined those businessmen who now recognize that something extra must be done to deal with pollution and anti-pollution costs.

"We aren't poor-mouthing about the costs of pollution abatement," says a spokesman of Scott Paper Co. "We recognize that controls have got to be." An executive of St. Regis Paper Co., says, "We are committed whether there are laws or not." After all, explains an official of General Foods Corp., "We live in the environment, too." But if non-market values are taken seriously, a company may have to reject a new product because it would create disposal problems. May says: "That would be a hard decision; that would require statesmanship."

Businessmen are in accord with Interior Secretary Walter Hickel's view, stated in January, that polluters will bear the cost of cleanup programs and will treat it as a cost of doing business. What this means is that pollution costs, like any costs, will turn up in the price or as a tax-deductible expense. "Environment simply becomes a new function to reckon with, alongside exploration, production, transportation, and marketing," says Benjamin I. Bragg, air and water conservation adviser at Standard Oil Co. (N.J.).

At Consolidated Edison Co. of New York, esthetics rate in new plans as they never did a few years ago, says W.E. Wall, vice-president. Perhaps that is a direct result of the company's five-year-long battle with the Scenic Hudson Preservation Conference, which spearheaded the move to kill Con Ed's proposed installation on Storm King Mountain. Rod Vandivert, executive director of the conference, says that this case was the first in which a court ruled that esthetics were a proper question in approving a plant location.

Exercises in restraint

There are a number of current examples of company investment in the anti-pollution fight. They illustrate why business is insistent on sharing the costs.

Jersey Standard is spending $200-million on two new Caribbean plants to produce low-sulfur oil. It sets no dollar figure on a possible approach to the oil-spill problem: a pollution-free tanker. Its domestic affiliate, Humble Oil & Refining Co., is midway in a five-year, $60-million program to upgrade its water pollution abatement at its refineries. The company will also have its share in the estimated $4-billion cost of de-leading gasoline. This change, says a spokesman, might amount to less than $10 a year for the consumer at the pump.

St. Regis Paper Co. expects to spend a minimum of $50-million on air and water pollution abatement over the next five years. Ford Motor Co., Henry Ford has said, is putting up half a billion dollars a year in the U. S. and Canada "to keep up with government standards and catch up with public expectations with respect to automotive safety and air pollution."

It took nearly $500,000 to bring to market Ingersoll-Rand Co.'s new quiet air compressor, the Whisperized Spiro-Flo, silent version of the excruciatingly noisy jackhammers used in construction. Environment costs average 5% of the total capital investment of American Can's Consumer & Service Products Div.; at its new super-clean paper mill at Halsey, Ore., they came to 10%. Union Carbide figures its anti-pollution measures average 3% of total capital outlays, but that average can include a hefty 20% in some instances. Standard Oil Co. of California spent $40-million through 1968 installing pollution abatement equipment at its large refineries at El Segundo and Redwood.

U. S. Steel Corp. spent $250-million over the last 10 years and sees no chance of a let-down. Scott Paper's outlays ran to $15-million in the late 1960s, and may total $75-million in this decade. Republic Steel Corp. spent around $30-million for air and water quality projects last year. It has others under construction that will cost some $50-million to complete. Southern California Edison Co. expects to be spending $6.5-million a year through 1975 to bury overhead distribution lines, and $1.7-million this year on landscaping and other esthetic matters.

One obvious result of the cost of cleaning up will be higher prices. Fearful that this will scare off customers, industry is looking for ways to offset the new costs. Bernard W. Recknagel, executive vice-president at St. Regis Paper, points out what may become a major route to balancing big anti-pollution budgets: slow down in expansion. He says that plans in the works will not be suddenly abandoned, but that perhaps those plans simmering on a back burner may be allowed to simmer a while longer.

Union Carbide officials say old plants need some work to

bring them up to antipollution standards. Sometimes a switch in the process will solve the problem. "In our processing work with chemicals and plastics, we used to concern ourselves with minimum investment and efficiencies of raw materials," says Leon Shechter, a research and development expert for the company. "Now we have a third ingredient, pollution costs. So we reassess the process. We trade off the original reactants for more expensive ones if the process results in fewer pollution controls costs."

While there are many points of view on how to attack the problem, on one point there is near unanimity: There ought to be a law.

"We are living in a fool's paradise if we think that industry will do anything until it is forced to," says Leo J. Weaver, president of newly formed Monsanto Enviro-Chem Systems, Inc. Every company shares the fear that the "good guy," who has raised prices to pay for cleaning up his operations, will lose out in the competition to the "bad guy" who has not bothered. American Can's May says that industry will go along readily if all live under the same rules.

What happened to Ingersoll-Rand's quiet air compressor illustrates the need for standards. W. L. Wearly, board chairman, explains that the "Whisperized" compressor, with a 25% premium on it, faced a competitive disadvantage—it does no more work for a contractor than a noisy machine. So, even though the Mayor's Task Force for Noise Control in New York, which inspired the development, rejoices in the soft-spoken machinery, sales are slow. Ironically, the city itself recently ordered 10 more noisy machines.

But now there seems to be a change of heart, or improved staff work. The city has challenged other manufacturers to give Ingersoll-Rand some competition by coming up with comparable compressors. And another antinoise device is being tested: GM's quiet sanitation truck. The city has bought 10 of them for a start.

Because there are no laws on the books that set noise levels for such equipment, standards fall to the discretion of city officials. Mandatory noise restrictions may come some day, Ingersoll-Rand hopes.

Juggling the politics

Local political leaders obviously recognize the political clout to be gained by grabbing a hefty pollution issue and running with it. But they frequently give the impression that pollution is too good a vote-catcher to be surrendered to a solution. Utilities such as Con Edison in New York could use encouragement from statehouses and city halls to find acceptable plant sites. But few elected officials have yet felt it safe to call for judicious weighing of alternatives in an issue involving power plants. That's one reason many companies conclude that this is the time for the federal government to step in.

Some would elevate the environment chief to Cabinet level to avoid bureaucratic entanglements. Centralization of authority would help speedy settlements of some problems. Con Ed's Wall suggests vesting the public utility commission with power to approve a plant location—which, cynics might say, eying the past performance of utility commissions, is tantamount to giving full authority to a utility itself. As it stands, Con Ed must get approval from some 30 agencies. Southern California Edison echoes the plea. To get approval for a nuclear power plant that it proposes, it will have to go through a maze of agencies having jurisdiction over water pollution, fish and game, water and parks, utilities, and atomic energy.

As for federal funds, Alan S. Cook, a vice-president of American Can, suggests an environmental Fannie Mae. It would be a corporation to receive and distribute special tax funds collected from industry. Cook says that the anti-pollution job is so great that we have to accumulate capital, and that a federal agency is best suited to handle it.

To some questions, the only answer seems to be: It is in the public good. "How do we convince a developer who wants to fill San Francisco Bay and put up a housing development on it that a mud flat would do more for the area?" asks Melvin B. Lane, publisher of Sunset Books, and the chairman of the San Francisco Bay Conservation & Development Commission. Sunset has put its money where Lane's mouth is. A few years ago, it lost advertising from timber interests when the magazine called for the preservation of the Redwoods. It also abandoned DDT ads last year.

Roger Hansen, chairman of the Rocky Mountain Center on Environment, says that businessmen will listen to discussions of how to preserve the locale. But, he says, few have gone so far as to consider not building that new plant. A Scott Paper spokesman answers that business does not have a "public be damned" attitude. "We operate by public consent," he says.

The quest for profits

Someday, there may be a more concrete answer. And that answer may be, in a word, profit. Every company dreams of making a profit from its anti-pollution programs; yet, sadly, most say economic returns amount to peanuts.

"Maybe we'll get back 10¢ on the dollar of our $200-million Caribbean investment," Jersey Standard officials say.

Time was, says Alan Cook, when pulp mills could get some economic benefit from selling sulfite wastes for chemical byproducts—and reduce water pollution at the same time. However, the sulfate process has pretty much made the sulfite process obsolete; besides, water pollution regulations militate against the sulfite. So the whole sulfite paper business faces a threat from ecology and technology. Oil refineries, which may recover sulfur or sulfuric acid for sale, report that sulfur is becoming a drug on the market.

A lot of experimental work—much with government backing—is going into recycling of wastes. This is a favorite solution of Richard D. Vaughan, the director of the Bureau of Solid Waste Management of the Health, Education & Welfare Dept. Recycling, as Vaughan points out, works two ways: It conserves resources and helps hold down the nation's waste management bill. The bill now runs to some $4.5-billion annually, and it would take an increase of 18.5% in expenditures over a 10-year period to do a really effective job, Vaughan estimates.

St. Regis Paper reports it has great faith in the recycling process. It has made excellent progress in recycling water and is working on chemicals and recovering fibers from packaging waste. Complete success might eliminate the need to raise prices to offset pollution control costs.

Many companies in packaging, chemicals, plastics, and related fields are deep in studies to ameliorate the waste disposal problem. General Foods Co. and Union Carbide agree that no feasible bio-degradable package—one that eats itself up—is ready for the market. Shechter of Union Carbide points out that there are technological difficulties in complying with regulations that demand that materials be both nonflammable and easily incinerated.

Efforts at recycling are not limited to packaging, though. Last December, the Bureau of Mines published a study on the possibility of dismantling a "typical junk" automobile to produce quality scrap: A cost evaluation showed that to process a composite car would require about $51 to produce about $56 worth of marketable ferrous and nonferrous metal products.

Technology's rewards

Occasionally, company efforts to clean their own house have had the happy effect of uncovering a new market. Monsanto Co. proudly displays as Exhibit A its fledgling subsidiary, Monsanto Enviro-Chem Systems, based in Chicago. Set up as a separate organization last October, it is expanding from an already profitable line the company had developed to handle some of its own pollution. The leading item Enviro-Chem sells is the Brink Mist Eliminator, developed by Monsanto to recover odorous or harmful "mists" from effluents from its chemical processes.

At the same time, Monsanto added a new line, its Biodize Systems for water treatment. Another new product eliminates sulfuric acid from flue gas, and still others are in the works. "People have begun to smell the rewards of technology," says Leo J. Weaver, president of Enviro-Chem.

Whatever unkind words the general public may have for technology, industry views it as the ultimate salvation. John O'Leary, until recently director of the Bureau of Mines, defends technology spiritedly. "There is nothing wrong with it. We have just told it to do the wrong things. We told DDT to kill the bugs and it did, but it poisoned the lakes. Santa Barbara citizens say: 'We don't need the oil, or at least, don't drill in our backyard.' Neither solution is sound. There shouldn't have been an oil spill in Santa Barbara. Technology should have prevented it." And more than one major competitor of Union Oil Co. agrees.

Considering that environmentalists are urging nothing less than a planetary housecleaning, it is little wonder that they disagree over procedure. Paul Ehrlich of Stanford preaches the doom of overpopulation. Others say that at least in the U. S. it is the distribution rather than the number that is harmful. "I am not afraid of people," Candeub said flatly. "You can handle people if you plan for them."

Right now one can say only that—clear down to the fourth-graders—people are asking uncomfortable questions. To business, they say: "What else have you done besides earn a profit?"

And they demand an answer, though they don't know what it should be. The militant young throw their gauntlets at business: Neither business nor government knows "where it's at," they say. Others would agree with the Caltech student who says, "The government should harness business's natural greed for the public good—business is no worse than any other group." The technology that put man on the moon can keep him alive and well and living on the earth, they feel.

Maybe man is powerless to stop the polar ice cap, says Hansen. "But you can clean up litter." To many consumers, thousands of small steps may provide the answer at last.

After all, what people want is essentially simple. Charles E. Little, president of Open Space Institute in New York, sums it up in his brochure, Challenge of the Land. He speaks of the American Dream in these words: "The flickering image of grass, trees, and 'a good place for the kids to grow up'."

Simple though it is, it will take a massive social, economic and technological effort to get us there. But maybe the oldest priority of all will enable us to keep the polar ice cap in place.

ConEd vs. the World

For all the good things electricity does for both the social and the natural environment, man has not yet found a way to produce and transmit electric power in the quantities people want without some impact on the natural environment.

Consolidated Edison Company of New York (Con Edison) and other utilities have taken steps to reduce this impact. Con Ed has spent more than $250 million in 1975 and 1976 annually for costs related to environmental protection. This includes the costs of burning very low sulpher oil, the extra costs of putting transmission and distribution lines underground, and other costs associated with meeting Federal, state, and local laws pertaining to the environment.

Most of these expenditures are essential for an energy company serving a city such as New York, but some may be costing consumers more than the value returned. Con Ed strives to strike a fair balance between the benefits of environmental protection and the high costs involved.

Particularly high cost are efficient precipitators, tall stacks, pollution monitors, and boilers which produce low amounts of nitrous oxides. Con Ed also has underway a $15 million five-year study of the Hudson River to assess, principally, the ecological effect of plant operations on fish populations and other aquatic life in the river.

Con Ed points out that insofar as water quality is concerned, the impact of the company's plants is small. The big water pollution problem in the river is sewage and storm water runoff. The sewage discharges come from local governments. The storm run-off comes from both city streets and upstate farmlands.

The Hudson river, heavily polluted for years with all manner of human and industrial wastes, is beginning to regain its old sparkle. Much credit is due the use of electricity in treating wastes before they flow into the river -- electricity produced by Con Ed. One company served by Con Ed has spent $8 million on equipment and uses 7 million kilowatthours of electricity a year to overcome the discharge of chemicals into the river.

In 1962 Con Ed came up with the idea of a hydro-electric plant on the Hudson River (the Storm King Plant). The idea has faced bitter opposition from environmentalists, who charge that the project would destroy the scenery and possibly damage fisheries in the area. Yet the single plant would allow the retirement of twelve older fossil-fueled (oil or coal) generators located in New York.

By 1976 the project was still contested. Con Ed had invested $34,329,891 in the pumped storage project, plus $1,714,257 for the land. "It remains the Company's conviction that Cornwall is the most economical and reliable source of peaking power...."

ABOUT CON ED

Con Edison's primary business is, of course, making and delivering electricity. The company's 2.8 million electric customers consume about 33 billion kilowatt-hours of electricity. This electricity is produced in conventional power plants (burning fuels such as oil and gas to make steam to turn the turbine-generators) nuclear plants, and gas-turbine installations.

One of the big problems Con Ed has faced in recent years has been a growing demand for electricity. The company wanted to build more plants to produce power for the people, but the people objected to the potential pollution that would come with the new facilities.

In 1973, demand had grown to just about match the generating capacity of the system. Those were the days of brown-outs when the weather was hot and air conditioners were going full blast.

Then came the oil crisis and the price of conventional fuels (mainly oil) went sky high. Con Ed wanted to use coal, but that has been banned for use in New York City. So what happened was that costs went up, and were passed along to consumers as higher prices. Revenue per kilowatthour shot up from 5.2¢ in 1973 to 8.2¢ in 1975.

As you would expect, consumers cut back on usage (in part due to a promotion campaign by Con Ed to "save a watt") and the major crunch of supply was eased for a while.

Con Ed is still in the middle, however, with the demands of consumers, stockholders, and the public to satisfy all at once.

Con Ed expects use of electricity to grow in New York, reaching a peak demand of 11,000,000 kilowatts sometime in the 1970's. The time may not be far off, though, because the total usage (at the summer's peak) is at 8,000,000 kilowatts now. Con Ed believes that this growing demand requires a new million-kilowatt generation station every two years.

The problem of finding suitable sites where people will let Con Ed build plants and the related problems of assuring environmental protection really slow down the building process and add significantly to costs.

THE PAST AT CON ED

Life wasn't always like this at Con Edison. The company has been on the scene since 1823, when the second gas company in the country was organized. It was the New York Gas Light Company, a corporate ancestor of Con Edison.

The electric part of the business dates to 1882, when the Edison Electric Illuminating Company of New York started supplying electricity from the country's first commercial central generating station for incandescent service. Thomas A. Edison, the inventor of the first practical light bulb, established the historic Pearl Street station in lower Manhattan.

Con Ed is in the steam business too -- to heat buildings in New York. That business also started in 1882, as the New York Steam Corporation -- and merged with Con Edison in 1954. If you're in the city today you may see steam coming up through manholes in the streets. It's an old, reliable system that still serves a lot of customers. The World Trade Center towers, the Empire State Building, several buildings in Rockefeller Center, Penn Station, Grand Central Station, and the Pan-Am Building are among those heated today by Con Ed steam.

Most of the steam is made at the electric generating plants. The rest comes from steam plants. The steam has the power equivalent to an electricity demand of almost 600,000 kilowatts, enough to serve a city the size of Syracuse, New York.

Of course, Con Ed also supplies natural gas to nearly half the people who live in New York City and Westchester County. The availability of gas is limited, however, and so this means sales are restricted. Sometimes service even has to be interrupted if supplies are short.

Con Edison has all the burdens of other utility companies plus special problems that the company gets by being in New York. It has been plagued by mechanical breakdowns, construction delays, political attacks, and cost pressures.

Con Ed is a big business, a strong private enterprise that carries its share of social responsibilities. The company regards itself as a leader in the fight against pollution even though many New Yorkers regard them as blatant polluters. The company has taken large steps toward reducing noise, pollution, and unsightliness, and at the same time has satisfied the city's needs for power. The company's profits are regulated by the government, through a process of approving rates charged.

Small Business Must Face Ecology

Environmental concerns have created important problems for managers of small business enterprises. Already hard pressed for cash to use in building their businesses, they must now comply with tough governmental regulations designed to preserve our environmental quality.

Small businesses are at a disadvantage, by comparison with large businesses, because they are less flexible, less influential, and they don't have the capability to plan ahead as large businesses do. Also, they often don't have the specialized expertise needed to respond to such demands.

Generally, small businesses don't have up-to-date facilities and equipment, and are hard-pressed to make them pollution free. That takes a lot of money, higher costs. Higher costs mean lower profits and possibly business losses -- or it means higher prices in a marketplace that was tough to compete in to begin with.

As a result, some small businesses have actually closed down operations because they couldn't afford to make the necessary changes.

EXAMPLES

An upstate New York food processor with sales of $15 million has been disposing of its waste product for more than two decades by channeling it into the municipal sewer system. This practice caused no particular problem until the number of homes in the town started to grow.

Now the combination of the residential sewage and the company's product waste has taxed the present sewer system to its limit. The town, with the backing of state health officials, has ordered the company to build and maintain its own primary treatment facility or cease operations that produce the waste. The initial capital costs and ongoing expenses of the treatment have placed a major hardship on the company, which was struggling to stay profitable all along.

A builder of vacation homes in Pennsylvania recently closed its doors after new health regulations made the costs of building prohibitive. Up until last year the company had built modest vacation homes in development style (only several basic styles, low cost, high volumes). However, the increasing number of homes built plus soil conditions in the area caused health officials to severely restrict new home construction.

"Goodness me! You mean my little pie shop is polluting the air?"

Drawing by Minter, © 1971. The New Yorker Magazine, Inc.

The direct costs aside, the larger company is usually better able to afford delays, interruption, or even cessation of operations which require retooling, installation of pollution control devices, or other changes. The loss of production and sales for only a few days is often critical to a small company. Larger firms may have numerous plants producing the same products at different locations. Small companies can't switch production to other plants when one plant faces environmental problems.

One could argue, as many people have, that a small company which fails to generate sufficient profits to operate according to the rules -- normally accepted standards including environmental quality standards, is a marginal operator at best and should be allowed to go out of business, if necessary. Indeed, many such small firms will do just that.

PROBLEMS AND SOLUTIONS

The costs of improvements for ecology may be great, even greater than a small business can bear. Small businesses, generally defined as enterprises having annual revenues of $25 million or less, have fewer resources, less access to credit, a weaker voice in industry and in government, and less flexibility in controlling their own destinies.

It may be possible for some small firms to convert wastes into desirable byproducts, which may be added to the product line or which will at least defray the costs of conversion. One company that made cider and vinegar from apples now sells the tons of residue remaining as cattle feed. Wood chips and particles left over from lumber mills are now collected and sold as garden mulch or pressed together as fire logs.

In some cases, small businesses may change products entirely, thus avoiding the waste or the pollution impact. Such changes are major, however, and are possible only if the company is in good economic health.

SPECIAL RIGHTS

A small business has no special right to continue to pollute just because the company is small and may not be able to afford the costs of pollution control. The need for action by a small business may be balanced in a small community that depends on the firms for jobs, products, or tax support. Society needs small businesses -- as producers but not as polluters.

WHAZZIT?

BANKRUPTCY

The condition of a person or an enterprise that is unable to pay its debts.

SOCIAL AUDIT

An evaluation of the social performance of the business. Its aim is to point out areas for future improvement that will serve the needs of society.

IMPACT REPORT

A written report of a project's potential effects on its surrounding environment, such as the proposed construction of a building or a dam.

DIVERSIFICATION

An attempt by a company to achieve stability in sales and profits by expanding the number and variety of its products and services.

What is an Impact Report?

As the name suggests, an environmental impact report is a written analysis of the potential effects of a new building, a power plant, an airport, a dam, a road, or other project on the ecology of the area.

The ultimate aim is to discover, long before the work on the building is begun, any potentially adverse effects the project would have on the area. Where possible adverse effects are found, the report offers recommendations for removing or reducing them.

The size and costs of impact reports vary widely, according to the size of the project studied. A builder of a small office building may pay $1000 or so for a brief report. A multi-million dollar power plant would require a study with a cost well into six figures.

Environmental factors studied usually include the physical, social, economic, and bilogical. Most impact reports follow a format devised by the federal government. The services of specialists are used in the various areas and in compiling the final report. For example, engineers would study the pollution-causing elements of a project. Aerial photographs using infrared film may be used to detect underground water, while on the ground geologists look for unstable soil and possible earthquake fault lines.

Meanwhile, biologists may investigate the variety of animal and plant life in the area, including the underwater exploration of nearby bodies of water, to study the possible effect of the proposed project on marine life.

Sociologists and economists would study the possible burdens the project would place on the local community -- from streets to schools -- and whether the tax structure would fairly cover the added social costs.

The impact report also considers the appearance of a project, examining the landscaping features and the ways the natural landscape of the area may be preserved.

Archeologists may study the historical value of the area to find ways of avoiding potential damage to important relics, ruins, or fossils.

All of the data are usually put into a computer, to provide a full analysis of the environmental data. The final report provides findings and conclusions along with the recommendations for project planning.

WHAZZIT?

TRUSTEE

An individual assigned by the court to control the operations of a bankrupt company while it is attempting to reorganize.

SMALL BUSINESS

An enterprise is considered to be small if in manufacturing it employs fewer than 250 people. In wholesaling yearly sales should not exceed $5 million or $1 million in retailing. Another rule of thumb that is used is any business with sales below $25 million.

Why Business Cares

"We travel together, passengers on a little spaceship, dependent on its vulnerable reserves of air and soil; all committed for our safety to its security and peace; preserved from annihiliation only by the care, the work, and, I say, the love we give our fragile craft. We cannot maintain it half fortunate, half miserable, half confident, half despairing, half slave to the ancient enemies of man, half free in a liberation of resources undreamed of until this day. No craft, no crew can travel safely with such vast contradictions. On their resolution depends the survival of us all."

-- Adlai Stevenson
   (1900 - 1965)

No business enterprise can isolate itself. We are all part of one community of man on one "spaceship". As the community we serve prospers or falters, we prosper or falter. For this reason and because it's the right thing to do, most businesses try their best to contribute to the well being of society and the physical environment.

Companies are working to improve the quality of life in their communities. They are involved in jobs, education, health, housing, recreation, and cultural programs.

Con Edison, for example, makes substantial contributions in each of these areas. In education, money is directed toward experimental programs which are trying to reach economically and culturally deprived youth with special educational needs. Other programs reach students from kindergarten through college -- including help to schools for extension programs reaching adults who couldn't afford to go to college.

Jobs are the heart of a community's well being. Not only does Con Ed see that everyone gets a fair shake in its own employment, but in addition is working with community groups to train and place minority group members on jobs.

A growing number of minority businesses are struggling to grow. Con Ed buys goods and services from these enterprises and often helps them obtain business.

Through its consumer affairs programs, Con Ed supports programs for improved housing, tenant education, consumer education and assistance, and health. Company contributions also support cultural programs, special events, and institutions.

The War Business Must Win

Robert Dehlendorf II, president of Arcata National Corp., remembers the day all too well. It was in August, 1965, and Dehlendorf was in a plane high over Los Angeles. "I couldn't believe what I saw below," he recalls. "It looked like a city being bombed. Pillars of smoke were rising block after block. Tanks moved up and down the streets, their hatches closed and turrets swiveling." What Dehlendorf saw were the violent beginnings of the Watts riots. When the flames and pillage subsided, 34 people were dead, $40-million worth of property was destroyed, and for the first time many Americans had come to realize that there were explosive discontents ticking away within their ghettos.

For Charles Luce, board chairman of New York's Consolidated Edison Co., the day that will long live in memory came in 1966. That June, a special city task force warned: "All the ingredients now exist for an air pollution disaster of major proportions." Sure enough, on Thanksgiving, pollution from two states filled the skies over New York City and poisoned the air beyond endurance. When the thick, sooty shroud lifted, 168 people were dead.

In Cleveland, Walter O. Spencer, executive vice-president of Sherwin-Williams Co., still shivers when he thinks about last June 22. On that day, the oily, oozing Cuyahoga River—a waterway so reeking of filth that it cannot support even leeches, sludge worms, and other common low forms—actually caught on fire and damaged two railroad bridges that span it.

Nationwide concern. Sherwin-Williams' Spencer, Con Ed's Luce, and Arcata National's Dehlendorf are typical of thousands of businessmen who are concerned about the deterioration of our social and physical environment and who are trying—though often with mixed results—to do something about it.

After the Watts riots, Dehlendorf organized the country's first small business investment company chartered exclusively to finance minority entrepreneurs. Partly as a result of New York's killer smog, Con Ed's Luce has mounted a major antipollution effort that one government official describes as a "model" for the industry. Following the Cuyahoga River fire, Sherwin-Williams' Spencer ordered a reassessment of some of his company's water

control measures, and made cleaner water almost a personal crusade.

Bread cast upon the waters

Many businessmen still shrug off such involvement and the torturous questions it raises as so much "do-goodism" or charity. They feel, as MIT Economist Paul Samuelson puts it, that "the business of business is business" and "under laissez faire, everybody's business [that is, the public weal is nobody's business]."

That may be true in the rare cases where companies are responding purely out of some lofty sense of mission. But increasingly, they are responding to something much more basic: the profit motive.

"There is no longer anything to reconcile, if there ever was, between the social conscience and the profit motive," Henry Ford II has said. "Improving the quality of society—investing in better employees and customers for tomorrow—is nothing more than another step in the evolutionary process of taking a more far-sighted view of return on investment." Often, the return is more immediate. As the president of a major job-training company says trenchantly, if somewhat earthily: "Whenever a human problem is solved, it's always because somebody has found a way to make a buck on it."

Public pressure. At the same time, business is also responding to stiff public pressures. A poll by Opinion Research Corp. shows that 65% of American stockholders feel that business should play an active role in the war on poverty. H. I. Romnes, board chairman of American Telephone & Telegraph Co., considers it a matter of basic survival. "We must remember," he notes, "that most Americans now live in the cities, and they constitute the great majority of our customers. The problems of the city, therefore, are our problems, and the future of the cities is our future."

Where the focus is greatest

If there are profits and pressures, there are also problems. And nowhere are the problems greater—or the stakes higher—than in the social or ghetto area, industry's biggest single focus of involvement. "This is the one area where business cannot afford to fail," says Dr. Courtney Brown, retired dean of Columbia University's Graduate School of Business. "Yet it is also the one area where business—because of the emotional intangibles involved—will never completely succeed." Consider the plight of the private organizations for social uplift:

The Urban Coalition, set out to mobilize all major urban institutions and map a coordinated attack on ghetto ills. Today, the coalition has blossomed out to 48 affiliates, has organized some laudable programs, and generated a dizzying array of facts, figures, and ephemera. But on both a national and local level, it is beset by factional disputes and proliferating bureaucracies.

The National Alliance of Businessmen, organized a few months after the Urban Coalition, now has 18,500 member companies, has placed more than 200,000 ghetto residents in jobs, and is shooting for 614,000 placements by June, 1971. However, large companies still dominate the hiring, partly because many small and medium-sized companies are not committing themselves. On a recent speaking visit to New York, NAB President Paul Kayser admitted that he found it "absolutely incredible, the number of people who don't know who we are."

Many local groups are also problem-plagued. Boston's Opportunities Industrialization Center, a three-year-old job training agency, set out this year to raise $900,000. It came up with only $225,000. The city's teen-age Youth Alliance hoped to drum up $150,000. It has raised less than one-third of that. Last summer, the New Detroit Committee—possibly anticipating some of the same problems—merged its money-raising effort with the local United Fund. In the future, the committee plans to concentrate more on performing a catalytic role and getting others to pick up the bill.

Reevaluations. Such problems are partly the cause, partly the effect, of a broad shake-out in the business commitment. "This was bound to happen," says Louis Winnick, an urban specialist with the Ford Foundation. "A businessman is a pragmatist. If he puts something in one end, he wants to see something else pop out the other end. And in this area you just don't get quick, clean results."

William Hart, manager of state and urban affairs for General Electric Co., claims the shake-out does not reflect a lessening sense of commitment so much as a growing sense of reality. "You have to go into this field with a full hand of cards," Hart stresses. "You're not just dealing with joblessness. You're also dealing with poor housing, poor schools, lack of training—people caught in an appalling web of frustration and despair. And you have to know what you're up against."

More than money. In some cases, what it takes is not so much money as hard business savvy and resourcefulness. Take the case of Smith, Kline & French Laboratories, which is headquartered in one of North Philadelphia's seediest and most ramshackle neighborhoods. To encourage a local developer to spruce up the area's housing, Smith, Kline offered to cover 40% of the interest on his renovation loans. By last week, 70 large houses had been renovated and converted into 200 modern, low-cost apartments. The cost to Smith, Kline: only $4,000.

Smith, Kline also helped the neighborhood convert a big, century-old limestone mansion into a community center at only a fraction of the normal cost. It pulled off this sleight-of-hand by helping arrange first and second mortgages plus long-term lease commitments from several tenants. "Government can outspend us," admits President Thomas M. Rauch, "but it can't out-talent us."

Frustrations of job training

Another quality just as important is patience, especially in the one area where industry is applying most of its muscle: job training. Equitable Life Assurance Society began a job-training program for high school dropouts in 1962. Within six months, 45% of its dropouts had dropped out. Turnover for the year stood at 67%—more than three times that of the company as a whole. "It didn't take us long to learn," one Equitable vice-president recalls, "that dropouts lived in a world outside our experience."

When Chrysler Corp. began hiring the hardcore unemployed, Chrysler's President Virgil Boyd thought he knew what "hardcore" meant. "I was wrong," he admits. "Hardcore refers not to those without steady jobs, but those who are not equipped for any job. Not the unemployed, but the unemployable—those who are unable to fill out even a simple job application." Some of Chrysler's applicants signed on for job training, then never showed up. Others who did report were notoriously late. As Chrysler registered those who did report, it found that many of them had never been counted in a census, had no Social Security number, had never registered to vote, and belonged to no organizations of any kind. "In most of the accepted senses," Boyd says, "they really didn't even exist."

Stark profile. From his experience in working with the disadvantaged, Stephen Keating, president of Honeywell, Inc., draws a stark portrait of the damp and subterranean world of the ghetto. "Among disadvantaged youths of 18," he says, "probably not more than 25% have lived with both parents all their lives. In their homes there is little tradition of work, education, family stability, community responsibility, or individual achievement." In fact, he adds, the average middle-class American probably shares more in common with his counterpart in France or Japan than with the disadvantaged family

living only a few blocks away. A Honeywell interviewer tells the story of offering a young, disadvantaged youth a job, and explaining that the shift started at 8 a. m. The applicant replied, without a trace of sarcasm or rancor: "I don't get up that early"—and out the door he went.

To help prepare the disadvantaged for the work-a-day world, many companies are even going into the classroom. In Cleveland's Hough area, GE donated a $5-million, 200,000-sq.-ft. building to the local school system, and helped set up a "school-factory" to educate and train high school dropouts. After seven months, the school-factory has trained and placed 335 workers (of an original 435 who signed up), and is now training another 36.

In Detroit, Chrysler "adopted" one of the area's largest and toughest inner-city high schools. "Too often in the past," says Lynn Townsend, board chairman and chief executive officer at Chrysler, "education has been designed to prepare young people for college." Chrysler refocused—with promising success—on the masses who never make it to college. It created special courses in clerical work and other basic business skills; it also installed an automobile service training center, complete with a one-ton crane, floor hoists, an engine analyzer and all the other appurtenances of a well-stocked service station.

To add a little incentive, Boron Oil Co. agreed to place advanced shop students into related jobs outside school. Boron and Chrysler also set up a savings plan at a local black-owned bank to encourage the students to salt away at least 10% of their wages every week. As seed money, each company kicked $5 into every account.

Across town, Michigan Bell Telephone Co. formed a similar partnership and even fashioned a remedial summer program for 60 students. Recalls Edward N. Hodges III, Michigan Bell's employment supervisor, the guiding godfather behind the "adoption," and a Negro who came from a broken home himself; "We told the summer school teachers, 'Be as innovative as you want. You're not under the auspices of the board of education.'" In the English class, students read such books as Claude Brown's incendiary Manchild in the Promised Land, and wrote "some rather raw" short stories. In math, the instructor invented a card game to teach fractions. After six weeks, the summer students boosted their achievement scores as much as two or three years. "I don't think we taught the kids that much," Hodges feels. "I think they were just turned on."

In most cities, the dark mood and decay of the ghettos has spread like some inexorable malignancy into adjacent downtown areas. For years, many companies responded by packing up and decamping to the suburbs, thus draining away precious

tax revenues. Increasingly, however, many downtown companies are now sticking fast and trying to breathe new life into their moribund neighborhoods.

The decision to stay is not always easy. "Economics have a lot to do with it," says Harry B. Warner, president of B. F. Goodrich Co. "But if the cost of renovating and rehabilitating is about the same as starting up in a new location, the decision to stay in a given community is fairly easy"—if only because companies today tend to get more involved with their communities and build closer ties.

Atlanta's example. Without doubt, one of the biggest single downtown revitalizations has taken place in Atlanta. In the late 1950s, Atlanta was a big, slumbering Southern city where lethargy hung in the air like Spanish moss. Then in 1961, the Chamber of Commerce kicked off "Forward Atlanta"—a brass-band campaign to lure more business and industry to the area. And slowly but perceptibly, Atlanta began to snap out of its doze. To get things rolling, the chamber asked the public for $1,500,000. Business immediately pledged $1-million, and 600 volunteers raised the rest. Since then, Atlanta has averaged 27,000 new jobs a year, and more than $1.5-billion worth of new construction has sprouted into the skyline.

Progress, however, has brought problems, or, as the city's late publisher, Ralph McGill, once cracked: "The fleas come with the dog." And the peskiest flea of all is the city's traffic mess. Many of the city's highways carry three times the traffic they were designed for. Some suburbanites spend two hours a day commuting 15 or 20 mi. To head off the threat this poses for downtown business, Atlanta merchants threw their support behind a proposed rapid transit system, and Richard Rich, chairman of Rich's, Inc., chaired the Metropolitan Atlanta Rapid Transit Authority. But last November, the voters, already overburdened with taxes, roundly defeated the system.

Mass transit pitch. In the half-dozen other cities where rapid transit systems have been proposed, businessmen are similarly trying to drum up support. They are also backing plans for improvement and expansion of existing systems—improvements long overdue.

Some of the improvements are already on the way—and stirring plenty of activity among manufacturers. To handle its expanding mass-transit business, GE recently set up a special Transit Systems Dept., and over the last 24 months has supplied propulsion equipment for more than 900 cars on five systems—a 50% spurt over the preceding 24 months. Westinghouse has also boosted its business; last July, the company's Transportation Div. picked up its biggest contract yet—covering the computerized controls for San Francisco's

Pollution: 'As the pressures continue to grow, businessmen are slowly—if reluctantly—stepping up their antipollution efforts. They moan and they gripe. But in the end, they comply'

sleek, $1.2-billion Bay Area Rapid Transit (BART).

Stepping up pollution control. More efficient mass transit would not only help clean up traffic jams. It would also clean up air pollution caused by traffic jams. And in the end, that might be one of industry's biggest contributions at a time when it is under mounting pressure to protect the environment.

Five years ago, California allowed new cars bought in that state to spew out as much as 900 parts of hydrocarbons per million parts of exhaust gases. Today, the law permits only 275 ppm and, after next year, that will drop to 120 ppm. So far, no other states have slapped such stiff regulations on auto makers. But the federal government is expected to follow suit, and is also talking a tougher line on pollution control in general. Last week, for instance, U. S. Steel Corp., Republic Steel Corp., Jones & Laughlin Steel Corp., Interlake Steel Corp., Eagle-Picher Industries, Inc., and the city of Toledo were all on federal notice to clean up their water pollution or face prosecution. The government plans to move on other polluters along the Savannah and Passaic rivers.

Cleaning tab. Then, of course, there is the thorniest problem of all: cost. Senator Jackson estimates that the total tab for cleaning up the nation's pollution over the next five years at $15-billion for air, between $26-billion and $29-billion for our lakes and streams, and some $15-billion for solid waste removal.

High cost of pollution. The cost of pollution goes beyond tougher government regulation and an outraged citizenry. Incomplete combustion in factories and power plants now wastes some $300-million worth of sulfur each year. Once in the air, these and other pollutants corrode metal, weaken and fade fabrics and leathers, crack rubber, discolor paint, eat away concrete and building stone, and destroy $500-million worth of crops and livestock each year. The total annual tab for air pollution: $12-billion. For water pollution: several billion dollars more.

By tightening its water control measures, the pulp, paper, and paperboard industry now recovers 1-million tons of reusable pulp fiber previously lost into rivers and lakes. American Can Co. converts its waste into a concentrate used for industrial adhesives and vanilla. Schenley In-

dustries, Inc., is turning its distillery wastes into cattle feed. The Tennessee Valley Authority and U. S. Public Health Service are converting raw sewage and municipal waste into soil fertilizer.

Last year, San Francisco was even considering a proposal for changing garbage into electricity. This would involve building a $20-million incinerator that could burn up to 2,000 tons of garbage a day. The energy thus created would produce steam which, in turn, would produce electricity for Pacific Gas & Electric Co.

Too big a bite. Partly because there has not been enough close local dialogue, business ended up promising far more than it could ever deliver. The result is that performance has not been everything it could be. In a recent National Industrial Conference Board survey of 114 cities, local officials related industry's urban improvement efforts as only "fair." "That doesn't mean," notes a member of the University of Chicago's Center for Urban Studies, "that business has not reacted and is not aware of the necessary change needed. What it does mean is that business certainly has much more to do."

The Social Audit

The idea of an audit of a business organization's activities stems from the accounting function. For years, companies have been required to submit their accounting records to open inspection by outsider "auditors", or public accountants.

An audit of a firm's social impact in its environment is taking this traditional practice one step further. The social audit is an evaluation of the responsible social performance of a business. That's different from the economic performance -- which is measured primarily by profits.

Recently, Chase Manhattan Bank retained an outside consulting firm to assess its social performance. IBM, Kimberly-Clark, and others have set up internal committees of directors and top managers to appraise how they're doing and how the company measures up to society's expectations.

An executive of Citibank noted, "It's just common sense that if any corporation operates in a social environment, it has to be attuned to it. Otherwise the employees aren't going to like the place, the customers aren't going to be satisfied, and the government's going to be on their back."

Of course, there is no consensus as to just what a corporation's social responsibility is, or how social performance should be measured. What should be the standards of appraisal? "How many unskilled minorities should be employed and trained; at what cost? How far should pollution control be carried? How involved should the company be in community programs and cultural activities? What is the company's responsibility in consumer affairs? Should officials take a stand and speak out on public issues, such as equal housing opportunity? What are reasonable profits? When are products of sufficiently high quality? The list is endless.

Like Chase, Bank of America (San Francisco) brought in outside observers to assist its own staff take stock of what it has done and what it should be doing. Exxon developed a policy statement along these lines for internal management use.

The aim of an audit is not to find fault with business practices, but to point out areas for improvement in the future that will better serve the needs of society. Thus an audit is more than a static study. It is an evaluation of a business enterprise's social responsibility.

Today there are no particular methods or approaches that are accepted as the standard way to do a social audit. Even the objectives of an audit may vary among firms.

What subjects have been included in social audits? At the top of the list are environmental protection, equal employment opportunity, and the impact of business decisions. Also considered are growth, efficiency, education, employment, labor relations, training, community involvement, conservation and recreation, culture and the arts, medical care, and government.

If the focus were to be broader, subjects may include poverty, urban development, prices, population growth, aesthetics, urban transportation, and research and development impact of the firm.

Through the social audit we may be able to build in to business certain reforms we feel will make business more able to serve our society's best interests. At the same time, businessmen feel that the net benefit comes back to the firm, as a strengthening self-evaluation and redirection effort.

Beyond business, the experience in social audits may stimulate similar audits in governmental, nonprofit, and other organizations.

A "Social Audit" by David Rockefeller

David Rockefeller is chairman and chief executive officer of The Chase Manhattan Bank.

Recent trends in business criticism differ from the Populist-Progressive-New Deal attacks of the past in certain significant respects that could have a profound bearing on the future role of business in our society.

Today's criticism focuses on performance. One frequent charge is that, through their performance, corporations are making our communities dirtier, more polluted and less congenial. Another, that corporations are too heavily oriented toward profits at the expense of service to the community. Still another, that corporate performance is too often flawed because minorities don't participate equally, because waste goes unchecked, and because output is sometimes unfit for human use.

Business must respond to these criticisms through consistently better performance effectively communicated. It should also devise incentive systems which will lead more private firms to serve public needs while at the same time making a profit. Encouraging steps in this direction have been taken in experiments with what has come to be known as "performance contracting." The most significant example is in the field of education where private companies have taken over public classrooms in some thirty cities and have tried novel teaching methods.

If private businesses could work out a sound basis on which they could get into the field of public-problem solving, they could not only contribute creatively to solutions, but would also respond dramatically to the critics' charge that business is failing "to relate and to help" in community service.

Many of today's critics—not all, to be sure, but many—appear to feel that the system is beyond reform, and that the only solution is to destroy the capitalist framework and start over. Considering the seriousness and growing prevalence in some quarter of this attitude, it seems to me that businessmen have no choice but to respond by becoming reformers themselves, making a conscious effort to adapt the market system to our changing social, political and technological environment.

The question really comes down to this: Will business leaders seize the initiative to make necessary changes and take on new responsibilities voluntarily, or will they wait until these are thrust upon them by law?

Some adjustments in the social contract, binding business to society, are inevitable. There may have to be new laws to force consideration of the quality-of-life dimension so that more socially responsive firms will not suffer a competitive disadvantage.

The allocation of scarce capital to meet social needs, even at the expense of greater economic efficiency, is another area that will come in for attention. Unless business and finance take the initiative in this area, government may decree that a businessman must be concerned not only to find the quantity of money he requires but also to obtain specific authorization to use the funds in the manner he proposes. Investment projects not sufficiently high on the "social agenda" may have to pay a premium or wait in line for approval. There are already prominent members of Congress who would favor precisely this kind of directed investment.

Because of the growing pressure for greater corporate accountability I can foresee the day when corporations may be required to publish a "social audit" certified by independent accountants.

It is up to businessmen to make common cause with other reformers —whether in Government or on the campus or wherever—to prevent the unwise adoption of extreme and emotional remedies, but on the contrary to initiate necessary reforms that will make it possible for business to continue to function in a new climate as a constructive force in our society.

How Companies React to the Ethics Crisis

An overly ambitious employee might have the mistaken idea that we do not care how results are obtained, as long as he gets results. He might think it best not to tell higher management all that he is doing, not to record all transactions accurately. . . . He would be wrong on all counts. . . . We don't want liars for managers."
—Clifton C. Garvin Jr., chairman of Exxon Corp. in a statement on ethics, 1975

Policy statements on business ethics pour forth from corporations in the wake of almost daily disclosures that some of this country's most distinguished executives were themselves "overly ambitious employees" who did not care how results were obtained, even if it meant breaking the law. Whatever companies do now, the image of America's business elite—shattered by too many illegal compaign contributions made and too many bribes paid—can hardly be repaired quickly. But along with the policy pronouncements,

Even now, the most that can be said is that at most companies the problem is no longer being treated as a joke. Executives who have privately contended that there is no other way to do business in many parts of the world than to pay bribes have been forced to look for alternatives as the Securities & Exchange Commission pressures companies for more payoff disclosure, as the Internal Revenue Service adds new procedures to sniff out slush funds, and as company auditors adopt new controls intended to make unauthorized payments difficult to cover up.

Clearly the pressure on executives will not ease. Shareholders will have their say when annual-meeting time rolls around this spring. Congress, aware that antibusiness sentiment remains at an all-time high, can be expected to try to find a way to legislate ethical practices into boardrooms.

Pressure is also building, from inside business and out, for a national or international code of business ethics. At least two international codes are already in the works, and they could have the advantage at least of prescribing the same principles for U. S. and foreign companies. Most executives, however, put little stock in codes other than the ones companies formulate for themselves. Last May Bendix Corp. Chairman W. Michael Blumenthal proposed that a group of businessmen devise a U. S. business code, but the idea seems to be foundering. "We've had several meetings," says Bendix Executive Vice-President William M. Agee. But those meetings saw the practicality of any national code seriously questioned.

One problem is that any general code would have to be so watered down to gain general acceptance that it would be all but useless. Says Fred T. Allen,

Edward Bailey

George Knight

Allen: We don't want a code to "refight the last war."

Blumenthal: His idea for a U. S. code is foundering.

Morison: Social responsibility is part of the ethics question.

which are not so different from the ones to which corporations have given lip service all along, there are welcome signs of tighter controls, of belated efforts to establish a higher moral tone throughout management and, in a few companies, of a serious grappling with questions of right and wrong that go beyond simple strictures against bribing politicians—questions like whether to buy safety by paying off racketeers or whether to close a plant that is endangering the health of a town.

At Foremost-McKesson Inc., says President William W. Morison, a special committee consisting of three outside directors is formulating a policy statement that deals with company policies in such areas of social responsibility as equal opportunity hiring and environmental protection, as well as with the conduct of business.

And Allied Chemical Corp. has been running managers through an innovative three-day business ethics seminar in which they discuss the obligations of the company to society at large. (Ironically, Allied has recently found itself under heavy fire for the apparent Kepone chemical poisoning of workers at a contractor's plant at Hopewell, Va.)

Embattled business. But getting business to own up to its sins and do something constructive about them is a slow process. To much of the public—and, indeed, to many businessmen—it seems that a hard fight still lies ahead merely to establish the principle that bribing politicians and government officials is no longer an accepted business practice.

chairman and president of Pitney-Bowes Inc.: "Writing a code that would be universally accepted means you would end up with a motherhood sort of thing."

In the final analysis, codes of good conduct—and enforcement of those codes—will be up to individual companies. And the unpleasant truth today is that many corporations, including some that have been in trouble, still seem to be ducking the job. Greyhound Corp., which gave special cash bonuses to executives who made contributions to the 1972 Presidential campaigns of either Richard Nixon or George McGovern (the bonuses were double the amount of the executives' actual contributions), pleaded guilty in federal court to violations of federal election laws. But its 1975 proxy statement concluded its report of the incident by observing, "No steps need to be taken to avoid illegal political expenditures by or on behalf of the company in the future."

Even companies that sincerely want to draft codes of ethics are finding the job difficult. "My primary concern," says Allen of Pitney-Bowes, "is not where to begin but where to stop. It would be fairly easy to draft a general policy and specific guidelines in a given area such as political activity or campaign contributions. But that would be analogous to a nation rearming itself to refight the last war."

Certainly the problem is not insoluble. Enough corporations are taking concrete steps against corruption, real and potential, to demonstrate that the situation can be confronted—and with more than platitudes.

Among the changes that can help restore credibility:

■ **Tighter controls** should go into place almost everywhere. Four years ago Exxon discovered that its Italian subsidiary had paid at least $46 million in political contributions over a decade. Although legal, the gifts were not reflected in the company's books. In response, uniform financial controls were instituted throughout the company, and communications among auditors was strengthened (a unit auditor who cannot get satisfaction from his manager can go to higher-level auditors—all the way to the audit committee of the board). Today, an auditor's first task when visiting an affiliate is to make sure that Exxon policy statements are being complied with.

■ **Codes of conduct** should be utilized to at least make clear what is expected of employees. Codes, in fact, are coming back into fashion, as they do after nearly every major business scandal. Unlike the proposed U.S. or international codes, the policy statements governing conduct in individual companies receive widespread approval. Heublein Inc. and Pitney-Bowes, for example, are drafting codes of business ethics for the first time. "If you have a formal code," says Wallace W. Booth, president of United Brands Co., a company that paid $1.25-million to Honduran officials before Booth arrived, "you have less chance of getting into trouble unknowingly."

■ **Penalties** for unethical conduct should be severe, especially for infractions at the top. Here the credibility gap between corporations and the public is perhaps widest of all. Many companies insist that unethical conduct, such as paying off politicians—both legally and illegally—and covering up with false bookkeeping entries, is grounds for dismissal. Yet many of the chief executives who have admitted making illegal contributions, such as Northrop Corp.'s Thomas V. Jones and Braniff International Corp.'s Harding L. Lawrence, continue at the helm. "I think a few more examples of board action, like at Gulf [where Chairman Bob R. Dorsey was fired last month in the wake of widespread political payoffs by the company] would help," says Thiokol Corp. President Robert E. Davis. "If a few more people like that get axed, people will fall in line."

Prevention. Guidance and direction must come from the top—and so it is at some companies. "You can't legislate morality in a corporation," says William F. Ballhaus, president of Beckman Instruments Inc. "Beyond procedures, it's a matter of climate. I have one simple rule: No one does anything intentionally wrong."

But even where the climate is right, infractions can occur. Accountants at many companies have sharpened their pencils to make sure there are no slips. American Airlines Inc., where George Spater resigned as chairman in 1973 after admitting he contributed corporate funds to President Nixon's reelection campaign, has eliminated procedures that allowed off-the-books cash funds to develop. "Under today's controls, they could not be reestablished," says Senior Vice-President Gene E. Overbeck.

A large number of companies, such as Pitney-Bowes, have recently demanded that managers sign annual pledges that they have followed the rules in the company's ethics code. Continental Oil Co. has gone a step further. "To detect any possible conduits [for illegal or unethical payments]," says Keith W. Blinn, senior vice-president and general counsel, "we have written to all of our law firms to which we pay more than $2,000 and asked them this year and last year for a certificate that they had not been used in any way as a

Dorsey: He was fired in the wake of political payoffs.

Jones: He still heads Northrop despite its illegal payments.

conduit for the payment of political contributions." Conoco also runs special auditing checks to detect potential sources of slush funds. "We've tried to pick those things we thought were the most fertile fields for this kind of thing," says Blinn. "Law firms are one. Investment bankers, maybe. Suppliers, maybe. Advertisers. Public relations firms."

At Northrop new policies, instituted at the behest of outside directors after the company's illegal campaign contributions came to light, include the elimination of such catchall expense account labels as "Northrop private," which were apparently covers for entertaining government officials. Special attention was also given to consultants' and agents' fees, an area of abuse in many companies that is coming under increasing scrutiny. Frequently such fees are thinly disguised bribes or are rebated to executives for slush funds outside the company books.

A blurred line. The whole question of whether a fee is a legitimate commission or a payoff gets hazy for companies doing business abroad, and most executives who have to deal with the problem say there are no easy answers.

United Brands' Booth says that a problem arises because in many countries where his company does business a "tip" (which is not necessarily a bribe) is simply part of doing business. "We want to identify payments case by case to see if it's proper, legal, and appropriate," he says. If the payment is illegal, it is not made. The "big hangup" is deciding whether it is proper, and Booth knows of no hard and fast rule to determine that.

And that, of course, is the ultimate problem—these gray areas, as opposed to the impropriety of illegal political payoffs by such companies as 3M, Phillips Petroleum, and Goodyear. They were plainly illegal—in violation of even the most rudimentary codes of business conduct. At the very least, the public must be assured that the episode of illegal campaign contributions will not be repeated.

What business must understand today is that the public has a right to demand much more. When executives at the summit of some of the nation's most prestigious and powerful companies fail such an elementary moral test, shareholders, workers, and customers can legitimately wonder what else is going on in the executive suite—whether antitrust laws are being violated, or whether American business is consorting with organized crime. As companies probe their ethical standards, they must accept that the question of illegal political handouts should not be the end of it but just the beginning.

CONSIDER

1. Who loses if Con Ed has to give up on the Cornwall plant on the Hudson River? Who wins?

2. Is it in the stockholders' interest for Con Ed to spend time and money in all of the varied community and public affairs activities?

3. How can a social audit be beneficial to a firm?

4. Who pays for pollution control?

5. Why should a firm be required to file an impact report for major projects?

6. Should small businesses be exempt from pollution control requirements?

7. What can a company do to ease unemployment in a community? How far should this help go?

8. Can business ethics be taught?

9. Do consumers realize that the prices they pay include the costs of pollution control and social actions?

10. Are there limits to corporate social responsibilities? What are they?

CHALLENGES

Look for a source of pollution around you and d develop a plan of action th that the company responsible may follow to correct it. Send your plan to a company executive or to your local newspaper.

Examine a firm in your area and evaluate how the four areas of the environment affect its operations (social, political, economic, and physical environment).

Develop a plan for a social audit of your college or university and present the plan to the administration.

ABT Associates, in Cambridge, Massachusetts, is a consulting firm that offers assistance to companies in conducting social audits. Write the firm and ask for details on how they approach such an audit.

Read George Steiner's book, Business and Society (New York: Random House, 1971) or some other text on the subject. Identify five points from the book you feel are interesting and important.

Read Howard R. Bowen's classic book, Social Responsibilities of the Businessman, published in 1953.

RECAP

Is ecology the business of business? Companies are finding that it is in their best interest to be responsive to the demands of their environment. It's a matter of short-term profit and longer-term survival and prosperity for business organizations. If they are to be around doing business in the future, their managers must act responsibly in areas of social, political, economic, and ecological concern.

In this chapter we have examined some of the issues involved in business and management in relation to the environment. We started with a view from TRW's President regarding a company's responsibilities. Then we examined in some depth the trade-offs which a company must make to have a better physical environment.

We see that large companies such as Con Edison and small companies both face similar kinds of problems and pressures, but in different degrees. The very process of serving customer needs in Con Ed creates problems that outrage the public, such as the pollution resulting from generation of power.

Both large and small companies must weigh their responsibilities to consumers, stockholders, and others in the community to ensure a proper balance for the maximum common good.

One specific tool used by management to consider this balancing act is the social audit. Such a report provides a basis for managers to make plans and decisions within a framework of social needs.

Another is the impact report, an in-depth assessment of the potential effects of a proposed project such as a new plant.

Business faces major challenges in today's society -- including such broad social concerns as overcoming poverty, providing employment and training opportunities, providing housing, public transportation, health, and issues in urban development and growth.

To meet these challenges companies are doing more than just paying taxes (although that alone is a very substantial role to play). They are getting directly into the act in their own communities and giving the time and energies of employees as well as financial support.

WORKSHEET NO. 2

NAME_____

INSTRUCTOR'S NAME_____

DATE_____

1. Do you agree with the following statements? Explain.

   a. Industry has to be forced to spend money to clean up the
       environment. It will not voluntarily do so.

   _____

   b. Businessmen will not do anything in the public interest
       if it reduces their profits.

   _____

   c. America's large corporations are insensitive to changing
       social conditions.

2. What are the major fronts in the "war" business is trying to win?

---

3. What steps can be taken by business to maintain credibility in the wake of problems in ethical behavior.

CHAPTER 3

Business And The Economy

Our economic system is based on exchange of goods and services in an open marketplace. As a result, companies prosper or fail according to their ability to compete effectively and according to other factors such as economic and social conditions.

Demand for a product or service interacts with the supply of the product or service to determine the price. A business can charge only "what the market will bear". Demand for a product changes as people's needs change. On the other side, the supply of goods may be limited due to productive capacity or simple scarcity -- as for precious gems.

Thus supply and demand are the two major forces that control our economy. The system benefits both business and the consumer in several ways: generally lower prices to consumers, better service (to attract customers), new and better services and products, elimination of the inefficient or un-ethical, and creation of opportunities for talented and industrious individuals.

Businessmen in our free market system have the right to acquire and own property, to choose their specialization, to make decisions freely, to sell goods and services in a free market at the highest price possible, and at the same time have an obliga-tion to incur the risks of doing business. Adam Smith, an 18th century English economist, described this system of "perfect compe-tition" as being the most efficient for a society. What was good for the busi-nessman was considered good for society. In his view, enterprise was regu-lated only by the "invisible hand" of competition. By definition, there would be no need for government control as those businesses that failed to serve the public good would not sur-vive competition. Thus, Smith described the economy as "laissez faire," meaning that the government would take a hands off attitude in its dealings with busi-ness.

While competition is a basic quality of our busi-ness enterprise system, ours is not necessarily free competition. Both by the behavior of busi-nessmen and by the inter-vention of government, representing public needs and attitudes, competition in the United States is regulated.

The measure of the eco-nomic condition of our society is the GNP, Gross National Product. The GNP is the sum of all the goods and servies produced in our society. Part of the goals of any economy is to have a continuously growing per capita real GNP. Unfortu-nately, we have business cycles, economic ups and downs, that represent changes in economic activity. When the economy is on the way up, we often call it a "boom." When it turns down, it is a recession, or if really bad, a depression. Government acts to dampen the economic cycles, taking direct action such as taxation and public expenditures to boost or hold down the rate of economic growth.

In This Chapter

Supply And Demand

We have said that the enterprise system is based on the satisfaction of needs. In the marketplace we describe needs in terms of the DEMAND for specific products and services.

Normally, consumers will buy more of a product that they desire if it is lower price. Conversely, as the price of a desired product rises, the demand for the product falls. There are a few products for which demand rarely changes, at least in relation to price, such as salt. You need only so much salt, regardless of how cheap it is.

The pattern of DEMAND is shown in the figure at the right (bottom). The line shows the relationship between the price of the product and the quantity of the product that customers will buy. The line is often called a demand curve.

Put an x on the line at any point you wish. Draw a line left to the side where it says PRICE. Then draw a line stright down to where it says QUANTITY DEMANDED. You have shown that at the given price, say $4.95, the customers will buy the given amount, say 350 of the products.

Put another x above the one you marked before. As you go through the same steps as above, you'll see that at the higher price, customers will buy fewer of the products.

Prices are set through competition, with prices going up when goods are scarce. When there is a glut of a particular good or service, the price falls. Eggs are a good example -- when eggs are in good supply, the price usually falls slightly; when they are short in supply, the price rises.

Or demand may change, too -- with a soaring demand for a popular new product. You've seen what tickets for a sporting event can sell for when the team's a winning one.

The fluctuations in demand and supply are key factors in our overall economic conditions. When the economy is "booming", there is lots of demand and prices tend to rise. In "bust" times, goods move slowly and so prices fall.

Between recession and inflation and the fickle desires of consumers for certain products, a businessman has a rough time trying to know just what to do. He or she has to apply good judgment and hope the decisions come out okay.

SUPPLY

If a demand curve represents the need for

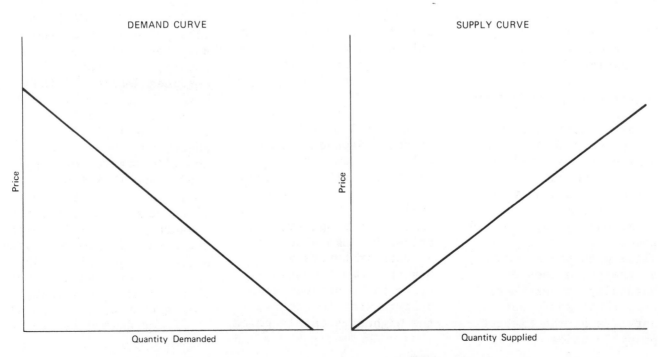

DEMAND CURVE

Price

Quantity Demanded

SUPPLY CURVE

Price

Quantity Supplied

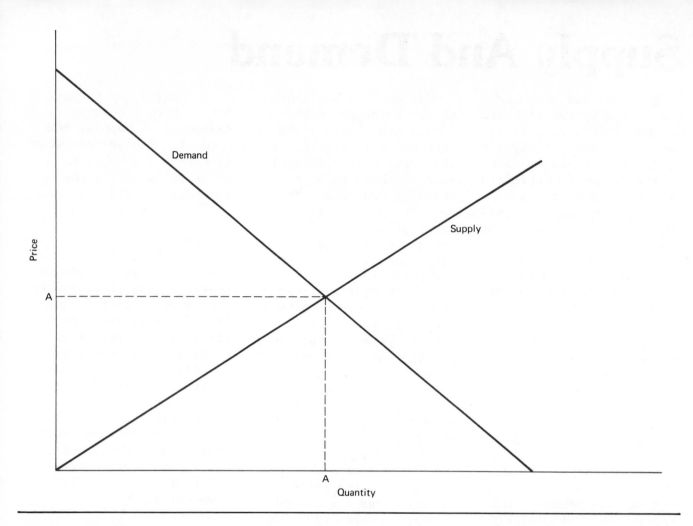

specific products at various price levels, the SUPPLY curve represents the willingness of the business to provide these products at various price levels.

Other than some so-called "free" resources such as air, goods are scarce -- and making them costs money. If labor is required to produce them, or transport them, or transform them into useful goods, someone has to be willing to do this work. (That's another supply curve -- the supply curve of labor availability.)

Normally, suppliers of goods and services are willing to provide more as the price goes up. Naturally, owners seek to sell their goods and services at the highest possible price.

There are a few goods that are in short supply -- and the quantity that can be supplied is limited, regardless of the price. That's exactly what's happened with regard to oil. There's only so much oil in the world and bidding the price up doesn't create more supply.

The prices where a seller will offer his products depend on the prices of raw materials, labor, and other resources needed to make the products available. Thus as costs rise for a supplier, the prices he asks also rise.

Because buyers want to pay the lowest possible price for a product and sellers want to receive the highest possible price,

there has to be some give and take, or bartering, for agreement to be reached. This is exactly what happens in the marketplace.

According to the law of SUPPLY AND DEMAND, there is a price at which the supplier will provide the quantity of goods or services desired by the buyer -- and at which the buyer will actually buy. This point is indicated where the curves cross in the illustration of supply and demand (Point A).

If the supply is great in relation to demand, the advantage tends to be with the buyer. If you're buying a used car you'll usually get a better deal when lots of used cars are sitting for sale on used car lots!

If the demand is greater

than supply, the seller has the advantage and a higher price results. If you're looking for a classic car in top condition, be prepared to pay for it!

In the marketplace, the resulting price is assumed to be fair for all of the parties involved. Competition provides for the allocation of resources with the maximum possible satisfaction for all.

Further, the working of supply and demand also helps plan for future production. If the price of a product is falling or is below costs, the supplier may pull back and stop selling the product. If prices are rising and demand is strong, the supplier may gear up to make more.

Examine the figure of supply and demand to consider what the price would be if the demand curve shifted (moved to the right for example -- meaning customers are willing to pay a higher price if they have to for the same quantity of goods.) Or if the supply curve shifted right (downward, meaning suppliers will offer the goods at a lower price for the same quantity -- maybe he's got a warehouse

full of the dogs he wants to unload).

What happens to the price in these situations? The "sticking point" between supply and demand moves. And we see that every day as prices we pay for goods and services change (usually up, it appears).

FIXING PRICES

Where there is competition and where government involvement does not influence prices, consumer demand determines the prices of goods and services.

A businessman sets the prices of the products he or she sells, but within bounds. He starts with the cost of the product as the absolute minimum. If the price were any lower, he would lose money. If the price is greater than the cost, he has a profit margin, but only up to the point where sales start to fall because of competition -- where someone else offers comparable goods at a lower price.

Only in rare cases, as in a monopoly, may a seller charge whatever the market can afford. In some industries, big companies may try to set prices with the hope that smaller

companies will "follow the leader" higher or lower. But the government usually intervenes in such efforts.

In many states, laws have been passed which give state agencies power to regulate the prices of given goods, such as liquor, agricultural products such as milk, and drugs. By the sheer purchasing power of local, state, or federal government, prices of many goods are affected. For example, when steel prices rise, the government may slow its purchases of steel to slacken the demand for steel and thus lower prices in the market.

Some taxes also make prices on goods and services higher than they would be in a free market. Liquor, cigarettes, gasoline, and leather goods are examples. But whether government action through the imposition of taxes raises the prices of some goods, as long as we have a free market economy, the price of goods will ultimately be set by what the consumer is willing to pay.

How About The Chocolate Bar?

REMEMBER THE NICKEL BAR

Hershey used to make a 5¢ candy bar, and then a 10¢ bar, and a 15¢ bar. A Hershey bar continues to be "the best chocolate bar in the world," according to Hershey Foods.

Though the candy has stayed the same, the price and size of the bar has changed over the years.

In the late 1960's the 5¢ bar shrank to 3/4 ounce before it was discontinued in 1969. Over the previous 25 years, the nickel bar had varied between 7/8 ounce and a full ounce, depending on the price of cocoa beans. The 10¢ bar was discontinued at the end of 1973 when it weighed 1.26 ounces. The 15¢ bar, introduced on January 1, 1974, weighed 1.4 ounces. Two weight reductions followed, but in 1976 the weight was increased to 1.2 ounces.

Year	Ounces
10¢ Hershey Bar:	
1950	2
1951	1 7/8
1954 (Feb.)	1 5/8
1954 (Aug.)	1 1/2
1955	1 3/4
1958	1 1/2
1960	2
1963	1 3/4
1965	2
1966	1 3/4
1968	1 1/2
1970	1 3/8
1973	1.26
1974	0

Changes in Typical Candy Bars *

HERSHEY'S MILK CHOCOLATE
Now—15¢ for 1.2 oz.
New—20¢ for 1.35 oz.
HERSHEY MILK CHOCOLATE

PETER PAUL Mounds
Now—15¢ for 1.5 oz.
New—20¢ for 1.65 oz.
PETER PAUL MOUNDS

3 MUSKETEERS MILK CHOCOLATE NET WT 1 13/16 OZ. 51g
Now—15¢ for 1 13/16 oz.
New—20¢ for 2 1/16 oz.
THREE MUSKETEERS

* These standard prices may be exceeded at many retail outlets.

Less than a decade ago, a candy-loving child on a tight allowance could budget a nickel for a daily chocolate bar. But those days have gone as the price of chocolate has steadily risen. Yesterday, the Hershey Foods Corporation and M & M/Mars announced new prices that raise the cost of chocolate bars by 5 cents.

Hershey and M & M, a division of Mars Inc., said that consumers in most parts of the country would pay 20 cents for a chocolate bar that now costs 15 cents.

Hershey's increase goes into effect no later than Jan. 1, while M & M's is effective Nov. 29.

Larger Bars are Planned

While prices are going up, however, the chocolate manufacturers said the increases would partly offset by larger bars. As a result, consumers will pay a net increase of 6.6 percent to 18.5 percent for their candy bars.

The Hershey and M&M announcements followed a notice Tuesday by another chocolate bar manufacturer, Peter Paul, that its prices would be raised by 5 cents, to 20 cents, in early 1977. Peter Paul said the weight of its bars would be increased, too.

The candy bar manufacturers said the higher prices of imported cocoa beans made it necessary to raise prices, because cocoa was the main ingredient in chocolate. Since last year, when cocoa beans sold for 75 cents a pound, prices have soared to record levels and earlier this week, cocoa beans sold for $1.41 a pound.

"We were faced with the choice of either raising prices," said Lloyd Elston, president of Peter Paul, which manufactures such candies as Mounds, Almond Joy and Power House bars, "or simply going out of business."

The price increases had been expected for several weeks, but industry sources said they did not come sooner because of the low current price of sugar. While cocoa prices have climbed 50 percent from last year, sugar has dropped nearly 90 percent in price from its record 1974 levels.

"Yes, sugar is down, but it is a less important cost factor than cocoa," said a spokesman for M&M., which produces such candy as Milky Way, Snickers, M&M's and Three Musketeers bars.

"Labor, packaging, energy costs have been creeping up, but cocoa is the one factor that finally threw us over the edge and made us raise prices."

In the weeks ahead, consumers will pay 20 cents for a Hershey Milk Chocolate bar that will be increased from 1.2 ounces to 1.35 ounces. This will mean an 18.5 percent price rise for consumers. A Hershey Rally bar will be increased from 1.2 ounces to 1.5 ounces, or a 6.6 percent price increase for chocolate munchers. An M&M-produced Three Musketeers bar will be increased in weight from 1 13/16 ounce to 2 ounces, which means consumers will pay an additional 13.8 percent.

The  Story

"I will build a motor car for the great multitude. It will be large enough for the family but small enough for the individual to run and care for. It will be constructed of the best materials, by the best men to be hired, after the simplest designs that modern engineering can devise. But it will be so low in price that no man making a good salary will be unable to own one -- and enjoy with his family the blessings of hours of pleasure in God's great open spaces."

-- Henry Ford.

Henry Ford was a great entrepreneur and a great innovator in American industry. He created a great industrial enterprise on the basis of the little black Model T. More importantly, his achievements have had a profound and lasting influence on the social, economic, and cultural values of our time.

"Any Customer can have a car painted any color that he wants so long as it is black."

-- Henry Ford

HENRY FORD

THE MODEL T

"As we see it, the Model T is the acme of motor car perfection. Although slight improvements are made from year to year as our corps of engineers discover them, they are not of sufficient importance to warrant the changing of the car's model. Therefore, since 1909, contrary to the policy of other companies, the Ford Company has made no yearly change in the model of its car."

-- Ford Motor Co., 1919

That's when the first real growth started in the automobile industry. Prior to 1908 there were a large number of small "garage" manufacturers of horseless carriages. The cars were largely custom made, by hand, with a good deal of experimentation and hand craftsmanship.

After the economic downturn of 1907 had ended and customers had new money to spend, Ford came out with his first Model T. This was the first mass-produced car priced for the masses -- under $1000.

In that year 65,000 of these vehicles were sold in the United States. In the following year, output doubled, reaching 130,986 vehicles. By 1915, production passed the million per year mark.

In this period of rapid growth, Henry Ford took the lead. Many of the small automobile builders dropped out of competition; some banded together to form larger companies such as United Motors, later General Motors. Ford's strategy was to build a car suited to the people and then build a large distribution network of dealers and regional sales offices. By 1913 Ford had branch houses in 31 American cities and 14 foreign countries. This strategy resulted in the torrent of orders for cars.

In fact, the demand for Model T Fords outpaced supply. Ford responded by pressing for new, faster and more efficient production processes, including the radical innovation called the assembly line.

By 1920 Ford had 50% of the automobile market; General Motors had 20%, and the market was still growing. Soon after,

1917 Model T Ford

however, the production capacity of the industry exceeded demand. At one point the industry could produce 6 million vehicles in a year while the public bought only 4 million.

As a result, attention turned to marketing and to aggressive competition, rather than production and growth.

While the Model T was certainly a very remarkable automobile, Henry Ford refused to recognize changes in customer demands taking place as a factor in the more competitive market.

He continued to concentrate on the production of the Model T, as cheap and efficient auto transportation. But the design of the Model T was getting old and the public wanted more in a car -- more comfort, more power, and more equipment.

After 1924 the demand for Ford's car began to drop. By 1926 the Ford Motor Company was in trouble. The company lost ground in the marketplace and eventually was forced to halt production altogether and redesign its product. Ford found it hard to keep up with General Motors, let alone ahead of G.M. and other competitors.

Today Ford is the second largest automobile company in the United States. Its primary competition comes from General Motors (the largest), Chrysler Corporation, American Motors, and major foreign manufacturers.

COMPETITION

The automobile industry sells around 12 million cars each year, but some observers don't think this level will hold up. They are worried about the costs of controlling pollution, rising labor costs, rising gasoline costs, and rising gasoline consumption in the face of limited supplies. The gasoline shortage accelerated a trend toward smaller cars -- a long term trend that is bound to persist.

In the short term, however, customers prefer to buy comfortable large cars, regardless of the price or gasoline consumption, as long as the economy is good and gas supplies are okay. Big cars are good news for automobile makers because they provide bigger profits than "economy" cars.

The worriers are wrong, says Lee Iacocca, President of Ford Motor Company. He says Ford is learning how to sell little cars AND big cars. A few years ago Iacocca set a goal: to cut operating expenses in four major areas so that net profits would increase by $200 million. The program aimed at improving productivity on the production line through improved computer programming and scheduling, improved model changes, and shortened changeover time. Plants can be shifted from one product model to another to meet changes in market demand.

Iacocca also seeks to increase Ford's share of the luxury market (G.M. has always dominated the market at this end -- with Buicks and Cadillacs -- while Ford has collected 70% of its sales at the low end). Ford has spent more than $1 billion on new product development and dealer expansion for its Lincoln-Mercury division, its luxury arm. The Ford Granada represents an entry in the market designed to compete head on with Mercedes touches.

What about federal safety and pollution requirements? "I don't consider them a problem," Iacocca has said. "I consider them undue harassment. You can't sell clean air as an option, so we need some regulation in that area. The question is how much regulation."

Is the automobile industry competitive? Lee Iacocca thinks so.

Competition in the Auto Industry

The role of large business in American life and in the competitive American economy long has been a subject of widespread interest. In view of the size of all automobile firms, and General Motors in particular, a question has been raised as to whether competition in the automobile industry has been replaced by planning and regulation of the market by these firms.

The purpose of this statement by General Motors is to show that competitive rivalry in the industry, far from being replaced by planning and regulation, has intensified. This rivalry has produced a steady improvement in quality, safety and value, and a greater variety of product choices for the auto buyer than at any time in history. The vigor of competition is reflected in the fluctuations in market shares as the companies strive to excel in every aspect of the business — superior products, lower prices, and better sales and service. The statement also shows the error in any claim that General Motors has market control.

Summary

Almost from its beginning, large size and vigorous rivalry have characterized the successful firms in the auto industry. Yet, Ford's high market share, which reached a peak of some 60 percent in the early 1920's, and its high profitability, which for several years exceeded 100 percent return on investment, did not insulate that firm from later loss of position to smaller competitors, such as General Motors and Chrysler, when they offered better product values.

The domestic passenger car companies which were brought into General Motors, the most recent approximately 50 years ago, gave it no competitive advantage in technology, products or markets and were of little significance to its ultimate success. At the end of 1920, General Motors was on the verge of financial collapse and in 1921 had less than 14 percent of the market. Since this turning point in its history, GM's growth

has been from within. Its success stems in major part from: (1) the development of new concepts of internal administrative management, largely pioneered by Alfred P. Sloan, Jr., and widely copied by many companies, including General Motors' competitors, and (2) its conviction that the American consumer wanted improved products and a variety of choices, not merely basic transportation in "any color as long as it's black."

Today, car buyers are increasingly knowledgeable. Aside from the home, the new car is the largest single expenditure of the average family. A wealth of information — such as road tests by independent publications — is available as to the performance characteristics of cars of competing makes. It is a rare prospective car buyer who has not driven —or ridden in—cars of several competitors. Innovations in engines, steering, suspension, seating, comfort, air-conditioning, visibility, safety and styling are well known to him. Product improvement and new product types are important and effective means of competition.

The car buyer is aware of the choices available and of his bargaining power. He can buy a new car—domestic or imported—or a used car, or buy no car at all and keep the one he is driving, if the products or prices do not meet his desires. Each year millions of car owners shift from one make of car to another. No customer can be regarded as a captive, and each firm must constantly compete to retain, as much as possible, the loyalty of its present customers and to win over new customers. Thus, statistics as to annual sales shares constitute a composite of innumerable choices reflecting many shifts in patronage, and indicate no power to control any portion of the market.

If further evidence were needed of the vitality of competition and its control of the automobile market, it is to be found in the several forms in which competition exists, particularly in the

areas of product, price and marketing competition.

The automobile industry has been characterized by product competition producing a steady stream of product innovations—some dramatic, some less so—but all contributing in the aggregate to producing automobiles of greater value, safety and reliability. All are the result of competition within the industry.

The other principal competitive areas in the industry are pricing and marketing. General Motors' 1969 model price announcements illustrate the forces of competition. While substantial labor and material increases applied to the production of all General Motors 1969 cars, price changes varied from a decrease of $1 to an increase of $144 reflecting the disciplines of market forces. During the last decade, when the Consumer Price Index rose over 20 percent, the Index of New Car Prices actually declined slightly as a result of competitive forces.

Another important means of evaluating competition in any industry is to examine its performance. Have the results benefited the consumer and the public? On this score, auto industry performance ranks high by any standard. For example, the number of months of average family income required to meet the average purchase price of a new car has declined from 7 months of income in 1959 to 4.9 months of income in 1967, a decline of almost 30 percent. The index of new car prices, from the base period of 1957-59 to August 1968, has remained unchanged and compares to increases of more than 15 percent in such categories as rent, meat and apparel, and more than 40 percent in the cost of medical care. In 1967, the American public was able to buy almost 2 million more new cars than in 1959 without increasing the portion of its aggregate disposable income spent for new cars.

The fact that the number of U.S. automobile manufacturers is small is of no relevance to the intensity of competition among them. Each year since 1921, except for a few years in the mid-1920's, the three largest producers have accounted for 75 percent or more of total U.S. new car output. Neither the quality nor the quantity of competition in the auto industry can be measured by counting number of sellers or by market shares. The small number of domestic competitors does not mean that General Motors can in any way control market supply and increase prices above competitive levels, the prime requisites for monopoly power.

In the automobile industry, the customer exercises a free choice and shifts from one manufacturer to another as he pleases. Thus the superior product, as determined by the consumer, captures the greater share of the market because there is no other means by which the manufacturer can "control" the customer's choice.

How Inflation Works

During wars and postwar periods there is usually substantial inflation. In these times there is a sudden increase in consumer buying power and a relative shortage of available goods. Until the supply of goods can catch up, prices soar.

In peacetime the situation is different. The problem is one of creeping inflation, or gradual inflation. Here prices rise unevenly and restlessly through the whole cost-price structure. This insidious process is more difficult to understand, to identify and, in some ways, to combat.

Since World War II, "wage-price spiral" has become a well-known term. Wages rise, prices rise, wages rise, prices rise.

During inflation, wages, costs, and prices move upward together like a dog chasing his tail up a stairway. But the crucial question is one of causal relationships. Can inflation be caused by the upward pressure of costs? Do wages lead to higher prices? Are businessmen forced to pay out higher costs, including wage costs or are they able and willing to do so BECAUSE prices are rising?

Except for brief periods of apparently fairly stable prices, there have been almost continuously upward adjustments in wages and prices. Successively, rounds of wage increases in unionized industries and a parallel pattern of rises in non-unionized sectors, joined by rising wholesale and retail prices, seem to fit an inflationary pattern that can be dramatic.

This wage-price spiral is coupled with other types of economic factors. Both individual prices and the general level of prices are determined, in part, by costs of production and, in part, by money demand. Neither costs or demand alone determines prices or price levels overall.

To come to grips with this thorny problem, it is convenient to make a distinction between two types of forces at work in an inflationary situation:

-- cost-push forces operate on the supply side of the market, and

-- demand-pull forces of excessive money running after goods and services on the buyers' side.

Higher wages, rising raw material costs, taxes, productivity decline, bottlenecks in particular lines of production, higher transportation costs, and diminishing ability to improve industrial efficiency all are factors that contribute to cost-push, and force a businessman to raise prices.

On the demand side, excessive spending by government, businessmen, and consumers, and competition among producers for scarce labor and other resources all contribute to increased demand and "pull" prices up.

We usually prefer to make excessive demand the chief villain in the case of inflation. Inflation of prices and incomes takes place when current supply (output) cannot be increased rapidly enough to meet the enlarged demand. As a result, prices are bid up and continue to rise until a new level of prices is reached where money value of aggregate supply does equal aggregate money demand. At the same time incomes derived from rising prices also become swollen.

So the question of the spiral boils down to whether "cost-push" forces can initiate or cause inflation or whether they merely aggravate the inflation already generated by excessive spending for available output. Are costs an active or passive factor in inflation? When we push for wage increases to be able to pay higher prices in living, are we just keeping up with

This Is No Fairy Tale

inflation or are we directly contributing to it?

We prefer to blame the demand-pull side because we would like to think we just are keeping up.

THE ROLE OF DEMAND

Aggregate demand, or the total expenditure for the output of the economy has three parts: consumer expenditures, investment expenditures, and government expenditures.

The principal source of money to finance these expenditures is current income earned in the process of production. But total demand can also be financed by borrowing, by drawing on past savings, or stretching out payments. Simply, business, consumers, and the government can spend a great deal more money on current output than the actual money being generated by current production. We can expand the supply of money and thus put a lot of pressure on the prices of the few goods available.

Inflationary increases in total spending can come from an expanded supply of money (credit, savings, etc.) or from an increased velocity of money or both. Velocity simply means how fast money changes hands. As you would expect, these conditions are both strong inflationary factors during war, postwar, or in any other period of rapid economic recovery.

THE ROLE OF COSTS

Costs contribute to inflation in three ways:

-- a general increase in business outlays,

Argentine June Infl. 2.8%

BUENOS AIRES. — Inflation in Argentina in June was 2.8%, the lowest increase of the year, economy minister Jose Martinez de Hoz said last week.

Government economists had been predicting June inflation would be less than 5%. Private economists attribute the decline to deepening recession rather than official anti-inflation programs.

The 1975 inflation rate was 334.8%.

---

especially as higher labor costs, expands money incomes and fuels demand;

-- during periods of economic expansion, shortages develop in some materials and in some segments of the labor market. In these areas, prices and wages are bid up;

-- increased costs in some industries (such as steel or the cost of electricity) spread directly and indirectly throughout the economic system, pushing costs (and prices) up at every step.

Increases in money wage rates may generate inflation when:

-- they are not offset by improved productivity

-- the rates are reflected in higher costs, which are added to product prices

-- wage increases are followed by other companies or industries, simply as the prevailing pattern

-- they are keyed to prices themselves, or the "cost of living". Here wage increases are cumulative and self-reinforcing.

CONTROLLING INFLATION

It makes sense that this sprial has to be broken somewhere if the dilemma of inflation is to be solved. Ah, but where?

Some countries have experienced inflation far more extreme than we have in the United States. Would you believe prices doubling and doubling again? By allowing labor costs (wages) to rise freely and prices also to rise, it is sometimes argued that everything works out okay. If bread costs $1 a loaf instead of 25¢, that's okay, if you earn $1 instead of 25¢. Nobody gets ahead, but everyone supposedly keeps whole. (People on fixed incomes such as pensioners or people living on savings can't cope with this approach, though).

Serious inflation is usually controlled through action of the federal government. Wage controls, price controls, or changes in government spending patterns are tools that are often used.

"Which came first—the wage hike or the price hike?"

Drawing by Dana Fradon; © 1970 The New Yorker Magazine, Inc.

The trouble with these tools is that they tend to put a damper not only on prices, but on economic growth. That means fewer goods are demanded, prices may even fall, employees may not receive wage increases, and few new jobs are created.

Political realities play an important role, then, in controlling inflation. As a rule, we would rather tolerate some inflation than have unemployment and a dragging economy. We like boom times -- and boom times usually mean lots of money chasing few goods. That means inflation.

Wage and price controls themselves are artificial clamps on certain costs and prices -- artificial because they don't arise out of competition, but from the hands of the government. We generally don't like government meddling with the workings of our competitive system, so we prefer to avoid that approach.

In recent years the approach has been to stimulate the economy while trying to hold down the rate of inflation.

What we got was STAGFLATION. What we ended up with was not the usual increase in unemployment and decrease in inflation that usually resulted from government actions designed to control inflation. With stagflation we got the worst of both. unemployment increased to over 7% and at the same time inflation stayed up. True, it was reduced from double digit inflation to about 6% a year, but the best efforts of the government were not able to get it below this level. Unfortunately, the efforts to control inflation reduced economic activity and increased unemployment It's tough for the economy to grow without prices getting out of hand. To hold down prices stagnates the economy.

It's a great problem we must learn to live with.

WHAZZIT?

BUSINESS CYCLES

Changes in business conditions over time.

DEPRESSION

The period of a business cycle when business is poorest -- production is lowest, prices are highest, unemployment is highest, and people are pessimistic.

RECESSION

A mild form of depression.

GNP

Gross National Product, the money value of the total output of goods and services in our country during a year.

Gross National Products And

We like to think we have a growing, healthy economy.

By economic growth we mean expansion of the total amount of goods and services produced in our economy, in "real" dollar values. Real dollars are constant dollars, with the impact of inflation removed.

We measure our economic growth in terms of changes in our GROSS NATIONAL PRODUCT. (Gross means total; national means all sectors; product means all final output produced.)

The GNP is the estimated dollar value of the total annual output of goods and services produced in our nation. Included in the measure (which is, of course, an estimate), are the values of consumer goods and services produced, private invest- ment (goods we produce but don't consume), government purchases, and net exports (what we make and sell

outside the U.S. over and above what we buy).

Only the value of final goods and services are included. For example, the clothing that you buy is included, but the cloth that was made or the cotton that was grown and processed for it are not included.

Our nation's GNP has steadily grown over the years, with the exception

of the depression years during the 1930's. As shown in the table below, which continues for several pages, our GNP has grown on a per capita basis. Combined with our population growth, it's easy to see we have a healthy economy.

We are more productive, through the use of our resources and technology, than people in many other

UNITED STATES GROSS NATIONAL PRODUCT

Billions of Dollars

Year	GNP	Year	GNP	Year	GNP
1946	209.6	1956	420.7	1966	753.0
1947	232.8	1957	442.8	1967	796.3
1948	259.1	1958	448.9	1968	868.5
1949	258.0	1959	486.5	1969	935.5
1950	286.2	1960	506.0	1970	982.4
1951	330.2	1961	523.3	1971	1,063.4
1952	347.2	1962	563.8	1972	1,171.1
1953	366.1	1963	594.7	1973	1,306.3
1954	366.3	1964	635.7	1974	1,406.9
1955	399.3	1965	688.1	1975	1,499.0

AMERICAN BUSINESS ACTIVITY FROM 1790 TO TODAY.

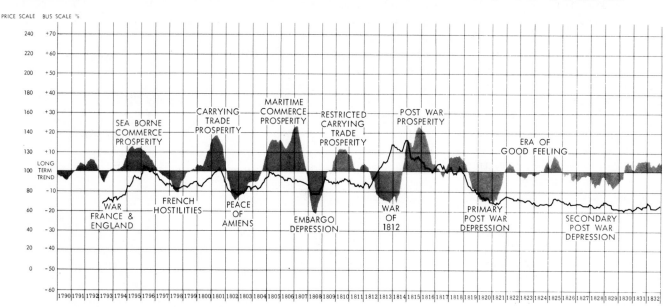

The Business Cycle

nations. No other nation can compare with our GNP record. Some countries have high rates of economic growth, but their total GNP and per capita GNP is not comparable to that of the U.S. A few countries, oil exporting nations with small populations may have exceeded our per capita GNP, but economically, the United States is still the dominant economic power.

It is the goal of our government to have our economy operate in such a way that there will be a steady, moderate growth in GNP. This type of growth would help reduce the problems of inflations and unemployment that plague our economy when growth is not steady.

Our economy has had its ups and downs through its history. These changes in economic conditions we call business cycles (or economic cycles). The general pattern of cycles in the American economy is shown in the chart below.

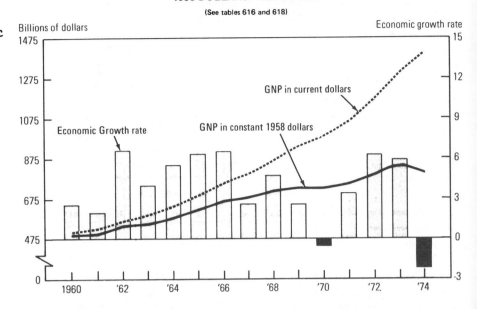

Fig. 13-1. GROSS NATIONAL PRODUCT IN CURRENT AND CONSTANT 1958 DOLLARS: 1960 TO 1974

(See tables 616 and 618)

Source: Chart prepared by U.S. Bureau of the Census. Data from U.S. Bureau of Economic Analysis.

The worst period in our economic history was from 1929 to 1940, a period we refer to as the "Great Depression".

During these years unemployment was widespread in the U.S., as shown in the sample statistics below:

Year	% of Labor Force Unemployed
1929	3.2%
1930	8.7%
1931	15.9%
1932	23.6%
1933	24.9%
1934	21.7%

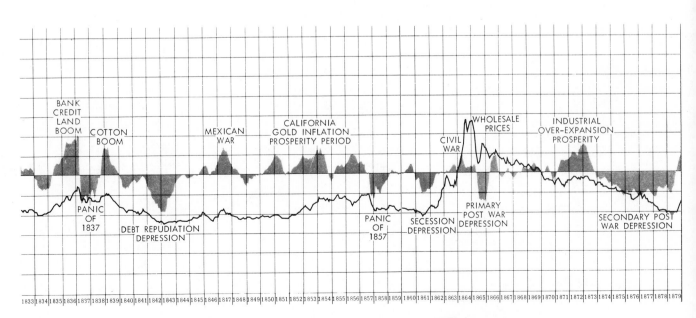

Unemployment persisted through the 1930's, not dropping below 10% until 1941, when the United States actively entered World War II. The war production effort during the late 1930's provided some earlier relief of unemployment.

The Great Depression was chiefly fought through a combination of monetary and fiscal policy. Controlling the supply of money, through MONETARY POLICY, helped spur economic expansion and strengthen the purchasing power of the dollar. Government FISCAL POLICY included direct expenditures to spur economic recovery and growth -- through public works programs to provide jobs in building parks, advancing the arts, conservation, and public construction.

To fund these massive economic programs, the federal government spent more than it received in taxes. This deficit spending has been commonly used ever since as a potent tool to stimulate or control economic activity and employment.

The use of monetary and fiscal tools to influence business cycles is not a precise, predictable process. We are still learning about the working of economics and the potential impact of alternative types of governmental action.

In fact, business cycles themselves are hard to define. You never really know what's happening to the economy until it has already happened. That makes economic decisions tough to make.

Governmental actions aim to smooth out the business cycles -- to prevent the level of economic activity from fluctuating as much as it has in the past. We want economic growth, but we don't want to pay the price of rampant inflation. We especially want stability without unemployment.

Hardships caused by loss of income during unemployment are not exclusively economic. The psychological impact of reduced purchasing power, lost job and career security, and demoralization of self respect are all

significant social losses. They must be added to the costs of depression and recession.

In times of rapidly rising prices, too, people may be discouraged. This time the loss of purchasing power of the dollars earned is the frustration.

Thus ideal economic conditions lie on a fine line between ups and downs. To get to this fine line between the ups and downs we shall have to learn a great deal more about what makes our economy tick. We shall try to develop an economy that will generate steady growth, low inflation, and reduced unemployment. The problem is that often we don't know that we are having problems until it is too late to do anything about them. Economists are hoping that by studying those indicators that appear before trouble comes we shall be able to do a better job of fine tuning our economy.

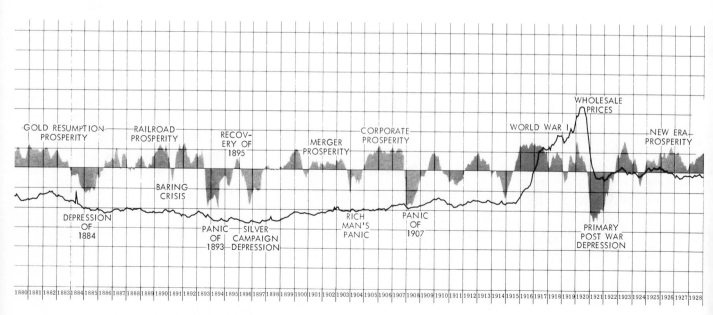

Recession

Since World War II the business cycle has produced four full-scale officially-recognized recessions.

The latest really began in 1970 and dragged on while inflation increased through 1974 and 1975. It began as a result of extensive deficit spending by the federal government for the Viet Nam war. When military and aerospace spending was cut back, unemployment and reduced demand for goods resulted in an economic downturn. Reduced demand and lower profits in turn led to further reductions in other companies.

In the economy there was prosperity and inflation in some areas and severe unemployment and hardship in others. Whatever the government tried to do for one had an effect on the other.

Unfortunately we never know whether a recession will become serious or will disappear with monetary or fiscal treatment. Often a recession is the signal of a depression in the making. On other occasions, downturns don't turn out to be much and are "mini-recessions". Some miscalls that made businessmen nervous were in 1967, 1962, and 1956.

The big difficulty is that there is no precise definition of a recession. When is a downturn a recession or just a slight hesitation in growth? Economics textbooks don't agree on a useful definition, so it's up to the National Bureau of Economic Research and governmental agencies to say when we're in a recession or not.

One rule of thumb is that we're in a recession when we have experienced two quarters (six months) with a decline in GNP (in constant dollars). But we can't wait that long to find out if we're in economic trouble. By the time we decided, we would be in the third or fourth quarter, and possible danger. So we react quickly at the slightest changes in GNP and other indicators.

Some indicators that seem to lead the economy, that is they move in the direction that the economy will move at some later date are: the stock market, manufacturer's inventories, help-wanted advertising, and investemnt in new plant. By watching the movement of these indicators, or the composite indicators that the government has developed, economists should be able to predict the onset of a recession. Whether the economists and the government can take the appropriate actions to head off a predicted recession is another thing. It has been our experience that the government often overreacts to economic problems causing other problems later on. It is hard to know how much is enough and not too much.

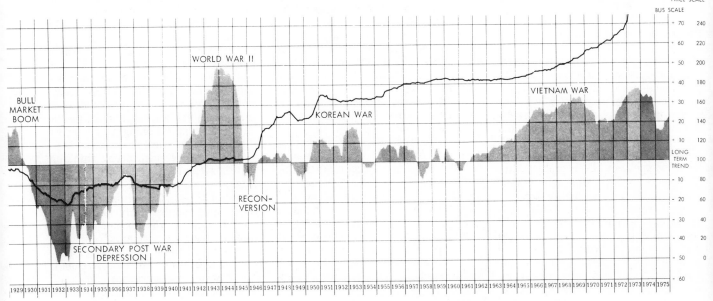

Small Business

The maddening struggle to survive

"I would be nuts to go through this another season," sighs Ben Blanc, president of Calliope, Inc., a Philadelphia manufacturer of children's wear. In the past year his volume has shrunk from $250,000 to $150,000, his material costs have increased 25%, and his labor costs have risen 20%. But pinched by heavy inventories ("I overbought last year when I thought prices were right") and the drop in sales, he has been able to raise his prices only 15%. Blanc complains that only his bigger competitors can survive these days.

"Take Oshkosh B'Gosh, Inc. They can make something that sells for $3.75," he says. "Hell, I can't even start to make it for that." Another big problem is accounts receivable. More than 25% of last year's sales are on collection, a situation Blanc calls "deadly." Says he: "The collection agencies charge you 20% to collect, but my margin is only 16%, so I'm losing money collecting money." Blanc, who has been in business 15 years, concludes: "If we have another bad season, I will shutter down."

Blanc's lament is repeated by small businessmen in virtually every industry in every part of the country. "The small businessman these days is like the guy in Las Vegas who prays, 'Please God, let me break even. I need the money,'" says Oliver O. Ward, head of the Smaller Business Assn. of New England. "Things are tough now, and it looks like they will be tough for a long time coming."

The tribulations of smallness

After months of devastating inflation and recession, many of the nation's smaller entrepreneurs are fighting for survival. Squeezed by tight money, rising costs, depressed markets, and uncertain supply sources, they find it tougher to cope with economic adversity than larger, more financially robust competitors. Their problems are compounded by growing government intervention. New occupational safety rules, environmental restrictions, product safety regulations, and increased minimum wages pose costly challenges that are more difficult for the small businessman. Just as significant, the harsh economic climate has created unprecedented barriers for new entrepreneurs eager to enter the marketplace.

These tribulations are vividly pointed up in the steady rise in bankruptcies and the decline in new business incorporations. Dun & Bradstreet's statistics on commercial and industrial failures, which essentially cover small businesses, last year reached a three-year high in numbers—9,915—and a record high in total dollar liabilities. Last March the rate was the highest for any month in eight years.

Dollar liabilities topped $3-billion for the first time in 1974, and included an unprecedented 427 bankruptcies in the million-dollar category. Increasingly affected are larger businesses, not just store-front "mom-and-pop" operations. Especially hard hit are retailers of general merchandise, building contractors, home furnishings retailers, and building materials dealers. Failures are also up in textile and apparel manufacturing and among transportation equipment producers. New business incorporations slumped to 319,149 last year from a record 329,358 in 1973. Early in 1975 the number dropped to the lowest level in four years.

To be sure, economic calamity is not universal among small businessmen. Many continue to thrive, and some even see strategic advantages in their size during a recession. "We can be more flexible, can move more quickly, and concentrate on smaller segments of markets," notes David Bigelow, president of R. C. Bigelow Co., a Norwalk (Conn.)-based specialty foods outfit that grosses about $10-million.

Bigelow's most successful product is a spiced tea, Constant Comment. General Foods had a competitive brand that was abandoned. Now Bigelow is battling GF again in spiced- and fruit-flavored instant coffees. This time, Bigelow concedes, General Foods has "flattened us out a bit."

Nevertheless, Bigelow is bullish about the future of small business. "I feel the large corporations are failing in this country, leaving opportunities for small specialty companies," he says. "Big manufacturers are making such bad products. The big, discount-type retail operators run stores where no one gives a damn about the customer. So there are opportunities for small businessmen. But it takes a strong individual to handle them."

How small is small?

Getting an exact fix on the life and times of small business is complicated by the question of definition. The official definition—employed by the Small Business Administration (page 100) on loans—ranges all over the lot. In manufacturing, it is based on numbers of employees and the industry. Apparel and textile companies are regarded as "small" if they have no more than 250 employees. For producers of aircraft and ammunition, the number is 1,500. In the service industries, the criterion is dollar volume: a maximum of $5-million for department stores, groceries, and auto dealers, and $1-million for most other retailers; $5-million for general contractors; and $5-million for most wholesalers. To reflect inflation, SBA is now revising the sales figures upward by as much as 90%.

The problems of size, however, are not limited to companies that fit neatly into the government's "small business" pigeonholes. Scores of companies with sales running into nine figures—"second-tier" corporations in industries dominated by billion-dollar giants—suffer the same kinds of disadvantages in a recession (page 99). Their difficulties in raising capital, lining up stable supply sources, and remaining competitively strong are likely to result in growing concentration of market shares among the giant companies.

The cost and availability of capital head the list of small business problems. Financing a small business is like a line from Gilbert & Sullivan, quips Oliver Ward. "The small businessman tries his sisters and his cousins and his aunts." Raising money to launch or expand a small enterprise is never easy. But business conditions, the collapse of the new equity market, and a possible nationwide capital drought have made it tougher than ever.

"Small businessmen aren't thinking in terms of growth," asserts Timothy Hay, president of First Small Business Investment of California. "They're thinking in terms of survival—getting their houses in order rather than increasing their commitments."

James M. McCarl, president of Perfection Furniture Co. of Claremont, N. C., who now performs janitorial chores in his own plant to cut overhead costs, says that "December and January were the two worst months I have seen in my 20 years in the furniture business. If you look at our balance sheet and P&L statement, if it didn't curl your hair, it would turn it white." He now operates his plant only four days a week, and with other executives, helps clean up on Fridays.

But things are looking up, says McCarl, with the entrepreneur's incurable optimism. "Business has gone from horrible to terrible." Long range, he believes, "the things we are trying to do will eventually turn this company around unless the economy just stays sour." For example, he is offering customers three weeks delivery on his medium-priced, special-order upholstered furniture. "A competitor asked me how I could do it, and I told him it wasn't hard at all with a two-week backlog," he says. "The slump taught me to take every adversity, and try to turn it into an opportunity."

McCarl's bankers helped with a loan extension, but other small businessmen paint a different picture of bank largesse. "The banks don't cooperate as they do with big firms," complains Edwin H. Stern, who operates a suburban Atlanta gift shop. "We pay higher interest rates, and credit is not as easily available."

Financial problems are by no means limited to gift shops, however. Sierracin Corp. of Sylmar, Calif., a $23-million producer of coatings, heating devices, and other highly specialized products, is sandwiched "between billion-dollar customers and billion-dollar vendors," says its president, John P. Endicott. "Many of our vendors will not give us fixed prices for any length of time, and some are strictly on price at time of delivery. At the other end, we have to give our customers firm commitments for much longer than our vendors are willing to give us."

Partly because of his track record with two other ventures, Endicott has been in the enviable position of having a good line of credit and not needing to tap it. Part of his success is sticking to product lines requiring narrow, intense skills, says Endicott, who proves the theory that entrepreneurs succeed less with pure invention than with perseverance.

The search for financing

Still another headache for small business is its inability to increase prices. Says Richard M. Bailey, an economist at the University of California at Berkeley: "Volume is more steady" for small than for large manufacturers, but "small business may have problems raising prices in inflationary times because it's closer to the consumer, and too substantial price rises might cut them out."

Premix, Inc., of North Kingsville, Ohio, is a case in point. President George H. Kaull started his reinforced plastics business with two partners on borrowed capital of $22,400. Fifteen years later, he does $20-million in sales and declares that "inflation and recession have played hell with us."

Kaull says polyester resin soared from 18¢ per lb. to 48¢ in one year, and some raw ingredients for his plastics went up 500%. "But the small supplier has a particularly difficult time passing inflationary costs on to his big customers," says Kaull. "A little guy making knobs for windshield wipers doesn't really know how to go to Ford and tell them that prices are going to have to go up 12½%. When Ford says absolutely no, the little guy often can't tell them to take their business elsewhere. He's caught in a tighter bind than a large corporation."

Kaull is equally bitter about increased government regulation. "OSHA [Occupational Safety & Health Administration] will probably destroy more businesses than lack of financing will," he says. "When OSHA regulations slipped through Congress, there was no coherent body that scrutinized what the effects would be. OSHA is the glaring example of how uncoordinated our government activity can be, and how punitive they can be on small business in a very unintentional manner. If OSHA had passed 10 years earlier, our company wouldn't exist."

Nicholas G. Polydoris, president of ENM Corp., a Chicago manufacturer of electrical counters, says his company has swallowed $100,000 in inventory on occasion when a big customer asked him to take it back. "We could sue, but the customer will remember you down the pike," says Polydoris, who in the meantime has to pacify his own banker's complaints about ENM's high inventories.

"You don't run the business on profit, you run on survival," says Polydoris, who last year netted $375,000 on sales of $7.5-million. Sales are off 15% from last year, and ENM has reduced employment mostly by laying off part-time workers.

Flexibility and tenacity are key ingredients in any small company's success. "The average small businessman has no investments outside of his own business, doesn't read business journals, doesn't understand the economy, and tends to guess wrong," says Henry Warren, head of SBA's management services section. Warren adds, however, that "one of the interesting things about small business is that it is very adaptable."

A classic example is Certron Corp., an Anaheim (Calif.) producer of blank cassette cartridges and precision computer parts. "There was simply no financing available for us," says Edwin R. Gamson, Certron's president, about a $600,000 operating loss reported last year when the oil crisis sent plastics prices soaring. "We stayed alive by trimming operations and keeping on a positive cash basis. The banks have been extremely cooperative with us, except in giving us money."

After its big suppliers, Du Pont and Monsanto, could not fill company orders during the shortage, Certron had to turn elsewhere for 50% of its materials. "Black market was out of the question," Gamson says. "Their prices were out of sight." So Gamson turned to the major airlines, purchasing their used plastic dishes, eating utensils, and cocktail glasses. "With help from the health department we learned to clean them, grind them up, and use them over again," he explains. "We also bought used Kodak Instamatic film cartridges from film processors."

Certron had been selling cassette cartridges to Ford Motor Co. in several different colors, but adding the new materials gave the batches a muddy color. Undaunted, Gamson added black to disguise the polyglot antecedents. "And we convinced Ford they would have any color they wanted as long as it was black," he says with a grin.

Byron L. Godbersen, president of Midwest Industries, Inc., of Ida Grove, Iowa, a manufacturer of farm and marine equipment, solves his financial problems by dealing solely with a factoring firm. Midwest's sales have grown from $600,000 in 1964 to $15.5-million last year, on which it netted more than 6%. To compete with the giants in its field, which offer promotions in the fall on spring items at reduced terms, Midwest sells its invoices to William Iselin & Co., of New York, for ready cash, permitting it to offer customers the same financial terms as its competition.

Other companies, such as Houston-based Big State Pest Control, report that business is still booming, but profits are not sufficient to provide for future expansion. "This company could be two to three times this size if we could get an attractive long-term loan," complains William J. Spitz, who launched the company 25 years ago with a $400 loan. "But we're not big enough to go to insurance companies and other long-term lenders."

Kaull of Premix is even more critical. "Discrimination is practiced in small business financing by financial institutions," he asserts. "It's called 'sound banking practice.'" Loans are smaller, terms shorter, and interest rates higher. A 16% to 18% interest rate on short-term loans was not unusual last year. "Small businesses normally can't withstand that type of interest expense when they invest in new equipment," Kaull complains. "They can't get the return on it to justify that interest. Either they can't grow or they don't survive."

Why banks are reluctant

For their part, most bankers insist that their basic lending policies are the same for all businesses regardless of size: They make loans only on the reasonable assurance that they are going to be paid back. But small businesses, which almost inevitably are woefully undercapitalized, do have a harder time than their bigger corporate brethren in convincing banks that they can repay.

For one thing, says Leonard O'Connor at the First National Bank of Boston, most small-business borrowing is term business ranging from 12 months to as long as 10 years, compared with the more common 90-day loans to larger corporations. And that, he explains, makes the small-business loan more risky at the outset. "We look at the cash flow of a small business to see if it will support monthly loan payments," says O'Connor. "In making a loan to a major corporation, we look at the balance sheet and assets and liabilities." In addition, his bank also probes for secondary sources of repayment that the small businessman might have—property, equipment, and even the personal assets of the owners.

Even so, many banks—especially those serving more limited local communities—actively cultivate small-business financing. Such business actually may be more profitable; sharp-pencil treasurers of large corporations can shop around for cut-rate banking deals. But as Luther L. Hodges, Jr., chairman of North Carolina National Bank, explains, the small firm often "has no other credit source" than his local bank.

Kenneth R. Keck, head of Chicago's Harris Trust & Savings Bank's small-business section, claims that "the banking community has become much more interested in small business in the past few years. People who thought that companies like the Penn Central were safe because they were big found out otherwise, and some banks also were badly burned on foreign commitments. Small businesses, other than the mom-and-pop ones, which are basically inefficient, are more stable because they don't have access to other money markets as do big ones."

Government loans are sometimes available, but a problem is that they make it easy for small businesses to fail by building in onerous debt loads, contends Brian Haslett, director of development for the Institute of New Enterprise Development (INED), a private consulting organization funded by both the government and foundations. To help remedy that situation, INED, which is based in Belmont, Mass., has launched a series of screening workshops from Appalachia to Salt Lake City to uncover promising new ventures. Those with the potential to become million-dollar enterprises within two years are recommended to local community development corporations, which can supply badly needed equity capital.

Traditionally, private venture capital companies have been the vehicle for raising seed money for new businesses. But tight money and the current economic slump have drastically shifted their method of operation. Venture capitalists take positions in fledgling companies, nurturing them until the enterprise can be taken public. But while $1.4-billion was raised for companies with less than $5-million sales in the equity markets during 1969 at the peak of the "hot issue" craze, such public financing now has dried up.

Undaunted by the scarcity of money, L. L. Durr, an Indianapolis engineer who has successfully run his own businesses before, started Interdyne, Inc., which designs and produces purification and recycling systems, in early 1974, with four partners and $100,000 equity. "I prefer a tough economic period to start a business," says Durr. "It eliminates the blue-suede-shoe boys, and customers are convinced you probably will last. The major reason most new firms fail is that management doesn't understand its true costs. They see a manufacturing cost of $10 per product, overhead of $5, add 10%, and think they are making money. But you must take the manufacturing cost and multiply it by six. You have to take all you can get, all the market will bear."

WHAZZIT?

COMPETITIVE MARKET

Many buyers and sellers in a market where prices and quantities are subject to negotiation and bargaining.

OLIGOPOLY

Only a few powerful sellers in a market; they can influence both the prices and the quantities of goods and services.

MONOPOLY

Only one seller in a market, who can control both the price and the quantities of goods.

CARTEL

An international agreement among businessmen to split up and control markets and the production of goods.

INFLATION

A period when a given amount of money will purchase fewer goods and services than in the past.

CONSIDER

1. Does the fact that similar products made by different companies are priced the same necessarily indicate collusion in pricing?

2. What advantages might a cartel have over firms operating in an environment of free competition?

3. Why did Hershey actually increase the weight of its candy bar without raising the price?

4. Thousands of new products are introduced each year. Some succeed and some fail. Explain why.

5. To what extent has the growth of Ford Motor been due to the sheer economic expansion in the country?

6. Can a company sell products that are no longer in demand by customers? Explain.

7. Would our economy be better off without marginal small businesses? Explain.

8. Should struggling small businesses be aided or subsidized by larger businesses? By the government? Explain.

9. Would we be better off with a larger number of smaller auto manufacturers? Explain.

10. What's so bad about inflation? Are there advantages to inflation? Explain.

CHALLENGES

Examine a HERSHEY bar today and compare the price and weight with the data presented for previous years in this chapter. Explain any changes.

A loss leader is a retail product priced low so as to attract customers into a store to buy normally-priced goods. Compare prices of featured items in several grocery advertisements in your local newspaper. Identify the loss leaders, if any, and explain pricing differences. Explain why several stores might feature the same loss leader goods.

Compare the total list prices of a new car from several manufacturers all with the same features (engine size, body style, accessories). Analyze and explain the differences.

Examine the prices charged for long-distance telephone calls. Explain why intra-state calls may cost less than calls across the nation. Why are special rates given? Are these prices based on a free market competition: supply and demand?

RECAP

In our business enterprise system, goods and services are provided through exchange in the marketplace. The demand for goods and the supply of goods interact to determine the prices and quantities of goods made available on the market.

The "free" competition and bartering principle is a key aspect of our economic system. When competition is reduced (one or more companies tend to dominate the setting of prices and the availability of goods), we may feel we are not getting the best price or the best goods.

Competition tends to be greater when there is a large number of firms in the marketplace. Yet one industry, the automobile industry, has only a few very large firms that compete vigorously. The automobile companies see no need for government influence or control to "improve" the competition.

Help is needed, however, to keep the overall economy on an even keel. Business cycles are normal changes in the economic activity, responding to changing supply and demand.

Inflation is a serious problem, represented by a spiralling upward of wages and prices. Nobody seems to get ahead. Rising costs reflect rising prices; prices rise to cover higher costs. Wages are but one type of costs in business, and may not be a major direct factor in inflation. We typically fight inflation by holding down prices and trying to reduce overall demand for goods -- to "slow down" the economy.

Recession is a period of lessened demand for goods and thus slower economic activity. Prices may fall, or at least don't rise as rapidly! A depression is the worst possible economic slowdown. When times get tough we try to spur the economy, usually through governmental spending and monetary policy actions.

In this chapter we also got acquainted with Ford -- the man and the company. Ford Motor Company is the second largest automobile maker in the nation. Founded by Henry Ford, the company jumped to the leadership of the industry in the early years through the development of the Model T and innovative production techniques. The company continues to be an aggressive competitor, both in the U.S. and internationally.

WORKSHEET NO. 3

NAME_____

INSTRUCTOR'S NAME_____

DATE_____

1. What would make a manufacturer decide to make more of a
    particular product? Identify the factors that would normally
    lead to this decision.

2. What factors might induce a buyer to purchase more of a particular
    product? Explain.

3. Who sets prices on products?

4. What is inflation and what causes it?

CHAPTER 4

Business And Government

Competition in the market-place is a basic quality of our economic system, but ours is not necessarily "free" competition. By the behavior of businessmen seeking to reduce competition and by the intervention of government, representing public attitudes and needs, competition in America is regulated.

Government influences supply, demand, and business practices in many ways. Yet we continue to enjoy a freedom of business enterprise that is significantly greater than that found in many nations, particularly planned economies such as Russia.

Wage and price controls are an example of the influence government plays in our business system. Here, controls directly affect supply and demand in the marketplace. In other more subtle ways, government regulates a myriad of business practices, ranging from advertising to taxes.

Public utilities are regulated by various federal, state, and local agencies because they operate with virtual monopoly power in their defined geographic areas. We feel that competition is not particularly desirable in electricity, water, gas, and telephone businesses. Con Edison is one of the largest public utilities and is heavily regulated in the things it does.

Railroads are a special case. First, the railroads found they could not provide passenger travel service on a profitable basis, so the government set up AMTRAK. Then some of the railroads found they were in deeper trouble financially and the government set up CONRAIL, a single, integrated rail system to handle freight transportation. Both are business enterprises, subsidized by the public.

In many other ways, government acts to help and maintain competition and a strong economic system. Attempts to limit competition by private businessmen may be quashed under our anti-trust laws. Price-fixing, attempts to limit output to raise profits, and other conspiracies are not tolerated in our society.

There are many other areas in which the government controls the activities of business. As a society we have decided that we want some controls placed on businesses, and government is the agent for enforcing those controls. As times change the aspects of business that government controls have changed to the point where now we have controls for pollution, discrimination, safety, pensions, hours of work, and hundreds of other aspects of business operations.

As well as controlling business, government works to ensure that our enterprise system remains strong. Federal fiscal and monetary policies are designed to ensure that our economy remains healthy. The government also stimulates business by its purchases and the money it spends on research and development that ultimately end up as improved products for the consuming public.

Government activities are paid for through taxes. Business pays a big share of this support of our "public enterprises". There can be little question that business and government are partners today.

In This Chapter

Uncle Sam's Hands

Businessmen are ideologically and emotionally committed to the idea that competition is good and **government intervention is bad.** Regulation, they say, discourages initiative, efficiency, and the profit motive.

But in this twentieth century, competition has been abridged by changing customs of doing business, monopoly and other natural limitations on free trade, trade unions representing employee interests, legislation, and changing public interests. While we don't really want monopoly by industrial giants, we tend to discourage free competition as well.

As consumers we may prefer brand name products, warranties that only large companies can provide, and efficiencies (thus lower costs) that only large-scale production can achieve. This encourages big business and discourages competition.

Consumer demands for reliable utilities (water, gas, power, telephone), public transportation, radio, television, banking, and other services has resulted in ever-expanding government intervention through regulation.

Early regulation of toll roads, canals, ferries, and gristmills was founded on the reasoning that competition in these industries would be uneconomical and not in the public's best interests. Railroads, air routes, utilities, broadcasting, and nuclear power are further modern-day examples.

Regulation is felt to be necessary in other industries for reasons of consumer protection. Examples include drugs, food, securities and investments, automobiles, and packaging. Also we regulate business practices to assure environmental protection, as in air and water pollution abatement and control, waste control, and building inspections.

Government intervention in our enterprise system is generally considered essential today -- for the mutual benefit of business, consumers, and the public.

It isn't a matter of taking away power from business. Rather, it's a matter of making the economic system work well for all.

FAIR TRADE

Government influences business activity through various forms of regulation. Trade is regulated by the Federal Trade Commission, established in 1914. The commission aims at controlling unfair trade practices such as:

-- false or misleading advertising
-- bribery of a customer's employees to gain secret information
-- misbranding or labelling of goods as to quality, ingredients, or other characteristics
-- using packages or containers to give a false impression of the contents
-- advertising free goods, but then requiring a purchase
-- using sales approaches involving gambling.

Under several laws, this Commission and other agencies are empowered to watch over competition to ensure that it is fair.

ANTITRUST

If a company grows too large, where the effect is to substantially lessen competition or to create a monopoly, the federal government may step in. There have been many cases where the government has required companies to spin off part of their business so as to promote competition.

In the late 1800's, some businesses took a "public be damned" attitude and exploited investors, employees, and customers. Outcries from farmers, small businessmen, and public users of railroads led to the first major federal law to regulate business: the Act to Regulate Commerce. That 1887 law made unlawful the charging by the railroads of any unjust, unreasonable, or discriminatory freight rates and prohibited collusion among the railroads in establishing rates. It also created an Interstate Commerce Commission to enforce the provisions of the law.

Other laws, including the Sherman Antitrust law and the Clayton Act soon followed, expanding the role of Uncle Sam.

While the federal government doesn't control the creation of businesses, that's the job of state governments, various federal agencies do control many of the activities of corporations. Since the Internal Revenue System collects taxes from all of us, including businesses, the IRS can have a great deal of influence on how corporations keep their books and report their profits. The Security and Exchange Commission keeps an eye on how corporations raise the money that they need to keep running and to grow. Other government agencies (OSHA) control working conditions to ensure employee safety, (EEOC) guarantees equal employment opportunity, and (EPA) controls pollution. There are hundreds of agencies that control aspects of business activity, but control is not the only relationship between business and government.

PARTNERS

Business leaders often play an active role in formulating public policies affecting business. They serve on various governmental commissions and committees, at federal, state, and local levels.

Other businessmen take time off to serve on governmental posts. Many men and women who hold key governmental positions have had extensive business experience and are sensitive to the potential impact of government actions.

Even the President of the United States seeks counsel directly from businessmen. The Council of Economic Advisors, the Cost of Living Council, and various special groups bring the business perspective to the White House.

Additionally, a large proportion of governmental expenditures are in the form of supply contracts -- purchases from business organizations and contracts for research and performance of services. This spending is an important source of revenue for private firms and spurs our economic growth.

So we see that Uncle Sam and business have a good two-way relationship. What is good for "General Motors" may be good for our economy and what is in the public interest may also be good for business.

ConEd vs. The World

Charles F. Luce, Con Edison's Chairman of the Board and Chief Executive Officer, has been trying to recast the company's public image. Investor interest, approval of rate increases requested, and continued growth all depend on a positive view of Con Ed.

This is difficult because realistic rates must be maintained for customers to pay, but costs have been soaring -- both for fuel and for construction of facilities and pollution control.

How to provide the electrical energy people need, at a reasonable cost, and to do so with minimum adverse impact on the environment, is the test for electrical utilities today.

No utility has more headaches than Con Edison. Its market is one of the least profitable because New York's old, cramped apartments consume only half as much electricity as the average American household. Yet costs are high because of the cost of maintaining old generating plants and fraying distribution lines.

Because Con Ed is ever present in the city, sympathy from the press and the public has been slowly increasing. Con Ed has a lot of buried transmission lines, so "Dig We Must" and the streets always seem to be torn up for construction or repairs.

Further, it's tough to find a "site" for a new power plant anywhere in the metropolitan area. Public outcries are heard in opposition to every proposed location that Con Ed finds. Pollution can be controlled, but nobody wants the plants in the backyard anyway. The "siting dilemma" will continue to be a difficult problem, and Con Ed will continue to be a polluter for some time because it is a side effect of making electricity.

Today, Con Ed needs to find sites for plants or transmission lines on crowded Manhattan and in Westchester county. Everywhere the company turns to build, there is a court, a commission, or an outraged citizens group standing in opposition.

Several facilities that are already under construction are in doubt. The Cornwall (Hudson River) pumped storage plant mentioned in Chapter 2 is one such plant. Others are being taken over by the state, with the expectation that completion will be easier.

"The realization is coming," says Luce, "that if you oppose every site, eventually it will have an effect when you try to turn on the light."

REGULATIONS

Con Edison is subject to regulation by the New York Public Service Commission, which regulates the company's electric, gas and steam rates, as well as the issuance of its securities (how it raises financial capital for construction, expansion, etc.).

The company is also subject in some of its activities to the jurisdiction of the Federal Power Commission under the Federal Power Act. Construction and operation of nuclear power plants are subject to regulation by the Atomic Energy Commission. In addition, various matters relating to construction and operation of the more conventional (coal and oil fueled) and nuclear plants require permits from, or are subject to regulation by, numerous other governmental agencies.

As illustrated in the figure below, permission to build a conventional power generating plant requires approval or licensing by a range of local, state, and federal governmental agencies.

Prior to the mid 1960's, Con Ed's relationships with the various government agencies that had an interest in electric utilities was a lot less complex than today. A decade or more ago, the business of agencies was to see that the company provided the power demanded by the public and broke no laws in the process. Little concern for today's environmental factors existed and public voices were rarely heard. Public hearings and governmental intervention focused on infrequent service or rate issues. Fuel was abundant and plants were built without hassle.

Utilities often benefited from close personal relationships

among utility executives and members of regulatory bodies. Common interests, backgrounds, and concerns facilitated smooth relations. Federal influence was small, thus local and state bodies assumed the power. Thus personal relationships and lobbying at the state and local levels paid off well for the utilities.

Power shortages (brown-outs and black-outs), increased awareness and concern about air and water pollution, and the soaring fuel costs (passed along in rates charged) all have attracted attention and closer regulation to Con Ed and other utilities.

Con Edison is now in the middle of diverse (and even conflicting) regulatory constraints. In the future we may expect utility-government relations to become even more formal and arms-length, requiring considerable time and effort to reach decisions satisfying diverse needs.

It is likely, too, that controls will become even more fragmented before any consolidation of regulatory forces occurs. Con Ed must deal with all of the agencies and interest groups simultaneously. At some point, improved coordination of these bodies will be needed, to provide an overall view and approach to utility affairs.

One solution may be for Con Ed to give up part of its responsibility to a public agency. In fact, this is being done now -- for the tough job of building new power generation facilities.

STATE POWER

In planning for future power supply, Con Ed has anticipated increased reliance on the state government to build new generation and transmission facilities. Having plants built wholly or partly by others reduces the pressure on capital financing and on rates.

The Power Authority of the State of New York (PASNY) is authorized by the legislature to construct power plants to supply the needs of the metropolitan transportation system (subways and trains) and of other governmental customers.

In 1975, Con Edison sold its partially-built Indian Point No. 3 plant to PASNY for about $384 million. In 1974 the state acquired Astoria No. 6. These sales were authorized in 1974 when Con Ed faced a severe cash shortage resulting primarily from the rapid escalation of fuel oil prices during the Arab embargo. The sales relieved Con Ed of about $800 million in construction costs, including the sale price plus further costs of completing the units.

CON ED in the Middle

AGENCIES INVOLVED IN APPROVING A FOSSIL FUEL GENERATING PLANT FOR CON ED

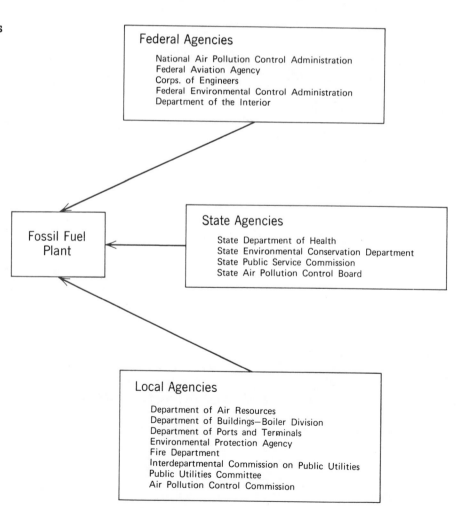

Federal Agencies
 National Air Pollution Control Administration
 Federal Aviation Agency
 Corps. of Engineers
 Federal Environmental Control Administration
 Department of the Interior

Fossil Fuel Plant

State Agencies
 State Department of Health
 State Environmental Conservation Department
 State Public Service Commission
 State Air Pollution Control Board

Local Agencies
 Department of Air Resources
 Department of Buildings—Boiler Division
 Department of Ports and Terminals
 Environmental Protection Agency
 Fire Department
 Interdepartmental Commission on Public Utilities
 Public Utilities Committee
 Air Pollution Control Commission

PASNY expects to build additional baseload plants and to establish an interconnection with Hydro Quebec (for exchange of power at peak periods) by 1984.

When the public is asked to pick up the tab for construction as well as rate increases, interest picks up in basic management issues: Is Con Ed managed efficiently? Could there be savings in costs?

At the direction of the Public Service Commission, a management study of the company was done by an independent management consulting firm. Results of the first phase of the study were reported in 1975 and received headline attention in the newspapers. The Wall Street Journal headline read, "Con Edison Management Gets Top Marks in Consultants' Study for State Agency."

The study pointed out possible areas for improvement and cost savings, but was generally favorable. "The system is, by and large, operated effectively with the limited capital available for new plant and system reinforcement," and "...there is little within direct control of management that would reduce ra rates to consumers signifi direct control of management that would reduce rates to consumers significantly or do much to limit the size and frequency of future rate increases."

The report said Con Ed had used "considerable resourcefulness" in buying fuel at favorable prices under severe market conditions. It commented favorably on the company's

"very genuine and widespread dedication to giving quality service to customers."

Thus government looks over the shoulders of executives and judges how well they are doing. But the judgments may be favorable. Con Ed will benefit from the study by learning where it may improve operations. Also, the public impression of Con Ed was given a positive boost.

WE LIVE HERE, TOO

Con Edison doesn't just work in New York and Westchester County. Its employees live within the service territory. Also, in a broader sense, the company is a corporate citizen of the community, with rights and responsibilities.

A substantial portion of the company's business comes from the city. When the city loses residents or businesses, Con Ed loses

customers. The municipal crisis -- the city's dire financial situation -- may mean higher taxes, layoffs, deterioration of municipal services, and related developments. These could lead to a lower level of economic activity in the city and have adverse effects on Con Edison's sales, receivables, and uncollectible accounts.

Con Edison's billings to City and State agencies alone (which could be affected directly by the situation) amount to more than $275 million and $80 million, respectively, each year.

As PASNY develops, the problem of services provided to government may be more clearly defined, with Con Edison merely receiving a fee for managing the facilities and transmission of the power.

Con Ed can't leave town. The company must learn to be a working partner with the city, the state, the federal agencies, its customers, and the public.

The Law

Back in 1787, Thomas Jefferson proposed that a provision be written into the Constitution to prohibit monopoly power in business.

The provision was not included and in the years that followed, as the American enterprise system took shape and grew, businessmen used various means to influence their competitive situations. Among the means used were price conspiracies among businesses, trust agreements to produce large combinations of businesses that could effectively restrain trade, and direct formation of holding companies to acquire smaller competitive firms.

Such companies as General Electric, General Motors, General Foods, Anaconda, McDonnell Douglas, U.S. Steel, Texaco, TWA, and others grew not as single business enterprises, but were put together through the device of the holding company.

By the last quarter of the 19th century, despite satisfying growth and prosperity in the economy, it was apparent that unregulated business had developed some inequities: price-setting, frauds on investors and customers, and exploitation of labor and suppliers. Many of the public felt that business had adopted a "public be damned" attitude.

It wasn't until 1890 that the federal government acquired power to combat restraints of trade. The Sherman Antitrust Act sought to abolish monopolies, monopolistic practices, or other practices restraining trade. The law was initially aimed at the massive Standard Oil Trust.

The act includes provisions that:

"Every contract, combination in the form of trust or otherwise, or conspiracy, in restraint of trade or commerce among the several states or with foreign nations is hereby declared to be illegal...."

"Every person who shall monopolize or attempt to monopolize or combine or conspire with any other person or persons, to monopolize any part of the trade or commerce...shall be deemed guilty of a misdemeanor...."

The Sherman Act proved to be not only late in arriving, but grossly underpowered to do its job. The law was extremely difficult to enforce in the face of such massive and powerful companies as Standard Oil, U.S. Steel, American Tobacco, and the mining interests.

Yet the courts did apply the law to break up two of the largest companies in the nation: Standard Oil and American Tobacco. But even with court action, it took nearly two decades to finally effect the breakup of Standard Oil Company into some twenty separate companies.

Many of today's active competitors in the oil industry were once part of the Standard Oil Trust. You may recognize their names today: Exxon, Sohio, Chevron, Mobil, Amoco (Standard Oil Co., Indiana), Atlas, and others. Each of these smaller companies, incidentally, is today larger than the original one that was deemed to be restraining trade. In fact, Exxon is the largest industrial firm in the world in terms of assets, sales and profits (See Page 18).

FURTHER LAWS

From 1890 to 1914 there was considerable dissatisfaction and controversy concerning the ineffectiveness of the existing antitrust law. Monopolies and trust agreements flourished through a rather liberal interpretation of the Sherman Act by the courts.

As a result, the Clayton Act was passed by Congress in 1914, making it unlawful for a company to acquire the stock of a competing company for the purposes of gaining a monopoly. It was further declared unlawful to set up interlocking directors (the same people serving on the boards of directors of two or more competing companies) or to discriminate in price between different purchasers where the effect is to lessen competition.

Also, Congress enacted the Federal Trade Commission Act to spell out unfair business practices and to establish an agency (the Federal Trade Commission – FTC) to enforce the laws. Since then (1914), the FTC has actively monitored business growth and activities such as proposed mergers or combinations and said "no" when trade was likely to be restricted.

In recent years, the FTC has initiated actions against IBM, AT&T, Goodyear and Firestone, among others, to break them up because they dominate their respective industries.

In 1936, the Robinson-Patman Act further amended the Clayton Act by prohibiting price discrimination and exclusinve agreements in the sale of goods for consumption in the United States. It prohibited price discrimination against small firms where discrimination substantially interfered with competition, except where such differentials were due to differences in quantity, quality or grade of goods sold.

Also in the 1930's the Congress established the Federal Power Commission (FPC) to regulate the building of facilities for power generation and the setting of rates for gas and electricity.

These Acts were followed by others in the Roosevelt Administration: a Federal Communications Commission, a Securities and Exchange Commission, and the Social Security Administration. We also got the federal recognition and support of labor unions, increased and more varied forms of taxes, and controls over food, drugs, and other types of products.

TRENDS

The legislation has continued to flow. We are governed by an increasing number of laws, enforced by an ever-expanding government organizations. We now have agencies for environmental protection, equal employment opportunity, control of atomic energy, and communications satellites to name a few. As a result of this growth in legislation and control, the federal government is by far the largest employer in the nation.

Few business actions may be made that do not involve considerations of some law. We take almost all of the regulation for granted, though, as it is now very much a part of American business life.

We have seen the federal government pass legislation concerning pollution control, equal employment opportunity, consumer protection, safety on the job, pension reform, and many other areas that traditionally were left to the discretion of businessmen to determine what they should or should not do.

The trend continues to be toward greater federal involvement in business affairs, providing more centralized, standardized legal requirements across the nation and replacing many varied local and state laws which are hard to keep track of. Our society is growing larger and more complex every day; our economic stability and growth depends in part on government regulation.

WHAZZIT?

Is John Sherman's Antitrust Obsolete?

The head of the major U. S. corporation spoke feelingly: "I would be very glad if we knew exactly where we stand, if we could be free from danger, trouble, and criticism." His plea could have been made yesterday, by executives at IBM, Xerox, GTE, General Motors, AT&T, Exxon, Standard Brands, Chrysler, or dozens of other large companies that have recently stood in the dock, accused of violating the nation's antitrust laws.

It was, in fact, said back in 1912 by Elbert H. Gary, chairman of U. S. Steel Corp. He was giving a Congressional committee his views on the need for updating the country's first antitrust law, the Sherman Act, to which Ohio Senator John Sherman gave his name in 1890. Echoing the sentiments of many executives, Gary complained bitterly of the restraints imposed by the antitrust law on his company's ability to compete in world markets. Business had grown too big and complex, Gary maintained, to be shoehorned into laws drawn from Adam Smith's economic model of many small companies competing in local markets.

Two years later Congress gave Gary an unwelcome answer to his plea. It passed an even more restrictive antitrust measure, the Clayton Act, and set up the Federal Trade Commission to police business practices and methods of competition even more closely.

Today business faces much the same danger, trouble, and criticism that disturbed Gary, and is raising much the same complaints against antitrust. The International Telephone & Telegraph Corp. scandal and corporate participation in Watergate has stirred up deep public distrust of national institutions, including business. In response, as in Gary's day, the antitrust wind is rising, blown up currently by the oil crisis and fanned by consumerists, such as Ralph Nader, who argue that antitrust weapons have been used like peashooters against dinosaurs. Business almost certainly faces even tougher antitrust enforcement and possibly even a new antitrust law aimed at breaking up the corporate giants in the country's basic industries.

This prospect points up the underlying question businessmen ask about antitrust: Are laws framed more than three-quarters of a century ago appropriate legal weapons in a market system grown increasingly large, complex, and multinational? In raising this basic issue, businessmen can point to a far-reaching, intricate web of laws and rules that has made the government the regulator, watchdog, and even partner of business. Wage and price controls, health and safety regulations, and disclosure laws, are all a far cry from the economy of Sherman's or Gary's day.

Businessmen complain of the unsettling vagueness of the antitrust laws, which permits antitrusters to attack many long-standing business practices in their effort to root out restraints of trade and monopoly. The FTC, for example, is now suing Kellogg, General Foods, General Mills, and Quaker Oats, alleging that such procedures as having route men arrange their breakfast cereals on supermarket shelves are anticompetitive. The Justice Dept. has a similar suit against tire makers Goodyear and Firestone.

Executives of International Business Machines Corp., caught by both government and private antitrust suits attacking pricing and promotion policies, privately declare that they are baffled over what they can legally do. Bertram C. Dedman, vice-president and general counsel for INA

Corp., echoes a widely held view: "We never really know precisely what antitrust means. It's frequently strictly a matter of opinion."

Enormous economic stakes are involved in antitrust enforcement. Such current cases as those against IBM, Xerox Corp., and other giants involve billions of dollars' worth of capital investment and stockholder interests. Executives fear that such suits give broad power to courts not schooled in business, economics, or industrial technology. This power was dramatically illustrated last fall when U. S. District Judge A. Sherman Christensen announced a $352-million judgment against IBM and then confessed error, sending IBM's stock into wild gyrations.

Many businessmen wonder whether their companies are often targets of antitrust prosecution simply because they are big and successful. Philadelphia lawyer Edward D. Slevin sums up this attitude: "If the free market is pushed to its fullest extent, somebody wins. But the Justice Dept. seems to say: 'Now that you've won, you've cornered the market. We're going to break you up and start over.'"

All this, say many executives, makes it increasingly difficult for American business to compete internationally. Douglas Grymes, president of Koppers Co., argues that "big corporations are the only ones that can compete with big corporations in world markets." He says that the antitrust laws seem to equate bigness itself with monopoly and thus hinder American corporations from reaching the size necessary for world competition.

Tougher enforcement likely

Despite all these deeply felt concerns, the antitrust laws are likely to become even tougher and more restrictive. Starting with the Sherman Act, antitrust has been a product more of politics than of economics. Today's rising populist sentiment has led to demands for tighter antitrust enforcement. Only a decade ago historian Richard Hofstadter wrote, "The antitrust movement is one of the faded passions of American reform." Today it is the darling of reform. As James T. Halverson, director of the FTC's Bureau of Competition, sums up: "The political atmosphere is very favorable to antitrust right now."

The many signs of stepped-up antitrust activity in the last one or two years make an impressively lengthy list. They include:

NEW INVESTIGATIONS. Last week three federal agencies—Justice, the FTC, and the SEC—as well as some congressmen, revealed that they are turning to a little-used section of the Clayton Act to investigate the complex of interlocking directorships among major oil companies.

NEW LEGISLATION. The industrial reorganization bill that Senator Philip A. Hart (D-Mich.) introduced in Congress last year would provide a new legal basis for breaking up leading companies in the nation's most basic industries: autos, iron and steel, nonferrous metals, chemicals and drugs, electrical machinery and equipment, electronic computing and communications equipment, and energy. It is given no immediate chance to pass, but its ideas could find their way into future legislation. Another bill introduced by Senator John V. Tunney (D-Calif.), already approved by the Senate and taking a back seat to impeachment considerations in the House, would increase the current maximum criminal antitrust fine from $50,000 to $500,000 for corporations and $100,000 for executives. It would also require the Justice Dept. to explain publicly its reasons for accepting a consent decree instead of preparing a case and actually going to trial.

BIGGER ENFORCEMENT BUDGETS. The Administration is seeking large increases, by usually puny antitrust standards, in the fiscal 1975 budgets of both the Justice Dept. and the FTC for their antitrust departments. If Congress approves, Justice's Antitrust Div. will pick up 83 additional staff slots, more than half lawyers and economists. At the last big increase, fiscal 1970, the division got only 20. The FTC is due for an additional $3-million, or a 20% increase in its present antitrust budget.

GROWING MUSCLE AT FTC. After a long hibernation, the FTC is stepping out as a feisty agency with a new esprit, a highly professional staff, and a taste for going after bigness. It filed the monopoly suits against Xerox Corp. and the four biggest cereal makers. It has a special unit with an extra $1-million appropriation to litigate its case to break up the eight leading oil companies. And it got important new powers from Congress last year, including the right to demand otherwise unavailable product-line sales and profit figures from companies without first clearing with the Office of Management & Budget.

REORGANIZING JUSTICE. If the Justice Dept.'s monopoly case against IBM, filed more than five years ago, is successful, it would give new spirit to the Antitrust Div., which at least until recently has been demoralized by the successive shocks of ITT and Watergate. Even so, the division reorganized and beefed up its economics staff last fall to enable it to undertake investigations and prosecutions with a sharper eye to the economic impact of its actions.

More and tougher antitrust enforcement is foreshadowed by more subtle changes in mood and belief as well as by these specific developments. One such change is a growing recognition that the government itself creates monopoly power. Several weeks ago Columbia Law School called together many of the nation's leading industrial economists and antitrust lawyers for a conference on industrial concentration. The participants examined what business concentration means both for the economy and for antitrust policy. About the only thing generally agreed on was that governmental attempts to regulate an industry often result in preserving the monopoly power of those being regulated. In line with this belief, insiders say that the Antitrust Div. will step up its policy of intervening in other government proceedings to shape regulatory policy consistent with antitrust principles. Last January, for example, the division formally intervened in FCC proceedings in an attempt to deny renewal of the broadcasting license of Cowles Communications, Inc., in Des Moines, and those of Pulitzer Publishing Co. and Newhouse Broadcasting Corp. in St. Louis. All these companies also own newspapers.

Another change has been the dramatic multiplication of private antitrust suits—those brought by one company against another. These include the 40-odd private business suits against IBM, ITT's suit to split up General Telephone & Electronics Corp., and the large class actions against plumbing and wallboard manufacturers. In fiscal 1973 the government filed 45 antitrust suits. By comparison, businessmen and other private parties filed 1,152, making the business community itself a significant factor in antitrust enforcement (box).

All this is leading to an antitrust Congress. Victor H. Kramer, director of Washington's Institute for Public Interest Representation and a leading antitrust lawyer, expects that "more supporters of an effective antimonopoly

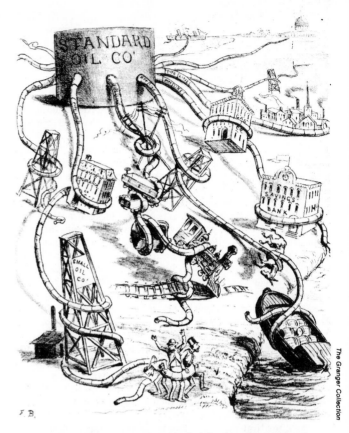

An 1884 cartoon strongly critical of the Standard Oil trust: As antimonopoly feeling grew in the U.S., and as populist politics picked up steam, Congress passed the 1890 Sherman Antitrust Act, but it failed to curb bigness or monopoly.

The Granger Collection

program are going to be elected to the 94th Congress than to any previous Congress in many years."

The alternatives

But as antitrust action steps up, so do the conflicts over the direction antitrust policy should take. The populists contend that antitrust enforcement in the past has been spineless. Businessmen complain that current policy paralyzes corporations because they are uncertain what practices are lawful and that they are being punished for being successfully competitive. Who is right?

The conflicts lead many businessmen to push for an updating of the antitrust laws. Richard L. Kattel, president of Atlanta's Citizens & Southern National Bank, which has been sparring with the Justice Dept. over the bank's expansion plans, feels that the antitrust laws "need complete revamping."

Major revamping, though, will not come because there is no general agreement on what form it should take. Most of the Columbia conference participants believe that the economic evidence for a change in policy is scanty and inconclusive. Suggestions ranged from doing nothing to pushing the tough Hart bill through Congress.

In approaching antitrust policy, there are alternatives:

1.) Abolish the laws altogether. A very few economists, such as Yale Brozen of the University of Chicago, talk as though antitrust laws are largely unnecessary. But as Robert L. Werner, executive vice-president and general counsel of RCA Corp., told a Conference Board antitrust seminar earlier this month: "There should be little disagreement by industry over the basic validity of the doctrine of antitrust. Certainly no businessman would seriously suggest that we scuttle that doctrine and return to a pre-Shermanite jungle." The courts have ruled that such practices as fixing prices, dividing markets, boycotting, some mergers, and predatory pricing designed to destroy competitors unlawfully impose restraints on the market.

2.) Clarify the laws by specifying precisely what business practices are unlawful. If various practices can be identified and prohibited through case-by-case litigation, why not draft a detailed code of conduct?

But the very difficulty of identifying such practices when business conditions are constantly changing led to the broad wording of the Sherman Act originally. No one has ever produced an all-inclusive list of anticompetitive conduct. No one can possibly delineate all the circumstances that amount to price fixing and other illegal practices. If publication of future prices by members of a trade association is unlawful, as the Supreme Court held in 1921, is dissemination of past inventory figures and prices equally unlawful? (No, said the Court in 1925. For other such cases, see box.) Moreover, as Thomas M. Scanlon, chairman of the American Bar Assn.'s 8,500-member antitrust section points out: "There's uncertainty in any kind of litigation. Laws intended to bring more certainty often bring less."

3.) Replace antitrust laws with direct regulation. U.S. Steel's Gary favored and Koppers' Grymes favors a business-government partnership with this approval. Its advocates agree with John Kenneth Galbraith that antitrust is a "charade," that it has not and cannot produce a competitive economy in the face of the technological imperatives of large corporations. University of Chicago's George J. Stigler concludes that antitrust has not been "a major force" on the economy to date. "The government has won most of its 1,800 cases," he points out, "and there has been no important secular decline in concentration." On the other hand, many economists and lawyers would argue that Stigler has drawn the wrong conclusion. As Almarin Phillips, professor of economics and law at the Wharton School of Finance & Commerce, puts it: "The success of antitrust can only be measured by the hundreds of mergers and price-fixing situations that never happened."

Moreover, in the view of an increasing number of observers, regulation that is designed to mitigate the effects of "natural" monopolies, such as telephone service, often winds up fostering them instead. Civil Aeronautics Board regulations, for example, have compelled higher airline rates than prevail on federally nonregulated intra-state flights. Wesley James Liebler, recently named director of policy planning at the FTC, says: "What the airline industry needs is a little competition. In the long run we should get rid of the CAB and let in some free competition." Liebler also wants to abolish fixed commission rates for stockbrokers.

Much of the energy of regulatory commissions seems to be devoted to anticompetitive ends. The Federal Communications Commission promulgated rules several years ago designed to stifle the growth of pay-cable television. Sports events, for example, may not be broadcast on pay-cable TV if similar events have been shown on commercial television any time during the previous five years.

Walter Adams, a Michigan State University economist, notes that regulatory commissions can exclude competitors through licensing power, maintain price supports by regulating rates, create concentration through merger surveillance, and harass the weak by supervising practices that the strong do not like. To combat this kind of government behavior, the Antitrust Div. itself has, for the past several years, been intervening or attempting to intervene in such

agencies as the ICC, CAB, and SEC to force decisions that spur competition in industry.

In support of their position, reformers make a further point: Large corporations have the political muscle to force the government to support their anticompetitive goals. Adams charges that the government has established an industrywide cartel for the oil companies through publishing monthly estimates of demand; through establishing quotas for each state pursuant to the Interstate Oil Compact, which Congress approved at behest of the oil companies; and through "prorationing devices" that dictate how much each well can produce. It is illegal to ship excess production in interstate commerce. Tariffs and import quotas protect only the producers, Adams says.

What this all amounts to is maintenance of shared monopoly power with the active cooperation of government. Only when the power of large companies is reduced, argue the populists, will the government be able to guide a competitive economy rather than serve as a prop for large interests. This was one of the original arguments for the Sherman Act in the 1880s.

4.) Move toward tougher enforcement. Populist critics of antitrust, such as Nader and Senator Hart, agree with Galbraith that antitrust has been all too ineffectual, but they move in the opposite policy direction. Since they believe that government regulation usually entrenches the power of big firms and concentrated industries, they favor a get-tough antitrust approach. They argue for two related tactics: extending existing law through the courts to curtail many practices of large firms in concentrated industries and getting Congressional legislation such as the Hart bill to attack the structure of these industries.

The Hart bill would permit the prosecution of companies because of their size alone. The history of antitrust has largely been to define and prosecute practices that courts would rule were restraints of trade, such as price fixing by agreement among competitors. But with increasing fervor, "structuralists" argue that size itself can be harmful.

Excerpts from the major antitrust laws

Sherman Act, Section 1: "Every contract, combination in the form of trust or otherwise, or conspiracy, in restraint of trade or commerce among the several States, or with foreign nations, is hereby declared to be illegal."

Sherman Act, Section 2: "Every person who shall monopolize, or attempt to monopolize, or combine or conspire with any other person or persons, to monopolize any part of the trade or commerce among the several States, or with foreign nations, shall be deemed guilty of a misdemeanor."

Federal Trade Commission Act, Section 5: "Unfair methods of competition in commerce, and unfair or deceptive acts or practices in commerce are declared unlawful."

Clayton Act, Section 7: "No corporation engaged in commerce shall acquire, directly or indirectly, the whole or any part of the stock or other share capital and no corporation subject to the jurisdiction of the Federal Trade Commission shall acquire the whole or any part of the assets of another corporation engaged also in commerce, where in any line of commerce in any section of the country, the effect of such acquisition may be substantially to lessen competition, or to tend to create a monopoly."

Cartels

Jerome Castle is an up-and-coming young businessman who doesn't particularly like antitrust laws. He is chairman and chief executive officer of a complex of construction and raw materials companies topped off by the Penn-Dixie Cement Corp. His company has acquired 52.4% of Continental Steel and other varied operations in rock, roadbuilding, and heavy construction. He'd like to buy other companies too, in closely-related fields.

"Right now," he says, "we're still small enough in the industry that we'll be able to make some acquisitions without running into difficulty." But sooner or later he will run into antitrust constraints, and that, he contends, shouldn't happen.

More major industries, he argues, should be organized along the lines of the auto industry, with a few giants dominating. That way, he argues, they can be effective, efficient competitors in a worldwide market.

Other countries tolerate, and even encourage, the formation of cartels -- and they are often very successful in taking our business away. So why shouldn't we compete with cartels?

WHAT'S A CARTEL?

A cartel is a business arrangement which has the purpose or effect of reducing or regulating competition in international trade. The objective is usually to secure higher net returns to the producers or sellers of goods in the cartelized industry -- and this means higher prices.

Some cartels are merely price-fixing arrangements, but most cartels are more concerned with dividing up the available market by territory, function, or technology. This means each member firm has to spend less money and effort to get the same or greater returns. It could be more efficient, but it means reduced competition. Function would mean taking a particular type of customer or category of business; technology would mean a particular type of manufacturing process or product category.

Cartels have existed in international trade covering such goods as rubber, petroleum, fertilizers, iron, cooper, tin, beryllium, chemicals, plastics, explosives, surgical instruments, machinery, paper, and aluminum.

They are formed through loose associations, informal understandings, written contractual agreements, patent licensing agreements, trade-mark agreements, joint selling practices, or even through government sponsorship in some cases.

Probably the most famous cartel today is OPEC, the Organization of Petroleum Exporting Countries. This cartel of oil producing nations meets on a regular basis to set the world price for crude oil, and determines how much each member country may produce if there is a surplus of oil that might threaten the posted price.

Our laws protect the "monopoly" of patents and trademarks, at least for a period of time, but other laws rule out further restrictive agreements affecting trade in the U.S. Generally, the public is opposed to cartels, a feeling against "big business," even though much business is conducted through cartels in the international marketplace.

NOTHING TO FEAR

Castle acknowledges that there are problems with his passion for bigness. Huge companies, unchecked, may try to use their vast size to force up prices and pad profits, rather than take advantage of their improved production leverage to drive costs and prices down.

Further, dominance of businesses that are so big may discourage brash newcomers, like himself, to try to build a business.

But the government has the power to slap regulation on any giant that gets out of hand. Being big alone isn't being bad.

We should not assume that leaders in large corporations are bent toward exploitation. In fact, the larger the businesses, the tougher it is to keep all the pieces working smoothly and profitably.

Castle has found this to be his big challenge: to try to make the benefits of being bigger come true.

AT&T And The Courts

The American Telephone and Telegraph Company controls 82% of the tele-communications networks in the United States, which makes it a near monopoly. AT&T also makes most of the equipment it uses, which one could argue makes it two monopolies in one.

The result is purely in the interest of the public, argues John D. deButts, the company's chairman and chief executive. The Bell System's customers get the best possible service at the lowest possible rates, he asserts.

THE CHARGE

In a move that rocked the business community, the Justice Department brought suit against AT&T, charging the company with monopolizing and conspiring to monopolize telecommunications service and equipment in violation of the Sherman Act. The 23 Bell Telephone companies which are part of the AT&T holding company, along with Western Electric (the manufacturer of the equipment), and Bell Telphone Laboratories.

The "relief" sought is the severing of the manufacturing arm -- a huge corporation in itself, with revenues of $7 billion. And then this company (Western Electric) would be broken into two or more parts, to provide a competitive market for equipment.

The government also demanded that AT&T sell its long-distance telephone network, which handles 90% of all United States long-distance calls or else sell off some of the 23 operating companies that now make up the Bell system.

THE RESPONSE

Said deButz, "Needless to say, we are going to do all we can to see that that doesn't happen. Indeed, we are confident that, when the consequences of the Justice Department's recommendations are made plain, it will <u>not</u> happen."

Mr. deButts dug in for a "fight to the finish", a battle that could well last until his retirement expected in 1980 and even beyond for his successors. He vowed, too, that the company would continue to operate as it always had run as a service and manufacturing monopoly.

The effect of the suit will be anything but business as usual, however, as many people are devoting time and effort to the fight. Also, state and federal rate regulators may be harder to persuade regarding rate increases as long as the suit is pending and AT&T is painted as the big bad giant. These problems, in turn, may reduce the company's profitability and ability to maintain its pace in providing modern equipment and technology.

KEEP A WINNING TEAM

AT&T has served the public without major problems for nearly a century. Costs of calls and quality of the service have markedly improved over the years. Many innovations are due to research and development by Bell Laboratories, paid for out of AT&T revenues.

There is also serious question whether a larger number of fragmented firms could provide the same consistent quality of communications services. Mr. deButts bets the quality of service would deteriorate as a consequence, and it would cost much more.

The third factor is that AT&T is regarded as well-managed. While under a consent decree to improve the equal employment opportunities of women and blacks, AT&T has made significant strides, ahead of other major companies. Management capabilities are strong, and the organization is taut and highly productive.

Why a breakup? The obvious reason is the firm's dominance, size, and control over services offered and the markets. Under our antitrust laws, this is clearly inconsistent with our usual philosophy of supply and demand in the marketplace.

A Landmark Law That Boxes in the Banks

Glass and Steagall were to banking what Mason and Dixon were to the drawing of boundaries—each taking what had been whole and dividing it into parts. The line that Charles Mason and Jeremiah Dixon drew divided slave from free states. The line that Senator Carter Glass (D-Va.) and Representative Henry Steagall (D-Ala.) drew almost two centuries later divided commercial from investment banking.

If the Glass-Steagall line seems anachronistic to many today, it appeared vital in 1933 to the salvation of the nation's banking system—or what remained of it. By the time the Banking Reform Act of 1933 (the formal title of Glass-Steagall) went on the books on June 16 of that year, 9,000 U. S. banks had failed, and the nation had gone through Franklin Roosevelt's bank holiday, aimed at stanching a hysterical flight of bank deposits.

The achievement. The act accomplished a great many things—creating the Federal Deposit Insurance Corp., for example. Most of its provisions were hotly controversial, and had it not been caught up in the whirlwind of Roosevelt's first 100 days, it might not have passed in the form that it did.

Glass believed that no single institution should do both commercial banking (taking deposits and lending money) and investment banking (underwriting and dealing in securities), and he got his position written into the Democratic party platform of 1932. The divorce was no easy matter because the two functions had been part and parcel of banking since the Civil War.

At their peak in 1930, commercial banks, through their investment banking affiliates, participated in 61% of all new bond issues. The banks were equally important in the underwriting of new stock issues. It was precisely this strong position in stock and bond markets that had gone bad that led Glass—and most of the public—to blame the stock market crash on banks in general and on big-city banks in particular. Glass's special villain was Charles E. "Sunshine Charlie" Mitchell, chairman of the National City Bank of New York (today's Citibank) and perhaps the greatest bond salesman who ever lived. Mitchell, said Glass, was "more responsible than all the others put together for the excesses that have resulted in this disaster."

The bill of particulars that Glass and Steagall drew up against the banks was a long one. The first charge dealt with country banks—hardest hit by the Depression—and their reliance on big-city correspondent banks for investment advice. To most observers it was the collapse of the agricultural sector that dealt the country banks so harsh a blow. But big-city banks were also happy to sell the country banks securities that their investment affiliates had underwritten. H. Parker Willis, a Columbia University professor, told Congress that "various banking superintendents have of late classified unsatisfactory bond holdings as a primary cause of failure."

Banks were also charged with lending money on very favorable terms to their own investment affiliates—and to customers wishing to buy securities underwritten by the affiliates. Corporations often found that their dealings with commercial banks went more smoothly when the bank was allowed to underwrite the company's public securities offerings. Finally, there were charges that banks stuffed their own trust departments with securities written by the bank's investment affiliate, and that the affiliate sometimes jumped in to help support the stock of the parent bank.

The misdeeds. Congressmen were awed to learn that Chase National Bank (today's Chase Manhattan Bank) had taken into its own portfolio $10 million in issues of dubious quality to help out its securities affiliate. And National City Bank apparently sold $25 million worth of speculative loans to its securities subsidiary, paid for out of new stock sold to the public.

In the end, it was evidence of self-dealing by bankers that put Glass-Steagall on the books. Bankers would often risk the bank's assets in the operations of the securities affiliate—and then share in the profits of the affiliate as though they were partners of a private banking house. In hearings before the Senate Banking & Currency Committee in 1933, counsel Ferdinand Pecora forced disclosure of a "management fund" at National City Bank, distributed to officers, that totaled "20% of the bank's net earnings after 8% of capital surplus and undivided profits had been deducted from the net operating expenses of the year."

The name forever linked with Glass-Steagall is that of Mitchell of National City Bank, which surfaced time and again during the hearings. In the end, Mitchell resigned from the bank and shortly afterward stood trial for income tax evasion. In 1929, it was alleged, Mitchell had a gross income of $3 million but reported a loss of $48,000 following the sale of National City shares at a loss to his wife. Mitchell later was acquitted of the tax charge.

Ironically, Glass-Steagall eventually picked up a degree of bank support, though for the most pragmatic of reasons. As the Depression deepened, the securities markets virtually dried up, leaving the banks with hundreds of idle employees. The imminent passage of the bill provided banks with an excuse for trimming employment rolls.

On Mar. 7, 1933, even before Glass-Steagall became law, National City Bank voluntarily liquidated its securities affiliate. A day later, Chase National Bank announced that it had spun off Chase Securities Co. (a trace of which remains today in First Boston Corp., along with the securities affiliates of First National Bank of Boston and Harris Trust & Savings Bank). When the measure finally became law, the grandest of all the banking names—J. P. Morgan & Co.—decided that it would become a commercial bank. Several partners then created Morgan Stanley & Co. as an investment banking house, quite apart from the Morgan bank.

Full disclosure. Other pieces of New Deal legislation dealt with some of the abuses uncovered during the Glass-Steagall and other hearings. The Securities Act of 1933 provided for full disclosure of material information to investors. The Securities Exchange Act of 1934 gave the Federal Reserve the authority to regulate the bank credit available to purchasers of new securities—limiting the extent to which bank loans could support speculative investments. The Federal Reserve now has the authority to regulate bank affiliates and to insure that the sort of dealings that were commonplace in the 1920s do not happen again.

Wage And Price Controls

Should we have wage and price controls?

"Yes, it's the only way we can restrain people from demanding more money. The manufacturer will have to raise his prices. This starts inflation more and more...there's no end to it."

   -- Albert Kean, chauffeur

"I feel we're better off not putting controls on anything. By having no controls, things find their own levels in the law of supply and demand."

   -- Susan Esterak, airline stewardess

Who's right? Who knows. We have had general controls over prices and wages at several critical times in our nation's history, and we felt they were needed. But we also have doubts as to their effectiveness or fairness.

In World War II, the Korean War, and during the period of 1971 - 1974 (post-Viet Nam war), we had broad systems for monitoring and controlling wages and prices.

Controls are government's most direct way of breaking the wage-price spiral. It can directly say "no" to companies who propose to raise prices in excess of a set guideline and to keep salary increases or union wages also within set guidelines.

Controls are intended to slow down the rate of inflation and to manage equitably the increases obtained by various firms.

1971-1974

As a first step, the government introduced "Phase I", a 90-day freeze on all wages and prices in November, 1971. During this period, the rate of inflation did level off, but the effect was not expected to last without further help.

Phase II introduced an elaborate government organization charged with analysis of price and wage patterns and to review and approve requests for increases. The organization is shown in the chart. The persons staffing this organization came from the public, labor, and from businesses.

In 1973 this system was replaced by a simpler, voluntary process (Phase III) aiming to keep wages and prices in line with guidelines based on patterns of growth and productivity.

When inflation continued, a freeze was again imposed, for 60 days. The Cost of Living Council and the IRS kept an eye on prices with the hope of breaking the spiral.

REACTIONS

Some businessmen feel that the controls actually spurred rather than reduced inflation. And the 1974 recession may have been caused by it as well.

"Controls may be a short-term remedy, but we should focus on the long-term implications.

"It is, in fact, profits which many seek to limit. But profits are the lifeblood of business; without them, business cannot expand, renew or replace the job-creating equipment of our society.

"America's experience with controls in 1971-1974 was not a happy one. We suffered distortions and inefficiencies in production, and shortages of such products as meats, canned foods, paper products, metals, plastics, and chemicals.

"Government has a role in the functioning of the economy, but another period of wage-price controls would do more harm than good."

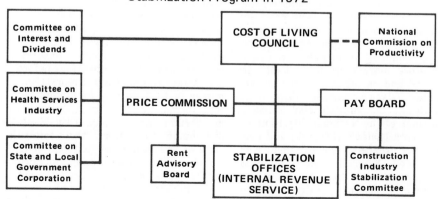

Organization of the Economic Stabilization Program in 1972

Bankruptcy

If you are unable to pay your debts to creditors as they come due, you may be a bankrupt. Corporations can become bankrupts, too, as long as they aren't railroads, banks, insurance, or municipal organizations. Those are special cases under bankruptcy laws that have to protect the public interest (continuing the services provided, protecting deposits, etc.).

How does it work? You simply file a petition to the court to be declared a bankrupt. Or the creditors may do this for you -- involuntarily for you -- if you get badly in debt.

Under involuntary bankruptcy proceedings, the petition is filed by a creditor (or three creditors if total claims are more than $500 and total creditors number 12 or more).

Liabilities must exceed $1000 and the debtor must have committeed at least one "act of bankruptcy" four months prior to the filing of the petition. The acts of bankruptcy, defined by the National Bankruptcy Act, include:

-- concealing or removing property with the intent of keeping it from creditors
-- transfering part of the property to one creditor to keep it away from others (preferential treatment)
-- allowing a lien on his property by the courts and not doing anything about it
-- asking for the appointment of a receiver or trustee to take charge of his property
-- admitting in writing his inability to pay his debts and his willingness to be declared a bankrupt.

Under bankruptcy, the court lets the person or company to "start over". You get out of legal liability for claims of creditors (except for taxes, debts related to a breach of trust or by wilful and malicious tort).

You get to keep some of your property (essentials to live with), and the right to get started again. (Although, admittedly it's tough to get credit!).

REMEDIES

A company may liquidate all assets to pay the creditors, or may reorganize the assets and management of the firm to become able to pay the debts.

For a reorganization, a plan is submitted to the court, hearings are held, and the plan is approved by the court and by the security holders. If everybody finds it "fair and equitable" and "feasible" it is ordered to be done. The steps are laid out in Chapter X of the law.

Liquidation is more common for individuals, proprietorships, or partnerships, where reorganization is not feasible. Title to all property covered is vested to a person assigned by the courts (trustee). This person allocates the property to the creditors on an equitable basis as settlement of the debts.

Property is allocated in the following priority order:

-- costs of operating and administering the bankrupt estate until everything is settled.
-- wages due, if earned
-- wages earned by employees during the three months prior to filing
-- taxes due
-- secured creditors (e.g., mortgage holders)
-- unsecured creditors
-- stockholders or owners

PENN CENTRAL

One of the biggest bankruptcy stories to he hit the news this century is that of the Penn Central Railroad.

For reasons of mismanagement and changing market demands, this company (actually more than just a railroad, but a holding company), started having all sorts of financial problems.

The company filed for reorganization and was managed for some time by a group of trustees. The public wasn't about to let the company liquidate, however, because we are dependent on good rail service. In fact, a number of other railroads were in a similar fix, although on a less grand scale.

Special federal laws were passed to make possible the merger of these various bankrupt railroads into a single consolidated rail system.

The following article describes the early days of ConRail.

A Tentative Start For ConRail

At midnight last Sunday the federal government's plan for restructuring railroad service in the Northeast and Midwest finally went into effect. With virtually no objections raised on Capitol Hill before the deadline, the "final system plan" developed by the United States Railway Assn. became the official guide for rescuing the Penn Central and six other bankrupt railroads.

For a while, rail service in the area will operate without change. But starting Dec. 9, bankrupt lines can file notice of service cutbacks for lines not included in the final plan. This service can be discontinued on Feb. 7, 1976, when the final plan must be submitted to a special court. On Feb. 27, the formal transfer of the selected bankrupt properties to the Consolidated Railroad Corp. will take place.

More legislation. But Congressional action designed to put the plan into operation is far from over. This week it became apparent that lawmakers fashioning the necessary legislation are struggling just to make sure the entire effort will stay on track.

"This is our last chance at developing a comprehensive program to keep the

Grant Compton—BW

railroad industry in private hands, to save it from further degradation and eventual nationalization," says Representative Fred B. Rooney (D-Pa.), chairman of the House subcommittee dealing with railroad problems.

Rooney and his Senate counterpart, Vance Hartke (D-Ind.), have drafted separate omnibus proposals designed not only to save the troubled railroads of the Northeast but also to aid the en-

tire industry and prevent the collapse of other carriers. The proposals include minor and major changes in federal rail regulations, a special government assistance fund for all railroads, a financing rescue plan for Northeast and Midwest carriers, and a financing package to upgrade passenger service in the Northeast corridor. Each of the bills provides more than $8 billion in government support for the industry.

The different approaches in the proposals demonstrate the still unsettled state of alternative solutions to the Northeast rail crisis and the problems of the railroad industry. There are four major areas of disagreement.

FINANCING. Although the USRA plan calls for an initial government investment of $2.1 billion in ConRail securities, most investment experts feel even more is needed. The House bill provides what the USRA asked for, but the Senate proposal would provide $3.4

There are four major areas of disagreement in the proposed bills

billion. Hartke wants ConRail to have sufficient federal start-up funds to make it viable later as a private corporation.

FEDERAL PROTECTION. Transportation Secretary William T. Coleman Jr. wants a review committee within the USRA to oversee government investment. The House bill provides for such review but the Senate version does not. Coleman also favors eventual transfer of certain ConRail operations to profitable railroads in the future. Representative Brock Adams (D-Wash.), a ma-

jor figure in drafting the ConRail legislation, opposes these moves. He says they would involve the federal government far more deeply in ConRail than it would be by merely supplying funds.

FUNDING MECHANISM. The House bill provides for a national loan guarantee program of $2 billion as part of the total $8 billion package. Funding would be from general revenues. The Hartke plan calls for a system of government debt instruments to raise money for ConRail and other roads. Proposals for a trust fund paid for by new carrier fuel taxes have been sidetracked by opposition from trucking and other interests, although the Hartke plan calls for the Transportation Dept. to develop a trust fund later.

REGULATORY REFORM. The House proposal, which calls for improved accounting and reporting standards, is opposed by carriers. But one House staffer says: "If anything should survive this process, it's the securities and accounting improvements."

To soften the impact of line abandonments, the Rooney proposal provides subsidies to continue service for up to four years. Such a program may cost no more than $180 million—a fraction of the total omnibus packages.

Luckily for the lawmakers, a potential crisis was averted last week when the Chessie System and the USRA agreed on the final terms for the Chessie's acquisition of most of the bankrupt Erie Lackawanna Ry. and parts of the Reading Co. The Chessie had until Dec. 9 to make up its mind, and while the purchase is contingent on passage of some technical legislation, it appears the Chessie will be part of the solution rather than part of the problem. That gives Congress until Feb. 26 to deliver its final package to the special court overseeing the bankruptcy so that the insolvent carriers can be transferred to ConRail.

What the bankrupt Northeast railroads...

	Route miles	Personnel	Freight cars	Locomotives
Penn Central	19,459	77,225	153,284	3,919
Erie Lackawanna	2,932	10,426	19,992	524
Reading	1,128	5,452	12,243	235
Lehigh Valley	988	2,534	3,965	143
Central RR of New Jersey	324	1,785	2,173	79
Ann Arbor	299	331	392	15
Lehigh & Hudson River	86	86	121	6
Total	**25,216**	**97,839**	**192,170**	**4,921**

...will contribute to the ConRail system

	Route miles	Personnel	Freight cars	Locomotives
Total	**15,000**	**90,000**	**159,000**	**4,162**

Data: U.S. Railway Assn., Interstate Commerce Commission

When Companies Get Too Big To Fail

The giant corporations have become so important to the U. S. economy that government does not dare let one go under

In the years before World War I, Germany invested so heavily in battleships that, when the war came, it did not dare let them fight. As the U. S. economy slides deeper into recession, the federal government finds itself in a similar position. The huge U. S. corporations have become such important centers of jobs and incomes that it dare not let one of them shut down or go out of business. It is compelled, therefore, to shape national policy in terms of protecting the great corporations instead of letting the economy make deflationary adjustments.

As many scholars have pointed out, the corporation is the institution that the capitalist nations have chosen to translate rapidly increasing scientific knowledge into jobs, goods, incomes, and consumption. Adolph A. Berle, Jr., lawyer, teacher, businessman, and part-time politician, perhaps said it best in his thoughtful little book *The 20th Century Revolution*, published just over 20 years ago. His theme was that the corporation was doing for the U. S. and other advanced countries what the Russians were trying to achieve with Communism.

Primitive nations such as Russia, said Berle, had to choose Communism as "an instrument by which a vast backward country could be mauled into industrialization." But "the capitalist revolution in which the United States was the leader found apter, more efficient, and more flexible means through collectivizing capital in corporations."

Losing control. The past two decades have confirmed Berle's argument that "it is justifiable to consider the American corporation not as a business device but as a social institution in the context of a revolutionary century." In the last five years, however, something has gone badly wrong. Caught in an explosive inflation and wracked by two painful recessions, an increasing number of giant corporations can no longer claim either flexibility or efficiency. They have lost control of their costs, lost their access to capital, misjudged their markets, and diversified into lines of business they do not understand. In desperation they turn to Washington for help, and if they are big enough and shaky enough, they get it. Neither the Administration nor Congress dares allow a major employer to go down the drain—any more than the Kaiser dared to risk one of his expensive battleships.

The mounting number of bailouts—loans, tariffs, import quotas, and tax cuts—blurs the distinction between the capitalist revolution and the Marxist version. A visitor from Mars might see little difference between the government and the ailing corporation it is propping up.

More important, the willingness of the government to shelter a big corporation from the pain of retrenchment takes the flexibility out of the system. A game in which there are no losers puts no premium on good management or good economic policy. This is one reason the U. S. has developed a chronic inflationary bias.

In the days when there were several hundred ambitious auto producers, it did not hurt the economy greatly if a Stutz or a Franklin dropped out. The market could ruthlessly penalize bad judgment, and the system emerged stronger than ever.

There are still industries—electronics is one—where competition can prune out the weak operators and force the strong ones to hustle. But each dropout increases the relative importance of the surviving companies, and in the end, each producer will be so important that its collapse would be an economic disaster.

Rescue operations. When Lockheed Aircraft lost control of its costs and teetered on the edge of bankruptcy, Congress saved it with a $250-million loan guarantee. And when the bankrupt Eastern railroads ran out of cash and threatened to stop running trains, the government bankrolled a federal corporation to take over their essential operations.

And now the auto industry—reduced to three huge companies and one small one—is stuck with acres of 1975 cars that the public does not want. It is following the well-trodden path to Washington. It suggests relaxing emissions and safety requirements, and vigorous stimulation of the economy. Chrysler has called for a cut in income taxes and easier credit for car buyers.

A bad year for autos is a bad year for everyone. But if the government guarantees a no-lose game for autos, it will have to provide some other mechanism by which the economy can correct the mistakes of management and government alike. When a big company brings out a bad product, or when it yields to a powerful union and writes an inflationary wage contract, its management should not end up just as well off as good management. If it does, the economy will have no built-in discipline, no way of confirming good decisions and revising bad ones.

The answer of the dedicated antitrusters is to break up the big companies, but the U. S. probably has gone far beyond the point where that could be done without paralyzing the economy. The real problem, therefore, is to make big corporations more resilient, more capable of correcting mistakes. Ideas for achieving this result are strangely scarce.

Perhaps the trouble is that Berle's forecast was wrong in another respect. "There is solid ground," he said in 1954, "for the expectation that 20 years from now the men of greatest renown in the United States will be the spiritual, philosophical, and intellectual leaders for the sufficient reason that they will be needed more than any other type of men. Society still tends both to produce and to honor the kinds of men it needs most."

He was an optimist.

The Individual And The Law

Business law isn't just for businesses. It's your business too.

Everytime you buy something or sign on a dotted line you are making a purchase contract that is just as real as any made by a purchasing executive at General Motors.

Or if you are the creative type, you want your work protected by the law -- whether copyright, patent, or trademark.

And if someone falls through on his or her side of a business bargain with you (even if it may be a major corporation or a department store) you have recourse under the law to sue and get the situation made right.

These are three basic situations where the individual has important rights under the law. You should know what these are and how they work on your behalf.

BEING INVENTIVE

If you invent something, write a book, or develop a trademark to distinguish your product from everyone else's, you have the right to apply for protection under federal law.

In the United States, a PATENT grants an individual exclusive right to use, own, and dispose of his invention during a period of 17 years.

After that time, the protection of the government expires and cannot be renewed. The holder is also protected against infringements abroad

through an international agreement.

To get a patent, your invention has to be new, useful, and an improvement over previous inventions of a similar or related nature.

For more than a century, Congress and the courts have struggled to define just what inventions meet these requirements.

The nation's first patent law, passed in 1790, required only that the inventions be novel and useful. Soon, however, inventors were obtaining patents for variations on well-known items. There even was an application for a patent for a door knob, this one made of porcelain, but in no other way different from other doorknobs.

In a landmark case, the Supreme Court ruled, in 1850, that the porcelain knob was too trifling an advancement of technology to be considered an invention, and therefore did not deserve a patent. A patented device must not be obvious and must contain "invention".

So then the courts debated what this meant, with one judge even ruling that the word "invention" cannot be defined.

In 1941, the Court declared that inventions must imbody a "flash of creative genius", a notion just as impossible to measure or define.

In 1950, the Court said that too many patents were being granted for

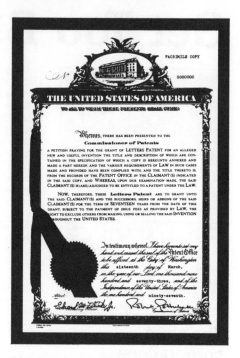

worthless gadgets, and that to justify a patent, an invention had to "serve the ends of science." Tougher standards were also laid out for items that are combinations of already patented devices. The applicant now has to prove the merits of a device for a patent.

If you obtain a patent and go ahead and sell your bright idea as a product on the open market, you will probably give it a brand and a name, and will adopt a trademark.

Most businesses use some type of trademark to identify its products or services. By registering your trademark (or "logo') with the United States Patent Office, you are given exclusive right to use it for 20 years, and a another 20 years by renewal. Applicants must submit a written application, five copies of specimens, and a $35 fee.

The same process holds for your patentable devices. Get a form, fill it out, and send it in with the money required. Sometime you'll hear back, either a rejection with questions or a certificate of Letters Patent.

Virtually everything you read these days is copyrighted. And if you have an inclination to write a book, a song, a poem, a play, or a computer program, you'll want to get a copyright on it.

A COPYRIGHT is a form of permission granted by the federal government to an author or publisher, giving him the exclusive right to own, sell, or otherwise use his written works. Such a right allows a person to earn royalties or payments for the use of copyrighted materials (just as you could for use of your patented inventions).

The holder of the copyright isn't selling the copyright, but rather is agreeing not to press charges for infringement. Further, the government does not enforce these forms of protection, but merely establishes rights through registration.

If an individual feels his or her rights have been infringed upon, he must se seek relief through the courts.

In fact, there is a widespread controversy on the rights of people to make photocopies (Xerox copies of articles, pages of this book, etc.). It is clearly a violation of copyright, but how the heck can copying be controlled? Or is making copies on a Xerox machine a right? It is a serious problem for libraries and publishers of limited edition books and technical journals.

BUYING

If you want to make a purchase and do it responsibly, you need to understand the impact of the law.

When you buy, you are really entering into a contract for sale of goods with certain stated or implied warranties.

A contract is an agreement, written or oral, between two or more parties that posess the following characteristics:

-- an offer by one party
-- acceptance by the other
-- competence of both parties (sane and sober)
-- legal subject matter (not illegal goods or gambling, etc.)
-- consideration (money)

When any of these conditions does not exist, the contract is not enforceable in the courts.

Otherwise, a contract is binding on the parties. Generally, if the value of the purchase is over $500, the contract must be in writing to be enforced.

The buyer promises to pay for the ordered goods; the seller promises to deliver the goods. Other conditions, such as timing, location, condition, or credit may be involved.

When you buy goods, you get a warranty with the goods. At a minimum, the seller warrants that he or she has title to the goods. There is implied merchantability: the goods fit the description purported, the goods are in average and usable condition unless otherwise stated, the goods are consistent in quality and quantity, and are as labeled.

In recent years, consumer demands have led to more extensive warranties on goods sold. These are discussed in later chapters on Marketing and Consumerism.

GOING TO COURT

If what you get isn't what you saw, or thought you were getting for your money, you can complain.

Most businessmen want to keep you as a customer and will replace the goods or refund your money. It's in his interest to keep you coming back with more money for more purchases.

It used to be "caveat emptor" (that's "let the buyer beware" in Latin). But increasingly, the seller is being held accountable for his end of the bargain.

One powerful tool you have available to you is the SMALL CLAIMS COURT. You don't need a lawyer in most small claims courts, and many won't allow them anyway. Court fees range from $2 to $15, and judgment in your favor usually includes recovery of fees from the seller.

You may state your grievance in plain words; you don't have to know the legal jargon. In most cases the judges don't insist on formal procedures or strict rules of evidence. You tell your side of the story and the seller tells his. Cases come to trial quickly and decisions are given immediately from the bench, or within a few days after the trial.

Of course, these courts serve the sellers, too, and many small businesses go to court to enforce payment for goods sold to customers. A college dean won $50 for breach of warranty against General Motors in a New York small claims case. A further case awarded $255 against a moving company for damage to goods moved, and another awarded $315 for faulty air conditioning service.

When you sue in small claims court, a summons is sent to the other party by registered mail or is served by a sheriff or officer of the court. This tends to get the attention of companies that may have ignored your previous complaints or attempts to get satisfaction.

Typically, 25% of the cases reaching this step are soon settled out of court. The company is ordered to appear in court, but isn't particularly excited about doing so -- again, a negative mark on its customer relations.

If the defendent does not settle out of court and does not appear in court on the trial date, you stand a pretty good chance of winning outright by default. The judge will probably ask you to tell your story and, unless it lacks merit, will decide in your favor. Then the court notifies the other party and orders

payment of the amount awarded.

At best, the courts can force repayment of money paid for unsatisfactory goods and services and for damage done to property. The businessman runs no risk more serious than that. Further, most small claims courts have a limit of $500 or less for each case.

People should use their small claims courts. It's a good opportunity to put the government to work on personal problems and make the law practical.

WHAZZIT?

CONTRACT

An agreement between two parties for exchange of goods or services for money or other form of consideration.

WARRANTY

An assurance, whether expressed directly or implied, that the goods are as described -- of reasonable quality, proper quantity, and consistent throughout.

SMALL CLAIMS COURT

Under state laws, a type of court permitting settlement of disputes between buyers and sellers regarding terms of contracts.

BANKRUPTCY

The condition of an individual or a corporation unable to pay debts to creditors as they come due.

Anti-Monopoly Takes On Parker Bros.

General Mills Inc. makes most of its money from cereals and cake mixes, but it also produces toys and games, and its Fun Group is deadly serious business to the company's management. As the world's largest game maker, the group in fiscal 1975 accounted for 12% of General Mills' $2.3 billion in sales and 14% of its $203 million in operating profits. Now, the company faces a court battle to preserve its trademark on the star of its business, that ageless board-game favorite, Monopoly, and General Mills executives could not be more concerned if an attack had been made on Betty Crocker herself.

A California professor is charging that General Mills has no monopoly on Monopoly, claiming that it was a widely played American folk game 30 years before the company's Parker Bros. subsidiary began selling it.

It all started because General Mills is so protective about the game. In 1971, for example, Parker Bros.—a unit of General Mills since 1967—sent a letter of protest to Northwest Mortgage Co. of Gresham, Ore., which had advertised a new apartment complex called "Marvin's Gardens." Marvin Gardens, of

Anspach: His game has not sold as well as it might, he says, because of Parker Bros.

course, is the name of a piece of real estate in Monopoly. The complex was built, and the name kept, but General Mills got across the point that it would challenge anyone who threatened Monopoly.

Earlier this year Anthony C. Hankins at Ghetto Toys & Games Co. in Albany, Calif., sent a copy of its new game, Ghetto—a takeoff on Monopoly—to Parker Bros. to see if the General Mills division might be interested in buying it. Parker Bros. wrote back saying no and adding that it would refer the Ghetto game to its lawyers for pos-

A challenger says General Mill's Monopoly trademark won't stand up in court

sible copyright and trademark infringement.

Countersuit. The company is willing to go to such lengths because Monopoly is considered the industry's most valuable trademark. In the past 40 years more than 80 million Monopoly games have been sold worldwide, and it is perennially among the top 10 best sellers, averaging 3.5 million units. Just how much profit there is in Monopoly is a carefully guarded secret, but in fiscal 1975, the Fun Group netted $28.4 million on sales of $287 million.

It is hardly surprising then, that three years ago, when an economics teacher at California State University, Ralph Anspach, 50, brought out a game called Anti-Monopoly, Parker Bros. lawyers again swung into action. But this time, not only is Parker Bros. suing Anspach for trademark infringement, Anspach is suing Parker Bros., claiming that it never had legitimate title to the trademark in the first place. "Parker Bros. could have lived with our game," says Anspach, whose case goes to trial in October. "Now they are jeopardizing something a lot bigger. They could lose their monopoly position with Monopoly."

Anspach, an expert on private enterprise, originally developed Anti-Monopoly as a bust-the-trust game. Unable to interest other companies in commercializing the game, Anspach formed his own company, Anti-Monopoly Inc., in 1973 with an investment of $5,000. So far, it has sold 280,000 games, grossing around $1 million, and generated enough cash to pay the legal fees connected with the Parker Bros. suit, already nearing $80,000.

To wage his battle against Parker Bros., Anspach has curtailed his teach-

ing and traveled the country to investigate the history of Monopoly. He says he has found many people who played Monopoly before it was supposedly invented by Charles Darrow in the early 1930s. Anspach says he has learned that the game was invented and patented as "the Landlord's Game" by Elizabeth Magie, a Virginia Quaker who developed the game around the turn of the century.

For 30 years afterward, Anspach says, the game was played on homemade boards and painted oil cloths under various names, from Auction Monopoly to Monopoly. Around 1933, says Anspach, an unemployed Darrow copied one version of Monopoly, right down to the odd spelling of Marven Gardens. In 1935 Parker Bros. took over the game and had Darrow patent it and trademark the name.

Confused buyers. Anspach in his suit charges that the Monopoly trademark is invalid because the term was used generically, like chess, before the 1930s; therefore, it belongs to no one. Further, the suit says that even if the trademark were valid, Anti-Monopoly does not infringe upon it. Anspach says Anti-Monopoly's "opposite" name does not increase the likelihood of confusion. A lawyer for Parker Bros., Robert S. Daggett, disagrees. He says Anti-Monopoly has hurt Monopoly's sales. Daggett asserts some buyers have been so confused that they have even ordered Anti-Monopoly from Parker Bros. "The most celebrated board game trademark in the world has been appropriated by someone without any right to use it," Daggett says.

Anspach says Parker Bros. tried to settle with him and offered a sum in "the high six figures" if he would sell them Anti-Monopoly. "It would have been a sell-out," he says. "The true history of Monopoly would never get out and I would be giving up a game with great sales potential."

Anspach says Anti-Monopoly has not come close to approaching its potential because Parker Bros. informed its own customers that it would be requesting an injunction and possibly be pressing a law suit against Anti-Monopoly. "Most accounts were unwilling to buy large numbers of our game," Anspach says, "because of fear that there would be a recall and we would be unable to refund money." But if Anspach wins his trademark case, he says he plans an antitrust suit against Parker Bros. and General Mills for harassment and anti-competetive practices. ∎

Taxes

WASHINGTON

"Taxation," said Colbert, chief minister of Louis XIV, "is the art of plucking the goose in such a way as to produce the largest amount of feathers with the least possible squawking."

Government is supported by taxes. Local, state, and federal governments all use different kinds of taxes to raise the money they need to pay for the public services they provide.

In general, local governments are primarily supported by real estate and other property taxes. State governments are supported largely by personal and business income, sales, and estate taxes. As shown in the table on page 110, the federal government is supported primarily by individual and corporate income taxes. There is some "revenue sharing", or returning of federal revenues to state and local governments, but this amount is variable according to the federal programs authorizing these payments.

The taxing power of the federal government is established in the Constitution. An article provides that Congress has the power to collect revenues to pay debts, and to provide for the common defense and general welfare. Providing for defense and welfare has taken steadily increasing sums of money, provided by our increasing taxes. The only way our taxes can go down is if the extent and variety of services provided are reduced by the government, and that does not appear likely, regardless of which political party is in power.

Over the years we have grown to expect and have received more and more benefits from our federal, state, and local governments. Today we enjoy welfare benefits, old age and survivor benefits, compensation when we are unemployed, medical aid, legal assistance, training and educational assistance, and many other services provided by government. At the same time, of course, we pay for them.

WHAT MAKES A GOOD TAX?

We believe that taxes should generate enough money to pay the bills. To do this they must draw money from a large number of people as income taxes and sales taxes do. We also believe that taxes should be fair and equitable, not placing undue burdens on particular citizens or corporations. Similarly, we believe that every taxpayer should pay the full amount due, and not avoid paying a reasonable share through "loopholes."

But it is difficult to be fair and equitable, because every taxpayer has a different financial situation. A tax of $1000 is a greater burden to a person with an income of only $10,000 than to a person with an income of $75,000.

Therefore we have various types of taxes, each type having a slightly different taxing basis and a different impact on individuals. In our income tax law we allow a variety of deductions and special exemptions that benefit different people. Overall we believe that the result is a fair taxation system.

To keep our system fair we make changes each year, through Internal Revenue Service practices and new legislation. There is talk of major tax reform, but that would likely only start the whole process of refinement all over again.

Some taxes are what we call PROGRESSIVE. That is,

they make people with more money pay more tax. The tax rate increases as the tax base increases. Our federal income tax is progressive, with tax ran rates ranging from 14% to 70%. Individuals with a taxable income of $100,000 or more (if single) or $200,000 or more (if married) pay a maximum rate of 70%.

Some taxes are REGRESSIVE. Sales taxes, for example, place a greater burden on low-income taxpayers who spend a greater proportion of their incomes on goods and services. Even a flat tax (e.g., 2% state income tax) has a harder impact on these taxpayers.

Few people enjoy paying taxes. Hence we try to find more satisfying ways to finance governmental activities. Lotteries emerged as a natural way to combine public pleasure with raising public revenues. Off-the-track betting in New York is another good example. revenues. Off-track

betting in New York is another good example. Here, activities that caused problems as an unofficial activity (and illegal in many states) is converted to a substitute for taxes.

We also pay high taxes (relative to actual costs) on liquor, cigarettes, gasoline, and amusement admissions. We don't seem to mind, or even notice the tax bite.

THE CORPORATE TAX

From an individual point of view, taxes are best when they are on someone else -- like a business corporation. A tax is imposed on the profits of a corporation at the rate of 48%.

In actuality, most corporations reduce the net tax burden by applying legal tax offsets (such as investment tax credits, depreciation allowances, tax-loss carry-forward allowances,

"IF EVERYONE IS HERE, WE'LL PROCEED WITH THE CORPORATE EARNINGS REPORT."

and foreign tax credits).

One study showed that companies actually pay an effective rate of 35% on corporate income, plus taxes on property and various other federal, state, and local taxes.

The further truth is that many of the taxes paid are reflected in the prices paid for goods and services. Hence the ultimate burden falls again on the individual taxpayer. Maybe it hurts a little less when you're getting goods in return for your money, but some of it ends up in the tax coffers.

When profit margins are squeezed, businesses seek more liberal tax provisions, to stimulate recovery and new investment in capital equipment. It's also thought provoking to realize that as government purchases from business increase (just think of

the aerospace, defense, transportation, and other spending through private industry), it's tax money going into businesses, showing up as profits, a portion of which comes back to the government as tax payments. It's a circular process. And jobs are created all along the way. The faster the money moves, the more expansive our economy.

Some states have offered a no-tax period for businesses which agree to move there or build new facilities there. The aim is to attract the jobs. To heck with the taxes themselves for a year or two. Regional economic development needs businesses.

VALUE ADDED TAX

A final major type of tax that should be noted is the Value Added Tax

(VAT). Like many taxes paid by businesses, this is an indirect tax. It is a tax levied on a business as a cost of doing business. It is thus built into costs and comes out before profits are calculated.

The unusual feature of VAT is that it is applied to the VALUE ADDED to a good at each state of manufacturing. Each business adds something to a product -- changing raw materials into something with more value.

Thus it is the total of the wages, salaries, rents, and interest paid by a firm for the use of labor, land, and capital. It's the difference between the cost of the raw materials themselves and the price that could be received for the same material to just cover the costs of working on them.

If a bakery uses up $10,000 worth of flour, butter, and other raw material and in the process of making bread and various delicious bakery goods, incurs costs of $3500 in rent, wages, etc., it had better sell the goods for at least $13,500 to cover costs. Thus the $3500 is the value added, the base on which the VAT is applied.

If a 3% VAT were applied, the bakery would pay $105 tax for the value added through this production, and would need to sell the bread and other goods for at least $13,605 to break even and more to make a profit.

It's a logical idea for a tax, but complicated to

apply. It would surely raise a lot of money, and this means that property taxes could be reduced (they're rather unpopular).

It would be a regressive tax, because it raises the price of goods purchased by lower income groups, but it would not be a noticeable tax. It would be another "painless" way to pay the tax burden.

VAT isn't used yet, but proposals have been made and are being discussed in Congress. It has been used in France, where it has a side effect: to hold down salary increases and thus fight inflation.

But taxes on profits or the value added to a product are not the only kinds of taxes that are used by governmental bodies to raise the money they need to carry out their public service. Businesses have to pay property taxes just the same as the average homeowner. Sears, for example, must pay property taxes on all of its stores and other properties. This comes to a tidy sum, all of which goes into the local communities in which the Sears' stores are located.

Licenses to do business can be considered as another way of taxing business. Often the reason given for licensing is to allow a governmental body to control the kind of business activity that is taking place in its community, but in reality the revenue generated by the licenses may be the most important aspect of requiring licenses.

There's a lot of ways to skin (or tax) a cat.

WHAZZIT?

TAX

A compulsory payment to the government to defray the costs of public services.

SALES TAX

A percentage paid on the price of goods and, in some states, services.

PROPERTY TAX

A tax paid periodically on property that you own, such as real estate, your automobile, or personal property such as home furnishings or a boat. Property taxes are state or local levies.

INCOME TAX

A tax based on the income of an individual, a corporation, or other business. It is a direct tax that is based on your "ability to pay." Income taxes may be federal, state, or local.

EXCISE TAX

A tax levied on the sale of certain goods such as jewelry, luggage, or furs. It may be levied on a wholesaler, retailer or consumer.

ESTATE TAX

A tax on the total value of property left by a deceased person.

VALUE ADDED TAX (VAT)

A tax based on the value added to a product at each step of the production process.

SOCIAL SECURITY TAX

A tax paid by an employer and an employee to provide old age and survivor benefits under provisions of the federal Social Security Act.

UNEMPLOYMENT COMPENSATION

Benefits paid to workers laid off, funded by taxes paid by employers.

SURTAX

A special tax over and above the normal tax, imposed on the amount due in taxes or on income level.

LOOPHOLE

Any perfectly legal maneuver that a taxpayer uses to reduce his or her tax liability.

REVENUE SHARING

Transfer of federal taxes to state and local governments.

Where The Taxes Go

UNCLE SAM'S MONEY -- WHERE IT COMES FROM AND WHERE IT GOES

Sources of Money:	1960	1970	1976
Individual Income Taxes	44.0%	46.2%	44.0%
Corporate Income Taxes	23.2	18.6	13.5
Social Insurance Taxes	15.9	22.5	31.1
Excise Taxes	12.6	8.0	5.6
Customs, Estate, & Gift Taxes	2.9	3.7	3.0
Miscellaneous Receipts	1.3	1.8	2.8
	100.0%	100.0%	100.0%

Expenditures and Net Loans:	1960	1970	1976
National Defense	49.8%	40.1%	24.8%
International Affairs	3.3	2.1	1.5
Science, Space and Technology	.4	2.0	1.2
Natural Resources, Environment	1.1	1.3	3.2
Agriculture	3.6	3.2	.8
Commerce and Transportation	5.2	4.8	4.8
Community Development & Housing	1.1	1.5	1.6
Education, Training, & Employment	1.4	3.8	5.1
Health	.9	6.7	8.6
Income Security	19.5	22.2	34.4
Veteran Benefits and Services	5.9	4.4	5.1
Interest	9.0	9.0	9.3
General Government	1.4	1.8	.9
Revenue Sharing			1.9
Undistributed Offsetting Receipts	-2.5	-2.8	-4.0
	100.0%	100.0%	100.0%

Source: The Budget of the United States, Executive Office of the President.

In examining the above table, you will see that individual income taxes pay the big chunk of the revenues for Uncle Sam. Don't think that the taxes haven't gone up, though -- because the total receipts have gone up a lot:

1960 -- $92.5 billion
1970 -- 193.7 billion
1976 -- 297.5 billion

In addition, there was a surplus of receipts over expenditures in 1960. In 1976 there was a deficit of $50 billion over receipts.

Even though corporate income taxes have gone down as a percentage, they have gone up in dollar terms.

The same logic applies on the expenditure side. National defense is falling as a percentage, but is holding its own in dollar terms.

Of course, these are dollars subject to inflation. If you take out the inflation factor, the budget has still nearly doubled since 1960 (in constant purchasing power dollars).

CONSIDER   CHALLENGES

1. Does business pay more
or less a share of federal
taxes than in 1960?

2. Do you think electricity
rates would be lower if
utilities such as Con Ed
were run entirely by the
government?

3. Compare the federal
expenditures in years 1960
and 1976. In what areas
have been notable increases?
What is the impact of these
increases on business?

4. If you had the power,
how would you shift the
expenditures of the
federal government? Why?

5. In 1981, the GNP is
projected to be 2,877
billion dollars. Does this
mean business will be better
off than today? Explain.

6. In some states, the
government sets prices for
such products as milk,
liquor, and wines. Is this
good for business? For the
consumers? Explain.

7. Should companies be
allowed to grow "too big
to fail?" Explain.

8. Who suffers from
bankruptcies? Who benefits?
Explain.

9. Should AT&T be broken
up into smaller companies?
Explain.

10. Is the anti-trust
law obsolete? What changes,
if any, do you feel would
be a good idea? Explain.

Investigate the source
of money and the areas of
expenditures for state and
local governments in the
United States and put
together a total picture
of government receipts and
spending in the nation.

Investigate the budget
of your local government.
Identify and evaluate those
aspects of the budget that
effect business.

Identify an issue affec-
ting business and govern-
ment in your community
(e.g., a tax issue, a proposed construction project,
an urban development plan)
and determine your position.
Express your views in a
letter to your local newspaper or a public official.

Find out what services
are offered by the Small
Business Administration
in support of businesses.

Interview a local re-
tailer and ask what local
laws regulate his pricing
or other business practices.

RECAP

Government influences businesses in a lot of ways. Taxes, regulation, purchasing contracts, etc. This chapter has reviewed some of these important links between business and government.

In a broad sense, business and government are partners. The inter-action of supply and demand is guided and nurtured by government actions in the economic area. Ours is a managed economy, not a wholly free competitive system.

We recognize monopoly power in business as undesirable. Hence we have laws that set rules for business behavior in the marketplace, such as trade laws and anti-trust laws. Our govern-ment acts to protect customers, to help young businesses grow, to preserve our natural resources, to protect the welfare of employees, and a host of other public interests.

Public utilities -- electricity, water, telephone, gas -- are more closely regulated than other businesses because of their direct role in the economy. We feel that large size is an advantage in providing good service at low cost: it is most efficient. At the same time, we set the rates these firms may charge for their services and review many types of the decisions they make in managing their operations. Con Edison and AT&T, both discussed in this chapter, are public utilities.

Laws often tell business what its future will hold. The Glass-Steagall Act is an example. This law had an important effect on banking by prohibiting direct investment banking by banks. The law also set up an insurance system for bank deposits, which has proven a boon for depositors when banks hit upon hard times.

The government may also govern wages and prices in business organizations, should the economic situation make it necessary. We have had wage-price controls several times, and may have them again.

Unfortunate companies may experience the benefit of the National Bankruptcy Act. Under this law, a business that can't pay its debts may find protection for reorganization or dissolution. ConRail is the result of government efforts to "save" the railroads.

Of course, all business firms are subject to taxes. In this chapter we took a look at various kinds of taxes and the fact that most end up back in the taxpayer's lap. Most taxes are costs of doing business, and are reflected in costs of goods and services. Some taxes seem to be less painful to pay, however, and they tend to be the more indirect ones.

Our government needs a lot of tax revenues to pay for its extensive programs. The programs, in turn, regulate and control and subsidize and do other neat things for businesses, just as they do for all Americans.

WORKSHEET NO. 4

NAME_____

INSTRUCTOR'S NAME_____

DATE_____

1. Is government control of business the answer to our economic problems?

---

2. Are there some areas of our economy in which cartels (or at least a very few, very large businesses) might prove more effective than a free merket system? If so, what are they? Explain.

3. What are the principal arguments for antitrust today? Why do some argue
   that big companies should be broken up?

4. What was the business effect of the passage of the Glass-Steagall Act?

PART II

CAREERS IN BUSINESS

CHAPTER 5

Careers

Your career is your own personal business, and you need to give it your attention if you expect it to prosper.

Managers, counselors, teachers, and friends may be helpful, but the big responsibility for career planning is in your hands. You've got to make decisions about what you want to do with your life and how you are going to do it.

You have to decide what kind of work you want to do -- what occupation you want to be in, at least for a starter. You have to decide what kind of organization you want to work in and where you want to live. Life style and personal interests have a lot to do with these basic decisions.

Then there's the small matter of a job -- what specific kind of job assignment in an organization, and subsequent job changes and promotions. You have to decide what you want your career path to be, and get prepared to make it come true.

Hunting for a job is a job in itself. Particularly when economic conditions are not good, jobs may be hard to come by. In this chapter you will get some hints about how to search for a job, handle yourself during an interview, and things to look for in any job you accept.

Once on a job, it is really up to you to decide what you will do -- how hard you will work, what you will try to achieve, what skills you will learn, and how you will spend your personal time to advance your career. Granted, your manager has something to say about all of this, but you have to be motivated -- and care about the job as a step in your career plan.

Sometime you may decide to change jobs, change the organization you work for, or even change occupation. Lots of people do that these days. Sometime, too, you may face the question of retirement -- will you want leisure, a second career, or will retirement be the "scrapheap" for you.

Career planning makes work more fun. It lets you see how your immediate work fits into your own long-range career plans. Your job isn't so much just a job anymore -- it is a step towards a long-range goal.

In this chapter some pointers are offered for effective career planning. Examples of careers and information from Sears and other sources are provided to help you get to know the terrain.

Most of the material in this chapter is directed toward those of you that might want to go to work for a large, or even not so large company. But what about those who want to go into business for themsleves, what should they do? As we shall see, starting and running a small business requires a different kind of commitment than does working for someone else. When you work for yourself, you must make a total commitment to the business or you are likely to fail.

The following chapters tell about the various types of jobs and careers that are available in business today. Marketing, production, advertising, accounting, finance, and other areas all offer challenges for careers.

In This Chapter

Where Are You Going?

What Will You Do?

You are the only person in the world who can answer these questions. You have to make your own career decisions. That doesn't mean you have to make them all now -- You may make them one at a time, as career opportunities pop up. But if you're going to get the most out of life -- challenge, meaning, and satisfaction through your work -- then sooner or later you'll have to give serious thought to your career.

It's helpful to have an idea of your long-term goals, or at least some personal values in mind. You don't need to know what specific jobs you may like, but you can at least think through just what you feel is important. What's worth your time?

Do you want to be in the middle of the action in big business? Or in a business of your own? Perhaps a fortune through inventing or investing is what you prefer, so you can retire at 35. It's been done, you know.

You may feel that business isn't for you at all, that you'd rather teach, be a musician, a composer, an artist, a lawyer, or a medical technician. Thought about a government career -- public service? There are lots of social problems to be tackled, and tax dollars to be spent.

Like Woodstock, you can aim your sights as high as you like. It's an essential first step in career planning. You can always change your mind. Your interests will change, and your aspirations, too, as you learn about different careers open to you. Your feelings and values will change, too, as you think about the purpose of your life and what you want to achieve while you're on Planet Earth.

Recall the wisdom of the cat in Alice in Wonderland:

Alice: Will you tell me, please, which way I ought to go from here?

Cat: That depends a good deal on where you want to get to.

Alice: I don't much care where...

Cat: Then it doesn't matter which way you go.

Alice: ...so long as I get somewhere.

Cat: Oh, you're sure to do that if you only walk long enough.

One big factor in your career planning besides direction and purpose is your achievement motive.

Some persons have a lot of drive -- a need to feel they are accomplishing something they feel is important. You've known "fireballs". Their goals and plans are different from those of others who feel achievement isn't so important. America tends to be an "achieving society", but that doesn't mean you have to be a tiger to be successful or satisfied in your career.

Since your career is YOUR career, you should try to develop a career plan that fits your particular life style and value system. While it is true that business and other major employers tend to be conservative in their attitudes, there is indication that these values and attitudes are changing. Fifty years ago the forty hour work week was just a dream, fifty years from now who knows what the work week will look like? In planning your career, do what you think is really important.

The Mobicentric Generation

A conversation with Dr. Eugene E. Jennings

Harris: The radicals of the New Left believe that the fabric *has* to be torn. They're afraid that people like you will head off their revolution—by teaching corporations how to adapt to the values of the young.

Jennings: Yes, but I'm not talking about the student radicals. My research is among the young people who go to work for corporations. They reveal fundamental changes not only in values but actually in what can be called personality or character structure.

And you haven't seen anything yet. The college generation is the ripple that is hitting the beach before the tidal wave. The high-school pupils are doing everything the college kids are doing, but more as a way of life. They are the center of the new generation. If you think the kids are coming along differently now, just wait until it all gets institutionalized.

Harris: What were the first signs you noticed? As an advisor to very large corporations and to executives who hit career troubles, you weren't a professional youth-watcher.

Jennings: No, I got into this field for a practical reason. We discovered that companies were losing these bright kids in numbers we never suspected, particularly those with bachelor's degrees in science or engineering, and master's degrees in business administration.

Look at these numbers: between 1948 and 1953, only eight or nine out of 100 were leaving their jobs in the first 30 or 40 months. Today, they are leaving four or five times as fast. Out of 100 new scientists and engineers—and you add in the M.B.A.s—it's unusual not to lose 33 or 34 of them in the first 40 months.

Harris: You found, didn't you, that a lot depends on what kind of boss the graduate happens to work for in his first job?

Jennings: There is one type of boss who drives away almost every young man or woman who comes his way. Unfortunately, he happens to be like the majority of my generation. He was taught to obey first and think second. If you diagram his character, you find that he operates more by rules of thumb and principles than by perception, learning and facts.

The younger generation is just the opposite. They are the *why-whys.* They distrust rules and suspect that men who shout principles are incompetent. They go for facts, for analysis of the problem. They were raised to think first, obey second. Not only have they been brought up permissively but they are the most stimulated generation we've ever had. The studies show it. They've had almost 12 times the information input by the time they reach college—compared to previous generations—and by the second half of sophomore year they get as much input as we got in four years. They are conditioned to gross and intense stimuli.

Harris: In a sense, their lives have been like listening to an acid-rock orchestra—they've been bombarded with sound and light, or with facts.

Jennings: You can see what happens to them on the job. You have a supervisor who believes in authority and a graduate who believes in facts, in competency. I tell my students that if they hit the wrong boss, they have no choice: get out, "leverage." By leveraging, I mean quitting one firm and joining another to advance your mobility opportunities.

Harris: You give the same advice to executives. In *The Mobile Manager* [published by the University of Michigan Bureau of Industrial Relations], you show that in the last few years business has come to reward the man who leverages from job to job in a hurry.

Jennings: I was surprised when your staff spotted that book. We published only a few hundred copies, to fix a copyright on the computer program we developed for the study of mobility. The popular version of the research will be published this year by McGraw-Hill as *Routes to Executive Suite.*

Harris: Friends at M.I.T. believe, as I do, that you have identified the successor to William H. White's *Organization Man.* The "mobicentrics" you describe are decidedly different from White's man. Instead of shaping themselves to the rules of a single organi-

The Crucial Subordinate may be the key to success or failure. When the manager moves up, he takes his crucials with him.

zation, they ride one organization like a bus, then grab a transfer to the next organization.

Jennings: George, the rules have changed. The old saw of devotion to a corporation is disappearing with the advent of mobility. Executives now think of themselves as highly educated professionals who hire on to a corporation for a specific project.

Again, the numbers show the change. In the past 16 years I have done case studies on 230 company presidents and 1,500 executives from 500 large firms. Let me cite a few of the findings from this large sample:

One: 70% of today's corporate presidents take just 20 years to make it from first-level management to the top. They average seven geographic and 11 position moves along the way—one of either kind almost every year.

Two: Education sets a specific pattern. Among the most mobile men, 75% have an undergraduate degree in science or engineering and a master's in business administration.

Three: An educational specialty, however, can be a trap. Most future presidents start out as specialists but spend about three years in technical, non-managerial work. Men who get out of the technical stage in two years are four times as likely to make the salary suitable to their age as are those who stay technical for five years or more. At 30, if you are going to run a company, you ought to top $30,000.

Four: The education payoff is rising. Today, 21% of the men at the top have earned doctorates. By next year, 60% will have master's degrees and 30% will be holders of doctorates.

Harris: I can see why you needed a computer program to study what you call "mobilography." But let's get at the causes of all this rushing around.

Jennings: The entire business system is in radical change. If we hadn't had such a long period of prosperity, it might not have happened. But companies, especially growth companies, have learned to search out and develop manager talent. And managers have learned to develop themselves. Most jobs can be mastered in a year and a half or two years, and from then on you are learning little. But if you move on to another job, master it and go on to a third, you get intensive training.

Executives today are products of compressed experience—learning. Even company presidents tend to be

Shelf-Sitters are invariably cases of arrested development. They suffer psychosomatic illness, heart attack and suicide.

"project managers," brought in to solve a specific problem. The average president holds his job only five years, half as long as the average at the end of World War II.

Harris: So corporate life at all levels induces millions to center their lives around mobility—to be mobicentric?

Jennings: Mobility has become an end, a way of life, rather than a means. You don't move to take a job; you take a job to move. Whereas the traditional manager believed that hard work made men better, the new manager believes that mobility makes men work better.

To the mobicentric individual, the most important activities in life are preparatory to mobility — school, college, marriage, social life and even religion and faith. Most young people join the church today to achieve activity — the watchword of the mobicentric generation.

The mobile manager not only manages differently, he lives differently. He gears his family and community relations to the pattern of arriving, performing and departing. His friends are usually members of his corporation, because they provide instant social friendship. He likes to be pleasant but a little distant and to avoid people who are unaccustomed to his style of living. He teaches his children the pleasures of mobility.

Harris: I got hooked on your *Mobile Manager* book because it told about so many people I've met as a business reporter. You developed a cast of characters, like the "crucial subordinate."

Jennings: Well, I was only describing the relationships that exist. When the mobile manager moves, he seldom goes by himself. He takes his crucial subordinates. As he moves up to higher positions he takes more and more with him. The crucial subordinate may be the key to success or failure in the task. He may possess a set of skills that complement those of his superior.

The crucial subordinate carefully cultivates his relationship to the superior. He is loyal and he is predictable in that his judgments can be trusted.

Harris: You also wrote about the "sponsor superior," the executive who is most likely to influence promotions.

Jennings: You've seen them in most corporations, George. They are known for their capacity to spot promising talent. The test of their power is their ability to influence promotions outside their own direct chain of command. For any given manager, a number of people may have the responsibility for appraising performance or recommending promotion. But the sponsor superior is apt to be the final judge. His recommendations are solicited, not

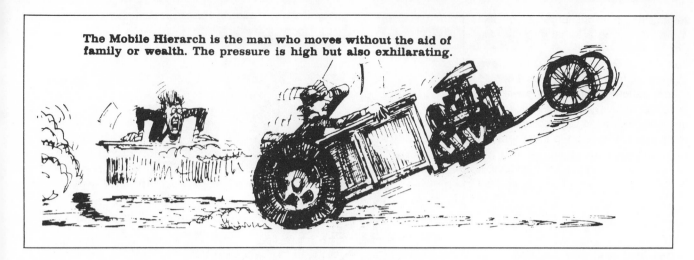

The Mobile Hierarch is the man who moves without the aid of family or wealth. The pressure is high but also exhilarating.

demanded, and when he offers advice it cannot be gracefully declined.

If a manager is mobility-bright, he will seek exposure to more than one sponsor. He may take a lateral move in jobs, not a promotion, so as to come in contact with a new sponsor superior.

Harris: I've also seen quite a few of your "shelf-sitters."

Jennings: The fast movement of young managers means that many older executives get passed over. Sometimes, of course, an intensely demanding project will cause a manager to find a shelf-sitting job for a while to recover from fatigue. He has to recover his physical and psychological energy. To be effective, a man has to do what he enjoys and find enjoyment in what he has to do.

But the greater number of shelf-sitters are cases of arrested development. They have reached their peak. The problem faced by a new president is to find out how to inspire the shelf-sitters to perform well, even though they know that they will not go on to a higher position. Shelf-sitters often use leverage as a way of managing disappointment. They go to another firm where their failure is less obvious.

Harris: The system generates higher pressure than traditional management.

Jennings: Yes, it does. Each job is an intense learning experience, and there's always a report card on what you do. But it is also exhilarating. The mobile manager has exploded the myth that ulcers come at the zenith. It's the shelf-sitter who suffers psychosomatic illness, heart attack and suicide. When a man has been passed over, the question is whether he will live to make 60.

Harris: You don't spend much research work on nepotism. Is it gone?

Jennings: No, but the emphasis on performance has reduced the power of family, wealth and social status. For the mobicentric, education counts far more. I tend to concentrate on those I describe as "mobile hierarchs," men who move through corporate structures without the aid of family or wealth.

Harris: Graduates going into business will soon spot your cast of characters, Gene, now that you've identified them. But I'd like to come back to your point about the mobility of young people who get out of their first jobs fast.

Jennings: You mean, I suspect, that they are acting like the men who have reached top management. These kids are even more mobile. They are the first true generation of mobicentrics. Geography doesn't mean much to them, and they can't be bluffed into staying in a job by a $5 raise. They are career-oriented, not job-oriented.

What haunts these bright kids is the fear of getting locked into something. They don't want to get trapped and they don't want to get screwed.

What Makes A Career A Career?

A career is a course of progress that you feel you are achieving through work.

By work, though, we may mean any kind of activity that is aimed at achieving personal or organizational objectives. So if we consider work to be any purposeful activity, you can really have a career in just about anything.

There are people who make careers out of pushing dope, leading Boy Scouts, helping out at the Red Cross, getting out the vote and supporting political causes, winning tennis tournaments, playing chess, playing bridge, writing books, eating in fine restaurants, growing lettuce, climbing poles, climbing mountains, going to college, inventing gadgets, talking with computers, counseling people, shopping, drinking, investing, and about anything else purposeful that you can imagine.

You can, therefore, have a number of careers at one time, and a number of careers during your lifetime. You may start a new organizational career every time you change jobs. You may have many different jobs in one or more organizations during your life.

You may have an OCCUPATION -- a career in a particular type of work, or even a PROFESSION -- a line of work that has particular standards and requirements for entry. You may have two or three or more occupational careers during your life, as you shift gears. As you graduate, you will end your career as a student -- a full time occupation, for sure.

Some careers may be avocational -- not your main line of work: your political, social, family, hobby, and other careers.

Have you considered a vocation? That's a career that you feel really strongly about -- such as political reform, teaching, religious ministry, or other "calling." Of course, even a vocation may turn to another kind of career, as the teacher turned insurance salesman.

Today it's a good idea to beware of limiting yourself to a particular type of career. It is becoming much easier to change gears and try a new career. Know your long-range goals and your interests, but be prepared to change plans when the opportunities appear.

So whatever you feel like doing, make a career out of it. There's a lot of career planning for you. Enjoy life.

"Here's to Harvey Corbel, the creative catalyst of the media development department of the J.H. Goggs Division of the Maco Company, a wholly owned subsidiary of Tele-computron Corporation of America, part of Computel Conglomerates, Ltd."

Joan Genovese

Systems Manager, Systems & Information Processing
College of Mt. St. Vincent '67· B.A. in Mathematics

I'm beginning to feel like an old-timer since I never planned on staying at Con Edison longer than two years. But here, seven years later, I'm still interested and enthusiastic about my job.

I was a math major at the College of Mt. St. Vincent, but by senior year, I knew I wanted a career in computer programming. After graduation, I looked to those companies with large computer operations and found Con Edison to be just the place for someone eager to learn computer science from the bottom up.

As a programmer in the Customer Service System department, I received my early training with the IBM 360 computer system. That has been replaced with the 370 system, and as a system analyst, I also designed, programmed and tested various applications on these computers.

The projects here require great detail. In fact, for the past five years I've been completely involved with the new computerized Customer Service System. My connection with it has been exciting and personally rewarding since I have seen it through from the design stages to programming and implementation. And even though all the Company divisions have been converted, our work isn't finished yet. It's a constantly changing system that requires altering of existing programs.

In my present job as systems manager, I supervise and oversee seven programmers. It's more responsibility and I've always welcomed that.

I don't feel that my advancement at Con Edison has come because of or in spite of being a woman. I can't speak for all women here, but for myself—I've done my job well and so I've progressed. I think the opportunities are here for everyone who is conscientious and willing to work for what they want.

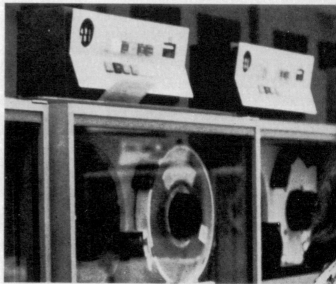

Colonel Sanders

You know the Colonel, don't you? He's the smiling gentleman will all that white hair and the good-tasting fried chicken.

About the time that most people are thinking about retirement, Harland Sanders began a whole new career-- franchising restaurants to use his "secret" southern fried chicken recipe. The Kentucky Fried Chicken Corporation is one of the largest and most successful food franchise operations in the nation and has diversified into other activities such as hotels.

Colonel Sanders (an honorary colonel) was born in 1890 in Indiana. His early career included work as a railroad fireman, farm hand, carriage painter, soldier, ferryboat operator, insurance salesman, service station operator, and motelkeeper. He also operated a roadside restaurant in Kentucky -- for a total of 25 years -- but when a new freeway was built, his business went bankrupt (in spite of the secret recipe with herbs and spices).

At this point, in 1955, the Colonel decided he would start all over. He had a $105 per month income from social security, a pressure cooker, and his secret recipe. This time, instead of selling chicken, he would sell the right to use his recipe and his name.

During two years of hard work, travelling all over the country in a 1946 Ford, he tried to sell franchises. However, he could only point to five successful sales.

He persisted, though, and by 1967 he had sold more than 700 franchises.

So after he had already turned 65, this entrepreneur started from scratch a second time and built, without financial capital, a large and profitable business.

In 1964 he realized that the company was getting too large for him to manage all by himself, and so he sold the firm to a group of investors for $2 million, plus a contract for life for $40,000 per year (since raised to $60,000 or more) to travel and promote the reputation of the business as a "goodwill ambassador." He retained ownership of about 200 of the franchises, located in Canada, the profits from which go to a foundation that he established to support education.

Heublein, a major food and liquor corporation based in Connecticut is now the owner of the Kentucky fried chicken business in the United States.

Heublein saw the possibility of exporting the popular Colonel's chicken, and outlets for Kentucky Fried Chicken began to spring up around the globe. Fried chicken outlets appeared in Europe and Japan as well as in Canada and Latin America. The Colonel's fame spread as he continued to act as the good will ambassador of Kentucky Fried Chicken abroad. As you will see in Chapter 17 on International Trade, the Colo-

nel's recipe and marketing proved to be successful.

Says the Colonel, "Anyone who has reached sixty-five years of age has a world of experience behind him. He ought to be able to gather something valuable out of that."

Other entrepreneurs have attempted to folow the Colonel's fine example, offering franchises in all varieties of fast food services, chicken included. During the 1960's, franchising became a major tool for building businesses quickly, as we discussed earlier in this book. But the businesses were rarely, if ever as successful as Kentucky Fried Chicken.

The same attribute applies to the men in charge -- there's no guarantee for career success. Why do you think that Colonel Sanders was able to build two careers so successfully?

Total Commitment

STARTING a BUSINESS as a WAY OF LIFE

by MIKE EDELHART

In *Zen and the Art of Motorcycle Maintenance* Robert Pirsig says that something strange happens when a man becomes involved with work he loves. The barriers between the man and what he is doing dissolve. He and his job become as one—growing, changing and deepening through their mutual experience.

If you ever become successful in a business of your own, something like this will happen to you. The creation and cultivation of a personal business—think about that, a business that's an extension of you—will grow so dominant in your life that after a while it will become impossible to separate you from what you do. You may run the business, but the business runs you, too.

That's a scary thought, but an important one. It's mighty easy to get so lost in up-to-the-minute details, statistics and theories when talking about launching a personal business that you forget the enormous long-range impli-

cations of what you are getting involved in.

If successful, your own business could set the tone for the rest of your life. If a failure, it will eat up many months or even years and most, if not all, of your savings. It will drain your strength and leave you—just maybe—with enough pride to bind your wounds and start over.

So, we get right down to the root of the matter. Why, if it's such a gamble and a hassle, would anybody want to start his own business in this age of raging economic uncertainty?

Good question. Maybe the best way to answer it is to look at the experiences and feelings of someone who has taken the gamble, accepted the hassle and come up a winner in the personal business struggle.

In the spring of 1970, John Shuttleworth invested $1,500 to start a newsletter for people who wanted to be self-sufficient. The editorial office was his kitchen. The first printing: 10,000 skinny copies.

Today, *The Mother Earth News* has a circulation of over 300,000. It has spun off a general store, a bookstore, numerous research projects, and syndicated newspaper and radio productions. Last year, receipts approached $1.5 million. John is still in charge and the whole operation still works to help those who want to become more self-sufficient get there.

A success, definitely. How did it happen? Well, first of all, it took more than money. Much more.

"Eight months after we began publishing, another magazine entered the alternative life-ecology field with a total backing of $1,300,000. It had a 'Big Name' editor. It had guaranteed circulation through a very large national distributor. It had advertising contracts signed before it ever printed the first page.

"That magazine was a guaranteed success, right? Wrong! It blew the whole one-million-three and went out of business two years ago."

"You may run the business, but the business runs you, too."

Money did play a major role in *Mother's* beginning, though. Primarily the lack of it. Because he started on an absolute shoestring, John financed *Mother* from his own savings. He ran the early *Mother* from his own home, with only himself and his wife Jane as employees.

Many businesses, however, simply can't get off the ground on $1,500. Other businesses require stores, staffs, special equipment and stocks of merchandise, which can raise the ante considerably. A children's clothing store, for example, can take as much as $80,000 front money to launch; a small pet shop only about $15,000; a mobile lunch counter operation around $5,000; a tiny craft shop could conceivably get started with as little as $1,000.

Would-be entrepreneurs often don't have the money they need. Where can they get it? Friends and relatives are one source. After all, if you can't convince your relatives that your business is a good idea, maybe it really isn't! Traditional loan sources—banks, savings and loans, finance companies, insurance companies and venture capital firms—also help new businesses. In addition, manufacturers and wholesalers sometimes help promising new retailers to secure good new outlets for their own products. One last source of cash, the factoring company, lends money against the value of your merchandise and store equipment.

One of the best loan sources for the beginning entrepreneur is the Small Business Administration, which offers moderately priced money to small firm owners who can't find financing elsewhere.

John Shuttleworth admits that like many first-time business owners he was terribly naive about money when starting *Mother*. Everything turned out to be more expensive and more complicated than he'd figured. He says that if he had known what was going on, he probably never would have started publishing. "We published all right," he says, "but we were defying the law of gravity all the way."

Figuring the amount of money needed to start a business requires the miserliness of Scrooge, the finesse of J. Paul Getty and the vision of Jeanne

---

Mike Edelhart, a former writer for Approach 13-30, has just joined The Mother Earth News *staff.*

Dixon. You can help yourself in this delicate undertaking by gathering every scrap of information and advice you can find; by talking with people who have already launched similar enterprises; by reading manuals, pamphlets and books on your specific business and on finance in general; by adopting a ruthless attitude toward your money needs (noting every possible expense but buying nothing you don't absolutely need).

When you've done all that, double the figure you've come up with (seriously!), so money will be available to cover the thousand-and-one things you forgot or underestimated.

Tips on getting information and advice: Anyone who might give you money in the future will almost certainly give you advice now, including banks and the SBA. Denude your library's business bookshelves. Pester the Chamber of Commerce and everyone within 50 miles who runs an operation at all like yours. Find out where successful business types in your area hang out and hang out there, too. Listen to them for tips and pump them for ideas.

When all is said and done, though, after you've figured out such esoteric items as start-up costs, operating ratios, risk capital and contingency funds, even after your financing has been nailed down, you may be no closer to success than when you started.

Money, properly applied in adequate amounts, is basic to getting a business going. But if money were all, that fancy magazine John mentioned would be nationally known today, and *The Mother Earth News* would not exist.

"Your business will survive or fail because of what you bring to it."

Beyond money, the key element in a new venture's success is the personality of the owner. Ecological magazines have come and gone by the dozens; *Mother* has survived because of John Shuttleworth. Your business will survive or fail because of what you bring to it.

John explains: "You have to go back far more than five years to understand how I came to found *Mother*. And don't be surprised that it might be more apt to say that *Mother Earth News* came to found me. I mean, given who and what I am, there was little chance that I wouldn't eventually wind up working with something like *Mother*. I was absolutely programmed by my early life to publish this magazine.... So many people, you know, seem to think that we just dreamed *Mother* up one day and went into business the next, but *Mother's* roots go back a long, long way."

Elmer L. Winter, founder of Manpower, Inc., the giant employment agency, has enumerated traits that a successful business owner should have. Winter feels entrepreneurs must be: leaders, not followers; able to delegate authority; able to roll with the punches; responsible; organized; personable; reputable; and healthy.

While these characteristics smack a bit of the Horatio Alger-Tom Mix syndrome, they reflect in a general way the "whole-person-ness" required of a self-activated business-person. But along with good character and the right background, a person who is going to motivate a business needs a clear and unshakable faith in the worth, practicality and wisdom of what he is doing. If, as John says, the owner isn't "programmed" for the work at hand, he may have a very difficult time bringing it off.

Nor is faith enough. The successful entrepreneur should have knowledge and experience in his field, as well. And he must have control of the fundamentals of the managerial craft.

Louis Allen of the Chase Manhattan Capital Corporation nicely sums up the qualifications for a successful entrepreneur. Allen lists three characteristics of the solid business owner: 1. He understands the gravity of what he is doing. 2. He is motivated enough to stick things out. 3. He knows his business.

After the problems of assessing yourself and gathering money, come the questions about precisely when and how an operation should be initiated. John Shuttleworth waited years for his ideas to take workable shape. Once he actually destroyed his manuscript for a large book dealing with the same kinds of topics *Mother* now handles because it didn't have the right feel. The question for a prospective entrepreneur is not just "Should I go to work for myself?" but also "When should I do it?" and "What form should I do it in?"

As Shuttleworth puts it: "It's one thing to have good intentions and to feel strongly about certain matters and to thrash about more or less in a particular direction. It's quite another to focus on the one most effective action you can take to further your ideals.

John waited to throw himself fully into a project until he was certain that the idea, the form, his own attitude and the social context were all ripe for it. This ability to be patient, to just wait and think the idea through, often marks the difference between success and failure for a new self-owned business.

"An extra two years of devoted planning and waiting until the time is right for your initial move might prove to be the best investment you ever made," writes Ernest Field in his book, *How To Make Money in Your Own Business*. Elmer Winter concurs: "If you are wise, you will take time to evaluate fully both yourself and your chances of success before making so momentous a decision."

"There's no glamor attached. Just staggering quantities of the hardest work you've ever done."

The months just after opening probably serve better than any previous hurdle to separate the winners from the losers in self-owned businesses. Those months bring mind-rending, bone-bending, head-pounding days of torturously long hours and constant attention to unforeseen problems.

Take, for example, the case of a frustrated young executive who chucked it over to start his own silver shop. Full of confidence but short on cash, he and his wife had a rough time during those first dry months: "Within two weeks, the car broke down and we found that we owed two months' security deposit plus a month's rent in advance on our new apartment. After deducting that, a month's rent on the store and living and moving expenses ... we had $100 left for the shop. We had hoped $1,000 would last two months.

"Cathy got a job which netted exactly enough for the two rents (home and shop). No food, no laundry, no gasoline; just rent. She drove a couple of other girls to work, which paid for gas, and since the shops in our area were staying open late every night, I offered to bring the shopkeepers a hot dinner for $1.50 each evening. Two of them accepted, and there was just enough left for us to buy our vegetables (we're vegetarian, thank God) six nights a week. On Sunday we fasted or ate popcorn."

When John started *Mother*, he became all but a slave to his invention. He found himself doing things 'like working all day, all night, all day, all night and halfway through the third day to get an issue out. Sixty hours straight ... after a solid two months of seven-day-a-week-eighteen-hour-a-day work.'

Looking back on that today, John says, "Whatever glamor you think is attached ... isn't there at all. What is there is simply staggering quantities of the hardest work you've ever done. Brutal, grinding, exhausting, devastating work.... This business just burns you out. Uses you up."

The J.K. Lasser Tax Institute estimates that a beginning business owner should expect to work at least 60 to 69 hours a week for several months.

John's description and Lasser's estimate could apply to nearly any new business—the endless hours, the constant press of responsibility, the gnawing tension of trying to bring something new into being. Here is where you must prove your love of the work itself. All too often, people go into their own businesses to escape the responsibility of wage-based jobs or to get out from under paper work and into something free from cares. The first couple of months weed them right out.

In fact, the red tape and paper work for small businesses have gotten so bad that even President Ford has commented on the situation. Ford said that if his father, who once owned his own tire store in Grand Rapids, were to try and start the same business today, he wouldn't have time to handle the required paperwork and still run the store.

As for when you can expect to get money back from a new business, J.K. Lasser's *How To Run a Small Business* states flatly: "It could be months before you realize a profit." And don't plan on spending that profit on filet too quickly either, because you'll probably need to put it right back into the business. The stock has to be improved; the shop fixed up; advertising started. Despite Horatio Alger's *Ragged Dick* and a hundred other unfortunate myths, no one ever gets rich overnight.

Maybe the idea of going into your own business intrigues you, but you don't have a specific field in mind. You've got to find a business that's suitable.

The first choice to face is: Do you want to start a new business or buy a going one? The new business will probably require less capital but involve more risk. The new business will come unencumbered by anyone else's reputation or habits. It will also, unfortunately, come unhampered by anybody else's customers.

Start watching the "business opportunity" ads in your newspaper to see what businesses are being sold. Also watch business columns and the major finance magazines, such as *Forbes* and *Business Week*, for trends in small businesses. Talk around to see if anybody knows of a business being sold or of a prime location lacking a basic kind of service. Confer with local SBA officials to find out what is involved for different kinds of businesses. Figure out what you can afford and what you want. Then stick as closely as possible to your conclusions, no matter how many extraneous temptations pass by.

In the case of retail stores, the question of location is probably the most vital. An ice cream parlor needs a lot of walk-by traffic. A grocery store requires sufficient parking space. A hobby shop ought to be located where kids walk by, not their parents, and if that's 10 blocks from downtown, fine. Also, you must consider the character of the town, the availability of advertising, the amount

and strength of competition, the rent and the ease of finding good help.

Keep in mind, as well, that the tone and style of the business you run can be as important as its product, both to you and your customers. David Steinberg, who founded his own successful alternative school in California says, "We tend to think too little about the environment in which we work. We pretend that our energy is unrelated to the inputs that surround us. When I think of work now, I look at the work environment and context as much as I do the substance. I measure my work as much by the process as by the result."

"Statistics can't tell what satisfaction a person gets from owning a business."

Let's assume, now, that you've picked the business, scrounged the money, satisfied yourself to your own suitability, and firmed up the location. What are your chances of making a go of it?

Well, Department of Commerce figures show that half of the new businesses started in a given year are still operating two years later. One-third are still at it after four years. After 10 years, only one-fifth of the original bunch have survived. Dun & Bradstreet, the corporate rating people, say that about 10 percent of small businesses remain open under their original owners after 10 years.

Sound bleak? Maybe, but reality and statistics don't necessarily jive. D & B, for example, temper their figure by saying the outlook is far better for "well qualified" persons. Which implies that the better you know your business, the less the figures mean for you.

And other batches of statistics put small business in a stronger light. For example, nearly 95 percent of all U.S. businesses can be considered "small." These small businesses account for 40 percent of the gross national economy each year. And every year 450,000 new small firms open.

As far as security goes, in the depression of 1932, 43 percent of the country's wage earners lost their jobs but only 20 percent of small businesses failed.

Figures just can't tell the tale about your own business, though, since so much of it comes directly from you. A million operations can flop, but the right man with the right idea will succeed. The problem, of course, is making sure you have the right idea before diving in with everything you own.

Neither can statistics tell what satisfaction a person gets from owning a business, what joy from working at something fulfilling, what pride at pulling together all the loose ends and

opening the doors on a place where "I am the boss."

Whether a business lasts six months or 60 years, it can be a deeply enriching experience. Sure you can make good money in your own business, but the entrepreneurial path offers more than that. It offers you control of your life, a chance to set up things according to your own rules (as much as is possible in today's regulated society), an opportunity to see yourself expressed in your surroundings, a position where your work reaches the public and benefits you without a lot of bosses and intermediaries to muck things up.

As a test, read these questions from the American Friends Services Committee booklet, "Working Loose." They may help you determine what you want, need and should expect from your own business. In addition, they sketch out the tremendous range you have in which to structure your environment when you take over your own livelihood:

- Forgetting about money, what would you like to do more than anything else?
- What physical and human environment do you find most comfortable?
- What's the most satisfying experience you've been involved with?
- What skills and abilities do you have?
- What do you need to learn and what can you do to learn these things?
- Really, what do you like to do?

If reading these over gives you a little tingle down deep somewhere because you know there's something you want to do and you know how you want to do it, then move ahead slowly. Be cautious. Get all the information you need. And keep in mind always that your own business will never happen unless you make it happen. The satisfaction received from being in charge will never be yours unless you take charge.

Recommended Reading

How To Finance a Growing Business, rev. ed., by Royce Diener (Frederick Fell Publishers, 1973; $9.95).

Working Loose, by the American Friends Services Committee (New Vocations Project, Random House; $2).

Your Future in Your Own Business, by Elmer L. Winter (ARCO Publishers, 1975; $1.95).

How To Run a Small Business, 4th ed., by J.K. Lasser (McGraw-Hill, 1974; $9.95).

101 Businesses You Can Start and Run with Less Than $1,000, by H.S. Kahm (Dolphin Books, 1973; $2.50).

The Federal Handbook for Small Businesses, available from the Small Business Administration, 1441 L. St., NW, Washington, DC 20416.

Career Development

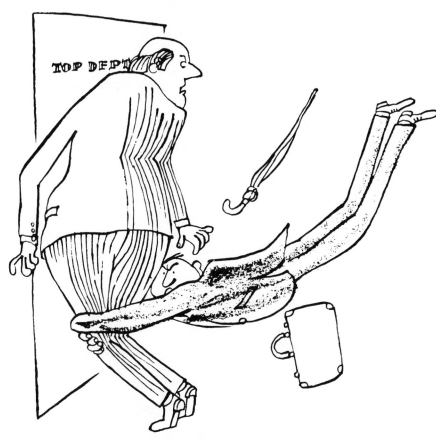

"*Aggression in job advancement is a necessary thing, Hoskins, but do try to be a little less blatant.*"

© 1971 Punch Publications

If you're lucky, you'll be working for a company that offers you new responsibilities as you are able to take them on, a company that will help you grow -- in terms of your personal interests, abilities, and aspirations -- both through job experiences and through educational programs.

By all means, pick a company to work for that cares about your career development. Regardless of the job and career opportunities, you cannot lose as long as you are developing your potential.

How do you know whether you'll have good developmental opportunities in a particular company? Sometimes you can tell from the experience of others. Other times you can tell from the information provided by the company (such as the material put out by Sears). Most likely, however, you will have to give the company a chance. Take a job and find out what the place can really do for you -- and what you can do for the company. If it turns out that it isn't your cup of tea, you can

always move on -- that's what is meant by the mobicentric man.

You should feel that your job does challenge your abilities and that it is contributing, at least a little, to your own longer-term career aspirations. Your immediate work may not always be just the kind of activity you like best, but if it strengthens your capabilities and enhances your future career opportunities, it's well worthwhile.

The developmental opportunities provided by a company should also tie into your career development plan. Does the firm provide training courses? How can you get into them? What would you get out of them? How about university courses or speical programs outside the company? Will they pay your way? Can you volunteer to go or do you have to be "sent"? Many companies have a tuition refund or tuition reimbursement plan whereby you can actually finish a college degree or even an advanced degree if you are able to spend the time on your own. Sometimes the company asks to approve courses in advance and sometimes the payment of the fees is dependent on a passing grade -- or a minimum "C". Frequently the firm will even pick up the tab for your textbooks. All in all, this can be a good tool for you -- even a "benefit" if you want to look at it that way.

Finally, you should know where you stand regarding your promotability. What can you look forward to as far as your next job is concerned? Can you ask for a transfer to a different division of the organization or bid for a job you know is open and you feel you can handle? (This system is often called "job posting."

Your career development depends in large measure on your own initiative and how well you plan for it. Some companies have concluded it is better to encourage its employees to work out their own developmental schemes rather than have them imposed on them.

In one large British company, an employee, given this opportunity, allowed his enthusiasm to run away with him: "When the training requirements he felt he needed over the next year were added up, it was found that they would take him 13 months of company time to complete."

And so goes the career development process in business. One U.S. corporation offers the following programs for career development to its employees:

1. Lower and middle level executives get the strongest dose of formal schooling. MOre than 90 specific training courses are open to them on company time, free, in everything from a two-day know-your-computer course to a 13-week dropout for advanced management training.

2. The most promising executives may go away to special seminars at prestigious graduate schools.

3. New college recruits come in through an orienatation course where executives try to sell the unassigned graduates on coming to work for them; recruits get an overview of the business.

4. Half of the company's supervisors and managers come out of the ranks within, so each plant has training programs for men and women freshly promoted to supervisors.

5. For production people without technical degrees, the firm has its own two-year technical school run in cooperation with a local university.

6. Employees may take non-credit courses at the same university or work towards a two-year "associate degree" at the firm's expense.

7. At the low-pay end of the work force, the company sponsors, under a federal grant, a reading-and-writing course for ghetto people, those in the box marked "functionally illiterate." The company is doing what was not being done in the public schools and is thus helping to let these people into entry-level jobs.

Lots of schooling, lots of courses. Is this all there is?

A company spokesman says, "We're going to have to plan for people just as we plan for our plant needs and our money needs. We can't just let the situation take care of itself."

"We'll have to develop career ladders so there aren't any dead end jobs. We have to help people develop aspirations, and not just within narrow limits; we have to help them identify their potential, then encourage them to develop it AND give them the opportunity to utilize it."

The knowledge explosion is blowing the old ways of working to pieces. "New knowledge is developing so fast in all fields," says the spokesman, "there is danger that managers may fall behind if they don't continue to learn throughout their lives."

At the same time our colleges and univeristies are going to have to develop the programs of continuing education that will be required to satisfy the growing educational needs of our society. If people are going to have to learn throughout their lives, the educational system will need to think about more than just degrees. This is not to say that a B.S. or M.B.A. will have less meaning, but it does mean that a whole new set of courses and programs will need to be developed to satisfy the educational needs of our society.

Sears | Merchant To Millions

We'd like you to spend a few minutes thinking about Sears. You might be surprised by what you find. We have more for you than you'd expect—including outstanding career options, salary growth and advancement. Sears has grown so fast that many of our own people are surprised by how quickly they can progress. They're surprised—and when you get to know us, you probably will be too.

If you haven't looked into Sears, we hope you'll do so now. If you've dismissed the possibility of a retailing career, take another look. Perhaps retailing isn't the field for you. But think twice about Sears before you make that decision. We've got a lot to offer.

Are you for us?

Sears isn't looking for a particular college degree. We're most interested in the person who earned it. Most important in our eyes are personal qualities: intelligence, curiosity, flexibility.

We want a person who can spot changes quickly—from fashion trends to new distribution ideas—and respond just as quickly. The person who won't settle for limited opportunity or limited salary potential. The person who's after a demanding career, as well as its rewards.

The retail store

Running a Sears store requires managers in several different areas. There is the store manager, of course, with a supporting staff. Managers are also required for such functional fields as personnel, display, merchandising, auditing, customer service and inventory control. And there are a number of people in division management—which would probably be your initial goal.

At Sears a *division* is a retail store selling department (such as infant's and children's wear or sporting goods). This is where all retail sales take place. Naturally, Sears' stores vary in size, but an average store might have 20 Division Managers.

The chart on this page should help put initial promotional paths—and how you would start with us—in better perspective.

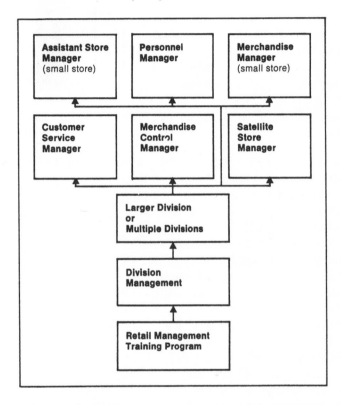

The pros and cons

We don't want you coming to Sears with any false impressions. So let's be honest. A career with Sears—like a career with any company—has some negatives.

Retailing can be a hectic business. There will be times when you wonder what it's all about. And while we don't want you to work more than 40 hours each week, you can be sure that those hours will include some evenings and some weekend work. You won't be sitting in an office—initially we'll expect you to spend most of your time out in the store getting things done. We'll also expect you to take on more responsibility, which often means moving to another city or another state.

Most of our people, however, have found ways to make these "negatives" work *for* them. For instance, working some evenings means you

131 CAREERS

have free time during the day to handle personal affairs. Moving to a new location means discovering new people and places—a growth experience in itself. As for the challenging pace of retailing—well, our people say they wouldn't have it any other way.

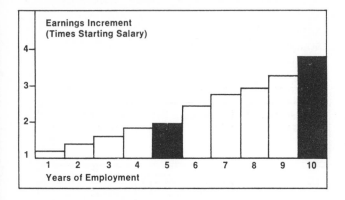

That's a question many companies don't want to answer. But we'll respond with some facts—facts that show how our people have progressed. The chart on this page shows the average salary growth for people who enter Sears' retail management program. While we're not guaranteeing this kind of growth—it will depend on your own performance—we thought you'd be interested in seeing how our management trainees have done, on the average, over a period of time.

In the long run

The retailing industry has long been regarded as exceptionally rewarding for those who move into executive positions. As Sears continues to grow, so do the rewards to our employees.

Obviously, your salary depends on your position as well as your performance. Since there are so many positions at Sears, it would be difficult to be specific about your long-term potential. So we'll simply say salary growth doesn't stop after 10 years. Sears' executives are good—and they're paid for it.

When you're deciding on a company, you should look at the *total* compensation package—monetary rewards aren't limited to salary. A generous benefits program, one which removes many of your financial burdens, is additional income.

Sears offers such a program. Some of the benefits include life and health insurance, travel-accident insurance, illness benefits, merchandise discounts, paid holidays and

vacations, and a highly regarded profit sharing plan.

Profit sharing that really means something

Sears' Profit Sharing Plan—perhaps the best known of our benefits—is designed to help all of our employees become financially independent upon retirement. Almost one-fifth of Sears stock is owned by our employees through this plan.

This is a plan that really means something to our people—so much, in fact, that more than 99 percent of all those eligible take part in profit sharing. To be eligible, you have to have worked at Sears for one year.

In 1950 the profit sharing fund totaled $350 million with 104,000 members. By 1970 this amount increased more than eight times (to nearly $3 billion) but the membership only slightly more than doubled (to about 217,000 people). And during those 20 years, over $2.5 billion was withdrawn by members at retirement.

Sears training varies slightly from one territory to another. Some areas have special training stores with training personnel. Others assign you directly to a retail store where local management is responsible for your training. Either way, you're given an in-depth understanding of retailing by Sears people—who have proven themselves to be the best in the business. This experience gives you the best possible start toward real professionalism in retail merchandising.

To be specific

Your own program depends on where you're located, your background and our needs at the time. Most programs last from eight months to a year, and consist of on-the-job assignments, informal discussions, films and outside reading. Initially you receive a series of rotational assignments in several sales supporting areas of the retail store. The accompanying chart outlines some of the areas covered.

Putting it together

After completing your training in these areas, you typically become involved in Assistant Division Management activities—in a selling department at one of our stores. Here you see firsthand the impact of the sales supporting departments in which you've been working. And by dealing directly with a Division Manager, you gain further exposure necessary for division management.

Your first goal after training is Division Management. Initially, this could mean managing your own small division or assisting the manager of a very large division. Both positions require the same amount of training—and both give you the opportunity to show what you can do. And in Division Management, you have to do a lot of things at once.

To supervise your sales staff, you must schedule hours and handle employee problems. You have to know your sales and inventory levels at all times. Division Management means working with the merchandise manager in deciding what items to select—and when to order. You work with the display department on the day-to-day arrangement of the merchandise in your division. And in helping plan and coordinate local promotions and advertising, you have to be sure you have enough merchandise to back up the promotion.

In short, it's your job to continuously improve the appearance and operation of your division—and, in so doing, to improve sales and earnings. You're given the tools to do the job, but it's up to you to get it done.

At this point you might think you could get lost. We're big, we have a lot of people, and we're always moving.

But Sears has developed a program specifically designed to keep track of your performance. It's called the *reserve group*—and it's an up-to-date file of promotable management people at Sears.

A detailed account of your performance and progress is recorded on reserve group record cards. These cards not only record your progress—they also make note of your personal career and development goals within the Sears organization.

So when you come up for your periodic reviews, we have many of the facts right in front of us. And when there's an opportunity that fits your background, performance and interests, chances are you'll be considered for it.

One more point. At Sears, your evaluations are objective to a great extent. Your performance on the job shows up in measurable and visible ways—such as increased sales in a division. And if you deliver that kind of performance, you will be noticed.

The paths you could take

After success in Division Management, you can move in several directions. If your goal is store management, you might first become a customer service or merchandise control manager. You might want to assume management responsibility in an appliance and catalog sales unit. You could advance later to merchandise manager (in charge of several division managers), or assistant store manager—many of whom have been with Sears less than five years. You'll also be able to move from one store to another, advancing to more responsible positions as you move.

Some people find they'd like to take on staff assignments in zone, group, or territorial offices. From there, they may look toward corporate staff positions or management positions at any of Sears' facilities.

In asking you to think twice, we tried to suggest an approach to job hunting, to getting beneath the surface, to asking the important questions. Naturally, we'd like you to consider Sears, and we've done our best to tell you why. We also think you should look at other opportunities and your own talents—in depth—before you decide. That could be helpful to us, and we know it will help you.

133 CAREERS

How Much Will You Earn?

That important question is tough to answer. How much you'll earn depends on your job, your training and education, your summer and part-time work experience, where you choose to work, and the policies of the company you work for.

Likely, though, you'll not consider your income enough. Americans (and many other peoples) tend to "want more" than they ever have. You'll find you have to borrow on credit to buy a car, a stereo, or take a vacation trip. You'll spend money you haven't even earned yet.

Inflation won't help, either, because your raises will at least partly be "gobbled up" by inflation. As prices of goods go up, your higher salary simply won't get you ahead of the game very easily.

AFFLUENCE

Overall, however, you will live well. You'll be independent and capable of paying your own way with your earned income. And as you progress in your career, your income will rise -- according to the responsibilities you take on. The increases will probably be faster than living costs so you'll get more from your paychecks. A bigger job gets a bigger check.

Also, educational area and level plays a role. If you're in a specialty that is in short supply, you'll get a higher starting salary.

In 1975, the oil industry recruited 4,885 college graduates. Many of the recruits were engineers, graduating in various engineering specializations. Starting salaries for these recruits ranged from $800 to $1600 per month.

Graduates recruited from other disciplines had starting salaries as follows:

Accounting	$775 –	$1,125
Biology	775	
Bus. Admin.	575 –	950
Chemistry	789 –	1,000
Economics	825 –	985
Ecology	900	
Finance	825 –	950
Geology	800 –	1,700
Geophysics	900 –	1,700
Liberal Arts	750 –	950
Law	1,050 –	1,300
Physics	800 –	1,275
Statistics	900 –	980

DOUBLE YOUR INCOME

Statistics show that college graduates are more likely to have much higher incomes. The surprise is that one key reason is that in many cases both husband and wife are employed, effectively doubling the family income. Income for college graduates' households is 50% above the income for other households on the average. The fact is that more than half of all wives who hold college degrees also work.

Further, the facts show that relatively few families have incomes over $25,000. Of those that do, many have two or more wageearners kicking into the family pot.

What will you earn? It depends on you. And whether you're satisfied depends on what you do with your income and whether you feel it's worth the effort to try to earn more.

You'll have to decide what income you need to fit your personal life style, and whether your career path will provide it. Balance your income needs with your interests. Some of the most satisfying job opportunities don't come with really big pay. You may feel they are more important than cash.

Of course, starting salary is not always the best indication of the level of income that a particular career may bring. For example, a sales trainee may not get a high starting salary, but if he or she is paid on the basis of the sales that they generate, the income level could easily reach very high levels.

Also, what about the salary levels of top executives? A look at the income levels of the top executives of major American firms shows that most earn well over $100,000 per year, with some earning as much as $500,000. Now clearly they didn't start at that salary when they first started working. But as a result of hard work, the average executive works at least 60 hours a week, and probably a little luck, the men who currently manage our major corporations have made it to the top. Some of the future top executives are just now beginning their careers. Is it possible you are one of them?

Where The Opportunities Are

You can readily see that most new jobs are in the "white collar" types of occupations. The greatest expansion of job opportunities is in the professional, technical, service, and clerical occupational groups. This helps explain why education is so important today.

You can also see the shift in employment away from farm jobs and most occupations requiring lesser skills and training.

Your choice of an occupation whould take into consi-deration the opportunities available. You can't just look around and see what people really are doing today -- patterns are changing. As our economy grows and changes, some occupations are expanding and others are contracting. occupations are expanding and others are contracting. You don't want to get stuck with special skills and no job to use them on.

The projections to 1980, shown below, suggest the changes taking place in job opportunities.

In Chapter 21 we shall talk further about where our society is going, but a look at the chart below should indicate something. Our society is moving away from one dominated by manu-facturing industries and toward one in which service industries and the profes-sions will grow in impor-tance. This doesn't mean that jobs in manufacturing will disappear, but the number of jobs in that sector of the economy will grow more slowly than in other sectors.

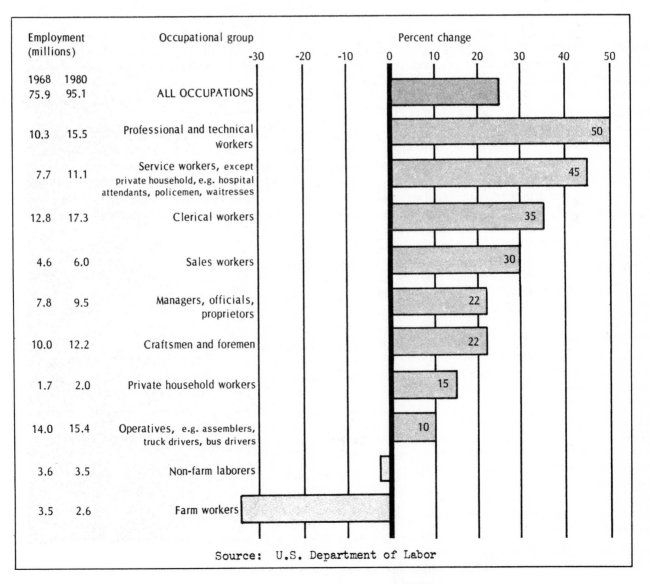

Source: U.S. Department of Labor

Sales Management — Sales Management responsibilities fall primarily into the areas of (1) business analysis and creative problem solving, and (2) personnel management. *These abilities are critical to our managers because they, in effect, run their own business.* You, as a P&G Sales Manager, must provide leadership and motivation in the hiring and development of your sales organization; accept personal sales responsibility for the key accounts in your territory; create and test new merchandising techniques; and provide the company with sales forecasts and market analyses.

The foundation of experience for this position lies in the beginning job of a Sales Representative. You'll be shown how to take responsibility for a sales territory — in your choice of locations, if we can arrange it — that has been producing up to one million dollars per year. As soon as you master the preliminaries, further training by your Sales Manager continues on a direct one-to-one basis to prepare you for management. Contact with upper management is an integral part of P&G's training.

Promotion is based strictly on merit and can come after less than a year in the field.

With it, you begin a concentrated learning experience that will involve you in the problems and opportunities of P&G sales management at various levels with the expectation that you will move forward again as you demonstrate leadership skills and problem-solving ability.

Advertising/Brand Management . . . is the management of ideas that create change . . . in the product itself . . . in the way we market it . . . so it will continue to gain consumer acceptance in a changing and highly competitive market.

The day you report to work you'll join a small (3 or 4 people) Brand Group which plans, develops and directs the entire consumer marketing effort behind its product. Each Brand Group develops an annual marketing plan, designs and executes advertising strategy, plans and selects media, designs and develops in-store merchandising events, and analyzes and forecasts business results.

Your Brand Manager will immediately assign you broad areas of responsibility and then look to you for creative ideas and recommendations in these and other areas. Your development will be highly individualized and take place exclusively on the job.

The objective is to put you on the fastest possible track to general management and move you up as quickly as your abilities will permit. This means that we must be very selective in choosing new people. The nature of our work demands an unusual combination of creativity, initiative, resourcefulness, leadership abilty and self-discipline. We value these basic talents and abilities more highly than specialized education or experience.

Field Office Management — You would be managing people engaged in administrative functions associated with sales activities in one of our regional offices. Following training, you would be given substantial responsibility and would progress on a merit basis. Responsibilities include order and shipment processing, credit management, mechanized system procedures, personnel management, and office operations. Your primary objective would be to manage one of our regional offices.

Procter & Gamble Careers

Finance and Accounting — The Comptroller's organization is the accounting and financial data information center for our worldwide operations. We seek people capable of staff and management responsibility in areas of cost accounting, financial analysis, cash and profit forecasting and budget control. We are not concerned with your academic specialization, assuming some basic exposure to finance or accounting. We are interested in your potential as a manager.

Industrial Purchasing Management — Purchasing is a major function involving the study of markets, negotiations with virtually every facet of industry, and contacts with most other P&G departments. Items purchased include chemicals, packaging materials, construction materials, equipment, and agricultural commodities.

At P&G, both Purchasing and Traffic (below) offer careers filled with variety, action, and a breadth of experience that can help qualify you for broader management assignments in these areas. Location is Cincinnati.

Industrial Traffic Management — In Traffic, you are concerned with getting raw materials into the plants and distributing finished products to cusomers efficiently and economically. You work closely with many other parts of the company and with carriers and regulatory agencies.

Market Research Management — You would have the responsibility for designing and directing total consumer market research programs that are the heart of successful marketing. The surveys you initiate are the vital bridge used to interpret the complex consumer. You would develop significant survey reports that are the indicators of future action. Initial training covers full range of interviewing experience while based in Cincinnati, Ohio.

in Business and Technical Management

Manufacturing/Plant Management — (ChE, ME, EE, CE, IE, Sciences, MBA or MSIA with technical BS). Because we manufacture more than 300 consumer, industrial and specialty products, manufacturing management is rich in opportunities for technically trained graduates who want broad, early responsibility. A 3-4 months intensive personalized training program prepares you to manage production, plant engineering or industrial engineering functions. The use of new management techniques applying the latest theories of organization and behavioral science makes this a dynamic field in which to work.

Product Development and R & D — (ChE, Chem). Chemical Engineers and Chemists at P&G create new products and improve existing ones — from fundamental research and upstream chemical engineering studies through applied development to actual start-up and shakedown of full-scale production units. You apply principles of math, chemistry, and engineering to develop processes and products such as detergents, processed foods, toilet goods, or paper products. You will be expected to manage your particular technical area and projects.

Engineering Division — (ME, EE, ChE, CE). Design and construction of new equipment and worldwide manufacturing facilities are managed by the Engineering Division. You would have complete responsibility, from preliminary planning through construction, installation, and start-up, for such projects as high-speed packaging systems, high-pressure fatty alcohol plants, complete paper-making machines and modern steam-generating plants. Starting assignments are matched to your general area of interest.

Engineering Development & Packaging — (ME, EE, ChE). As part of Procter & Gamble's Research & Development organization, this division is responsible for mechanical, electrical, and packaging input to new products. Developing unique equipment to produce and package these products is the primary function, supplemented with work on the mechanical features of products and with creating new packaging systems. You will have the aid of a design staff, technician support, a complete machine shop, and computer facilities.

Management Systems — (BS or MS in Comp. Sci., Eng. Sci., Eng., or Math and MBA, MSIA, MSIE or similar degrees). This division is in Cincinnati, and offers an exciting opportunity to use and expand technical and managerial skills in designing systems, operating computer facilities, internal consulting in many areas, and in developing creative technology in all these fields. Staff support is provided to all areas of the business, including administration, advertising, distribution, finance, manufacturing, purchasing, sales and technical staff. Here, also, is the responsibility for development and operation of corporate information systems. Use is made of the latest behavioral science, computer, analytical and quantitative technology to create systems for improving the managerial process. Involvement with all phases of the company's rapidly changing operations offers a continuous stream of challenging and stimulating projects which result in growth of the individual and the company.

International—Citizens of other countries interested in employment with one of our International subsidiaries in your home country are invited to write to the address below for specific information on opportunities in your field of interest.

If the department of interest to you visits your campus, you can easily arrange an interview with our representative through your Placement Office. Literature describing beginning opportunities in some detail will be available there.

If you cannot interview a P&G representative because we do not visit your campus, or because you are finishing your military service, or for any other reason, write directly to the address below and your letter will receive immediate attention.

Address: Recruiting Coordination
The Procter & Gamble Company
Hillcrest Tower
7162 Reading Road
Cincinnati, Ohio 45222

We are an Equal Opportunity Employer

A Young Liberal Meets The Payroll

Oliver Williams

By RICHARD J. SIROTA

I believe my generation is unprecedented for its liberalism and activism in America. And I earned my credentials. Beginning with volunteer work in the Presidential campaign of Senator Robert F. Kennedy and Eugene Nickerson's gubernatorial race in New York, I have worked my way up the ladder of political involvement. Included in those years was a stint in Mayor John V. Lindsay's abortive 1972 Presidential race, service as one of McGovern's California coordinators as well as work for the Senator at the Miami Convention and a year as national president of the College Young Democrats.

From my secure position at Cornell University, 1970-74, I viewed our economic system in terms of black and white—the good guys and the villains. Now a year and a half after graduation, I find myself enmeshed in the business world — working daily with the individuals I would have called "villains."

Yet today whenever conflicting worlds meet, issues become undefined and black and white becomes an undistinguishable gray.

Upon graduation from Cornell I joined my father's company in New York City. It is mostly a color-separation and offset printing business but with subsidiary work in industrial research and development.

The change in my views has occurred through many incidents both large and small. However, a few stand out as representative of the problems I confronted.

One of the first was during the quest for my first big sale. After a brief indoctrination into the technical aspects of the business, I was sent out to learn the ropes in the sales end. I spent a great deal of time and money wining and dining the print buyer for a large publication. She told me how impressed she was with our quality and said she would give us the "opportunity" to quote a price for the next issue. I was excited and, after discussing it with my father, I came back with our lowest possible price confident that we would start doing their work. When she told me that our price was 35 percent higher than our out-of-town competitor, I was flabbergasted.

This was my first, and somewhat rude, awakening to the fact that things like an 8 percent sales tax can have a deleterious effect on your sales, and that when you are competing for big jobs things like quality and service are sometimes secondary. Price is the name of the game.

I never really understood the old adage that "time is money" until I was assigned the task of setting up one of our research and development companies, from the drawing of the incorporation papers to the first day of operation within the confines of a budget. I felt that we could save money by carefully looking for the best buys in equipment and keeping the construction to a part-time operation with people we already employed.

The company took twice as long to get into operation as it should have, costing a great deal more than I anticipated. The money I tried to save became money lost because of the delay. Then there were the "hidden" costs involved in setting up a corporation that I had not counted on: incorporation costs, occupancy tax, payroll taxes, unemployment compensation, private sanitation costs.

As a liberal activist I found it somewhat incongruous to be sitting on the management side when it was time for contract negotiations. However, in labor relations— as in most other things—no one group is always on the side of the angels, and a settlement was worked out between our company and the union. I discovered that to be part of management does not mean that you have to be antilabor; what it means is that you look for that middle ground in which both sides can survive.

My respect for anyone who can run a small business in New York City is beyond measure. I am convinced that such people must be part genius and have the patience of Job. There are so many things outside your control that can add on to the cost of running the business.

For example, if the 7:05 train on the Long Island Rail Road's Babylon line is delayed 45 minutes you might have 15 of your key employees arriving late, ruining your entire production schedule.

One morning we discovered that there was no water in our plant on West 32d Street. After hours arguing with our landlord, we discovered that the city was making repairs on a water main and had not bothered to notify anyone about it. We lost nearly a full day's production.

Add to these such problems as voltage reductions during the summer months (which foul up delicate machinery), sanitation strikes, frequent rate increases for utilities and the likelihood of increased corporate taxes by the city and the state and it is a wonder that any businesses survive in New York.

It seems I've come full circle. My conscience and my heart tell me that we must retain all the programs that help the poor, the aged and the infirm, but what will be the price over the long run? Overburdening our city's businesses will in the end be self-defeating: almost 200,000 jobs were lost last year.

The hard truth is that colleges must start to emphasize that one should get out into the real world; As the song goes, "There ain't no easy run."

WHAZZIT?

CAREER PATH

A perceived course of progress in jobs or responsibilities

OCCUPATION

An individual's primary type of work or trade

MOBILITY

An individual's ability to move from one company to another, one job to another, or one occupation to another

Job Hunter's Survival Kit

STRATEGIES...FACTS...SUGGESTIONS
TO HELP YOU WEATHER THE JOB SEARCH

Job Hunt Strategies

Although every job hunt situation will be unique, here are some practical techniques to use:

WRITING LETTERS. For most people this is the only way to get an employer's attention, especially if the company doesn't send recruiters to campus. If the employer is in another city or state, the only way to let him know you exist is to send a letter—with resume. When you do this, you are competing with dozens, maybe hundreds, of people who have the same idea. So your letter has to be good.

There are two schools of thought about letters. One holds that it's better to write 300 standard letters and get maybe six interviews. The other school believes that it's better to write 10 individually-composed letters tailored to each employer's needs and then get maybe two sure-fire interviews.

The second approach has several advantages. If your letter shows that you've researched what a company is and needs, then the employer may feel that you've done some prescreening, that you're only writing the firms you're truly interested in. With a form letter, an employer is bound to wonder, "How can anyone be truly interested in so many companies?" The carefully composed letter usually merits more attention unless a firm has a large personnel staff which can afford to do lots of screening.

WALK-INS AND TELEPHONE CALLS. Dropping in to ask for an interview is terribly unprofessional. Personnel managers have hectic days and tight schedules, and an unwanted intrusion will do little to further your job prospects. Don't expect to get an immediate interview from a walk-in. You may be lucky if the receptionist asks you to leave your resume or fill out an application.

Telephone calls are much more professional than walk-ins. You're more likely to reach the person with whom you need to speak and less likely to disrupt his schedule. In a brief conversation, an employer may be able to judge if he wants to see you in person, needs a resume and letter before further consideration, or can reject you on the spot.

PERSONAL CONTACTS. If you have friends who are employed, it can't hurt to ask about job prospects where they work. Employers want good people, and a recommendation can save a lot of interviewing. Remember, though, that personal contacts will rarely win you a job unless you're also qualified.

WANT ADS. The space limitation of a want ad means that the results are often disappointing. Employers get all sorts of applications from people they don't want, as well as those from people they might consider. Situation Wanted Ads? Again, the sapce limitation hinders your ability to communicate your talents. Most classified ads are for accounting, clerical or secretarial jobs. However, do look under C for "College Graduate" in the classified section; this may have some good leads for generalists.

So much for strategy. There really isn't much to it beyond being yourself. In interviews be frank, be courteous, be spontaneous, be as relaxed as you can (the interviewer will allow for some nervousness). Above all, be prepared. The most common mistake new graduates make is not being prepared. If you enter an interview without a resume, with no knowledge of the company and without knowing who you are or what you want from life, how can you expect to convince an interviewer that you should be hired?

Job Hunt Methods That Work

What is the best method for finding a job? If the class of 1972 is any indication, direct application to employers, use of the school placement office and help of friends or relatives are your best bets. According to a Bureau of Labor Statistics Survey (conducted in October, 1972), college graduates of '72 used the following job hunt methods:

Method	Percent Using
Direct application to employer	79%
School placement office	68%
Friends and relatives	46%
Newspaper advertisements	38%
Public employment service	21%
Private employment agencies	20%
All other methods	38%

Nearly 40 percent of the grads got their jobs through direct application, while 20 percent found work through school placement offices and another 20 percent, through the help of friends and relatives.

When the number of grads using a particular method is compared to the number actually obtaining a job through that method, an "effectiveness" rate can be isolated. Direct application and asking friends or relatives had the highest effectiveness rate—about 52 percent each.

The Best Dressed Job Hunter

ENTER JOB APPLICANT A: male, college senior, majoring in accounting, 3.5 average. Bearded, he is dressed in a brown polyester suit, plaid shirt and green tie. His brown shoes sport large gold buckles.

ENTER JOB APPLICANT B: male, college senior, majoring in accounting, 3.5 average. He wears a gray wool suit with a solid blue shirt and a rep tie. His shoes are plain black slip-ons.

Who is more likely to get the job? According to New York City clothing consultant John T. Molloy, Applicant B is the overwhelming favorite.

Molloy believes that clothes do make a difference, and his 15 years of study—plus scores of satisfied clients—suggest that he's right.

What kind of clothing is most impressive in an interview? For both men and women the word is conservative. In addition to being conservative, though, attire should be well tailored and of good quality.

Suits should always be wool (avoid polyester doubleknits) and should be in sedate colors—blues and grays. Shirts should be white or a solid pastel (some stripes are okay). Good neckties are the rep, club, polka dots and other repeating patterns. Shoes: black, brown or cordovan slip-ons. Beards, according to Molloy, are taboo.

For female job hunters, conservative, highly tailored, expensive clothing is the choice in such colors as blue, gray and maroon. Makeup and perfume should be worn with restraint and jewelry should be unobstrusive.

If you don't believe Molloy, try this test. Have your picture taken in several outfits. Give the pictures to a friend and have him show them to several people who are in the same age group and socioeconomic category as the people who will be making decisions about your life. When he shows the photos, have him say, "These are identical twins. Which one is the brightest? When 90 percent of them pick one outfit over the other, you know it's better.

Putting together a job-hunting wardrobe Molloy's way can be expensive, but it may be worthwhile. As he argues, why short-circuit a career by trying to save money on clothing after spending thousands on an education?

For more about dressing for the interview and on the job, read Molloy's new book: *Dress for Success* (Peter H. Wyden, 1975; $8.95).

Recruiter Insights

The basic thing to remember about recruiters is that they are human. *The Graduate* sampled campus recruiters visiting a large state university during one week and found that 72 percent of them spent less than 25 percent of their time recruiting.

These part-time recruiters, while knowledgeable in other areas, may be as nervous about the interviewing process as you are. They know that if they choose the wrong man or woman for the job a lot of valuable company time and money is lost. Besides, they may have to see their choice regularly or even work with him or her. The pressure's on them, too.

What are recruiters looking for? Well, they're still interested in things like past performance (academic and extracurricular) and overall appearance. However, in *The Graduate's* survey, the ability to communicate and inquisitiveness during the interview were mentioned more times than any other attributes as qualities recruiters look for in a candidate.

Recruiters surveyed by the *MBA Journal* also stressed their admiration for the candidate who has done enough research on their company before the interview to ask intelligent questions about it.

One reason the recruiter is impressed by the candidate who has done some homework is that it makes his job much easier. His job is to sell the company to you, just as your job is to sell yourself to him. If you already know a lot about the company, then his approach can be on a higher level of understanding. The result is a refreshing, stimulating interview he's more likely to remember.

Listen to Your Biorhythms

You find yourself falling asleep right in the middle of a big interview. The recruiter, who seems nauseatingly energetic to you, makes a note that you appear lethargic and disinterested. Once again an "owl" meets a "lark" before noon and the results are disastrous.

Whether you've heard the terms before or not, you are probably familiar with both owls and larks. The lark is out of bed before the alarm rings because he heard its preparatory click. He takes his shower in the morning and has read the newspaper and run three errands before arriving at the office 10 minutes early.

The owl, on the other hand, spends his morning in a daze groggily downing cup after cup of coffee. By mid afternoon, he begins to remember his goals for the day. By dinner time, he's a real ball of fire. Unfortunately, there is no one left in the office to appreciate his brilliant ideas.

The distinction between owls and larks stems from differences in the endogenous biological rhythms, or biorhythms, which exist in every metabolic function—heart rate, cell division and so on. These rhythms are either "ultradian" (short-term)—such as the rapid eye movements (REM) which occur about every 90 minutes during sleep—or "circadian"—reproduced approximately every 24 hours and dictating our up and down times of day.

The effects of these biorhythms are endless. They are responsible for the "jet-lag" feeling we experience after a long flight overseas. Due to biorhythms, a person may feel the effects of alcohol more during one time of day than another, or gain more weight from eating a big meal in the evening than in the morning.

The greatest indicator of body rhythm—the clock which can tell you what time your body wants it to be—is your temperature. It reflects the sum total of your energy production on the one hand and your loss of energy on the other as your temperature rises and then falls. The lark's temperature may be rising before he even wakes up, while the owl's temperature rises more gradually during the day.

The traditional nine-to-five work day common in our society is obviously kinder to larks than to owls. The owl's performance often does not peak during the time when he is expected to do his best, and as a result he suffers stress. Of course larks who work overtime or who are on a four-day extended-hours work week tend to tire visibly toward the end of the day.

Once you begin to understand your biorhythms you can start to adjust your environment to accommodate them.

You may have been unconsciously doing so in college by scheduling classes at 7 a.m. or 7 p.m.

In the working world you may not be able to control your mental activities so closely, but you can still schedule the most important mental exercises—job interviews, important decisions and conferences—for the time of day during which you are likely to be at your best. Owls should make notes each night to get them through the following morning. Larks should concentrate on luncheon engagements rather than elaborate dinners they might sleep through.

It makes sense to listen to your body and schedule activities accordingly!

Understanding Fringe Benefits

Salary can obviously make the difference between two jobs, but so can indirect compensation or "fringe benefits." Such extras can sometimes add from 25 to 40 percent to your base salary.

While the number and amount of fringe benefits vary from company to company, these are the five basic categories and what they can include:

1. EXTRA PAYMENT FOR TIME WORKED—Found in almost every company on the blue-collar level and sometimes on higher levels, also. These include premiums for work done on holidays and weekends, as well as overtime and shift-change premiums.

2. NONPRODUCTION AWARDS AND BONUSES—Such extras as Christmas bonuses, suggestion and safety awards, quality bonuses and anniversary awards fall into this cateogry.

3. PAYMENT FOR TIME NOT WORKED—Included here may be severance pay, vacation pay, and payment for job absences due to such things as reserve military duty, jury duty, illness or death in the family. Some companies reserve the paid vacation as a reward for employees who have been with the company for several years.

4. PAYMENT FOR EMPLOYEE SECURITY—Such benefits as workmen's and unemployment compensation, health and welfare funds, retirement plans and prepaid medical and life insurance plans (insurance coverage can vary greatly, so be sure to see what a policy covers).

5. EMPLOYEE SERVICES—These may include free meals, trips, parties, libraries, educational assistance, recreational facilities, parking spaces, etc. Many companies even offer personal financial planning services to young executives.

Every job you consider won't include all these benefits. Therefore, it is important for you to set your priorities and then judge accordingly. Even a job with a modest salary can become attractive with the right fringe benefits tacked on.

The Sales Option

Everybody has sold something. Doughnuts. Girl Scout cookies. Raffle tickets. We've all been there. If you usually went home with the prize, maybe you should consider a career in sales.

Sales is an excellent way for a liberal arts graduate to gain entry into a business. A job in sales may prove productive in itself or may lead to a managerial or executive position in the company. And even in poor times, employment opportunities are good for top sales talent. The outlook is especially promising for women.

Sales occupations generally fall into five main categories: securities, real estate, insurance and brokerage, manufacturer's and wholesale representatives, and retailing. A college graduate will find the most opportunities in insurance sales and in manufacturer's or wholesale representation. Full-time salespeople are usually given specialized training by the company.

If you just want to supplement your income or earn some money while looking for a full-time job, part-time direct selling is an opportunity. When you're selling items like brushes, magazines, Tupperware, greeting cards, plants, etc. you can make your own hours, work out of your home (often with no large investment) and meet many people.

Even if you aren't the type to push a product, you can perhaps sell a service on your own for profit. Talented artists and craftsmen can work on commission out of their homes for extra income; accounting and tax services can be profitably sold by the qualified individual.

Try Going Temporary

If you have trouble locating the full-time job of your preference after graduation, why not consider working for a temporary service firm? Such national firms as Manpower, Kelly, Western and Olsen—plus numerous local and regional firms—fill the needs of other companies for short-term workers. The temporary service firm, rather than the client company, pays such short-term workers. Although most of the jobs are clerical, a growing number are in the industrial and professional occupations.

If you work for a temporary service firm, you can expect that 1) you will seldom make more than minimum wage, 2) you'll have few, if any, of the usual job benefits, and 3) you can't necessarily count on steady employment.

There are, however, certain advantages to such work—especially in a tight job market. First, you can practically set your own schedule and take your

"Good evening. I'm George Graham, Harvard '71. I have an A.B. cum laude in physics, and I can recommend the roast duck unreservedly."

Drawing by Weber, © 1971 The New Yorker Magazine Inc.

choice of assignments. This means that you can continue your search for a full-time job while bringing in some money. Second, you can pick up varied work experience, renew old skills and learn new ones. This experience can be valuable as you try to gain permanent employment. Third, you'll get to see the internal workings of a variety of companies, which may help you learn more about just what kind of work you really want. And fourth, you may make contacts that can later lead to full-time employment.

What You Should Know About Discrimination

With the passage of the Civil Rights Act in 1964, an important step was made toward diminishing job discrimination in the United States. Title VII of that act protects more than 75 percent of the work force from discrimination by private employers; employment agencies; labor organizations; joint apprenticeship committees; Federal, state and local governments; and educational institutions.

The following year, President Lyndon B. Johnson issued Executive Order 11246 requiring Federal contractors to take "affirmative action: to ensure that hiring practices were not discriminatory because of race, color, religion or national origin." In 1967, the order was amended to include "sex."

With the passage of The Age Discrimination in Employment Act of 1967 (and its amendments in 1974), people between the ages of 45 and 60 also gained protection against discrimination by both employment agencies and employers.

Since the Johnson legislation, nearly every organization which employs workers has 1) developed an affirmative action plan to demonstrate its commitment to equal employment opportunity and 2) moved to eliminate any possible overt or covert discrimination.

The affirmative action plans are monitored by the Office of Federal Contract Compliance (OFCC) and the Equal Employment Opportunity Commission (EEOC). Most state employment agencies employ a counselor who represents the EEOC and advises applicants on discrimination policies.

An individual may report discrimination by calling the local district office of EEOC, calling EEOC in Washington, D.C. at (202) 634-6930, or writing to the Office of Public Affairs, Equal Employment Opportunity Commission, 2401 E. Street, N.W., Washington, D.C. 20506.

In addition, interest groups such as the American Civil Liberties Union, National Organization of Women, National Association for the Advancement of Colored People or the National Education Association help in filing complaints of discriminatory practice if an employee or job seeker feels that he has been unjustly treated.

Government officials reiterate that affirmative action plans should only assure that a proper search of all qualified candidates is made before hiring or admission. The plan should not endorse preferential treatment of any groups.

CONSIDER

1. Have you considered a career in civil service? Why might you like or dislike such a job?

2. Why did Colonel Sanders do so well while other fried chicken franchisers remain unknown?

3. Why did the Colonel decide to start over at 65 when he could have retired?

4. Is a college degree important in a management career? To be an entrepreneur in business?

5. Do you think that mobility will become more or less common in the future? Explain.

6. What advantages and disadvantages do you see in a career with Sears?

7. What are the possible advantages of working in a small organization?

8. Why is so much emphasis placed on getting ahead (promotions and salary increases) in American society? Do you feel this is right? Explain.

9. What kinds of jobs will emerge in the years ahead that don't even exist today? Could you prepare for them today? Explain.

10. Does the employer have the responsibility for career development or do the individual employees? Explain.

CHALLENGES

Ask any successful person in business why he (she) chose his or her career. Ask how he or she happened to get into a business career and what has been good and bad about it. Also ask what importance is placed on education in the career.

Assuming that a truck driver earns $9 an hour plus time and one-half for overtime, does he earn more or less than a starting college graduate in business administration?

Interview a business executive and trace the career path that he or she followed. What changes in location, jobs, and employers were involved. Were these moves necessary? Could you follow this path?

Determine a style of living to which you would like to become accustomed and figure out how much income would be needed to support that life style. Develop a career plan for achieving that level.

RECAP

A job may be just another job. To a person who plans his or her career, however, it is a step toward an important objective. A job is an opportunity to develop toward one's full potential. It expands one's personal capabilities and lets you accomplish something as well.

To advance in a career, a person may strive to get ahead in one particular organization or may be "mobicentric" and jump jobs in order to progress. You'll have to decide whether you're mobicentric. Mobility represents a career strategy even within an organization -- as you opt to take on new jobs and relocate to progress. There are some advantages to staying put -- your talents may be recognized on the job. You'll receive recognition, in the form of raises and new responsibilities.

We don't say that one career strategy is better than another. It depends on what you want as an individual. Some people just don't want the hassle of trying to get ahead, moving, and changing jobs. Others consider it the focus of their lives.

But even individuals who "drop out" of the system have careers -- personal careers: families, art, writing, gardening, and other activities that are seen as progressing. You can have a career in just about anything.

Work in business takes on a greater, more significant personal dimension when viewed in the context of personal career planning. It isn't just work for a company or a paycheck. It's mutual. Companies support this view by providing career development resources (programs, counseling, etc.) and counseling regarding personal careers and on-the-job performance matters.

You can strike out on your own, too, as an entrepreneur. But that takes a lot of hard work and some special skills to achieve success. It's one challenge that's still a risk -- you have to work to make it come out okay. And a heck of a lot of people are in business for themselves today. Risk or not, it offers a satisfying career.

If you are going to be a career-oriented person, you'll have to stake out your aims, even though you know they may change later on. You look for the kinds of occupations, jobs, and organizations that will allow you to achieve your goals. That calls for planning.

Get with it!

WORKSHEET NO. 5

1. What kinds of things do you think you want to accomplish through your career (whether in business or not)? Why are these things important to you?

2. In many families both husband and wife work. What implications does this fact have for your possible plans and income aspirations?

3. Are you likely to be a "mobile manager"? Explain.

4. What makes for success in starting your own business? Identify several key ingredients that you would need, personally.

PART III

MARKETING ACTIVITIES IN BUSINESS

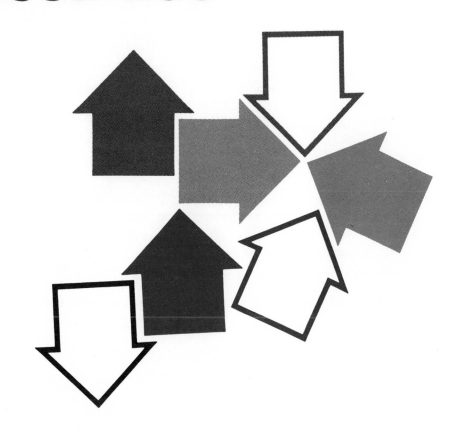

CHAPTER 6

Marketing

Marketing involves planning of products, their distribution, product promotion, and pricing. In this chapter we will examine these important marketing practices and concepts used in business.

In marketing, four basic elements are important -- the "four P's". They are:

Product -- to develop the right goods and services for the market. This includes developing or selecting a product or product line, adding or dropping items, branding, packaging, and grading.

Place -- getting the right product to the right markets. This includes determining where, when, and by whom the goods are to be offered for sale.

Promotion -- communicating to the market about the product. This includes sales promotion, advertising, and the training and development of a sales force.

Price -- determining the right price to move the product to the market with the right promotion. Competition must be considered, as well as practices regarding markups, discounts, terms of sale, and legal restrictions.

These basic elements aren't easy matters. There are many complicating factors affecting marketing today -- management, consumer, social, and environmental factors.

Introducing a product to the market, for example, is a difficult process. Considerable study and planning, involving both market research and product planning and development, are necessary if the goods are to be priced, promoted, and presented properly.

Of course, new products become old products as competing products come on the market. Products have life cycles, involving stages of growth, maturity, and decline. Product cycles, affected by environmental conditions, can play havoc with a company's profit expectations.

Understanding buyer behavior, special promotion tools such as warranties, market segmentation (appeal to different types of consumers), and other tools may be used to improve marketing effectiveness.

An then, of course, there is franchising -- whereby responsibility for marketing is contracted to independent businessmen, as in McDonald's. Franchising makes growth easier for many marketing organizations.

But no matter how you might decide to market the product or service that your business produces, the four P's of marketing, product, place, promotion and price will all have to be considered. If one of the four is neglected, the manufacturer may find lots of goods produced, but all sitting on his shelves. Those goods must be sold and distributed to the people who will use them. Without marketing and physical distribution, there would be little purpose in manufacturing anything. It is the function of marketing to get the goods to the people who want and can use them.

In This Chapter

What is a Market?

A beer is a beer is a beer is a beer -- or is it? Some people like light beer, others dark. Some like it warm, others cold. Some like it with a rich, frothy head, others prefer none. And people drink beer for all sorts of reasons, and link beer to various personal preferences and attitudes.

The market for beer is best tapped by approaching it as a number of smaller markets. People will buy the very same beer for different reasons. So breweries package, price, and promote their beer in different ways to stimulate the maximum sales.

-- Is it the working man's beer?
-- Does it have "old time" flavor?
-- Is it fun at suburban barbeques?
-- Is it the "champagne of beers" or is it cheap?

Market segmentation involves analysis of the market -- of sales today and tomorrow -- by different groups of buyers. By doing this, a marketer is able to better forecast sales, anticipate shifts in buying patterns, and adapt pricing, promotion, and even product design to increase sales.

Henry Ford originally saw one, homogeneous market for automobiles. When the preferences of the buying public changed, the Model T did not. General Motors and other Ford competition introduced different cars to satisfy the wants of different market groups.

Similarly, Procter & Gamble offers a varied line of soaps and detergents aimed at different segments of the market. Some soap consumers put emphasis on price, others on how "white" the wash becomes, and others on the ecology impact of the product.

The various additives, such as whitener, bleach, softener, and anti-cling liquids, are used by consumers with different degrees of enthusiasm. Small companies have actually prospered by appealing to particular areas of the market. The major firms, like P & G, seek to increase sales by offering varied combinations of additives.

Of course, planning for different products requires a great deal of market research. Major companies have the resources to do this.

Sometimes new products are introduced which catch on as fads. Their life cycles are short, but sales may turn out to be significant, nevertheless. Companies often introduce new products knowing well that the cycle will be short. The whole fashion business is geared to short product life cycles.

It's tough to know, of course, what will be a fad, what production will be required, and how long the demand will last. Who could tell how many customers would buy "pet rocks", a fad a few years ago.

Knowing that their cycle is short, some companies intentionally make their products obsolete. They bring out new products to replace existing ones, or new models with minor feature changes. Kodak has successfully introduced a prolonged series of Kodak instamatic cameras, each with new innovations that consumers "can't resist." Automobile makers, too, have created new models to generate demand -- to make the older models "obsolete."

1915

FORD
Coupelet

A car of style—beautiful in design—rich in detail of appointments. Fully equipped f.o.b. Detroit. **$750**

Ford
THE UNIVERSAL CAR

How to Introduce A New Product

Many of the rules that follow will seem glaringly obvious. Yet new product after new product is launched with sublime disregard of these basic truths. They almost always fail.

"Those who do not remember the past are condemned to relive it."

I. The Product

Beware of launching a new product unless it has a real point of difference which can be perceived by the consumer.

If a particular market category is growing by leaps and bounds, or has very few brands in it, it is possible to introduce a "me-too" product successfully. But the risks are great.

"Second" brands in a market typically get only half the share of the pioneer—unless the second brand spends outrageously more. It is usually better to wait until you have a product with a real difference.

Soap _dries_ your skin, but

DOVE _creams_ your skin while you wash

New toilet bar is _one-quarter_ cleansing _cream_

DOVE

1957: Dove is launched.

The difference may be in terms of better _performance_ or better _quality_. Dove Beauty Bar was easily recognized as a better _quality_ product. Better looking, better lathering, better for the skin.

The difference may be better _value_. It may be in providing a new _use_ or a new _service_. It may consist of _solving a problem_ which other brands do not solve.

For example, the Shell No-Pest Strip eliminates flying insects, without cumbersome spray bottles. Max-Pax Ground Coffee Filter Rings filter out messy grounds and sediment, and give a less bitter tasting cup of coffee.

Too many new products have only minor technical differences which can only be perceived in a laboratory.

Use research to make sure that consumers can see what's different about your product when they _use_ it, and that this difference means something to them.

II. The Package

Your package should help position your product and express its promise and personality.

1. Make sure your package is working _with_ the personality you are trying to build for your product—not against it. For example, Pepperidge Farm Old-Fashioned Cookies come in an old-fashioned paper sack, _not_ a fancy box.

2. Make your package reflect the taste of the _customers_ you are trying to attract. Hershey's new Special Dark Chocolate Bar is intended for grownups, not children. So the Special Dark package is sophisticated and contemporary looking.

3. Put your advertising promise right on the package, in _the same words your advertising uses._

The Shake 'n Bake package says "For crispy chicken without frying"; so does the advertising Dove Dishwashing Liquid says "Leaves hands feeling soft and smooth"; so does the advertising.

4. It helps to make the product _visible_ through the package—like Contac Capsules.

5. Don't skimp on package design, graphics, or quality. It will cost you more in the end.

Start worrying if your package is indistinguishable from your competitor's. It will get lost on the shelf. A "me-too" product in a "me-too" package is an invitation to disaster.

III. The Name

The name should help position your product and spell out its promise.

A good name can reinforce your advertising. It can give your brand meaning on the shelf. Your product is less likely to get into trouble if you follow these guidelines:

1. Choose a name that will help position your brand. Like Swanson's new Hungry Man Dinners.

2. Put your product promise in the name. Like Shell No-Pest Strip. Roast 'n Boast. Sears Powermate Vacuum Cleaner. And Sears Dial-Easy Sewing Machine.

3. Make your brand name memorable. Like Tijuana Smalls.

4. Don't pick a name that's so vague that it could apply to almost anything. Names like NoDoz, Electra-Perk, Spray 'n Vac all identify the product category quickly.

5. Make your brand name easy to pronounce. Especially if it's a product the customer must ask for, out loud.

To be sure the name you are considering avoids the pitfalls listed, *test it*. Product formulas can often be changed. Packages can be redesigned. But once your product is launched under a certain name, that is its name, forever. *So test.*

Test *alternatives* to see which name makes your product sound most effective. And most convenient. And safest. And most appetizing.

IV. The Price

1. The price of a new product should be consistent with the image you are trying to build. An elegant perfume almost *has* to be expensive. A special food for lap dogs can be expensive. But a food for large dogs had better be reasonably priced.

2. If your new brand is a "me-too" product — never price it above competition. But if your new brand has a real difference, people will usually be willing to pay more for it. Another reason for waiting until you have a product with a difference.

V. The Advertising

In his book "Confessions of an Advertising Man," David Ogilvy listed principles for creating advertising that sells.

The following principles are vital when it comes to advertising *new* products:

1. The results of your advertising will depend less on how it is written than how it is *positioned*. The positioning must be decided before the advertising is created.

2. Unless your advertising is built around a BIG IDEA, it will flop. It takes a BIG IDEA to make the consumer notice your advertising, remember it, and act on it in the market place.

3. Your product will only be new once. *Say it is new — loud and clear.* And be sure you say *what's new about it.*

4. If possible, put the *price* in your advertising. It answers the first question every consumer is sure to ask.

5. Tell your customer how to *use* the product. Tell her how it will fit into her life. Show the product *in use*.

6. Be sure to hammer home the *name* of your new product. Don't be shy about repeating it in your advertising — *many* times.

7. Don't be afraid to state the obvious. The benefits of your new product may be obvious to you. You have been thinking about them for years. They may not be so obvious to the consumer.

8. Don't overclaim. Today's consumer is an intelligent and skeptical woman. If you make exaggerated claims, she will turn you off.

If you have done your homework, and have a well-researched strategy and good executions of that strategy, you should be able to live with your advertising for years.

Maxwell House Announces

Maxim Freeze-Dried Coffee

Now, an entirely new process called freeze-drying actually makes it possible for you to brew **real** percolated coffee...*without a percolator!*

1968: Maxim is launched.

Product Life Cycles

Products have life cycles. They are born, they grow, they mature, and they die.

The buggy whip, a classic example, is dead. The wringer washer, innertubes, and churns to make butter are virtually dead. The markets for these and many other products has declined to a negligible level.

Other products are just catching on and are growing in sales, such as trash compactors, miniturized television sets, electronic watches, and dishwashers.

As shown in the figure below, each product has saturated the market to some degree. Basically, when everyone has one who wants one, the market is saturated, and sales decline.

When a new product is introduced, the consumer is made aware of the product and acceptance is being gained. As a product's sales rise, promotion and consumer repurchases (for newer models or to replace wearing products) push sales up. Consumer acceptance widens to a mass market.

At some point, however, growth slows down. There are continued gains, but at a lesser rate as the backlog for customer orders disappears. Then, as a product matures, a plateau is reached, where the market is reaching saturation.

Finally, newer or better products replace the old product, resulting in declining sales. At some point, the product disappears entirely, except aa a curiosity item.

To plan for marketing and ensure continued company growth, management must recognize the cycles and timing of them for the various products sold.

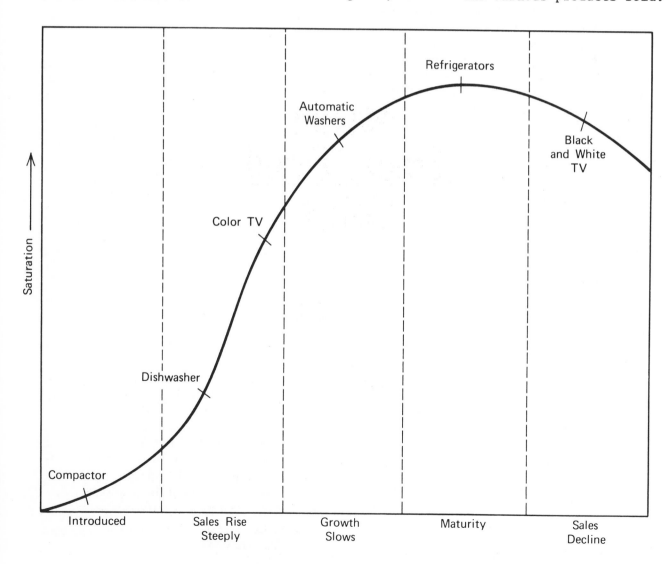

Market Experimentation

☐ From product conception to consumer acceptance, there stretches a chain of vital questions, all of which must be satisfactorily resolved before a new product joins the firm's regular market offerings. Can it be produced to sell at marketable prices? Will it be compatible with current marketing channels and methods? Can sustained volume be anticipated? These are typical of the problems that arise. Moreover, under "time compressed" development, the preparation of alternative designs, promotional materials and packaging proceeds simultaneously with product and process engineering. Such accelerated development schedules are aimed at reaching the market early enough to capture a good share and enjoy a full period of growth and maturity.

Test marketing

As part of the development activity, a product model may emerge that is believed to have considerable appeal. Some pilot quantities may be on hand. But before going into the expense of large-scale production and promotion, it will be advisable to check how the consumer will react, and whether modifications are necessary or desirable. The test market, representing a small geographic area which is considered to be typical of the nation-wide market, will serve as a kind of laboratory in which the new product can be evaluated. Figure 3 describes the functions of the test market.

Test marketing permits a further time compression in the race to get promising new items to market. For example, if there are three possible versions of the product with two likely package designs, then a total of six product-packaging combinations can be checked simultaneously in six geographically separated areas.

Marketing experimentation

Test marketing represents experimentation, since trials can be made of various modifications in the design and packaging of the product.

The particular method of handling market perturbations will vary with the type of problem encountered. For example, assume that a competitive promotion occurs somewhere in the middle of the 15-week test market period. We may compute a mathematical trend-line for the initial and final periods and then bridge the gap by means of a linear interpolation from the two trend lines. In place of trend lines, long-term moving averages—such as covering 8 weeks—might be suitable.

On the other hand, assume there is deliberate jamming. Chances are that it will take the competitor some four weeks to discover our test situation and develop his own competitive promotion—let us say in the form of a price cut. We can then do several things: (1) We can reduce our price and note the proportional changes during the unperturbed period as against the competitor's price cut and our own subsequent cut. The percentages so obtained may be aspects, such as pricing, can also be studied in relation to consumer demand. Since only small areas are involved, there will be neither large quantities nor large promotions, and costs can be kept relatively low. But the information gathered in this process will be tremendous value in formulating the final marketing plans on a nation-wide basis.

Limitations

It is admittedly difficult to find areas that are typical of the market as a whole, but localities that come close to this goal have been identified. And in time, with experience, a firm can usually develop adjustment factors to modify local percentages of sales volume when making total market projections.

As the popularity of test marketing has increased, however, new problems have arisen, such as conscious or accidental "jamming," when a competitor's special prices or premiums "muddy" the test results. With some additional testing and relatively sophisticated statistical "filtering" used as adjustment factors to more or less remove the effect of this "jamming." (2) We can start a smaller trial market in some other area, and utilize the experience in this experiment to make adjustments in the major market area. (3) We can interview selected purchasers by means of random sampling, both of our brand and the competitor's. From the data gained, adjustments in test market sales may be made to allow for the effect of jamming.

Despite the elaborateness, care and sophistication that may go into any corrective procedures, there is no denying the fact that we are dealing with approximations and estimations. It would be better if there had been no perturbation of the test market in the first place.

A further flaw in test marketing is the gradual emergence within the test area of consumers' awareness that they "live in a laboratory" as regards their market behavior. This knowledge can sometimes markedly affect their purchasing actions.

Giving due consideration to such pitfalls, however, the following benefits of test marketing seem assured:

1. Even though volume predictions for a new product may turn out to be relatively inaccurate, it is highly unlikely that a poor seller will show up erroneously as a promising product to market.

FIGURE 3. FUNCTIONS OF TEST MARKET

Action	Purpose
Selection of a Test Market	Utilize a restricted geographical area, which is representative of the national market, in which to test market new products.
Projection	Observe the marketing achievements in the test area and project them nation-wide. For example, if monthly volume in 2 per cent of the country is $500, then the total volume projected is 500/0.02 = $25,000.
Check of Demographic Validity	Assure, from careful review of all available data, that the test area is generally representative of the broad scale market in terms of social classes, age structures and other demographic conditions.
Check of Behavioral Validity	Assure that area is representative in terms of consumption of similar or substitute products.
Check of Competitive Validity	Assure that competitive strengths in area are approximately similar to market as a whole. Also check that no "jamming," as a result of competitors' promotion campaigns for their products, invalidates test results.
Check Marketing Mix	Test many factors, such as sizes, prices, promotion method and size-price-promotion combinations.
Filtering	Use sophisticated statistical methods to "filter out" the effects on "jamming" and other factors affecting validity of results.
Final Evaluation	Answer questions: (1) Will the product sell? and (2) At what probable volume rate?

2. When several versions of a product are tested in different market areas, using design, packaging or price differentials, the most appealing combination is likely to be readily identifiable. In instances where this process fails, it usually turns out that there is little real difference in appeal among several designs or packagings.

Thus, while market researchers continue to encounter problems and to devise means for minimizing the effects of test market deficiencies, they also recognize that there are few readily useable alternatives.

WHAZZIT?

PRODUCT

The good or service provided by the firm to the buying public.

PROMOTION

Communicating to the market about the product offered for sale.

PRICE

The price to be charged for the product. This is a function of the costs of production, legal restrictions, and competition.

FRANCHISE

An agreement between a manufacturer or other type of company and a private distributor allowing the franchisee to sell the franchisor's product or service in a specific geographic area or market segment.

MARKET SEGMENT

A portion of the market which has specific characteristics which makes that segment different from others.

WARRANTY

An assurance of the quality of the goods sold by the manufacturer or seller.

Is The Soap Leader Getting Soft?

In the eyes of most people in the consumer package goods business, Procter & Gamble Co., Cincinnati's colossus, is the model marketer and model manager. Its products dominate most of the markets in which they compete, and P&G has been the spawning grounds for consumer marketing men in many other companies.

Lately, though, some unexpected things have been happening. P&G ignored the developing market for tooth paste that does nothing but whiten teeth, and one of its own products took a deep slide in the tooth paste market. Similarly, other companies have been far ahead in pushing aerosol deodorants, and P&G's non-aerosol deodorants have lost market position. And there have been just enough other incidents of that sort to nurture a brand-new crop of P&G critics.

Their question is whether the P&G formula of conservatively paced growth is in tune with today's times. President Howard J. Morgens thinks it is. "You don't want to grow faster than the organization itself—its people—can grow," he says. "If you do, you get sloppy. That's why we pace our growth."

Some critics say that P&G has paced itself too much—that its emphasis on discipline is shackling executives and hampering the company's growth. "Procter has reached middle age," says a former P&G executive. "It is full of guys aged 35 making $35,000 who have to ask permission to go to the washroom. Elsewhere, they'd be running their own show."

Victor Bonomo, another alumnus and now president of United Vintners Div. of Heublein, Inc., recalls "layer after layer of executives rewriting memos. Hearsay suggests it's still true today." Bonomo, who in his last job as a General Foods Corp. divisional vice-president and general manager took on P&G toe-to-toe, adds: "General Foods is more malleable. Procter continues to be highly proceduralized."

Big lead. Few of P&G's critics expect the company's earnings to drop off. They simply see competitors rapidly narrowing P&G's huge lead.

Last year P&G earned $182.6-million on sales of $2.5-billion, for a 7.2% margin on sales and 16.5% return on invested capital. Both figures have moved up over the last 10 years. Soap and detergents make up 58% of P&G's volume; food, 18%; industrial products, 10%; toiletries, 9%; paper, 5%.

It would be no mean feat for P&G to improve on its own performance. Its prime competitor, Colgate-Palmolive Co., netted just 3.3% on sales and 11.7% on investment last year. Third-place Lever Bros. did even worse.

A brand-by-brand, market-by-market analysis of P&G gives no hint of pending difficulties in profit or growth. In fact, two products—disposable diapers and enzyme detergents—are shaping up as short-term runaways, further brightening P&G's outlook. But a host of legal problems (a consent decree severely hampering acquisitions of household products and a huge private antitrust suit) cloud the picture.

All told, P&G has cornered almost 60% of the market in heavy detergents and more than one-third of the markets in liquid detergent and bar soap. It also leads in automatic dishwasher detergent, fabric softener, and household cleaning products. In foods, the company still dominates the solid shortening and cake mix markets, and is about to introduce a stack-packed, stay-fresh potato chip after a highly successful market test. P&G's vacuum-packed Folger's coffee leads in the half of the country where it is marketed, and the company plans to step up its invasion of the instant coffee market. In paper, P&G's Charmin toilet tissue leads in the parts of the country where it is marketed. Bounty towels are tied for first in their marketing area, and P&G continues to lead in toothpaste and shampoos.

P&G's successes follow a pattern. Crest, Bounty, Charmin, Head & Shoulders shampoo, Tide, Duncan Hines, and now enzyme detergents and Pampers diapers have been product improvements. "The greatest misconception is that we're just great marketers," says Morgens. "If I had to put my finger on just one thing it would be product development."

Morgens' feelings on the subject notwithstanding, the marketing side consistently gets all the glory. But P&G has sometimes succeeded when marketing was unenthusiastic about a product's prospects. Pampers, which did poorly in the first test market, is a case in point. Says Harry Tecklenburg, manager of research and development: "It is much to the company's credit that it let the technical group go their way. There was no marketing evidence that it would work."

Likewise, the product development team pushed to get the American Dental Assn.'s endorsement for Crest toothpaste. "The public was cynical of claims in this

Where P&G leads

[Estimated share of retail sales]

Heavy duty detergents

Tide	P&G	25%
Bold	P&G	8.0
All	Lever	8.0
Dash	P&G	6.0
Cold Power	Colgate	6.0
Cheer	P&G	5.0
Ajax	Colgate	4.5
Gain	P&G	4.0
Wisk	Lever	4.0
Fab	Colgate	4.0
Oxydol	P&G	3.5
Breeze	Lever	2.5
Duz	P&G	2.0
Bonus	P&G	2.0

Light duty liquid detergents

Ivory Liquid	P&G	19
Palmolive Liquid	Colgate	14
Joy	P&G	13
Lux	Lever	11
Dove	Lever	6
Thrill	P&G	5

Deodorant soap

Dial	Armour	15.5
Zest	P&G	9.0
Safeguard	P&G	6.5
Phase III	Lever	5.5
Lifebuoy	Lever	5.0

Solid shortenings

Crisco	P&G	48.5
Swiftening	Swift	6.0
Snowdrift	Hunt	5.5
Spry	Lever	5.5
Fluffo	P&G	2.0
Private Label Brands		25.0

Toothpaste

Crest	P&G	38
Colgate Dental Cream		23
Ultra-Brite	Colgate	10
Gleem	P&G	9
McLeans	Beecham	6

Shampoos

Head & Shoulders	P&G	21
Prell	P&G	15
Breck	American Cyanamid	15
Johnson's Baby Shampoo	Johnson & Johnson	10

Mouthwashes

Listerine	Warner-Lambert	43
Scope	P&G	15
Lavoris	Richardson-Merrell	11
Micrin	Johnson & Johnson	10
Colgate 100		3

area with the ammoniated and chlorophyll talk going around," Tecklenburg recalls. "This inhibited the marketing people."

Misses. Like the triumphs, the errors at P&G can be shared. Colgate's Ultra-Brite recently bumped P&G's Gleem into fourth place, and that happened because P&G knew the dental association didn't like the "whitener" tooth pastes and the company thought it couldn't afford to buck the ADA. Both marketing and product development people misjudged aerosol deodorants. Marketing didn't think a product directed at all members of the family—such as Gillette' Right Guard—would sell; product development wouldn't put together a deodorant that did not contain an antiperspirant.

P&G's real bloopers of recent years were in deodorant soaps and in peanut butter.

P&G people don't like to talk about the fact that they were first offered the formula for Dial, the soap which is such a large part of Armour & Co.'s earnings. It was turned down, says Morgens, because "at that time we had our hands full introducing Tide. Toilet soaps took second priority and probably wouldn't have fitted into our marketing schedule."

P&G bought a peanut butter manufacturer to get into a growing part of the food business. Then its product development people tinkered with the formula and wound up in a labeling dispute with federal authorities. And at the same time, the marketing people found out that selling peanut butter was not the same as selling, say, cake mixes. So, while the product is still on grocery shelves, it is lagging.

Hard sell. To compete against P&G, says a marketing executive who has done so, "you have to take risks." Colgate recently moved its enzyme pre-soak Axion into national distribution with almost no market research backup. Unflustered, P&G continued to test its Biz. It entered the product late but is now relentlessly chopping away Axion's early lead.

P&G rarely deviates from the time-tested method of hammering away at the housewife via soap operas and other saccharine TV fare—stressing the "slice of life" approach in its commercials—plus piles of cents-off coupons. Its competitors, by contrast, must innovate. "Competitors? My gosh, 99 and 44/100ths% are spending more proportionately than our brands," says Morgens. The percentage may be lower, but outside estimates indicate competitors are sometimes obliged to put 20% or more of a brand's volume into promotion while P&G, with its good time slots on TV guaranteed by the high level of its spending, gets by on half that.

For years, P&G was consistently No. 1 in advertising expenditures. But in 1968 the company slipped to second place (behind General Motors) with expenditures of $198.7-million, with probably about 90% earmarked for TV.

The advertising is backed up by an 1,800-man sales force that is often as irritating to the merchant as the commercials are to the discerning TV viewer. "We are controversial with the trade," confesses Owen B. Butler, vice-president for sales.

Talent search. The P&G machine operates with such precision because it is probably more scrupulous than any large U. S. company about matching its pegs and holes. After exhaustive screening, only men with time-tested qualities are hired. (Less than 1% of the applicants in the marketing end make it.) "We don't care if a man has straight As or is in the top 10% of his class," says Francis Dinsmore, Jr., creative services manager in the advertising department. "How does he rub minds with other people?"

P&G promotes exclusively from within. Earlier this month, this trait showed up again when Edgar H. Lotspeich, former managing director of P&Gs British subsidiary, was elevated to the vital post of general advertising manager. His predecessor, Albert N. Halverstadt is retiring after 38 years with the company. Lotspeich joined P&G right out of Princeton 32 years ago.

P&G is known to string along with executive laggards longer than most companies. But it doesn't get saddled with many because the passed-over executive soon gets the message. "When a P&G man is promoted, his children immediately change their friends," says a Cincinnati housewife. Adds a prominent hostess in the city: "It is always said that you shouldn't invite P&G people of different levels. The lower man will always be uncomfortable."

Tough standards. Inevitably, the outgrowth of such rigid guidelines is a big dose of conformity—despite all of P&G's denials. "We have nothing against beards," Morgens insists—but it's a safe bet that the only two a visitor will see side by side are those of William A. Procter and James N. Gamble (sons of the founders) whose portraits peer down imperiously on top executives occupying the 11th-floor offices of the company's headquarters.

To Morgens, the tough job is keeping a balance. "This company lives on creativity, but it has to be disciplined as hell," he says. It's the discipline that chafes. "We're criticized about being too particular. Why do I have to change this memo? Why is it so awfully important if the typist makes a little mistake?" muses Dinsmore. "It's important because accuracy means 100% accuracy."

This is where the managerial swingers and P&G part company. "Oh, that damned thoroughness," groans a former associate brand manager. "You can innovate, but only within the Procter tolerances. And the walls are very high." This executive once kept track of personnel moves in the advertising department: 60% of the executives had been there less than 5 years and 95% less than 15. P&G won't say what the turnover is. But the company admits that it is high, and that some people use P&G as a training ground. "Harvard, Stanford, and Procter & Gamble," chuckles Morgens.

Parameters. Morgens says his biggest managerial achievement has been to give his brand managers more power. But P&G is probably still not so decentralized as other large companies more solidly wedded to the profit-center concept. A P&G brand manager is responsible for "success" of a brand in volume, but not profit. Only at the division manager level does one man have production, R&D, and accounting people reporting to him.

The larger decisions come up to P&G's 25-man administrative committee. But P&G is so inbred that most matters are a foregone conclusion. "This is our advantage," Morgens says. "Communication is easy. Everybody has spent their entire lives with the company. I have yet to see a matter actually come to vote."

In their zeal to be different, P&G's competitors have tried to give their brand men more autonomy. "Our man is screaming and yelling with R&D people, screaming with packaging," boasts a Colgate executive. "It's not just brand management. Each is a president of a corporation."

But a top official of another large consumer goods company, who in a long career has beat heads with all the big ones, puts it this way: "The problem is there are few good brand managers around. Sure, you may give him more autonomy, but he is more likely to make an awful blooper. If I had to bet, I'd go with P&G. Colgate goes by guess and gee-whiz. Lever is even worse. You don't find P&G with big national flops."

Is P&G's approach out of date? The swingers may think so, but not all the alumni. George Mihelic, an account supervisor in the Chicago office of J. Walter Thompson, says, "I didn't prosper at Procter. I tried to do things outside the parameters. But I hope my kid goes to work for that firm, even if he only lasts six months."

And a former production man adds: "Procter fall down? Lord, no. There's no question it's a tremendously effective, well-run organization. It's an institution. It's a religion."

Problems in Business

Most products have life cycles in which they progress from being new to the point where they have wide acceptance. But there are some products that really don't have that fate.

Generally, foods don't have life cycles that are the same as manufactured goods. It is true that tastes and eating habits of the public change, but people always need to eat, and as long as they are eating, the food producers and processors have an assured market for their goods. Granted, there are some "fad foods" which come and go, but most foods are stable in their market demand.

What happens if the market starts to disappear? Gerber, the baby food people discovered this can happen.

Faced with a birth rate that has declined, Gerber is beginning to feel the pinch of a reduced market for baby food products. Further, many mothers are fixing "natural foods" at home for their babies. While Gerber may be hit first, other companies will feel the dip, as the growth for their products slows.

The Bad News In Babyland

With the nation's birthrate down, there are too few mouths to feed.

Wherever John C. Suerth turns these days, someone is giving him bad news. In recent months, the 59-year-old Chairman of Gerber Products Co., Fremont, Michigan, has had to grin and bear government figures that show the national birth rate trending downward over the past decade. He has done a slow burn at charges by everyone from Ralph Nader to *Consumer Reports* that the nutritional values in prepared baby foods are not all they are chopped up to be. And he has smarted at reports that a mini-movement is afoot among some mothers to forsake the little glass jars for fresh foods they cook and strain themselves.

"There is not too much being said that is favorable," says Suerth with characteristic understatement. Especially, it should be added, on Wall Street, where "GEB" has been dragging like a loose diaper and trading at eleven times earnings. As one apathetic baby-food industry analyst puts it, "I've seen the birth rate figures. That's enough."

Moreover, the baby bust is not the only problem Suerth (pronounced "sue-earth") is facing. He has also been having trouble with his profit margins. Even though Gerber won a 2% price increase from the Price Commission, it must buy 50 million pounds of non-price-controlled fruits and vegetables a year. Then, too, the baby food industry has just gone through a six-month price war as H.J. Heinz and the Beech-Nut Division of Squibb Corp. attempted to wrest some of Gerber's big 60% share of the baby-food market.

As a result, Gerber has stumbled from its record $282.6-million sales and $2.40 a share profits of last year, which ended March 31. For the first half of its current fiscal year, profits of $1.10 a share were off last year's pace of $1.25 for the same period, and sales fell by some $2.7 million to $140 million. Gerber will be "lucky," says Suerth, to equal last year's profit this year.

But for the coming years, Suerth thinks that Wall Street "is a poor barometer of the company's prospects. Sitting where I am sitting," says the chairman, "things are coming along pretty well." Together with encouraging changes in pricing practices, Suerth has been gleaning signs that the birth decline is leveling off. Such statistics are vital to Gerber's business, of course, so the company maintains a staff of demographers "who do nothing else" but collect, correlate and contemplate figures pertaining to population growth. They point out that by 1980, the number of women in the prime fertile years between twenty and 29 will increase by 20%.

Even so, the big baby-food company is keeping its family growing beyond baby foods. Gerber Life Insurance Co., which it set up in 1969 to sell low-priced policies to young parents by mail, already operates in 44 states and has written more than $118 million in coverage for some 59,000 policyholders. Gerber also operates six day-care centers for children, has three more under construction and five in the planning stage. Neither project has yet made any contribution to earnings (the turnaround for insurance is expected around 1974-75), but Suerth contends that "These are the businesses we think we ought to be in."

Even the baby-food business (which accounts for 88% of Gerber's sales) itself could show some solid growth—at least for Gerber. Recently, Squibb confirmed that it was discussing the spinoff of Beech-Nut baby foods. And as long as it does not fall into the hands of a superb marketer such as Procter & Gamble, Suerth thinks that the prospective sale could only help Gerber "pick up additional market share." Suerth has yet to hear anyone yell "Break up Gerber," but adding to the 60% of the market it already holds would be quite an accomplishment.

The Re-Honing of Gillette

William Salatich, president of Gillette North America, points proudly to the speed with which the company got out its Trac II twin-blade razor last fall. Salatich says that Gillette has developed great skill in the new-products area, introducing 19 others besides Trac II in the past 18 months —and new products are the name of the game in branded goods.

"These 20 new products will produce 20% of Gillette's North American sales and earnings this year," Salatich says. They are, in part, the fruit of a stepped-up research and development program; R&D expenditures have more than doubled since 1968 to $22 million in 1971.

Trac II has become an immediate success. The new razor has recaptured the initiative in the razor and blade field for Gillette from an aggressive Wilkinson, which had grabbed a healthy 6.7% share with its bonded razor in less than a year.

Now President Joseph Turley of Gillette's Safety Razor division claims, perhaps a bit defensively, that Wilkinson has peaked and is losing its share of the razor market. "We expect its blade share to begin to decline soon," he adds, "because blade shares always follow razor shares. On the other hand, Trac II's share of the razor market is up around 25%, on average, and over 40% in some cities where we delivered samples."

Isn't Trac II hurting Gillette's other brands? "Not as much as we expected," says Turley. "Gillette's total share of the razor and blade markets is increasing because of Trac II."

One of Gillette's problems has been that there is little real growth left in the U.S. razor and blade market. A company can only get growth by increasing its share of the market at someone else's expense; this is even more difficult for Gillette, which already has 70% of the razor and 60% of the blade market. Trac II is not only doing this; it is also trading the razor and blade user up to a higher-priced model. Once production is in full swing and start-up costs are amortized, its unit profit should exceed that on all other razors and blades.

Even with Trac II, the growth in the razor and blade end of Gillette's business will not be great, so the Safety Razor division has been pushing into new areas. Turley regards the Cricket disposable lighter as the division's most promising new product besides Trac II. Almost 9 million disposable lighters were sold in the U.S. last year, double the figure for 1970.

Though Gillette's toiletries operation can be dated back to 1936, when it introduced the first brushless shaving cream, its breakout from the shaving mold did not come until its intro-

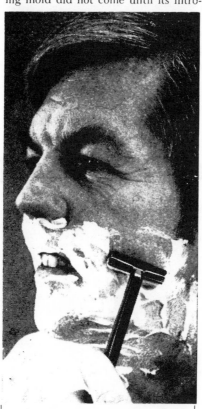

The Trac II twin-blade razor has given Gillette an edge on the competition, but Britain's Wilkinson is rumored to be working on something sharper.

duction of Right Guard in 1960. Right Guard, sold in both deodorant and antiperspirant form, quickly became the No. One product in its field, and was the item around which Gillette in 1968 grouped all its men's toiletries —including shaving foams and men's hair sprays—into a separate toiletries division, with domestic sales of more than $110 million in 1971.

But what division President Edward Schultz prefers to talk about is his *new* products. "This division was born in 1968, and by the summer of 1969 we had a new product, Soft & Dri antiperspirant, on the market nationally. We went without any test-marketing because we knew we had a good product. That shows the willingness of the company to take risks." Soft & Dri is now No. Four in its $500-million market. All told, the division has launched six new products, five of which are variations of existing items and one of which, Foot Guard, is a brand-new product aimed at the $60-million foot-care market.

The Personal Care division, renamed last year and built around the old Toni home permanent operation acquired in 1948, is the women's opposite number to the basically men's toiletries operation. For the last five years it accounted for some 15% of overall sales (about $110 million last year); and back in the late Sixties it accounted for an equal share of profits. Then came a major mistake: Divisional net slipped badly in 1969 because of the cost of introducing the Eve of Roma cosmetics line, and was sliced almost in half in 1970 by the cost of dumping it after it flopped. The 1971 results were hurt by a badly timed move into the wig business.

In spite of these setbacks, Personal Care, too, has been hitting the new-product trail; it has nine. Among them are three small electrical appliances, two hand-held dryers and a detangler, which are expected to produce more than $20 million sales this year—"four times as much as we had estimated," claims division head Marcel Durot. "I think that within five years our appliance business will be at $100 million a year, and may eventually be bigger than our toiletries." Meantime, the division is getting a lift from its new Lemon Up line, its balsam-based hair care products and a new specialty called Hosiery Guard that cleans and strengthens women's hosiery.

Besides these new products, the company is excited about the prospects for Braun, the premier German appliance maker, acquired by Gillette for $50 million in 1967. But last year, on sales of about $125 million, it contributed only a trifling 2% of earnings. With Braun has also come a

special headache in the form of a still-outstanding U.S. antitrust suit, filed because Braun is Europe's top maker of electric shavers. The Braun shaver is not sold in the U.S. because of prior licensing agreements with Ronson, but those agreements are scheduled to expire at the end of 1975. A complete restructuring of Braun's European marketing operation last year and better cost control should result in much better earnings this year.

Less than half the size (about $50-million sales last year) of Braun but twice as profitable is Paper Mate, Gillette's second major acquisition, dating from 1955. It too is in the new-products game on a major scale, following the success of its Flair line of porous-tipped pens introduced six years back. Because Flair, with about 50% of the market and growing at an estimated 30% a year, has been so successful, the company is bringing out a whole new line of low-priced pens under the name of Write Bros., aimed at the market now dominated by France's Bic.

As a household name overseas long before most U.S. products were, Gillette has been expanding its bridgehead, and foreign operations now account for about 45% of sales and a bit better than half of profits. Gillette now sells in 170 countries and neglects few opportunities overseas. "We're negotiating with India," says Stephen Griffin, president of Gillette International, "and we're building a miniplant in Indonesia for blades that will help us reach that market of 130 million people."

With all this new product development going on, Chairman Ziegler felt he could use more marketing help. In July he lured Ed Gelsthorpe

(FORBES, Aug. 15) away from Norton Simon Inc., where he had developed a name as one of the best new product marketers around. This move took courage in a company once so ingrown as Gillette: Bringing in a top man from the outside is a frank admission of weakness within. Vice Chairman Gelsthorpe will coordinate all new products, a most important role in the kind of company that Gillette has become. It is no secret that he expects to become president when Ziegler, now 62, gives up one of his two titles.

All these successes cannot change the fact that Gillette is less profitable than it used to be. The simple fact

Alexander the Great banned beards as a threat to his troops because they offered the enemy a convenient handle. But beards don't bother Gillette, because they have never noticeably affected razor sales. Most bearded men do some shaving; beards are tough on blades; and only 4% of shaving-age men wear beards.

is that Gillette does not—and cannot—dominate its other businesses the way it has dominated razors and shaving. After all, you can't push around Procter & Gamble the way you can push around, say, Schick or Wilkinson.

The desire for growth, moreover, has kept Gillette busy in the acquisition market, and acquisitions have a way of going wrong. Gillette has had some especially bad luck the past few years. No less than three acquisitions turned sour: Besides Eve of Roma there were Colton (men's fragrances) and Sterilon (hospital supplies). All turned out to be expensive mistakes. Eve died, and without her Gillette didn't have the industry knowhow to guide it in the mysteries of women's cosmetics; in men's fragrance the boom peaked just as Gillette was getting into the highly competitive field.

Two recent acquisitions, Buxton, the leather goods company, and Welcome Wagon, are new directions for Gillette and as yet unproved. And, inevitably, some new products fail: X-Hydra, an extra-strength deodorant, and three hair coloring products.

Right Choice

To get back to the original question: Should Gillette have expanded as fast and as widely as it did? Examining the evidence in the light of the company's situation, the answer must be: Management made the right decision—although the changeover was neither as smooth nor as unanimous as management likes to claim. Its expansion kept it from being permanently locked into the narrow, static razor market—and freed it from the risks a one-product company always faces.

Moreover, is Gillette really less profitable than it was? The 40% return is gone, possibly forever, but this year it will probably show a return on equity of nearly 30% and a 9.1% margin on sales of some $820 million. That should serve easily to place it among the top dozen U.S. companies in profitability, ranking with Coca-Cola and other such money machines.

And Gillette's margins are not necessarily preordained to stay at their present levels. In fact, they are already showing signs of improvement. "As you change the kind of business this was," says Ziegler, "to the kind of business it is and the kind it's going to be, the continuing problem of margin improvement is one you pay a lot of attention to."

Has Gillette got problems? Yes, indeed. But everything is relative. Such "problems" as Gillette has, most U.S. businessmen would consider a positive pleasure.

Moving Cereal

By PHILIP H. DOUGHERTY

Ralston-Purina, which has already delivered Freakies and Fruity Freakies to an eager young populace, has now developed Grins & Smiles & Giggles & Laughs. This, too, is a presweetened ready-to-eat cereal. Its special benefit is that on each crunchy, round, corn-based piece are two eyes and a smiling mouth.

The new cereal is being prepared for market now, and its advertising agency is Wells, Rich, Greene. Next comes the battle to get and keep the product's segment of shelf space in the supermarkets of America—space that depends strictly on survival of the fittest.

Other recent national cereal entries are Punch Crunch from Quaker Oats and Frosted Rice from Kellogg, which is also understood to have Corny Snaps in test market. General Foods is testing a C.W. Post brand.

The new entries have joined the more than 150 brands of ready-to-eat cereals that, according to Sales Area Marketing Inc., are available in two or more market areas.

(There are also 83 brands of hot cereals.)

The space devoted to them by the retailers has been steadily growing, according to the A.C. Nielsen Company. It calculates that the average supermarket devoted 91 linear feet of shelf space to them in 1972 and 107 feet last year. That compares with last year's 169 feet for soft drinks and 182 feet for dog food and cat food.

Nevertheless, according to a supermarket source, the retail food chains like dry cereals because, although they are in the medium-price range, there is very fast movement, bringing in a lot of dollars. "Fast movement"

is probably the key phrase; the chains certainly don't want to stock a brand that gathers dust.

Usually the chains make their judgments on the basis of data available from SAMI and Nielsen on best-selling brands, their own historical sales data and, in the case of new products, the national advertising and promotion plans.

The big companies with proven track records have an edge.

More than $118 million was spent on advertising in all measured media for cold and hot cereals in 1974, with $105 million of that figure in television.

Television advertising in the first nine months of last year was $76.2 million, down $2 million from the similar period of 1974.

That might reflect an earlier softness in part of the cereal market — specifically the presweetened segment—catching up with advertising budgets.

However, Wall Street and industry sources say the cereal market for the whole year was very good, with sales (on a weight basis) up 5 percent in 1975 to 1.82 billion pounds.

Earlier, rising sugar prices drove up the cost of the presweetened brands. But in 1975 for the most part, industry sources say, the consumer apparently considered most dry cereals a more economic alternative for breakfast than many other types of food.

Presweetened cereals accounted for 30.9 percent of the tonnage in 1975, about the same as in the previous year. The all-family brands, however, showed a 14 percent growth to a 63 percent share of the market. The natural cereals, which at their height had about a 10 percent share, were down to 6.1 percent last year.

The negative comments of consumer advocates about presweetened cereals seemingly have not affected their sales. "Mothers buy what their kids will eat," an industry source said.) However, positive stories about the need for high-fiber diets apparently gave a lift to sales of bran-based cereals.

Retail sales of ready-to-eat cereals are put at $1.7 billion by Sales Area Marketing Inc., which estimates Kellogg's share at 41.6 percent, General Mills at 19 percent, General Foods at 17.8 percent, Quaker at 8.3 percent and Ralston-Purina at 3.4 percent.

There seems to have been no slackening in the use of premium promotions, despite the proposed banning of advertising of such promotions by the Federal Trade Commission a couple of years back. That proposal is still going through regular channels. It may even be in limbo.

RICE KRISPIES® **Cheerios** **CREAM OF WHEAT** **RAISIN BRAN** **CORN FLAKES**

Kellogg: Target For Today

ANYONE who looks only at the annual reports would never suspect that Kellogg is a company with problems. Or that Kellogg's problems are problems that may some day beset many another company with equally glowing sales, earnings, market share and return on equity. The company's very success has made it a target for consumer groups, nutritionists and government agencies.

Along with the rest of the ready-to-eat cereal industry, Kellogg was the subject of hearings by the Consumer Subcommittee of the Senate Committee on Commerce in 1970 and again last year. In the U.K., where it boasts 50% to 60% of the market, the Monopolies Commission has ruled that Kellogg cannot raise prices despite rapidly rising costs unless Her Majesty's government approves. And in the U.S., the Federal Trade Commission has filed a complaint against Kellogg and three other manufacturers of dry cereals—General Mills, General Foods and Quaker Oats—charging them with monopolistic practices. In the ordinary sense of the word, Kellogg is not a monopoly. It has an estimated 43% of the market in the U.S.; the other three divide 45% to 50%. But if the FTC prevails, Kellogg and the others may be judged a shared monopoly—with fearsome implications for many other manufacturers of branded goods.

Commit Suicide?

Children cry for Kellogg's Corn Flakes in 156 countries in nobody has ever counted how many languages; Kellogg sells 2.3 billion packages of corn flakes and other dry cereals a year. Its history is a history of steady growth. Year after year, sales have kept rising, not spectacularly—8%, 9% a year—but steadily to $699 million last year. Over the years, the stockholders have enjoyed, on the average, a 23% return on equity. They also have enjoyed unusually high dividends for a growth company, 52 cents last year (62.7% of earnings, up from 19 cents in 1962). Despite this, Kellogg generates so much cash it has always been able to finance expansion without going into debt. It will spend $40 million this year, all from cash flow.

In the first quarter of this year, sales were up 24.8% and profits 15%. According to E.J. (Jim) Swan, financial vice president, dividends should reach 54 cents this year. Yet Kellogg's brass is still worried.

Of all the attacks, the FTC complaint raises by far the greatest threat. The FTC wants the four companies to break up their cereal operations, divesting themselves of assets, including plants, "for the formation of new corporate entities." It also wants the companies to license "existing and future brands or trademarks on a royalty-free basis for a specified period of time." This would hurt all four companies, but for Kellogg it would mean death. The others are highly diversified, getting only a fraction of their revenues from dry cereals (in Quaker Oats' case, 8%). Kellogg derives about 80% of its revenues from dry cereals. The FTC is asking Kellogg to cut off its arms and legs and then commit suicide.

How serious is the FTC suit? Under a generally pro-business administration it might easily be shunted aside. But Watergate may well have changed the atmosphere.

Beyond the dry-cereal industry, the FTC complaint has serious implications for other consumer industries. Says J.E. (Joe) Lonning, Kellogg's president and chief executive officer: "We believe every businessman should be concerned about what the FTC is doing. If the courts uphold the FTC, that will set a precedent." Professor Jesse Markham of the Harvard Business School, former chief economist for the FTC, agrees. "Along with cereals and soaps and detergents," he says, "I think it will affect proprietary drugs, toothpaste, anything that is marketed in the same way."

One has only to read the FTC complaint to understand why. Among other things, the FTC charges that "meaningful price competition does not exist in the RTE [ready-to-eat] cereal market." This, of course, is true. Mothers buy one dry cereal in preference to another because their children have learned about it from watching television and are clamoring for it. Once the children eat the cereal and decide they like it, they clamor for more. Advertising, not prices, is the key to sales. Last year Kellogg spent around $31 million advertising its cereals.

The FTC, in fact, is especially incensed at cereal advertising. It says: "Respondents' RTE cereals do not enable children to perform the physical activities represented or implied in their advertisements."

Nor does the FTC like the "profusion of RTE cereal brands. During the period 1950 through 1970," it says, "approximately 150 brands, mostly trademarked, were marketed by respondents.... Respondents have used advertising to promote trademarks that conceal the true nature of the product.

"Respondents artificially differentiate their RTE cereals. Respondents produce basically similar RTE cereals and then emphasize and exaggerate trivial variations.... Respondents also use premiums to induce purchases of RTE cereals."

Finally, the FTC declares that "respondents ... have erected, maintained and raised barriers to the entry to the RTE market through unfair methods of competition...."

The complaint, in effect, names Kellogg as the leader of the alleged oligopoly. It says: "Kellogg is the principal supplier of shelf-space service for the RTE cereal sections of retail grocery outlets. Such services include the selection, placement and removal of RTE cereals and allocation of shelf space for RTE cereals to each respondent and to other RTE cereal producers."

Ponder for a moment the implications of this case. They strike at the foundations of many of the most consistently profitable companies in the U.S. Companies that, like Kellogg, are dominant but not monopolistic companies, that maintain a strong consumer franchise by superior advertising power and by their ability to grab a major share of scarce supermarket shelf space.

"It's Good Business"

Kellogg's alleged control over shelf space is a key element in the FTC charge. President Joe Lonning says that Kellogg does make surveys of how much of each dry cereal brand is sold in every area of the U.S. On that basis, Kellogg does make suggestions to supermarket chains and supermarket managers on how much shelf space to allocate to each brand and where to place them. Asked, "Doesn't Kellogg's dominant share of the market make these suggestions, in effect, orders?" he replies: "No. They don't have to accept our suggestions. We put no pressure on them. Most of them do because they realize it's good business."

Shelf space is all-important in the supermarket business. Scores of surveys have shown that products displayed at eye level in heavy traffic aisles will sell better than products displayed elsewhere.

What the dry-cereal manufacturers are accused of doing has long been standard operating procedure throughout U.S. industry. Price competition doesn't exist in the cigarette industry. Or the detergent industry. Or the proprietary drug industry, for that matter. Few people buy a particular brand of toothpaste because it's a couple of cents cheaper than other brands. They buy the brand they prefer.

The proliferation of brands also is a commonplace. There is *Fud*. There is the *New* Fud. There is the *New New* Fud. There is *Superfud*. And there is the *New* Superfud. All the products are basically the same. All are sold by TV, just like dry cereals.

Kellogg was among the first companies in the U.S. to supply shelf-space service, but it's not the only company. Philip Morris, Campbell's, Procter & Gamble, General Foods and Coca-Cola, to name just a few, also do, though not in exactly the same way. Says a former P&G employee: "In some ways, P&G is more overt in using its muscle than Kellogg, in other ways, more subtle. They're more subtle in their approach to chain management, and much, much more overt in their dealings with the individual stores. A salesman will tell the manager his shelves are a mess and why doesn't he let the salesman fix them. The manager probably will, and the salesman will arrange the shelves in P&G's favor."

There's even a name for the practice. It's called "space management." Says an expert on the subject: "Selling has gotten to the point where you have to try and help the retailer and you get together. You say, 'Look, here are ways we both can make money.' You can't screw your competitors because the retailer knows what he sells in his store."

The FTC's Aim

What are the FTC lawyers driving for in the dry-cereal case? Among those with knowledge of the FTC's philosophy, there is general agreement: It's to make dry cereals a commodity. The same thing could happen to other branded products. Right now, the name "Rice Krispies" is the property of Kellogg; the name "Wheaties" of General Mills. If the courts uphold the FTC, anyone will be able to put out a product that looks and tastes like Rice Krispies and has the same ingredients and call it by that name. There can be a Smith's Rice Krispies, a Jones' Rice Krispies,

an O'Reilly's Rice Krispies, not only a Kellogg's Rice Krispies.

The FTC believes this will make for price competition. Perhaps it will, but nobody really knows.

What chance does the FTC have of persuading the courts to uphold its complaint? On this, experts on antitrust laws are guarded, for one thing, because the complaint has not been fleshed out with facts, for another, because the complaint has a couple of unusual aspects.

First, Kellogg and the other three companies are charged not with conspiring to fix prices but with being an oligopoly that simply fails to engage in price competition. This is a concept, the legal experts say, on which there is no clear precedent. No conspiracy. Just an existential situation.

Second, the objection to Kellogg's space management. Again, says a former Justice antitrust lawyer, "There's no precedent that can be applied to a company that sets not only its own space but space generally."

Third, the demand that Kellogg and the other companies make their trademarks available to all comers without fee. There is a precedent for this in private trademark litigation, says a leading professor of law. Companies have brought suit to make a trademark public property on the grounds that it has acquired "a secondary meaning." And they have won. A notable example is cellophane. Originally, nobody could call a product cellophane except du Pont. Now, anyone can do so if the product is essentially the same.

Civil antitrust suits have set precedents for government action in other cases. Right now, Eastman Kodak is facing three such suits, in which the remedies sought, if not all the charges, are quite similar to what the FTC wants in the dry-cereal case. In one suit, GAF Corp. is asking that Eastman Kodak be divided into ten separate companies. It wants the company's trademark, Kodak, made public property. And it demands triple damages for alleged monopolistic acts. Bell & Howell and Berkey Photo, Inc. are the other two companies that have filed suits against Eastman Kodak.

Consumerists' Complaints

The FTC assault on the dry-cereal industry, while a deadly threat, is not an immediate one. Meanwhile, the industry has the rising tide of consumerism to cope with, a tide already strong enough to force the Senate Committee on Commerce to conduct hearings.

The industry even has a Ralph Nader, Robert B. Choate Jr., chairman

of the Council on Children, Media & Merchandising. A self-taught nutritionist, Choate has been attacking the industry on the grounds that most dry cereals have little nutritive value and cost too much for the nutrients they do provide. Choate claims to have forced the dry-cereal industry to improve the nutritive value of its products, a claim that Kellogg officials scoff at. Says William E. LaMothe, executive vice president: "Nutrition has been a driving force behind our company since its founding."

Kellogg officials say that Choate, in his attacks on dry cereals, overlooks a basic fact: Most people eat them with milk, and many with fruit—sliced bananas, strawberries. No one can talk about the nutritive value of dry cereals without taking this into account, they insist. And besides, they say, cereals have never been promoted as a complete diet.

Presweetened dry cereals are a particular target of the consumerists, who claim they are just as bad for children's teeth as is eating candy for breakfast. Kellogg points out that normally children dump sugar on unsweetened cereals. In rejoinder, the consumerists point out that many children do eat presweetened cereals as candy.

The dry-cereal television commercials aimed at children also have come under attack. Action for Children's Television has said: "The advertiser . . . uses all the wiles of trick photography, fantasy, animation and promises of 'free gifts' and 'surprises' to sell his cereal to children. Of course, the sell is easy; children still believe what they are told. . . .

"The parent is naturally caught in the middle. . . . If the parent refuses to buy a cereal, the child is unhappy; if the parent buys the cereal, the child is usually disappointed with the promised 'free gift' and . . . blames the parent."

So far, consumerism has not visibly hurt sales of dry cereals in the U.S. On the contrary, consumption, which had been on a plateau for several years, last year inexplicably rose by 6.8%, says Financial Vice President Swan. However, Kellogg officials are well aware that Nader's attacks on the auto industry didn't have any immediate effect, either. They are no more complacent about the consumer movement than they are about the FTC complaint.

Why People Buy

Consumers buy goods and services to satisfy various needs. These needs may be grouped as "rational" and "emotional" buying motives. When a person is hungry he attempts to satisfy his hunger by getting something to eat. This is considered rational behavior. The man who starts nibbling peanuts, potato chips, and drinking beer at a football game after a big lunch is satisfying an "emotional" rather than a "rational" need.

The rational buyer responds to his desire for economy, quality, and dependability by considering the following factors when buying goods and services:
-- the price
-- dependability
-- durability
-- efficiency
-- availability
-- availability of repairs and maintenance
-- potential benefits to be gained.

The emotional buyer responds to the following motives:
-- sensual pleasures (comfort, beauty, smell, taste, sound)
-- distinction or pride
-- social standing
-- achievement or desire for success
-- desire for safety (fear)
-- curiosity
-- impulse, buying for its own sake.

More than one of these types of motives is usually involved in any purchase. Market research and the product development and advertising that follow must take all of them into account for effective marketing decisions.

Figuring out why people buy is a tough and important marketing task. Why does a customer buy Brand A and another buy Brand B?

To find out more about the buying behavior of their customers, companies spend a great deal of money on opinion polls, test panels, market sampling, and other forms of market research. There is also extensive use of computers to explore buying patterns.

But whether individuals are asked what they like about products or computers are used in an attempt to predict buyer behavior, one major problem remains: some of the consumers' motives are not easily determined. It is not necessarily the case of consumers not wanting to tell why they do what they do, but they simply may not realize why they are making the buying decisions they do. This is because there are both conscious and dormant motives that affect buyer behavior.

Conscious motives are easily seen and can usually be described by buyers in terms that are useful to the market researcher. Dormant motives, on the other hand, are usually hidden even to the consumer, and as such are very difficult to determine. It seems that buyers are motivated by multiple motives, and to market effectively, the businessman must understand them.

But until recently there was no handy all-purpose system of thinking which any educated, intelligent businessman could use to determine whether his product will be a winner or a loser. This tool, a special theory of buying behavior, has been proposes by Columbia University Professor John Howard and his co-author Jagdish Sheth.

These men view the buying decision as the result of a stream of actions -- as problem solving by individuals. When an individual buys a car, for example, he has given the matter consider-able thought and has already decided many of the qualities he is looking for. With a new product, however, a buyer knows little, and thus the problem is a tougher decision.

The theory is based on the view that buyer behavior is influenced by:
-- the person's environment
-- whether he or she is married and has a family
-- what he or she feels about prices in relation to quality
-- what someone tells him or her about the product.

These and other factors stimulate the buyer to choose and reject various influences, resulting in a clearer picture of what the buyer wants. Thus if a lady who has bought a new refrigerator sees an advertisement for a refrigerator, whe will usually blank it out of her mind.

J.C. Penny: Getting More From The Same Space

Midway through a routine store tour, Donald V. Seibert scowls at an empty shelf in the infants' department. "Let's fill up that space with some of those plastic kiddie chairs I saw in the toy department," says the 51-year-old chairman and chief executive of J.C. Penney Co., the country's second largest retailer behind Sears, Roebuck & Co. With his store manager in tow, Seibert moves on to the menswear department, where he pulls out a drawer stuffed with undershirts. "This drawer unit takes up too much room," he tells the manager. "You need a higher fixture here, and you should get all this merchandise out in the open to create more excitement."

In the big new Penney store in Charlotte, N.C., last week, Seibert (pronounced sy-bert) saw some things that he did not like, yet much that he did like. The 178,000-sq.-ft. unit, one of eight new prototypes, belongs to a new generation of Penney stores that makes better use of space and rings up the same volume of sales as older stores that are 15% larger. Penney is also redesigning the interiors of many existing units and trying to wring more sales and profit out of them.

With its emphasis on "space economics," as Seibert calls it, the Penney program is part of a massive efficiency drive that is beginning to sweep the $65-billion general merchandise industry and alter its whole approach to growth. Traditionally, retailers expanded their businesses by simply building more stores. Just as surely as "white sales" follow Christmas, a big boost in volume also boosted profits.

"This strategy worked fine when the economy was booming, consumers were on a buying spree, and there was always volume growth to cover up any mistakes," says Seibert, an affable, onetime shoe salesman who moved into Penney's top job last October. Today, adding stores is no longer enough. "You've got to get far more productivity out of your space," Seibert stresses. "For a lot of retailers, this means a radical change in thinking. But then again, these have been radical times."

Seibert is referring, of course, to the recession, which hit merchants harder than anything since the Depression. Caught between spiraling costs and a sudden slump in consumer spending, more than a score of major discount op-

erations went broke or teetered on the brink. Department stores, stuck with huge inventories, had to slash prices as much as 40% or more. Hardest hit of all, however, were Penney and the other big, mass-merchandising chains. Because they buy in far larger quantities and much further in advance, they took the worst beating on markdowns. So after a steady and sometimes spectacular growth through the 1950s and 1960s, the five largest chains reported a sharp drop in earnings last year: Sears 24.8%, Penney 32.7%, S. S. Kresge 24.2%, Woolworth 30.7%, and Montgomery Ward 9.6%.

Segmented markets

More significantly, the recession exposed some major weaknesses in chain-store selling and raised some serious questions about the whole concept of mass merchandising in today's fast-paced retail environment. From the first, mass merchandisers depended upon a mass market that could be served by centralized purchasing and partly centralized management. Within the last 8 or 10 years, however, the mass market began giving way to many different "class" markets or segments and to individual, highly demanding local markets. This requires far more flexibility and speed than chains normally bring to their business. By its nature, the "chain" concept also depends upon the addition of new stores. Yet soaring energy, construction, and real estate costs—plus a stepup in zoning and environmental pressures—are making a shambles of many new-store programs. Chain operations rely, as well, on self-service. Today's customer, however, is demanding more—not less—help.

Then there are the more standard miseries that bedevil every merchant: a consumer who is shorter on money and harder to reach, tougher competition at all retail levels, and the near-saturation of many primary markets.

Confronted by such pressures, Penney and other merchants are moving in several important directions:

■ Merchandising speed and flexibility, always crucial in retailing, are becoming more urgent than ever. "You can no longer build a store with solid, inside walls where everything stays the same," says Arthur J. Emma, president

of G. Fox & Co., a Hartford (Conn.) division of May Department Stores Co. By shifting quickly to today's hot movers—citizen band radios, prewashed denims, "gauze-look" fashions, and leisure suits, for instance—an aggressive merchant can often double or triple the volume of a given floor area. "Even more important, you can also end up with higher margins," says Thomas M. Macioce, president and chief executive of Allied Stores Corp.

■ A denser and more concentrated use of display space can raise over-all selling floor capacity 20% to 40% and reduce merchandise handling and storage costs 50% or more—while creating more merchandising excitement. This involves tightening up aisles and backroom space, switching from standard 54-in. displays to 72-in. displays, and getting more merchandise out of the storeroom and in front of the customer. At Carter Hawley Hale Stores, Inc., President Philip M. Hawley predicts that fully half of the industry's future growth will come from this type of "internal expansion."

■ Computerized point-of-sale registers, which began filtering onto selling floors before the current productivity push, promise to cut some administrative costs by 60% or more while making more and better information available faster. Eventually, electronic-register systems will handle everything from credit authorizations and billing to inventory control, reordering, and sales payrolls. One leading chain-store executive estimates that "lost sales" caused by items being out of stock now run 10% to 15% of his company's total sales. "We think the computer will bring that down to 3% to 5%," he says.

■ Store expansion is getting away from the old "race for space" idea, as Edward S. Donnell, chairman and chief executive of Montgomery Ward & Co., describes it. For every 100 sq. ft. of new store space that Ward's opens today, it closes 50 ft. of less productive space. "We're being much more thoughtful," says Donnell. "For the first time, retailers are giving far more consideration to return on investment." This means they are closing more marginal units, entering smaller markets with smaller stores, and building fewer giant stores that try to be all things to all customers.

Space economics calls for 72-in. fixtures vs. 54-in. for ties, a wall display for shoes (left), and greater use of floor capacity to display jeans (below).

In its drive for greater efficiency, Penney probably faces the industry's biggest, single challenge—and opportunity. On the one hand, the 73-year-old company has more stores than any other general merchandise retailer: 2,039 vs. 851 for Sears and 1,326 for S. S. Kresge Co. At the same time, Penney has some growing pains that come from an extraordinary corporate transformation. Up to the early 1960s, Penney was a small-town, middle-American purveyor of softgoods, home furnishings, and the folksy merchandising ideals and homilies of founder James Cash Penney (Of any transaction: "Does it square with what is right and just?"), who died in 1971 at the age of 95. Today, Penney has grown into a highly diversified multinational and a leading force in retailing.

From its lofty headquarters building at 52nd Street and Sixth Avenue in New York City, Penney now operates 354 full-line department stores, 1,289 smaller soft-line stores, 31 Treasury discount stores, 255 Thrift drug stores, 24 supermarkets, a mail-order catalogue business, and a life, health, and casualty insurance company. Abroad, Penney has four stores in Italy and owns Sarma, a Brussels-based chain of 82 food and general-merchandise stores. During the past 10 years, the Penney expansion has doubled net selling space (to 54.5-million sq. ft.), while increasing total sales 188% (to $6.9-billion) and net income 54.6% (to $125.1-million).

Behind this heady growth was a 1959 "Merchandising Character Study." Launched by Seibert's predecessor, William M. Batten, the study laid out a whole new direction for a company that was beginning to find itself languishing on the industry sidelines. At that time, Seibert was a Penney district manager in Minneapolis.

In one of the most dramatic refurbishings in American corporate history, Batten broadened Penney's product line, added a bundle of new services, built bigger stores in more major markets, introduced sophisticated computer controls that were years ahead of the field, and put far more emphasis on fashion and aggressive merchandising. Above all, Batten gave Penney both a big-city image and new stature within its industry.

Leapfrogging to the top

Early on, Batten brought Seibert into New York in a succession of key management assignments: planning and research, the Treasury stores, international operations, and then the spot where Seibert made his biggest mark–catalogue sales, which Penney acquired in 1962. Running the catalogue business for nine years, Seibert guided it into the black in 1971, a full year ahead of schedule. Last August, on Batten's recommendation, the Penney board skipped over President Jack B. Jackson, Executive Vice-President Walter J. Neppl, and several other senior executives and picked Seibert to succeed Batten, who retired on Oct. 1.

When he talks productivity, Seibert is like a buyer with a hot, new fashion item: He can almost taste the results. "With 54.5-million sq. ft. of selling space that returns well over $100 per sq. ft.," he says, "just raising our sales $1 per sq. ft. would bring in more than $54-million in additional sales. A $10 increase would add more than $540-million, and $20, $1-billion." Unlike a new store, which has big startup costs, most of the gross profit added in an existing store also goes straight to the bottom line as net profit.

Describing greater productivity as Penney's "No. 1 management priority," Seibert named a special task force on productivity last month. It will analyze company-wide efficiencies and report directly to a senior steering committee, consisting of Seibert, Jackson, and Neppl. "Traditionally within Penney," says Seibert, "productivity has been based on two measurements: sales per man hour and sales per sq. ft. These measurements are fine as far as they go," which, Seibert makes clear, is not far enough. So the task force will "analyze the productivity of all areas and resources of our operation: human,

material, financial, and technological." Adds William R. Howell, director of domestic development and head of the new task force: "There is absolutely no part of the company that will be 'hands-off.'"

Improved productivity, of course, starts with simple cost cutting. Penney and most other leading merchants have always been skilled at that. With a new computerized system that helps consolidate shipments from suppliers to stores, for instance, Penney saved 43.9% on a typical shipping charge from a Boston supplier to the Fresno (Calif.) store. In the same way, a special energy conservation program trimmed Penney's total power consumption last year by 20%—despite a 5.2% increase in square footage of net selling space. "What we're trying to do now, however, goes beyond simple savings," says Jackson. "The industry must get more out of less."

With Penney's entry into full-line department stores, the merchandising trick is to balance or optimize the low end of the hardlines business with the high end of softgoods. Margins on softgoods fashions may run 50% or higher, while those on refrigerators, stoves, and television sets may average only 18% to 20%. Major appliances also are more expensive to handle, package, and inventory, which explains why more and more conventional department stores are yielding that part of their business to discounters.

The major competition

So far, Penney has moved cautiously on big-ticket hardlines, which still rep-

resent only 7% of its business or roughly $483-million last year. Ward's Donnell concedes that Penney has "done well in some of their hardgood lines. But I still don't think they're very strong. The major competition in hardgoods is still Sears." Admits a Penney merchandiser: "We aren't scaring Sears by any means. But you have to remember that the first time Penney ever sold a refrigerator or washing machine was just 12 years ago. And furniture didn't come along until 1964."

On the other hand, Penney is moving far more aggressively in higher-margin fashions, which are more immune to competition and economic ups and downs. Penney now employs 290 apparel fashion buyers in New York, Miami, Dallas, and Los Angeles and last year launched an ambitious "Women's Fashion Project." This brings together 15 Penney "associates," as employees are called, from display, merchandising, finance, and other areas of the company. They work on project teams to analyze all aspects of the fashion business and are trying to promote what Penney hopes will be "a quantum leap forward" in fashion. "Penney has become very, very fashion-aware," says New York fashion consultant Terry Mayer. "In the middle range of the market, a lot of people are watching Penney fashions."

Penney is also moving deeper into its own higher-margin, private-label fashions, as well as other private label merchandise. Penney's private labels now account for some 85% of the more than 100,000 items carried by the giant merchant. "And Penney is promoting its private brands much more aggressively, too," says one competitor. A few weeks ago in one of Penney's Eastern stores, a shelf-sign compared the 69¢ cost of a quart of Penney's Foremost premium motor oil with Quaker State (78¢) and Pennzoil (73¢). During the 30-day promotion, Foremost Oil sales jumped nearly 30% from the same period the year before.

To milk the same kind of productivity out of its new-store construction, Penney is following the lead of other merchants and is thinking small. Five years ago, most new Kresge K marts ran 94,500 sq. ft. Today's average is closer to 84,500 sq. ft., and last year Kresge began opening its first "mini" K marts of 40,000 sq. ft. Penney is doing the same thing with its eight new prototype stores, ranging from 12,500 sq. ft. in selling space to 130,000 sq. ft. In Atlanta, Penney's new Cumberland Mall prototype with 85,000 sq. ft. of net selling space is 32% smaller than an older Penney store nearby, yet gets 30% more sales per sq. ft.

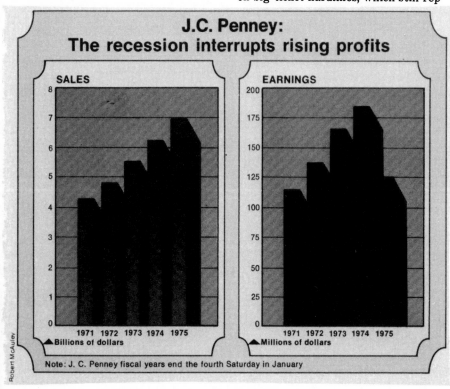

**J.C. Penney:
The recession interrupts rising profits**

SALES

Billions of dollars

EARNINGS

Millions of dollars

1971 1972 1973 1974 1975

Note: J. C. Penney fiscal years end the fourth Saturday in January

Robert McAuley

Another alternative to new construction: the purchase of cast-off stores from all the merchants who went out of business in the last few years. Kresge recently picked up three discount stores in Pennsylvania. Ward's bought two discount stores in Florida and another in California. In Altus, Okla., Penney vacated a cramped 6,000-sq.-ft. downtown store and switched to a 10,800-sq.-ft. mini-department store on the edge of town. "And we doubled our sales and profits for that unit," says one Penney executive. In Weslaco, Tex., Penney moved across the street into a former Safeway supermarket. This raised its selling space from 4,500 sq. ft. to 11,000 sq. ft. "There, we tripled our sales," says the same executive, "and it looks like the profits will grow as much."

In some sections of the country, Pen-

So Penney dumped its pharmacy and home-improvement sections out of its three large Houston stores. It also eliminated some nurseries and outdoor garden shops from stores in Missouri, Kansas, and Colorado. "This is just not the kind of business that Penney should be in," says McDermott. "We tried very hard. I would be embarrassed to tell you the number of man-hours and the effort and energies that we direct at trying to make a program like that work. We ran at a brick wall awfully hard, and I think all of us around here have a few lumps on our heads to prove it."

In the name of productivity, Penney and other merchants are cutting back the same way on sales help, since salaries and fringe benefits can make up 60% to 70% average industry operating costs. In Penney's new stores, many

90,000-sq.-ft. Penney store in Marysville, Calif., and came away unimpressed. "They have checkout stands just like Safeway," says M. G. Morris, founder of Mervyn's, a 24-unit chain. "I think that detracts from service and prestige." While Morris admits he has hired "some good people" from Penney, he is not high on Penney's run-of-the-mill employee. "They're a unique breed and don't necessarily fit in with other stores," he says. "They're very restricted and, because of Penney's private label policies, don't get the entrepreneurial spirit we like to see."

As an occasional Penney customer, New York suburban shopper Mary Pszczola is equally unimpressed. At Penney's 255,000-sq.-ft. unit in Long Island's Roosevelt Field, she complains that, "Service is worse here than in

Where J.C. Penney ranks among the chains

	Sales* [millions of dollars]	Cost of goods sold [millions of dollars]	Percent of sales	Selling, general & administrative expense [millions of dollars]	Percent of sales	Net income [millions of dollars]	Percent of sales	After-tax return on average common equity
Sears, Roebuck	$13,101.2	$8,144.9	62.2%	$3,821.3	29.2%	$511.4	3.9%	10.0%
J. C. Penney	6,935.7	4,979.9	71.8	1,533.8	22.1	125.1	1.8	9.2
S. S. Kresge	5,612.1	4,208.4	75.0	1,150.5	20.5	104.8	1.9	10.8
F. W. Woolworth	4,177.1	2,947.9	70.6	1,007.4	24.1	64.8	1.6	7.1
Montgomery Ward	3,622.7	2,579.7	71.2	799.7	22.1	44.3	1.2	NM**

*Fiscal 1975   **Not meaningful

Data: Investors Management Sciences, Inc.

ney miscalculated and overbuilt. Now it is retrenching. John McDermott, sales and merchandise manager for Penney's nine-state Southwestern region, notes that Penney opened its first full-line unit in the Southwest in 1963. "We started out with a store that had about 80,000 sq. ft. of net selling space," he says. "And then like the navies of old, we decided that if battleships were good with nine guns, they would be great with 16." Before long, some Penney stores ballooned to 135,000 sq. ft. to 140,000 sq. ft. of net selling space.

Battling labor costs

"When we opened them," says McDermott, "we had a complete pharmacy, drug, sundry, and—in one of the major departments—almost a variety-store-like merchandise mix. Besides that, we had a home improvement center similar to those at Sears. But that isn't something the average customer buys with enough regularity for us to stay in that business."

service areas have been eliminated, and customers now take merchandise to a central "wrap" or counter where three or four clerks ring up sales and bag the merchandise. Even in the shoe department of some new stores, shoppers fill out a small order slip and turn this into a "service desk" for help.

"This kind of reallocation of people," Penney's Neppl insists, " is aimed at improving customer service and making it easier to shop and buy with us. Sales training and service are very important to us." In fact, Penney now operates three special training centers with courses running up to five days. "Training used to be done exclusively by manual," says Robert R. Van Kleek, vice-president and Western regional manager for Penney. "We relied on the ability of the different stores to see that the information got to the individuals. Now we have 60 people a week going through our Buena Park (Calif.) training center."

Yet some customers and competitors are less enthusiastic about Penney service. One competitor toured the new,

Korvettes." With that, she drops a blouse on the counter and stalks out of the store.

A challenge in Europe

Abroad, Penney's battle with labor costs and other operating expenses takes on special urgency. In Brussels, where the company bought the then-deteriorating Sarma chain in 1969, Penney pulled the chain back from a nearly $7.5-million loss in 1972 to its first profit last year in several years. The Penney formula: more merchandise planning and control, the closing of out-of-date stores, and expansion of nonfood sales. However, Penney faces bigger problems in Italy, where the company operates four stores. There, a recently enacted law requires local and regional approvals before new Penney-size stores can be built. And local merchants are determined to keep the big chains at bay.

Because its Italian base is too small to absorb the high costs of administration, merchandising, and so on, the

169 MARKETING

Italian operation has been a money-loser. So Penney is taking the same course in Italy as in the U. S.—broadening store lines, tightening merchandise displays, and crowding more items in front of the customer. This way, the company hopes to minimize its losses and—with higher profits in Belgium—turn its first European profit this year.

While the challenges in Europe and the U. S. are big—and growing—Seibert is moving slowly in whatever change he brings to the Penney organization. "His approach," says Van Kleek, "is not what more can we get into, but how much better can we do the things we're already in." Or as another executive notes, "Penney is just too big to jerk around by the reins."

Yet some outsiders claim that both the times and the nature of the Penney management system may demand some jerking around. Seibert himself gets high marks among outside managers and merchandisers who know him. A crack tennis player, he runs the company the way he plays his favorite game: He is thorough, analytical, and as someone who has seem him on the court puts it, "He is very fast on his feet."

Sociology of success

However, Penney's over-all management environment elicits more mixed comments, despite the modern management techniques and the worldly outlook that Batten introduced into Penney. "The management atmosphere has always been a little stuffy and conservative," says Alan Posner, a former member of Penney's public relations department and now an executive at Gulf & Western Industries, Inc. "You still get some of that Bible Belt, middle America feeling. At the higher levels, it is rigid and monolithic and a part of the sociology of anybody who gets ahead at Penney. There tends to be an unwillingness to accept any ideas except those produced by 'the system.'" Another former Penney executive points to "Penney's almost suffocating sense of togetherness and familyhood. If you move up in management, it means your father probably worked at Penney before you and your son or daughter is probably there, as well. There is an awful lot of low-grade nepotism."

At the crucial field level, outsiders claim that the "Penney mythos," as one Penney supplier calls it, has also tempered the initiative and imagination of store managers. To promote more management flexibility at the store level, Penney has decentralized a big chunk of decision-making on local merchandising, inventory maintenance, advertising, and promotion. Some industry members claim that Penney store managers may now be too independent.

"It's difficult with Penney store managers to find anybody who is managing," says one Southern department store executive. "We work with them in shopping centers, and you just can't get them to make a decision as to 'Yes we will,' or 'No, we won't.' When we retailers have a meeting or the newspapers have a meeting and invite the advertisers, nobody ever shows from Penney." He pinpoints the problem as "a lot of oldtimers" in Penney store management and a corporate headquarters that hesitates to tell them how to run their operations. "So you have all these autonomous stores that may or may not be headed in the corporate direction," he says. "That's why you have corporate management. There's no way that a store manager can have all the insight into money management, inventory, and everything that the corporate management has. This is the problem of the retail industry as a whole: In what areas should the store manager act autonomously, and where should he receive higher-level direction?"

Seibert is already beginning to wrestle with that question. As part of "shortening communications" between New York and the store level, he has logged nearly 50,000 miles and visited dozens of cities since taking over last October. One of those trips included four days in Los Angeles. "He was very concerned not to spend those days as part of an entourage," says Van Kleek. "He wanted to be dropped off at a store and left alone." During the visits, Seibert had a series of luncheons and meetings—one each for store managers, trainees, and district and regional personnel. "He didn't want to inhibit conversation by having the different groups together," says Van Kleek.

A friend in New York

Shortly after the trip, Van Kleek received a phone call from the manager of the Glendale store. The manager wanted to know why Penney never sponsored a float in the Rose Bowl parade. Van Kleek suggested that he call New York directly. "About 20 minutes later," Van Kleek says, "he called me back and said, 'I just talked to Don, and he's going to look into it.' 'Don who?' I asked, and he said, 'Don Seibert. I met him when he was out here on a visit, and I felt I knew him well enough to call.'"

The Southwest region's McDermott describes his own meeting with Seibert during Seibert's Dallas stopover. "I asked for more urgency on the part of other departments in keeping us abreast of the marketplace," McDermott says. Shortly thereafter, the merchandise managers for several buying offices arrived in Dallas to help the region's field merchandisers develop special merchandise for their markets. "I know this was a direct response to my comment to Mr. Seibert," says McDermott, "because I was told on several instances, 'You mentioned to somebody that you had a need that wasn't being fulfilled, and we were told to get into it right away.'"

"These trips and this kind of contact are very important in a company like ours," says Seibert. "Somewhere along the line, productivity ultimately comes down to people and motivation. And increasingly, that's what this whole business is going to be about."

All About Franchising

Marketing comes alive when an entrepreneur opens a franchise business. A franchise is a type of business arrangement between a manufacturer or other type of company and a private distributor -- the entrepreneur. The big company provides the merchandise, promotion, and backup support and guidance that the business needs to make it a success.

Thus, a popular way to start a business today is to open a franchise. For an investment as small as $1000 you can buy a franchise to open a "fast-food" business, a gas station, a coin-operated laundry, a dance studio, or practically any other type of business. Of course, you might have to put far more money into the business, for buildings, equipment, merchandise and supplies, and to get the operation started. How much money is required and how much you might make depend on a number of factors: your location; your product; the competition; your abilities; but most of all, your franchise.

That's what a franchise is -- an agreement (otherwise it would be a small business) between a manufacturer or other type of business (known as the franchisor) and you, a private distributor (known as the franchisee) allowing you to sell the company's product or service in a specific geographic area. The company gives you an exclusive selling territory, provides a line of products and necessary supplies, equipment, and materials, all at a presumably competitive price. The franchisor also provides backup advertising, trademarks, and promotions for the product and may provide direct training and assistance to you in starting the business and effectively running it.

In return, you agree to invest the necessary funds, to purchase all (or part) of your stock and supplies from the franchisor, to pay the franchisor a share of your revenues, and to identify your business and manage your operations exactly the way the franchisor prescribes.

A franchise provides a big advantage in attracting business because customers recognize the name and see your business as part of a nationwide chain that has consistent quality and service. Chuck's Burger House just doesn't make it like a McDonald's.

In many franchise agreements, the franchisor has built in a trial period, or an option to terminate the agreement at some future point in time. His logic is to have a chance to replace ineffective franchisees. The franchisor may also view the arrangement as a transitional distribution and financing technique rather than as a permanent situation. It is often a quick way for a company to expand as a national organization with limited captial. Howard Johnson, for example, pioneered in franchising highway restaurants. By the end of 1969, however, 64% of the familiar orange-roofed restaurants were owned and operated by the company, and the company was opening new ones at a rate of 3 to 1 over franchised units.

There is, then, a risk assumed by the individual entrepreneur who sees a franchise as a long-term business opportunity. Further, he is facing the risk of losing his shirt should the franchise not achieve its promoted potential. In the recession years of 1969 and 1970, when franchising was at a peak, failures among fledgling franchises were frequent. On the other hand, if he is associated with a good company, has a good location, and follows the franchisor's directions, the franchisee may learn a great deal through the arrangement, and hopefully also become quite prosperous.

For Ray Kroc, Life Began at 50, or was It 60?

MOST PEOPLE think they want to be rich, but Ray Kroc sincerely did. And we mean *sincerely*.

From the time he came back from World War I (at 15 he falsified his age), Kroc was working at getting rich. Dance bands. Early radio. Florida real estate. Selling paper cups. Promoting a patented milk-shake machine. But at age 50, Kroc was just about getting by. His net worth couldn't have been much over $100,000. This was in 1952.

Kroc kept right on trying, long after most men would have given up.

Today, at 70, he is one of the dozen or so richest individuals in the U.S., with a paper worth of over $500 million.

Of his adventurous and varied life, Ray Kroc says: "I was a dreamer, but I was also a doer."

Kroc's dreams, indeed his fantasies, finally came true through McDonald's hamburgers.

Luck at last, you say?

Luck played a part. But like a lot of lucky people, Kroc made his own, because he never stopped trying. When a man fails, when a company fails, Kroc says, "It is inner breakdown, inner rotting, dying, going to hell." Ray Kroc is obsessed with the idea of perseverance. You see it in his personal credo, reprinted on page 111, which has been published in almost every major newspaper in the country.

Kroc is not a placid man. His hates (among them, people who talk about market saturation, and above all people who get so rich they want to slow down) are as violent as his enthusiasms. Says Kroc: "It's dog-eat-dog, and if anyone tries to get me I'll get them first. It's the American way of survival of the fittest. There's always someone trying to cut you down.... As long as you're green you're growing and as soon as you ripen you start to rot." All delivered in rambling monologue in the style of Casey Stengel.

Now Ray Kroc was in no sense the actual founder or creator of McDonald's. The concept was worked out and the first restaurants established by two New England brothers (Richard and Maurice McDonald) who had moved to California. The financing and real estate brainpower came from Harry Sonneborn, now retired, who joined Kroc in 1955.

But Kroc was the dynamo who drove the company relentlessly. One

by one, the others departed, rich men, but unable or unwilling to keep up with Kroc's goading ambition.

Kroc's first job was in Chicago where he played piano with various bands, then became music director of a pioneer Chicago radio station (where he first hired, for $5 a show, the team that went on to become "Amos 'n' Andy"). Then off he went to become a lot salesman in Florida, until the collapse of the Florida land boom in the late Twenties sent him scurrying back to Chicago with barely enough money to pay his fare. He rode out the Depression selling paper cups for Lily Tulip. By the late Thirties, he had risen to Lily Tulip's midwest sales manager.

At that time he struck out on his own, after acquiring the rights to a machine that would mix six malted milks at a time. Says Kroc: "I wanted adventure." All he got, however, was a modestly good living and a certain amount of freedom.

Kroc discovered the McDonald brothers in 1954. He was surprised to find that one drive-in restaurant in San Bernardino, Calif., owned by two transplanted New Englanders named Richard and Maurice McDonald, was

using eight of his milk-shake machines: Whatever the McDonalds had, Ray Kroc knew he wanted part of it; you don't hustle for 35 years without getting to recognize a good thing when you see it.

"The Volume Was Incredible"

"I was amazed," Kroc says. "This little drive-in having people standing in line. The volume was incredible: I figured it at about $250,000 in that single store. I began to do some figuring. If they could have 100 stores like that one, I could sell them 800 multimixers. The deal would put me in clover."

Kroc approached the McDonalds, proposing to sell franchises for them. The brothers had already franchised six other stores in California. They were by no means thrilled by Kroc's offer. They had already turned down an even bigger deal.

As Dick McDonald now tells the story, another man, already a franchisee, had proposed a vast expansion of the chain by means of company-owned stores. The McDonalds said no. "A few years before we would have jumped," Dick McDonald told FORBES, "but by now we were netting $75,000 a year from our San Bernardino store, and we were selling franchises without any trouble. The idea of big expansion didn't much appeal to us. It would have entailed a tremendous amount of traveling, and we would have had to neglect San Bernardino."

And that, says McDonald, is why Ray Kroc got the deal. It wasn't that his proposal was better, but only that it would involve less trouble for the McDonalds. Even so, the negotiations almost fell through several times. When the deal was finally closed, Kroc hit the road again, selling McDonald's franchises—and multimixers.

"It goes to show," Dick McDonald muses, recalling how he nearly turned Kroc down, "what a big part fate plays in a man's life. After all, what would Ray Kroc's future have been in the milk-shake machine business?"

Perhaps, but Ray Kroc was right in there, helping fate along.

At the time, in fact, Kroc concedes he was chiefly interested in expanding the chain in order to sell more multimixer milk-shake machines. He had no alternative, because the deal with the McDonalds didn't give him much leeway. Recalling those days, Kroc says: "I made the mistake of letting their damned attorney dictate to me what I could charge for the franchise, a lousy 1.9% of revenues. Of that I had to give the McDonalds 0.5%." Even after Kroc had franchised some 200 stores, doing over $37 million annually, his *gross* franchise income was only about $700,000 a year. He was subsisting on the milk-shake machine business. Kroc had taken a partner, Harry Sonneborn, a former vice president of Tastee Freez; Sonneborn was drawing $100 a week. Kroc's secretary was taking her wages in stock.*

The Land Beneath

As the McDonalds showed Kroc how to run a hamburger stand, Harry Sonneborn showed him how to get out of the franchising bind.

Sonneborn worked out a whole new approach. It involved both company-owned stores and franchisees, but the latter no longer would be just franchisees; they would be *tenants,* too. Kroc's company would frequently lease a site and have it developed, then *re*-lease the whole operation to the franchisee. McDonald's would now enjoy a profit from the lease as well as from the franchising fees.

It was a great plan. Unfortunately, it required money, or at least credit. Kroc had neither. His main source of

*Mrs. June Martino, like most of Kroc's other early associates, has dropped out of the company, but what a dropout! Now retired and living in Chicago, Mrs. Martino owns an estimated 1 million shares of McDonald's stock.

income dried up in 1960 when Kroc had to sell his mixer business for $100,000 to pay for a divorce from his wife. The minimum amount needed for Sonneborn's plan was $1.5 million. Kroc remembers going to see David Kennedy of Chicago's Continental Illinois Bank.

"My total assets, including my house, were $90,000," Kroc recalls, "not much for a man of my age. Kennedy said: 'You won't find a bank in the country that will make you a loan in your condition. If anyone were willing, you'd have to give him a big slice of the company.'"

Kroc's luck held. In 1960 Sonneborn wangled an appointment with the investment officers of several Worcester, Mass. insurance companies. One of them, John Gosnell of Paul Revere Life (since merged into Avco Corp.) sniffed something interesting. Gosnell later told FORBES: "We looked hard and saw that there was more here than a chain of hamburger stands. They had operations under tight financial controls." Paul Revere and another insurer came through with a loan of $1.5 million for 15 years; as a premium on the loan, they took 20% of the company.

Like the McDonalds and like Sonneborn, Paul Revere no longer has an equity position in McDonald's Corp., although part of the loan is outstanding. Gosnell sold his stock for around $7 million—pure profit. A lovely deal for Revere. But if it had stayed with the stock—if it had Ray Kroc's faith—Avco would now be sitting with a paper profit of around $500 million.

So here was Kroc, 60 years old in

1962, having gambled all his life and now finally having enough money for steady, profitable expansion. And what did he do? He pulled out all the stops. As he recalls it: "I wanted to go public, but I couldn't because I wasn't showing a profit. I couldn't because I was pouring everything in, everything we made. I used to drive my accountant crazy because I would anticipate the next three months' profit and I would obligate it in the way of debt for expansion.

"I was going for broke. Don't get me wrong. I'm not a gambler. But when I like something, if I'm sold on it, I'll go all the way."

On Top at Last

Not for several years did McDonald's show real profit. By 1964 it owned 87 stores, franchised 570 more and was grossing $26 million.

Ray Kroc has never liked inactive partners. He wanted to get the McDonald brothers out. "They didn't make one move," Kroc complains, "and they had checks pouring in." Kroc claims the brothers were drawing $200,000 in royalties alone, and he had a further worry: Suppose they sold their rights to the name to someone who would try to squeeze Kroc out? The answer was to buy them out. But money was the problem.

Harry Sonneborn raised $2.7 million in 1961, which was what the McDonalds demanded for selling out. A very shrewd venture capitalist, New York's John Bristol, was willing to put up the money, but he wanted stock. Kroc didn't want to give any stock; he was down to 52% now. Bristol

settled for a straight five-year loan plus, when that was paid off, the 0.5% Kroc had been paying the McDonald brothers. Good-bye McDonalds. Bristol's clients, college endowment funds, ended up with about $14 million for their $2.7-million loan.

Harry Sonneborn was the next to go. When his health began to fail, he wanted to take life easier, and this miffed Kroc. Of Sonneborn, Kroc now says: "He was letting up, showing signs of age, and he wasn't that old; he's 15 years younger than I am. Harry was an aggressive guy who all of a sudden when we went public felt secure. He quit pushing. And here we were just getting started. I do have to admit he did us a lot of good."

Sonneborn sold his 11% of the company and retired to Florida. He took with him an estimated $10 million in cash plus $100,000 a year from the company for life and after his death $50,000 for his wife.

Today there are 600 company-owned stores and 1,600 franchisees. McDonald's netted an estimated $36 million last year. Ray Kroc still owns 20% of the stock.

Kroc has no more major partners, but he does have a very capable right-hand man, President Fred Turner. Turner, now 40, is very much in the Ray Kroc mold. "Fred didn't finish college," Kroc says. "He has what we need: spirit and guts and dedication and integrity. Forget the brains. Fred is a multmillionaire, but it hasn't slowed him down."

Turner, too, *sincerely* wants to be rich.

What McDonald's Had, the Others Didn't

How do you identify a growth stock in its early stages? You could do worse than check to see whether they keep the toilets clean.

WALL STREET is littered with the debris of so-called growth stocks. Technicon and Telex. Memorex and Ampex and Stirling-Homex. Four Seasons. We could go on with the list, but why be morbid?

What did these ill-fated stocks have in common? A concept. A concept that was going to revolutionize something: home-building or the care of the aged or the way information is processed. These companies were at the frontiers of technology and of service.

Oh, there was a bit of a flurry over the franchising concept, but it was short-lived. How long could you be excited about frying hamburgers and chicken? McDonald's Corp., the hamburger outfit, did fairly well, and in 1969 it had a total market value of about $500 million; Four Seasons had $800 million.

In the end, homely McDonald's has turned out to be the greatest concept stock of the whole period. Four Seasons is bankrupt and so is Stirling-Homex. Investors in most of the others have been clobbered. McDonald's now sells for close to 80 times earnings and has a total market value of $3 billion. An investment of $5,000 in McDonald's just six years ago is now worth close to $100,000.

Instead of playing at technology and spinning fantasies about retailing revolutions, The Street's analysts would have been better occupied peering into the washrooms at McDonald's to see how clean they were. Or noting how consistently McDonald's employees said, "Thank you. Come again." Or recognizing that real estate rather than franchising was the heart of the McDonald's operation.

Now, of course, Wall Street *has* caught on, and McDonald's stock is in the stratosphere. What made McDonald's rather modest concepts work brilliantly while more brilliant concepts turned out to be dismal failures?

The only way to answer the question is to start at the beginning.

After World War II, Richard and Maurice McDonald were having trouble staffing their San Bernardino, Calif. carhop restaurant; there was the usual parade of drunks and drifters. A problem familiar to all restaurant men. "We said," Dick McDonald recalls, "let's get rid of it all. Out went dishes, glasses and silverware. Out went service, the dishwashers and the long menu. We decided to serve just hamburgers, drinks and french fries on paper plates. Everything prepared in advance, everything uniform. All geared to heavy volume in a short amount of time." In short, the

---

The Fast-Food Chains—Fewer but Hardier

After the shakeout of a host of fast-food operators in the last few years, there are fewer but hardier survivors.* Most have resumed or accelerated their growth, but none has really succeeded in overtaking McDonald's.

Company	Number of Units	Revenues** Latest 12 Months (millions)	Revenues** 5-Year Compounded Growth Rate	Earnings Latest 12 Months Per Share	Earnings 5-Year Compounded Growth Rate	Recent Price	1967-72 Price Range	Price/ Earnings Ratio
Bonanza Intl	260	$ 20	52%	$ .20	d-p	15⅝	47½-1¾†	78
Church Fried Chicken	350	60	86	1.25	62%	21⅞	53⅜-7¾††	18
Denny's Inc	770	141	51	.60	6	16¾	52⅝-4¼	28
Friendly Ice Cream	330	67	25	.70	18	35	38¼-7†	50
Gino's	330	123	33	.97	22	30¾	48¼-2⅛	32
Hardee's Food	580	97	40	.76	9	19⅛	36½-3½	25
McDonald's	2,200	345	47	.88	35	73⅝	73⅝-2⅜	83
Pizza Hut	855	52	45	.94	31	34⅞	35¾-3¼††	37
Sambos	203	16	47	.89	36	41½	43 -4⅞††	47

*Burger King (Pillsbury) and Kentucky Fried Chicken (Heublein), major factors in the industry after McDonald's, do not break out figures separately from those of the parent.
**Excludes franchise system revenues.　d-p Deficit to profit.　†1968-72 Price Range.　††1969-72 Price Range.

brothers brought efficiency to a slap-dash business.

It was a simple formula, but no one else did as well as the McDonald brothers. Ray Kroc (*see preceding story*) recognized this as soon as he cut back for nonrush hours.

Most of these employees get the legal minimum wage, $1.60 an hour, with no fringe benefits. Without such flexibility, McDonald's and other fast-food chains couldn't combine fast service with low prices. Thus, it is hardly surprising that Ray Kroc, who is an enthusiastic backer of Richard M. Nixon, lobbied hard and long against the recent proposal to raise the minimum wage to $2.

If McDonald's had contented itself with franchising a name and a system, saw the McDonald's operation. Two thousand stores later, the basic principles have not changed.

Big as it is today, McDonald's still has a low ratio of labor costs to sales. It has 30,000 employees today, its franchisees another 82,500. But the labor is used with superefficiency.

Most of McDonald's labor force consists of high school and college students and housewives, 90% of them part-time. This enables McDonald's to do something most employers can only dream of: staff heavily for rush hours, however, it would never have grown the way it did. Ray Kroc was dissatisfied with simply franchising. An alternative was to do what most franchisers do, force the franchisees to buy certain products or equipment on which the franchiser makes a nice profit. But Kroc wasn't enthusiastic about these arrangements; too much potential for legal hassles, kickbacks and the like. What to do?

Why Not Be a Landlord?

Harry Sonneborn, Kroc's former partner, hit upon the idea of putting McDonald's into the real estate business. That is, the franchisee would have to lease the ground and/or store from McDonald's. As its franchises have become more and more desirable, as volume climbed, the rents have steadily mounted, from 6.25% of the store's gross income to 8.5%.

The arithmetic of being a landlord is very handsome from McDonald's point of view. In 1968 rental income was $17 million. Last year it was about $58 million. Over the same period its lease *costs* (interest, ground rents, etc.) grew only $14 million to about $21 million. As a consequence, Mc-Donald's profit from leasing went from $3 million to $37 million.

In fact, rentals, while they account for only about 15% of the company's gross income, account for 33% of net profits. Profits from company-owned stores account for another 45%, leaving franchise and royalty revenues, 16%, the smallest part of the pie.

Those who regarded McDonald's as just another hamburger franchiser overlooked these vital differences.

Nor did they allow for the great and growing role that advertising promotion would make on McDonald's success. The company is today the second-biggest national retail television advertiser in the U.S., spendng $40 million last year.

But growth brings its own problems. McDonald's system sales last year were already over $1 billion. In the three years 1971, 1972 and 1973, McDonald's alone will have opened nearly 1,000 new stores.

This cannot go on forever. Nothing grows to the skies. Howard Johnson's once looked as irresistible as McDonald's, but now has slowed to a growth rate of about 10% a year. Somewhere, somehow, the same thing will happen to McDonald's. (To which Kroc replies: "That's a lot of crap," and goes on to talk about a world-wide potential of 12,000 stores, six times the current figure.)

Can McDonald's keep it up? Only if it can continue to produce internal growth; getting more out of existing stores. In 1968 McDonald's began to renovate its existing stores and increase the size of new stores to provide for tables and chairs inside. This has attracted customers who were unwilling to eat in their cars. Also, after an earlier unsuccessful attempt to introduce breakfast items to the menu, McDonald's has come up with what appears to be an extremely successful breakfast, the Egg McMuffin. The 900 stores testing it are approaching $100 a day in extra revenue, and Turner says that will build.

The second answer is: Move into new areas. Naturally, McDonald's has tackled the ripest territories first—suburbs and heavily trafficked roads. The company now is moving into the inner cities.

"We were scared about the cities," says President Fred Turner. "We are well aware of the problems in the cities, like getting good help and theft and bribery and high fixed costs. But we think we can handle it. The answer is that our city stores are producing enough volume to take care of the problems." So far McDonald's has opened about 50 big-city stores. Fred Turner claims the inner city stores are averaging about $1 million a year, twice the volume of the typical store.

Turner has also tested Mini-Macs,

smaller stores for smaller towns. He is also getting ready for a big push overseas. There are two stores in Paris, 19 in Japan; and stores will start to open in Britain this year.

Hurdles Ahead

The stock market is saying that McDonald's growth can go on almost forever. It prices McDonald's at 78 times earnings and 30 times book value. McDonald's, to justify its current price, will have to be earning something like $5 a share, and be selling $5 billion worth of hamburgers.

Are such numbers achievable? Perhaps, but the odds are against them. They won't stop the growth. But they may slow it.

The cities, for example, where 31% of the U.S. population lives. Howard Johnson Jr., president of the famous chain, has this comment on doing business in the cities: "They are a can of worms. We would never think of trying to crack that market." But crack it McDonald's must to keep up its growth rate.

In one city, at least, McDonald's is taking its lumps. McDonald's has filed an antitrust suit in San Francisco against restaurant trade associations and unions alleging that these organizations have kept McDonald's from opening more stores there.

Foreign expansion looks good on paper. How will it work out in practice? Admittedly McDonald's is packing them in on the Champs Elysées and the Ginza, which are superhigh-volume stores. But the Champs Elysées and the Ginza aren't the world. Japan looks promising, but it poses problems. Even Canada proved a tough nut for McDonald's to crack. "Our subfranchisee there did a lousy job," says President Turner. "We bought it back from him and it was a real headache for a few years."

How big a headache? Try $15 million in unforseen costs to straighten out the Canadian operations, just to get them into the black.

There are two questions to ask about McDonald's. Is it really worth $2.9 billion, close to 80 times 1972 earnings? The answer is: Can *any* company be worth 80 times earnings?

The other question concerns management. Here the answer is easier. This still youngish company in a cut-throat business has turned out to have some of the best management in the U.S. Its secret, if secret it be, is simply a fanatical attention to detail and a willingness to try new approaches to old problems. Which is a "concept" in a way, but it is the oldest concept of them all.

Horatio Hamburger
and the golden arches

Franchising waxes in times of prosperity, perhaps because consumers then are freer to spend, and the eternal longing of a man to run his own business brings the spare greenbacks out of the savings account. So, if one believes the recent encouraging economic news, a new period of popularity for franchising should be just ahead. In which case, *Big Mac*—an irreverent romp through Ray Kroc's McDonaldland—is a timely reminder of who makes the big loot in franchising: the promoter and, to some extent, the early bird.

Ray Albert Kroc, a Chicago-born salesman of almost anything, was 52 years old in 1954 when he discovered the McDonald brothers selling hamburgers from a single stand in San Bernardino, Calif. Kroc's first move was to negotiate a licensing deal with the brothers. Then, in 1960, he acquired all rights to the McDonald name for $2.7 million. Today Kroc's stock is worth about $500 million, he owns a major league baseball team, the San Diego Padres, homes scattered about, and a $4.5 million jet airplane, and he contributes vast sums for political causes he favors. Kroc's bookkeeper took her pay in stock rather than in cash in the early days and, when she had worked long enough, retired with stock worth $70 million. Kroc's crisp valedictory: "Get out. Make room for someone else. The business is for the needy, not the greedy."

Having discovered some years back that there is more profit in owning a McDonald's store than there is in franchising it, the corporation has been busily buying out its successful franchises—sometimes, the authors hint darkly, with muscle. So McDonald's Corp. now owns about 30% of the 3,500 stores and in 1975 had revenues of $941.5 million, on which it netted $86.9 million. Not bad for selling less than 4 oz. of ground beef and "fixin's" on sesame seed buns.

Ray Kroc did not invent franchising; neither did he invent the hamburger. What he did was to develop a system for serving a burger, a milk shake, and french fries in record time. He established a system for training employees and a way of policing it. And he managed to con millions of Americans—including a lot of small town mayors—into equating McDonalds with the American Way of Life.

The franchise system, at its simplest, is the way an entrepreneur finds a substitute for capital. He has the product or the service but lacks the money to build and equip the outlets. So he lets others finance the stores and lets them sell the product or service for a fee or a royalty or a combination of both.

McDonald's, however, has gone far beyond the simple form of franchising. It sells a 20-year license for about $200,000, picks the site, buys the land, builds the store, equips it, and rents it for 8.5% of gross annual revenues, plus a 3% annual franchise fee.

The glue that holds any franchise system together is standardization and promotion. A motel chain's furniture, for example, will be built to certain specifications and in enough quantity to make the price so attractive that a franchise holder would be a simpleton not to buy it. Franchisers are forbidden to force franchisees to buy anything from them. But they can stipulate approved suppliers. Ray Kroc made a lot of friends rich that way. And owning the real estate, as McDonald's does, makes it all the easier to buy out a franchise holder when the franchiser wants to own the business.

Above all, a McDonald's franchiser gets from the corporation advertising support—to the tune of more than $60 million a year, the authors assert—that makes the names Ronald McDonald, McDonaldland, Big Mac, and the Golden Arches so well known to the American consumer that a book about them makes very good sense.

The authors subtitle their book "The Unauthorized Story of McDonald's," perhaps to escape the stigma that usually attaches to company histories. They certainly seem to have had all the access they required to McDonald's executives and facilities. I would have liked more of the raw meat of money and management, but the authors concentrate on the sizzle. And not just of McDonald's. They pan over the franchise landscape to provide a view of rival franchise operations, often by recording Kroc's recollections or estimates of his competitors, particularly of the white-suited Colonel Harland Sanders, whom Kroc remembers from the days in the 1950s when both men were out peddling franchises.

But the authors do dig into the less joyful times of McDonald's: the fights in New York over store locations, the exhausting battle with the San Francisco unions, the continuing controversy on Capitol Hill over legislation that would interfere with the McDonald wage rate for its hordes of teen-age workers.

It is the sizzle that sells the book. The description of what goes on at corporate headquarters—the 11-story building in Oak Park, Ill., dubbed Hamburger Central—is well worth reading. Not only does headquarters have one of the first open offices, with "work units" separated by cabinets and plants, but it also has a think tank equipped with a device that projects the thinker's brain waves on a screen and a room filled by a nine-ft.-diameter water bed. The authors note that Ray Kroc has never visited the think tank—although McDonald's president, Fred Turner, frequently does—and that the think tank is open to male and female employees

Big Mac

by Max Boas and Steve Chain
Dutton ▪ 212 pages ▪ $8.95

"but never at the same time. Heterosexual thinking is strictly prohibited."

There is also Hamburger University, which awards the degrees of B.H. (Bachelor of Hamburgerology) and M.H. (Master of Hamburgerology), and the Golden Hat to the student most helpful to his classmates. Don't snicker. Hamburger U. is the key to McDonald's growth and the maintenance of the system that has been so successful. It trains the managers who train the kids. The only reason McDonald's does not buy back its franchises more rapidly, says Ray Kroc, is the lack of managers. Says the dean of Hamburger U.: "The majority of [McDonald's] people have the same philosophy toward the hamburger. That is, it is not a joking matter to us but a damn serious business."

It surely is. Ray Kroc is not around the place much any more, so Fred Turner is the master of the mystique surrounding that thin pat of meat on the sesame seed bun. And his wife's name is Patty.

—William Kroger

Joan Sydlow—BW

American symbol: Big Mac

Distribution

Manufacturing doesn't make much sense unless there is some setup for moving the goods produced from where they are made to where they are sold or used. The transportation, or physical distribution, of goods from one place to another is an important business activity.

Physical distribution involves the movement of materials into a plant, movement within the plant, and the movement of finished goods out of the plant, all in an organized, systematic manner.

Moving materials costs money. In fact, physical distribution costs represent a major element in the overall cost of goods produced. For many types of products, distribution costs equal one-fourth or more of the total sales dollar.

Thus, any possible savings in distribution costs may result in greater profits, product improvement, or lower sales price. Efficiency is desirable.

What are the major elements of distribution costs?

- Warehousing
- Materials handling
- Transportation
- Shipping

Modern methods for minimizing these costs and moving goods as rapidly and efficiently as possible are illustrated in the following discussion of Sears' distribution system.

How a lack of planning for these elements destroyed a new business is discussed in another article -- about San Diego's TeleMart venture.

TRANSPORTATION

In transporting goods, there are a number of trade-off factors influencing the best type of carrier. Whether to send goods by railroad, truck, water, or air requires analysis of these factors.

Railroads can haul bulky goods long distances at low cost. But they are often slow and not always reliable. They are also rather inflexible for small shipments and in terms of where goods can be transported.

Truck transportation offers quick and convenient shipping of goods to any community. Trucks may be adapted to particular needs and may be loaded and moved when desired. Thus trucking is more flexible than rail transportation. For heavy or bulky goods, however, it may be more expensive.

The oldest and cheapest method of transporting goods is by water -- by ship or barge. Coal and heavy ores are often shipped by water.

Air transportation is the fastest, but it is also the most expensive. Thus it is used for high priority items that must be moved safely and quickly, such as perishables or electronic goods.

For some special goods, such as oil, gas, powdered coal, and wood pulp, pipelines are used. As we have seen with the Alaskan pipeline, the construction costs of pipelines are high, but they do ensure a continuous flow of materials once they are completed. A vast network of pipelines has been built in the United States to connect sources of raw materials with users.

Merchant to Millions Sears

A semi-automated distribution system

It took more than five years to develop the merchandise control and handling systems that are being used and refined in Columbus. Under the new concept, Columbus is "attached" to the Chicago Merchandise Distribution Center for purposes of inventory control. Buyers at the Chicago center are responsible for determining the quantities and for ordering the merchandise that will be carried at the Columbus site, and computers in Chicago record the inventories of the Columbus operation.

When merchandise is received in Columbus, it is loaded onto a mechanized routing system—composed of programmed in-floor conveyor carts and automatic conveyor belts— which transports the merchandise to a designated storage area.

At the same time the goods are being fed into the routing system, information on their arrival is being keyed into the Columbus computer by a CRT (cathode ray tube) operator who is in touch with receiving via communications link. The computer updates the merchandise-on-order file, places the merchandise in inventory and notes its storage location.

All customer orders are received on line by the Chicago computer, processed and then transferred via high-speed data link to the Columbus computer for filling, shipping and billing.

Customer orders are released from the computer in the same sequence in which the merchandise is stored, thereby enabling a merchandise selector to make one trip through each storage aisle and fill the orders efficiently. The merchandise selector places the packages on a mechanized shipping system; they are moved to a central point, key coded for destination and automatically sent to a consolidation area. Simultaneously, the computer creates a bill of lading for the shipment and completes the accounting for each transaction. Once merchandise is consolidated, it is loaded onto trucks for overnight delivery to Sears facilities for customer pick-up throughout a six-state area.

Highly trained people make it work

While the high degree of automation at Columbus has enabled the company to shorten the time involved in manual merchandise handling and inventory control, it has also pointed dramatically to the importance of Sears people. Without highly trained personnel to maintain the systems and provide the information required to carry out the day-to-day functions of the Distribution Center, it could not operate at the level of efficiency for which it was designed.

The advanced technology utilized in this, our first all-new catalog facility in 25 years, is already creating operating efficiencies that will help us to maintain our position in the marketplace. Many of the lessons we have learned at Columbus are being implemented in our other catalog centers. They are being used in the development of plans for future facilities, such as the 1.6-million-square-foot Jacksonville, Florida, center which will be in operation in 1975.

Bill Bailey, Where Are My Groceries?

by Tom Leech

■ Few people living in San Diego within eye or earshot of radio, television, newspapers, or even only slightly loquacious friends, have not heard of a business enterprise known as TeleMart. It burst upon the San Diego scene with all the flair a Barnum or Bailey at their best might have engineered. In the year 1970 there wasn't a Barnum, but there sure was a Bailey.

Bill Bailey of Volkswagen and "finger lickin' good" Kentucky Fried Chicken fame was the ringmaster behind the show called TeleMart. From the first of the year right up to the day he opened for business and became so successful he went broke in less than two weeks, he kept the whole city enthralled. TeleMart was the wave of the future, the "Service of the Seventies." Who else but TeleMart would sell their stock on TV and send you their "screaming yellow prospectus" if you called while the idea was "hot, new and happening!"

"We intend to deliver TeleMart to the world," Bailey said. Before he could do that, however, he had to accomplish a less grandiose feat. He first had to deliver groceries to San Diego. And, aye, there was the rub.

He spoke of TeleMart doing $20,000,000 in business the first year. All he was after was a measly four percent of the grocery sales in San Diego County, a business worth nearly $700,000,000 last year. The giants of the industry were such names as Safeway and Food Basket. But, said Bailey, "The time has arrived when we believe TeleMart will have its place." Maybe he was right.

What was going to provide TeleMart that place? The magic formula was an idea that had faded away during the '40's with the advent of second automobiles, freeways, and, yes, supermarkets. The key to TeleMart's place in the mart would be home delivery, an end to all that waiting around in those long shopping lines. An end to lugging those "sixteen tons" of groceries out to your car and into the house. With TeleMart, the groceries would be delivered to your door and unloaded right on your kitchen table. TeleMart would be exciting, the "young way to shop." The customers would see the products advertised on TV, then they'd refer to a *Shopper's Guide* and phone in their orders. And they'd even talk to a computer; no more pushing, shoving, waiting, or carrying. "And never a minimum order!"

You could even read about TeleMart in *Business Week*. A few thousand San Diegans and a major supermarket chain from the East became partners in the venture. Local giants like Rohr and Pacific Telephone put their money, talent, phone lines and computer know-how on TeleMart's future. The world breathlessly awaited the grand opening, scheduled for Sunday, September 13, 1970.

The crash

Bill Bailey didn't sleep well the night before the grand opening. "I lay there for quite awhile, thinking about tomorrow. One question kept nagging at me. What if nobody calls?" Well, somebody called. About 2,600 somebodies called the first day. "We need TeleMart!" they proclaimed loud and clear. "I am tired of those long lines. Bring over those groceries."

Apparently TeleMart had made it. For as Bailey had said, "Our main problem is a marketing one. Our Wheaties are no different than anyone else's." Now that the market had spoken all that remained was to fill the orders, load them on the waiting fleet of trucks, deliver them, and then get back on TV with some more enticing commercials to make sure they'd buy again.

TeleMart's "exclusive distribution conveyance systems and special collateral mechanisms" now went to work to fill the orders. This order-filling system was designed to fill 3,000 orders per day. It never had to. TeleMart didn't receive that many orders on any day—which is just as well since the system never could get above 600 in actuality. The scene in the picking area has been described by various of those who served there as "chaotic," "a madhouse," and "unbelievable." It became quickly apparent that TeleMart was in deep trouble, with all that business and no way to serve it.

Rumors about TeleMart's troubles drifted out. And then the word came that a decision had been made on Friday, September 25 to close down the shop. Every new venture must expect some setbacks, was a typical public reaction. Four days later, on September 29, TeleMart filed for bankruptcy. The public was stunned. To go bankrupt after only being open 13 days was unbelievable. But true. Bailey was given time to reorganize and obtain more financing, but this effort was fruitless. On December 10, TeleMart was declared legally bankrupt. In the words of Bill Bailey, TeleMart had proven "a sociological success and a technological failure."

How?

"Who knows?" Bailey once said, "I might turn out to be TeleMart's Colonel Sanders." It didn't work out that way, but it easily might have, based on the consumer interest shown in the TeleMart concept. The road to either success or a 13 day bankruptcy has lots of hurdles and false turns to throw off the unwary, or unwise, or unschooled.

Set up an organization

TeleMart was originally incorporated in July, 1968 by Bill Bailey under the name Alexander-Bailey. One year later its name became TeleMart and Bailey began forming a team in earnest. Bailey was to be the Chief Executive Officer and Chairman of the Board of Directors. His credentials as an advertising man and TV pitchman were excellent. For President he selected Paul Thanos, a steelman of many years and Bailey's brother-in-law. Food Baron, operators of Kentucky Fried Chicken and H. Salt, esq. franchises, held three more spots on the board, along with another Kentucky Fried man. The lone grocery man on the board was Robert Palmer, a past President of the Western Association of Food Chains.

The board was to change its makeup a few months before TeleMart opened when Food Baron sold its interest to Pueblo International, the eastern food chain. Pueblo then held controlling interest of the board with four seats, with Bailey, Thanos, and Palmer holding the other three.

The pessimists saw a lot of promotion but not much grocery expertise on the top level. The key management level, however, was spotted with names that should have offered assurance that Tele-Mart did indeed have some top people familiar with groceries and retailing. Experienced men from places like Fed Mart, 7-Eleven, Bradshaws, and Cost Less Imports held down key slots. As TeleMart progressed from the paper stage to a Kearny Mesa warehouse, a variety of people were hired to handle the many facets of business. Travel agents, pharmacists, food handlers, order takers—about 370 employees in all. For many it was a good learning experience. One veteran grocery man said he learned more in a few months at TeleMart than in the previous ten years with a large chain. And it was great fun. Employee spirit and loyalty were high right to the end.

Why wasn't all this experience and zest able to foresee and warn about the impending disaster? Two factors might have been involved. First, TeleMart's mode of operation was really different from that of almost all standard supermarkets. High speed, theoretically automated grocery-filling was far removed from either the shopping center or warehouse supply operations where orders are moved on pallets. Second, an atmosphere of euphoria existed around Tele-Mart that might have caused normally astute powers of observation to dim amid the glamour of the enterprise. Who notices flaws in Raquel Welch? One top executive recalls being concerned early about a particular facet of the warehouse. He said, "It was stupid. There was so much TV and press conferences and Hollywood that I actually forgot all about it." In such an atmosphere it is questionable would internal doubters have even been seen by those at the top, where the critical decisions were made.

Sampling of opinion was easy; everybody had one. "It'll never work," wasn't too uncommon. "Those women have got to squeeze the tomatoes," said many observers. Skeptics questioned Bailey's claims that his prices would be competitive. In an industry noted for small profit margins, TeleMart would have to pay employees to do what the housewife does for free. And how would housewives react to ordering their groceries from a catalogue?

A more scientific view of the potential consumer was sought from Business Behaviorial Research Associates, a La Jolla research firm. Their findings showed TeleMart would meet overwhelming approval from consumers. The primary shopper would be the 40 year old housewife, with a couple of teenagers, and with middle to upper income. And she'd order about like she'd order from a regular supermarket, which was plenty. National surveys showed that nearly 70 percent of American homemakers spend $21 or more per week for supermarket expenditures. This pattern of the likely customer was at variance with TeleMart's original theory, that the younger working women would be the primary market.

According to Dr. David Feldman of BBRA, "the point we made very clearly was that the critical thing to TeleMart success was the ability to deliver within five to six hours from the time of calling in the order."

The TeleMart membership drive began in August; 30,000 to 40,000 members was the stated goal. Television was the major medium, with Bailey always the pitchman. The format was basically the same as had proven so successful for Bailey in the past—folksy, personality, humor, a little music and a little corn. Home again on the farm or the range—TV style—with "This is TeleMart Territory." Catchy slogans high-lighted the predominant themes.

TeleMart means service—"quit all that carryin' on," and savings. TeleMart "ding-a-ling" shopping is smart, and for "the beautiful people." "It's the young way to shop." The T's were rampant, TeleMart is Terrific, Territory, 292-two-two-two-two. And the phone lines were nearly always open.

Bailey apparently worried the newspapers with his emphasis on TV. The typical supermarket relies almost exclusively on newspaper advertising. Bailey's words must have seemed like heresy: "Television is truly our store. People will see our products come *alive* in their most appetizing and appealing manner. As our products crunch, steam, pour, and beckon—there can be instantaneous sales reaction just by picking up the phone." The Union-Tribune was so concerned they quickly extended Tele-Mart credit.

Under the Bill Bailey by-line a chatty one-column newsletter ad was begun. In "TeleMart Talk" Bailey talked to Mom about how grocery shopping was in the old days, when "you used to call up Faquar's grocery down on Main Street." He got in the assurances about the meat and fruits and vegetables. "Remember how you always used to wonder…whether dogs had been sniffin' 'em?" Bailey also had a memorable dialogue with himself in that first ad. "When did you say you were gonna open?" "September 13" "That's a Sunday. You sure you know what you're doin'?" "I hope so. I'm tryin' awful hard."

Shopper's Guide was a work of art. It featured beautiful, original photography—a dozen grocery items arranged around San Diego's most photogenic spots. Beef stew and chow mein in front of a Balboa Park fountain. *Shopper's Guide* was included free with a membership, and available otherwise for $1.00. It was planned for replacement quarterly.

September 13. "TELEMART IS OPEN" in red letters all over a full page newspaper ad. To ensure everyone possible got the word, "TELEMART AHORA ABIERTO," said an ad in a Spanish-language paper.

When the TeleMart phone lines opened, 19,080 families had signed up. And, they did call—the campaign to woo the consumer was an overwhelming success. Bailey said 28,907 calls came in during the entire 13 day operation. Many more calls would undoubtedly have been received under less chaotic conditions.

Was the market research substantiated? According to Bailey, "We hit nearly every target. We were so right sociologically. We said we'd do $20 million volume a year. The experts said we were out of our gourd. We were *low*." One area in which the reality was not in agreement with the research was that oft-mentioned trouble spot, produce and meats, the perishables. TeleMart had estimated the average caller would order about nine perishables per order. This was the value used in the design of the warehouse, in setting up conveyors, timing, locations. The actual number of perishables per order was 21.

A warehouse worker was startled at the meat orders. "We thought people would be cautious, try just a little bit at the start. Wow! Right off they took more meat than I've ever seen people take in a regular supermarket."

Says Bailey, "Beware of research. It can lead you down a tragic path." Says Feldman, "Bailey ignored the research. We said the average order would be around $30. He didn't believe it. He still kept thinking in his mind of the single shopping girl, and that's what he was advertising to, and expecting to happen."

Was the marketing of TeleMart a success? Unfortunately, no one really knows. The test period was probably too short and chaotic, to provide a basis for projecting order size, makeup, frequency of purchase, and product preference. Key questions about customer satisfaction and reorders were not answered.

Speaking of the fickle market, Bailey said, "We can't conclude because the factor in marketing any product is, when boredom set in....boredom changes patterns and changes human behavior. We did establish that delivery time was the last thing they were concerned about."

Set up a system

Assuming a TeleMart was able to line up some customers, how could they give home delivery, be competitive with regular supermarkets, and make a profit?

The answer seemed to lie in technology. Why couldn't the technology of the 60's that put a man on the moon be applied to making the TeleMart concept work in the 70's? Technology like computers and automation. This was the direction toward which TeleMart headed.

Clara

Rohr Corporation was given a contract to develop the computer system. The computer was an IBM 360 named Clara, and like a true woman, she talked. Clara was the key to receiving and processing the orders.

In practice, a customer would make out her grocery list, using the glamorous *Shopper's Guide.* For each product she found a four-digit number, such as 21 19 for a box of Wheaties. When she had her list completed she would call 292-2222.

One of 60 "TeleShoppers" would answer. The TeleShopper, essentially an order taker, would bring the computer into the conversation. Clara would greet the customer with a friendly hello and ask for her order. As the customer gave the number for each item, the TeleShopper punched it on her touch-tone telephone. Clara would instantly tell if the item was in stock and its price. When the order was complete, Clara would sum up the total price. A delivery time would be arranged and the order process was completed. Clara would bid the customer

goodbye, then arrange the items in the proper picking order and printout the order invoice at the TeleMart warehouse.

Eight weeks before opening day Rohr and TeleMart started the testing of the computer system. The TeleShoppers started training in July. "A good training program," one girl recalls. Art Phelps, a former 7-Eleven markets' ad man, and the Director of TeleShoppers said the girls had no trouble catching on to the computer operation.

Rohr conducted an extensive test program of the computer setup, from TeleShopper through the computer to the order printout. Tom Barnard of Rohr recalls, "We tried to overload the system, subjected it to volumes above the 3,000 per day expected, and varied the expected peak times."

The results were no surprise to Rohr. "The first day we operated for 16 hours, with zero down time," said Barnard, "No software problems at all." Phelps said the TeleShoppers were very quick to adapt to real customers. "They were able to spot most of the customer item errors within the first couple of days." One TeleShopper found the customers to be fascinated with talking to the computer and "especially pleased with the meat and produce."

The order-filling system

TeleMart contracted with Rapistan, Inc. of Grand Rapids, Michigan to design and develop the system to fill all those orders Clara had printed out. The system was to be able to handle 3,000 orders per day.

Their system consisted of two independent lines, one for mainly perishable items and one for "hard" items such as canned goods. The order from Clara would be separated into perishables and hards and each part processed independently. They would then be joined to make up a completed order in a matching area.

The perishable side consisted of a long conveyor, on which an empty box (a tote box) was placed. It went through a large refrigerated section where pickers selected the perishable items noted on the list—produce, dairy products, meats—and placed them in the box. The conveyor then rose to the second floor where drug and cosmetic items were added, and then led back down to the matching area.

Meanwhile a warehouseman was pushing a second tote box through the hard goods section on a pushcart. As he went, he pulled products like canned goods from numbered bins on his right and left and placed them in the tote box. He then rolled the cart to a conveyor, placed the boxes on it for transport to the matching area, where theoretically, the perishable order had just arrived. The combined order would then be sent out to the delivery trucks.

When a truck was loaded, the driver would deliver the orders to each customer's home, carry the order into the house and unload each item. The customer either wrote a check or charged the order to his TeleMart charge account. A delivery charge of one dollar per order was included in the total.

The system was completed one to two weeks before opening date. Late delivery of the refrigeration system reportedly caused further delays in having a ready system. Most of the time before opening day was occupied in stocking the shelves.

A popular question concerns dry runs. Several employees in the picking area said that few dry runs were made, to their knowledge, and these only were done the last day or two before opening. Testing seemed to be fairly low pressure and concentrated on the hard goods side. Bill Bailey said that batches of 300 orders were run through the system and out onto the trucks. It's possible they were all correct—communications were undoubtedly hectic the last day or two before opening.

Reality replaces utopia

So they opened the doors, wide open. Some wag had remarked, "It's either going to be a Mustang or an Edsel." Bailey had chuckled and then asked, "Why am I laughing?" The observation is still valid. Was it an Edsel, since it failed, or a Mustang, since it succeeded?

The scene inside the warehouse became pandemonium in short order. Pickers on the hard goods line found the numbering system extremely inefficient to work with, a "fiasco" as one recalled. The planning had said the pickers would push their carts down the aisles neatly spaced. The reality was pickers nearly running into each other as they went down and back and forth across the aisles.

Bailey told of how the perishable line was thrown for a loop by a much greater number of perishable items ordered than had been expected. And one problem begat another problem. Said Bailey, "Perishables started piling up back there like a Mexican Hat Dance."

Things became rather chaotic in the matching area as the problems in both of the lines were passed on. Here they apparently multiplied. Lou Decker was loading trucks the first day. "I had one truck with orders that came out at 4:30 in the morning that was still on the loading dock at 4:30 in the afternoon, waiting for the rest of its orders."

Very quickly a new numbering system was derived that made locating items much easier. But this fix wasn't enough. Material handling experts were called in. They pulled out their stop watches and studied all the operations necessary to fill the orders. Bailey rolled up his sleeves and spent hours on the line, trying to figure out where the problems were and what might be done to fix them. Nothing seemed to work well enough. The customers kept calling in and the orders kept

piling up, and getting lost, and mixed up. The system had been designed to fill 3,000 orders per day, but they were never able to achieve more than 600, according to Bailey.

He finally threw in the towel on Friday, September 25.

"At three a.m. I called in the chief engineer and warehouse manager and said, 'You have 100 percent of the stock in the company, think like that for a moment, would you open up in the morning?' He said, 'I don't think so, I'm scared to death of it. We're getting deeper and deeper in problems and we're not coming out of them.'"

Of the nearly 30,000 people who called in an order, about five to six thousand of them received one.

What went wrong with the system? This is a question that will probably take months to resolve, as legal action by TeleMart against Rapistan has been strongly suggested in the press. Bailey in court hearings said that the two major problems were related to the loading

dock area, with only one exit, and to the single matching area. A fundamental question that seems sure to be asked concerns the feasibility of a system with two independent lines and a matching area. The form of the specifications and the proof of achievement are sure to be questioned. What is an order? $20 or $30? All meat and no potatoes?

The wake

It turned out that the 13th day was to be the last in the brief and tumultuous life of TeleMart. The following Tuesday, September 29, 1970 they filed a petition under Chapter XI of the Bankruptcy Act. The bubble had burst. The patient had died.

Now the skeptics really appeared. Everybody had known it couldn't work six months ago. "I was right," said one local broker, "but for the wrong reason." He wasn't alone.

Careers In Marketing

If you decide marketing is a career for you, you'll probably start out with direct customer contact. This means you'll be a sales representative for a particular product or line of products in a specified area or for a group of customers.

You'll get essential experience in sales techniques, product knowledge, and the behavior of customers. That will prepare you to take on additional responsibilities, such as product management, sales management, promotion or advertising management, buying, or unit management.

You may find that you like customer contact. Companies are eager to have capable, career-oriented marketing personnel. Incidentally, direct sales is a good way to earn a lot of money. It's one of the few types of jobs where rewards directly relate to the work you put in. (Look for a commission arrangement that pays for the volume of sales.)

If you want to be relatively independent, you may go into a franchise or other small business. Most involve selling products and, frankly, selling yourself. While the risk of failure is high, such a career can be quite satisfying.

In some companies you may be able to move fairly rapidly into a product management responsibility. Here you have direct influence over the success or failure of a specific product. The following article describes what's involved in this challenging type of career.

Becoming a product manager

Product or brand management—complete responsibility for a product or a line of products—can be one of the most interesting jobs in industry. To a large extent, a product manager is an entrepreneur within his organization.

Some of the best-paid and most coveted jobs in product management are with big, dynamic companies that package goods for consumers—General Foods Corp. of White Plains, N.Y., for example, or Procter & Gamble Co. of Cincinnati. P&G, as it is respectfully called, invented the modern system of product management. A product such as Head & Shoulders shampoo or Folger's coffee is put in the care of a group including a manager (called a brand manager at P&G), an assistant manager and one or two assistants. The group, says a P&G recruiting pamphlet, "is expected to know more about its brand and how to increase its acceptance than anyone else in the organization."

Case studies and computers

The admission ticket to product management—and on to broader responsibilities in marketing—is a master's degree in business administration. Marketing companies seek out M.B.A.s for two reasons: the new graduates have selected the type of work they want to do and presumably are motivated, and they already have had some highly relevant training. The case study system, in use at most graduate business schools, immerses students in practical problems. Many business schools also offer courses in such subjects as market research that involve extensive use of computers.

This year General Foods will hire about 25 M.B.A.s for product management. Typical starting salaries are $17,500 to $18,000 a year; those with business experience get more. At other companies that sell nationally advertised brands of soft drinks, detergents, razor blades, cosmetics, blue jeans and such, the story is much the same. Even in 1975, a drab year that saw college job placements decline by 18%, graduates of leading business schools averaged two to 3½ offers each. Marketing, which includes product management, was the fourth most popular job category among this year's 774 graduates of the Harvard Business School, ranking after finance, general management in the field and staff work at corporate headquarters.

Beginners in product management work as assistants until they know the whole job. "Three years is generally the soonest that anyone without prior ex-perience can become a brand manager," says a cigarette executive at R.J. Reynolds Industries; this is true at most companies.

Once a person becomes a competent product manager, he can switch companies readily; the jobs are somewhat interchangeable. Though turnover in the field has been at a minimum lately because of the recession, in ordinary times it is high.

The advent of women

Marketing jobs other than product management have been opening in new areas. Banks are hiring more marketing M.B.A.s to gain increased sophistication in dealing with consumers. So are auto makers. Since the oil crisis wrought havoc with sales of large cars, Detroit has stepped up its market research to learn what kinds of cars it should be manufacturing.

Another change in marketing is the advent of women. When Linda Hagen, now of General Foods, received her M.B.A. from Northwestern in 1970, she was one of ten women who made up 5% of a class of 192. This June there were 29 women in a class of 299. In the coming year, a fourth of the first-year students will be women—75 in a class of about 300.

CONSIDER

1. What motives do you think the average buyer has?

2. Why do you think Procter & Gamble has eight (count them) different brands of heavy-duty detergents?

3. Do Lever Brothers and Colgate-Polmolive have a chance of knocking down Procter & Gamble?

4. What effect would a ban on detergents have on Procter & Gamble?

5. Why do some people buy Tide and others Bold, both made by Procter & Gamble?

6. Why do some people buy deodorant hand soaps while others buy "beauty" or regulat soaps?

7. Try to explain why you dislike certain products: like liver, grapefruit, or buttermilk.

8. Since gasolines are all basically alike, why do customers have brand preferences?

9. Why does Gillette continue to develop new products when their old products are doing so well?

10. What is J.C. Penney doing to attract more customers?

CHALLENGES

List a dozen products and ask ten people at random whether they like them or dislike them. Then ask their reasons. Tabulate the results to show the various influences behind their preferences.

List a number of your own unsatisfied desires for products and services. Estimate the annual income you would need to satisfy those wants. Do you think you would be happy if you had such an income?

Look at automobile advertising on television, in magazines, and in newspapers to determine whether emphasis is on safety features, styling, gasoline milage, price, or other factors.

Look in the MART section of THE WALL STREET JOURNAL for a franchise opportunity. Evaluate whether you think it is a potentially good one.

Go to a department store and compare the warranties or guarantees provided on two or more brands of a product, such as toasters or televisions. Ask about any differences you may find.

Check the ingredients listed on a box of cereal. Identify the sources of these materials and the means of distribution likely used to make them available.

RECAP

Marketing is the process of providing the right products at the right places with the right promotion and at the right prices to satisfy the needs of the market. The four key elements of marketing, then, are Product, Place, Promotion and Price.

In this chapter we have examined the various tools, concepts, and issues of concern to businessmen in marketing. To introduce a new product is a fundamental task, an important step in approaching the market. We discussed five basic truths about launching new products. Each of the four elements of marketing are considered in the task.

Once launched, a product -- whether a good or a service -- follows a life cycle pattern in the marketplace. Sales of a product normally grow, level off, then decline. The pattern is reflected in the various products of Gillette. The new Trac II razor, for example, is in the "newborn" stage of the cycle.

There are cases where the market itself declines, not the product. Gerber faces a declining market as fewer babies are being born. In response, the Company has introduced new products -- in diverse areas.

In order to properly launch and market a product, a company needs to examine the behavior of the buyer in the marketplace, to project sales, and to plan the best marketing strategy. Through market experimentation, surveys, and other forms of market research, management gains useful information.

To sell more of a product, many companies attempt to identify segments in their markets -- so that promotion, product design, pricing, and other factors may be tailored to consumer preferences and motives. Segmentation is a useful tool in sales forecasting and planning. We discussed how this tool is applied by Procter & Gamble.

One particular form of marketing organization, the franchise, provides valuable backup support for small businesses. Franchising offers a number of definite advantages to individual entrepreneurs -- promotion, supplies, product development, management and operations know-how. In many instances, however, franchise arrangements aren't the whole answer to the problems of a business. There is no guarantee of success through a franchise business any more than there is through an independent business enterprise.

Once products are made, the job of getting them to the customer must be performed. As discussed in the case of TeleMart, an inadequate distribution system can prove to be disasterous for a business enterprise. Computerized distribution systems can be effective if well planned, as in the case of Sears. But whether computerized on not, this is an important aspect of business that cannot be neglected.

WORKSHEET NO. 6

NAME_____

INSTRUCTOR'S NAME_____

DATE_____

1. What is the key factor in McDonald's success?

2. How has Gillette attempted to cope with the rapid life cycle of some of its products?

3. How does J.C. Penney attempt to increase the productivity of
   its stores?

4. What were the first signs that TeleMart was in trouble?

CHAPTER 7

Advertising

Marketing moves a company's goods and services "out the door", resulting in profitable business operations. Advertising is at the heart of marketing, bringing products to the attention of customers.

Advertising is any form of communication through various media used to present goods or services to the public and to induce the public to buy.

It used to be that products were shown to potential buyers on a personal, face-to-face basis. We think of the local merchant and the traveling salesman both talking directly to us as customers. In today's complex mass-market society, however, most companies cannot rely solely on personal communications. The scale of business, the importance of television and other media, and the changing buying behavior of the public all make advertising increasingly important.

Coke, 7-Up, Schaefer beer, and Chevron gasoline all rely on advertising to stimulate consumer demand. Various techniques are used to make advertising effective, including the use of brand names, positioning of advertisements, and use of special ad themes. In this chapter we will examine these and other advertising techniques, as applied to these particular products.

Sears uses a catalog to present its many products to its customers. The target of this form of advertising is the mail order segment of Sears' market, but it also supports the marketing efforts of Sears' retailing operations. At the time Sears published its first catalog, it was just about the only way to reach the public, particularly the farmers, who comprised Sears' primary market early in the century.

J. Walter Thompson is the largest advertising agency in the United States, and has served Sears for years. An advertising agency helps a company such as Sears plan and implement programs for introducing and promoting its products. An agency provides a wide variety of services including research, creative work, media buying, and public relations.

In conjunction with advertising, other promotional tools and techniques may be used by a company, such as contests, special offers, incentives to salesmen, coupons granting discounts, and premiums or prizes. The automobile industry has traditionally relied on special promotional campaigns and on sales incentives to spur sales. When you buy a car, for example, you may be able to get a vinyl top or an air conditioner included without additional cost.

In This Chapter

Understanding Advertising

The demand for a product (a good or a service) is influenced by a wide variety of factors including prices, availability and prices of substitute products (such as margarine for butter), consumer incomes, shifts in population, geography, tastes, religion and customs, as well as advertising.

The total demand for consumer products and the patterns of spending among different products are most significantly influenced by total consumer incomes. As incomes rise, for example, expenditures shift toward more expensive convenience foods and luxury goods. Advertising only slightly affects overall consumer buying patterns, such as toward dairy products as promoted by the American Dairy Association.

Within a particular industry, different companies or brands share the consumer demand for a given product. Advertising influences changes in company shares of the market and may also extend total demand to some extent, particularly when new or improved products are available to the public.

Advertising is only one selling tool, of course. It is part of a broader ma marketing effort which includes product planning, pricing, personal selling, planning for distribution (whether by mail order, franchise, or other

There are no simple solutions. Only intelligent choices.

"FOR TWO YEARS AFTER DELIVERY WE'LL FIX ANYTHING THAT'S OUR FAULT."

Warning: The Surgeon General Has Determined That Cigarette Smoking Is Dangerous to Your Health.

means), packaging, displaying (as in store windows), and servicing. For some products, personal selling or packaging may be more important in stimulating sales than advertising (clothing, for example). While these different marketing techniques are generally used together in combination, the role of advertising depends on the product and the market characteristics.

The obvious aim of advertising is to inform the public about a product and to promote its sale. Advertising is paid promotion; non-paid (free) promotion is a type of publicity -- an aspect of public relations. The latter is generally concerned with building a favorable image of the organization or product in the market and the relationship of the company with its customers, stockholders, suppliers, dealers,

employees, and the community at large.

Advertising urges people to try a product, to buy more of it, and to use it for more purposes. One example is the promotion of cereal as an in-between meal snack. To accomplish these ends, a variety of different media are used, including
- newspapers
- television
- magazines
- direct mail
- radio
- business journals
- free samples
- coupons in magazines
- skywriting
- billboards
- display advertising (at the point of sale)

There may be a fuzzy line between advertising and sales promotion for some products, such as automobiles. Special promotions for cars are focused on price reduc- tions, new product innovations, and sales incentives to dealers.

The media for advertising depends on the impact desired. Whether you pay $100,000 for a page in a national magazine such as Playboy or $1000 for a page in a local newspaper depends on the type of advertising planned.

Five types of advertising may be generally identified (You may look for an example of each):

1. National advertising - usually urging customers to buy the product at local stores

2. Retail advertising - usually specific regarding price and urging the customer to shop at a

3. Industrial advertising - aimed at producers and manufacturers, such as ads for pumps and other equipment that may be used as part of a larger product or process

4. Trade advertising - urging retailers and distributors to handle the particular line of products

5. Institutional advertising - designed to enhance the image of the business or industry that makes the product.

As we have seen, some firms specialize in making or selling the products; others make advertising their own business. These ad makers, the advertising agencies, serve to link the companies to their consumers.

Dan Seymour, President of J. Walter Thompson, one of the world's biggest agencies, notes: "Between people and business our Company acts as a bridge, the pipeline, the connection. Our historic role has been to bring to people the news of the market, to tell them what business has made."

The media, in turn, is the place where these "bridges and pipelines" are built. Commercial television, for example, survives on advertising revenues. A recent New Yorker article noted that commercial TV is not primarily an "artistic endeavor, or even primarily an entertainment medium, but an industry that sells its products (the attention of audiences of varying sizes and demographies) to its customers (corporations with advertising budgets). The latter are motivated, in turn, by a primitive desire to sell their products (headache pills, Cordobas, floor wax, etc.) to these same hapless audiences." The case in point was the heavy editing of the Monty Python special show broadcast on American commercial television after serial broadcasts on public television in the U.S. and the U.K.

The article continues, "Paradoxically, the networks' fear of their audiences is as exaggerated as their contempt for them is limitless, because the real objects of that fear (and, if the truth be told, that contempt, too) are the advertisers, who want only to do business in a predictable atmosphere unmuddied by bohemian irrelevances."

The Pythons may have forgotten these realities, if in fact they are the "way it is" in the television world.

MARKETING SHIFTS

Advertising follows and sometimes leads the way in changing consumer patterns. Advertising changes with the tides. Among recent changes have been:
-- the growth and dominance of television and its total influence on communications as well as the general life style of the American public. Magazines, so big in the past, fell in importance (what ever happened to Life, Look, and the Saturday Evening Post?)
-- the growth and use of the computer as a tool for planning and advertising
-- dramatic changes in distribution patterns, and concentration of merchandising leadership in the major chains
--governmental intrusion in advertising. Regulatory agencies have assumed new power from new laws and today new standards are being applied for product safety, corrective advertising, labeling, codes, ad documentation, environmental challenges, and nutritional and health warnings all color brand messages.
-- rising costs of advertising services. Agencies used to think of ten staff people per $1 million billings to clients. Staffing is now down to about five.

There are also some new, more positive trends in advertising. These include a trend toward a fee structure related to services provided rather than a flat 15% based on the value of media purchases.

Related to this trend, there is more interest in media-buying services, as a special fee-based service. Similar services are growing for creative specialists -- fee paid assignments for small creative groups and independent teams of advertising experts working for a client company.

Overall, however, the major trend is toward the self-reliance of the clients to develop and place their own advertising. As a result, many agencies have had a hard time holding their own, let alone growing. The people in the agencies, then, have to become more broadly rounded to maintain strong client relationships.

COMPANY	ADVERTISING SPENDING
1. Procter & Gamble Co.	$274,569,000
2. General Foods Corp.	149,713,000
3. Bristol-Myers Co.	133,822,000
4. American Home Products Corp.	120,576,000
5. General Motors Corp.	103,840,000
6. Lever Brothers Co.	85,722,000
7. Ford Motor Co.	83,264,000
8. Sears, Roebuck & Co.	83,215,000
9. R.J. Reynolds Industries, Inc.	82,056,000
10. Colgate-Palmolive Co.	78,488,000

Source: Advertising Age.

Advertisers And Agencies

A few years ago, an analysis was made of the percentage of advertising expenditures to the sales of the 125 largest advertisers in the United States. Of these companies, only 32 reported they paid out 10% or more of their sales dollar on advertising:

- 17 sold drugs and cosmetics
- 4 sold soaps and cleaners
- 3 sold soft drinks
- 2 sold gum and candy
- 6 were in other fields

Among the products for w which companies spent 5%-10% of their sales dollar on advertising were food products, liquor, cigarettes, and beer.

AGENCIES HELP

Over $26 billion is spent each year by advertisers for services and ads appearing on everything from television to matchbook covers. Ad agencies provide the know-how to get this job done.

Of 650 largest ad agencies, ten control about 40% of all of this spending. These large agencies have the staff and resources needed to serve large accounts that do a lot of advertising.

These large agencies are:

J. Walter Thompson
McCann-Erickson
Young & Rubicam
Leo Burnett & Co.
Ted Bates & Co.
Ogilvy & Mather

BBDO
Doyle Dane Bernbach
Grey Advertising
SSC & B

Agencies such as these are retained by companies to handle particular products. As you can imagine, the competition is keen for accounts.

As noted in the last section, agencies receive a commission based on a percentage of total media costs. Actual charges for agency services vary considerably from one agency to another. Some now charge special fees for research and design work in lieu of or on top of commissions.

Some companies are s setting up their own media buying services and doing their own research and creative work as well.

Advertising is a business of persuasion, and the ad makers are the professionals. There are three major functions served by agencies: research, creative work, and media buying. An agency that provides all of these services is termed "full-service".

RESEARCH

Research involves the planning of the entire advertising campaign, based on data obtained regarding customer attitudes and a thorough understanding of the company and the products.

At J. Walter Thompson research is reflected in a "T Plan" -- "T" stand-ing for "Target". Who is to be reached by the advertising? What is being offered that is different? How is a detergent, for example, different from other detergents? How can the product be best "positioned" in the market?

CREATIVE WORK

This function involves the development of the advertisments themselves, including design of copy, graphics, television scripts, and any other material that must be prepared for the ads. In recent years, advertising has benefited from expansion of humor, satire, animation, and even self-mockery (Avis, Hebrew National, Alka Selzer, Listerine, etc.) Copy today is generally more literate, specific and detailed, graphics more innovative, and productions more lavish than ever before. In many cases the ads are more carefully prepared than the television programs or written copy they interrupt.

MEDIA BUYING

The actual purchase of space in newspapers and magazines, and of time on radio and television is another agency service.

The price of media space varies directly with the size of the audience and other factors. Also, the choice of media depends on the specific audience to be reached and the impact desired. Thus media buying is a specialized task for which an advertiser needs the expert assistance of an agency.

Frequently, agencies also provide specialized counsel and services in public relations --

company communications not restricted to specific products, but concerned with the overall image and reputation of the firm.

Public relations is increasingly important to companies as consumerism and general public attitudes toward business turn more critical. The public needs to have

facts upon which to develop opinions about prices, pollution, alleged monopoly power, excess profits, etc.

The need has grown so rapidly that many agencies specialize in public relations and corporate image services.

Space-Age Spokesman

Leonard Nimoy is now appearing in television ads for the $1.3 billion asset Atlantic Bancorporation, Jacksonville, Fla.

Mr. Nimoy is remembered as the actor who portrayed Mr. Spock, Science Officer of the Starship Enterprise in television's space adventure series, Star Trek. His personal recognition by consumers and the long-standing popularity of the space-age series were pluses for casting him in the role of the bank's principal spokesman introducing Atlantic Bankaround and Atlantic Bankcard -- new computer-based banking services.

"Very early in the planning for Atlantic's entrance into the field of automatic banking, we felt very strongly that the introduction of a totally new service had to be carefully tied to our brand name, Atlantic Bank," said the VP-Marketing of the 31-bank corporation. "Through research, we learned that Florida consumers were interested in 'space-age technology' and how it could improve

"I have here, gentlemen, a personally prepared and signed statement, to be included in all our advertising, declaring that everything we claim to be true is true."

their daily lives."

In addition, consumers responded best to a recognizable spokesman introducing and explaining the new service in a straight-forward and direct manner.

The space-age theme was carried out in a variety of marketing materials, all displaying a galaxy or starry night scene. Advertising copy for television and print media heavily emphasized the term "space-age technology". Mr. Nimoy,

with his strong tie to space and technology, strengthened the message to the Jacksonville area.

The automatic banking system is available around-the-clock to customers at eight suburban shopping center and supermarket locations. Atlantic Bankaround is activated by a magnetically coded plastic card -- Atlantic Bankcard - and a manual registration of a four-digit number known only to the customer.

195 ADVERTISING

How To Make A Brand Popular

Lest alert competitors get advance notice of an upcoming campaign, most television advertisers guard their commercials with CIA-level secrecy between the time the films are shot and the time they go on the air. But this month, Foster Grant Co., which holds some 20% to 22% of the $300-million retail U.S. sunglasses business, proudly began showing off two new TV ads that viewers will not see until next year.

The ads have already been shown to 200 company salesmen and executives. Now they are making the rounds of major customers and buyers who help get Foster Grant sunglasses into 100,000 retail outlets. It is basic to the company's marketing strategy that its customers see the ads early, for it relies on its lavishly produced TV blurbs to convince buyers that Foster Grant sunglasses are superior to those of its primary competitor: Cool-Ray, Inc., a division of American Optical Corp.

Like a producer of bread, milk, or aspirin, Foster Grant sells a product that is inherently similar to its competitors'. Moreover, Cool-Ray, holding a virtually identical share of market, outspends Foster Grant: Television Bureau of Advertising reports that in 1971 Foster Grant bought $1-million worth of TV-network time, while Cool-Ray spent $1.6-million. And while both companies use polarizing lenses in some of their styles, only Cool-Ray can use the magic name, Polaroid, in its advertising.

A decision. Facing such a tough opponent, Foster Grant decided in 1965 to move from a program of exclusively trade advertising to see if consumer advertising could help establish its brand name. It has since doubled its volume in sunglass sales—they now account for about 25% of the giant plastic manufacturer's estimated $110-million gross in fiscal 1972. It did it by creating product differentiation through advertising and styling, by changing the idea of sunglasses-for-protection to sunglasses-as-a-fashion-accessory.

In so doing, Foster Grant has raised the average price per pair of the glasses it sells from $1 in 1965 to around $3.50 today. Thus, while volume has held steady—"around 200,000 gross a year," estimates Harry C. Richards, vice-president for marketing and sales—profits have soared.

After listening to several overly flamboyant Madison Avenue agencies pitch for his tiny account seven years ago, the late Joseph C. Foster settled on Geer, DuBois & Co., Inc. One factor in the decision, says an associate, was agency President Peter Geer's low-key, thoughtful approach to the problem.

The campaign. The deliberations of the youthful Geer (then 33) and those of creative supervisor Rea Brown produced a much-heralded print campaign that used top-name film stars. The stars were photographed in several dif-

'We had a much-talked about campaign, and with little expenditure'

ferent styles of sunglasses. "Is that Raquel Welch behind the Foster Grants?" asked a typical headline.

Full-page ads ran in *Life, TV Guide* and other big-circulation magazines. "The best thing," says Richards, "is that we had a campaign everyone talked about and remembered—with very little expenditure." The ad space cost $1.5-million to $2-million over four years. The "sunglasses of the stars" campaign won important space for Foster Grant displays in stores.

"We still meet people who think they saw the Raquel Welch ad in a recent magazine," says Mauri Edwards, director of marketing and advertising. But the company has not used print ads since 1969 when it switched into TV. Realizing that its budget would not permit a heavy schedule of commercials, it decided to opt for a few memorable spots starring its sunglasses, rather than movie stars.

Geer, DuBois called on Howard Zeiff, a top TV commercials director, who began turning out two or three one-minute ads a year. In *The Sunfighters*, a group of rugged, dirty cowboys outfight a rival gang after adjusting their Foster Grant clip-ons to ward off the desert glare. In *The Coup*, an aide to a South American despot takes over the throne by simply disguising himself with the dictator's sunglasses.

The two new spots now making the rounds are only 30 seconds long, but they pack a punch. In *The Boss*, an attractive young secretary picks up her female employer's sunglasses from a desk and playfully imitates her boss barking orders into a phone—only to be squelched by the boss's sarcastic applause behind her. (For verisimilitude, the agency modeled the office after that of famed ad woman Mary Wells Lawrence). In the second ad, a young boy and girl, fashionably wearing sunglasses indoors, stare lovingly into each other's eyes—for 30 seconds without a word.

Youth market. "The young viewer is who we're after on TV," says Richards. "These are the people who buy more than one pair of glasses a year."

The company's success has persuaded most of its customers to let Foster Grant make the decisions as to which styles will sell, and pre-pack displays accordingly. Six-week tests just getting underway in 150 markets give Foster-Grant the key to which of 50 or 60 new styles should be manufactured for sale next spring. "Such a test three years ago," says Edwards, "tipped us off to the demand for aviator glasses. We got them out first, and the style sold $3-million last year. It may sound chauvinistic, but we did as much for the 'Gloria Steinem look' as she did."

Is That Raquel Welch Behind The Foster Grant's?

'Positioning' Ads:
Why Is Schaefer the One Beer To Have When Having More . . . ?

Secret Is in Ads, Not Brew, And It's Part of Latest Trend on Madison Avenue

A New Name for an Old Idea?

By JONATHAN KWITNY
Staff Reporter of THE WALL STREET JOURNAL

NEW YORK--Ever wonder why Nyquil, the night-time cold medicine, claims to fight the sniffles only after dark, while rival remedies such as Contac and Dristan claim to work all day long? Why Miller's High Life is recommended for leisurely beer-sipping and Schaefer's for big-quantity guzzling, while most other brands claim to be best under any circumstances? Or why Correctol is a "woman's laxative," even though its only two active ingredients are the same ones contained in rival brands recommended for everybody?

According to one theory, disputed in varying degrees by the manufacturers, these products are distinguished less by their inherent features than by the way they are promoted. Nyquil, Miller's, Schaefer's and Correctol are considered prime examples of the latest trend in advertising. It's called positioning. And while some admen say positioning is overrated, and others say it's really old-hat (indeed the Schaefer campaign is 10 years old), almost everyone in the industry is talking about it these days.

Advocates of positioning say the best way to sell a product that isn't already the clear leader in its field is to concentrate on one segment of the market. In other words, rather than struggle head-to-head against dominant brands like Budweiser, Ex-lax and Dristan, a rival product stands a better chance trying to outspecialize the competition. If this means surrendering a large number of potential users

--if Schaefer has to abandon the sippers in order to dominate the guzzlers--so be it.

Of course, if you're clever and first on the spot, you pick the largest available segment of the market to specialize in. For example, women use laxatives more than men, half of all cold suffering occurs at night, and most beer drinkers quaff in quantity.

Having More Than One?

Vick International, which makes Nyquil, and Plough Inc., which makes Correctol, both decline to release figures on how much headway their products have made against the dominant brands. But both are believed to have carved out a profitable niche in the market.

Hunter Finch, the Vick vice president who supervised the development of Nyquil, also declines to say why his product is supposed to work better at night than in the daytime. A Plough spokesman says Correctol is recommended for women because it contains a little less of the same ingredient that powers Ex-lax. But the spokesman acknowledges it's also "a matter of product positioning."

Jim Jordan, vice president of the Batten, Barton, Durstine & Osborn agency, gives a much more explicit account of why he switched Schaefer's advertising campaign from the former, position-less theme of "What do you hear in the best of circles? Schaefer all around" to the current, "Schaefer is the one beer to have when you're having more than one."

"Beer commercials used to be the same as soft-drink commercials," Mr. Jordan says. "There were guys and girls on beaches, swirling around, presenting pilsner glasses to each other." He adds: "We went out and talked to a lot of beer drinkers." And it turned out that "15% of the people of this country drink about 85% of the beer." These 25-to-49-year-old middle-income men routinely down three or four bottles an evening, but they complained that "the flavor seemed to fade a little" as they sloshed further through a six-pack, Mr. Jordan says.

"We thought, gee, we ought to address ourselves to the problem they were talking about." Although Schaefer didn't change its beer formula, the admen found a couple of quirks in the brewing process that they felt would justify a new claim: Schaefer was uniquely designed to taste the same after you were tight as it did when you were stone sober. The result: Lowly Schaefer quickly passed Ballantine, then Rheingold, and now—Mr. Jordan says—it is neck-and-neck with Budweiser as the largest selling beer in the East.

Excedrin or Anacin?

Which doesn't surprise Jack Trout and Al Ries, two New York advertising men who articulated the theory of positioning in three long articles last April and May in Advertising Age, the industry's major trade magazine. "Unless an advertisement is based on a unique idea or position, the message is often put in the mental slot reserved for the leader in the product category," Messrs. Trout and Ries wrote. They cited research showing that "a David Janssen Excedrin commercial was associated with Anacin twice as often as with Excedrin."

The Trout-Ries articles spawned a debate that has raged in Advertising Age and on Madison Avenue ever since. Some critics claim "positioning" is just a new name for an old idea—the Correctol campaign is also nearly 10 years old. One outraged adman dusted off copies of old publications to show that the "soap market was engaging in positioning advertising as early as 1901."

Messrs. Trout and Ries have been accused of gimmickry to bring attention to their own obscure firm (Ries Cappiello Colwell, which ranks 136th among U.S. agencies). The charge may very well be true. But even some of their severest critics concede that Messrs. Ries and Trout have made an impression on the clients of rival firms. "It seems like every time I walk into a guy's office he has those articles on his desk," one member of a major Madison Avenue agency complains.

The articles acknowledged there is sometimes room for a "number two" brand in a product category, but only if the "number two" comes right out and admits it. Examples included not only Avis, the well-known rent-a-car underdog, but Sports Illustrated, which claims to have upped its business and industrial ad lineage 30%-40% since it started calling itself the number three newsweekly instead of the number one sports magazine.

While citing the success stories of Schaefer, Avis and Sports Illustrated, the Trout-Ries articles toure the graveyard of products they say failed for lack of a unique position. Bristol-Myers, they wrote, has "run through millions of dollars trying to launch me-too products against strongly dug-in competition." They

cited F ct, an anticavity toothpaste similar to Procter & Gamble's Crest; Vote, a cosmetic toothpaste launched against P&G's Gleem; and Resolve, a fizzy blahs-battler that couldn't dent Alka-Seltzer. (Bristol-Myers says it doesn't know exactly why the three products failed.)

The largest debacle Messrs. Trout and Ries attribute to poor positioning is the failure of RCA and General Electric in the computer field, where IBM is entrenched. RCA and GE, they say, should have established a beachhead by claiming to specialize in some particular kind of computer associated with their traditional fields of expertise.

"It made little difference how clever the ads of RCA, General Electric and Bristol-Myers were. Or how well the layout, copy and typography were executed. Their strategy of attacking the leaders head-on was wrong," according to Trout-Ries. Better, they say, is Honeywell's position as "the other computer company."

Alka-Seltzer vs. Alka-Seltzer

When a manufacturer enters more than one field, the positionists advise a totally different brand name for each product. Trying to carry a successful brand name from one product line to another dilutes the position, they say. For example, they argue that Miles Laboratories flubbed its entry into the cold tablet derby by naming its tablet Alka-Seltzer Plus, trying to capitalize on the $20 million a year Miles was spending to promote Alka-Seltzer. "Lo and behold," Messrs. Trout and Ries wrote, "instead of eating into the Dristan and Contac market, the new product turns around and eats into the Alka-Seltzer market."

The same mistake, they said, cost Scott Paper its preeminence in certain product lines. "The housewife could write, 'Charmin, Kleenex, Bounty and Pampers' on her shopping list and know exactly what products she was going to get. 'Scott' on a shopping list has no meaning. The name 'Scott' exists in limbo," they said.

When a competitor has established a solid position, Messrs. Trout and Ries advise adopting a contrary position. Mr. Trout, for example, argues that United Air Lines has monopolized the friendliness position. So rival American Airlines, he says, should abandon the vacationer to United and appeal to the businessman with a speedy, no-nonsense approach. He says American's current advertisements go partway, but not far enough, toward the man-in-a-hurry position. "American's afraid they'll give up too many trips to Disneyland," he says. "They want to have their cake and eat it too."

Sometimes a manufacturer creates a product to fill a predetermined position, as Plough did with Correctol. Other times, as with Schaefer, the advertising agency develops a position after the product already exists. Sometimes a product outgrows its position. Gillette created Right Guard as the man's deodorant; research showed wives and kids were using it, too, so the ad campaign turned 180 degrees and Right Guard became a family deodorant.

Positioning alone can't guarantee success. No-Cal seemed to have a strong position as the first diet cola, but when competition developed, No-Cal lacked bottling and distribution facilities to fight Tab (a Coca-Cola product) and Diet Pepsi. Gablinger's seemed to have a strong position as the first diet beer, but it tasted awful.

The Champ: P&G

But positionists say their theories work when all other things are equal. And they also say that all other things usually are equal. In fact, the whole notion of positioning seems to rest on a belief that competing products are similar. The old days, "when advertising people focused their attention on product features and customer benefits," have been washed away in a deluge of "me-too products," say Messrs. Trout and Ries. The positionists predict that marketing in the 1970s will be dominated by companies that compete with themselves by launching multiple entries in the same product class, each advertised to appeal to a particular psychological type of buyer.

"Any manufacturer who actively, aggressively and continually promotes two or more functionally equivalent brands is run by people who know how to position products," wrote management consultant Jack Springer, joining the fray in Ad Age.

The company most admired by the positionists in this respect is Procter & Gamble. "P&G makes seven or eight soap products for washing machines," Mr. Springer says. "Sometimes they say you should use a tablet, sometimes a liquid, sometimes a powder. The function of them all is to get your clothes clean in a washing machine." Messrs. Trout and Ries marvel over how "Tide makes clothes 'white,' Cheer makes them 'whiter than white,' and Bold makes them 'bright.' Although the advertising for each Procter & Gamble brand might vary from year to year, it never departed from its pre-assigned role or position," they say.

Mr. Springer elaborates: "These products may have different ingredients, more phosphorescents or whatever, but that's not what people buy. They buy the image, or positioning. I contend that blindfolded consumers couldn't tell the difference between Marlboros, Benson & Hedges and Virginia Slims (all Philip Morris Inc. cigarets), or between Busch Bavarian,

Budweiser and Michelob (all Anheuser-Busch beers). They're buying the position.

Understanding Your Cigaret

"Marlboro is a masculine cigaret. Benson & Hedges is for people who want to feel guilty about smoking and want to lessen their guilt—it's positioned as being fun. And Virginia Slims is for the segment of people who happen to be female and who also think of themselves as being *au courant,* or modern. This brand of cigarets says, 'If that's the way you feel, this brand is for you. Wear it like a badge.' " In beer, Mr. Springer says, Busch Bavarian is for people who want to be athletic, Michelob is for people who want to look and feel rich, and Budweiser is the dominant beer brand.

"I can think of lots of other (examples), but they happen to be my clients," adds Mr. Springger, a partner in The First Team Inc., a marketing consulting firm. He says his clients include General Foods Corp., Reynolds Metals, Brown & Williamson Tobacco and Miles Laboratories, among others.

James Morgan, assistant director of brand management for Philip Morris, says he "wouldn't basically disagree" with Mr. Springer. Mr. Morgan acknowledges that the cigaret industry is "dependent on advertising to separate brands. Cigarets basically look the same." As for what's in them, Mr. Morgan says he doesn't know. "There are only two or three people in the entire company who know exactly what's in the product. That's very competitive information," he says.

Procter & Gamble declines to comment, and Anheuser Busch hasn't responded to an inquiry.

Perhaps the greatest tribute to positioning's importance is the growing number of advertising agencies that claim to have discovered the theory. Neal W. O'Conner, president of N. W. Ayer & Son, said in a recent newspaper article that the "Ayer New Product Model" blazed the positioning trail long before Messrs. Trout and Ries did.

And Ogilvy & Mather, a large New York agency, bought full-page advertisements in several publications, including this one, earlier this year, in which founder David Ogilvy stated:

"We have learned that the effect of your advertising on your sales depends more on this decision than on any other: How should you position your product? . . . In Germany, Sanella Margarine has been advertised for years as a table spread. We repositioned it as a superior cooking margarine. . . . A 13-year share decline was arrested four months after the repositioning. Sales turned up dramatically."

Coke's Formula: Keep The Image Fresh

Ira "Ike" Herbert, vice-president of advertising for Coca-Cola Co., enjoys leading visitors to his office window overlooking Atlanta and asking them to count the Coke signs they can see. "There are 11 signs down there," he says. "But most people can find only two or three, and they know what they are looking for. In our way, we have become a part of the environment. The

Despite its success, the giant soft-drink maker is changing its pitch

public is so accustomed to seeing Coke that it literally isn't seeing it."

In the next few weeks, if you could peer out of Ike Herbert's window, you would see 11 eye-catching Coke signs that will be both distinctly different and visible. They will be part of a giant image renovation that the 83-year-old company has undertaken to help fizz up its sales and to maintain its commanding leadership and momentum in the $5-billion soft-drink industry.

Coca-Cola's facelift—dubbed "Project Arden," after Elizabeth Arden cosmetics—comes at a time when the industry is quaking with change. Private label brands are spurting ahead in sales, and promise to give Coke and other national brands some fierce competition. With the growing trend toward cans and other one-way containers, franchised bottlers are also up against a sharp rise in costs. Largely as a result, more and more of them are merging, and what has long been an industry of local operations is now consolidating and becoming more regional. At the same time, the market itself is going the other way and increasingly fragmenting—by race, ethnic background, geography, and age. This, in turn, creates new challenges for soft drink makers who must come up with catchy slogans and campaigns that appeal to a national audience.

Perhaps the greatest challenge of all is coming up with a slogan or campaign that keeps appealing month after month and year after year—when the fact is that modern communications and its saturation of the market has steadily reduced the life expectancy of any campaign. "And as major campaigns get shorter and shorter," says J. Paul Austin, president and chief execu-

tive officer of Coca-Cola Co., "your costs must inevitably go up."

In Coke's own case, "Project Arden" came six years after the company kicked off its previous big campaign—built around the slogan, "Things Go Better with Coke." The new campaign goes much further, and incorporates a whole new look. The company will retain only the "Coca-Cola" script and "Coke" trademarks, the bright red color long associated with Coke, and its famous, green hobble-skirt bottle. Coca-Cola introduced these specific changes:

- A new slogan, "The Real Thing—Coke," replaced "Things Go Better with Coke." The old slogan thus joins 73 other retirees, including the famous "The Pause that Refreshes," and some lesser-known, better-forgotten cre-

ations, such as "Enjoy a Glass of Liquid Laughter."
- A new graphic image features a flowing white ribbon underscoring the "Coca-Cola" and "Coke" trademarks, and suggests the curve of a Coke bottle.
- All Coke signs will be standardized and limited to two colors—red and white. Heretofore, they assumed hundreds of shapes, colors, and designs.

Today, of course, scores of companies are changing their image. But none of

them has an image quite as indelible, and thus as challenging to change, as that of Coca-Cola. Since that historic day in 1886 when pharmacist John Pemberton came up with his famous formula and then spent $46 for a sign that said "Drink Coca-Cola," the Atlanta company has grown into the General Motors of the soft drink industry.

Under 54-year-old Austin, Coca-Cola Co. runs the world's second largest truck fleet (after the U. S. Post Office), the world's largest retail sales force, and one of the world's largest franchise systems, consisting of 1,700 bottlers. Coke alone controls 34% of the soft-drink market, and the company's com-

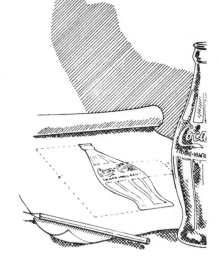

the pause that refreshes

plete line of 17 soft drinks runs its share to 41.3%, a bigger hunk than its next six competitors combined. Besides its carbonated beverages, which represent 75% of its business, Coca-Cola has also become the world's largest producer of private-label instant coffees and teas, as well as the world's biggest processor and marketer of citrus concentrates and drinks. All told, the empire added up to $1.3-billion in sales last year, with profits of $121-million—more than twice those of its nearest rival.

New look. Around company headquarters in Atlanta, however, it is clear that Coke is the principal fuel that drives the company engine, and Coca-Cola executives look to their new marketing strategy to provide a fresh, high-octane boost. The brainchild of Lippincott & Margulies, Inc., a New York industrial designer, Coke's image change is designed, to "position the product" in the coming decade. The mood and momentum of the country, as Coke executives read it, is toward "relevance" and vital "life-styles," and that is what "The Real Thing" is supposed to signify.

Obviously, the new slogan is open to more mundane interpretations. It could be taken as a direct slap at PepsiCo, Inc., No. 2 in the field, and Royal Crown and 7-Up, the distant third and fourth. Coke was the first to make it big in the soft-drink league, and the feeling is unanimous among company executives that other soft drinks are only imitations. "I want to say in a statesmanlike manner that, yes, we're being mean," concedes Richard D. Harvey, vice-president of marketing. "We're building on the work a lot of people have done in the past 83 years, and that does not call for us to relinquish our place in the market. Let me say that we're not going to be anybody's patsy." In fact, industry figures show that Coke—despite its proportionately larger sales base—is growing at a faster percentage rate than most of its competitors (charts), and is steadily increasing its share of the market roughly 1.5% a year.

Whatever the slogan does or does not mean, it will get heavier and heavier exposure in months to come. The bulk of the company's $75-million to $100-million advertising budget will go into television promotion of "The Real Thing." Special messages will be keyed to specific audiences. In the Midwest, the camera will zoom in on barns, open farmland, and

picket fences. In larger metropolitan areas, viewers will see the swinging side of city life. On the radio, youth commercials will carry more of a rock beat than before. Others will range from Sousa-like oompahs to Broadway musical-type orchestrations. And all

world's landscape. Herbert says he does not even like to think of the mammoth job ahead. He estimates that it will take four to five years to make the complete change. No one will even guess at the total expense. "The cost to the company and the bottlers is something we don't know," Herbert admits. "It costs more to put a sign up than to tear one down. We do know that. And,

	Rank		Millions of cases		Share of market	
1969	1966	Brand	1969	1968	1969	1968
1	1	Coca-Cola	1,390	1,250	34.0%	32.6%
2	2	Pepsi-Cola	575	550	14.1	14.3
3	3	7-Up	237	211	5.8	5.5
4	4	Royal Crown Cola	147	140	3.6	3.7
5	5	Dr. Pepper	120	107	2.9	2.8
6	8	Sprite	90	78	2.2	2.0
7	6	Diet Rite Cola	89	100	2.2	2.6
8	7	Fresca	60	80	1.5	2.1
9	9	Diet Pepsi	57	65	1.4	1.7
10	—	Canada Dry Ginger Ale	43	40	1.1	1.0

Top 10 drinks

Data: Soft Drink Industry Magazine

of them, says Austin, will reflect Coke's awareness of minority and other social sensitivities by stressing the product rather than people.

While all this is going on, Coca-Cola bottlers, who will bear the brunt of the broader changeover cost, will be repainting their trucks and replacing the 2-million or so Coke signs that fill the

to be honest, no one knows where all the signs are."

Policy. Behind the change of theme and image is a long-time company policy. One Coke executive describes it simply as "quitting while you're ahead." Says Charles W. Adams, senior vice president, "We have always switched themes while they

"I'd like to buy the world a home
And furnish it with love;
Grow apple trees and honey bees,
And snow white turtle doves.

"I'd like to teach the world to sing
In perfect harmony;
I'd like to buy the world a Coke,
And keep it company."

were at their peak. We are continually weighing the effectiveness of our advertising. As the consumer changes, we change."

At a far subtler level, the image change is also part of a growing recognition that Coca-Cola faces stiff competition, and that it is bound to get stiffer. That awareness began to dawn in the mid-1950s when Coca-Cola's share of the market suddenly started slipping after Royal Crown and PepsiCo introduced family-sized bottles. Reluctantly, Coca-Cola stopped relying on its classic, wasp-waisted 6½-oz bottle, and began offering family-sized bottles as well. From there, the company went on to cans and a variety of other containers, including a 2-gal. keg with spigots, designed to fit into the family refrigerator.

Coca-Cola also began diversifying into new beverages. It brought out the Fanta line of flavored soft drinks, then Sprite, a lemon-lime drink competing with 7-Up and PepsiCo's Teem. It began producing ginger ale, soda water, and quinine water. It bought Minute Maid Corp. and started selling orange juice and other citrus blends.

Amid all this diversification, Coca-Cola was again brought up

short in 1961 when Royal Crown and PepsiCo introduced diet colas to the world—one of the hottest developments ever to hit the soft-drink market. Not until two years later did Coke finally follow with Tab, a diet soft drink that never moved higher than third place, an unusual spot for any Coke product. Coca-Cola followed Tab with another sugar-free drink, Fresca—though held off promoting it as a diet drink, figuring that one in the house was enough. "At that time," says one Coke executive, referring to the early 1960s, "we had some serious problems—one of them being that Coke did not recognize that it indeed has aggressive competitors who are talented. We finally got off our duff and decided that it was a competitive world after all."

Slim pickings. Just how competitive, Coca-Cola discovered when the government moved against cyclamates six months ago. Diet sodas then accounted for $420-million a year in retail sales and fully 15% of the carbonated soft-drink market. And all three leaders—Coca-Cola, PepsiCo, and Royal Crown—felt the lash.

Hardest hit was Royal Crown's Diet Rite, which had 24.1% of the diet-drink market and accounted for 25% of Royal Crown's total business. Before the year was out, according to *Soft Drink In-*

dustry Magazine, Diet Rite sales slumped 11%. Because of this and other internal problems, Royal Crown's earnings plunged from $5.3-million in 1968 to $1.7-million in 1969. PepsiCo, which accounted for 15.4% of the diet-drink market, saw Diet Pepsi sales plunge 12.3% for the year.

Ironically, it was Coca-Cola that suffered the biggest percentage plunge of all. Tab, which had a bare 10.8% of the diet market, dropped 33.3% in sales. And Fresca fell 25%, even though it was never billed as a diet drink. Coke officials still have high hopes for Fresca, and claim that it is weathering the transition from a cyclamate to a non-cyclamate beverage.

The bottlers. As part of its effort at a look-ahead strategy, Coca-Cola is also trying to effect another transition of sorts. It is encouraging consolidation among its 867 domestic bottlers—all but a handful of whom, like their more than 800 counterparts abroad, are independent businessmen who buy syrup or concentrate from Colca-Cola Co., mix it with carbonated water, and then distribute the finished drink in their exclusive franchise territories. Right now, many of these bottlers are feeling a profit pinch, which can only get worse as they begin forking out money to replace all those Coke signs and repaint all those trucks. The danger, of course, is that the squeeze might ripple back to Coca-Cola itself.

In the good old days when the returnable bottle was king, the bottler could make a fortune—and often did. His problems began when nonreturnable bottles and cans came along in the early 1960s, and sharply raised his costs. Today, 40% or more of soft-drink beverages are sold in one-way containers. The result is that smaller bottlers are being forced to shave their profits, while larger, more efficient companies such as General Tire & Rubber Co., Westinghouse Electric Corp., Rheingold Corp., and General Cinema Corp. are moving deeper into the market. From a peak of 8,000 bottling plants a few years ago, there are now only 3,500. And of these remaining plants, some 450, or slightly more than 10% of the total, do more than two-thirds of the industry's volume. "The ones which remain," says Richard A. Smith, president of General Cinema, now the country's second largest Pepsi bottler, "will be larger, sell more and a greater variety of products, and will be more efficient as well as more profitable." In the last two years, General Cinema has spent $38-million to acquire 17 bottling plants covering five major marketing regions.

Private labels. At the same time, franchise bottlers of all sizes face growing competition from private soft-drink brands sold by the large supermarket chains. So far, private brands represent slightly over 1% of total soft-drink sales, but they are expanding steadily. Last year alone, according to *Soft Drink Industry Magazine*, Kroger Co.'s Big K brand jumped 24% in sales, A&P's Yukon moved ahead 30.8%, and Safeway Stores' Cragmont finished 30% higher.

To sharpen the competitive edge of its franchise bottlers, Coca-Cola would naturally like to see them consolidate into larger, regional organizations. The hitch is Coca-Cola's franchising agreement, which dates back almost to the dawn of the company. Unlike several other soft drink franchisers, Coca-Cola cannot cancel a franchise if the bottler does not suit the company, nor can Coca-Cola buy back a contract without the consent of the bottler. A Coke franchise is an iron-clad, perpetual agree-

---

The company cannot revoke a franchise even if a bottler doesn't suit it

---

ment. What Coca-Cola has attempted to do, therefore, is encourage its bottlers to merge and consolidate, and in the past 10 years it has managed to cut the number of domestic franchises from 1,000 to the present 867. "This year," says one Coke executive, "we went a step further than just urging, and established a specific department within the company to assist in mergers and consolidations."

New directions. For the future, Austin sees several other important new growth areas for Coca-Cola. One of them is in water treatment and pollution control. Next month, the company's stockholders and those of Aqua-Chem, Inc., a $30-million manufacturer of pollution control equipment and steam and hot water generators, will vote on a merger of the two companies. Under the merger agreement, already approved by the company boards, Aqua-Chem would become a wholly-owned subsidiary of Coca-Cola. Fred W. Dickson, president of Coca-Cola USA, the company's American division, feels Aqua-Chem is a logical move for Coca-Cola. "After all," he says, "we've been in the water-technology business longer than anyone else. It is only natural that we expand in this area."

Closer to home, Coca-Cola is also at work on another facet of pollution control—the roadside blight created by nonreturnable containers. As one possible solution, Coca-Cola is experimenting in New England with a new plastic bottle that incinerates without causing smoke or fumes, or can be dumped into any home disposal unit. PepsiCo is conducting similar experiments in Las Vegas. "The question that remains," says Austin, "is that one big one—will the consumer go for plastic?" In the likelihood that he will not, Coca-Cola is experimenting with glass-crushing machines and also plans to launch a campaign to bring back returnable containers. It will carry the slogan: "Wouldn't you rather borrow our bottle than buy it?"

The slogan does not have quite the snap or catchy ring of "The Real Thing." But as they are wont to say around Coca-Cola headquarters: "Give it time."

WHAZZIT?

ADVERTISING

Any form of communication through the various media used to present information about goods and services to the public and to induce the public to buy.

MEDIA

The instrument used to get the advertising message to the consumers. For examples, newspapers and televisions are media.

CATALOG

A listing of articles that a company is offering for sale (often illustrated) including descriptions of the articles and the prices. The catalog is usually used in mail-order sales operations.

F.T.C.

The Federal Trade Commission. A five-member board charged with investigating any illegal activities involving interstate commerce. Fraudulant advertising falls in this category, and the agency can force the offender to stop what he is doing or impose other penalties.

A Splash of Whimsy

FIRST they called it Bib-Label Lith-iated Lemon-Lime Soda. A year later, in 1930, they renamed it 7-Up. In private, some skeptics at the company's St. Louis headquarters dubbed it "holy water," poking fun at its alleged medicinal and curative virtues and the seriousness with which they were taken. By the mid-Sixties, however, solemnity seemed out-of-date. Seven-Up's sales and earnings were growing because the soft drink market was growing here and abroad. But the market share was shrinking: U.S. food store sales, 7-Up's biggest market, were 7.2% of the market in 1965, fell to 6.7% in 1966 and to 6.2% in 1967. It was a passive kind of situation: Seven-Up was being carried along by the momentum of the market rather than by its own efforts.

Ben Wells, who became president and chief executive officer in 1965, decided to go over to the offensive. He felt he needed an image change. Seven-Up should be fun. It also should deal frankly with the problem that the soft drink business was fast becoming a cola business. In 1968 his advertising agency, J. Walter Thompson, came up with a slogan and 7-Up became the Uncola.

For the first time 7-Up wasn't slinking around but was offering itself as a true alternative to cola. Things started to move. Earnings per share climbed from 29 cents in 1966 to $1 in 1971, and in the first six months of 1972 jumped another 22%.

Once an English teacher at a St. Louis prep school, Ben Wells went to work in Seven-Up's advertising department after marrying the daughter of one of the founders. When he became president in 1965 he commissioned a study that showed a problem of definition. "People were buying 7-Up for indigestion, as a mixer, for little children off their feed," says Wells. "Our problem was we weren't a soft drink."

Now that it is accepted as a soft drink, Seven-Up still has a problem. It spends $24 million a year, 22% of sales, on advertising and promotion. No major soft drink company spends that high a percentage, and yet Seven-Up's money is a drop in the barrel by comparison with what Coca-Cola or Pepsi-Cola spend. To make sure of getting noticed amidst all this advertising flash and din, Seven-Up leans heavily on humor and whimsy.

By gently poking fun at its own image —in everything from its annual reports to its TV spots—Seven-Up has built a distinct image. It also has built its stock to a price/earnings ratio of 45.

The moral is: If you can't be big, be different.

Think Negative. **Ben Wells' new Uncola approach reversed 7-Up's market slide.**

Chevron's F-310 Gas: How Not To Promote A Product

SAN FRANCISCO—Standard Oil Co. of California, as the biggest industrial company based here and the fifth largest oil company in the country, isn't accustomed to attacks by its local Better Business Bureau.

Early in 1970, however, Charles R. Thurber, BBB executive vice president in San Francisco, wrote a private letter to the company chiding it for its promotion of F-310, a gasoline additive. Mr. Thurber recalls that he warned Standard that the additive "seemed to promise a miracle" in reducing air pollution—particularly in a now-famous television commercial featuring Astronaut Scott Carpenter.

In the ad, Mr. Carpenter shows how a plastic bag attached to a car's exhaust pipe fills with black smoke before using F-310. The car's gas tank is subsequently filled six times with Standard's Chevron gasoline, containing F-310, and the bag appears to be crystal clear.

"We suggested that Standard play down the black bag bit," Mr. Thurber says. He adds that the company politely agreed to consider the idea and gave him a tour of its Chevron Research Co. laboratories. Following the tour, Mr. Thurber says, he was convinced California Standard could "substantiate its ad claims."

But a number of persons are not convinced. In the 13 months since Standard began its televised trumpeting of F-310's virtues, a succession of news stories has noted critical response from powerful quarters, including, among others, the Federal Trade Commission.

Firm Vows to Fight

The FTC has charged in a proposed complaint that F-310 advertising is deceptive and fraudulent. Moreover, the commission has made it clear it considers the case a key one in which it will seek to establish a novel penalty: An order requiring that all Chevron ads for one year devote 25% of their print space or 25% of their air time to proclaiming the falsity of original F-310 ads.

Perhaps even more significant for Standard —and for industry in general—is the fact that a number of conservationists consider the promotion of F-310 to be corporate exploitation of public concern about the environment. At least two private suits—as class actions on behalf of the public—have been filed against the company seeking to halt F-310 advertising. And the Sierra Club, a prominent and powerful conservationist organization, hints it may also file a legal action.

California Standard has responded by intensifying its advertising and vowing to fight the FTC charges. Chairman Otto Miller, in fact, told San Francisco security analysts recently that F-310 is "an exceptional breakthrough in gasoline technology," and has been "an outstanding success in the market." Standard, Mr. Miller said, has "extensive, documented evidence" of F-310's effectiveness, which it will use "in court, if necessary."

How Not to Promote a Product

The case against F-310, of course, is far from proven. Indeed, many sources agree that the additive does appear to work, albeit to a modest degree, in reducing emissions of two key pollutants: Unburned hydrocarbons and carbon monoxide. While Standard's most extensive test to demonstrate this reduction has been called flawed, most scientists familiar with the experiment say it was more careful than similar research by other oil companies.

Nevertheless, an examination of F-310's evolution and history to date suggests that California Standard may be hard-pressed to defend every aspect of its additive. And while much of the controversy clouding the substance's introduction and promotion has been previously aired, a careful study of the F-310 saga seems to illustrate how not to promote a new product.

The story of F-310 begins in 1968, when Chevron Research came up with a gummy substance described as a polybutene amine. The new substance, Chevron scientists say, seemed to have an unusual ability to dissolve or prevent deposits that clog carburetors, intake systems and certain automotive valves. The additive was then given to Scott Research Laboratories Inc., an independent auto-testing concern, for further experimentation.

Scott ran 13 cars—all containing Chevron with polybutene amine, which the company had dubbed F-310—on a 17-mile city-and-country driving course. The results were impressive: After less than 2,000 miles of driving, each car was said to have shown a dramatic decline in exhaust emissions.

Armed with the Scott results, along with additional observations of certain taxi fleets using F-310, California Standard on Dec. 18, 1969, unveiled what it termed a "revolutionary" new product. The Scott tests, a press release declared, demonstrated how F-310, under "typical city driving conditions," could reduce unburned hydrocarbons by "more than 50%."

The Criticism Begins

So far, so good. California Standard, however, neglected to inform newsmen and prospective consumers that cars used in its F-310 tests had been artificially "dirtied up" by using a specially formulated low-quality gasoline supplied by Chevron. Furthermore, it was soon noted by critics that Scott Research didn't compare Chevron with F-310 with competitive gasolines.

By March 1970, less then three months after F-310's introduction, California Standard had become a target for conservationists and government agencies. An official of the Los Angeles Clean Air Council called F-310 promotion "misrepresentative" and "a false advertising campaign." And the Federal Trade Commission, among others, began studying California Standard's claims.

Particularly enraging some television viewers were props used in F-310 ads. "They purposely confused what air pollution is all about," says the Sierra Club's Mr. Berry, citing the "black bag" commercial. The bag, Mr. Berry asserts, is black because it's full of carbon particles from an abnormally dirty car. But these particles are a minor part of air pollution, he says, and the "clear" bag is full of invisible pollutants—including hydrocarbons and carbon monoxide.

Another advertising prop that soon came under fire was an "air-pollution meter" that registered "90" for Brand X and swung back to "20" for Chevron with F-310. Critics noted the numbers on the dial weren't explained and therefore meant nothing. Moreover, they said a reduction from 90 to 20 was nearly 80%—far more than the emission reduction indicated by published F-310 tests.

Criticism shortly became more concrete. In May, the California Air Resources Board issued research findings that cast doubt on the value of F-310. Use of the additive, the state agency said, didn't result in any "significant changes in the emission of pollutants." In fact, one of the board's studies found that cars using F-310 released slightly more unburned hydrocarbons than cars using other brands. The F-310 cars, however, released slightly less carbon monoxide.

The Rose Bowl Test

California Standard's rebuttal was lengthy and well publicized. The state tests, the company said, didn't use F-310 for a sufficient period of time. The company's big barrage, however, came in August when it released the results of experimentation subsequently christened the "Rose Bowl Test."

The Rose Bowl test began and ended in Pasadena's famed stadium and was duly chronicled in the press. Regulatory officials, FTC representatives and newsmen were informed that California Standard and an independent testing laboratory had experimented with 455 cars of all ages and makes. Each car's driver left the Rose Bowl with a Chevron credit card and returned 2,000 miles later. And when they returned, the company said, the cars were averaging 13.9% less hydrocarbons and 11.6% carbon monoxide than when they started.

The Rose Bowl Test was also criticized. For one thing, some researchers said, California Standard didn't use a control group of test cars with other gasoline brands. And the Air Resources Board subsequently said that almost one-third of the cars tested emitted more, rather than less, pollutants after using F-310. "There are so many loose ends," complains Frank Bonamassa, a board official.

Whom can one believe? A state senate committee in Hawaii has chosen not to believe California Standard, and last year, after bitter public hearings, criticized the company's ad claims for F-310. The FTC, meanwhile, isn't commenting on its investigation, but it's believed the agency is focusing on anti-pollution claims of all kinds from all companies. California Standard, however, is the only company yet named by the FTC for making possibly misleading clean-air claims.

Some Embarrassment

California Standard, in the face of such consistently heavy criticism, hasn't remained entirely unmoved. "They've backed off in some of their claims," says an Air Resources Board official. And the company was clearly embarrassed when the FTC complained a building labeled "Chevron Research Center" in an F-310 ad was, in fact, the Palm Springs courthouse.

Whatever the outcome, the year-long brouhaha will undoubtedly leave its mark. Even granting that F-310 is beneficial, California Standard's promotion of the additive—with early factual omissions and later corrections—has if nothing else, served to confuse the public.

But Frank Fenton, assistant advertising manager for California Standard, is philosophical. "We don't think the public is misled by F-310 advertising," he says. "In our professional judgment, we think the public understands no product is a cure-all for everything. Obviously, no one really thinks the guy using a certain advertised deodorant is going to get all those pretty girls because of the deodorant."

Sears Merchant To Millions

At Sears, the catalog has always been the number-one promotion tool. At the turn of the century, when Sears was predominantly a mail-order house supplying the needs of farmers across the country, the catalog was the only means of communicating with buyers. This was true not only for Sears but for its competitors, including Wards.

When the 1902 catalog was published, Sears was not among the largest firms of its type and was much less widely recognized than Wards. The aggressive approach used by Sears in this 1100-page paperback put Sears in the number one position, where it has remained ever since. Other companies gave their catalog away free, but Sears charged 50¢, a high price at that time. What made it worth it to the customers? Sears made the catalog very personal -- with anecdotes, household hints, comments on the merchandise, and general editorial comments. To the readers he argued that the 50¢ charged made lower prices for merchandise possible.

Famous in catalog history is the plan Richard Sears used to put his wish books into the hands of thousands of potential customers. In 1905 Sears wrote to the company's best customers in Iowa, asking each to distribute twenty-four catalogs among friends and neighbors. The customers sent Sears the names of the people who received the catalogs. When these people, in turn, sent in orders, the original customers received premiums for their work. A stove, perhaps, or a bicycle, or a sewing machine. With success in Iowa, the system was applied in other states.

In 1902, before "Iowaization," approximately 600,000 copies of the spring catalog were distributed. In 1905, after Iowaization had started, more than 2 million copies of the spring catalog went to potential customers. Little wonder Sears spring catalog, in 1907, could say: "We will forfeit ten thousand dollars ($10,000) in cash to any worthy charity if anyone can prove that any other five (5) catalog houses in the

Today you can order from Sears catalogs direct by mail, by telephone, or in person at order desks of retail stores, catalog sales offices, and independent catalog merchants.

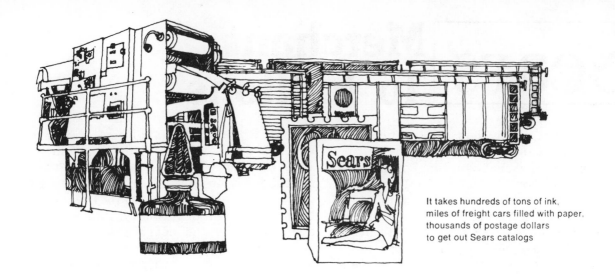

It takes hundreds of tons of ink,
miles of freight cars filled with paper,
thousands of postage dollars
to get out Sears catalogs

United States, selling general merchandise exclusively to the consumer, the same as we do, can show combined sales for the twelve months ending July 30, 1907, aggregating as much as $53,188,901."

As people moved to the cities in the decades that followed, Sears relied less on mail-order sales and turned to retail stores. Advertising continued to emphasize the company's strong identification with its customers and the importance of product value for price. Steadfast adherence to a policy of customer satisfaction is a factor believed to have been significant throughout Sears' history.

The catalog, of course, is an important promotion tool even today. It brings in a steady 22% of Sears' total sales volume, and the major fall and spring "wish books" go to 12 million families. There are about 1700 relatively small catalog, retail, and telephone sales offices around the country, as well as a catalog desk in every store. There are executives at Sears, as in other retail businesses, who see catalogs adaptable to the future, fitting perfectly into the future of at-home electronic shopping.

The balance, and majority of Sears' advertising is devoted to newspapers and magazines. Like most retailers, Sears uses radio and television to a lesser extent (less than 5% of its budget in 1968), although there is a trend toward greater use of these media.

In recent years, Sears has aimed its advertising toward the higher income and more youthful (21-35 year old group) market through advertising programs and adaptation of its product line and store decor. You may have noted its fashion-oriented series of ads in PLAYBOY, expansion of fashions and home furnishings in its stores, and extensive redecoration in many of its stores to appeal to this group of customers.

The Corporate Image And NBC's 'N'

By WALTER LANDOR

We must break through with new directions in expressing corporate image.

When a major broadcasting network produces a logotype similar in design to one developed by a small television station in Nebraska and a bank in Kentucky, it's not too difficult to see how the viability of the entire design profession could be questioned.

The focus of attention, however, primarily has been on trademark research and seemingly high overall costs. It has not centered on what I feel are the real problems brought out by National Broadcasting Company's embarrassment, a greater understanding of which would lend enormous perspective to the role of corporate visual communications today.

Lacking this perspective, it seems to me many business leaders' instinctive suspicion of creative people in all fields would appear to be warranted.

Actually, the NBC logo controversy may be a blessing in disguise as now the need for renewed dedication to the expression of corporate uniqueness becomes apparent.

Uniqueness can only be portrayed effectively by reflecting a corporation's true personality. This character cannot be fabricated. Personality, in most cases, can be discovered only after thorough research and analysis; examination of heritage and equity already existing in present design system; avoidance of abstract symbology lacking meaning; and dedicated effort on the part of designers skilled in both artistic and psychological communications.

Absolutely vital is a mutual commitment on the part of design firms and clients to expend sufficient energy and funds to execute a total design system rather than relying merely on a symbol.

It has been the lack of both orientation and dedication to portraying corporate personality that has led to an environment which, if not changed, will produce more NBC-type problems.

Also manifest in this environment has been a tendency, since the early 1970's, to follow design fads—to be 'trendy' instead

Business personality is best expressed through a total design program—rather than simple reliance on a 'trendy' symbol.

of concentrating on expressing corporate uniqueness. The best of all executions, in any communications attempt, is useless if the basic concept is not on target. Corporate symbolism, beyond just identifying, must trigger positive response and be appropriate to expressing the corporate purpose.

The void of personality that has formed today is leading to a kind of corporate unisex. This is reflected in an unfortunate sameness, a condition we see everywhere: hotel rooms, supermarkets, airplanes; even television commercials!

Corporate unisex dates back to the mid-1950's when companies first tried, en masse, to personify themselves through the use of initials as indentifiers, emulating I.B.M., G.E., PPG, and other well-established abbreviations. It didn't take long for alphabet soup to emerge.

Emphasis later shifted toward highly abstract symbolism. In this fad, many designers and clients literally threw away the corporation's past and denied themselves benefits of equity built from images used previously. The NBC peacock may be an example of this.

Subsequently, some designers began to discover the value of "wordmarks"—conversions of actual company names into symbolism — and "tie-lines" — well-chosen image-building phrases, positioned near the wordmarks.

Yet, with abstract symbolism still predominating—much of it lacking feeling—it becomes easy to see how a major network and design firm, both of which, I'm sure, were determined to develop a very basic new corporate mark, could have arrived at symbology so vulnerable.

What may have happened at NBC was that out of probably hundreds of logotypes shown, the design firm and the corporation mutually hypnotized themselves into believing the simple geometric shape of the "N" to be a unique, protectable mark, which of course, it was not.

Secondly, the N, rather than NBC, is somewhat defensible when visual tie-ins with local stations are considered. The N probably was thought to be abstract enough to bear juxtaposition with other letters and names without causing visual confusion.

On cost, I doubt if NBC paid the reported high price for a symbol alone. This price is far above price-value relationship standards in the design profession and is completely non-competitive. Further, it is highly unlikely NBC would be so unsophisticated that it would accept such services without full understanding of market values in design. Clearly, the cost must have covered a total design communication system involving numerous applications throughout the corporate structure.

I feel strongly that the NBC situation proves abstract symbolism, however pure, is a risky road on which to travel in the future. The airlanes of visual communications are already overcrowded and the more totally abstract — and meaningless — symbolism is used the more danger exists of similarity, overlap into others' visual expression, and lack of ultimate effectiveness.

Within every corporation, there are well-defined resources available to be tapped in order to put across, visually, a unique message to that corporation's various publics (customers, potential customers, financial community, top management, and employees), in spite of the fierce competition for attention today. A major challenge to business, therefore, is to derive maximum benefits, over a period of years, from the vast marketing potential inherent in effective visual communications.

In our profession, the best talent, whatever the cost, usually proves to be the best value in the long run. Our work is affecting billions of dollars of communications and there is no question that many of the world's companies envision corporate image - building through identity systems as being essential for their growth.

I have seen too many boards of directors approve too many major investments in new and periodically improved corporate identity systems to make the design business one of ego massaging.

Industry today, as never before, is realizing design-inspired benefits through improved cost savings, greater efficiencies and more accurately reflected images to various publics. With far-flung enterprises, increasing steadily in their complexity, there is a need now, as never before, to both communicate well and to keep costs low for media and all the inflation-prone materials used in visual communications.

Many corporate boards know that identity systems save money through coordinated worldwide executions which consolidate purchasing, avoid duplication of expenses, and assure greater efficiencies through standardization. Even if there were no cost savings, industry has found that improved image building is available through its influence on internal and external publics.

Also today more than ever, we are dealing with overly bombarded publics, communications-wise, and the challenge to project true corporate personalities has placed our profession into many new arenas.

A program of design research and systems application may require thousands of man hours from teams of marketing, research and design specialists. Expressing corporate personalities through identity systems must be carefully planned and executed through subsidiaries' names, signage, architecture, interiors, stationery, business forms, and sometimes packaging.

Implementation also involves development of manuals and handbooks which explain precisely how programs are to be carried out at all levels and in all offices of corporate empires, nationally and worldwide.

Finally, while all other factors are important, corporate visual communications can be only as good as both the professional advisor's creative ability and understanding of human psychology. The client, in the end, is buying his design firm's skill in translating research into creative solutions which capture attention and communicate in the most effective way.

All of these factors combine to make the effective symbols or logotypes merely the "tip of the iceberg" in truly resultful corporate identity planning.

Careers In Advertising

About a third of people working in advertising are employed by agencies. Of these, more than half are employed in the New York and Chicago metropolitan areas. The other half work for independent or branch agencies. The best opportunities used to be only in New York, but now you could build a career in advertising anywhere in the United States.

The two-thirds of advertising people who don't work for agencies work for corporations, retail stores, banks, newspapers, magazines, broadcasters, mail order houses, printers, engravers, art studios, designers, or others who service the profession.

Let's consider a product such as Forsythia Fragrance. The Forsythia people may have their own small advertising department which develops a budget and works closely with an advertising agency and the employees assigned to that account. When a local department store runs a special sale on Forsythia, the store's advertising staff prepares the material; if a special mailing is enclosed with monthly bills, bearing Forsythia's aroma, the work is probably done by a direct mail company. Meanwhile, representatives of the various media are soliciting the advertising staff at Forsythia, urging them to use a particular publication or station. (The media themselves are advertising their

own space and time). All along this complex route there are men and women using creative, analytical, technical, and managerial skills to keep the ideas and information flowing.

JOBS IN AGENCIES

The 5,000 ad agencies in the country employ some 75,000 people. Some people feel that an agency job offers a more creative challenge because the same product must be handled over a long period of time. "It's a matter of establishing a total concept," explains an agency executive, "rather than describing a single item."

Some advertising people are ACCOUNT EXECUTIVES, who maintain day-to-day contact with the client. They act as liaison between the client and the departments of the agency. The account executives must be familiar with every aspect of the account and interpret it clearly to the agency people, while using the agency facilities to provide the best possible service to the client. It's a job of policing a two-way street, a job that usually pays well. Some executives started their careers writing copy; others came up through training programs emphasizing the financial and management aspects of the work.

COPYWRITERS write the headlines, slogans, and

text to convey the client's message in clear, attention drawing language. Like a reporter covering a story, the writer looks for an "angle" -- an original approach -- on the story to attract and convince the reader. Beyond a skill with language, copywriters need to understand people and what will evoke a response in them.

Women often excel as copywriters, perhaps because of their familiarity with many consumer products and their audiences. It's a good starting job, particularly in retail stores. A well-known book by Bernice FitzGibbon, Macy's, Gimbels and Me, tells the story of the author's remarkable career as a copywriter.

ART careers involve working with design and layout, graphic and photo-graphic presentation. These jobs may lead to jobs of art director or television director.

MEDIA BUYERS help decide, after studying the client's sales and distribution patterns and results of research, which media will reach the largest number of potential buyers for the limited money available to spend. Media selection is not a simple matter -- the coverage costs and selling influence of the various 1,900 newspapers, 6,500 magazines, 700 TV stations, and 5,300 radio (AM and FM)

211 ADVERTISING

stations are always in a state of change.

RESEARCHERS assemble and analyze the data needed to plan a campaign and to evaluate its effectiveness. People have to be interviewed, data are processed, and statistics are examined. Today a lot of the research data are processed and statistics are examined. Today a lot of research is contracted to research firms -- specialists in data collection and analysis.

Competition is fierce in the advertising field, and good entry jobs are hard to get. Creative jobs are the plums, and are given to the top talent after above average perserverance and skills are demonstrated. So much learning has to take place on the job, it is best to find a position which enables you to squeeze in and soak up experience. Sometimes you can get into advertising careers after starting in publishing or broadcasting jobs.

A survey of new hires by a group of advertising agencies during a recent year indicated that 4% of hires had junior college degrees, 83% had bachelor's degrees, and 13% had graduate degrees. Major area of study did not seem to matter. Major area of study didn't seem to matter, although business graduates tended toward management jobs.

MARKET RESEARCH CAREERS

People who enjoy the research end of advertising may find careers in research organizations. Some of these firms are "syndicated" -- that is, they provide an ongoing service of collecting and providing data for clients. An example is the Nielson service, rating audiences of television programs. Others are firms that conduct special studies such as readership, image, recognition, audit of sales, consumer attitudes, or media rates.

In these firms, jobs are available to people with varied backgrounds. The jobs include interviewer, statistician, coder, editor, research analyst, all leading to project director, supervisor, or research director positions.

There are at least 300 market research firms, and a journal called the Journal of Marketing Research.

PUBLIC RELATIONS

PR is a closely related field with similar career opportunities. Well over 125,000 people are employed in public relations today. 7000 are members of the Public Relations Society of America (PRSA), the professional society.

Of PRSA members, 60% work on PR staffs of business firms, 30% for PR agencies (some of which may be related to advertising agencies), and 10% for nonprofit organizations including universities, professional associations, and health and welfare agencies. 12% are women.

The best career bet is in a corporation, as 60% of all large companies have PR departments. The rest use outside firms for any PR help they need.

Because writing is an essential skill in public relations work, many professionals come from a journalism background. Either journalism training or newspaper experience provides an advantage in developing the skill needed.

In fact, many of today's leading professionals followed a similar pattern of advancement: a few years with a daily newspaper as a reporter, a stint with a wire service such as UPI or AP, a public relations agency spot to learn other facets of the business, and finally, an executive position in a company.

CONSIDER

1. What would competition be like without advertising of any kind?

2. Is there any other way for Coke to promote its product?

3. Are advertising agencies necessary?

4. Does public relations and "image" advertising pay off?

5. How could you evaluate the cost of advertising a product as opposed to its effectiveness

6. Compare the images that Coke and 7-Up project to the public. How do they do this?

7. Is there psychological meaning to various forms of symbols, used in logos and trademarks?

8. Does advertising take unfair advantage of human psychology? Explain.

9. If you were the advertising manager for Ford Motor, how would you position ads for a new luxury car?

10. If you were the advertising manager for Standard Oil of California (Chevron), what would you do to build the image of Chevron gasoline?

CHALLENGES

Pick two television commercials that you think are particularly good and two that are not. Analyze why you think they are good and bad.

Analyze the promotion of two or more brands of gasoline. How do the companies differentiate their products from all others?

Pick two ads from Newsweek, Time, Playboy, or other large circulation magazines. Determine exactly what market is being targeted.

Examine a copy of the Sears catalog and evaluate it in terms of its advertising impact.

Examine a company's annual report and evaluate its advertising impact, if any.

Investigate the outcomes of the suits involving Chevron's F-310 advertising. Do you agree with these decisions? Explain what they mean to the company and the public.

Have a friend pour a glass of Coke and a glass of Pepsi into unmarked glasses. Drink them and see if you can tell which is which. Explain the advertising relevance of your finding.

RECAP

Advertising is any form of communication through the various media used to present information about goods and services to the public and to induce the public to buy. It is a critical aspect of marketing and is essential to competition. It is through advertising that the public learns about new products and gains the information needed to make intelligent buying decisions.

Different companies use different approaches to advertising suited to their needs and differences in their products. A company needs to tailor its advertising to the behavior of its customers and to the competitive situation it finds itself in. Different products require different types of promotion. A bottle of Coke must be advertised in a different way than a Cadillac. Only a very small segment of the population is in the market for a Caddillac, while practically everyone is a potential buyer of Coke.

In this chapter we have seen the techniques used by Coke and by its competitor, the Uncola, in advertising. As the number-one soft drink, Coke seeks to keep its market position by keeping a "fresh image". The Uncola, 7-Up, seeks to gain a stronger market position by being creative in its advertising.

Sears uses a catalog as one of its promotional tools, complementing its advertising and its image created by the retail operations. The catalog originally was aimed at farmers and other customers who made purchases by mail order. Today, over 12 million catalogs are distributed each year and help generate about a quarter of Sears' total sales.

Sometimes advertising backfires. Chevron's F-310 gasoline prompted strong charges that the product wasn't what it was claimed to be. Cereal makers have long touted the nutritional value of their products ("Wheaties -- the breakfast of champions"), but critics have charged that this advertising isn't the whole story.

Advertising agencies play a major role in helping business organizations promote their goods and services. Agencies provide three major types of services: research (planning the advertising campaign), creative work (developing and producing the advertising), and media buying (the actual purchase of media space and time).

Most careers in advertising involve work with an ad agency, usually with some work in copywriting. Advertising is a stimulating and challenging area of professional work. You might consider possible opportunities in the field -- advertising, public relations, or one of the support functions.

WORKSHEET NO. 7

1. Why do companies spend money on advertising?

---

2. Why do companies use advertising agencies?

3. What does "positioning" mean?

4. Why does Coca-Cola feel a need to "keep its image fresh?"

CHAPTER 8

Consumerism

There's communism, socialism, patriotism, and now, consumerism. Is consumerism good or bad? Thinking makes it so. For the customer who feels that product quality isn't always what it should be, consumerism is long overdue. For the company the "ism" may mean a lot of expense in examining and possibly redesigning products, gearing up for expanded public and customer relations, researching charges made by critics and reporting findings.

Can a company ignore the best interests of its customers? We would like to think not. In many cases this has been shown to be true. Paying attention to changing consumer demands has been a key to the management of Con Ed, Sears, and other companies we have studied.

Yet companies easily become so excited about the products they are pushing and their processes of manufacturing and selling that the true feelings of their customers may not be recognized until it is too late.

Large companies may be able to bear the penalty of insensitivity to consumer wants and needs, but will in fact be penalized as consumers stop buying their products and turn to competitors.

In the long run, sensitivity to customer desires is a critical factor in the survival of all business enterprises. For small businesses that don't have the cushion of product diversification it is particularly important, even critical, for short-range survival.

Some companies try to make up for problems in their marketing and product design by providing special communications with customers. But good communications with customers. But good customer relations, and thus good marketing, begin with good product design and market research. Good public relations and communications cannot brush away basic problems.

Also, governmental regulations relating to product safety, marketing practices, credit, and other consumer interests require companies to adopt positive practices. Frequently, therefore, management responses to consumer demands and desires are not entirely voluntary. Increasingly, the government is extending its hand into this aspect of business activity. Through product inspections, consumer education, class action suits, standards for government contracting, and other means, governmental agencies are having a strong influence on the manner in which businesses relate to their customers.

In This Chapter

What About The Consumer?

SEN. WARREN G. MAGNUSON
(D., Wash.)

"Consumerism" is a word used to describe the phenomenon whereby purchasers of goods and services are trying to attain a marketing system which makes the consumer sovereign—which guarantees to him the right to safety, the right to be informed, the right to choose, and the right to be heard.

Consumerism is based upon that basic tenet of the free enterprise system which says that the consumer (rather than government) should control, through rational purchasing decisions in the marketplace, which goods and services are produced. But consumerism looks to government to control producers who would interfere with rational choice and thereby destroy the free enterprise system.

If consumerism is a fad, why isn't it passing? A number of ambitious laws have been put on the books, including laws on auto safety, packaging, and consumer credit. Vocal consumerists have had their days in court, in the media, and in the corporate board rooms as well as in the stores.

Instead, there seems to be more and more grumbling about the quality of goods and services today than ever before. Ralph Nader has become a major and permanent institution on the consumer scene. Circulation of consumer-oriented publications, such as the Consumer Reports, have swelled. Public polls and the activities of congressmen indicate that consumers want more protection.

To some degree consumer dissatisfaction may be directly linked to inflation. With prices going up all of the time, consumers are getting less for their dollars, and are taking a closer look at what they are getting. Prosperous times have also put burdens on business. Telephone service, power service, back-orders on furniture and automobiles, shortage of service personnel, and other common problems rub consumers the wrong way, regardless of the reasons why things aren't the way they should be. Changing employee attitudes and hiring individuals with marginal job qualifications have made it tough for managers to keep production standards up where they should be. Defective products coming off the assembly lines give consumers the impression that "nothing works anymore."

Actually, there is no objective evidence that there is a general decline in workmanship. A lot of dissatisfaction may stem from the improvements made in products. Appliances and gadgets add convenience, but they are subject to repairs and they make life more complicated. The typical consumer is no match for a modern machine -- whether it is an automatic can opener, a color television, or an automatic garage door opener. Something's bound to go wrong sometime and the buyer can't fix it.

Expert repairmen are in such short supply that consumers have to be grateful for small favors. And often these small favors come at high repair fees. Manufacturers' warranties haven't helped this situation, as many are confusing or misleading as to what is covered and what is not. Some, in fact, are not so much promises of quality or service as disclaimers to protect the manufacturer from the buyer's common law right to insist that a product do what it is advertised to do.

LEO BOGART
Executive Vice President and General Manager
Bureau of Advertising, American Newspaper
Publishers Association

Consumerism is a catchword in current vogue among marketers to describe a variety of distinct phenomena. These include (1) the long-term evolution of a more sophisticated and better educated buying public; (2) public skepticism about business practices, a reflection of deeper malaise with all established institutions in the aftermath of the Vietnam war; (3) organized activism (led by a handful of articulate advocates with a following among university students) to correct product deficiencies and advertising claims, and (4) legislative moves to increase consumer protection and an intensification of actions by government regulatory agencies.

CONSUMER RIGHTS

Generally, a consumer may be deemed to have four basic rights:

- the right to safety
- the right to be informed
- the right to choose
- the right to be heard

First, a consumer expects a product to perform its intended function without incurring any harm or damage to its user. There's a lot of concern about product safety, yet most products are far safer and more reliable than ever before. Automatic washers must comply with over 350 safety requirements of Underwriter Laboratories Standard No. 560. UL is an independent testing and certifying organization relied on by major manufacturers of electrical products. Toasters must comply with over 250 requirements and electric space heaters, with about 500 safety requirements. Further, actual injuries and accidents are less frequent today because of the care given product design and production.

Second, consumers have a right to be informed about products and to choose among alternative available products on the basis of this information. Today companies provide more printed information on products than consumers could ever read. Business experience shows that consumers simply don't read the user manuals, specification sheets, and other materials carefully drawn up and published by manufacturers. Perhaps what is needed is better communications with consumers, better training of retailers to provide the information consumers want, and more third-party assessments of products to guide consumer choices.

Third, consumers do have the right to choose products they feel are "right" for them. This is basic to our enterprise system -- and yet time after time, consumers reject the better quality product for one with some advertising or promotional gimmick. G.E. once came out with an advanced refrigerator design with thinner walls and more interior space. Consumers rejected it because it wasn't as ostentatious or as large in looks as the other makes. The consumer can buy what he wants, but

BETTY FURNESS
Former Special Assistant to President Johnson
for Consumer Affairs

"Consumerism" is a word originally coined by industry to make the burgeoning consumer movement sound like a dangerous threat. Business loved the word. Consumer advocates didn't, but they were too busy doing their work to bother about it.

Today, the movement by any other name would smell as sweet. We'll take the title.

Consumerism is an effort to put the buyer on an equal footing with the seller. Consumers want to know what they're buying. What they're eating. How long a product will last. What it will and will not do. Whether it will be safe for them and/or the environment.

That's consumerism.

Consumers do not want to be manipulated, hornswoggled or lied to. They want truth, not just in lending, labeling and packaging, but in everything in the whole vast, bewildering marketplace.

HERBERT S. DENENBERG
Pennsylvania Insurance Commissioner

Consumerism is not merely putting safety into cars or taking fat out of hot dogs. It is much more than improving the physical environment, creating safer products, and protecting the public from fraud and other consumer abuses.

Consumerism should have more basic purposes. Consumerism should aim for government and institutions "of, by, and for the people" instead of government and institutions "of, by, and for special interest groups."

Consumerism has been focused on some of the obvious symptoms of lack of responsiveness to the public interest. But consumerism is moving toward a more fundamental definition which is in fact a reaffirmation of our basic democratic concepts: Consumerism seeks to give representation to all interests, especially the individual buyer, consumer, and citizen who now has no adequate voice in the power structure.

who's to say that the consumer really knows best? Consumers are human and make human mistakes in judgement when making purchases.

Finally, the consumer has the right to be heard -- heard by businesses from which he has purchased goods or services. As businesses grow larger, it is often difficult for the individual customer to complain or get a problem solved. It really is amazing what a person has to go through sometimes. Companies have responded by setting up special customer service departments, special telephone numbers, or simplified procedures.

Companies say, however, that consumers have an obligation to have their facts straight, to be sensible and practical. Ever-higher standards are being imposed on businessmen concerning their business and their products -- with penalties for misrepresentations, omissions, and inaccuracies. With class actions and triple damages, consumers are encouraged to join up with the SEC, the FTC, and other governmental agencies in monitoring these statements. Nowhere does there appear to be any reciprocal responsibility on the consumer or his representative critics at large (like Ralph Nader).

We are likely to see continuing strong consumerism because the problems and needs of consumers are continuing ones. However, we are likely to see more governmental participation in consumer-oriented activities and increased demands from businessmen for more temperate, reasonable, and responsible consumer actions.

SENATOR CHARLES H. PERCY
(R., Ill.)

To me, the consumer movement represents a broad public reaction against bureaucratic neglect and corporate disregard of the public.

It is a repudiation of misleading advertising, empty warranties and guarantees, deceptive packaging, anti-competitive conduct, unfair pricing and bait-and-switch merchandising.

It is a check on sham, misrepresentation, deceit and fraud. And it is a control against monopolistic behavior by some corporations and the abuse of authority or discretion by certain agencies of government.

The fight for consumer protection is a battle for quality in goods and services, for fairness in advertising and promotion, for honesty in the marketplace. In its broadest sense, I believe that the consumer movement amounts to a yearning for an improved quality of life—for an America that works again, for people, products and governmental institutions that support the society rather than tear it apart.

Consumers Aren't All Angels Either

BY ROSE DeWOLF
Columnist for the Philadelphia Bulletin.

Oh, I know whose side I'm on . . . I'm a consumer. I bow to no one in my antagonism to useless warranties, fraudulent claims, garbled instructions, hidden flaws, and ridiculous computers which threaten to have me arrested if I don't pay $0.00 right away. If I feel affronted, I can holler for

fully cheat, steal, lie and/or behave with incredible stupidity. There, I've said it and I'm glad.

Take the "switchers," for example. Those are the people who take the price tag from a cheap item and put it on an expensive item before taking the expensive item to the sales-

housewife slip a pound of butter into an oleomargarine box, assuming that the check-out clerk would never check. She assumed wrong. All check-out clerks know that trick.

One time I merely mentioned the word "consumer" to a friend of mine who works for a

Ralph Nader as loud as anyone.

And yet . . .

Every once in a while, much as I try to fight it, I feel a twinge of sympathy for merchants, manufacturers, and providers of service. Every once in a while, though I feel like a traitor, I want to jump up and say: "You know, consumers can be pretty rotten, too."

Consumers are not all angels. They include in their numbers those who would quite cheer-

clerk. They hope the clerk will be too busy to notice and will sell the goods at a "bargain" price the store hadn't really counted on.

Switchers are everywhere. I once saw this very dignified-looking gentleman craftily switch the lids on a jar of peanuts and a jar of cashews. The prices, you see, were stamped on the lids. The man intended to buy his cashews, quite literally, for "peanuts."

And I have seen a dear little

supermarket and the poor guy went bananas. (On special, that week.)

"Consumers!" he wailed. "I'll tell you about consumers. They buy magazines, take them home and read them, then return them for a refund claiming their husband bought duplicates . . . they demand to get five cents back on the five-cents-back coupon without buying the product first . . . they finish off bars of candy or bottles of soda while they walk through the store and then don't mention it when it comes time to pay . . ."

Did you know that baby food manufacturers deliberately seal their jars so they'll open with a loud "POP". That, says my friend, is so that a consumer who gets a jar that opens only with a little "poof" knows it has been opened before. Seems some mothers want to taste the food at the store to make sure little junior will like it, but then don't want to buy the jar they tasted.

Do you know why most cereal manufacturers don't give away prizes in the cereal boxes anymore? That's because so many women used to pry open the package, snitch the prize, and leave the unsalable torn box on the shelf. Nowadays, if you want to get that super-spy ring your kid has been crying for, you have to buy the box, clip the coupon, and send 25 cents in coin.

Suburban stores tell of women who "buy" a fancy dress on the Friday just before the Country Club dance and then return it ("I just changed my mind.") on Monday. They get indignant if the clerk says the dress looks as if it had been worn.

There are those who carry on loudly when the billing computer makes a mistake and claims they owe a bill they know they don't owe—but keep awfully quiet when the computer gives them credit they know they don't deserve. That makes it tougher for the store to straighten out the error.

Don't we all know people who brag about how they got the "whole car fixed" on the insurance of the guy who merely dented a fender?

My local laundryman claims that if he ever loses a shirt

(Heaven forbid), it invariably turns out to be (a) "very expensive" and (b) "just purchased."

"How come I never lose last year's cheap shirt?" he asks. "No. Those are the ones I manage to return. Right?" He is skeptical.

There are, of course, those who cheat the stores even more forthrightly. Shoplifting is at an all-time high. Do you know why manufacturers often pack such little items as batteries, pencils and razor blades in plastic bubbles attached to huge pieces of cardboard? That's because the cardboard is larger than the average consumer's pocket where many batteries, pencils and razor blades used to just disappear.

People who deal with consumers sometimes lose patience with them not because the consumers are greedy or dishonest but because they sometimes simply cause problems for themselves.

A local weights and measures inspector told me of pulling a surprise raid on a local butcher shop where the butcher was suspected of resting his elbow on the scale while weighing meat. Did the consumers appreciate the inspector's arrival? They did not.

"They were angry because it was close to dinner time. They started yelling at me," the inspector said. "They said I was holding them up . . . they had to get home to start cooking. They called me a city hall drone. They said I was annoying the butcher who was their friend. Some friend!"

Consumers can be funny. Recently, a spokesman for a national meat canning company

told a convention of food editors that consumers persist in sending an open can of meat back to the company to illustrate whatever complaint they're making. The fact is, that after days of travel in the unrefrigerated mail, the product *always* looks awful and smells worse. How can the company possibly tell if the complaint was justified in the first place?

Consumers complain about high food prices and then insist on buying every convenience food on the market. They yell about too loud commercials and then don't buy the products advertised on soft ones.

The government says motorists will be safer if their cars buzz until the safety belts are fastened. But car-buyers by the hordes are threatening dealers with mayhem unless the buzzers are unhooked. (The dealers are prohibited by law from complying.)

Consumers are just not always happy with what is being done *for* them. Frankly, I have to admit that *I* was a lot happier before packages of hot dogs had to admit right out in public that they contain ground-up cow's lips. Ycchh. Do we have to know EVERYTHING?

I'm not trying to say that the fact that the consumer can be, in his turn, greedy, dishonest, unappreciative, and just plain stupid, in any way excuses commercial interests for being the same. As my mother used to say, "Two wrongs don't make a right."

Still, fair is fair and somebody had to speak out. And now that I have gotten that out of the way, I can get to all these complaint letters I'm preparing for Ralph, and Virginia, and my local office of Consumer Affairs.

Government And The Consumer

Getting effective consumer laws and regulations on the books is a tough battle, both on the legislative and the administrative sides of government. One reason is that consumers don't agree about what they want. Consumers are a varied group.

Bankers, retailers, manufacturers, travel agents, oil producers, trial lawyers, and insurance executives are all consumers, but at the same time they feel they have good reasons for resisting new laws and regulations. Controls create problems and expenses for businessmen and cut into profits. Businessmen, as consumers, care about product quality, safety, and fairness, but their different standards and their significant power often lead them to oppose governmental action on consumer affairs.

It took seven years to pass the landmark truth-in-lending bill in 1968 after it had gone through a labyrinth of obstacles. When it was finally passed it was hailed as a breakthrough, which it was. Yet the record since then shows a smattering of relatively small successes of which few were of such major impact. Most dealt with peripheral problems or corrected blatant consumer deceptions without getting to the root of the problem.

Each piece of legislation and each successful action represents a step in the right direction. As public concern for consumer rights is heard in Congress, we will see increased governmental participation in consumerism.

At least six major concerns are emerging in new laws or regulations today. The first is the establishment of an independent Consumer Protection Agency -- a permanent agency to look after the consumer's interests. Other topics of concern are no-fault insurance for automobile owners, warranties and guarantees, fish inspection, drug pricing (and disclosure of drug prices for comparative shopping), and drug safety and labeling.

A bill establishing the Consumer Protection Agency has been proposed in Congress on several occasions. Each time it has gained support but has not yet passed. The agency is to be the consumers' advocate within the federal government, designed to give the consumer a voice adequately balanced against business, with its trade associations, the Department of Commerce, and its large complement of lobbyists. The creation of such an agency would mean that consumers could be heard on decisions affecting their pocketbooks,

"It's my observation that more and more consumers are looking after their own interests these days."

Drawing by Booth, © 1972. The New Yorker Magazine, Inc.

their health and their safety -- before the Food and Drug Administration, Federal Trade Commission, or the Departments of Commerce, Agriculture, or Transportation. If these agencies failed to meet their responsibilities, the CPA would be able to bring them to court, a procedure already available to other federal bodies.

The no-fault auto insurance proposal would provide by federal law that an auto insurance policy holder would receive immediate and equitable compensation in an automobile accident without having to go through long procedures to establish who was at fault. While the facts indicate that the benefits of such a law would be great for the consumers, and maintaining profits for insurance companies, the proposed law is opposed by the American Bar Association on behalf of the many trial lawyers who would lose billions in litigation fees. Nevertheless, no-fault insurance may be on its way. Numerous states have enacted such laws, and the public seems to support the concept.

The question of consumer warranties and guarantees is an old one, but the need for legal clarification and support continues. The problems with present warranties and guarantees include meaningless small-print exclusions, burdensome duties and expense for consumers, unreasonable delays or failure by the manufacturer in making good on promises to repair or replace goods, and the use of a specific limited warranty as an excuse to disclaim responsibility for other product defects not covered. Too often, the guarantee is a sales gimmick, not a true consumer protection. Sooner or later, the government will step in to strengthen warranties and guarantees, if business doesn't make desired changes first.

In summary, consumers have the potential power to bring about changes in business practices, either through direct pressure on enterprises or through the enactment of federal laws and regulations.

Drawing by J. Mirachi; © 1976 The New Yorker Magazine, Inc.

"If it gives you any trouble, don't let us know. We hate trouble."

The Pressure Is On For Safer Products

When the final report of the Public Land Law Commission arrived at the White House last week, President Nixon received it in person in front of photographers. The same day, he got the final report of the National Commission on Product Safety. But for all the attention that report received, it might, as one wag suggested, "have been slipped between the bars of the White House fence."

The ho-hum reaction was not due to any lack of vigor in the commission's recommendations. After a two-year study, the group, headed by New York attorney Arnold B. Elkind, concluded that the country needs an "omnibus" consumer product safety act and a new, independent federal agency to set and enforce safety standards. Consumer products, the commission said, injure 20-million people a year—four times as many as are hurt in highway accidents.

Government, consumers, and the law are forcing industry to change

---

The Administration does not favor a new agency, but Congress may have other ideas. The Democratic leadership is already running against the Administration on consumer issues. Senator Frank E. Moss (D-Utah), chairman of the consumer subcommittee of the Senate Commerce Committee, expects to start hearings soon on the proposed safety act and seems determined to get some action by Congress this election year.

Proponents of a new, independent agency for product safety may have to reconcile it with other proposals that would make a product safety agency subordinate to a new consumer protection agency. Another question is whether Congress will be willing to give up the power to set standards, industry by industry, that it has exercised in the past.

Mandate. The safety agency recommended by the commission would have wide-ranging powers. It would set mandatory standards, enforce them through civil and criminal sanctions, enjoin distribution of products that violate federal standards "or are unreasonably hazardous," and inspect manufacturing facilities to implement compliance. It would also:

- Require consumer notification or recall of defective products.
- Conduct public hearings, with power to subpoena.
- Disseminate information about hazardous products and ways to reduce hazards.
- Require products to be tested, and accredit private laboratories to do such work.
- Operate its own facility for research and development of testing methods and for analysis of consumer products.

In addition, the commission recommended that injured consumers be permitted to file treble damage claims in federal courts against manufacturers who "intentionally violate" safety standards; that class-action procedures be made applicable; and that state and federal courts adopt the principles of strict tort liability. The commission said the Small Business Administration should be authorized to make low-interest loans to help small businesses meet stiffer product safety requirements.

The commission did not concern itself with products such as autos, tires, pesticides, and paints, which are already under federal safety regulation. It found fault, however, with a long list of everyday products, including glass bottles, color television sets, household chemicals, architectural glass, power tools, and rotary lawn mowers.

How companies are reacting

Hoover Co. has set up a corporate product safety committee. Toro Mfg. Corp. watches customers operate its power mowers. American Machine & Foundry sends its "leisure time" products to be checked at a company test center.

Each of these companies, in its own way, is responding to the changing climate surrounding product safety. Together with managements throughout industry, they are taking a closer look at the things they make, spurred by a rash of public inquiries, newspaper and magazine articles, new and proposed legislation, court decisions, and rising insurance rates. And though some are reluctant to admit that product changes are needed, even manufacturers of top-quality goods concede that the clamor has had an effect on the way they do business.

Not all the changes are substantive.

Hoover's new safety committee "hasn't increased the safety of our products," says G. P. Daiger, engineering vice-president. "It tells the people we are conscious of safety, and when we get in trouble on it, the committee provides a better public image." That image—of a company with specific, centralized control over safety—can close off a main line of attack in liability suits, he says.

Daiger hastens to add that Hoover has reviewed its production procedures since the clamor began, but found no changes needed. Even so, Hoover is doing some things differently. It is putting together all of its product safety standards—some not previously written down—and will make them part of top management policy. And it is taking more trouble to warn customers against improper use of its products. "Now we say, 'Don't pick up puddles of water with the vacuum cleaner,'" says Daiger. "In the past, we would just wonder who in their right mind would do that."

New experience. Concern over misuse of products is new to most manufacturers. It comes as the result of court decisions that increasingly hold the manufacturer responsible for injury not just by a defective product used normally, but by a product misused in any way that might reasonably have been foreseen.

One consequence is that manufacturers are paying more attention to the way customers behave. Toro, for instance, tested customers as well as machines in developing its new fall line of power mowers. "First we orient them on how to operate the machine safely, and observe how they do it," says Chairman David M. Lilly. "Later we come back, and, as they are more familiar with the machine, we find out what shortcuts they are trying to take which lead to accidents."

Some manufacturers do not hide their concern over the trend of the law and what degree of foresight may be called "reasonable." Lilly claims he once saw two men trying to cut a hedge with a power mower. "It's impossible to invent an idiot-proof machine," he says.

Improvements. On the other hand, Keith Pfundstein, director of product safety for Deere & Co., concedes that "we've upgraded our requirements for what is reasonable." The company's riding lawn mowers, for example, now are fitted with a longer discharge chute, a

ISSUES IN BUSINESS **226**

motor brake that will stop the blades more quickly, and controls relocated away from the discharge side of the machine. Engine vibration has also been reduced to cut operator fatigue.

The effort to cope with the ingenuity of users could be part of a broader trend toward viewing safety as a system problem. The "system" takes in not just the design and production of the hardware, but also initial planning, software (labeling and instructions), marketing, shipping, and servicing. The concept is well established in the aerospace industry. In the consumer goods industries, it can be seen only in patches and is seldom articulated.

There are signs, though, that companies increasingly are seeking safety solutions outside the normal spheres of design and production. More warnings like Hoover's are going out to users. Tappan this year listed 15 safety tips in its owner's manual for electric ranges. And Hunt & Wesson is using TV jingles to warn children about the sharp edges on the lid of its Snack-Pak container.

The trend to more wide-ranging consideration of product safety could be bolstered by the trend to establish corporate safety directors or committees. Motorola's Consumer Products Div., for example, recently matched some of its competitors by appointing a director of consumer affairs; the post went to Carl Heisig, formerly director of engineering. Critics say some such appointments have been window dressing. But theoretically they are useful for coordinating the safety efforts of distinct corporate groups—product planning, design, production planning, quality control, marketing, and servicing—whose individual efforts sometimes nullify one another.

Autonomy. Coordination is a favorite word in the safety world, but so is autonomy. Many safety experts believe strongly that quality control, for example, should be a separate function and not, as it often is, merely an adjunct of the production department. Many product defects, they insist, originate not in design but in sloppy fabrication or assembly.

A West Coast product safety director sees pressure building up for such autonomy. Quality control, which started out as a fancy name for an inspection station, is becoming firmly established as an engineering discipline. And the insurance industry, he feels, will increasingly insist on quality control groups with "more of a say." Ultimately, he believes, an autonomous quality control group may be answerable not only to top management of the company but directly to a regulatory authority.

AMF makes its own audit of quality control. At its corporate test center in Springdale, Conn., a six-man engineering staff tests company products "the way a consumer would." They include bicycles, motorcycles, lawn mowers, snowmobiles, snowblowers, power boats, and diving equipment. The center, says the company, is "completely autonomous."

The idea of separating the checkers from the doers is not confined to the production phase. At Motorola, a separate safety group reviews the work of the design group. It gets a fresh look at the product, says Heisig, and is much more likely to ask tough questions than if it were involved in the design.

How much? Few of these extra efforts on behalf of product safety are made without extra costs. For industry, the question is whether they can be recouped in the marketplace.

Hoover, which spends 2% to 5% of its production cost on safety, feels it is compensated for "by customer goodwill, fewer service calls, and reduced liability." Toy maker Mattel, Inc., whose safety bill includes stuffing its toys with material as clean "as a piece of white bread"—which accounts for 15% to 20% of the material costs—feels cutting corners can mean lost sales and "loss of confidence by big buyers." Some companies, notably power tool makers, have been able to add safety features while reducing prices because of expanded volume.

At that, the price of voluntary controls is likely to be cheaper than that of regulation. Philco-Ford's vice-president of consumer affairs, Armin E. Allen, figures that the record keeping that the government wants on TV sets will cost Philco $150,000 a year, and the industry as a whole $4-million to $5-million a year.

Under these circumstances, some manufacturers are taking a fresh look at the possibility of merchandising safety. Toro, for instance, is planning a major campaign on the safety theme for its fall line of power mowers. Market testing has shown that customers would be willing to pay 10% more for new safety features; company officials have their fingers crossed.

At Libbey-Owens-Ford, Vice-President James M. Ashley figures safety consciousness is good for his company, too. The demand for safety glass, he says, has produced much of its sales growth in the past four decades.

But there are still doubters. Hoover's chief engineer, D. C. Krammes, believes safety is too complicated to explain well to consumers. "There's no way of selling safety," he says bluntly.

Emphasis. Some manufacturers and safety experts think the safety angle on products has been overdone. Baron Whitaker, president of Underwriters' Laboratories, has pointed out that only 1,071 of the nation's 108,000 accidental deaths in 1965 were due to electricity. The figure does not take into account the injured. But the death rate of 5.5 per million population was lower than that in 1940 (7.6 per million), despite an increase of 440% in total consumption of electrical energy.

Still, some leading manufacturers of consumer products welcome pressure for product safety. They hope it will result in voluntary standards that will force their low-price rivals to compete on a more equal cost level. What they fear is that the self-imposed standards will be too weak or too late to stave off government regulation. They also face increasing odds that their customers may sue them.

Why legal hazards are growing

A growing tide of product liability claims, suits, and adverse judgments has been engulfing manufacturers—and there is no respite in sight.

Though the volume of claims for auto accidents caused by driver negligence still leads the pack, product cases "are crowding them cheek by jowl," says Thomas F. Lambert, editor-in-chief of the American Trial Lawyers Assn. Along with autos and bottles, the products getting zapped in court run from power tools to soaps and bleaches, from pesticides to pure drugs.

In one case last fall, an Illinois housewife, Frances L. Moore, was awarded $930,000 by a Cook County jury after she was blinded by an exploding can of Drano. The manufacturer, Drackett Co., which was charged with negligence, has appealed.

Such huge verdicts have alarmed corporate counsel and insurance companies. Otis Elevator Co.'s lawyer says frankly: "The payout in liability suits has increased faster than our increase in sales. It's a substantial cost of doing business." Insurers, who have watched product liability losses mounting each year since 1966, are upping their rates and toughening their standards. And along with corporate counsel, they are riding herd on their clients' quality control and safety programs.

Much of the blame—or credit—for this phenomenon can be pinned on the increasingly liberal legal climate for consumers. As sympathetic juries have inflated their awards, plaintiffs' lawyers have become more aggressive in bringing product suits. And changes in legal doctrine—particularly the evolution of "strict liability"—have eroded industry's traditional courtroom defenses and made it easier for consumer lawyers to prove their cases.

Earlier this month, supreme courts in three more states—Hawaii, Indiana, and Nevada—adopted the strict liability rule, bringing the total to about 40. And just last week, the National Commission on Product Safety recommended that all state and federal courts follow suit.

Landmark. Before this latest trend in tort law, a plaintiff had to prove that a manufacturer was negligent in order to recover damages for injury by a defective product. Under strict liability, proof of negligence is not necessary. In recent cases, the doctrine has been extended to include injured bystanders and the victims of side effects from otherwise pure drugs. Some courts are even telling manufacturers that they must design their products to anticipate situations beyond the product's intended use. Thus, in the landmark case of Larsen vs. General Motors in 1968, an appellate court said that GM was responsible for designing cars so as to make them safe in the event of a collision. GM says other high courts have taken the opposite view.

With the trend to strict liability, there have been developments in contract law that make it easier for a consumer to recover from a manufacturer under breach of warranty. Today, no more than 10 states retain the doctrine of privity, which shields the manufacturer from liability if he is not a direct party to the transaction.

Other formerly iron-clad defenses have also withered under the brunt of the consumer movement, some under a broader interpretation of the doctrine of foreseeability. If a product is judged "unfit" for its intended use or a use that could reasonably be anticipated by the manufacturer, he can be held liable under a breach of implied warranty, even, in some courts, if he has disclaimed liability.

Where a manufacturer's failure to give adequate warning creates an unreasonable risk of harm, some courts are finding him negligent, even in cases of abnormal or unintended use, such as a child swallowing a bottle of furniture polish. More courts, too, are holding industry liable under breach of express warranty for the contents of its advertising, whether misleading statements have been "consciously, negligently, or innocently made," according to Lambert.

Nor is compliance with government standards much help to a manufacturer in the courtroom. Such standards are often seen as the minimum, not the maximum, requirements, and may therefore be judged inadequate. In a Massachusetts case, a herbicide maker was held liable for the injury and death of some illiterate tobacco farm workers, although his label bore a written warning in compliance with Agriculture Dept. standards.

The future. Industry may face a whole new ballgame if federal class-action procedures are made applicable to safety standards, as the Product Safety Commission recommends. The prospect of one injured consumer suing on behalf of thousands—or millions—of others is one that chills industry. "The only people who will gain from this are the plaintiffs' lawyers," groans Don Blenko, counsel for Philco-Ford.

Other issues still unresolved are whether people who use products to perform services, such as beauticians or doctors, could be held strictly liable for defective products which cause harm, and how far a manufacturer's liability extends in the case of new drugs or cosmetics which cause side effects.

Now there is a new puzzle for business and trial lawyers: If a link can be established between industry and pollution-caused injuries, the stakes would be enormous. Several such cases are working their way to trial.

Do We Need All That In The Bread?

Additives:

WASHINGTON — In pre-historic times the Cro-Magnon man learned to smear saltpeter on his mastodon steaks to help preserve their shelf life in his cool cave. Today, many of his descendants are wondering if that first use of food additives was such a smart idea.

Food additives, which represent a $50-million-a-year business in the United States, encompass a collective term indicating not only the 3,000 chemicals added to groceries but also to their containers. These additives have greatly enhanced the business of eating. Flavoring agents may make a bland product more palatable; antioxidants may prevent some foods from becoming rancid; dyes may produce more eye appeal; preservatives may prolong the item's shelf life and thus lower its cost by reducing spoilage; indeed, extra vitamins may benefit some consumers who either have poor eating habits or an incomplete knowledge of nutrition.

Take bread as an example. A loaf might well contain a bleach to make the flour less dark (lighter bread appeals to some consumers), vitamins as nutritional supplements, buffers to even the acidity, surfactants to keep liquids apart in the baking process, sequestrants to inactivate tiny amounts of possibly harmful metals, as well as preservatives to prevent spoilage.

But increasingly over the last decade two searching questions have been asked about these additives: Are all the extra chemicals really needed in foods? And are some of the added ingredients in fact harmful to health?

Such questions were raised anew last week during three days of hearings by the Senate Select Committee on Nutrition and Human Needs which kicked off a legislative investigation into additives that is due to continue into next year. The reason: Concern that the regulation of existing statutes may be too lax and thus hazardous; concern that the maze of agencies and regulations dealing with additives may be unfathomable to both manufacturers and consumers; concern over a rush of bills that would alter current Federal additive laws.

"I don't want all the preservatives in my bread—if the loaf goes stale after three days I'll throw it away and buy a new one," said one committee witness who should know—Dr. William Lijinsky, a chemist and cancer researcher at the Atomic Energy Commission's national laboratory in Oak Ridge, Tenn.

Dr. Lijinsky pointed out that some nitrates and nitrites, including saltpeter, could, under certain conditions, form toxic substances in the stomach that are believed to cause cancer. Other witnesses outlined scientifically supported arguments against a red dye, commonly used in foods, that Russian researchers have linked with cancer. Another expert expressed alarm that the flavor-enhancing chemical MSG, which is under suspicion as causing brain damage to infants, is still finding its way to children despite the fact that it has been withdrawn from use in baby foods.

Some of the witnesses went so far as to charge that the Food and Drug Administration, one of the most prominent of several Federal agencies regulating food additives, had dragged its feet on enforcing the letter of the law and relied too heavily on advice from the National Academy of Sciences. The witnesses believe that too many members of the academy's advisory panels are linked in some way with the food industry.

Dr. Charles C. Edwards, the head of the F. D. A., retorted in testimony that his agency was trying to overcome its problems by seeking more impartial advice and was pushing forward on the testing of additives for safety. In fact, in the last two years the F.D.A. has either banned completely or proposed restrictions on seven common food additives such as cyclamates, MSG and saccharin.

But Dr. Edwards pleaded that a key act that prohibits the use of cancer-causing additives in foods should be modified because increasingly sophisticated analytical techniques now are finding such chemicals at levels as low as one part in one trillion, an amount that hardly could be toxic. Enforcing the letter of the law might lead to the banning of many common foods, he said, even some natural

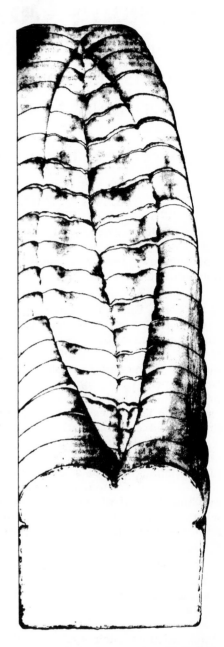

foods such as sugar and coffee that also contain traces of such chemicals. Some critics, however, said a relaxation of the law "would open the floodgates" to increased use of additives.

Whoever wins the escalating fight between the consumers and the manufacturers, an increasing number of people have already begun voting with their wallets. The size of the so-called natural food business—products free from additives—is expected to almost double this year.

—RICHARD D. LYONS

Iowa Money Maker:
Maytag Co. Prospers By Stressing Quality, Selling AT High Price

Washers Once Were Sideline; But Is the Company Dull Or a Really Shrewd Place?

Country-Boy Image Prevails

By LEWIS M. PHELPS
Staff Reporter of THE WALL STREET JOURNAL

NEWTON, Iowa—Stand behind your product. Give your customer his money's worth. Hoe your own row, and ignore the flashy city slickers out for a fast buck.

Such homespun homilies sound like pure Iowa corn. But they make up the corporate credo of Newton's Maytag Co., a company that offers one of the more unusual success stories in American manufacturing. Simply by building high-quality washing machines and selling them at premium prices, Maytag has prospered. It has ignored the temptation to cash in on its success by selling out to acquisition-minded conglomerates, or by turning into a conglomerate itself, which its asset-rich balance sheet easily would permit. Instead, Maytag's management has preferred to tend the store here in Newton, known as the "Washing Machine Capital of the World" during a time when, through an accident of history, it served as home base for no fewer than seven washer manufacturers.

Only one, Maytag, survived, but it has done more than merely survive. In the past decade the company consistently has chalked up earnings of 13% or so on sales, nearly triple the average in its fiercely competitive industry, which includes such appliance giants as General Electric, McGraw Edison, Westinghouse, Norge, Hamilton, Frigidaire, Bendix and Kelvinator. Even in troubled times, Maytag outperforms most firms; a crippling five-month strike last year knocked it down to number 623 from 486 on Fortune's list of the 1,000 largest U.S. industrial corporations ranked by sales, yet Maytag still managed to earn 9.1% on sales and a 14% return on shareholders' equity—among the highest percentages in the country. Since the strike's end, Maytag has fared even better.

No Hicks Need Apply

The Maytag approach to the washer game isn't everybody's cup of Tide. For one thing, says a former executive, Maytag is dull. "You shouldn't do anything (there) to rock the boat," he says. Another former executive complains that "nobody will listen to really bold, creative ideas." But James Magid, a New York security analyst and Maytag watcher, defends Maytag management. "Even though they're out in the cornfields," he says, "those people aren't hicks. They're sophisticated, talented managers."

Neither the Maytag company nor the town of Newton set out deliberately to get in the washer business. The company was founded in 1893 to make farm implements. Its founder was F. L. Maytag, who had come to Iowa as a farm boy in a covered wagon. After a local tinkerer invented a washing machine, the Maytag company and other local firms began making their own washers to offset the seasonal nature of the farm-implement business.

The Maytag company introduced a swinging, reversible wringer on its washing machines in 1910, and an electric motor the next year. Maytag gradually eased out of the farm-equipment business to concentrate on the faster growing and more profitable washer market.

The company owes its tradition of high-quality engineering to its founder, who always was trying to improve his products. After four years of fiddling, he introduced, in 1919, an aluminum-tub washer and eliminated the serious drawbacks in wooden washers. A son, L. B. Maytag, president of the company from 1920 to 1926, imposed on the company his commitment to conservative financing—the avoidance of debt and the accumulation of cash.

No Place Like Home

It fell to E. H. Maytag, another son of the founder, to guide the company through the Depression. He did it so well that the company remained profitable, though squeezed; Maytag was forced to discontinue dividends on its common stock for a while, and to create two issues (since retired) of preferred.

Not until the mid 1960s did Maytag again run into serious problems. The company had been selling commercial laundry washers in Germany for several years, and it decided to get into the home laundry market there, too. However, Maytag washers weren't very suitable for home use because the typically small European home water heaters couldn't supply the large quantities of hot water that American-made washers needed. To make a suitable machine for the German market, Maytag bought an interest in a German manufacturing concern—competently, but autocratically, managed by its aging principal owner. He died, "and we were stuck with literally no management to handle our interest there," recalls Maytag chairman E. G. Higdon.

While Maytag tried to get the German company moving again, Italian producers invaded the German market with low-priced washers and staked it out for themselves. Maytag threw in the towel and wrote off its $4 million foreign investment.

Although the company's basic domestic business has fared enormously well, other Maytag attempts at diversification, too, have come croppers, albeit minor ones. Fred Maytag II, son of E. H. Maytag, presided over some of them; he ran the company from 1940 to 1962.

Fred Maytag had the company make private-label products for other marketers, for a brief time, but there was little or no profit in them. He also tried to expand into some non-washer appliances like ovens and refrigerators; with no special technology or reputation in the manufacture of those appliances, Maytag's efforts sputtered out. And when Fred Maytag contracted to have other firms make some Maytag products, the other firms couldn't match Maytag's quality specifications.

Today, no Maytag is still active in company management, though L. B. Maytag (known universally as Bud), a son of the late L. B. Maytag, is a director. He owns about 34,000 Maytag shares, only one-quarter of 1% of the outstanding shares. No other surviving Maytag owns a big proportion of the company, either. Bud Maytag has spent most of his business career running National Airlines.

More often than not, of course, Maytag's decisions have turned out well. Its cautious, even plodding approach, generally has paid off. Only last fall did the company begin selling a full line of dishwashers, for example, and it took nearly 20 years to do it. Company engineers began tinkering with designs back in the 1930s, but they didn't start serious development until the mid-1950s. "We had no intention of rushing into the market with just another dishwasher," says Mr. Higdon, a vice president at the time. "We wanted to develop a product that was significantly better than anyone else's."

Not until 1961 did the company come up with an improvement deemed important enough to give Maytag dishwashers a competitive advantage in engineering; this was a fine-screen filter to trap food particles in water circulating through the washer. The engineers spent still another four years testing hundreds of different designs.

Some large companies selling in national consumer markets introduce new products in big nationwide advertising and promotion campaigns. Maytag won't do it that way, and for a reason. It took three years for the company to get national distribution of its one portable dishwasher model introduced in the late 1960s. Maytag just didn't want to sell the product helter-skelter until its servicemen and dealers had learned its ins and outs. "We had a team from the factory that went around to service and dealer organizations in one marketing territory at a time and said, 'Look, this is our new product, and this is how it works, and this is how you fix it if it breaks'," a marketing executive recalls.

By focusing on quality—and not changing models until an important improvement is possible—Maytag has had no trouble persuading consumers to shell out more than $350 for its top-of-the-line washers, nearly $100 more than the price on the top models turned out by most other makers. Competitors, as well as independent product evaluation groups like Consumer Reports, concede the high quality of Maytag products.

Retailer Loyalty

Besides relying on quality, Maytag's marketing strategy has aimed at maintaining high profit margins. That's why the company handles most of its distribution itself, eliminating an outside middleman's profit. It sells through a network of independent dealers who are carefully cultivated. "We don't sell directly to home builders," observes Ralph L. Nunn, marketing vice president, "partly because there's not enough profit in that business and partly because it would undercut our dealers."

Because Maytag salesmen deal personally with the independent dealers—and because Maytag's products fetch those dealers higher profit margins—the dealers have a high regard for the company, and they push Maytag models extra hard. "Maytag is one appliance company that truly understands the problems of the independent retailer and works hard to help overcome them," says Sol Polk, president of Polk Bros. Inc., a big appliance retailing chain in Chicago.

To get executives who are committed to the Maytag way, the company promotes entirely from within; of all the officers of vice presidential rank or higher, only one, Paul A. Stewart, manufacturing vice president, has had any significant outside business experience. Maytag does nearly all its recruiting from college campuses. "We used to try hiring people from other companies," says Mr. Higdon, "but it never seemed to work. They had a hard time adjusting to the Maytag philosophy, because they had gotten used to doing things some other way."

The conservative Maytag philosophy crops up in small ways here in this company town. Although brightly colored shirts and wide lapels have made inroads, along with mustaches and beards, most Maytaggers still wear coats all day long in the office; and Mr. Higdon still wears white shirts.

Rolling Up the Sidewalks

The small-town atmosphere of Newton, dominated by Maytag, bores some employes and their families, but others find its compensations rewarding. Lunchtime sends some executives home; most live only five minutes or so from the office. But many also lunch at the local country club, where the busy dining hall often is more than half filled with Maytaggers. (Drinks are to be had, but it's considered very bad form for Maytaggers to indulge at lunch.)

Newton pretty much rolls up the sidewalks at night. There is one movie theater in town, and swingers can enjoy a rock band, starring the daughter of a Maytag plant guard, that plays nightly in the cocktail lounge of a motel at the edge of town. And that, says a Maytag man, "is just about it."

To avoid morale problems, Maytag recruits almost exclusively at Midwestern colleges and universities, concentrating on hiring employes with rural backgrounds, accustomed to the quiet small-town life. Although this effort appears to have been rather successful in some respects, it has its drawbacks. "We tried very hard for several years to recruit some black college graduates," says an executive, "but let's face it, they're in demand, and they'd rather live in a big city. Nobody wants to be the one to start a black community in Newton, and I don't blame them a bit." (The town now has only a handful of black residents.)

Employing about half Newton's work force, Maytag naturally swings a lot of weight. Maytag executives serve as directors of every civic and charitable group in town. Two Maytaggers are on the six-man city council.

In the past, the company was blatantly paternalistic. Founder Maytag and his family helped finance a hotel, a golf course, a park, two churches, a hospital, the Young Men's Christian Association and the Salvation Army. Today, the company's profile is a little lower—partly because some Maytag wage earners, since founder Maytag's death, have become rather militant unionists.

Employes generally are happy at Maytag; they are the highest-paid workers in the appliance industry, with wages averaging $4.28 an hour, 13% above the industry average. What angers some workers, however, is a complicated incentive pay system, a major target of the prolonged 1971 strike. The United Auto Workers, which represents the Maytaggers, lost on that issue. Company officials insist they'll never give up the incentive pay plan because it's largely responsible for the work force's high degree of productivity-though Maytag's modern, highly automated facilities are a big help, too.

WHAZZIT?

NO-FAULT INSURANCE

Auto insurance that provides immediate payment to a policyholder who has been involved in an accident, regardless of who was to blame.

CLASS ACTION SUIT

A legal suit by one or more individuals on behalf of all individuals affected.

TRIPLE DAMAGES

Three times normal payment for damages in a legal suit.

BAIT-AND-SWITCH

Offering an item for sale, but intending to sell the buyer another, more expensive item.

DECEPTIVE PACKAGING

Presenting the product in a way that it appears to be something that it isn't.

Sears | Merchant To Millions

The improvement in the quality of Sears' goods goes hand in hand with the story of Sears' laboratory. As early as 1905 some Sears men were insisting not only on accurate catalog descriptions but on quality merchandise as well.

Not until the laboratory was opened in 1911 did the campaign for high-quality merchandise get a real push. With a laboratory, buyers no longer had to guess about quality. They could have tests.

Interestingly enough, Sears' laboratory wasn't started with merchandise testing in mind. The company had a grocery business as part of its operation. Wishing to comply fully with the spirit as well as the letter of the new Pure Food and Drug Act, Sears started the laboratory only to test food. Its first boss was a food chemist.

After a few days on the job, the head of the laboratory reported that Sears groceries were of extremely high quality. What Sears needed, he said, was a laboratory that would bring all Sears merchandise into harmony with the spirit of the Pure Food and Drug Act.

Sears executives bought the suggestion. In time the laboratory was to be called the "watchdog of the catalog"...was to suggest minimum standards for some merchandise...was to spot test merchandise mail-order plants were shipping...was to start scientific comparisons between Sears' and competitors' products...and to help develop new products.

Today the Merchandise Development and Testing Laboratory occupies approximately 75,000 square feet in the Chicago location and operates three smaller, somewhat specialized laboratories in New York, Fort Myers Beach, and Los Angeles. The New York and Los Angeles laboratories are specially designed to serve the buyers in those particular locations. The Ft. Myers Test Base is used primarily for year round testing of products such as marine equipment, lawncare equipment, motorcycles, and other similar products. The Florida Test Base is also used for testing products which must withstand extensive exposure to sunlight.

Each year Sears spends about $3 million to operate the laboratory. The value of the merchandise tested each year adds another $500,000 to the cost of operations. Nearly 80 per cent of the staff of 200 scientists and technicians hold one or more college degrees. Among them you'll find mechanical, electrical, and chemical engineers; physicists; textile chemists and production engineers; industrial designers and home economists; pharmaceutical chemistry experts and an architect.

The laboratory has different divisions concerned with different operations:

- the textile division evaluates textiles, textile finishes, and wearing apparel.

- the chemical and materials division examines a range of products including candy, mugs, mufflers, and paint. The division's work includes chemical, structural engineering, and materials-finishes.

- the electro-mechanical division evaluates such products as guns, appliances, cookware, engines, garbage disposal units, and space heaters.

- the home economics division tests Sears home appliances just as they would be used at home.

-the electronics-physics division evaluates televisions, radios, binoculars, clocks, and cameras.

-the industrial design division has responsibility for making Sears products aesthetically appealing.

Product development at Sears is a continuous process, a process that begins months or years before the product can be offered to Sears customers.

Often product development begins with the buyer of the Sears merchandise line. He knows what the merchandise can do and what it can't do. He knows what the customer would like it to do.

With these ideas in mind, the buyer calls on the laboratory to appoint a development team, typically composed of a product engineer, an industrial engineer, and other specialists.

The team tackles the problem -- on a rigid time schedule. How much will the new product or feature cost? What are the production problems? Are there any new technological breakthroughs that can be used? How will the product stand up in use? These and countless other questions must be investigated and answered.

Thus through its many and varied testing and development projects the laboratory makes a continuing contribution to Sears and Sears customers.

From small beginnings in food testing,
Sears laboratory grew
to where it now tests thousands
of merchandise items yearly

Disgruntled Customers Finally Get a Hearing

Last fall, a Middletown (Pa.) couple checked into the Holiday Inn Penn Center in Philadelphia. The two had planned a relaxing weekend. What they got was 48 hours of hassle and irritation. There were not enough towels, the bathtub drain was clogged, and the shower sprayed the ceiling. To add to their frustration and agony, the telephone clerk forgot to awaken the couple at the appointed hour so they had to pay an overtime charge in the inn's parking garage.

Quite naturally, they stormed out the motel, vowing never to darken the doors of another Holiday Inn. Upon returning home, the couple fired off a hot letter to Holiday Inns in Memphis and cited in detail the various offenses. The company responded immediately and pledged an investigation. Shortly, another letter followed from Vincent deFinis, general manager of the Philadelphia motel. He, too, extended his apologies and offered the couple two free night's lodging.

William G. Lanham, assistant vice-president of Holiday Inns and head of its customer relations staff, points out that the company is not in the habit of doling out free rooms to everyone who complains, but the motel giant, like hundreds of other companies, is now at least listening to the people whom they serve and sell products to. This has not always been universal. Until the consumer revolution of the late 1950s and early 1960s, only a handful of companies bothered to spend much time or money in the consumer affairs area. In fact, most did not set up formal departments until the early 1960s and then only after the consumer movement became so heated that the department became a necessity.

New corporate rung. Even though most companies entered the consumer affairs area under duress, most have come to recognize that they are fulfilling a needed function. While the recession has brought about belt-tightening all across the board, most consumer affairs departments have remained untouched by the corporate hangman. Corporations are not acting out of compassion for the employees in these positions. Rather, they recognize that sales are harder to come by, and this is not a climate in which to kick the consumer. "Customers are more value-conscious than ever," says Norbert W. Markus,

Jr., vice-president of Scott Paper Co.'s packaged products division. "Shoppers are very adept at equating price and consistent quality. This makes our consumer relations vitally important."

The advent of the professional consumer affairs manager has created another rung in the corporate structure. In addition to adding to the payroll, many companies have discovered that the information flowing into these departments is yielding valuable data that is being sent to its marketing, sales, and quality-control departments. The Conference Board says that more than 300 corporations now have formal consumer relations departments and that the large companies have led the pack in moving into this area.

The responsibilities and effectiveness of consumer affairs departments vary greatly. Some are staffed by managers who have no real say in the corporations and simply serve as a convenient buffer to keep the customers away from the brass. Other departments, such as that of Coca-Cola USA, have delegated wide authority. Dianne McKaig, a Harvard law graduate, was hired by Coke in 1973 to head the company's consumer affairs unit. She has the title of vice-president and reports to President Donald R. Keough. Ms McKaig reviews all Coke ads and frequently recommends changes when she feels the consumer is not getting a fair representation of the product. She recently had a Tab ad altered so that it read "less than one calorie per 10-oz. serving." Originally it was written "1/16 of a calorie per oz." "We don't want to talk in fractions of calories," says Ms McKaig.

However, Ms McKaig is in a minority. Most consumer affairs managers are several tiers away from top management. The Conference Board says that only 17% hold the title of vice-president. Nevertheless, the consumer affairs fraternity is becoming more visible and effective.

Pioneers. The idea of a department to deal directly with the customer is not new. General Motors Corp. established its Owner Relations Dept. in 1937. Now the department has 475 employees.

Glen Warren, manager of the GM customer relations unit, provides the divisions' marketing groups with statistics on complaints every 90 days. Every 10 days, GM executives get samples

of the letters that have come into Warren's department. The same letters are routed to quality control.

When a GM auto purchaser complains, the letter is sent to the zone office involved, which then contacts the dealer. Once the complaint has been handled, the process is reversed. If the customer is not satisfied, the Detroit office reviews the file and determines whether everything possible was done to satisfy the aggrieved party. A letter to Warren's office often gets satisfaction where dealings with the dealer have not. Warren recalls a woman who complained that her $246 bill for transmission repair was too high. Investigation revealed that she was correct, and the dealer agreed to refund $71.

Warren maintains that GM customers receive a fair hearing at the company. "In the auto business, a good 70% is repeat business," Warren claims. "If it isn't, you're a dead duck. At GM, the complaint trend has been going down as a percent of sales."

Despite the establishment of departments to handle consumer complaints, most of the consumer advocates find little good in what has been done. But one company official declares: "If they finally admitted that something positive is being accomplished, then the reason for their existence would be debatable."

Carol Tucker Foreman, executive director of the Consumer Federation of America, maintains that consumer affairs departments are window dressing. "They are owned by the other side. They are quite literally in an untenable position," charges Ms Foreman, adding that she has never met a "consumer affairs person who gives me confidence that they can do anything."

In 1972, Chrysler Corp. learned the hard way that a company's consumer relations is not established by advertising and promotion alone. With much fanfare, Chrysler dubbed a vice-president, Byron J. Nichols, the "Man in Detroit" who, the ads said, would be available via phone and letters. However, as scores of customers found out, the Man was never in, and the company found itself tangling with the Federal Trade Commission. Chrysler now has a lower-keyed approach, and a Detroit staff of 20 handles customer grievances. "Steps have been made toward handling the customer's problem in seven days," says John L. Freeman, manager of customer relations.

Others in the consumer advocate camp are somewhat more benevolent. Peter Barash, staff director of the House subcommittee on commerce, consumer, and monetary affairs, holds that the average consumer affairs department is nothing more than an extension of the marketing department and has little influence on actual policy. "They can serve, however, as a focus for consumer complaints, cut corporate red tape, and, in this capacity, they have some impact," asserts Barash.

Mona Doyle, consumer affairs director for Pantry Pride, believes that the

Some consumer affairs people have real clout, but others are just buffers

role of the company consumer activist is to find a balance between the demand of advocates such as Ms Foreman and the "actual concerns" of the day-to-day consumer. Pantry Pride established its department two years ago. One of Ms Doyle's first moves was to create seven regional consumer boards that are made up of a cross-section of supermarket shoppers. From these meetings came the demand for nutritional labeling, which Pantry Pride has placed on all of its house brands. Minutes of the board meetings are channeled to all Pantry Pride officers.

Ms Doyle, who has a reputation for being one of the more hardnosed and outspoken company consumer affairs heads (she is described as "brassy" by one chain executive), has also pushed her idea of roving "hostesses" in some of the Pantry Pride Stores and hopes to expand the concept in the coming months. The hostesses report to Ms Doyle—not to the store manager.

Opponents. But, as the consumer advocates charge, there are companies—large and small—that continue to buck the idea of consumerism. One major television manufacturer—despite efforts from within—has steadfastly beaten back all attempts to create a professional consumer affairs department. Says an officer of the TV maker: "I recommended that we immediately respond to complaints by telephone so our customers knew someone was listening. We had a girl come in the evenings to call and acknowledge letters and to tell people we were asking our local district representative to contact them and send a service person. This way, at least the customer knew someone was paying attention. After three weeks, the director of consumer affairs killed the program without telling anyone. He felt it was not worth the cost."

One who disagrees with Ms Foreman's assessment is Niki Singer, president of Niki Singer, Inc., a New York product publicity firm. Ms Singer gives the consumer advocates full credit for getting the ball rolling but says that the companies are now in the forefront.

"Spearheaded by the active, organized groups, the general attitude of the consumer movement has become part of the ideology of the middle-class consumer," says Ms Singer. "Americans, as they should, are questioning value, questioning product makeup, and questioning sales practices. Without a doubt, the major firms, particularly consumer goods companies, are responding with conviction."

Losers. But some companies are doing little more than fueling the fire to enrage the consumer. One needlepoint-kit company in Illinois is one of these. A Washington (D. C.) woman, after buying a kit, ran out of yarn and wrote the company asking whether she could buy additional yarn to finish her product. The reply, a poorly written and reproduced form letter, advised the customer to buy another kit. Says the needlepoint buff: "Customarily, needlepoint suppliers are very accommodating about sending extra yarn if you run out. I guess they figure repeat business is the name of the game, and it surely is. Needless to say, it'll be a cold day in hell before I ever buy a kit from this outfit."

Naturally, those serving in consumer affairs jobs are reluctant to minimize their importance in policymaking, and corporations do not admit that their consumer programs are window-dressing. However, many departments are just that—public relation fronts.

Joyce Loding, formerly consumer affairs director of Grand Union Co., who saw her job "consolidated" out from under her, says that she never possessed the clout to make decisions. "Whether the company chose to act or not was a decision made by other members of management," asserts Ms Loding. "We didn't have the kind of clout needed to get things done."

Grand Union, in what was said to be a belt-tightening in the corporate structure, last month released Ms Loding and another consumer affairs assistant and consolidated the department under public relations. "I think it's pretty sad only because this seems to be a time when more and more companies are spending more and more time developing better customer relations," she says.

More authority. But the number of companies that have instituted quasi autonomous consumer affairs departments is growing. Companies are now rou-

tinely routing reports from their consumer affairs department to quality control. Letters from consumers that paper napkins emitted a strange odor resulted in Scott Paper Co. finding a well-concealed valve that had worked open and was causing the smell.

Quick action can prevent large-scale consumer desertion of a product

At Richardson-Merrell, Inc., Virginia Woodward checks all advertising for misleading or confusing statements. She also has the responsibility of monitoring packaging. Recently a 20-cents-off coupon was packaged in a product after the offer had expired. When the unhappy consumers complained, Ms Woodward saw to it that each was given a package of the product.

At a Southern foods company, buying carpets for customers has become an unpublicized routine. The company switched from a glass to a plastic nonbreakable container. The result was an avalanche of letters from customers who had stained carpets when the nonbreakable container broke.

Consumer affairs departments, in addition to monitoring the customer's reactions, are also being credited with solving situations before they become widespread problems. Alexis Cole Shantz, a former writer for the *Newark Evening News* and now director of consumer affairs for Chesebrough-Ponds, Inc., provides top management with confidential reports. "I work very closely with research and development and with legal. If there's a letter that asks for information about formulas or ingredients, I go to R&D. If a customer writes saying a product caused damage to clothing or property, I go to legal," says Ms Shantz. As a result of acting quickly on consumer letters concerning Wipe 'N Dipe—a chemically treated cloth—the company averted a major exodus of consumers from the product. Letters began to filter in that the oil was settling on the bottom of the packages. As a result, Ms Shantz recommended that the package labels be reworded to warn the customer to periodically turn the package over to redistribute the oil.

"We are a barometer," Ms Shantz says. "As soon as a product is shipped, the following month is a very clear indication of how the consumer feels about the product." ∎

CONSIDER

1. Should a cigarette manufacturer be liable for injury to a consumer's health resulting from smoking, when the label clearly admits that the product is injurious? Explain.

2. How safe should automobiles be made, and at what consumer price? Explain.

3. To what extent do you feel Maytag's success is due to its product quality emphasis? Explain.

4. Can you trust Sears' laboratory to give an objective evaluation of the products that Sears sells?

5. Should the government represent consumers in dealing with businesses? Explain.

6. Are class-action consumer suits fair?

7. Is it economically feasible to build an automobile that can withstand a 20 mile per hour crash? Explain.

8. Should companies be able to sue consumers who make a lot of noise without having the facts straight? Explain.

9. Would you be willing to pay 20% extra for a product, in order to have a full guarantee of its quality and useful life? What would a full guarantee be worth to you?

10. What career opportunities are there in the consumer affairs field?

CHALLENGES

Identify a product you think is unsafe for some specific reason. Write a letter to the manufacturer to tell about it.

Examine the label on a loaf of bread produced by a major bakery in your area. Identify the additives and check with the company to find out why they are used. If additives are not indicated, find out why.

Visit a local bakery, a small business in your area, and find out what inspections or controls affect the business. Find out why the bakery goods are not labeled as to contents, as major brands are.

Visit a local health foods store and find a product advertised as having no additives. Compare the price (for the same quantity) with that of a comparable product (with additives) at a regular grocery. If there is a difference, explain.

Compare several boxes of laundry detergent in a grocery store. Compare the size of the boxes of competitive brands in relation to the amount of detergent (by weight) indicated on the label. Also note the box sizes. Explain any differences.

RECAP

Companies are not only listening to customers today, many are actually doing something. Many are making changes in the design of their products, changing their warranties, and upgrading customer services. They are looking more closely at their pricing, labeling, packaging, and advertising of products.

Contents of products and details of warranties and guarantees are being written in plain English for customers to read and understand, and often in Spanish or French as well. Quality of products and services is being more closely examined and controlled. Product safety is of major concern and is being improved as far as possible within economic and technological constraints.

More intensive public relations or public-consumer affairs efforts have been put into action in many companies, to tell the story of company empathy for consumer needs. There is a lot of controversy and criticism among consumers who feel that business is not putting their interests first -- and this discussion is leading to new legislation regarding consumer welfare. Overall, even the affected businesses agree that consumerism is healthy and is contributing to solutions for many problems.

Increasingly, the government is becoming involved in consumer protection activities. Consumer rights -- to safety, to be informed, to choose, and to be heard -- are being protected by an increasing number of laws and administrative regulations. New agencies and expanded governmental staffs are monitoring business practices that have an impact on these consumer rights.

Some companies have been successful in part because of a strong commitment to consumer satisfaction. Sears, for example, has operated a laboratory for many years to test the quality and safety of products being considered for sale. Another company, Maytag, has built a reputation for high-quality products. It definitely can be in both business' and consumers' interests to emphasize product quality, safety, and durability.

WORKSHEET NO. 8

1. What rights do consumers have?

2. Who has responsibility for protecting these rights?

3. Is it in the best interest of business to provide the
   safest possible products? Explain.

---

4. What was Maytag's marketing strategy?

PART IV

FINANCIAL ACTIVITIES IN BUSINESS

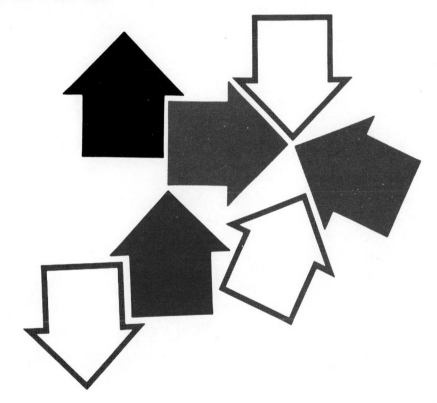

CHAPTER 9

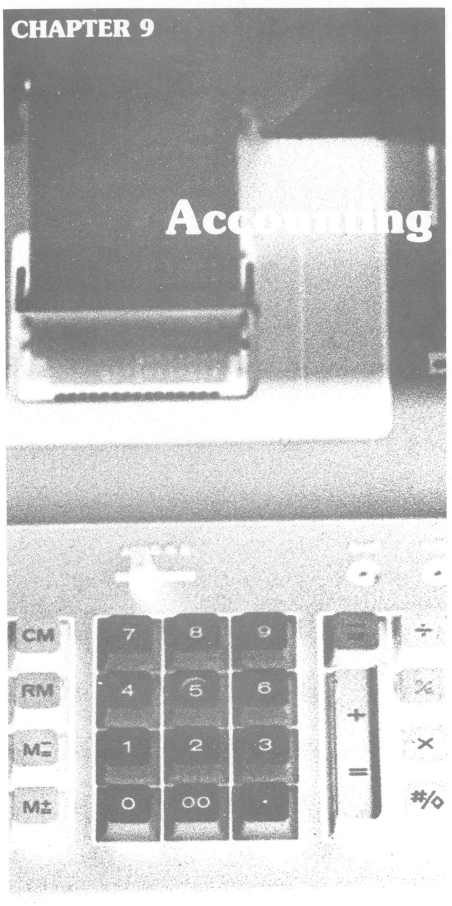

Accounting is a means of expressing in clear, understandable, financial terms the results of complex activities in business, government, and other institutions. It gives us the information we need to make meaningful decisions regarding future activities.

The way accounting is practiced is guided by a generally accepted set of rules and principles developed by the Accounting Principles Board (APB). The accounting profession attempts to develop and maintain consistent, meaningful accounting practices in American business.

But this does not mean that all accountants are in agreement as to accounting principles and policies. On the contrary, there is considerable debate on a variety of issues that are of importance to management. For example, in recent years here has been a re-examination of the matter of accounting for mergers. This has resulted in changes in conventional accounting practices in this area.

Guidelines for accounting practices are announced by the APB in bulletins designed to provide standards. These don't hold the force of law, but do generally have the respect of the accounting profession and corporate management.

One of the key roles of the accountant is to ensure that investors have a complete and accurate picture of a company's financial situation. In very large business organizations and with accounting principles applied in different ways in different situations, this role is difficult to fulfill.

The application of accounting principles depends on an organization's circumstances. Simply, there is more than one way to keep the books of a company. How a company accounts for an acquisition, records sales, keeps track of inventory values, depreciates assets, and values marketable securities and other assets are all matters of judgement. Accounting principles provide broad guidelines, not hard and fast rules.

The most prestigious member of the accounting profession is the Certified Public Accountant (CPA). Less than 20% of all accountants are CPAs, and to become one an individual must have appropriate education and experience. The prospective CPA than must pass an examination in accounting practice administered by the American Institute of Certified Public Accountants.

When accountants are on the company payroll, accounting practices are applied to present the company in the most favorable light to investors and the public. Even CPAs are frequently subject to pressures from management (who pay the fees) to allow accounting practices that are favorable to the company's position.

In short, the accountant is being pulled by two forces: professional standards on the one hand and the practical desires of management on the other. The role of the accountant is essential in our society; it is not easy to fill.

In This Chapter

The Accounting Process

Accounting provides quantitative information about the results of a firm's activities. As such it is often thought of as the language of business. It provides management with the information needed to run the business enterprise. It is also used by potential investors to determine the investment potential of a firm. The accounting system in a business keeps track of all kinds of business activities and reports the results of those activities to interested parties.

In a recent statement by a group designated to develop basic definitions about the accounting function, accounting was defined as: ". . . the process of identifying, measuring, and communicating information to permit informed judgements and decisions by users of the information."

Just who are the users of accounting information, and how do their needs differ? In general, there are two major users of accounting information: the management of the firm and investors. To satisfy the needs of these two groups there are two types of accounting, MANAGERIAL and FINANCIAL.

Managerial accounting is designed to assist management in making the complex decisions that must be made to keep the enterprise functioning. Management uses accounting information as the basis for planning and to control operations by comparing actual performance against that which was planned. The accounting system reports to management the results of past activities which can then be analyzed to determine if any significant trends are evident.

Management needs information about sales, the revenues derived from those sales, the cost of producing the material that was sold, the amount of material in inventory available for use, the costs of labor, and much more.

Since management must make hundreds of decisions every day about all aspects of the firm's activities, the accounting system must be capable of collecting data about just about everything that happens. This data must then be in a form that is understandable and available when it is needed by the appropriate decision-maker. As such, the information generated by the accounting system can be considered to be an important part of the firm's management information system.

Financial accounting presents information about the business to stockholders and potential investors. This information is presented to investors through the use of financial statements. These statements, some of which will be discussed in detail later in this chapter are issued periodically, usually quarterly, with a major publication of the firm's activities presented yearly in the ANNUAL REPORT. The information contained in the Annual Report is checked by outside auditors whose function is to insure that the firm has used generally accepted accounting practices in the preparation of the financial statements enclosed in the report.

Other groups outside of the corporation are also interested in the accounting information generated by a firm. The one most interested is probably the government since taxes are based on the profits and other activities of a firm. The government is also interested in the financial reports of an organization from the point of view of regulating business activites.

Creditors also use the financial reports of a firm to determine if the organization is strong enough to pay back borrowed money or pay for material that might be sold to the company.

But no matter whether the accounting data is to be used to assist in making managerial decisions or to assist a potential investor decide about the financial health of the firm, all accounting follows basic accepted principles. These principles are set forth by the Accounting Principles Board (APB) and guide all accountants in the pursuit of their profession. While there is some discretion given to accountants in how they apply the principles, we can be reasonably assured that the records we see are prepared according to the APB standards.

Getting Accountants 'Involved'

API's Levy feels it's time for accountants to display concern for social problems.

"If API had been a nationwide organization last year, half the environmental battles that were lost would have been won," says San Francisco conservationist Gil Bailie. Bailie is talking about Accountants for the Public Interest, an 18-month-old nonprofit organization that provides accounting and financial analysis to help consumer, environmental, and community groups, mostly in California.

Now API is going national, and environmentalists and their fellow advocates in many parts of the country will be getting more of that kind of expertise. This month, 65 accountants from 12 states and the District of Columbia flocked to API's first national convention in San Francisco to learn how to set up local chapters.

"There's a feeling that it's about time the accounting profession displayed a real concern for public and social problems," says Morton Levy, API's bearded and jovial executive director. Up to now, most CPAs have avoided controversial issues. "Accountants for the most part are concerned with making money," says API President Esmond Coleman.

Getting involved. Many CPA firms allow employees to do some free or low-cost bookkeeping for nonprofit organizations, just as law firms have given time for *pro bono* work, but most duck cases that could bring them into the public spotlight. API is out to change that. So far it has deployed 40 volunteer accountants, some from the Big Eight accounting firms, to examine 25 public issues ranging from utility rate hearings to airport expansion.

Many who attended API's conference represented accounting aid societies, which have sprung up around the country in the past few years to provide tax assistance to minorities and the poor. Levy believes that a number of these groups will widen their mandates to include the API kind of investigative and analytical services.

API has tapped several national CPA firms for volunteer help and has received recognition from professional accounting societies. Accountants from Coopers & Lybrand; Peat, Marwick, Mitchell; Haskins & Sells; Ernst & Ernst; and Alexander Grant are helping. Some firms are going along with the idea, Coleman says, because they feel that this kind of public service will help them attract and keep bright young persons on their staffs. But other CPA executives are skeptical. "It's difficult to separate the individual from the organization," says the San Francisco manager of one major CPA firm. "That's why most firms have strict rules against moonlighting."

Some accounting firms undoubtedly fear that public interest involvement may present conflicts of interest with corporate or government clients. Many of the cases that API has taken concerned challenges to large private or governmental institutions—the bread and butter of major CPA firms. The passions stirred up by, say, a gas utility rate hearing are fierce. And if an accountant made a particularly telling analysis on behalf of public clients, that might well blacken the firm's image in the eyes of the utility.

Absolutely objective. API tries to avoid a taint by insisting on careful objectivity. "The financial community accepts the accountant's independence in dealing with corporate clients," Levy says. "There is no reason why it shouldn't be true in broad public issues."

He cites API's handling of two hospital cases as a model of the objectivity his group is seeking. In one case, federally funded poverty lawyers sued seven New Orleans hospitals over their failure to provide free or low-cost care for the poor, as required for hospitals receiving government funds under the Hill-Burton Act. The hospitals claimed that such care was not financially feasible. But an API analysis showed that it was, and the case was quickly settled.

When another legal services group asked for help on a similar case against a New York hospital, however, API turned it down. "We told them we thought they were wrong," Levy says.

But the appearance of independence is hard to come by, particularly for a fledgling organization. After API produced a model accounting system for San Francisco's tough new campaign spending ordinance, one candidate accused it of trying to pressure him into using its services.

A newspaper attack on a proposal for city acquisition of Pacific Gas & Electric's San Francisco facilities castigated API's report—without even mentioning the legal assistance group that actually sponsored the plan. (API's analysis of the projected operating results had noted that the city would profit by an estimated $15-million to $22-million a year.)

A new approach. If API can win acceptance because of its objectivity, Levy believes, it will bring a unique contribution to many social problems. Bailie, a founder of the San Francisco Ecology Center, agrees wholeheartedly. "Many decisions with environmental implications are intimately involved with complex economic problems," he notes.

The Ecology Center recently commissioned an API study of proposed expansion plans for the San Francisco airport. Bailie says that the report contains enough material "to give us grounds for an interesting battle before the Board of Supervisors."

Among other points, the API analysis indicated that bond repayment for the projected expansion would depend heavily on fees from expanded parking facilities. And such facilities, Bailie contends, do not seem likely to win Environmental Protection Agency approval under that agency's present policies. ∎

The Annual Report

The annual report is an account of an enterprise in action -- a picture of the life of an economic organization. The report, a statement of activities and results to the public and the stockholders, reflects the past actions of the business, the present condition of the business, and prospects for the future.

Corporate financial statements in an annual report portray a corporation's financial progress growing out of the soundness of its operations. Investors are interested in this information to aid them in making sound investment decisions. We are all interested in the progress of corporations because they have such a great impact on our economy and our lives.

All corporations with securities listed on the national stock exchanges, regional stock exchanges, or over the counter listings are required by law to publish extensive information on their activities and financial condition. The corporations listed on the New York Stock Exchange are the most important in terms of their economic impact. These firms, over 1200 in number, earn almost 70% of the profits earned by all American corporations, pay stockholders more than half of all the dividends paid in the nation, and pay a vital portion of the taxes that support our government.

Until modern times there was little need for elaborate annual reports. Corporations such as banks and mills in the early days of American business were largely local enterprises with only a handful of stockholders. In most cases the major stockholders were also the managers of the enterprises or were closely acquainted with the managers.

But as times changed, more complete annual reports were needed, to assure the stockholders that the business was sound and appropriately managed. Corporations expanded, capital needs increased, the number of stockholders grew, and the firms became regional or national in scope. The expense or trouble of attending an annual meeting of stockholders, especially for individuals holding few shares of stock, was impractical.

So, the printed annual report was born. It is a report to the stockholders on the results of the year's business and shows where the company is headed in the year ahead. Of course, some reports are very short, with only financial tables presented; others are very elaborate, with four-color photographs of company products, facilities, individual executives, and with detailed information on business operations.

As you can see from the following table of contents from a typical annual report, most start out with

Contents

a message from the top corporate officers, followed by information about company operations, the financial statements, and a five or ten year summary of operations. The financial statements that go into an annual report are explained on the following pages of this chapter.

More Meat In Annual Reports

Investors who have grown accustomed to seeing at least one or two major new revelations about corporate operations in each year's annual report will be disappointed when they read the 1975 crop. For the first time in years, the Securities & Exchange Commission asked for no big piece of new data. But corporations are using the respite to do a better job of presenting what already is required, and more of them are voluntarily revealing helpful bits of company information that could be required in the future.

BUSINESS WEEK's yearly survey of annual reports from 100 of the nation's larger industrial companies indicates that 84% now give investors a breakdown of both sales and earnings by broad product line, about the same number as in 1974. These data used to be available only in the 10-K reports that corporations must file with the SEC. Beginning in reports for 1974, the commission decreed that the same information had to be spelled out for shareholders, too.

Unless the SEC or the Financial Accounting Standards Board changes the rules, the percentage of companies reporting that kind of data is expected to remain about the same in coming years. Many large corporations, such as Scott Paper, Burroughs, McDonnell Douglas, Kraftco, Merck, and Eastman Kodak, still consider themselves to be in just one line of business. While these companies do report sales data about various major product lines, they still do not have to tell just how much profit each line contributed to the company's net earnings. But Coca-Cola, long known for its bare-bones annual reports, makes no product-line or geographical disclosures of any kind to shareholders.

New rules coming. That could change a bit if recently proposed FASB rules are approved this year. One-product companies—those that have 90% or more of their sales, earnings, or assets concentrated in a single line of business—still would not have to make additional product-by-product disclosures. But all companies would have to give sales, earnings, and asset data about foreign operations, disclose revenues from export sales, and reveal their dependence, if any, on just a few major customers or suppliers.

In anticipation of this new requirement, 59% of the companies in BW's current survey volunteered information about foreign sales and earnings, compared with only 48% in 1974. And last year, after the SEC required all companies to carry quarterly data on the price of their stock in their annual reports, almost half also took the opportunity to give quarterly sales and earnings data to shareholders. This year that percentage climbed to 60%.

Almost 70% of the big corporations are telling shareholders what they spend for research and development, compared with only 40% a year ago. That revelation long has been required in 10-K reports.

Less history. In one key area, though, investors are getting less information these days. In past years, two-thirds or more of the big companies surveyed gave shareholders financial statistics for 10 years or more, although a few still clung to the minimum requirement of two-year comparisons. For 1974 reports, the SEC mandated a five-year breakdown, together with a detailed management analysis explaining the significant changes for the two most recent periods.

As a result, sometimes to save space in overweight annual reports, only 45% of the companies continued to provide 10-year statistics that year. And in 1975 only 48% gave investors the longer-term picture in addition to the five-year analysis required by SEC.

In the early 1970s, when "corporate social responsibility" became a management buzzword, most companies felt obligated at least to pay lip service to the idea in their annual reports. In recent years fewer corporations have been playing up this theme. But those that do are getting away from the more general "God, mother, and country" approach and are making far more factual analyses. Norton, for example, issued a separate eight-page special report this year, detailing its corporate social philosophy and progress. Ford, Celanese, Merck, and Shell Oil all gave detailed employment data on women and minority groups.

This year a few companies, such as General Electric and Koppers, took special pains to explain to investors how to interpret each line on the income statement and balance sheet, while Kraftco carried a special guide inside its front cover on how to read an annual report.

Although surprisingly few companies picked up the Bicentennial theme for 1975, it was a year for "message" annual reports. Armco Steel, Standard Oil (Indiana), Du Pont, Caterpillar, and Union Carbide took the opportunity to complain about excessive government regulation. Owens-Illinois expressed concern about the capital crisis, while Pan American made its

What companies are telling shareholders this year

Sample of 100 companies	1970	1971	1972	1973	1974	Percent 1975
Sales and earnings by product line	32%	51%	57%	58%	83%	84%
Sales only by product line	24	19	21	22	10	14
Financial statistics for 10 years or more	67	63	67	73	45	48
Research and development expenditures	17	24	35	26	40	69
Concern for corporate responsibilities	30	60	64	22	35	33
Foreign sales or earnings	NA	NA	NA	38	48	59
Quarterly earnings or sales	NA	NA	NA	26	47	60

NA = not available
Data: BW

The year of the 'message' about federal regulation, financing, and economics

brief for regulatory reform. Both Koppers and Greyhound carried prominent essays about the role of corporate profits in the economy.

Inflation factor. While the rate of inflation has cooled, many companies still are concerned about its distorting effect on profits and assets. Again this year Shell Oil presented supplementary financial statements adjusted by a general price-level index to measure inflation's impact. Compared with Shell's traditional financial statements based on historical cost, these "purchasing power" calculations show the company's 1975 net income to be $438 million rather than $515 million and its property, plant, and equipment to be $5.8 billion rather than $4.4 billion. Shell concludes that adjustment of its accounts for inflation brings its return on shareholders' equity in 1975 down from 14.5% to 8.4%.

Similarly, General Electric says that if it had used the index adjustment in 1975, its depreciation charge, reported under historical cost accounting at $419 million, would have been about $140 million higher.

While conceding that inflation adjustments need to be made, critics charge that using a single general price-level index may be misleading. They prefer an adjustment of each individual asset to something more akin to current value. One approach is to show inventories and assets such as plant and equipment at replacement cost, and the SEC has just decreed that the nation's 1,000 largest companies will have to make that kind of disclosure in their 1976 annual reports. At least one corporation, Rocky Mountain Fuel Co., went even further this year and gave shareholders current-value estimates for all its mining properties and mineral rights (story below).

A few companies already are beginning to make replacement cost calculations. Koppers, for example, states the original cost of its plant and equipment at about $500 million but indicates that when "generally accepted construction cost indices" are used, the replacement cost is about $900 million.

Accounting methods obscure the revenue necessary to provide for replacement, GE complains. It cautions shareholders that until accountants can get together and decide how to devise financial statements that reflect the ravages of inflation, "financial reports must be read with care to avoid drawing conclusions that are incorrect in terms of 'real' earnings." Warns GE: "Such conclusions have contributed to the anti-profits bias held by many today." ∎

Making a virtue of full reporting

A tiny Denver energy company that has been in liquidation for 30 years has come up with a way to show the current value of its assets to shareholders. Enclosed with Rocky Mountain Fuel Co.'s annual report, which contains the traditional balance sheet based on historical costs, is a special supplement detailing all property and mineral rights owned by the company in 10 Colorado counties, their value as carried on the books, and their current market value compiled from estimates made by geologists, engineers, and real estate appraisers.

Many observers believe that before long all U. S. companies may be required to make the same disclosure. The difference between the two sets of numbers is sizable. Book value of land and mineral rights, set in 1946 when the company was reorganized, is only $376,149. But estimated market value is $10.7 million.

Wide differences. Coal rights on 3,812 acres that have been fully depleted for accounting purposes (and have no balance sheet value) are valued at $822,400. A 160-acre farm, appraised in 1946 as agricultural land at $7,273, is now suitable for residential development and has a market value of $400,000. Oil and gas rights on 2,400 acres are listed as having no book value because there were no known reserves in 1946. But oil and gas were discovered three years ago, and the mineral rights now are valued at $1.3 million.

The supplement is the idea of Gerald R. Armstrong, a shareholder rights advocate who led a proxy fight to get on the company board in 1972 and a year later was named president. Last year the company made an after-tax profit of $300,681 and paid out half of it in dividends, compared with pre-Armstrong profits of $10,000 or less.

"Shareholders are entitled to more information," says Armstrong. Many shareholders of the "Rocky" have held their stock since the 1930s, when the company was the second-largest coal producer in the state, before it defaulted on bond payments, was declared insolvent, and agreed to a gradual liquidation of its assets.

"This is our answer when they ask if they are being realistic or sentimental to continue their investment," Armstrong concludes.

WHAZZIT?

GOODWILL

In accounting, this is an intangible asset representing the value of good relations with customers and the public, the firm's trademarks, and the firm's future earning power generated by past operations.

BIG EIGHT

The largest eight public accounting firms in the United States.

CPA

A Certified Public Accountant. In Great Britain and Canada, the equivalent designation of an accounting professional working independently of any one company is a Chartered Accountant (CA).

SEC

The Securities and Exchange Commission.

Behind The Scenes

You are cordially invited to attend the 1975 Annual Meeting of Stockholders on Saturday, May 3, in the corporate offices of our Company, 6301 Lincoln Avenue, Morton Grove, Ill. The meeting will begin promptly at 11:30 a.m., Central Daylight Time.

So begins the printed notice of our Company's Annual Meeting. However, before notices are sent, and before the Annual Meeting can ac-

tually take place, a multitude of details must be handled. Our law and public relations departments coordinate all Meeting arrangements.

The law department begins preparing in January. Assistant Secretary of the Corporation, Phil McKinsey, records all topics to be voted on, in addition to the election of Directors.

Once legal materials are obtained, proxy voting statements and notices

of the Annual Meeting are printed. The Securities and Exchange Commission lists information which must be included in the forms.

The actual mailing of materials begins in late March. Proxy statements and cards are sent to every direct shareholder of common stock. Those shareholders who own **Baxter** stock through a brokerage firm will receive proxy materials through their brokers. Georgeson & Co. in New York help Baxter solicit proxies from brokers.

In mid-April, if proxies have not been returned, a second mailing is made with a blue, instead of a white, proxy card. Also at this time, the Company begins contacting major brokers, nominees and shareholders if their proxies have not been received.

"Generally, we receive an 85 to 90 percent return of proxies," McKinsey said. "When proxies are counted, they are first verified manually for correct stockholder identification. Then, votes are tabulated by a computer. On broker tabulations, all votes must be tabulated manually, as the broker may submit proxies for several shareholders, which results in partial voting."

above: Product displays are arranged in the Meeting room. right: Joan Schmerschneider, B/T marketing, holds microphone for shareholder posing a question during the Meeting.

At The Annual Meeting

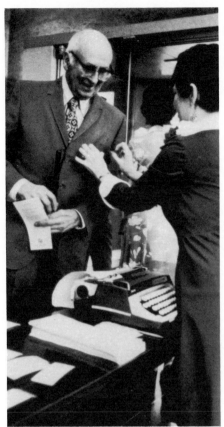

During this vote solicitation period, the public relations department starts its preparations. It prepares an agenda and has it printed. It contracts a caterer to prepare the light buffet luncheon which follows the Meeting. It arranges for personnel to work as typists and guides. Public relations contacts Divisions to arrange for product displays to be set up for the Meeting. It assists executives scheduled to speak at the Meeting in preparing their notes. It contracts sound systems equipment and arranges installation. It arranges for floral arrangements for the lobby and serving tables. It contracts a photographer for the Meeting. Public relations writes a news release about the events of the Annual Meeting for release that day.

"As far as the meeting room preparation is concerned, we begin the afternoon before the Meeting to co-ordinate the physical aspects of the room," said Mimi Trangsrud, public relations specialists. "We make sure everything is in order, right down to the pencils on the directors' table."

Soon after the stockholders arrive and register, the final tabulation of voting begins. Few shareholders vote at the actual Meeting, but for those who do, proxies are manually verified and the votes are added to the computer count. At the close of the Meeting, voting results are announced in percentage form. Shortly after the meeting, votes are tabulated by a computer for an exact count.

The business meeting concluded, shareholders adjourn for a light lunch, a look at product displays, and maybe a chat with a Baxter executive. The votes are computed, news releases are dispatched, and the shareholder's meeting is over—until next year.

above: Betty Stromquist, public relations, helps a shareholder with his nametag at the registration area. below: the caterer completes the buffet arrangements for a light lunch. right: Chairman William Graham talks with a shareholder following the Meeting.

How To Read A Balance Sheet

When a company goes broke where does the holder of common shares stand?

Answer: at the end of the line. In general, as we noted last month, secured bondholders get first claim, followed by the unsecured bondholders, general creditors, preferred stockholders and finally, if there is anything left, the common shareholders.

The very nature of equity investing implies a degree of risk. In certain cases, stockholders could be required to "kick in" additional sums to meet corporate liabilities.

The key to the relative safety of your equity investment lies in the company's balance sheet. Unfortunately, reading a balance sheet isn't simple, and a surprisingly large number of investors do not understand what it's all about. The three most important clues to your degree of protection are assets, liabilities and stockholders' equity.

Assets are listed in the balance sheet on the left and are divided into three parts 1) current; 2) fixed; and 3) "other."

Current assets include cash, holdings of U.S. government and other marketable securities, accounts and/or notes receivable and inventories. In the event that they are easily collectible, investments in and advances to unconsolidated subsidiaries and affiliates are also included in current assets, although more conservative practice is to list them under "other."

While the amount by which current assets exceed current liabilities is a vital indicator of financial health, even this figure may be deceptive. Sometimes the current assets are inflated by accounts receivable. It may be a sign of danger if the accounts receivable amount to more than a third of the total.

A further danger signal could be in notes receivable, which are generally signed promises by customers to pay their debts and which may have been arranged when payment became overdue or if payment is long-term. Obviously, if accounts and notes receivable constitute a disproportionately high percentage of total assets, this could impair the company's ability to meet its short-term commitments. In boom times, this may not be serious, but in a recession or a period of illiquidity the incidence of bad debts increases, lessening the credibility of weighty receivables as current assets.

Cash and marketable securities are definitely "current" assets, but marketable securities are carried "at cost, which approximates market value" or simply "at cost" and therefore the figure may be deflated in a bear market.

Fixed assets pose an analytical problem. They include property, plant, buildings and equipment and are usually carried at cost, less reserve for depreciation. The fixed assets figure, then, may be above or below actual value. In the case of older companies, the figure is generally conservative, since property bought several years ago can be safely assumed to have appreciated in value over the years.

"Other assets" are less important as an indication of financial health or otherwise, since they include intangibles such as trademarks and patents as well as investments in subsidiaries.

Liabilities are listed on the right of the balance sheet and consist of two categories: current and long-term. Current liabilities are usually payable within one year and include accounts payable, income taxes, dividends payable, bond interest payable, long-term debt becoming due within one year, salaries, wages, commercial paper, bank loans and "other" short-term debt.

In general, current liabilities should not exceed half of current assets, for an asset-to-debt ratio of two-to-one. In times of illiquidity, conservative analysts become nervous if the ratio falls below three-to-one. A shareholder in a company whose ratio fell below two-to-one would be justified in asking management if it had any lines of bank credit open, as a cushion, or what alternative arrangements it had in mind.

The degree of danger in a close current assets/current liabilities ratio depends, of course, on the general state of the economy and the capital markets. For instance, a company with a heavy load of current liabilities could go to the bond market to translate some of the short-term debt into long-term debt if it felt a danger point approaching—assuming a receptive bond market. Otherwise, it might spread it with long-term bank credit—assuming, once again, an availability of money.

Long-term liabilities are debts which are due after a year's time and should be analyzed for maturity. Ideally, maturity dates should have a good spread to avoid the danger of a liquidity crisis.

So, at the bottom of the left-hand page on the balance sheet we have a total for assets. On the right, above the item "shareholders' equity" is the total debt. The figures do not balance but, when the equity is added to the debt, the total should equal the assets total. If the company were liquidated and the creditors paid out of sale of the assets, the shareholders would get the difference, viz. their equity.

Measure your security armour

Here are some general yardsticks which many financial analysts use to measure protection: current assets to liabilities, no less than two-to-one; cash to current liabilities, one half-to-one; quick assets to current liabilities, about even; debt to total capitalization (capitalization is the sum of the funds in the business) 35% to 65%, depending on the type of company—utilities on the high side and industrial companies on the low side.

One of the reasons for the recent liquidity crisis has been the fact that many companies have drastically exceeded these yardsticks, borrowing in some cases over 80% of their worth. This degree of "leveraging" demands tremendous growth and puts a company in jeopardy during a period of economic slowdown.

A couple of years ago, a company using heavy leverage was admired as a go-getter, growth-oriented enterprise. Today, the investor is seeking out companies with little or no debt—and these are few and far between. At time of writing, only about 6% of the companies with shares listed on the New York Stock Exchange (which in itself offers a degree of protection) had no long-term debt.—**J.W.Day**

The Balance Sheet

Sears, Roebuck And Co.

STATEMENT OF FINANCIAL POSITION

$ in thousands	January 31 1976	1975*
Assets		
Current Assets		
Cash	$ 277,437	$ 192,015
Receivables....................	5,200,660	4,979,355
Inventories (note 3)	1,877,609	1,979,280
Prepaid advertising and other charges	97,904	97,827
Total Current Assets	7,453,610	7,248,477
Investments (note 1)		
Allstate Insurance Company (cost $61,874 and $54,600)	1,148,915	839,418
Other investments and advances	645,025	531,795
	1,793,940	1,371,213
Property, Plant and Equipment	2,322,556	2,223,930
Deferred Charges....................	6,467	5,409
Total Assets	$11,576,573	$10,849,029
Liabilities		
Current Liabilities		
Short-term borrowings (note 11)		
Commercial paper	$ 1,706,286	$ 2,300,742
Banks	217,567	227,181
Agreements with bank trust departments....................	634,384	539,615
Current maturity of long-term debt	125,000	—
Accounts payable and accrued expenses....................	1,119,604	844,876
Unearned maintenance agreement income....................	221,562	203,240
Deferred income taxes....................	782,673	781,620
Total Current Liabilities	4,807,076	4,897,274
Deferred Income Taxes....................	140,804	105,362
Long-Term Debt	1,326,252	1,095,120
Total Liabilities	$ 6,274,132	$ 6,097,756
Shareholders' Equity	$ 5,302,441	$ 4,751,273

Balance Sheet Items

THE BALANCE SHEET

This statement presents the financial condition of an enterprise as it appeared on one particular day, January 31 in the case of the statement on page 253.

The statement is a picture of the company, with two parts:

-- Assets
-- Liabilities and Stockholders' Equity.

These two basic parts of the statement are always in balance -- they have the same dollar totals. That's why a "statement of financial position or financial condition" is often called a balance sheet.

ASSETS

These represent all of the goods and property that the business owns, and all claims against others yet to be received (money owed to the business). Simply, assets are anything of value owned by a company.

LIABILITIES

These represent all of the debts of the business, the claims of other businesses and individuals and the government on the firm's assets.

SHAREHOLDERS' EQUITY

This represents the amount of the shareholders' (or stockholders')

investment in the business, the amount for which the firm is accountable to the owners of the business. It includes the money that investors paid in for stock, plus the value of any past earnings retained by the business.

We may look at this section of the balance sheet in a different way. Assume that a company were to go out of business, and that its assets were sold for a million dollars cash. After all the debts are paid to creditors and lenders, the remainder is left for the stockholders:

$1,000,000	Assets
825,000	Liabilities
$ 175,000	Shareholders' Equity

Theoretically, the shareholders would divide up this money according to how many shares of stock each of them holds.

WHERE ARE THE ASSETS?

Companies don't sit on big piles of money, though. The dollars shown on the financial statements are actually tied up in goods and property used to run the business. Below are the types of assets that you might find in a company (and on the balance sheet).

CASH

Cash is just what you think it is -- money on hand and in bank accounts.

MARKETABLE SECURITIES

This asset is money the company has invested in stocks and bonds of other businesses, government bonds, notes, or other financial investments for the purpose of earning dividends and interest.

This is a temporary investment, intended to put idle or excess cash to use while it is not needed for other business purposes.

They are called "marketable" securities because they may be sold on the market for cash at relatively short notice.

The general practice is to show this asset at its original cost, with an explanation to show the present market value.

RECEIVABLES

Sometimes called "Accounts Receivable," this asset represents money not yet collected from customers to whom goods and services were sold prior to payment.

INVENTORIES

This asset represents raw materials to be used in the product, particially finished products, and finished goods or merchandise ready for sale to customers.

You will note that in the case of Sears, receivables and inventories are quite high dollar amounts. You would expect this to be the case for a large retailing business, wouldn't you?

PREPAID CHARGES

This asset includes payments for services not yet used, such as advertising charges not yet applied to actual services.

INVESTMENTS

Stocks, bonds, and property owned by the company for the purpose of earning a satisfactory return with a reasonable safety factor for the money invested. This asset differs from marketable securities in that the investment is viewed as a long-term, rather than a liquid asset.

PROPERTY, PLANT, EQUIPMENT

Often referred to as fixed assets, this item represents those assets used in conducting the operations of the business, but not intended for sale.

DEFERRED CHARGES

This asset is similar to prepaid charges, but includes benefits that will be received over a period of future years rather than in the current year. As the benefits are received, the charges are deducted from the total. One example is

LIABILITIES

On the other side of the balance sheet are the obligations of the business enterprise. The liabilities that might appear on a balance sheet

include payables, debt, accrued expenses and taxes, and deferred taxes.

These are briefly described below.

NOTES PAYABLE

Money owed to banks or other lenders which must be paid in the upcoming year. Notes payable appear on the balance sheet as evidence of the fact that a written promise to pay has been given by the company to the lender.

CURRENT MATURITY OF LONG-TERM DEBT

The portion of the company's long-term debt that will mature in the year ahead.

ACCOUNTS PAYABLE

Money owed to regular business creditors for goods and services purchased on an open account (without a note signed). This item represents the company's "charge accounts".

ACCRUED EXPENSES

These are expenses that have been incurred but that have not yet been paid, nor have bills been received as yet.

FEDERAL INCOME TAX ACCRUED

Federal income taxes that are owed to the government, but are not yet due to be paid.

DEFERRED TAXES

Taxes that are due at some future date, but are, nonetheless, an obligation of the company.

LONG-TERM DEBT

Under the heading of long-term debt are listed the liabilities of the company that are due after one year from the date of the annual report.

Long-term debt may include bonds, debentures, and mortgage bonds issued

SHAREHOLDERS' EQUITY

This section, also called Stockholders' equity, includes all of the items that represent the equity interest of the owners of the business.

For accounting purposes, the section is often broken into three sections:
-- capital stock
-- paid-in surplus
-- retained earnings.

CAPITAL STOCK

This represents the total value of the shares of stock issued by the company. These shares are backed by printed stock certificates issued to each stockholder.

There may be different types of stock issued, such as common or preferred stock, and different levels or classes within these (e.g., A,B,C). Sears happens to have only common stock.

The statement usually indicates the number of shares of stock that is authorized to be issued and the par value, in addition to the amount actually issued.

PAID-IN SURPLUS

A Capital Surplus is often listed to indicate the amount of money paid in by shareholders in excess of the par or legal value of the stock.

RETAINED EARNINGS

Earnings of the company that are kept for internal use in running or building the business. These funds may be used to help the company grow or to satisfy any other financial commitments, such as repayment of debts. When a company is founded, it has no earned surplus. When there are earnings, it is possible that they could all be paid out as dividends to shareholders, also resulting in no retained earnings.

In general, however, this is an important source of capital funds and represents money that might have been paid out to stockholders in the form of dividends. If the company were to be dissolved, the retained earnings would be distributed among the stockholders.

To an extent, then, the retained earnings are reflected in the market value of the stock.

USING THE BALANCE SHEET

A generation or more ago, before present accounting standards and principles had gained wide acceptance, considerable imagination was used in preparing such statements. This naturally made the public skeptical of financial reports.

Today there is little need for skepticism, as companies are very consistent in their accounting and reporting practices.

Of course, many of the items on the balance sheet continue to be based on estimates (like the value of property, inventories, or accounts receivable), but companies generally fo follow similar procedures in making these estimates.

AUDITS

Further, balance sheets and other financial

Report of Certified Public Accountants

To the Shareholders and Board of Directors of Sears, Roebuck and Co.:

We have examined the statement of Financial Position of Sears, Roebuck and Co. and consolidated subsidiaries as of January 31, 1976 and 1975, and the related Statements of Income, Shareholders' Equity and Changes in Financial Position for the years then ended. Our examination was made in accordance with generally accepted auditing standards, and accordingly included such tests of the accounting records and such other auditing procedures as we considered necessary in the circumstances.

In our opinion, the aforementioned financial statements present fairly the financial position of Sears, Roebuck and Co. and consolidated subsidiaries at January 31, 1976 and 1975, and the results of their operations and changes in their financial position for the years then ended, in conformity with generally accepted accounting principles consistently applied during the period except for the change in the method of valuing inventories, and after restatement for foreign currency translation and marketable securities, all as described in note 2 to the financial statements and with which we concur.

Touche Ross & Co.

statements are examined or audited by independent accountants that are licensed by the state.

These audits, by CPAs, provide assurance to the directors, stockholders, and the investing public that the company has used generally accepted accounting practices.

This does not mean that the auditor's guarantee that the company hasn't done something illegal, or that an individual might have embezzled money from the firm. The audit simply indicates that generally accepted accounting principles were followed in the preparation of the company's financial statements, and that the methods used were applied consistently.

There are also principles for auditors to follow in the course of their audit. A short list of the generally accepted auditing standards is shown in the next column.

Generally accepted auditing standards.

General standards

1. The examination is to be performed by a person or persons having adequate technical training and proficiency as an auditor.
2. In all matters relating to the assignment, an independence in mental attitude is to be maintained by the auditor or auditors.
3. Due professional care is to be exercised in the performance of the examination and the preparation of the report.

Standards of field work

1. The work is to be adequately planned and assistants, if any, are to be properly supervised.
2. There is to be a proper study and evaluation of the existing internal control as a basis for reliance thereon and for the determination of the resultant extent of the tests to which auditing procedures are to be restricted.
3. Sufficient competent evidential matter is to be obtained through inspection, observation, inquiries and confirmations to afford a reasonable basis for an opinion regarding the financial statements under examination.

Standards of reporting

1. The report shall state whether the financial statements are presented in accordance with generally accepted principles of accounting.
2. The report shall state whether such principles have been consistently observed in the current period in relation to the preceding period.
3. Informative disclosures in the financial statements are to be regarded as reasonably adequate unless otherwise stated in the report.
4. The report shall either contain an expression of opinion regarding the financial statements, taken as a whole, or an assertion to the effect that an opinion cannot be expressed. When an overall opinion cannot be expressed, the reasons therefor should be stated. In all cases where an auditor's name is associated with financial statements, the report should contain a clear-cut indication of the character of the auditor's examination, if any, and the degree of responsibility he is taking.

Source: John & Marlene Buckley, The Accounting Profession.

WHAZZIT?

AICPA

The American Institute of Certified Public Accountants, a professional organization of accountants.

APB

The Accounting Principles Board of the AICPA, which makes rules to guide accounting practices.

PROXY

A statement signed by a stockholder allowing some other person (usually the company management) to vote for the stockholder at the annual meeting.

TRUST

A legal device that puts title and control of property in the hands of one party (called the trustee) for the benefit of another party (called the beneficiary).

The Income Statement

Sears, Roebuck And Co.

STATEMENT OF INCOME

$ in thousands	Year Ended January 31	
	1976	1975*
Net sales (including finance charge revenues—note 10)	$13,639,887	$13,101,210
Cost of sales, buying and occupancy expenses	8,543,844	8,200,465
Selling and administrative expenses	3,941,369	3,830,027
	12,485,213	12,030,492
Operating income from sales and services	1,154,674	1,070,718
Other income (loss)	96	(4,022)

Equity in income of (note 1)
  Allstate Group
    Insurance companies
      In accordance with prescribed standards, unrealized increases (decreases) in the market value of equity investments of $271,803 and ($421,079) are not included in the determination of net income.

Underwriting and investment income	52,606	156,375
Realized capital gains	11,847	10,830
Allstate Enterprises, Inc.	11,464	536
	75,917	167,741
Other unconsolidated subsidiaries and affiliates	40,216	12,456
Other companies (dividends)	1,799	1,977
	117,932	182,174
Income before general expenses	1,272,702	1,248,870

General expenses

Interest (less capitalization of $7,411 and $19,570)	271,169	361,347
Contribution to Employes' Profit Sharing Fund	86,442	87,783
Income taxes (note 4)	392,500	303,842
	750,111	752,972
Net income...	$ 522,591	$ 495,898
Per share (average shares 158,034 and 157,473)	$3.31	$3.15

Income Statement Items

An income statement is a report of a company's operations over a period of time, providing an accounting of profit and loss.

While the balance sheet shows the basic soundness of a company, reflecting its financial position at a given date, the Income Statement shows the record of its operating activities for a whole year. As a result, it is often more valuable to investors because it provides a guide in anticipating how the company may perform in the future. It is not assets alone that makes a company great -- it is the company's earning power.

This statement matches the amount the company receives from selling its goods and services and other forms of income against all of the various forms of costs and other expenditures made in order to gain those revenues.

The result is a Net Profit (or Net Loss) for the year. For example:

$6,500,000 Revenues
6,200,000 Expenditures
$ 300,000 Net Profit

Net Profit is, of course, the important figure at the "bottom line" on an Income Statement. If a company doesn't earn a profit, the company must dip into its retained earnings to cover the year's losses.

CONSOLIDATED STATEMENTS

This means that the financial statements report the operating activities of the whole company, including all of its subsidiaries, even though the company may have only a partial ownership interest.

That's why there is often a line that says, "Income before minority interests." Minority interests are the equity in subsidiary businesses only owned partially by the company.

Sears, for example, has a consolidated statement, plus separate statements for its Allstate Insurance subsidiary.

SALES

The most important sources of revenue are generally number one on the Income Statement: Revenues. This represents the money received from customers for goods and services provided. Net Sales is the amount received after deducting any allowances for returned goods or reductions in price. A railroad or a utility would use the term operating revenues instead of sales.

COSTS AND EXPENSES

These are expenditures incurred in the process of producing and selling the firm's goods and services.

Only those expenditures that relate to present year sales or revenues are counted as costs and expenses.

If expenditures have provided a type of benefit that lasts over several years, such as the construction of a new plant or design of new machinery, only that part of the expenditure that applies to the current period is charged off as costs and expenses.

COSTS

In a manufacturing company such as Ford Motor, costs of sales represent all of the costs in curred in the factories in order to convert raw materials into finished goods.

These costs include the costs of raw materials, direct labor costs, and such costs as supervision, rent, electricity, supplies, maintenance, and repairs, which we generally call overhead or indirect costs.

DEPRECIATION

Depreciation represents the cost of an asset, such as a building or a machine, that is applied to the process of producing the goods. It is an estimate of the decline in the useful value of the asset due to wear, tear, and obsolescence.

As depreciation is charged as a cost of direct, current operations, that amount is deducted from the value of the asset as listed on the balance sheet. Sometimes the original cost of the asset is listed, with a special listing of the amount of depreciation taken up to the time of the statement.

AMORTIZATION

Depreciation on tools, special designs, patents, or other assets that are used in operations is called amortization. These costs, too, are allocated over several years of production, according to their estimated useful life.

SELLING AND ADMINISTRATIVE EXPENSES

These expenses are listed separately to indicate the extent of selling and administrative costs. Included are salesmen's sala salaries, commissions, advertising, promotion costs, travel, entertainment, executive and office costs, office payrolls, and other items of this type.

EMPLOYEE RETIREMENT PLANS

Sometimes the costs related to maintaining a pension plan for employees is listed specially, because of the specialized nature of such a cost. Payments are made into a special fund for future pension payments to employees, according to a formal pension plan.

PROVISION FOR SUPPLEMENTAL COMPENSATION

This item represents an allocation of funds, as a cost item, for special compensation such as bonuses.

MEASURES OF INCOME

On the Income Statement you'll find several income figures reported.

OPERATING INCOME

This figure represents the difference (net) between operating revenues and operating costs and expenses, that is, all profits directly related to the production of goods and services.

OTHER INCOME

In addition to its basic operations, a company may earn additional income through dividends on its marketable securities and investments, interest on money loaned, royalties, and patent payments. In the case of Sears, you will note that in 1975 the Other Income was negative, therefore a deduction from income.

INCOME AFTER MINORITY INTERESTS

As noted earlier, part of Sears' reported "consolidated" income comes from operations of subsidiaries that are fully owned by Sears, thus there is no minority interest to deduct from the income generated by those subsidiaries.

NET INCOME

This is the "bottom line" item that represents the actual return to the company from all of its activities during the period reported.

Quarterly Results $ in millions

	FIRST		SECOND		THIRD		FOURTH	
	1975*	1974*	1975*	1974*	1975*	1974*	1975	1974*
NET SALES	$2,836	$2,894	$3,314	$3,209	$3,503	$3,360	$3,987	$3,638
NET INCOME	54	127	110	141	119	109	240	119
Per Share	.34	.81	.70	.90	.75	.69	1.52	.75
DIVIDENDS PER SHARE	.40	.40	.40	.40	.40	.40	.65	.65
MARKET PRICE OF COMMON SHARE HIGH-LOW	69–58	90–80	74–62	90–67	72–57	70–45	74–64	66–42

Careers In Accounting

Ask some people what they think accountants do, and they will turn out an image something like this: a man wearing a green eyeshade and armbands to keep his shirtsleeves out of the ink, sitting high on a stool in a dark corner of a room, adding up columns of numbers.

Of course, this picture is far from the truth -- accountants today are specialized professionals who work with management to assure that important financial and operating decisions are based on sound examination of alternatives. Accounting is an analytical way of measuring the progress of many types of business activities, so that costs may be held down and profits increased.

Accountants may be involved in setting up cost control systems, figuring tax implications of management plans, providing timely information for management, checking on and controlling theft or fraud, and a multitude of other activities.

Many accounts have progressed to top executive positions -- in such large companies as Allegheny-Ludlum, Caterpillar, Greyhound, ITT, 3M, Chrysler, Sun Oil, Xerox, and Western Union.

There is a need for more scientific, rigorous cost controls and other accounting services in today's complex organizations.

Accountants help management use budgets, planning, investment analysis, and other modern tools for running a business.

Further, there are diverse opportunities in accounting. There's corporate work in finance, systems, and cost accounting, credit management, and other areas. In addition, there is the world of public accounting.

In total, there are more than 100 specialities in the accounting field.

PUBLIC ACCOUNTANTS

Public accountants are either self-employed practitioners who work on a fee basis for businesses or individuals, or are members of public accounting girms. In either case, their clients consist of a number of outside concerns.

In public accounting, you are certified by your state to offer such professional accounting services, including independent audits, to the public. Your certificate is comparable to a doctor's license or a lawyer's admission to the bar, permitting independent, professional practice.

An accountant with this certification may use the letters "CPA" as a title after his or her name, meaning "Certified Public Accountant."

There are further accounting opportunities in government, civil service, and in teaching.

NEW OPPORTUNITIES

Accounting is growing as a career field, because the profession is changing.

Computer systems are replacing manual records systems. This reduces the need for manual work, and junior-level accounting jobs. Instead, the jobs for individuals who can use the computer systems effectively are wide open; as the systems grow and become more common, the career opportunities are increasing for experienced, computer-oriented accountants.

Also, new governmental laws and regulations are calling for more and more accounting activity -- through systems and through expanded reporting. Tax laws, health and insurance plans, pension plans, pricing and competitive data, cost data, and other areas all have expanded in government-mandated accounting demands.

EDUCATION NEEDED

You may prepare for a career in accounting through coursework in college or a university. Graduate work is more and more important for advancement in the profession. Four years of college with a a

college with a major in accounting (or the equivalent in individual study and experience) is a minimum requirement in the field today.

After you have completed your studies in accounting you may take the CPA examination, which comprises a number of sections. When you pass this exam, you are certified as a CPA.

Of course, you may work as an accountant before you attempt the CPA examination. In fact, many people feel that practical experience in business, government, or a public accounting firm is an important step in preparing to become a CPA.

MONEY

Accountants are generally well paid for their work. Starting salaries for college graduates in accounting are often higher than for other business majors. With a continued high demand for accountants, salaries may be expected to continue to be high in the years ahead.

JOBS

One specialty is auditing. This consists of checking and testing the accuracy of an organization's accounts and determining whether established procedures and systems are being followed properly. Auditors, whether in private practice (paid a salary by a company) or in a public accounting firm, travel widely and have to manage a number of assignments.

A budget and forecast accountant is concerned with providing information for planning. This includes figuring out the organization's cash requirements, estimating future costs, planning for future profit budgets, and advising management on the findings.

Cost accountants work mostly with production records and inventories. A manufacturer needs to know not only how much of a product has been sold, but how much is left, and how much it cost per unit.

A controller (or comptroller) directs a company's overall accounting program. A tax accountant prepares tax returns or advises on tax matters for the company. Systems and Procedures accounts are concerned with building and maintaining the accounting systems needed for a growing or changing organization, in a never-static legal environment.

General accountants may work in all or some of these job areas.

Distribution of accountants and auditors by industry classification, 1970.
SOURCE: Modified from data provided by the U.S. Bureau of the Census, Publication C3.223/10.970/V.2/Pt.76, October 1970.

	Men		Women		Total	
	Number	%	Number	%	Number	%
Public accounting and professional services	149,342	28.0	40,323	22.4	189,665	26.6
Manufacturing	136,493	25.6	29,846	16.6	166,339	23.3
Public administration	64,713	12.1	31,960	17.7	96,673	13.5
Finance, insurance and real estate	45,897	8.6	22,893	12.7	68,790	9.6
Wholesale and retail	43,924	8.2	23,069	12.8	66,993	9.4
Communication, transportation and other utilities	30,539	5.7	10,529	5.8	41,068	5.8
Business and repair services	18,933	3.5	9,882	5.5	28,815	4.0
Construction	12,994	2.4	3,806	2.1	16,800	2.4
Mining	8,292	1.6	1,218	0.7	9,510	1.3
Personal services	6,001	1.1	2,932	1.6	8,933	1.3
Entertainment and recreation	2,035	0.4	910	0.5	2,945	0.4
Agriculture, forestry and fishery	1,438	0.3	477	0.3	1,915	0.3
Other	13,441	2.5	2,233	1.3	15,674	2.1
Total	534,042	100.0	180,078	100.0	714,120	100.0

Source: John & Marlene Buckley, The Accounting Profession.

CONSIDER   CHALLENGES

1. Should the government audit all corporate financial reports?

2. Do companies "hide" accounting mistakes?

3. To whom are accountants accountable?

4. Does an accountant's "opinion" mean the annual report is true?

5. What impact have computers had on accounting practice?

6. Does the Balance Sheet give a picture of the entire year's operations of a firm? Explain.

7. What is the relationship between the Income Statement and the Balance Sheet?

8. Why do we have both Managerial and Financial accounting?

9. Why should the government be interested in the accounting system used by a firm?

10. On the Balance Sheet Assets are balanced against Liabilities and Stockholder Equity. What is the difference between Stockholder Equity and Liabilities?

Read the financial notes and statistical supplement to a major company's annual report. Identify two or more disclosures of accounting practices that are out of the ordinary.

Compare the balance sheets of an insurance company and a manufacturing company. How do they differ in the types of assets and liabilities they have?

Write a major company for minutes of the last stockholders meeting, and read them.

Read the Sears or Ford annual report to identify company actions regarding key management decisions or management philosophy.

Interview a CPA and find out what is involved in public accounting work.

Interview an accountant and identify one or more controversial accounting principles.

RECAP

Information about the operation of a business is gathered, stored and reported through the accounting system. Accounting is a means of expressing in clear, understandable, financial terms the results of complex business activities.

The people who fulfill this function for organizations are accountants. Accountants working within a business ensure that accounting practices provide complete and meaningful information, consistent with accepted accounting principles. These standard practices are set by the APB (Accounting Principles Board). Another type of accountant who may work either for a company or for a Public Accounting firm is the Certified Public Accountant (CPA). This individual, trained in accounting and licensed by the state in which he works, examines corporate financial statements and attests to their fair representation.

There are two basic types of accounting, each directed to the needs of specific groups. MANAGERIAL accounting provides information to the managers of the firm to assist them in making the complex decisions that are a part of every business day. The purpose of the reports to management is to show trends and point out potential problem areas that may need the attention of management.

FINANCIAL accounting provides people outside of the firm the information they need to make decisions about investing money in the firm, lending money to the firm, and checking to make sure that the firm is paying its fair share of taxes. The information is provided in the form of financial reports, often contained in the Annual Report of the corporation.

Two basic types of financial reports are prepared by companies: the Balance Sheet and the Income Statement. All companies listed on the various stock exchanges are required by law to provide them, and other small businesses, such as your neighborhood drugstore, may not make up the statements as formally as the major corporations, but must have some form of these statements for tax purposes.

A company's balance sheet shows the state of a company's financial condition as of a given date. An income statement shows how the business fared during the year. Both statements are useful to investors and managers, but the income statement is often more revealing because it shows what the company is actuall doing over the period of a year.

A number of interesting and well paying careers are available in the accounting profession. There are positions both within companies and with Public Accounting firms.

WORKSHEET NO. 9

NAME_____

INSTRUCTOR'S NAME_____

DATE_____

1. What do annual reports tell stockholders?

2. What does an Income Statement reveal that a Balance Sheet does not?

3. If you owned and operated an ice cream shop, what would be
    your principle assets? Your principle liabilities?

---

4. Why are company accounting records "audited" by public accountants?

CHAPTER 10

Finance

All organizations need money to use as capital for financing operations and expansion. Capital is the lifeblood of businesses -- the money available for investment in land, factories, machinery, and new jobs. It finances inventories and carries the business over the gap between payments out and payments in.

Short-term capital is needed to finance purchases of inventories and raw materials, to pay wages and salaries, and to pay other current operating expenses. It is usually acquired through accounts receivable (which may be sold to other companies for collection), short-term loans made by banks, purchases made from suppliers on credit, and through various other means.

Long-term capital is needed to finance purchase of land, capital equipment, plants, stores, buildings, and other assets. It is usually acquired through long-term loans (bonds), issuance of capital stock (sell more shares in the ownership of the business), and by saving part of the profits that are earned through the company's operations (retained earnings).

Securities (stocks and bonds) are bought and sold through exchanges such as the largest, the New York Stock Exchange. The exchanges are the markets where prices reflect the basic law of supply and demand. There are about 3000 different stocks and bonds traded on the New York Stock Exchange alone, representing a total of about 1200 business organizations. Additional stocks and bonds are traded on other exchanges (Midwest, American, etc.)

All the companies with securities sold on these exchanges are required by law to publish annual financial statements. Most also publish quarterly statements to stockholders.

The 1200 companies listed on the New York Exchange earn about 70% of all the profits reported by American corporations, pay stockholders more than half of all dividends paid in the country, and employ a large sector of our total workforce.

Because of the major impact on our society, corporations need to keep stockholders, employees, and the public well informed regarding its operations and financial condition. Companies in the 19th century were largely local enterprises with only a handful of stockholders and employees. The owners were generally on close terms with managers, or were managers themselves.

Further, the need for large amounts of financial capital has impelled companies to provide more complete information and to look more widely for sources of money. Hence accounting and financing have become increasingly important business functions.

In This Chapter

Financing

Each year, businesses search for more capital. The process of financing business is itself a big business, supporting a large number of financial experts on Wall Street who counsel businessmen on the most effective ways to get the money they need.

Where do businesses get the money they need? The key sources are lenders, stockholders, and earnings. Which sources to use depends on the availability and the cost of funds from each.

Recently, for example, A.T.&T. offered 12 million shares of common stock worth $655 million to the public. U.S. Steel sold $400 million in convertible debentures, bonds which may be exchanged for shares of stock. DuPont settled on $300 million in bonds and $100 million in short-term notes (loans) to raise capital.

Normally longer-term borrowing is less costly to businesses and guarantees a fixed rate of interest for the period. On the other hand, a long-term borrowing may restrict the firm's flexibility in financing and the use of property which may have been pledged as security.

To obtain money from stockholders, a business may issue additional shares of stock. This type of financing, called equity financing, has the effect of diluting the value of previously issued shares of stock. But there is no commitment to pay for the use of this money (as in borrowing) because stock-holders are owners of the firm. Further, no property is pledged as security, thus providing continued freedom of business action.

So both debt financing and equity financing have their disadvantages and their advantages. Further, both are dependent on the condition of the economic market at the time the money is sought. If the prevailing interest rates are high, debt financing is undesirable. If the stock market is down, or at least the price of the company's own stock on the market is down, then issuing new stock shares would not be desirable. Simply, the cheapest source of funds, with the least constraints placed on the business is the one that should be pursued.

The third primary source of funds for business is earnings. As a business earns profits, only part of them are passed on to stockholders in the form of dividends. The remainder may be reinvested in the business. The only cost to the firm is the possible "opportunity cost" -- the money that might have been earned by simply putting the money in the bank at interest or investing the money in another business.

The company may also use idle funds, such as money in bank accounts for checks that haven't been processed yet (float), current accounts payable (hold off on paying bills), taxes withheld but not yet paid to the government, and special reserves and funds such as pension funds.

Of course, business is not alone in competing for capital. Individuals need money, such as for home mortgages and automobile financing. State and local governments issue bonds to finance activities, drawing capital from the market that might otherwise go to businesses. The amount of money available for business use is influenced by the amount of money made available for home mort-gages and for government financing. Sometimes government bonds look good to investors because of high interest rates or the low risk. Some government bonds are also tax free on interest earned. On the other hand, the federal government makes money available, through several agencies. The amount of this money influences the supply of money on the open market for business needs.

There seems to be a bottomless pit of capital demand, but a limited supply of financial capital available. Financing a business enterprise is a difficult and increasingly complex task. Debt or equity -- that is the question for raising capital.

THE SALES DOLLAR

Where does a sales dollar go? Many people have the vague idea that the money a company receives goes directly into the profit pocket.

Distribution of each $1 of Sales & Other Income

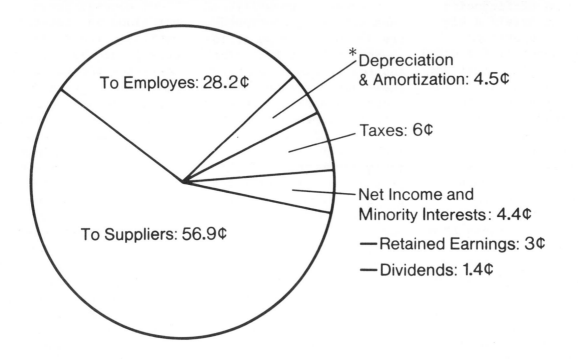

To Employes: 28.2¢

*Depreciation & Amortization: 4.5¢

Taxes: 6¢

Net Income and Minority Interests: 4.4¢

—Retained Earnings: 3¢

—Dividends: 1.4¢

To Suppliers: 56.9¢

*Provisions for depreciation and amortization are charges to income for usage and obsolescence of plants, equipment and special tools.

As shown in the chart above, this is not the case. The Ford story is typical of industry: more than half of Ford's sales revenues are passed along directly to suppliers. Another quarter of the revenues go to pay for employee wages and salaries. Five cents of each dollar is used to pay for the use and replacement of plants, equipment, and special tool tools. Six cents go to Uncle Sam and state and local governments.

Of the total sales dollar, only about four cents represents net income. This represents the money available to Ford to help make the company grow and to pay dividends to stockholders.

Business organizations that are not industrial firms like Ford would have somewhat lower supplier costs and may have higher labor costs (e.g., banks, insurance companies, service firms). Some firms are more profitable because of their efficiency or the demand for their products. But for all non-financial corporations, after-tax profits on the sales dollar are less than half a nickel -- 2.3¢ on each dollar sales. In wholesale and retail trade, profits come to 1.4¢ on each sales dollar.

In construction it's about the same.

Profit is not a four-letter word, but many people have the mistaken idea that it is a "dirty" word. Profits are essential for the financing of a healthy business, and are hard to obtain.

So, regardless of the type of business, the sales dollar is split up and spent buying goods and services needed by the firm and for paying the wages of the employees of the firm. Then come taxes, and if there is anything left, these may be a profit.

Why Coors Finally Had To Take Public Money

Where most companies would give an arm and a leg to get equity capital from the public, and can't, Adolph Coors Co. is one of the fortunate very few that could do so almost any time—but would rather not. The Colorado brewer's only reason for going public, which it did this spring, was to pay inheritance taxes. Even then, it decided to offer only nonvoting stock. "We decided to go public," quips William K. Coors, chief executive, "when we got a bill from the IRS for $50-million in inheritance taxes."

Most companies would have solved such a problem by going into debt. Not Coors. It has always paid for every cost it could out of revenues. Between 1970 and 1974 it spent $276-million on plant expansion—and paid out of cash flow. At the time it went public, Coors had only $2-million in long-term debt on its books—against $375-million in equity.

But even for Coors, the raising of equity in today's public markets in the amount required was not accomplished overnight, and the offering itself was not done without a great deal of drama. It didn't even start by seeming a simple task. Arthur B. Treman, Jr., a managing director of Coors' investment bankers, Dillon, Read & Co., recalls a January meeting with the client at which the $64 question came up: How much could be raised? The Dow Jones industrial average was then moving between 620 and 690, and hardly anybody was sure it was not going back down. "Some of our people felt $75-million would be appropriate," says Treman, "and when I said $100-million, our lawyer's face fell."

Inside track. In fact, the markets improved dramatically, with brewery stocks standout performers, and when Dillon, Read actually marketed the issue on June 10, it was able to raise $127-million. But by then the preparations had been going on for the best part of a year. Ever since the early summer of 1974, investment bankers had been descending in droves on Coors' headquarters in Golden, Colo. "I've no idea how many offered their services," says "Bill" Coors. All the principal ones did, he adds. "I'd have been flattered if Coors had then considered us their investment bankers," says Treman, but Coors—who is extremely complimentary about the way the offering was handled—says that because Dillon, Read had performed valuation services for the brewer in the past, "they had the inside track."

The question now became, "How soon can we go?" The decision to go public taken, after 102 years of private ownership, Coors wanted to get the offering done as soon as possible. But the preparation of three years' complete audited financial statements made it impossible to go before the spring or summer of 1975. The alternatives, recalls Treman, were to go in June or wait till August. "If we waited beyond June 15," he says, "we would have then had to wait till the second-quarter's figures would be ready—and audited—for the prospectus."

Coors did not like the idea of sitting and contemplating what, to the company, was an unconscionably large amount of debt—that huge estate-tax bill. And neither Coors nor Dillon, Read wanted to take the market risk of waiting another three months, even though they anticipated having better earnings to report in 1975 than in the equivalent months of 1974. They were all very conscious, says Treman, that while brewery stock prices had jumped 50% in six weeks in early 1975, they could easily fall back 50%—or more—again.

Government factors. The underwriters did not come up with the final price of $31 a share without a lot of heart-searching, however. "I picked certain people to be involved because I knew they would be advocates of widely different pricing policies," Treman reports. And there were hot discussions: "I prefer to call them constructive differences of opinion," he says with a grin.

Among the factors Dillon, Read had to consider were some that would have stopped many stocks from selling at all. Coors plans to pay no more than 5% of its net income as dividends. And the nonvoting shares it offered raised three drawbacks. First, the shares cannot be listed on the New York Stock Exchange. Second, a lot of investors, especially institutions, do not like the idea of holding nonvoting stock. Third, nonvoting stock cannot even be offered for sale in many states.

The first drawback—the impossibility of listing—proved no problem. "To be blunt," says Treman, "it may have helped"—because so many firms planned to make dealer markets in the stock. The other difficulties were more serious. At the beginning, it looked as though underwriters could not sell Coors stock in 17 states. At the end, Dillon, Read was able to get the num-ber down to 10—but one of these was California, not only a huge reservoir of investment dollars, but a state in which Coors stock could otherwise have expected a great reception: No less than 49% of the company's product is sold there.

Against this, though, was the spirit of Coors—what Treman calls "the company's attitude of hard work, saving money, devotion to the quality of the product, caring about the environment, giving people something to believe in."

Heady interest. Because of this Coors spirit, which infects almost everyone who has anything to do with the company, Dillon, Read eventually set a price just about on a par from a price-earnings viewpoint with that of the leader in the industry, Anheuser-Busch, Inc. They began with a price range of 26-30, but found so much interest in the stock that, in the last days before the offering, they were able to raise it to 30-32. "If we'd left it at 26," Treman explains, "it would have been a riot, and the price could have gone to 36." But not only would that have given some "free riders" a very easy lift, it would have deprived Coors of a lot of money. By raising the price to 31, other Wall Streeters say, Dillon, Read was taking quite a chance. Not only did they squeeze out the free riders, but they also squeezed out some "legitimate" investors—people and institutions that planned to hold on to the stock.

In the end, Dillon, Read's strategy worked, though not without some heart-stopping moments. When they raised the price range, one major bank withdrew a very large order, another reduced its "indication of interest," and rumors ran around the Street that the deal was falling apart. Dillon, Read used a stratagem to check this. The bank that had reduced its order had done so at another underwriter, while leaving intact an order for 8,000 shares with Dillon, Read itself. The investment firm got the bank to reduce its order by 4,000 with Dillon, Read—and to reinstate its 4,000 order with the underwriter where it had canceled before. Rumors raced around the Street that the deal was "hot"—and it was a sellout the first afternoon.

Investing

The aim of investing is to make money, and the more the better.

Investing is the process of putting money to use to obtain profitable returns. It differs from savings in that a risk is assumed by the investor that is not assumed by the saver.

How an individual goes about investing depends on his or her particular objectives. Objectives may include one or more of the following:

- To keep the money readily accessible (liquidity).
- To earn a fairly stable and reliable income.
- To gain an increase in the value of the investment
- To keep the money safe.
- To protect against loss of the money's purchasing power due to inflation.

To achieve his or her objectives, an investor may invest in short-term or long-term securities. These would be as follows:

common stock, preferred stock, bonds or notes. An individual may invest in commodities, future contracts for commodities, or other assets such as coins, stamps, or real estate. Any of these may represent short-term or long-term investments. Further, each represents different risks to the investor.

When you invest in a business enterprise there is always the risk of business failure. While some firms prosper, others fail. Companies that at one point are booming may suddenly turn sour. Penn Central, TeleMart, and Boise Cascade are such companies. This risk is greatest with common stock, least with bonds secured with property.

There is also market risk -- the chance that the general market for securities will decline. Business cycles make future investment values uncertain.

You can minimize your investment risks by knowing what you are

doing. Knowing business trends, particularly within particular industries, may be helpful in making wise investment decisions. Knowing about the particular companies you are investing in may also help. You may analyze the financial and operating data available to you. Finally, you may reduce your risk by spreading your investment among a number of companies and industries, and among different forms of investments (stocks, bonds, and real property).

Above all, the key to success in investing is to "buy low, sell high."

YOUR NEST EGG

There are many tales about men and women who have built small or large fortunes in the stock market. But for each success story there may be dozens of sad stories that are not told. In the stock market, for someone to make a dollar, someone else must lose a dollar.

DOONESBURY   **by Garry Trudeau**

It's a matter of buying and selling shares of stocks, bonds, and other securities, as discussed in this chapter.

A retired postal worker had put away part of his pay check into stocks each month for 42 years, building a wealth of about half a million dollars. Unfortunately, he neglected to pay income taxes on his investment earnings and was arrested.

If you wanted to have $200,000 today, you should have been born not with a silver spoon in your mouth, but with $1000 in Polaroid stock. That's how much it has increased in value in about twenty years.

And there are always hot tips to help you invest your money -- like "buy electronics," or "there's this unknown little growth company," or "this stock is going to take off next week so buy it quickly."

Investing, particularly in the stock market, can be made to sound ridiculously easy and profitable. Stop and think about the advice you may find so attractive. Consider your own investment objectives and the risks you are willing to bear. It is far easier to part with money than it is to double it, triple it, or even earn a fair return on it.

Before you even consider investing any money you should evaluate your living needs. You should invest money only if it can truly be considered "extra." This means it is money you have above and beyond your needs for living expenses and potential emergency expenses. You might start investing by buying life insurance that features both protection and "savings" elements.

Some people say you should not enter the stock market until you have about one year's income put away in a savings account (or other liquid savings such as government savings bonds). How much you should have is up to you, buy you should avoid spreading your financial condition too thin.

Should you borrow money to invest in the stock market? Or in ventures such as a business your brother-in-law is starting? It's inadvisable because you would be risking your own financial security.

WATCH YOUR MONEY GROW

So how can you "get rich" if you have to follow all these rules? Do you have to "have money to make money?"

An inheritance from a wealthy aunt or a salary big enough to permit regular savings and investments makes the job of building financial assets a lot easier. But you can make financial headway even if you have little money to put away.

Even if you set aside a few dollars a week, you will soon find that you've accumulated a small nest egg that you are "free" to invest. Many employers provide payroll deduction programs for purchase of savings bonds or even matching programs ("thrift plans") in which they will kick in some cash for each dollar you agree to save. You can set up a monthly payment plan yourself for investing -- such as in a mutual fund or special stock investment plan offered by a stock broker or investment service.

Many people view the purchase of a home or other property as a type of investment, particularly in time of rapidly rising prices. They reason, if you buy property at a low price and watch the prevailing market prices rise, you have earned a return on the "investment." Once you save up the initial down payment, you may be on the way to building your "small fortune."

The question that should be considered in building that "fortune" is whether you are considering the short-run or the long-run in your calculations. It is accepted that people invest for a number of reasons, but even if capital appreciation is the goal, the investor must consider the time frame in which the investment is to grow. Some investors move into and out of the market quite quickly, often on a daily basis. But the majority of investors take a longer term view of the stock market and what they expect to gain from their activities in the market.

The federal tax laws tend to benefit the long-term investor over his short-term brother. Current tax laws only tax long-term gains (stock held over six months) at about half the rate that short-term gains are taxed. But whether investing for short-term or long-term returns, investing is one way to make your "fortune."

An Unacademic Course In Stocks

In the gloomy stock market atmosphere of 1973, quite a few investors have concluded anew that outsiders don't have much of a chance against Wall Street's mighty pros. In fact, however, most professionally managed portfolios have fared much worse than the market indexes this year. There's no reason why you can't expect to do at least as well as the pros—and you may do a lot better.

Academic researchers find that even over the long pull the experts have by and large done no better than the averages. That's not bad, since the long-run return on common stocks has amounted to something over 9% a year including dividends and capital gains. But stocks selected at random would have done just as well—which is the lesson of the "random walk" theory.

"Random walk" is an obscenity on Wall Street because it suggests that a blindfolded chimpanzee throwing darts at the newspaper's stock market pages can pick a portfolio that would do just as well as stocks carefully selected by the professionals. In essence, the random walk theory reflects the belief that future stock prices cannot be predicted. It's not that prices move erratically or irrationally. Just the opposite: the theory says that any news about the earnings or dividends of a company gets reflected in its stock price immediately, not gradually. But such news occurs randomly. If it did not—that is, if it were dependent on past events—then it wouldn't be news at all, the theory goes.

Investment advisory services, earnings predictions and complicated chart patterns are all useless, the random walkers say. The market professionals retort that the academics are so immersed in equations and Greek symbols, to say nothing of excruciatingly stuffy prose, that they couldn't tell a bear from a bull even in a china shop.

The random walk theory is a perfectly reasonable approach to the stock market, and it's a good one for people who are content to do no better than the averages. Suppose

Burton Malkiel, professor of economics at Princeton and a director of the Prudential Insurance Co. of America, was an investment analyst for Smith, Barney & Co. from 1958 to 1960. This article is adapted from his book, A Random Walk Down Wall Street, to be published this month by W. W. Norton & Co.

you believe in the random walk theory. What do you do? For most people, especially those with little capital to invest in the stock market, a mutual fund is the only practical choice. You buy proportionate shares in a diversified portfolio of stocks suited to the degree of risk you want to take—flyers for those able and willing to bear risk, more stable blue chips for the chickenhearted. You should pay as little in sales charges as possible. Avoid load funds, which have a 9% sales charge. Some individual funds do better than others. On the whole, however, load, no-load and closed-end funds don't differ in their performance—so there's no reason to pay extra unless you believe in capital punishment.

But if you are like most hardened players of the money game, you are unlikely to be swayed by the argument of the random walkers that no one can achieve consistently above average investment returns. Telling an investor he can't beat the averages is like telling a six-year-old there is no Santa Claus. It takes the zing out of life. Thus there will always be investors who will never stop dreaming that they can beat the market, even if it is an impossible dream. For such investors, I offer a sensible and low-risk strategy that may produce substantial rewards. The method has worked splendidly for me.

Four rules for successful stock selection

I am a random walker—with a crutch. My four rules are inconsistent with a strict application of the random walk theory, but they are based on sound principles of stock valuation. Like the random walkers, I think that the stock market is a tremendously efficient mechanism for translating information about a company into its price. But I don't believe that valuations always reflect the news about a stock precisely. Some stocks can be overpriced and others can be underpriced for long periods. Because the market's collective judgments are often fickle and ill-founded, investors should not always take the current tableau of market prices as the best estimate of the values of stocks. The pros can be faddish or hypnotized by charts, and they trade more actively than an investor should. I prefer to stick to fundamentals.

☞ **RULE 1.** *Confine stock purchases to companies that appear able to sustain above average earnings growth for at least five years.* An extraordinary rate of earnings growth over the long run is the single most important element in the success of most stock investments. IBM, Xerox, Avon Products and practically all the other really outstanding common stock investments of the past were growth stocks. Consistent growth not only increases the earnings and dividends of a company, but it may also increase the multiple that the market is willing to pay for those earnings. Thus the purchaser of stock in a company whose earnings begin to grow rapidly has a chance at a potential double benefit: both the earnings and the multiple may increase. Suppose, for example, you buy a stock selling at $15 in a company that is earning $1 a share. If the earnings grow to $2 a share, and if the price/earnings multiple increases from 15 to 30 (in recognition that the company now can be considered a growth stock), you don't just double your money—you quadruple it.

Your $15 stock will be worth $60 (30, the multiple, times $2, the earnings).

RULE 2. *Never pay more for a stock than can reasonably be justified by a firm foundation of value.* A time-honored principle of investment selection is to buy stocks whose prices may temporarily have fallen below realistic estimates of their intrinsic value. Value is a function of the stocks' prospects for earnings and dividend growth.

I don't think anyone can tell you precisely what the proper value is for any stock, but I do feel that you can roughly gauge when a stock seems to be reasonably priced. Generally, the earnings multiple for the market as a whole is a helpful bench mark. (An approximation of that figure is the price/earnings ratio for the Dow Jones industrials, which appears every Monday in the Wall Street Journal. Recently that multiple has been about twelve.) Some companies pretty consistently grow faster than the general run of corporate earnings, which average a 4% to 5% growth rate. They deserve to sell at a higher multiple than most. So growth stocks that sell at multiples roughly in line with the overall market usually rest on a firm foundation of value.

There are special risks involved in buying growth stocks when the market has already recognized the growth and has bid up the price/earnings multiple to a hefty premium. The extremely high multiples may already fully reflect the growth that is anticipated, and if the growth does not materialize and earnings in fact go down (or even grow more slowly than expected), you will take a very unpleasant bath. When earnings fall, the multiple is likely to crash

as well, but the crash won't be so loud if the multiple wasn't that high in the first place.

RULE 3. *Buy stocks whose stories of anticipated growth are ones on which investors can build castles in the air.* Stocks are bought on expectations, not facts. Individual and institutional investors are not computers that mechanically calculate objective values for stocks and print out buy-and-sell decisions. They are emotional human beings—driven by greed, gambling instinct, hope and fear in their stock market decisions. This is why successful investing demands both intellectual and psychological acuteness.

Stocks that produce "good vibes" in the minds of investors can sell at premium multiples for long periods even if their growth rate is only average. Those not so blessed may sell at low multiples for long periods even if their growth rate is above average. Ask yourself whether the story about your stock is likely to catch the fancy of the crowd. Is it a story on which investors can build castles in the air—but castles in the air that rest on firm foundations?

RULE 4. *Trade as little as possible.* In general, hold on to the winners and sell the ones that don't work out. Frequent switching does nothing but subsidize your broker and increase your tax burden if you have realized gains. I do not say, "Never sell stock on *continued*

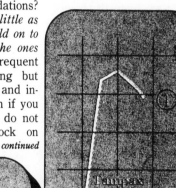

Three hits and a miss

Following his rules for picking stocks with promise, Professor Malkiel bought Tampax Inc. at just under 10, A.C. Nielsen Co. at about 12½, Masco Corp. at around 7 and Giddings & Lewis, Inc. near 28 (all the prices have been adjusted for splits).

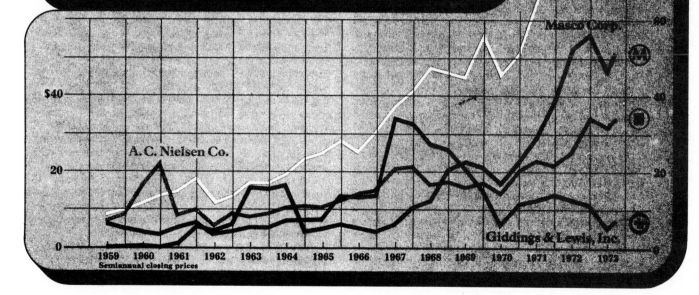

which you have a gain." The circumstances that led you to buy the stock may change, and many of your successful growth stocks may get way overpriced. But I doubt that investors can recognize the proper time to sell. I think most of my serious mistakes in the market have come from selling successful investments too soon. Now I seldom sell a successful investment.

I am merciless with the losers, however. With few exceptions, when I have a loss on a stock I sell out before the end of each calendar year (and usually within six months). The reason is that up to a point losses are tax deductible or can offset gains you may already have taken. Unless you have very strong reasons for holding on (such as that your stock is down only 15% while the market is down 20%, and the earnings are coming in right on schedule), sell out when the stock falls below your purchase price. Let the U.S. government subsidize part of your loss.

There are a number of companies available today, in a variety of industries, that offer both reasonable earnings multiples and good growth prospects. Indeed, at present there are dozens of companies selling at about ten times earnings that have a good chance at well above average growth. One that fit my rules this summer was John Deere & Co., a lead-ing manufacturer of farm equipment, which I bought in the low 40s at eight times earnings. (Recently it was at 56 with a price/earnings ratio of ten.) Others that appealed to me at the same time were Ingersoll-Rand, a major machinery manufacturer, selling in the mid 50s, or twelve times earnings (recently 66½ with a multiple of 14), and Allied Chemical, which has a large stake in energy-related activities, at just over 30 with a multiple of eleven.

If you have the talent to recognize stocks that represent good value and the art to recognize a story that will catch the fancy of others, it's a great feeling to see the market vindicate you. Even if you are not so lucky and, like most investors, do no better than the averages, my four rules will help you limit your risks and avoid much of the pain that is sometimes involved in the playing.

Investing is a bit like making love. Ultimately it is really an art requiring a certain talent and the presence of a mysterious force called luck. And like lovemaking, it's much too much fun to give up. Even if I were convinced that my past record was sheer luck and that I couldn't do better than average in the future, I would continue to play the game with relish, and I'm sure all of you with speculative temperaments would as well. **END**

WHAZZIT?

PROSPECTUS

A brochure that describes securities being offered for sale to the public by a company.

P/E RATIO

The ratio of price (current market price) to earnings for a company's stock.

DIVIDEND

Earnings or profits that a corporation pays its stockholders. It may be cash, stock, or other property.

CONVERTIBLE

Generally, a bond that may be exchanged for shares of stock.

PAR VALUE

The value printed on the face of a stock or bond certificate. It may be any amount and may have no relation to market value.

INTEREST

Payment to a lender for use of money. A corporation pays interest on its bonds to its bondholders.

WARRANT

The right to buy a stock at a given price.

Ratios: Keys to Analysis

If you were going to invest in a firm you would probably start out by getting hold of the financial reports of that firm. But once you had them, what would you do with them. You could probably determine if the firm was making a profit, but that would not be enough information for you to make an informed investment.

An investor needs some basis for evaluating the numbers that are given to him the corporate financial reports.

One approach that is commonly used by security analysts, brokers, and investors is the use of financial ratios.

The ratios listed below are applicable mainly to industrial organizations, but are sufficiently basic that they may be applied to most businesses. When properly used, these ratios allow the investor to obtain an in-depth picture of the financial condition of a company.

The ratios that we shall examine are: (1) profit margin, (2) net profit ratio, (3) inventory turnover ratio, (4) current ratio, (5) acid test ratio, (6) earnings per share, (7) dividends per share, (8) debt to ownership ratio, and (9) the price-earnings ratio.

PROFIT MARGIN

The ratio of net income before interest and taxes ("operating income") to sales or revenues. If the financial reports showed net income of $100,000 on sales of $1,000,000 the profit margin would be 10%.

Comparison of this ratio over several years and with the same ratio in similar companies will suggest to management and investors the reasonableness of operating costs and expenses. Depending of supply and demand, a price increase will improve this ratio.

NET PROFIT RATIO

The ratio of net profits (after taxes and interest) to sales and revenues. If after paying $50,000 in taxes and interest the firm had $50,000 remaining on its sales of $1,000,000 the net profit ratio would be 5%.

This ratio provides a guide to how well the company has performed during the year, taxes and other considerations counted. It shows how many cents of each sales dollar ultimately ended up as profit to the company. It is thus a more general analytical tool than the profit margin.

The ratio varies widely among different industries. Comparison, then, must be made from year to year and with similar firms. For example, this ratio ranges from 5%-6% in the steel industry and from 14%-16% for utilities.

INVENTORY TURNOVER RATIO

The ratio of inventories to sales. If the average inventory was $250,000 on sales of $1,000,000 the inventory turnover ratio would be 4.

This ratio indicates how effectively capital tied up in inventories is being used.

CURRENT RATIO

The ratio of current assests to current liabilities. If the firm has current assets of $350,000 and current liabilities of $100,000 the current ratio would be 3.5:1.

This is probably the most widely used financial ratio among industrial companies. A gradual increase in the current ratio is usually a sign of improved financial health. A current ratio of 2:1 is considered a standard.

ACID TEST OR LIQUIDITY RATIO

The ratio of cash and marketable securities to total current liabilities. If cash and marketable securities amounted to $150,000 and current liabilities are $100,000 the acid test ratio would be 1.5:1.

This ratio shows the company's ability to meet its current obligations or to raise cash. It is a useful complement to the current ratio and shows a company's need for more working capital.

EARNING PER SHARE

The ratio of net profits after taxes, interest and preferred stock dividends to the number of shares of common stock outstanding.

If the firms net profit was $50,000 and there were 25,000 shares of stock outstanding, the earnings per share would be $2.00.

This ratio indicates the increase in equity earned through company operations during the year.

DIVIDEND PER SHARE

The ratio of dividends paid on the common stock divided by the number of shares of common stock. If $12,500 was paid out in dividend on 25,000 shares of common stock, the dividend per share would be $.50.

Dividends are a matter of policy set by the board of directors. Dividends actually paid out of earnings depend on their decision and upon the availability of funds.

OWNERSHIP TO DEBT RATIO

The ratio of total liabilities to total capital. If total liabilities are $200,000 and total capital $350,000 the ownership to debt ratio would be 1.75:1.

This ratio shows the relative amounts of capital obtained from owners and from borrowing.

PRICE-EARNINGS RATIO

The ratio of the market selling price of the common stock divided by earnings (net profit after everything) per share. If the earnings per share are $2.00 and the stock is selling for $22.00 per share the price-earnings ratio would be 11:1.

This ratio varies with economic conditions, corporate performance, investors' expectations of the future, buyer confidence in the stock's growth, and other factors. It is thus an extremely important ratio to investors.

Dividends Reported September 26

Company	Period	Amt.	Payable date	Record date
Airwick Ind Inc	Q	.04	11–15–73	10–31
Amer Gen Bond Fd	M	.16	10–31–73	10–15
Atlantic City El 5⅞%pf	Q	1.46⅞	11– 1–73	10– 9
Brooklyn Union Gas	Q	.43	11– 1–73	10– 9
Campbell Soup Co	Q	.29½	10–31–73	10–11
Canadian Ind Gas & Oil		b.07½	10–19–73	10– 5
Chase Group of Boston:				
Shareholder's Tr Boston		h.08	10–31–73	9–28
City Investing Co	Q	.15	11– 1–73	10– 9
City Invest $1.31pf A	Q	.32¾	11– 1–73	10– 9
City Invest $2pfB	Q	.50	11– 1–73	10– 9
Cutler-Hammer Inc	Q	.35	12–14–73	11–30
Div Earth Sci Inc	Stk	(n)	...	...
(n)-Co rescinded a previously announced stock dividend.				
Dymo Ind Inc	Q	c.07	10–25–73	10–12
Esquire Inc	Q	c.08	10–31–73	10–16
Foursquare Fund		h.08	10–19–73	10– 5
Glatfelter (PH) Co	Q	.20	11– 1–73	10–15
Glatfelter (PH) Co 5%pf	Q	.62½	11– 1–73	10–15
Golden Flake Inc	A	c.3461	11–23–73	11– 2
Gov't Empl Fin pf	S	.42	11– 1–73	10– 9
Greater Jersey Bancorp	Q	c.32	11– 1–73	10–15
Heritage Bancorp	Q	.27	11– 1–73	10–19
Heritage Bancorp	Stk	5%	11–23–73	10–19
Hoover Ball&Bearing Co	Q	.32	10–31–73	10– 9
INA Corp	Q	k.33½	11–15–73	10–18
k-Co reduced fourth quarter dividend to conform to federal guidelines.				
Insilco Corp	Q	.17½	11– 1–73	10–10
Insilco Corp 2ndpfA	Q	.31¼	11– 1–73	10–10
Kaiser Cem & Gypsum	Q	.12½	10–31–73	10–16
Kaiser Cem & Gyp 5%pf	Q	.62½	10–31–73	10–16
Kaiser Cem & Gyp $1.37½	Q	.34⅜	10–31–73	10–16
Kellwood Co	Q	c.20	12– 4–73	11–15
LngIslandLight 5¾%pfI	Q	1.43¾	11–10–73	10– 5
LngIslandLght 5¾%pfII	Q	1.43¾	11–10–73	10– 5
LngIslandLght 8.30%pfK	Q	2.07½	11– 1–73	10– 5
Mammoth Mart Inc	Q	.05½	11– 1–73	10–12
MerleNormnCosmtcs	Sp	.02	10–31–73	10–10
Montana Pwr	Q	.45	10–26–73	10– 5
Otis Elevator	Q	c.55	10–29–73	10– 8
Penney (J C) Co	Q	.28	11– 1–73	10–10
Price Co Ltd		b.10	11– 1–73	10– 5
Raytheon Co	Q	.17½	10–26–73	10–12
Ronson Corp	Q	.05	10–24–73	10–10
RTE Corp	G	.04	10–22–73	10– 8
St Mut Investors SBI		.55	10–31–73	10–15
Tejon Ranch Co	Q	.05	11–15–73	10–15
Texas Instruments	Q	c.17	10–29–73	10– 9
United Brands $1.20pf	Q	.30	12– 1–73	11– 2
Veeco Instruments	Q	.06	11–14–73	11– 2
Victor Comptometer	Q	.12½	10–26–73	10–11
VWR United Corp	Q	c.16	12–10–73	11– 9
Wash Gas Light	Q	.47	11– 1–73	10–10
Wiley (John) & Sons	Q	.11	10–22–73	10– 5

c-Increased dividend. d-Reduced dividend. h-From income. j-From capital gains. b-Payable in Canadian funds. A, annual; Ac, accumulation; E, extra; F, final; G, interim; In, initial; Liq, liquidation; M, monthly; Q, quarterly; R, resumed; S, semi-annual; Sp, special.

Third Quarter Dividend Increased

Stockholders of record at the close of business on July 30, 1973, will find enclosed with this report a payment of dividends totaling $1 a share. The payment consists of a third quarter dividend of 80¢ a share (an increase of 10¢ a share from the 70¢ dividend paid since the first quarter of 1973), and an extra dividend of 20¢ a share, both declared by the Board of Directors on July 12.

September dividend

On July 25, Union Carbide's Board of Directors declared a dividend of 52½ cents a share, payable September 4 to stockholders of record on August 3. The last quarterly dividend, also 52½ cents a share, was paid on June 1.

Standard Oil Company of California

On July 25, the Company's Board of Directors declared a quarterly dividend, No. 190, of 75 cents per share, payable on September 10 to stockholders of record August 10.

Stocks Ex-Dividend September 28

Company	Amount	Company	Amount
KnightNewspapers	.08	(k) 5% stock.	
PolaroidCp	.08	UnitedCorp	.26
SSP Ind	.10	UniversalLeafTob	.44
Seligman&Latz	.10	VestaurSecur	.101
Seligman&Latz	(k)		

The Stock Market

On May 17, 1792, a group of merchants and traders met under an old buttonwook tree on Wall Street in New York City. At this meeting they decided to meet daily at regular hours to buy and sell securities. This "exchange," they felt, would ensure that buyers and sellers of stocks and bonds would receive the best possible price.

Today, membership in the New York Stock Exchange numbers almost 1400. These individuals are partners in brokerage firms across the country which, by virtue of their membership are called member firms.

How does the stock exchange work? How do you go about buying and selling securities?

Let's take an example. Bill Phillips of Chicago has some extra cash on hand, and decides he wants to buy some stock. After a talk with this stockbroker, he decides to buy some common stock in American Telephone and Telegraph Co. He asks his broker to find out for him what AT&T shares are selling for on the Exchange.

The broker may go to his firm's office computer terminal -- that has instant access to the Exchange's Market Data System -- and find out that AT&T stock is being quoted at "50 to a quarter." This means that, at the moment, the highest bid to buy AT&T common stock is $50 a share, while the lowest offer to sell is $50.25 a share. Phillips figures out

that the 100 shares he is interested in will cost him approximately $5000 plus a commission to the broker.

He tells his broker to go ahead with the purchase. The broker writes out an order to buy 100 shares of T (the symbol used to indicate AT&T common stock) "at the market" and has it wired to his New York office where it is phoned or wired to his firm's partner on the floor of the Exchange. "At the market" means at the best price available to his broker at that time on the trading floor.

Each stock is assigned a specific location at one of the eighteen trading posts in the New York Stock Exchange and all bids and offers of a stock must take place at the location. The American and other exchanges are operated in a similar manner. The floor partner hurries over to Post 15 where T is traded and meets with a representative of a Seattle hardware store operator who wants to sell his AT&T stock.

Phillips' broker would like to buy at the lowest price possible at that time, 50. The seller's broker would like to sell at the highest price, at that time, 50¼. Since nobody is selling at the lower price, Phillips' broker bides 50 1/8. The Seattle man's broker hears the bid and instantly shouts "Sold 100 at 50 1/8."

Over and over again every day this auction procedure is repeated on the floors of the stock exchanges.

The brokers complete the agreement by noting each other's firm name and reporting the transaction back to their phone clerks so that the customers may be notified.

A clerk at the post notes the transaction "T 50 1/8" on a card that goes directly into the Market Data System computer.

Usually, within minutes, the transaction has been reported on the market ticker tape which records all transactions that take place on the Exchange. The ticker is one way that information about the market is transmitted all over the country. If Phillips were sitting in his broker's office in Chicago, he would see T 50 1/8 go by on the ticker, and while he might not know that it was his purchase, he would know that the latest price paid for AT&T was 50 1/8.

In the past, the final part of the transaction would take place when the man in Seattle delivered his stock certificate to his broker's office and had a check issued to him for the proceeds of the sale. Meanwhile, Phillips would have sent his broker a check for the purchase of the stock and would receive the stock certificates sometime in the future. Now, most stock transactions are recorded on computers and no stock certificates are issued. Phillips would have to be satisfied with a computer notation.

Common Stock

There are two basic types of stock that a company may issue: common stock and preferred stock. Preferred stock is discussed on the next page.

If a company has only one type of stock, it is usually common stock, also called "capital stock" in some cases.

A common stockholder is an owner of the business in a broad sense of the word. He almost always has the right to vote for the directors of the company. The directors, in turn, select the top management of the company. The directors, in turn, select the top management of the company.

If the majority, or a well-organized minority, of the common stockholders become dissatisfied with the way the company is being run, they can elect a new slate of directors to replace the current group.

The holder of common stock receives dividents from the company as a payment for the capital he has put into the firm. Dividends on common stock, which are determined by the board of directors, may be increased when the business is doing well. If business is bad, or if the board wished to keep the profits in the firm in the form of retained earnings, dividends may be cut or omitted.

For some investors the promise of a steady stream of dividends is the major reason for purchasing common stock. Many companies have a record of paying dividends on their common stock that stretches back almost one hundred years. For other investors the interest in common stock is the fact that it is traded on one or more of the stock exchanges. These investors are hoping that the market value of the stock will increase and that they will profit from selling the stock for more than they paid for it.

For the companies whose stock is listed (bought and sold) on the New York Stock Exchange, the number of shares of common stock per corporation varies from around 500,000 shares to many millions of shares. AT&T, the largest, has more than 500 million shares outstanding.

Currently, the common stock of approximately 1250 different corporations are listed on the New York Stock Exchange.

Preferred Stock

Preferred stock is so named because it is given certain preferential treatment over the common stock.

For instance, holders of preferred stock are usually entitled to their dividends before the owners of the common stock are paid theirs. However, preferred stock normally pays dividends at a fixed rate; a holder of such stock can expect no more than his specified dividend even if the company becomes more and more prosperous. If the company runs into hard times, the dividend may be postponed, or in some cases, reduced or omitted entirely. If the preferred stock is "cumulative," any dividends omitted must be paid at a later date, before any dividends are declared on the common stock.

In the event the company is liquidated (goes bankrupt), preferred stockholders have a prior claim against the assets (resources) of the company over the common stockholders.

Because of these advantages, preferred stockholders are usually limited in their participation in company affairs. They generally have no voting privileges as common stockholders have.

Currently there are about 360 preferred stocks listed on the New York Stock Exchange.

Bonds

Bonds are issued by corporations as a source of capital funds. A bond is basically an I.O.U. or note, usually issued in multiples of $1000, although $100 and $500 bonds are not uncommon.

A bond is evidence of a debt on which the company promises to pay a specific rate of interest for a specific period of time (7 7/8% until the year 2001 in the example below). The debt must be repaid on the expiration date.

The bondholder is a creditor of the corporation and not an owner, as is a stockholder. So long as the company meets its obligations, such as paying the bondholder the interest due, the bondholder has no voice in the running of the business.

Some bonds are issued by corporations with property as collateral or "mortgage." That is, the land, buildings, machinery, or equipment owned by the company backs up the loan much in the same way that a house or car backs up loans made by banks to individuals.

Companies issue bonds in order to obtain long-term financing, with a redemption date twenty-five or thirty years in the future a common event. While the organization must pay interest on the money obtained through the sale of the bonds, the firm does not have to repay the principal amount until the redemption date.

By selling bonds instead of stock, the management of the corporation is able to prevent the dilution of ownership of the corporation. On the other hand it does increase the liabilities of the firm, but when large amounts of cash is needed, bonds may be the only answer.

This is not an offering of these bonds for sale, or an offer to buy, or a solicitation of an offer to buy, any of such bonds. The offering is made only by the Prospectus.

$40,000,000

Pacific Power & Light Company

First Mortgage Bonds, 7⅞% Series due 2001
(Due February 1, 2001)

Price 99.714% and accrued interest

These bonds are redeemable prior to maturity as set forth in the Prospectus, copies of which may be obtained from such of the undersigned as are registered or licensed dealers or brokers in securities in this State.

Blyth & Co., Inc.   Halsey, Stuart & Co. Inc.   White, Weld & Co.

Hornblower & Weeks-Hemphill, Noyes   Dean Witter & Co.
Incorporated

E. F. Hutton & Company Inc.   Dominick & Dominick,   W. E. Hutton & Co.
Incorporated

R. W. Pressprich & Co.   Wood, Struthers & Winthrop Inc.
Incorporated

First California Company   Foster & Marshall Inc.
Incorporated

Shuman, Agnew & Co., Inc.   Sutro & Co.   Davis, Skaggs & Co., Inc.
Incorporated

D. H. Blair & Company   Herron Northwest   June S. Jones Co.
Incorporated

Blakely, Strand & Williams, Inc.   Daugherty, Cole Inc.

Wm. P. Harper & Son & Company

Debentures

A bond for which no property has been mortgaged or put up as collateral is called a debenture.

The person who holds a debenture has only the company's promise that it will pay back the loan. In the case of large, well-established corporations, this promise to pay is good enough so that investors are willing to lend money on an I.O.U. basis.

The general credit rating stands behind the debenture, and if there are no other bonds with claims on the assets of the corporation, the debenture holders would be able to make a claim on the assets of the corporation if the debentures are defaulted on. Basically, the buyer of a debenture has to have a higher level of confidence in the corporation than does the regular bondholder.

PRICE 99 3/4%

That is not the interest rate. The interest rate is 8 3/8%.

The price for the bond being issued is 99 3/4%. This means that the bond with a redemption value of $1000 will sell for $997.50.

There is a small discount on the sale of the bond because there is some interest due that will not be paid the bondholder.

You'll recall that a sinking fund is an allocation of a company's earnings each year that is for the eventual repayment of the bonds.

"What's a debenture?"

Drawing by Stevenson, © 1967: The New Yorker Magazine, Inc.

Why Bulls Shun Bunnies

They just can't see the numbers for the bodies.

REMEMBER THE DAYS when Wall Street was skeptical about Disney? After all, it was nothing but a Mickey Mouse company.

This time Wall Street is skeptical about bunnies—Playboy Bunnies. But then, the difference between Mickey Mouse and Playboy's Bunnies is the difference between apple pie and loose living.

Should Wall Street look more closely at the percentages in sin—just like the ancient sect whose members decided to worship the devil, since he clearly had the upper hand? This is a company that has gone from nothing to $159 million in sales in 19 years—with record sales and earnings every year. Return on equity last year was 24%; operating margin, 16.4%.

Wall Street remains skeptical. At a recent price of 16, Playboy Enterprises sells at nearly one-third below its original offering price. Can it be that investment committees are embarrassed to have Playboy listed in their portfolios? Or that some analysts are embarrassed even to pass it up for the committee to consider in the first place? They can't all be, because some 20 institutions *do* own the stock and hold around 25% of the 2 million or so shares in public hands. It seems to be the public itself that is reluctant. Some analysts complain that they recommend the stock, but the customers aren't always interested.

"It's the same problem with advertisers," says Robert S. Preuss, Playboy's executive vice president and chief operating officer. "There are still managements too staid to allow their products in *Playboy*. We would love to have them, but we are doing handsomely without them." Handsomely, indeed. The magazine took in $37.9 million in gross advertising revenues in the last fiscal year, and if this is nothing like the $92 million *Life* did in its last year of life, *Playboy* has something *Life* never had: high circulation revenues, $52 million last year. Nor does *Playboy* cost anything like what *Life* did to produce. On revenues of $83 million in 1972—just over half the company's total—the magazine itself accounted for almost all of pretax net, $19.4 million. By contrast, in its last year *Life* lost an estimated $5 million on revenues of well over $100 million.

True, there are other potential problems, such as Playboy's hotels. They have so far soaked up $80 million in capital and are still losing money. (Preuss predicts that they will start making money in 1974.) In fact, since nearly half of Playboy's revenues yield almost no earnings, there are obviously a lot of hefty but unprofitable operations. On the other hand, the company could get a windfall from legalization of gambling throughout the U.S. Preuss' eyes must glitter at the very thought.

Meanwhile, apparently Playboy stock does have at least *some* appeal to the average investor. The company reports that about 1,000 of its estimated 8,500 shareholders own only one share. Obviously they didn't buy it for an investment, but for the handsome reclining nude gracing the stock certificate.

Reading The Market

1. A recap of the prior day's activity, including: the total number of shares and warrants traded and information about the most active stocks for that day.

2. The abbreviated name of the company issuing the stock is given -- in this case, ABBOTT LABORATORIES. It is a common stock unless,

3. "pf" follows the name -- indicating a preferred stock.

4. Columns showing the highest and lowest prices paid for the stock during the year. In this case, a low of 4 5/8 and a high of 9.

5. Number following the names show the rate of annual dividends -- for this stock, 80¢. The amount may be changed but is an estimation based on the last quarterly or semi-annual payment. The letters following the dividend indicate other information about the dividend. For example,

6. The "b" indicates that in addition to the annual dividend rate shown (45¢ for this stock) a dividend of stock was paid. Other symbols used are explained in a table appearing in each newspaper.

7. This column shows the Price/Earnings Ratio for the stock. In this case the P/E Ratio was 14.

8. This column shows the number of shares, reported in hundreds, traded during the day. In this case, 3900.

9. The preceding number doesn't include stocks bought and sold in odd-lots, that is in quantities less than 100 shares. The "z" means the actual number of shares traded, in this case, 60.

10. The highest price paid for this stock during the day was 15, the lowest was 14 3/4.

11. The closing or last price paid for the stock on that trading day was 25 1/4 per share, closing up 1/4 from the previous day.

THE WALL STREET JOURNAL,
Wednesday, March 14, 1973

Tuesday's Volume
14,210,000 Shares; 216,900 Warrants

Volume since Jan. 1:	1973	1972	1971
Total shares . . .	854,966,303	967,367,220	934,966,130
Total warrants . .	9,739,700	12,922,600	

MOST ACTIVE STOCKS

	Open	High	Low	Close	Chg.	Volume
EastnAirL	13⅞	14½	13⅝	14½	+ ⅝	166,300
Gulf Oil	25½	25⅝	25⅜	25⅜	. . . .	161,400
Magic Chef	15¼	15¼	11	12⅜	−3	158,300
Kresge SS	42¾	44	42¾	43⅜	+ ⅜	141,700
Atl Rich	68½	69⅜	68	69¼	+ ½	134,900
Comw Edis	34½	34⅝	34⅜	34⅝	+ ⅛	127,500
Va ElPow	20⅝	21	20½	20⅝	.	121,800
Am Medical	17¼	18¼	17¼	17⅞	+2⅛	118,700
Am Tel&Tel	50⅞	51¼	50⅞	51⅛	+ ⅜	118,100
Southern Co	19	19⅛	18¾	18⅞	. . . . .	108,600

Average closing price of most active stocks: 30.80.

A-B-C

—1973— High	Low	Stocks Div.	P-E Ratio	Sales 100s	High	Low	Close	Net Chg.
78¼	69¼	AbbtLb 1.20	26	59	76½	75⅛	76⅛	+ ¼
49⅜	40½	ACF Ind2.40	13	190	45	43¾	44¾	+ 1¼
17⅛	14⅝	AcmeClv .80	13	15	14⅞	14⅝	14⅞	+ ⅛
26	23⅛	AcmeMkt 1	22	19	23⅜	23¼	23⅜	+ ⅛
14¾	12⅞	AdmE 1.15e		x23	13⅛	12⅞	13	
8½	7	Ad Millis .20	32	3	7⅛	7	7⅛	+ ⅛
34	22¼	Addrsso .60	11	84	24	23⅝	24	+ ½
18	12¾	Admiral	6	59	13⅞	13¼	13¾	+ ½
76¾	61	AetnaLf 1.72	10	98	64¼	63¾	63⅞	− ⅝
60¼	54¼	AetnaLf pf2		2	54⅞	54⅞	54⅞	
31⅛	21¾	AhmanHF	8	20	22⅛	22	22⅛	+ ¼
9	4⅝	Aileen Inc	15	43	5⅞	5¾	5⅞	+ ¼
78¼	68¼	Air Prd .20b	25	85	75	74⅝	74⅞	+ ¼
18¼	13½	Airco .80	8	100	13⅞	13⅝	13¾	− ⅛
3⅝	2½	AJ Industris	7	60	2⅝	2½	2⅝	+ ⅛
31¼	27¾	Akzona 1.10	16	6	30½	30¼	30½	+ ¼
17	15	Ala Gas 1.10	8	6	15¼	15⅛	15⅛	− ⅜
37⅞	24⅜	Alaska Intrs	19	108	31⅜	30⅛	31	. .
29¼	19	AlbertoC .32	14	50	19¼	18¼	18⅜	− 1⅛
17⅜	15¾	Albfsn .36a	12	27	16⅞	16⅝	16⅝	− ⅛
26⅜	22⅞	AlcanAl .80	14	82	25⅝	25⅛	25⅝	+ ½
10⅞	8⅝	AlcoStd .36	7	18	9⅛	9	9	
40½	34⅝	AlconLb .6	54	21	37⅞	37¼	37½	− ¼
9½	6¼	Alexdrs .10e	27	12	6½	6⅜	6½	. . .
31⅞	28½	AlisnM 2.91e	10	25	29⅜	29	29¼	+ ⅛
14⅝	11½	AllALfe .24	10	5	12	11¾	11¾	− ¼
14½	10⅝	AllegCp .28e	10	7	10⅞	10⅞	10⅞	− ⅛
29⅞	23¾	AllegLdlm 1	10	33	26¾	26	26⅜	+ ⅝
44⅛	39	AllegLd pf 3	. . .	3	40⅛	39¾	40⅛	+ ⅛
24½	20½	AllgPw 1.44	8	49	21⅛	20¾	21	+ ⅜
19⅜	13⅛	AllnGp 1.04t	11	12	15	14½	14¾	− ⅝
33⅞	28⅛	Allied Ch1.20	14	214	33¾	33⅛	33½	+ ⅜
44⅞	35¼	All Mnt .45b	26	42	37¾	37¼	37¾	+ ⅝
24¾	22⅛	AlldMills .75	14	2	23½	23¼	23¼	− ¼
22	16¾	Allied P .68	9	39	20⅞	20	20¼	− ¼
49¾	46	AlliedP pf 3		7	57⅜	57⅛	57⅛	+ 7⅜
39⅝	27	AlliedSt 1.40	10	14	29¾	29	29¾	+ 1
62	60	AlliedSt pf 4	·	z60	61	61	61	. . . . . .
5½	4½	Allied Super	14	30	4¾	4½	4⅝	. . . . . .
12⅝	9⅝	AllisChl .20e	13	222	9½	9⅜	9½	. . . . . .
15½	11½	AllrgtAt .48	11	2	12	12	12	. .
17½	13	AlphaPl .48	8	39	15	14¾	15	+ ⅛
60	50	Alcoa 1.80	11	149	53	52⅞	52⅞	− ⅜
28⅜	24½	AmalSg 1.60	8	3	25¼	25¼	25¼	+ ¼
14¾	10¾	AMBAC .50	11	31	11⅞	11⅝	11⅞	+ ½
46	40¼	AmEs pf2.60		2	41	41	41	+ ½
50½	36¾	AmHes .30r	30	313	39	38	39	+ ½
112½	82	AmH pf3.50		117	86	84½	86	+ ¾
40	25	AAirFilt .42	26	58	28⅛	28	28⅛	+ ⅛
25⅜	17⅛	Am Airlin	93	904	18⅞	17⅞	18⅝	+ ½

Market Information

Most investors do a considerable amount of reading and studying before buying or selling securities. They want all the facts and opinions that they can get before putting their money on the line. Others rely only on the recommendations of their brokers -- they do little or no research on their own.

Corporations with securities listed on a registered exchange are required by law to disclose certain financial information to their stock-holders periodically. About 95% report this information quarterly.

Most corporations also publish annual reports that are readily available to the public. The scope of an annual report may vary from company to company, but a typical report includes the following types of information:

- Financial statements
- Research activities
- New developments and plans
- Information about the company's management and employees
- Outlook for the company and its industry or industries.

A number of the articles featured in this book have been drawn from such annual reports. Your library may have a file of annual reports for major corporations.

In addition to these reports, many newspapers and magazines carry business and financial news. Many of the articles featured in this text have come from leading business news journals and papers. The leading sources of business and financial news are:

- The Wall Street Journal
- Business Week
- Forbes
- Dun's Review
- Barron's
- Fortune
- The Commercial and Financial Chronicle.

Even your local news-paper probably reports daily trading activity, prices and news about companies of local and major national interest.

If you want to dig more deeply, you may consult one or more of the investor information serv-ices that are available. Moody's, Standard & Poor, or any that may be avail-able at your library will give you:

- An historical profile of the company and its financial growth
- Its current financial structure
- Stock behavior patterns
- Recent developments
- Prospects

In fact, you may request a tear sheet for a parti-cular company you may be interested in from your local broker. This is normally one of your broker's services. He may also have his own firm's analysis of the stock available for your con-sideration.

Men Who Get Ahead Read The Wall Street Journal

By a WALL STREET JOURNAL Staff Reporter

The numbers game, a popular gambling form in ghettoes, is essentially a lottery based on a three-or-four-digit number. Gamblers seek a number that can't be fixed and that is also easily accessible to their clientele.

In Cleveland, the numbers operators have chosen an Establishmentarian num-ber. It's the last digit of the numbers of stocks that advanced, declined and closed unchanged in the previous day's trading on the New York Stock Exchange. (Today's winner is 016.) Judging from the calls received by The Wall Street Journal's Cleveland office, the authority appears to be this newspaper's "Market Diary."

One caller not long ago, for instance, was concerned about a one-digit discrep-ancy between the winning number as it ap-peared in The Wall Street Journal and an-other paper. "I need to know because, heh heh, well, I guess you know why. I might lose some, uh, privileges if there is a dif-ferent number." He declined to give his name, and it was never learned if he'd won or lost his, uh, privileges.

Brokerage firms should be able to provide the needed information about a particular stock, but should also have industry profiles. By analyzing the industry as to its growth potential, the investor can make a more informed decision concern-ing a particular firm in that industry.

Most brokerage firms also have in-depth anal-yses of many issues which their advisory staff con-sider for their clients. These reports usually give advice about investing for income or growth and make recommendations about buying or selling a particular issue.

The Dow Jones Average

The Dow Jones Industrials Average represents the movement of the prices of thirty selected leading industrial stocks. Among the companies included are General Motors, General Electric, Woolworth, Allied Chemical, Du Pont, AT&T, Exxon, Sears Roebuck, Union Carbide, Proctor and Gamble and Eastman Kodak.

When the Industrial average was first compiled in 1896, it had only twelve stocks and was computed by adding the market prices of the stocks and dividing by twelve. Later, there were twenty stocks, and the sum of their market prices was divided by twenty. But them the companies began splitting their stock or issuing sotck dividends, and also more stocks were added to the Dow-Jones average. So today, to get the Dow Jones Industrials Average as it is published every day, you divide, not by thirty, but by 2.245 (called the "divisor"). This periodically adjusted number provides for changes such as noted above, so the average reflects as accurately as possible the realy movement of prices.

The Industrials Average represents only industrial corporation stocks on the New York Stock Exchange. Similar Dow Jones averages are compiled for transportation, public utilities, and all three groups of stocks combined. There are also other market averages, such as the New York Stock Exchange Index, which compile prices of larger numbers of stocks.

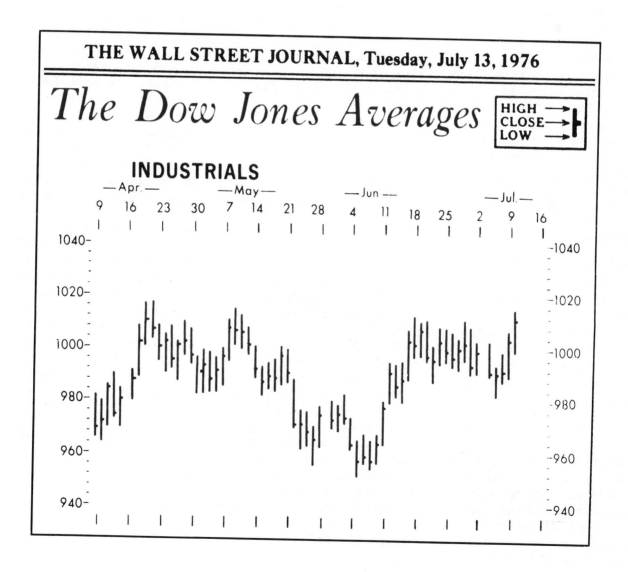

THE WALL STREET JOURNAL, Tuesday, July 13, 1976

The Dow Jones Averages HIGH → CLOSE → LOW →

INDUSTRIALS

Mutual Funds

To minimize the risks involved in owning particular stocks, an investor may put money into a mutual fund.

A mutual fund is a company that sells stock to obtain money for investment in the securities market. It makes possible the pooling of money from a large number of people and the investment of the money in a large number of stocks. In this way, an investor gains flexibility that a larger investment fund can have in trading stocks on the market.

Profits realized from the investments by a mutual fund are distributed to the mutual fund shareholders or reinvested in the market, thus increasing the value of the fund and its stock.

Funds may specialize in particular types of securities, such as utilities, electronics, growth stocks, or stocks of "socially responsible" companies.

The fund is responsible for making its investments and thus must do its own homework in studying the merits and potential of alternative investments. It is widely believed that the better the management of the fund, the better the growth and profitability of the fund.

One such fund is the Axe-Houghton Stock Fund, managed by E. W. Axe & Co. This is an investment firm housed in a 75-year old castle overlooking the Hudson River in New York state. If you invested $10,000 in the fund ten years ago, you would now have an investment value of $30,000 or more (with dividends and capital appreciation reinvested by the fund).

Says the president, Justin S. Dunn, "We have daily reports on over 800 stocks and maintain about 1300 charts on economic indicators. I'd rather see our analysts keeping up on changes in industry trends and calling companies primarily to find out why reality may have differed from what we anticipated, than making the routine security analyst's tour and asking the usual questions where you already knew the answers. A lot of what's called field work in the investment field is really ritual."

Each day the head of research gets a computer-produced list of risk-reward ratios on each of the 800 stocks Axe follows. This enables him to sell stocks more quickly where the upside potential has become realized and the downside risk potential has increased.

The computer, for example, said once that U.S. Steel stock had an upside risk potential of 75% over the next 12 months and a downside risk of only 9%. Bethlehem Steel shares looked even better, with 90% on the upside and 3% on the downside. The estimates change, of course, as the stock price and market conditions change.

TYPES OF FUNDS

Mutual funds became popular several decades ago. In 1940, the funds that existed had total assets of about $450 million. By 1970 the total assets were up to $55 billion, a considerable jump. Then in the 1970's, mutual funds became accepted as a stable part of the investment scene. There are more than 600 funds today, of diverse quality and purpose. Some funds have been formed and then disbanded because of failure. Funds, of course, ride with the stock market unless they are managed more effectively to counter trends.

Shares in most funds are sold by brokerage firms or special sales organizations. A commission, or "load", is charged on every sale. In addition, the investor pays an annual management fee, deducted from the earnings of the fund.

These funds are called "load funds." Some funds charge no sales commissions at all, and are called "no-load funds". Many people feel these funds are a "better deal" because all of your money is working.

In selecting mutual funds, the investor must consider many of the same factors that are considered in the purchase of other types of security: income, growth, security, diversification and the impact of inflation. Purchasing a mutual fund does not solve all of the investor's problems.

Commodities

Cash Prices

Monday, July 12, 1976
(Quotations as of 4 p.m. Eastern time)

FOODS	Mon.	Fri.	Yr. Ago
Flour, hard winter KC cwt	$8.70	$8.90	$9.30
Coffee, Brazilian, NY lb	n1.50	1.50	.69
Cocoa, Accra NY lb	n1.06	1.10	.75
Potatoes, rnd wht, 50 lb, NY del	y3.85	3.65	6.15
Sugar, cane, raw NY lb del	n.1520	.1555	.2100
Sugar, cane, ref NY lb fob	.2150	.2150	.2845
Sugar, beet, ref Chgo-W lb fob ..	.1925	.1925	.2380
Orange Juice, frz con, NY lb ...	b.5230	.5200	.5250
Butter, AA-93 score, Chgo., lb.	b1.07	1.07	.96¾
Eggs, Lge white, Chgo doz. ...	.61½	.61½	.51
Broilers, Dressed "A" NY lb ...	x.4593	.4526	.5342
Beef, 600-800 lbs, Midw lb fob ..	.57¾	.59¾	.85¼
Pork Loins, 14 down Mdw lb fob	n1.08	1.07¾	1.01½
Hams, 14-17 lbs, Midw lb fob ..	.80¼	.80¼	.83¼
Pork Bellies, 12-14lbMdw lb fob	.77	.78½	.89¼
Hogs, Sioux City avg cwt	e51.65	50.50	56.00
Hogs, Omaha avg cwt	e50.85	50.10	55.20
Steers, Omaha choice avg cwt .	37.60	38.60	50.25
Steers, Sioux City ch avg cwt ..	37.25	39.00	51.25
Pepper, black NY lb	a.90½	.90½	.91½
GRAINS AND FEEDS			
Wheat, No. 2 ord hard KC bu	3.64½	3.74	3.63¾
Wht,No.2 dk Nthn 14%-pro Mpls	4.30	4.39½	4.54
Wheat, No. 2 soft red Chgo bu ..	3.31½	3.45	3.52½
Milo, No. 2 KC cwt	4.95	4.95	4.85
Corn, No. 2 yellow Chgo. bu ..	h2.99½	3.03	2.93
Oats, No. 2 milling, Mpls bu ...	1.90	1.94	1.60
Rye, No. 2 Mpls bu	3.40	3.40	2.65
Barley, top-qlty. Mpls bu	3.70	3.70	4.15
Soybeans, No. 1 yellow Chgo bu	7.07½	7.27½	5.59½
Flaxseed, Mpls bu	n7.70	7.70	8.25
Bran, KC ton	95.00	96.50	74.00
Linseed Meal, Mpls ton	162.00	164.00	128.00
Cottonseed Meal, Memphis ton	188.00	190.00	120.00
Soybean Meal, Decatur, Ill. ton	200.00	210.00	119.00
Corn Gluten Feed, Chgo ton ..	98.00	98.00	80.00
Hominy Feed, Ill. ton	n91.00	91.00	79.00
Meat-Bonemeal 50%-pro, Ill.ton	n255.00	255.00	155.00
Brewer's Grains, Milw ton	97.00	96.00	81.00
Alfalfa Pellets, dehy, Neb., ton	89.50	89.50	65.00
FATS AND OILS			
Cottonseed Oil, crd Miss Vly lb	n.26½	.26½	.29
Corn Oil, crude Chgo lb	n.26	.26	.29½
Soybean Oil, crd Decatur, Ill. lb	n.2215	.2273	.2695
Peanut Oil, crd Southeast lb	.34½	.34½	.43
Coconut Oil, crd Pac Cst lb ...	n.24	.25	c.19¾
Lard, Chgo lb	n.2300	.2300	.3700
Tallow, bleachable, Chgo lb ...	.16¼	.16	.15¾
Tallow, edible, Chgo lb	n.20½	.20½	.25
Grease, choice white, Chgo lb	n.16¼	.15⅞	.14
Linseed Oil, raw Mpls lb	.25	.25	.39
Palm Oil, crude, per lb.	fa.20¾	.21¾	.18
TEXTILES AND FIBERS			
Cotton, 1 1-16 in. mid Memphis lb	.8845	.9045	.4675
Print Cloth, 64x60 45-in. NY yd	d.39	.39	.27
Print Cloth, 78x78 48-in. NY yd	d.54½	.54½	.43
Sheetings, 56x60 40-in. NY yd	d.51	.51	.38
Burlap, 10 oz. 40-in. NY yd	n.1730	.1730	.1790
Wool, fine staple terr. Bstn lb	1.83	1.83	1.58
Satin Acetate, NY yd	d.40	.40	.32
METALS			
Steel Scrap, 1 hvy mlt Chgo ton	95.00	95.00	60.00
Copper per lb.	p.74	.74	.63¾
Copper Scp, No. 2 wire NY lb.	n.58½	.59½	.42
Lead, NY lb.	p.23-.25	.23-.25	.19
Zinc, per lb.	p.37	.37	.38¾
Tin, NY lb, composite price	s4.2903	4.3191	3.2850
Aluminum, ingot, NY lb	p.44	.44	.39
Quicksilver, NY 76 lb flask	n110.00	110.00	145.00
MISCELLANEOUS			
Rubber, smoked sheets NY lb	n.40⅞	.41⅛	.32
Hides, lt native cows Chgo lb ..	n.36	.36	.27
Gasoline, 92 Oct. Mid-Cont gal	.35	.35	.29½
Fuel Oil, No. 2 Mid-Cont gal ..	.29¼	.29¼	.24
Newspapers, old No.1 Chgo ton	30.00	30.00	4.00
PRECIOUS METALS			
Platinum, NY troy oz	p165.00	165.00	155.00
Silver, troy ounce			
London, spot (in pence)	278.9	282.15	214.4
3-Month	288.2	291.10	219.95
6-Month	296.5	299.40	226.2
One year	313.0	315.50	239.7
(The U.S. equivalent for spot was $4.971 based on the $1.7825 London rate for sterling yesterday.)			
Handy & Harman base price	4.975	5.045	4.72
Engelhard Minerals & Chemicals			
Industrial bullion	4.975	5.045	4.72
Fabricated products	5.099	5.171	4.838
Gold, troy ounce			
Engelhard Minerals & Chemicals			
Industrial bullion	122.35	123.00	167.25
Fabricated products	125.41	126.08	171.43
Handy & Harman base price	121.85	122.50	166.85

	--Fixings-- Morn.	--Fixings-- Aftn.	Prev. Aftn.	Year Ago
London	122.20	121.85	122.50	166.75

a-Asked. b-Bid. c-Corrected. d-Dealer market. e-Estimated. f-Near-term shipment, C.I.F. delivered U.S. ports. h-In hopper railroad cars. n-Nominal. p-Producer price. s-Source, Metals Week. x-Less than truckloads. y-Virginia origin; varies seasonally. z-Not quoted.

Let's face it -- most people don't know what commodity futures are!

Through the mercantile exchanges (the largest is in Chicago), individuals and companies buy and sell contracts for future delivery of carload lots of agricultural and mining products. These include pork bellies (uncured bacon), live cattle, hogs, potatoes, eggs, sugor, coffee, wheat, oats, and other products. Also included are metals such as silver, lead, copper, and zink, and fibers, textiles, rubber, gasoline, and other products.

There are two kinds of prices quoted for commodities -- cash prices and future prices. Cash prices (shown on this page) are the prices that would be paid for delivery of the goods today. Future prices show what the price would be for delivery sometime in the future, at a specified date.

All futures contracts describe specific characteristics of each commodity, thus the basic value of one contract for a commodity is identical to another contract for the same commodity. That is, contracts don't vary very much at all.

Nearly all of these contracts are offset before the actual delivery date. That is, the seller usually repurchases the contract or a buyer sells his initial contract. Less than 3 in 100 of the commodities contracts traded on the futures market ever reach delivery to the initial buyer. When you buy a contract on potatoes, you would not expect to have the carloads delivered to your doorstep.

Rather, investors buy and sell commodity contracts as a way to take advantage of the price fluctuations. It is a dynamic market, and money can be put to good use.

These investors are takin taking on the risks of growers, processors, and marketers of farm products.

At the same time, large food processors, to insure the price they will have to pay in the future, buy futures contracts. This is known as hedging.

By examining their own costs, hedgers can buy or sell futures contracts at a price where they can assure themselves a profit regardless of the actual cash prices in the future.

On actual commodities (the produce or material), trading is in terms of cash price. A sample quotation was 62¢ a pound for coffee a few years ago. You can check today's newspaper for current cash prices and see the changes.

On the sample list, you will note that closing prices are given for two days and for the day a year before. Cwt, by the way, means hundredweight, or hundred pounds.

Investors and hedgers know that the exchange, the federal government, brokers, and the general supply and

Futures Prices

Monday, July 12, 1976

—GRAINS AND FEEDS—

WHEAT (CBT)—5,000 bu.; cents per bu.

	Open	High	Low	Close	Change	Season's High	Season's Low
July	368	371	355½	356-355½	−13to13½	464½	334½
Sept	376	378	363	364-363	−14to15	438	342
Dec	390	393	375	378-375	−14¾to17¾	423	354½
Mar 77	401	405	387	387	−18½	433	365
May	405	408½	391	391	−17½	437	391
July	403	410	394	394	−15	440	394

Sales Fri.: 16,300 contracts.

WHEAT (K.C.)—5,000 bu.; cents per bu.

	Open	High	Low	Close	Change	Season's High	Season's Low
July	375	375	367¾	369	−8½	458	342½
Sept	383	383¾	373½	375½-374¾	−9¼to10	420	350½
Dec	394	395½	384	386-385½	−10to10½	419½	364
Mar 77	406½	406½	394	398-399	−9½to8½	431	373½
May	405½	406½	399	404-403	−8½to9½	432	399
July	402	406	402	406	no comp	406	402

Sales Fri.: 2,484 contracts.

WHEAT (MPLS)—5,000 bu.; cents per bu.

	Open	High	Low	Close	Change	Season's High	Season's Low
July	414½	414½	401½	402½-403	−11¾to11¼	442	369
Sept	418	418½	405	407-408	−11½to10½	438	372
Dec	423	424	411	412	−11	441	380
Mar 77	428	428	415	419	−13	451	401

Sales Fri.: 1,186 contracts.

CORN (CBT)—5,000 bu.; cents per bu.

	Open	High	Low	Close	Change	Season's High	Season's Low
July	305	306½	298¼	304½-306	−2to½	342	248
Sept	298½	300½	292½	295-296	−4to3	305¼	260
Dec	288	290	281¼	284½-285	−3½to3	297	254½
Mar 77	296½	298¾	291	294-295	−3to2	305¾	262½
May	302	304	296	299	−3½	309½	269¾
July	307	307	300	303	−4¼	312	292

Sales Fri.: 24,590 contracts.

SOYBEANS (CBT)—5,000 bu.; cents per bu.

	Open	High	Low	Close	Change	Season's High	Season's Low
July	738	751	724½	724½a	−20	757	466
Aug	745	752½	725½	725½a	−20	760	469¼
Sept	750	757½	730¼	730¼a	−20	763	475
Nov	760	766½	740	740a	−20	777¼	483
Jan 77	761	772	743	743a	−20	782½	490
Mar	766	776	747½	747½	−20	788	504½
May	766	775	747	747	−20	784	511½
July	770	774	745	745	−20	794	619½

Sales Fri.: 37,340 contracts.

SOYBEAN MEAL (CBT)—100 tons; $ per ton

	Open	High	Low	Close	Change	Season's High	Season's Low
July	216.00	219.00	206.50	207.50	−9.30	228.00	127.00
Aug	218.00	220.50	208.70	208.70a	−10.00	230.00	129.00
Sept	218.00	221.00	209.30	209.50-210.	−9.80to9.3	231.00	131.00
Oct	218.00	221.00	210.00	211.00	−9.00	231.00	133.50
Dec	220.00	223.00	211.00	212.50	−8.30	231.70	137.00
Jan77	220.50	222.00	212.00	213.00	−9.00	232.00	139.70
Mar	222.00	223.00	212.00	213.00-.50	−8.20to7.7	233.50	142.00
May	222.00	222.00	213.50	215.00	−6.00	234.00	143.50
July	220.00	220.00	213.00	215.50-216.	−6.00to5.5	237.00	185.00

Sales Fri.: 9,233 contracts.

SOYBEAN OIL (CBT)—60,000 lbs.; cents per lb.

	Open	High	Low	Close	Change	Season's High	Season's Low
July	22.75	22.95	21.65	22.15	− .58	26.65	15.27
Aug	22.70	23.05	21.75	22.20-.30	− .52to.42	26.00	15.33
Sept	22.70	23.25	21.90	22.35	− .50	23.25	15.55
Oct	22.95	23.45	22.05	22.45	− .60	23.45	15.65
Dec	23.40	23.65	22.33	22.70-.80	− .63to.53	23.65	15.80
Jan 77	23.75	23.75	22.40	22.80b	− .60	23.75	16.31
Mar	23.60	23.85	22.52	22.85	− .67	23.90	16.48
May	23.55	23.55	22.55	22.90b	− .65	23.95	16.60
July	23.85	23.85	22.65	23.00	− .65	23.85	18.30

Sales Fri.: 9,298 contracts.

OATS (CBT)—5,000 bu.; cents per bu.

	Open	High	Low	Close	Change	Season's High	Season's Low
July	191	192	187	187a	−6	202½	134½
Sept	184	185½	178¾	178¾a	−6	196½	135
Dec	182	184¼	177¼	177¼a	−6	194½	146
Mar 77	180½	183	176¾	176¾a	−6	193¾	153
May	182	182½	175½	175½	−6	192	169½

Sales Fri.: 766 contracts.

OATS (WPG)—1,000 bu.; cents per bu.

	Open	High	Low	Close	Change	Season's High	Season's Low
July	149½	149½	148¼	148¾	−1¼	169	148
Oct	149¾	149¾	148¼	148½	−1¾	169¾	146

Est. sales 240; sales Fri.: 678 contracts.

RAPESEED (WPG)—1,000 bu.; cents per bu.

	Open	High	Low	Close	Change	Season's High	Season's Low
Sept	652	654½	632	633½b	−18½	679	458
Nov	648	652½	628½	630½a	−18	672	485
Jan 77	647	650	627	628	−19	672	491½

Est. sales 465; sales Fri.: 2,224 contracts.

RYE (WPG)—1,000 bu.; cents per bu.

	Open	High	Low	Close	Change	Season's High	Season's Low
July	310	313	302	302½b	−10	321½	231
Oct	305½	308	297	297½-298	−10to9½	318¾	231
Dec	303½	306½	296¾	297-297½b	−10to9½	317	249

Est. sales 450; sales Fri.: 269 contracts.

BARLEY (WPG)—1,000 bu.; cents per bu.

	Open	High	Low	Close	Change	Season's High	Season's Low
July	219¼	220	217¾	219	−1¼	243¼	217¾
Oct	220	220½	217¾	219½a	−1½	232	216
Dec	220	220	219	219½a	−1½	230½	216

Est. sales 520; sales Fri.: 522 contracts.

ICED BROILERS (CBT)—28,000 lbs.; cents per lb.

	Open	High	Low	Close	Change	Season's High	Season's Low
July	42.55	43.00	42.55	42.60	+ .05	43.80	38.50
Aug	41.65	41.95	41.40	41.45-.40	− .10to.15	43.40	38.00
Sept	41.55	41.75	40.80	40.95	− .40	42.85	37.75
Nov	40.50	40.50	39.70	39.70	− .72	41.10	36.90
Jan 77	41.50	41.50	41.00	41.00	− .50	42.20	38.50

Sales Fri.: 380 contracts.

—FOODS—

FRESH EGGS (CME)—22,500 doz.; cents per doz.

	Open	High	Low	Close	Change	Season's High	Season's Low
July	54.75	56.25	54.75	56.00-.15	+1.50to1.65	56.25	47.90
Aug	55.60	56.50	54.80	54.80	+ .25	56.50	50.25
Sept	59.00	59.10	58.00	58.70-.85	− .25to.10	59.65	50.25
Nov	60.50	60.60	59.75	60.25	− .25	61.00	50.20
Dec	62.50	62.80	61.50	62.-61.80	− .50to.70	63.50	54.00

Est. sales 457; sales Fri.: 384 contracts.

MAINE POTATOES (NYM)—50,000 lbs.; cents per lb.

	Open	High	Low	Close	Change	Season's High	Season's Low
Nov	5.65	5.68	5.35	5.40	− .19	6.56	4.87
Mar 77	6.83	6.83	6.51	6.58	− .15	7.30	5.85
Apr	7.70	7.70	7.42	7.44	− .24	7.75	6.60
May	8.43	8.50	8.17	8.17	− .23	8.90	7.40

Est. sales 1,012; sales Fri.: 1,282 contracts.

IDAHO POTATOES (CME)—80,000 lbs.; cents per lb.

No sales.

SUGAR, WORLD (CSE)—112,000 lbs.; cents per lb.

	Open	High	Low	Close	Change	Season's High	Season's Low
Sept	14.15	14.20	13.75	13.80-.88	− .24to.16	19.08	11.05
Oct	14.60	14.60	14.09	14.18-.15	− .28to.31	18.95	11.05
Jan 77	14.60	14.63	14.45	14.50n	−13	15.98	13.40
Mar	15.00	15.01	14.32	14.60-.51	− .23to.32	16.07	12.82
May	14.97	14.98	14.30	14.45	− .32	16.02	12.79
July	14.85	14.85	14.35	14.40n	− .26	15.85	13.30
Sept	14.65	14.65	14.05	14.23n	− .23	15.55	13.27
Oct	14.52	14.58	14.10	14.16n	− .26	15.50	13.28

Est. sales 6,010; sales Fri.: 4,714 contracts. Spot: 13.80n.

COFFEE (CSE)—37,500 lbs.; cents per lb.

	Open	High	Low	Close	Change	Season's High	Season's Low
July	135.00	135.00	130.60	131.00b	−9.00	158.30	55.60
Sept	138.15	138.15	138.15	138.15a	−3.00	158.40	77.00
Dec	136.15	136.15	136.15	136.15a	−3.00	153.10	82.10
Mar77	132.00	132.00	132.00	132.00a	−3.00	148.30	94.86
May	131.50	131.50	131.50	131.50a	−3.00	147.00	121.50
July	130.85	130.85	130.85	130.85a	−3.00	144.00	130.85

Est. sales 81; sales Fri.: 851 contracts.

COCOA (CEX)—30,000 lbs.; cents per lb.-s

	Open	High	Low	Close	Change	Season's High	Season's Low
July	95.40	95.40	93.25	91.85	−4.80	102.45	41.65
Sept	93.75	94.00	91.00	91.00	−4.00	100.10	43.46
Dec	88.55	89.05	86.38	86.65	−3.00	92.40	45.20
Mar77	83.76	87.51	82.36	82.75	−2.25	87.50	48.50
May	81.00	81.25	79.50	80.05	−1.95	84.25	52.45
July	78.10	78.10	76.70	77.50	−1.65	81.35	58.10
Sept	75.50	75.75	74.10	74.90	−1.75	78.75	57.10
Dec	71.75	71.75	70.50	71.05	−1.65	75.05	70.50

Est. sales 2,514; sales Fri.: 1,274 contracts.

ORANGE JUICE (CTN)—15,000 lbs.; cents per lb.

	Open	High	Low	Close	Change	Season's High	Season's Low
July	54.50	55.25	54.25	54.25b	+ .05	68.50	51.25
Sept	55.25	55.90	54.00	54.00b	− .80	69.50	51.20
Nov	55.80	57.00	54.90	54.80b	− .60	69.20	52.30
Jan 77	57.00	57.80	55.85	55.80b	−1.00	70.20	53.30
Mar	58.80	58.80	57.80	56.80b	− .95	69.90	54.40
May	60.25	60.25	58.40	57.90b	−1.00	69.75	56.35

Est. sales 400; sales Fri.: 190 contracts.

—METALS—

COPPER (CMX)—25,000 lbs.; cents per lb.-s

	Open	High	Low	Close	Change	Season's High	Season's Low
July	75.40	75.50	74.70	75.00	− .90	77.30	55.30
Aug	74.90	74.90	74.90	75.30	−1.00	77.30	72.20
Sept	76.30	76.40	75.40	75.90	− .90	78.60	56.30
Dec	78.00	78.30	77.20	77.70	− .90	80.50	57.60
Jan 77	78.00	78.70	77.60	78.20	− .90	80.90	58.20
Mar	79.50	79.70	78.70	79.20	− .80	82.00	59.90
May	80.30	80.40	79.40	79.90	− .80	82.60	66.20
July	81.00	81.00	80.00	80.60	− .80	83.20	73.00

SILVER COINS (NYM)—10 $1000 bags; $ per bag

	Open	High	Low	Close	Change	Season's High	Season's Low
July	3442	3453	3390	3375a	−135	3960	2745
Oct	3502	3502	3420	3430a	−140	4010	2810
Jan 77	3571	3600	3475	3480	−145	4164	2861
Apr	3635	3635	3535	3540	−145	3757	2915
July	3694	3694	3694	3605	−140	3824	3050
Oct	3713	3713	3713	3670a	−140	3881	3460

Est. sales 59; sales Fri.: 84 contracts.

PLATINUM (NYM)—50 troy oz.; $ per troy oz.

	Open	High	Low	Close	Change	Season's High	Season's Low
July	178.70	178.70	175.50	175.50	−4.00	193.70	136.30
Oct	182.00	182.20	178.80	178.80	−4.20	196.00	138.6[illegible]
Jan77	185.60	185.60	181.40	181.60	−4.80	198.50	141.80
Apr	188.00	188.00	184.20	185.30	−4.40	196.50	145.00
July	189.90	190.10	187.70	187.70	−5.30	201.50	148.00
Oct	195.00	195.00	195.00	191.60a	−4.90	204.00	170.70

Est. sales 1,435; sales Fri.: 557 contracts.

GOLD (CMX)—100 troy oz.; $ per troy oz.-s

	Open	High	Low	Close	Change	Season's High	Season's Low
Aug	122.40	122.40	121.90	122.20	− .60	191.00	121.90
Sept	123.30	123.30	123.30	123.00	− .50	125.70	123.30
Oct	123.30	123.60	123.20	123.40	− .40	193.00	123.10
Dec	124.80	125.00	124.40	124.70	− .80	185.70	124.40
Feb77	126.40	126.40	125.70	126.20	− .80	162.00	125.70
Apr	128.00	128.00	127.20	127.60	− .80	150.80	127.20
June	129.50	129.50	129.00	129.10	− .80	141.50	129.00
Aug	130.50	130.50	130.30	130.60	− .80	140.80	130.30

Est. sales 849; sales Fri.: 552 contracts.

GOLD (IMM)—100 troy oz.; $ per troy oz.

	Open	High	Low	Close	Change	Season's High	Season's Low
Sept	122.70	122.90	122.30	122.70-.80	− .60to.50	195.00	122.30
Dec	124.50	124.90	124.30	124.50-.60	− .90to.80	193.00	124.90
Mar	126.90	127.00	126.30	126.70	− .60	164.00	126.30
June	129.00	129.00	128.60	129.00b	− .70	142.10	128.60
Sept	130.70	131.50	130.60	131.10	− .60	143.00	130.60

Est. sales 802; sales Fri.: 511 contracts.

GOLD (WPG)—400 troy oz.; $ per troy oz.

	Open	High	Low	Close	Change	Season's High	Season's Low
July	122.00	122.00	121.50	121.50b	− .70	190.00	121.50
Oct	123.40	123.60	123.00	123.60	− .60	187.90	123.00
Jan77	125.60	125.60	125.00	125.60b	− .80	151.00	125.00
July	130.10	130.20	130.10	130.20b	− .90	140.00	130.10

Est. sales 25; sales Fri.: 21 contracts.

—FIBERS—

COTTON (CTN)—50,000 lbs.; cents per lb.

	Open	High	Low	Close	Change	Season's High	Season's Low
Oct	93.95	93.95	89.95	89.95a	−2.00	93.95	47.80
Dec	89.25	89.25	85.65	85.65a	−2.00	89.25	50.00
Mar 77	87.20	87.20	83.95	83.95a	−2.00	87.20	56.25
May	84.50	84.50	81.25	81.25a	−2.00	84.50	58.90
July	80.30	80.30	77.25	77.25a	−2.00	80.30	60.58
Oct	72.00	72.00	69.75	69.90	−1.30	72.50	63.35
Dec	66.35	66.35	64.90	65.10	−1.02	67.40	62.00

Est. sales 3,850; sales Fri.: 3,950 contracts.

WOOL (CTN)—6,000 lbs.; cents per lb.

	Open	High	Low	Close	Change	Season's High	Season's Low
Oct	184.0	184.0	184.0	179.0b	....	186.5	150.0

Sale: 1; sales Fri.: 10 contracts. Spot: 180.0n.

—WOOD—

LUMBER (CME)—100,000 bd. ft.; $ per 1000 bd. ft.

	Open	High	Low	Close	Change	Season's High	Season's Low
July	155.50	155.50	152.30	152.50	−3.20	183.30	139.20
Sept	154.80	154.80	150.50	150.80-.70	−4.40to4.5	182.80	150.50
Nov	157.50	157.50	153.00	153.50	−4.10	178.00	153.00
Jan77	163.50	163.50	160.00	160.30-160	−3.70to4.0	179.00	160.00
Mar	168.70	168.70	164.80	165.70	−4.00	176.90	164.80

Est. sales 1,923; sales Fri.: 1,138 contracts.

PLYWOOD (CBT)—76,032 sq. ft.; $ per 1000 sq. ft.

	Open	High	Low	Close	Change	Season's High	Season's Low
July	145.50	146.00	144.00	144.80	−4.70	169.30	125.50
Sept	150.20	150.20	145.00	146.80-.50	−4.10to4.4	170.40	127.00
Nov	152.80	152.80	148.00	149.20	−4.60	169.20	127.50
Jan77	153.00	153.00	150.50	151.00	−5.00	171.00	140.00
Mar	155.00	155.00	152.60	153.10-153.	−4.90to5.0	172.50	151.50
May	157.50	157.50	154.00	154.80-.40	−4.20to4.6	172.50	152.00
July	155.50	156.00	155.50	156.00b	−4.20	167.00	155.00

Sales Fri.: 805 contracts.

—FINANCIAL—

MEXICAN PESO (IMM)—1 million pesos; $ per peso

	Open	High	Low	Close	Change	Season's High	Season's Low
Sept	.07848	.07875	.07848	.07875	+ .00031	.07944	.07037
Dec	.07700	.07753	.07690	.07726	+ .00011	.07919	.06622
Mar 77	.07510	.07510	.07390	.07410	− .00070	.07510	.06140
June	.07210	.07210	.07095	.07116	− .00047	.07210	.05925
Sept	.06948	.06948	.06850	.06880	− .00038	.07056	.05685
Dec	.06850	.06850	.06735	.06755	− .00021	.06850	.05762

Sales Fri.: 370 contracts.

SWISS FRANC (IMM)—125,000 francs; $ per franc

	Open	High	Low	Close	Change	Season's High	Season's Low
Sept	.4067	.4069	.4058	.4059	− .0010	.4239	.3765
Dec	.4108	.4109	.4104	.4104	− .0011	.4287	.3867
Jun77	.4218	.4218	.4210	.4210	− .0005	.4253	.4168

Sales Fri.: 101 contracts.

BRITISH POUND (IMM)—25,000 pounds; $ per pound

demand situation provide information that permit intelligent trading decisions. The margin (per cent down payment) is small, often as small as 10% of the contract value. Further, the commission ($20 - $35) for a round of buying and selling is also small. So it doesn't take as much money to invest in commodities as it does in other financial actions. But the risks are high, and some consider commodity trading to be speculating, not investing.

Forward pricing provides market opportunities for the alert producer to plan ahead and for the housewife to thereby have food products available throughout the year at stable and reasonable prices. The market helps smooth out the peaks and valleys of pricing of these goods.

Careers In Finance

During the past several decades, the securities industry has been one of the fastest growing and rapidly changing employment fields in our economy.

Companies have expanded their staffs for finance and control activities. Securities advisors, brokerages, and information services have grown.

While opportunities on Wall Street tend to go up and down with the market, career opportunities do exist and future potential for people with financial specialization are good.

BROKERS

Registered representatives are the securities workers best known to the public. Stockbroker, account executive, and customer's man are other common names for this career.

As a broker you are an agent for buying and selling securities. You have no personal financial involvement in the outcome of a transaction, but take a commission for your services. You provide your customers with information about the quality of an investment, quote prices, and handle orders. A broker is basically a salesperson and overall performance is based on the number of transactions generated.

Stockbrokers may specialize in certain types of investments: some may concentrate on listed stocks, others on over-the-counter trading. Some are specialized in mutual funds, annuities, municipal bonds, or commodities. They also specialize by the type of client -- individuals or large institutions.

ANALYSTS

Financial analysts are the other side of the industry: researchers and decision makers. They are the jobs for evaluating stocks and bonds, providing information to brokers and investors. Most analysts specialize in particular industries, such as chemicals or cosmetics, and follow the activities of key companies in them. Economists work with the analysts to keep them up to date on conditions and trends.

INVESTMENT COUNSELORS

Counselors work on a fee basis and advise clients on the management of their investments -- their portfolios. Drawing on the work of analysts and economists, they evaluate a client's portfolio and suggest appropriate investments. A counselor may also be a portfolio manager -- which means he or she has power to make purchases directly. A manager may control a small trust for a bank or multi-million dollar funds, such as a pension fund.

CAREER PATHS

You could start out as a research assistant and work toward an analyst job. In turn, you could move into a counselor role.

You'll start out doing statistical work, keeping up on the literature on certain industries, and update economic charts.

Banks are often a good place to get training in these skills, and get useful experience for career development.

To get into sales jobs, you need to start in a training program. Often lasting six months or more, brokerages provide basic training that will prepare you for the examination for registered representatives.

Being registered doesn't mean you have a job -- you need to have clients, and a firm to work with. Your pay will be based largely on your actual sales, on a commission fee basis. Of course, this means you could make a lot of money, and some brokers do -- in six figures. You can find out more from the National Association of Securities Dealers (888 17th St. NW, Washington, D.C. 20006) or a local broker.

CORPORATE JOBS

Companies provide careers in finance, too, from the client point of view. Finance and control usually go hand in hand, with planning, budgeting, financial management, investor and banking relations, and accounting all linked as the company staff function looking after the money.

Financial Careers At General Mills

While operations in General Mills are decentralized by product line and groups, there is a strong, integrated financial control. The finance and control organization plays a vital role in day-to-day managing and in shaping the future of the Company.

Our several activities and the range and diversity of the Company's operations foster an environment in which starting positions and subsequent career routes are almost infinitely variable. Business graduates can start in almost any sector of finance and control and move up as their individual interests and experiences develop. Each of the beginning positions offers exposure to a broad range of activities in the Company.

Career paths are relatively unstructured. Since we have no formal training programs here, each new employee receives immediate responsibilities and individual attention. In this way we encourage people to develop rapidly and to take on increased responsibility.

Most of the beginning positions are located in Minneapolis but, since we have operations throughout the United States and in several foreign countries, the choice of subsequent geographic locations generally is quite flexible. We encourage people in their first few years with us to gain experience at both the corporate level and in division or subsidiary operations.

There are a wide variety of finance and control activities at the Corporate headquarters in Minneapolis:

Corporate Planning has responsibility for developing and guiding the long-range planning process. This includes an accountability for counseling with all levels of management on major strategic issues. Our *Corporate Growth* has the mission of building new business growth opportunities through acquisitions and venture development.

The *Treasurer's Department* manages the Company's financial resources on a world-wide basis, handles foreign exchange, credit policy, insurance, and the monitoring of pension fund investments. In *Corporate Analysis*, we establish and monitor the annual operating programs for profits and capital expenditures, analyze capital investment opportunities, and perform operating studies for top management. *Corporate Accounting* is where the broad corporate accounting policies are established and where the estimated and actual operating results are consolidated and analyzed. Appropriate reports are issued to management, stockholders and others.

The General Mills *Audit Staff* functions as an independent corporate group, providing management with objective appraisals of accounting, controls and operations. Auditors visit all principal domestic and foreign locations. In *Information Systems* they assist divisions and subsidiaries in appraising computer equipment and in the design and implementation of data processing systems. The *Tax Department*, in addition to the preparation of tax returns, serves a vital role in providing counsel on tax laws, legislative interpretation, and acquisition studies.

● ERICA WHITTLINGER

Erica Whittlinger graduated from Beloit and received an MBA from Vanderbilt in 1973. She started with the Company as a financial analyst in Corporate Planning and was promoted after two years to Manager of Administrative Services for the Consumer Center. Erica directs the daily financial affairs for the Center and its showpiece—the Betty Crocker Test Kitchens.

● TED BRAGGANS

Ted Braggans received his BA in Accounting from St. Cloud State in 1968. He joined the Company as Supervisor in the Cash Disbursement Section and moved into Corporate Analysis. He is currently Manager of Planning for the Sperry Division of the Consumer Foods Group.

● CHARLES HORTON

Charles Horton graduated from Hampton Institute in 1974 with a BS in Accounting and began his General Mills career in Data Control- Order Processing. He is now involved in the Common Files section of Data Processing, responsible for the total maintenance of department computer systems.

CONSIDER

1. How might investors learn about a company's performance if no annual reports were published?

2. What would be the impact on corporate finance if government bonds offered a significantly higher interest rate than corporate bonds?

3. Is the price of a stock solely determined by the earnings of a company? What determines price?

4. What determines the price of a share in a mutual fund?

5. Is a mutual fund that specializes in socially responsible companies likely to make as much money as other funds? Explain.

6. Why do we have a Securities and Exchange Commission?

7. Could we do without stock exchanges?

8. How does a farmer benefit from a futures market?

9. If you had $10,000 to invest, what factors would you consider in selecting securities?

10. Why do prices of some stocks rise at the same time as prices of other stocks fall?

CHALLENGES

Select five stocks and trace their progress over a period of two or three weeks. You might figure your gain or loss on a total investment of $2500.

If you don't have time, you might look up the price of one selected stock in the Wall Street Journal for a few months back in time. Assuming you had invested $2500, what would be your gain or loss?

Contact a stock brokerage and find out the terms of using the services offered. What are the costs involved? Are they fair? How are they based?

Make a balance sheet on your personal financial condition. How do you stand? Would you be a good investment? Develop a plan for the future development of your financial health.

If you were to place a dollar value on your personal worth as an asset in the business of going to college, what factors would you consider? How much is your "goodwill" worth in dollars? Do you have a future earning power that is worth considering?

Compare the commodity prices for a good (wheat, coffee, copper, sugar, etc.) for a two-year period. Why did the prices vary? Ask a grocer if the retail prices (if a grocery good) varied in the same way?

RECAP

Business organizations need money to finance operations and expansion. This financial capital may be acquired through internal financing (hold back some of the earnings), by borrowing (issue bonds or short-term notes), and by increasing stockholders' equity (issuing more shares of stock in the company).

In this chapter we have examined the different types of securities that a company may issue to raise financial capital: common stock, preferred stock, bonds, debentures, convertibles, etc.

We discussed how the stock market works and how individuals make investing decisions. We have also considered various types of careers in finance.

A lot of information is available to the prospective investor, including accounting reports and published data. We discussed how to read stock prices and bond prices, and how to find other information on securities.

A number of ratios were described that are often used in the process of analyzing the information given on companies. Ratios are helpful when they are compared for a company over several time periods or with ratios of other similar companies.

Mutual funds are a way to balance investment decisions, to reduce risk by pooling individual money into a fund that holds a large number of different stocks. Funds are usually open-end, that is, they expand to take in new fund members. Fees are paid for the management of the fund (out of gains), plus some funds (load funds) also require commission fees for joining.

One area of investing is not widely known -- the commodity trading area. Investors buy contracts for commodities such as farm produce, metals, and textiles either at current cash prices for the contracts or contracts for future delivery. Futures trading allows the suppliers to reduce risk by selling contracts for goods not yet delivered. Investors gain the opportunity to make money by buying and selling at changing price levels.

1. What collateral (assets backing up a debt) is provided by a company that raises financial capital through:

(a) a mortgage?

(b) a debenture?

(c) a short-term note from a bank?

_____

2. How are dividends different from interest?

3. If you were buying a stock, what information would you want to know about the company? Where could you find that information?

---

4. Why do companies use a variety of ways to raise capital? Why not just use one method?

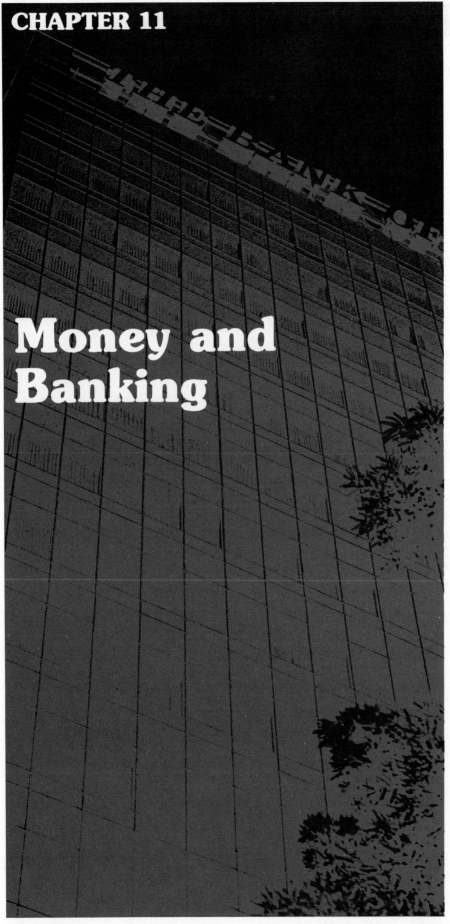

CHAPTER 11

Money and Banking

If business is the machine that makes America go, then money is the lubricant that keeps the machine humming. Our economic engine would grind to a halt without a constant and generous supply of cash and credit.

Money serves as the medium of exchange for goods and services. In addition to currency (the paper money and coins we use), we rely on credit to keep our economy alive.

Our government can print more money as currency and coins, but credit can expand as our economic activity expands. Credit provides the money that businesses need to operate and individuals need to purchase goods and services.

Banks facilitate the flow of money through a variety of services. They keep money moving in an uninterrupted flow from the lender to the borrower. As money moves through a bank, payment (interest) is made to the lender or the depositor who provides the money and charged to the borrower. Naturally, the bank charges the borrower more than it pays the depositor; the difference is the bank's profit.

Other financial services include checking and savings accounts, safe deposit boxes, trust assistance, transfer of money from one location to another, administration of estates and pension funds, and consumer credit cards.

Other types of financial institutions include mutual savings banks in which depositors share profits -- savings and loan associations.

"S&Ls" primarily serve the individual consumer market, providing most home mortgage loans in America.

The bankers have a bank too, The Federal Reserve Banks. This system of public banks facilitates and controls the flow of money in our economy. Checks are cleared through the "Fed", currency is issued by the Federal Reserve Banks, and member banks may borrow money to use in lending or to meet demands of depositors.

As we shall see, currency and checks are not the only form of money in our society. Of even more importance is credit. The business firm that wants to expand its operations and the individual family that wants to buy a new television set often use credit to make their purchases.

Banks actually create money by making loans to individuals and businesses. They expand the supply of money, within the limits set by the policies of the Federal Reserve System.

In general, credit benefits everyone in our society. It makes money available to individuals and businesses that would otherwise be idle. Money in use acts as a spur to the economy, leading us to build our economy on the basis of credit.

Currency, coins, checks, and credit all combine to give our economy the money supply it needs in order to preosper and grow.

In This Chapter

How Money Moves

Money is such a routine part of our lives that we ordinarily take its creation and acceptance for granted. Although a user may sense that money must come into being automatically as a result of economic activity or, perhaps, an outgrowth of government actions, just how this happens may be a mystery.

Many things -- from stones to cigarettes -- have been used as "money" through the ages. Today, in the United States, there are only two kinds of money used in significant amounts: CURRENCY (paper money and coins) and DEMAND DEPOSITS (checking ccounts in commercial banks).

Since currency and demand deposits are freely convertible into each other at the option of the holder, both are money to an equal degree. However, one may be more convenient than the other. When a depositor cashes a check, he reduces the amount of deposits and increases the amount of currency in circulation. Conversely, when more currency is in circulation than is needed, some is returned to the banks in exchange for deposits. Currency held in bank vaults is not part of the money supply available for spending by the nonbank public.

While currency is used for a great variety of small transactions, most of the dollar volume of money payments in our economy is made by check. Approximately eighty per cent of our total money supply is in the form of demand deposits.

Neither paper currency nor deposits have value as a material (gold coins did). A dollar bill is just a piece of paper.

Flow of Money

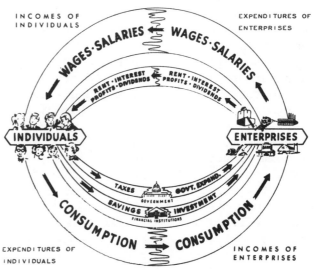

Deposits are merely book entries. Coins do have some value as metal, but much less than their face value. It is, then, the confidence people have that money can be exchanged for goods and services that makes it valuable.

Money, like anything else, derives its value from its scarcity in relation to its usefulness. Money's usefulness is its unique ability to command other goods and services and permit a holder to be constantly ready to do so. How much money is needed depends on the volume of transactions in the economy at any given time and the amount of money individuals and businesses want to keep on hand to take care of unexpected or future transactions.

In order to keep the value of money stable, it is essential that the quantity be controlled. Money's value can be measured only in terms of what it will buy. Therefor, changes in its value vary with the general level of prices (as prices go up, the value of the dollar falls). If the volume of money rises faster (assuming a constant rate of use) than the production of real goods and services grows under the limitations of time and physical facilities, prices will rise because there is more money per unit of goods. Such a development would reduce the value of money even though the monetary unit were backed and redeemable in the soundest assets imaginable. But if

the growth in the supply of money does not keep pace with the economy's current production, etiher prices will fall or, more likely, some resources and production facilities will be less than fully employed.

Just how large the stock of money needs to be in order to handle the work of the economy without exerting undue influence on the price level depends on how intensively the supply is being used. All demand deposits and currency are a part of somebody's spendable funds at any given time, moving from one owner to another as transactions take place. Some holders spend money quickly after they get it, making these dollars available for other uses. Others hold dollars for longer periods (stuffed into mattresses for example). When dollars move more slowly, more of them are needed.

Changes in the quantity of money may originate with actions by the public, the commercial bands, or (most significantly) by the Federal Reserve System. The "Fed" is our country's central bank, or banker's bank, that controls the supply of money through the commercial banks. The system, established by a 1913 act, includes a Board of Governers, 12 Federal Reserve Banks, and 24 branches in different sections of the United States.

The actual process of creating money takes place in the commercial banks. The demand

liabilities of the banks (what they owe) are book entries that result from the crediting of deposits of currency and checks, as well as the proceeds of loans and investments to customer's accounts. Banks can build up deposits by increasing loans and investments as long as they keep enough currency on hand to redeem whatever accounts the holders of deposits want to convert into currency.

Banks, then, can lend more money than they have in deposits. Further, they may borrow directly from the Federal Reserve Bank and lend that money. In these ways, banks can "create" money.

CALIFORNIA $50 GOLD PIECE — *1851*

Banking Services

Bank woo savers -- so that they will have the deposits needed to make loans. At other times, when savings and checking accoutns have a lot of money in them, banks woo borrowers -- so that the deposits can be earning interest.

As shown in the savings cycle shown on this page, depositors and borrowers are the key players in our banking system. Accepting depositors and lending money are the two basic activities of banks and non-banks.

Depositors put money into bank accounts and receive interest or dividends on it. The financial institutions lend this money to users and receive payments of interest on it. Banks make a profit on the difference between the rates of interest paid on deposits and the rates of interest charged.

In many instances, of course, depositors are also users. You may have money in the bank, yet take out a loan for a major purchase, or use a credit card.

In recent years banks have added to its traditional functions of receiving deposits and lending money.

It was natural for banks to issue credit cards in the 1960's as a means of offering a short-term credit account to its customers on a convenience basis. Further, however, it put banks in the business of processing customer accounts for local businesses such as retailers, resturants, and motels.

Banks also provide advice regarding personal finance, wills, and estate planning. They manage investment trusts for individuals and estates, and for businesses (such as pension funds).

They offer Christmas and vacation "clubs" as forms of savings accounts, give away merchandise and colorful checks to attract new customers, and sometimes even sell them directly for profit.

Banks rend safety deposit boxes in their vaults to customers for safe keeping of valuables, arrange credit for persons traveling abroad, and will sell traveler's checks for convenient use.

In the next decade, we may see even more diversified activities in banks as they expand their definition of their role in society.

The Savings Cycle

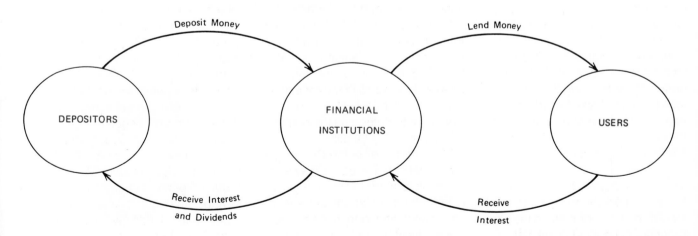

What Bank Of America Does

The California Division of the bank continued to be the largest financial unit of the corporation, providing a strong and stable base for much of the bank's activities. It is responsible for all the commercial banking services in California, involving commercial, consumer, real estate, and agricultural lending in addition to deposit functions, and it maintains banking relationships with the vast majority of businesses in the state. In 1975, it accounted for approximately 46 percent of BankAmerica's net earnings, about 40 percent of its deposits, and 80 percent of its employees.

In the increasingly competitive California market, Bank of America holds an impressive lead with 7 million deposit accounts, including 3 million checking accounts and 4 million savings and time deposit accounts. Effective last July 1, the bank raised the rate of interest paid on regular passbook savings accounts from 4½ percent to 5 percent. Bank of America currently pays ceiling rates of interest permitted by the Federal Reserve Board on all categories of domestic savings and time deposits.

The California Division's regional administration was restructured in August with a reduction in the number of regions from eleven to nine. Each geographic region is headed by a senior vice president responsible for all bank functions in his area.

New community offices were opened in California at 17 locations during 1975, bringing the domestic total to 1,057. These include the bank's first on-campus office at California State University, Los Angeles, opened in September.

New Services: Several new services, aimed at both consumer and business markets, were introduced in 1975, further strengthening the bank's preeminent position in the state.

In June, Bank of America introduced PersonaLine® Credit for qualified individual borrowers. The service makes available unsecured revolving

BANK OF AMERICA

lines of credit from $3,000 to $15,000. With just one commitment, a customer obtains funds for automobile purchases, home improvements, education, emergency medical expenses, and other long-term personal needs. It saves the borrower time and inconvenience, eliminating the negotiation of separate loans for each need and the waiting time for each credit approval.

From the bank's point of view, PersonaLine Credit eliminates duplication of paperwork in the processing of different types of loans for the same individual or family. It also provides a vehicle through which the bank may well obtain a larger share of the credit business of qualified individuals who might otherwise choose to diversify their banking requirements.

By year's end, 13,447 lines of credit had been extended, representing a total commitment of $102.2 million. Of these lines, 8,736 were active with total outstandings of $33.9 million.

On-line, automated, self-service BankAmeritellers were placed in three supermarkets and two community offices in Southern California. These teller machines can perform 11 different types of banking transactions. Together, the five machines have been averaging 15,000 transactions a month. The pilot system is being evaluated to determine the bank's future use of this banking innovation. (The Comptroller of the Currency's ruling that national banks may establish such terminals without regard to branching limitations of state law has been challenged in the courts. The ability of banks to continue to offer this type of service may require favorable action by the courts or by enabling state or federal legislation.)

In recognition of the growing

importance of the senior customers market, the bank initiated two programs designed to encourage people of senior years to become customers. Service 62 offers free checking accounts to people 62 years or older who maintain savings accounts or hold certificates of deposit with Bank of America. The plan offers free checkwriting and commission-free BankAmerica Travelers Cheques, as well as free personalized checks and, for qualified customers, a courtesy check guarantee card. A second service, incorporated as part of the plan, guarantees direct deposit of Social Security checks into customers' bank accounts on regular payment dates, with the bank guaranteeing the deposit after the initial transaction. The program now services 55,842 such accounts, 18,100 of them new to the bank.

The bank also introduced a new individual retirement account, designed for people not covered by qualified pension plans. It allows them to make deposits in interest-bearing, but tax-deferred, accounts in order to build a fund from which to obtain income during their retirement years.

In another significant first in the California market, the bank is now paying interest to home mortgage borrowers on loan trust account funds which are being accumulated for payment of taxes and home insurance premiums. This change affects approximately 70 percent of the more than 220,000 California mortgage accounts financed by the bank.

Following a change in regulations, Bank of America began offering a business savings account. Under this new arrangement, business establishments may deposit up to $150,000 in regular 5 percent interest-bearing savings accounts, thus earning income on idle funds. By the end of the year, 3,243 businesses, representing total deposits of $108 million, had availed themselves of this more flexible money management tool.

Customer Information and Assist-

ance: A booklet, written in layman's language, entitled Facts about Bank of America's Checking and Savings Program, was sent to more than three million account holders in 1975.

In May, Bank of America also introduced a special large-print embossed check for use by its blind and vision-impaired customers. The checks are available free of charge, and their development represents the result of two years' work with the Braille Institute of Southern California.

The bank's Loan Adjustment Department shared its expertise with 13 non-profit consumer credit counseling organizations in California, providing a wide range of assistance to people with personal financial problems.

Agriculture: Higher earnings and improved liquidity reduced California farmers' and ranchers' loan demands during the year. Loans made totaled $2.0 billion in 1975, compared with $2.3 billion a year earlier. But even though the 1975 figure was below the record highs of 1973 and 1974, it was above the more typical 1972 level.

Crop loans were down 2.2 percent from $601 million in 1974 to $588 million; livestock loans decreased 20 percent from $1.5 billion in 1974 to $1.2 billion in 1975; and loans for farm equipment were off 6.4 percent from $47 million in 1974 to $44 million last year.

The bank lent money to finance the breeding of approximately the same number of cattle and other livestock in 1975 as in the year before, but the animals' value declined sharply from the 1974 peak. Harvest receipts generally exceeded forecasts for the year, placing California farmers in a stronger cash position.

The bank has experienced an early rush by California farmers to set up 1976 lines of credit. Indications are that while costs of some items, such

as fertilizers and tractors, may decline, most farming expenditures will continue to rise. As a result, farmers will need more capital than in recent years, creating a stronger loan demand

To encourage careers in agriculture and related fields, Bank of America works with youths throughout California at state, regional, and local levels, supporting organizations such as the 4-H Club, Future Farmers of America, and the California Young Farmers Association with their award programs, livestock auctions, and other activities. In addition, for the past seven years the bank has awarded scholarships to encourage members of minority groups to complete college-level studies leading to agricultural teaching careers. In total, some $37,500 is awarded each year to about 30 students. The bank also awards scholarships annually to seven vocational agricultural teachers, enabling them to pursue their studies further.

Real Estate: Bank of America maintained its position as the nation's largest real estate lender in 1975, recording well over $1 billion in new loans. More than two-thirds of these are secured by California residential properties, the remainder by income properties and agricultural real estate. The bank's real estate loan portfolio now stands at nearly $6 billion. Over recent years, the bank has sold to investors an additional $1 billion in loans which it continues to service on a fee basis.

Net portfolio growth amounted to $360 million after principal amortization, prepayments, and loan sales to investors in the secondary marketplace. Portfolio yield on real estate loans outstanding increased by 32 basis points. Delinquency ratios compare favorably with industry averages and parallel the previous year's experience.

Unlike 1974, competing thrift institutions were able in 1975 to attract funds for real estate loans, thus relieving loan pressure on the bank and permitting the sale of loans from its portfolio to investors in the secondary market.

The bank has consistently been the largest real estate lender in California and expects to continue its well-established commitment to California homeowners and builders.

BankAmericard®

BankAmericard billings in California increased 18 percent in 1975 to $1.79 billion from $1.51 billion in 1974. At year's end, outstandings reached $754 million, up 13 percent from $667 million in 1974. The number of cardholders in the state rose 11 percent to 4.1 million. Merchants accepting BankAmericard and affiliated bank cards numbered 161,000 at year's end, an increase of 16 percent.

The rate of delinquencies dropped to 3.88 percent of dollars outstanding at the end of 1975 from 4.59 percent at the end of 1974. Responsible for the reduction were an improved state economy, greater selectivity in the issuance of BankAmericards, tighter requirements for credit limit increases, and improved collection procedures.

In an effort to control and offset rapidly escalating costs facing most bank card programs, BankAmericard made two major changes during the past year. First, the bank adopted the average adjusted daily balance method of calculating finance charges and altered the upper-dollar ranges to which different interest rates are applied.

Later in the year, Bank of America became the first bank card issuer in California to adopt the descriptive billing method. This more efficient system provides cardholders with a monthly statement detailing all transactions for the billing period, in lieu of copies of the original sales drafts. Descriptive billing minimizes the handling, and eliminates the mailing of an estimated 62 million pieces of paper per year. Cardholders also receive their statements sooner, giving them more time before payment is due.

Countries and those international areas accepting BankAmericard and affiliated bank cards numbered 116 at year's end. The card was accepted for the first time in Yugoslavia, El

Salvador, Surinam, Tunisia, Morocco, and Macao.

Corporate and Specialized Activities

BankAmerica Corporation continued to expand bank-related activities during 1975. It strengthened management, increased capitalization of existing subsidiaries, and provided guidance in the opening of several new subsidiary offices, though no new acquisitions were made. In addition to Bank of America community offices in California, the corporation's subsidiaries have 341 offices in 31 other states, offering a variety of financial services. These include consumer finance, leasing, data processing, mortgage banking, credit-related insurance, BankAmerica Travelers Cheques, venture capital and real estate investments, and investment management.

In February, 1975, BankAmerica Corporation completed the sale of $150-million 8⅞ percent 30-year debentures. Of the proceeds, $50 million was employed to increase Bank of America's equity capital base, $25 million was invested as additional equity in BA Mortgage Company, Inc., the corporation's mortgage banking subsidiary, and $25 million was advanced to FinanceAmerica Corporation, the corporation's consumer finance subsidiary. The remaining $50 million was available for general corporate uses.

Finance Activities: Finance-America Corporation, with headquarters in Allentown, Pa., operates 311 offices throughout the eastern, midwestern and southern parts of the country. Services offered include direct loans, financing and credit control for floor planning and distribution of consumer products by manufacturers and distributors, the financing of inventory and accounts receivable, and the purchase of retail instalment contracts.

The corporation's acquisition of FinanceAmerica, formerly GAC Finance, Inc., was approved by the Federal Reserve Board in 1973 on the condition that certain GAC Finance accounts receivable be sold together with the firm's offices in the western states. The major part of this divestiture was completed by the end of 1975.

Applications for new Finance-America offices in the western U.S. have been filed with the Federal Reserve Board. The first of these additional consumer finance service centers is expected to open in early 1976.

Mortgage Banking: BA Mortgage Company, Inc., with eight offices in primary real estate markets across the country, makes and sells loans while continuing to service them. The company emphasizes the financing of commercial and multi-family developments, but also plans to finance construction of single-family dwellings. Its aim is to provide a full range of mortgage banking services to real estate investors, developers, and mortgage lenders. Although the company is national in scope, its offices are staffed with mortgage bankers who have considerable experience in the various local markets served.

Computer Leasing and Data Processing Service: Decimus Corporation, a BankAmerica subsidiary, offers computer leasing and data processing services. Decimus manages a sizeable number of IBM computer systems and provides lease financing for manufacturers of peripheral computer equipment. In 1975, the company opened new data centers in Piscataway, New Jersey, and Chicago, its third and fourth such facilities, and expanded the range of data processing services it offers to business customers.

Other Leasing: The bank's leasing department and BA Leasing Corporation are engaged in many types of leasing, including those related to transportation, manufacturing, agricultural equipment and other kinds of machinery. In 1975, total leasing assets outstanding grew by 12.6 percent. BA Leasing opened lease processing offices in New York and Chicago, and others are planned.

Insurance: BankAmerica Corporation provides life and disability insurance for Timeplan and real estate loan borrowers of the bank through its subsidiaries, BA Insurance Company, Inc., and BA Insurance Agency, Inc.

Realty Advisory Services: BankAmerica Realty Services, Inc., a wholly-owned subsidiary of Bank-America Corporation, supplies advisory services to BankAmerica Realty Investors, a publicly-owned real estate investment trust.

A new subsidiary, BankAmerica International Realty Corporation, has been formed to provide real estate portfolio investment services to governments, institutions, and private capital sources in foreign countries.

Investment Advisory Services: BA Investment Management Corporation (BAIMCO), formed to manage major pools of investment, acquired significant new clientele in 1975. BAIMCO provides investment management and advisory services to the bank's Trust Department and to Montgomery Street Income Securities, Inc., a publicly-owned, closed-end investment company. During the year, BAIMCO strengthened its fixed income securities management programs to better serve clients seeking such services.

Venture Capital: Equity investments in and loans to new and growing business enterprises are made by Small Business Enterprises Company and Bamerical International Financial Corporation, subsidiaries of the bank. BankAmerica Capital Corporation, a subsidiary of BankAmerica Corporation, serves as advisor to these funds. In addition, BankAmerica Corporation is the general partner of WestVen Management, an advisor to venture capital funds. The corporation believes many interesting venture capital opportunities will exist in 1976, because of the present state of the economy and capital markets.

Travelers Cheques: Banks in the West African nation of Mauritania began selling BankAmerica Travelers Cheques in 1975, bringing the number of countries where cheques are obtainable to 153.

Our Banking System

Banking is the business of managing money. Banks serve individual customers, business organizations, and our economy as a whole.

Through banks you may write checks, which are payable for goods and services. These checks draw upon your money which is held in the bank. You may borrow money, plan investments, establish an estate or trust, seek personal financial advice and find other services through banks.

Through the banking system, our economy has a means of exchanging money -- millions of transactions every day -- in a highly efficient manner. Through the Federal Reserve System, banks also influence the stability of our economy.

Our banking system operates through a

variety of types of financial institutions: commercial banks, Federal Reserve banks, savings and loan associations, insurance companies, and other credit agencies.

COMMERCIAL BANKS

Commercial banks operate under state and federal government laws to (1) accept deposits; "demand deposts" in that they may be withdrawn by the depositor without advance notice, and (2) to make loans to individuals and businesses.

Banks that are chartered by a state are called "state banks" while those chartered by the federal government are called "national banks." To obtain a charter, a new bank must have a minimum amount of capital and demonstrate that there is a real need for the bank in the community.

From a depositor's point of view, it doesn't make much difference which way a

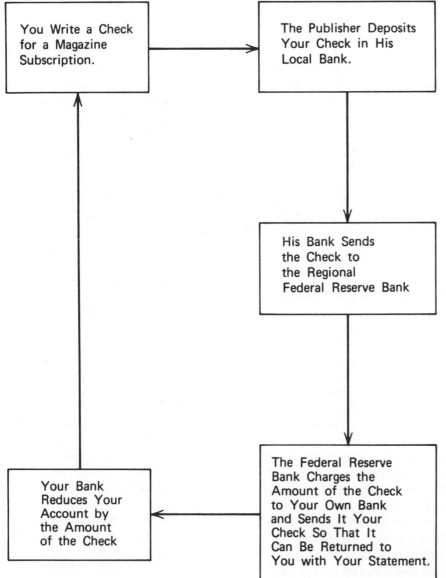

You Write a Check for a Magazine Subscription.

The Publisher Deposits Your Check in His Local Bank.

His Bank Sends the Check to the Regional Federal Reserve Bank

Your Bank Reduces Your Account by the Amount of the Check

The Federal Reserve Bank Charges the Amount of the Check to Your Own Bank and Sends It Your Check So That It Can Be Returned to You with Your Statement.

MONEY -- WHERE IT'S KEPT

NUMBER AND TOTAL ASSETS OF BANKS AND NON-BANKS

	1960	1965	1970	1975
Banks:				
Number	13,500	13,800	13,700	15,000
Assets ($ Billions)	260.7	382.9	545.3	940.0
Savings and Loan Associations:				
Number	6,300	6,200	5,700	5,100
Assets ($ Billions)	71.9	129.6	176.2	300.0

Source: Statistical Abstract of the United States

---

bank is chartered. Deposits in most banks are insured by the government through the Federal Deposit Insurance Corporation (FDIC) up to $40,000 per account.

All national banks in the United States (4600) and those state banks that wish (1200 of about 9000) are members of the Federal Reserve System. Through the Federal Reserve banks, Federal Reserve System members may expand their "reserves" and adjust the extent of their loans and investments.

MUTUAL SAVINGS BANKS

A type of bank that is more limited than the commercial bank is the mutual savings bank. These banks are chartered by states to accept savings and invest those savings in relatively safe investments. Mutual savings banks do not have stockholders and as a

result, any gain from operations accrue to the depositors who are, in effect, the owners of the bank. Mutual savings banks typically pay higher interest on deposits, but they cannot provide other banking services such as checking accounts. Depositors in mutual savings banks are protected by the FDIC for accounts up to $40,000.

FEDERAL RESERVE SYSTEM

The Federal Reserve System, founded in 1913, provides a central banking service for our commercial banks. The checks that you write, for example, may go through a Federal Reserve Bank on the way to your own bank for payment (see the illustration on how this might work).

Federal Reserve Banks serve other important functions in our banking system. First, they determine, through

rulings by the Board of Governors, the size of cash reserves that member banks must have to bak up the deposits of their customers. In doing this, the Federal Reserve System regulates the percentage of deposits that the banks can lend. This regulation of bank reserves, combined with the FDIC insurance, protects depositors from bank failures such as were experienced during the Great Depression during the 1930"s.

Second, the "Fed" adjusts the rate of interest, called the "rediscount rate" for money it lends to member banks. This indirectly influences the supply of money in the United States by regulating in an alternative way the amount of money a commercial bank has available to lend.

The "Fed" also buys and sells federal govern-

ment securities (the government promises to pay an amount of money owed with interest at a specified future time, loans to the government, really) on the open market (to the public). So when the Federal Reserve System buys such securities it is expanding the money supply; when it sells, it is reducing the supply of money, because money is taken out of circulation.

All three of these activities of the "Fed" have an impact on our economic conditions because they can either stimulate or retard economic activity. These are examples of Monetary Policy, one of the two basic tools used by the government to control our economy. The other tool, Fiscal Policy will be discussed later.

SAVINGS AND LOAN ASSOCIATIONS

In addition to commer-

cial banks, we rely heavily on another type of financial institution, the Savings and Loan Association. Regulated by a different set of laws, these organizations serve more limited purposes than do banks. Through an association, an individual or business may save and invest money. The money is pooled and lent to borrowers for five to twenty years, often in local home mortgages. These mortgages (a type of loan that is secured by a house or other type of property) are retired on a monthly installment plan, hence the home mortgage payment.

Savings and loan associations are privately managed organizations that are owned by stockholders or by the depositors. Depending on the type of association, stock or mutual (owned by the depositors), state or federal laws govern the operations. Deposits

are insured by the Federal Savings and Loan Insurance Corporation, a counterpart of the FDIC.

CREDIT UNIONS

A credit union is a co-operative organization designed to receive deposits from members and make loans to members. The members of the credit union are the owners and any profits from operations are shared by the membership, usually through dividends. While credit unions provide a form of banking service for their members, there is much more risk in a credit union since there is no federal insuring agency such as the FDIC for credit unions.

Other types of financial institutions include sales finance companies (businesses that specialize in financing the sale of automobiles and other consumer goods), consumer finance companies (they make small loans for any purpose), and insurance companies (they invest insurance payments in real estate securities and other investments).

Our banking system makes possible the use of credit. Because we have the opportunity to borrow money, we may make large purchases (like a house or a car) before we actually earn the money. Wisely used, credit is a valuable personal asset as well as a significant factor in building and maintaining our country's prosperity.

Bank Competition

The San Francisco headquarters of California's second largest bank, Security Pacific National Bank of Los Angeles, was actually built with money borrowed from California's largest bank, Bank of America.

Does this mean that California banks help each other and don't compete? On the contrary, California is very much a banking battleground. B of A simply viewed the Security Pacific building project as a good investment.

Security Pacific and about 150 other commercial banks in California view Bank of America as a lovely target. B of A, which grew from a hole-in-the-wall bank to the world's largest, has no monopoly or competitive clout, although it can be expected to shoot back. Even though B of A has improved its share of the lush California market, a half dozen other banks have been taking bigger bites, too.

A decade ago, only B of A could claim state-wide coverage. The others, all in the billion-dollar class, were clustered around either Los Angeles or San Francisco. Now all seven of the leading rivals boast state-wide coverage. B of A, Security Pacific, Wells Fargo, Crocker, United California, Bank of California, and Union Bank each has at least a sturdy leg in the two main population centers.

How did they establish their competitive positions with Bank of America? The competition for depositors and for borrowers has been keen -- involving advertising, aggressive marketing, physical expansion, and promotional activities.

Part of the growth of the larger banks is at the expense of smaller banks. A number of banks have merged in California, either voluntarily, or as a result of bank failure in the face of competition. For every ten commercial banks which existed two decades ago in the U.S., there are only six today. The result is fewer alternatives for those individuals and small companies who must meet their financial needs locally. Accordingly, the larger banks in California have a large number of local branches, serving communities across the state.

NON-BANK COMPETITION

Competition has also come from financial institutions such as mutual savings banks (MSBs) and savings and loan associations (S&Ls). In recent years, these non-bank institutions have grown more rapidly than commercial banks.

Commercial banks can offer a wider range of services than can these other institutions. Many customers prefer the "full service banking" that banks offer. On the other hand, some people prefer to bank with an MSB or S&L because they don't need all the services and feel that the service is more attuned to personal banking needs (savings, loans, payment orders). Further, savings institutions can offer better rates of interest (or dividends) on deposits, hence are more attractive to depositors.

The services that can be offered and the interest rates that can be paid and charged are all regulated by the government.

It used to be that only commercial banks could offer checking accounts. Then in 1972 a court in Massachuestts ruled that a certain type of draft (like a check) could be drawn on an interest-bearing account without violating the legal prohibition against interest on depand deposits. Specifically, the court ruled that a "negotiable order of withdrawl" drawn by a household on an interest-bearing savings account could function as a check without having to be classified as a "check". These "NOW" accounts have spread among MSBs and S&Ls in other states. In New York, a law was passed which made the special arrangement unnecessary -- these institutions can offer regular checking accounts.

So the banking market-place is changing, and the competition is keen. Watch what's happening in your state.

Dangling Less Bait For Savers

A friend of Harold Scales, president of $305-million Anchor Savings & Loan Assn. in Madison, Wis., called him with $30,000 to bank and asked if he were giving away any wristwatches. When told that the list of premiums for new deposits did not include watches, he took his money elsewhere to get one.

Soon, however, Scales' friend will have to look outside his own state for a wristwatch or any other gratuity in exchange for his deposit. Wisconsin's S&L commissioner, R. J. McMahon, last week asked all S&Ls in the state to refrain from giving premiums as of Nov. 1 so his office can study their effect. He is concerned that premiums may be contributing to lower earnings and higher-cost mortgages as the costs of promotions escalate in continuous competition throughout the state.

Wisconsin is one of the most competitive premium states in the country, says Harold L. Jenkins, executive vice-president of the Savings Institutions Marketing Society of America. But if Wisconsin decides to ban premiums permanently, it will be joining a growing number of states now discouraging what was once a popular marketing gimmick. California and New York have already placed severe restraints on premium promotions, and Texas has banned them altogether.

In New York, state law limits thrifts to two premium promotions per year. In California, S&Ls are limited to paying no more than $2.50 per premium item, and the item must be educational in nature and in printed form.

Nationally, the Federal Home Loan Bank Board limits S&Ls to premiums of $5 for deposits of less than $5,000 and to premiums of $10 for deposits of $5,000 or more. But there are no specific limits on how many premiums can be given during the year or how much can be spent promoting or advertising the premium.

From TVs to Cadillacs. "This whole premium business just vanished like a bad dream, and we haven't been troubled by it since," says W. Sale Lewis, savings commissioner of the Texas Finance Commission. It had reached the point, concedes Lewis, "that it didn't matter whether you were giving away a gold Cadillac or a television, everyone was on a parity. Once in a while, someone would come up with some-thing that gave them an advantage for a little while, but generally, it had gotten ridiculous."

In some cities, such as Detroit, premiums have been used sparingly and are not considered a necessary marketing tool. But in others, like Philadelphia, premiums have become a way of life. "Savers in the Milwaukee metropolitan area have been well indoctrinated to expect something," observes William P. Podewils, president of the Wisconsin Savings & Loan League.

Wisconsin has joined the states restricting giveaways for new deposits

William G. Schuett, president of Security Savings & Loan Assn. of Milwaukee, the largest state-chartered association in Wisconsin, says that he spends about a quarter of his ad budget on premium promotions (more than double the 9.5% average for similar-sized institutions around the country), and that they have been "super-successful. The customer will always choose 7.5% interest with a blender or a toaster over just 7.5% interest." Continues Schuett, "I was not sent here to preside over a sorority but to bring funds into the S&L, and premiums do bring in funds."

However, Scales, who spends a third of his $600,000 advertising budget on such promotions, complains, "you can't concentrate on being a savings and loan if you've got to concentrate on being a retailer. It's cheapened our business and gotten out of hand."

Even if a premium ban were made permanent in Wisconsin, however, there are still potential problems. A ruling by the state commissioner has force over state-chartered institutions, but not over federally chartered S&Ls or banks. Federal S&Ls and banks could put the state institutions at a real disadvantage if they continued to offer premiums, although this has not happened in Texas. Savers could also begin to send large deposits out of state to institutions that still offer premiums, but bankers do not expect this to be a major problem.

Expensive alternatives. Finally, S&Ls may scurry to develop other marketing strategies to attract depositors that could cost even more than premiums. At the University Savings Assn. in Houston, bill-paying services and free travelers' checks have replaced the old ice cream freezers and two-dollar bills. Although the S&L cut its expenses drastically after the premium ban, saving "tens of thousands of dollars" a month, Vice-President Mary Jane McLaren says it is difficult to trace the impact on mortgage rates and company earnings.

Even without such impact, other states are watching the premium bans with interest. In Pennsylvania, William J. Nice, vice-president of the Benjamin Franklin Federal Savings & Loan Assn., thinks it's "a damn good idea." And in Georgia, Edward W. Hiles, executive vice-president of the Georgia Savings & Loan League, says that although there is no move afoot, one would "get much industry support." An earlier attempt to ban premiums in Georgia failed. Said Hiles: "It seemed legislators feared their grandmothers wouldn't get blankets."

New York institutions can offer gifts less often.

Toy Giveaway Unbearable For Bank

LOS ANGELES, Aug. 28 (UPI)—Only now is the full story emerging of the great "Teddy Bear Caper" at Crocker National Bank, but it carries a message for those who would mix bears, money, children, depositors, tellers and bank vice presidents.

The heroes of the piece (or villains, depending on how one looks at it) were those little stuffed animals with bright button eyes and stitched smiles that have long been the companions of countless girls and boys.

Just before the Christmas season last year, the promotion department at Crocker—the nation's 15th largest bank, with 358 California branches — came up with "Sunny the Bear."

The deal was that anyone who opened a new checking account of $100 or more would be given a bear.

'Everyone Wanted One'

Angela Bohning, then handling new accounts at the Palos Verdes branch, remembers that "it started out great but then problems began to arise."

She added: "There were the bears sitting on the counters, cute as could be, and everyone wanted one. Customers who already had accounts insisted they should get a bear. One man who had a $50,000 savings account threatened to take out his whole deposit unless he got a bear."

"We tried to tell them to just withdraw $100 and open another account and some of them did," she continued. "Mothers would come in with two or more kids in tow and each child wanted a bear, of course. But it was one account, one bear, no more and no less, so they had to open two or three checking accounts."

On top of everything else, a shortage of bears began to develop. Bank officials sent down the word that there must be a strict accounting for each bear.

"It got so at our branch that we had a bear count at the end of business every day," Mrs. Bohning recalled. "The tellers had to balance their bears before they balanced their drawers.

"We finally had to appoint one of the assistant managers as 'the bear man.' He was in charge of bears. He would count them and then lock them up in the vault at nights."

As the shortage worsened, various branches tried to wheedle more "Sunnies" from banks that still had a reserve and the Palos Verdes branch, for one, sent a pickup truck to an office in Orange County.

Finally, Crocker ran out of bears some time early this year, but it took weeks before the outcry subsided.

"I remember one woman who marched in with a teddy bear she had bought at a department store," Mrs. Bohning said. "She said her son would have nothing to do with it because it didn't look like Sunny. She wanted to trade it in on a Crocker bear, but the bears were all gone."

In all 100,000 Sunnies went to bank customers. David Sanson, a spokesman for the bank, said that although it may try other promotions, "we will never come up with anything like the bears."

The bear

Getting Along Without Money

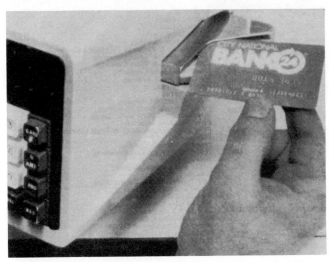

An Ohio bank's customers, using this simple card, will be able to charge merchandise, or pay for it from their checking accounts, at 60 stores in the bank's area.

A computer terminal verifies and records a sale in seconds. The customer can have the price of the merchandise transferred from her bank account or be billed later.

A bank that tried substituting a computerized credit card system for cash and checks pronounces the experiment a success—for itself and its customers

A nine-month experiment has convinced a Columbus, Ohio, bank that a cashless, checkless way of life not only is desirable but that it can mean money in the bank for bankers willing to try it.

City National Bank & Trust Co. is now installing a computer system that will make it possible for its customers throughout the Columbus area to buy virtually anything they want with a single credit card.

The customer can either have the amount of the sale transferred immediately, electronically, from his checking account or be billed for the merchandise later.

Merchants like the system because the bank credits all sales to their accounts at the end of each business day.

"We believe the credit card, not the personal check, will be the principal means of doing business in the future," says John G. McCoy, chairman of City National. "In my grandparents' time they used cash. When my parents came along they started using checks. And now my wife and I use credit cards."

Americans are now writing almost 25 billion checks a year and the cost of processing them is monumental.

In the 1971-72 experiment, the bank set out to show it could wean customers from using cash and checks and at the same time cut down on its own expensive paper work.

It selected the prosperous suburb of Upper Arlington, where its customers were writing an average of 29 checks a month against only 18 checks by its other Columbus area patrons.

Thirty businesses—supermarkets, pharmacies, department stores and the like—jumped at the chance to participate.

BankAmericard designed a special magnetized credit card for City National customers who wanted to take part in the test. IBM installed computer terminals in all the stores and these in turn were linked by phone line to a master computer at the bank.

Customers pay nothing for this convenient banking service. Participating merchants pay the bank 2.2 per cent of the amount of sales.

In a typical transaction—say, at a

Supermarket customers use a special BankAmericard to charge groceries during a test period. City National Bank & Trust Co. is now making the system permanent.

City National has opened the first drive-through Bank24 Service Center in the country where a customer can bank day or night without leaving his automobile.

supermarket—a housewife checked out her purchases as usual and handed the clerk a card instead of cash. The clerk placed the card in a small computer console next to the cash register and punched out the sales total on a keyboard.

In an actual voice response, the computer confirmed the amount of the transaction and either authorized the sale or rejected it if the customer had insufficient funds or if the card was stolen. The entire procedure took less than 15 seconds.

"The merchant and customer reaction was almost wholly favorable," according to C. Gordon Jelliffe, the bank's president. "We felt that if we could knock out 50 per cent of all the paper work involved in processing checks this would be a tremendous achievement. I think we have proven it can be done."

Many in the banking industry— and others—have been generally skeptical about this approach to everyday buying.

Some of that skepticism is being dissipated by what happened and is happening in Columbus.

"Everybody has talked about the

checkless, cashless society," Chairman McCoy says. "They said it would be here 10 years from now. We think it's here today."

During the Upper Arlington experiment, $748,918 in sales were rung up on the computer. This involved 46,803 individual transactions, and only 2.8 per cent of the sales were rejected. Significantly, bank officials note, there was a saving to the bank of from seven to 10 cents per transaction.

The bank estimates that the buy-by-computer system being installed throughout its marketing area—initially in 60 stores—will become profitable in about three years, when the cost of necessary equipment will have been paid off.

City National's experiment has captured the attention of bankers around the world. Some 280 banks, many overseas, have sent representatives to watch the system in action. Five banks from Japan alone had observers in Columbus. Recently, President Jelliffe was invited to England, Spain and France to talk to bankers about this breakthrough in procedure.

It's not difficult to understand why some businesses like the system. In the Upper Arlington experiment, a merchant could make a sale shortly before closing in the evening and write a check against it the first thing the next morning.

Prodded by the Federal Reserve Board, more and more banks are moving toward electronic transfer of funds to cut down on paper work. George W. Mitchell, a member of the Board who visited City National during the test period, noted that "paper in the form of currency and checks" is threatening to "overwhelm" the nation's banks.

Similarly, the American Bankers Association has warned its members that "to remain static with the present payments system and rely too heavily on the check processing method of funds transfer would be a costly mistake for our industry.

"Rising labor expenses will continually expand the relative cost of bank operations. These additional costs will either reduce profitability, which is already a concern, or increase the expense to our customers."

City National takes pride in the

Eleven types of transactions—from depositing cash to making payments from a checking account—can be made at this "total teller" computer terminal.

City National Board Chairman John G. McCoy (left) and President C. Gordon Jelliffe believe electronic banking is the way to cut down on the rising costs of processing checks.

fact it is not afraid to try new approaches. It was the first bank to acquire a BankAmericard franchise and its customers use the card to pay everything from county real estate taxes to the price of tickets for Ohio State University athletic contests.

Some of its public service promotions have been applauded by President Nixon and former Treasury Secretary John B. Connally.

Three years ago, the Columbus bank became one of the first in the country to launch "Cash 'n Carry" 24-hour banking service. Again, the "Bank24" system, as it is called, uses a special BankAmericard. A customer can call at any of City National's 20 branches and use the card to make deposits, withdraw from a checking or savings account, pay utility bills or mortgage payments and even obtain a cash loan.

City National is still thinking away off in the future. John B. McCoy, a bank officer and son of the chairman, says: "We're always looking for ways to improve what we're doing."

The elder McCoy, explaining the "Bank24" system, asks:

"Why shouldn't we have one of these machines at your apartment door? That way when you come home on payday and want to deposit money, you can."

City National President Jelliffe believes the services bank credit cards are able to perform are developing much faster than many banks are willing to admit or are prepared to handle.

Looking down the road, he sees the day when banks can install "total teller" equipment at a factory or large downtown office so workers can conduct all their banking business right on the site.

"The time is coming when we will have to presell our services," Mr. Jelliffe says. "Look what happens when you buy an automobile. It has to be financed. The dealer generates an installment loan and the bank buys his paper.

"Why not establish a reserve line of credit to buy a car or a major appliance? The homework can be done before the loan application is made, instead of afterward. That's prearranged banking."

Some banks are now doing this, but only on customer request.

"I see the day when we will do this for all our customers without their having to ask for it," Mr. Jelliffe says. "Then we can have the money immediately ready when it's needed."

The electronic transfer of funds is becoming a major business.

Some California banks are letting their customers authorize employers to deposit their pay in their checking accounts automatically. The employee does not have to be a customer of the bank used by his employer. Money deposited by the employer in one bank is transferred automatically to the employee's bank.

This automated transfer of funds is handled by Federal Reserve system clearinghouses in San Francisco and Los Angeles.

The Fed itself is taking a giant step to reduce paper work clutter. It has begun building what will eventually be a network of 44 highly automated computer centers around the nation. The aim: To uniformly cut the time it takes a check to clear from three or four days to a single day.

These improvements cannot come fast enough, according to banking experts. Those 25 billion checks now annually being written and processed are expected to increase to 75 billion by 1980—unless a better way is found.

Credit, Charging Ahead

If you have bought any merchandise on a time payment plan, borrowed money, or used a credit card, you have used your credit. Credit is your ability to obtain money, goods, or services in return for a promise to pay for them in the future.

You have this ability because someone trusts you, believing that you will fulfill your promise. It makes sense, then, that your track record in paying for goods on credit has a major effect on your credit standing.

For the privilege of using credit, you pay interest. Interest payments are based on a percentage of the total amount of money or value of goods or services obtained. When you borrow $100 for a year at 12% interest, you pay $12 interest for the use of the money.

A simple 12% loan, then, means that the borrower must pay the lender the principal (the amount borrowed) plus $12 for every $100 borrowed for each year that he has use of the money.

When interest is compound interest, the interest due is added to the principal each period. Future interest is then figured on the total. Interest may be calculated annually, quarterly, monthly, daily, or even continuously. An interest rate of 12% compounded quarterly means that 3% interest becomes due and is added to the principal

every three months.

A retail credit account typically bears an interest rate of 1½% per month. This comes out to 18% per year, a high rate related to most prevailing bank rates for personal credit.

Different borrowers pay different rates of interest, depending on their ability to fulfill their promises to pay. A person with a poor credit record would normally pay a higher rate of interest than a person with a good repayment record and a good ability to pay. The rate of interest also depends on the credit period -- the amount of time the money is to be used. Generally, the longer the time period, the lower the rate of interest charged. If a borrower has a lot of collateral (property or other resources) to back up his credit, the interest rate may also be lower. These are some of the factors that influence the availability of credit.

Why are these factors important? Lenders offer money or credit to make a profit. If there is a risk that the amount will not be repaid, with interest, the lender would lose money. So credit is based in part on the calculation of risk. The time factor reflects the lower administrative costs involved in longer-term loans.

Credit benefits everyone in our economy. It

makes money available to individuals and businesses that would otherwise be idle. Thus, it spurs our economic growth. That's why monetary policy is a useful economic tool, as we discussed in a previous chapter.

Credit also is a useful medium of exhange, replacing currency or checks in our monetary system. Using credit, as you may have discovered is an easy way to buy things!

In some cases it is too easy and as a result some people get themselves into debt without really understanding what is happening to them. When you use a credit card, it seems as though you are not really spending money, but when the bills come in the facts of life must be faced.

A special law, the "Truth in Lending Act," helps you determine the terms of credit most favorable to you. The law, The Consumer Credit Protection Act, requires firms to provide detailed information on the actual dollar amount and annual percentage rates for charges on credit extended. It applies to credit sales, and loans to individuals for personal, family, household, or agricultural uses that do not exceed $25,000. Look for this information the next time you borrow money or buy on credit. Know what interest charges you are paying for your credit purchases.

Digging Out The Dirt In Your Credit Report

The Fireman's Fund Insurance Co. ordered James C. Millstone's new automobile insurance policy cancelled after an adverse credit report from O'Hanlon Reports, Inc. Millstone's insurance agent appealed the cancellation order, pointing out that Millstone held a responsible position as Assistant Managing Editor of the St. Louis Post-Dispatch.

Although Fireman's Fund withdrew the cancellation order, Millstone was determined to find out what the credit report contained. He asked O'Hanlon Reports for a copy. The firm would provide only an oral description, represented as a synopsis. The synopsis indicated that Millstone had been described as a suspected drug user and as a generally disreputable, "hippie-type" person. Millstone denied the allegations, and O'Hanlon ordered a recheck of its sources for the report. The firm determined that there was no substance to its original allegations, but it still refused to give Millstone a copy of the report and to disclose the contents of his file.

Millstone sued, charging that O'Hanlon had violated the Federal Fair Credit Reporting Act. The Act requires credit bureaus to "follow reasonable procedures to assure maximum possible accuracy" and to "clearly and accurately disclose to the consumer" the information in its files.

A U.S. District Court judge found in Millstone's behalf and awarded him $27,500 in damages and $12,500 for legal fees.

O'Hanlon appealed the award, contending that credit reports were protected by the First Amendment to the U.S. Constitution. The District Court had ruled that, to the contrary, credit reports have no constitutional protection. The Eighth Circuit Court of Appeals upheld the original decision, saying that O'Hanlon "willfully violated both the spirit and the letter of the Fair Credit Reporting Act" by "tramping recklessly" upon Millstone's rights. In its decision, the court indicated that O'Hanlon "sought at every step to block Millstone in his attempt to secure the rights given to him by the Act."

However, by carrying his case through the courts, Millstone has established an important check on irresponsible credit reporting.

WHAZZIT?

COMMERCIAL BANK

A bank that accepts deposits and creates credit by making loans, primarily to businesses.

MUTUAL SAVINGS BANK

A bank in which the depositors are the owners and share in the earnings.

SAVINGS AND LOAN ASSOCIATION

An institution that finances through mortgage loans the building and purchase of homes with money invested by stockholders.

CREDIT UNION

An association (not a bank) whose members usually belong to the same occupational group or are employees of the same company, organized to pool savings (deposits) from members and make loans to members. Originated in Germany in the 1800s.

MONEY

Any medium of exchange for buying or selling goods and services

INTEREST

Payment for use of funds, as for the privilege of credit.

CURRENCY

Money which by law must be accepted when offered in payment for goods and services.

CREDIT

The ability of an individual or a business to obtain money, goods, or services in return for a promise to pay for them in the future.

CREDIT ANYONE?
The Trick Is Managing Money

This is the start of the boom season for American Express Co., the company that extracts more money from more travelers than anyone else. By the time the summer ends, more than 10-million tourists the world over will have bought American Express Travelers Cheques, taken one of its guided tours, or at least planned a trip through one of its 94 domestic and 700 foreign travel offices.

But the day is past when American Express just sold Travelers Cheques and tours. Chairman Howard L. Clark, chief executive officer of the 120-year-old company since 1960, has seen more change in the 10 years he has been there than occured in the 110 preceding years. Lately, the changes have been coming faster than ever. And though Clark may writhe when American Express is called a financial conglomerate, there are few financial areas that it is not in today.

Clark hopes that this year, travelers, and other people as well, will have bought their insurance from one of the Fireman's Fund American companies, and their mutual fund shares from one of the American Expresss funds. Both the insurance companies and the Commonwealth group of mutual funds came to American Express in a 1968 merger with Fund American, the big insurance holding company. In return for some $550-million in stock, American Express gained 11 U. S. and Canadian insurance companies with $1.7-billion in assets at the end of 1969, and four mutual funds (since expanded to six, and renamed the American Express funds) with $572-million in assets at the end of April.

Clark further hopes that customers will join the three-million holders of American Express' credit card; buy their stocks and bonds from Equitable Securities, Morton & Co., a brokerage and investment banking house which American Express owns; book their hotel rooms and rent their cars through the new American Express computerized reservations system; learn a foreign tongue from the Institute of Modern Languages, Inc., an American Express subsidiary since early 1969; and faithfully read *Travel & Camera* magazine (nee U. S. Camera), now published by American Express.

Beyond that, American Express nowadays does a big and growing commercial banking business, though only overseas and for corporations rather than for the average tourist. American Express International Banking Corp. has 53 commercial banking offices overseas and 189 military banking offices at U. S. installations around the world. It does a portfolio management business in Switzerland, with seats on the Zurich and Basel stock exchanges, and it deals in gold under a U. S. Treasury license.

In short, American Express has stretched out every which-way over the past decade. Yet there is a common thread that runs through the whole diversification program. Everything the company has built or bought still fits into one or another of its two basic businesses: travel and finance. Moreover, its gut business remains today what it has been for many, many years: managing money.

The float. "American Express," says security analyst Donald Kramer of Oppenheimer & Co., "is only in two businesses, credit cards and float." This is certainly true if you include in the float the investment of premium income by the insurance companies (as Kramer

> 'American Express
> is in only two businesses—
> credit cards and float'

does). Income and capital gains from investment of the float do provide by far the largest share of earnings.

The company used to make almost all of its money from the float on its Travelers Cheques—money paid in for checks that have not yet been cashed. Last year, more than $4-billion in U. S.-dollar Travelers Cheques were sold through 60,000 outlets in 131 countries. Since there is a six-to-eight-week lag between the time the Travelers Cheque is sold and the time American Express has to pay off, the float can be enormous—from a low of $700-million near yearend to $1-billion and more during the peak summer months.

There is always some money in the float—at least $700-million—and this permanent float is invested long-term by Senior Vice-President Robert L. Stillson. Mostly, this money goes into

municipal bonds to limit American Express' tax liability. Seasonal bulges in the float are invested in a variety of short-term securities by Senior Vice-President Charles A. Cuccinello. Apart from this, American Express invests its retained earnings in equities. That portfolio, which amounted to $76-million at the end of 1969, is managed by John S. Anderson, president of a subsidiary called Rexport Corp.

Last year, of course, a number of ventures made money for American Express: its credit card, international banking, its mutual funds. And for the first time in many years, its travel business showed a profit. Even so, the lion's share of 1969 earnings still came from its float—all those invested Travelers Cheque dollars plus the investments of its insurance companies. The investment income from the $1.2-billion insurance portfolio came to $57-million last year, while the $1-billion portfolio built up from its other businesses (but mostly from Travelers Cheques) brought in at least $30-million. Nor does that include another $17-million in capital gains from the two portfolios.

In all, American Express earned $75-million last year—$39-million from its travel and financial services and $36-million from its insurance business—up from $9-million in 1960 when Clark took over. Clark is tenaciously close-mouthed when it comes to breaking down last year's earnings. It seems likely that American Express earned around $17-million from Travelers Cheques, $13-million from its credit card, and $6-million from its international banking business. The remainder came from travel, mutual funds, investment banking, from the equities in which it invests retained earnings, from capital gains—and, of course, from insurance. On the other hand, American Express lost some money last year on the magazine and the language school, and on its Equitable Securities, Morton operation. And Express Reservation Services, Inc., the computerized reservations system, is still operating in the red.

Surviving Tino. The great salad oil swindle of 1963, which sent Anthony (Tino) DeAngelis to prison, nearly brought American Express' growth to a screeching halt. A subsidiary, American Express Warehousing, had a thicket of storage tanks in Bayonne, N.J., that were supposed to be filled with salad oil belonging to Allied Crude Vegetable Oil Refining Corp., of which DeAngelis was president. Millions of dollars in warehouse receipts, some put out in good faith by Warehousing, but some stolen from Warehousing and forged, were issued against the salad oil as collateral on loans. Actually, the tanks were mostly empty. When that was discovered, stricken creditors filed nearly $150-million in claims against Warehousing.

The fraud was pulled off by DeAngelis; Warehousing was an innocent, if naive, victim. Nor, in theory at least, was American Express liable for claims against its subsidiary. But American Express realized from the start what would happen to its name if it let the Warehousing creditors go hang, so it stepped in to satisfy the claims; a perilous move because American Express in those days was a joint stock company, meaning its shareholders could be held liable for debts of the company. Almost overnight, its shares plunged from 62 to near 30.

Today, American Express is out of the woods. It has switched from stock company to conventional corporation and has settled virtually all claims at an after-tax cost of $31.6-million.

It was, says Clark, "a big wound." But American Express survived it.

Moving out. Obviously American Express isn't the same company it was before 1963. While the groundwork for diversification was laid before the salad-oil mess, most of the big moves have come since and, far from being crippled by the swindle, American Express is growing today faster than ever before.

Its earnings, Clark observes, grew at a 17% annual rate through the 1960s. He thinks they can keep growing at around that rate with the businesses it already has, "plus natural extension," for a good while to come. Last year, the company added the two new mutual funds to the four funds that came as part of the 1968 merger with Fund American, one a closed-end fund offered in the U.S. and the other an international fund sold only abroad. The computerized reservations service, says Executive Vice-President George W. Waters, "has the potential of making a significant profit contribution to the corporation." The system already covers some 400,000 domestic and foreign hotel rooms; hotels pay a monthly fee for the service plus a fee for each room rented through it.

At the same time, Clark is also look-

ing at new areas, and one possibility is real estate. He says that the next time the company has to build somewhere, it

---

'The DeAngelis fraud was a big wound, but the company survived'

---

may buy some extra land and use it for development. In that way, he says, we could "get our feet wet with our own property . . . build our own organization and work from there." The company might then stretch into mortgage banking and resort development.

On the other hand, American Express is pulling back from some areas that have not worked out as planned. Clark is not enchanted with the retail brokerage business that came with Equitable Securities Corp. when it was acquired in 1968. "If you are going to be in the retail business," he says, "you ought to be a Merrill Lynch." Since Equitable is not in that league (it is not, says American Express President William H. Morton, "a nationwide securities supermarket") the decision was made to sell the Equitable part of the business back to its original owners. That plan fell through and now, says Morton, Equitable will concentrate on dealing with institutional investors, with the retail part of its business being gradually phased out. So far this year, seven of the 15 Equitable branch offices have been shut down.

Shedding the past. Several years ago, American Express got out of the international car rental business it had operated jointly with Hertz because it figured it could make better use of the capital that was involved elsewhere. Last year, it sold Uni-card, a New York area retail credit card, to Chase Manhattan Bank, because it had decided there wasn't much hope of making it into a national card. It got out of the domestic express business more than

half a century ago and out of the armored car business in 1967. And early this year, it cut its last ties to the historic past by selling its international freight business to Pacific Intermountain Express. Those ties go back to 1850, when American Express was formed through a consolidation of three freight companies: Wells & Co., Livingston & Fargo, and Butterfield, Wasson & Co. Today, it has no stake at all in the express business.

Considering the pace at which American Express has moved during the past few years, the pace of its first hundred years was one of glacial slowness. The first Travelers Cheque, for instance, appeared in 1891, but not until 1915 did the company take the next logical step and get into the travel business. And not until the early 1960s did it begin to emphasize its own tours, in addition to selling the tours of other travel companies. For all of its unique financial position overseas, it did not move into international banking in any organized way until 1959.

American Express could afford to stick close to home base for so long because home base—the one-two punch of travel and Travelers Cheques—was so profitable. Tourists booked tours and collected mail at American Express outposts the world over (the Paris office handles one-million pieces of tourist mail a year), and became converts to Travelers Cheques.

American Express sold only $9,200 worth of Travelers Cheques in 1891 but more than $4-billion worth of U.S. dollar-denominated Cheques last year, not to mention Cheques denominated in Canadian dollars and British pounds; a Swiss franc cheque was introduced at the start of this year. The company built the market from scratch and has dominated it down through the years. Senior Vice-President Michael E. Lively claims that American Express has two-thirds of the dollar check market today, an estimate that most Wall Street analysts endorse but one that some rival bankers insist is high. Its nearest rivals are Bank of America and First National City Bank, with Thos. Cook & Son, Republic National Bank of Dallas, and Barclays Bank, Ltd. far, far behind.

Travelers Cheque sales this year, says Lively, "are running at a high rate of increase over last year."

Pre Clark. Things began to boil at American Express in the late 1950s, just as Clark was getting ready to take over from Ralph T. Reed, who had headed the company since 1944. There was, says Clark today, no single event that prompted American Express to reach into new fields. Rather, he says, there was "a different attitude at the top . . . a willingness to take new chances . . . a different way of wanting to see the company grow."

The first really dramatic move came in 1958, when American Express moved into the credit card business. It was a chancy decision on two counts: Not only was the American Express going against two established card plans, Diners Club and Carte Blanche, but growth of its card plan could hurt Travelers Cheque sales.

The American Express card finally began earning money in 1962 and today it dominates the travel and entertainment card field to the same extent that Travelers Cheques dominate their field. More than three-million American Express cardholders charged $1.8-billion worth of goods and services last year, against two-million cardholders and $1-billion for Diners Club, and 650,000 and $200-million for Carte Blanche. And there is not much evidence that the credit card has cut very deeply into Travelers Cheque sales. American Express gets its money through the $15 annual fee that cardholders pay, plus the discount it levies on items charged through the card. That discount averages a little over 4%—or $70-million or more on the $1.8-billion worth of charges in 1969.

The rivals. The T&E cards, American Express included, have a new, tough rival today in the big bank credit card plans, BankAmericard and Master Charge. There are 10 times as many bank cards as T&E cards out and banks are signing up establishments that used to take only T&E cards. Of the three T&E cards, the American Express plan is the biggest and most profitable, and seems in a good position to withstand the bank card assault. Says Clark: "We've been competing with Bank of America in California for 12 years and they haven't knocked us out of the box yet."

In 1959, American Express welded together its various international banking operations into American Express International Banking Corp. As it turned out, this was just in time to catch the international business boom of the 1960s. At the end of 1969 AEIBC had $1.1-billion in assets, up 23% from 1968. One problem is that AEIBC has no banking operation back home, as do most of its rivals. Still, as AEIBC's president, Richard F. Blanchard, observes: "It forces you to be profitable. You can't run as a service to your domestic bank." Moreover, American Express has a niche in international finance that few rivals can match. "We grew fast because we were sponsored by American Express," says Blanchard.

Since Clark took command, the pace of diversification has quickened. In 1962, for instance, American Express plunged into wholesale travel, and while its retail travel business does not make money, its new wholesale business has proven quite profitable. Travel tends to be cyclical, and the economic slowdown could yet cut into this part of American Express' business. So far, says Senior Vice-President Stephen S. Halsey, who is in charge of travel, the company's retail business is running 10% ahead of last year and its escorted tour business 80% ahead.

American Express picked up W. H. Morton & Co. in 1966 and added Equitable Securities in 1968. Today, the Morton Div. does municipal bond underwriting, while Equitable Securities, Morton handles corporate securities.

The big diversification move, the one that really changed the scope of American Express, was the 1968 merger with Fund American. Fund American, says Clark, "was about the right size and it wanted us."

The merger obviously did a great many things for American Express—putting it into both insurance and mutual funds, and, of course, doubling its

---

Fund American was the key merger. 'It was the right size and wanted us'

net income. Because Fund American, like American Express, manages a great pile of money, the two companies fit together very nicely. While the two investment pools will not be joined together, there will be increased coordination of investments.

Property-casualty insurance companies typically lose money on their underwriting, while earning money on their investments. Last year, for instance, the Fireman's Fund companies posted a $19.5-million underwriting loss. Now, according to a report by brokerage house H. C. Wainwright & Co.: "Fireman Fund's investment policies stand to benefit from affiliation with American Express to the extent that tax-exempt bonds could be used in place of taxable bonds, which formerly were used to offset statutory losses. Such underwriting losses can now be applied against the operating profit of the company's travel and financial businesses." Last year's underwriting loss by Fireman's Fund cut American Express' tax bill by $10-million—a clue as to how the companies do mesh.

Careers In Banking

Banking offers a broad range of positions, and thus many individuals with different backgrounds and interests are attracted to the field.

Banks often look for well-rounded individuals, including liberal arts graduates. Further, with more than 33,000 banks and other financial institutions around the country, location won't be a restriction.

To work in banking you need to have a knowledge of people, the customers; of finances and the customers' businesses; and of the community, the industry, and the wider economy. The kicker is making sound decisions on loan requests -- you have to be able to weigh the information relating to each decision.

Of course, there are many supporting roles and specialized careers in banking that accompany the basic lending function. Banks include accountants, economists, lawyers, marketing and public relations specialists, personnel people, analysts, operations people, and information specialists.

New banking markets and services are continually emerging, and employment opportunities for the college educated individual are increasing in number and variety. Management and professional positions now account for one-fourth of all banking jobs.

There are many areas in banking, each one of which requires special aptitudes and knowledge.

OPERATIONS

One of the key areas in banking is operations. This staff, including clerical, data processing, and managerial staff, keeps the organization functioning.

Operations include processing of daily transactions, bookkeeping, check handling, data processing, and various support functions such as accounting, systems management, security, and distribution services.

Often careers begin as a TELLER. The job is essentially clerical, but involves a significant responsibility for handling large sums of money and handling of customer transactions. Tellers cash checks and handle deposits and withdrawals.

Often, teller jobs may be part-time, as large banks like to staff operations to meet peak times of customer demand. Over time, the job serves as good training, and may qualify you for other banking jobs. In fact, at Citibank in New York, 80% of the officers in the personal or retail department began at the level of teller.

There are advanced steps in operations, including SENIOR TELLER, TELLER SUPERVISOR, and OPERATIONS OFFICER. Also, there are jobs specializing in credit analysis -- involving research on the credit worthiness of a particular customer. This means personal contact with people outside the bank to get information on the finances of an individual or business customer.

CONSUMER CREDIT

Anyone seeking a loan is interviewed by a loan officer or manager. After the interview, the manager reviews credit information and verifies employment and residence. Based on the data, the loan is made or refused.

Lending is at the heart of the banking activity and thus is an important career area. With this experience, a career may lead to branch management, corporate lending work, or work in trust or other banking areas.

Leading to the lending officer position are jobs as "platform assistants", as aides to lending officers and branch managers. This person may assist in opening new accounts and processing loans. The work may include approving checks for cashing, issuing travelers' checks, supervising teller operations (in small branches), and general branch responsibilities.

CORPORATE BANKING

In large banks, careers may specialize in services for corporate clients -- meeting the banking needs of businesses. The work is essentially the same -- handling accounts, processing loan requests, and providing other bank services. In large banks, there are often individuals who spend all their time taking care of particular companies' needs.

Corporate banking work involves a greater amount of financial and economic analysis abilities and knowledge. It may also require specialization in a particular industry or geographic area. Often, therefore, graduate business education is a prerequisite to work in this area, although the paths through the bank may be available.

TRUST

The trust department is responsible for managing trusts and estates. Trusts protect the property of individuals who, because of age or health, cannot manage their own affairs. A trust manager frequently manages investments, disbursements, and offers advice to customers who lack the time or expertise connected with financial affairs.

Trust departments provide administration and investment services. One important area is care of pension funds and profit-sharing funds established by unions or companies. Often the work includes management of farms, buildings, and other real property held in trust.

In Corporate trust work, banks also get involved in issuing shares of stock, serving as "transfer agents" when shares are sold, and keeping track of the owners of each share of stock.

Careers start with clerical jobs, leading to trust administration jobs, leading to various trust management or officer jobs. You could be an executor or administrator of estates -- a major function of a career in estate administration. Here you collect the assets of a customer who is deceased and determine how to sell them, pay all expenses, prepare tax returns, handle the estate's accounting, and distribute remaining assets to the beneficiaries.

TRAINING

One way to get into these banking careers may be through a formal training program. Many banks hire individuals directly into training -- whether for retail (branch) jobs or for other types of banking jobs.

While admission to such programs usually requires a college degree or MBA degree, it can shortcut the longer job-to-job route up through a bank's ranks.

Banks encourage self education, and usually pay for courses related to a banking career. The American Institute of Banking offers courses in virtually every area of banking. Courses are offered in most large cities, through 369 chapters, through study groups, and even through correspondence study. Such education is beneficial in seeking advancement in a banking career.

INFORMATION

For more information on banking careers, write to the American Bankers Association, 1120 Connecticut Avenue NW, Washington D.C. 20036.

You may also read issues of the magazine, BANKING and other industry journals, or the daily newspaper, THE AMERICAN BANKER. Here you'll get an idea of trends and opportunities in this field.

For information on the roles of women in banking, you may write the National Association of Bank Women, Inc., 111 East Wacker Drive, Chicago, Illinois 60601.

CONSIDER

1. What would we use for money if we didn't have currency and checkbooks?

2. Could we get along without any kind of money?

3. How does American Express earn its profits?

4. What are the advantages in having a credit card?

5. What risks go with credit cards? Who pays for a customer's failure to pay for charges charged on the card?

6. What would you lose by putting your money under a mattress instead of in a bank?

7. Home mortgages used to bear interest of 3%. Why have mortgage rates climbed so high (upwards to 9% today)?

8. Should banks give away toasters and other premiums to savers?

9. How will banking careers be different in a cashless society?

10. How does inflation affect the value of your savings? Do interest rates "beat inflation"?

CHALLENGES

Examine the annual percentage rates charged for credit at a local store (such as Sears) and compare the rates with those charged for a personal loan at a local commercial bank. Explain the difference in rates.

Find out what services are included under the label "full service bank." Are any of the services free?

Look for advertisements by two or more financial institutions. Compare the features stressed and evaluate them.

Find an article in the Wall Street Journal on changing interest rates as charged by a large bank or as set by the Fed. Explain why the change is being made.

Examine an application form for obtaining a credit card. Explain why each item of information is being requested.

Examine the markings on the back of a check that has been cancelled, preferably one that was sent out of your state. Trace the route your check followed.

RECAP

In our economic system, management of the money supply is a broad-scale, complex task. Banks and other financial institutions help create money by making loans to individuals and businesses. They expand the supply of money within the limits allowed by the Federal Reserve System. It is the responsibility of the Fed to regulate interest rates, deposit requirements, and other banking practices. Through these measures, the Fed controls the amount of money available through banks.

Banks also provide an important means of exchanging money through the processing of checks, through credit card systems, and other financial services. Some financial institutions offer limited services -- accepting deposits and lending money. Together, banks and savings and loan associations in the U.S. have assets approaching $1 trillion. Based on these assets (outstanding loans, investments, and other income producing properties owned by the companies) they are able to grow and effectively serve their customers.

Through the privilege of credit, individuals and businesses obtain the money, goods, and services they need in return for a promise to pay in the future. The kicker in credit is interest -- the charge for the use of the money. Interest is based on a percentage of the amount of money borrowed and may be calculated on a simple or a compound rate.

Even non-bank credit companies such as American Express are in the lending and deposits business. When you buy travelers' checks you are depositing cash which the company can invest, at least for the time until you cash the checks when you make a purchase. Similarly, when you make purchases using an American Express credit card, you are borrowing from the company (You pay an annual fee, and the retailer accepting the card pays a percentage rate on the amount charged). Hence the company is in the finance and credit card business.

In the future we may see increased use of credit cards and computers and far less use of cash and checks. This will be the age of the "cashless society" made possible by communication networks among banks and other businesses. Electronic funds transfer systems will reduce the burdensome flow of paper in business and will speed up the rate our transactions are completed.

Money is nearly always a subject of interest to people. If you are interested in a career that helps keep money flowing in our economy, you may consider a career in banking. There are lots of possibilities, depending on your education and your specialization.

WORKSHEET NO. 11

NAME_____

INSTRUCTOR'S NAME_____

DATE_____

1. What services do banks provide?

_____

2. How do banks help our economy?

3. What does the Federal Reserve System do?

_____

4. What are the advantages of a cashless society?

CHAPTER 12

Insurance

Insurance is protection. For money, an insurance company or insuror agrees to share the risk that something will happen that will result in a financial loss. Some of the risks that are commonly covered by insurance are:
- death
- injury, accident, illness
- property damage by fire, hail, flood, vandalism, explosion, or earthquake
- theft of money or property
- spoilage or deterioration of merchandise
- liability resulting from negligence, as in an automobile accident or personal injury

You could overcome the financial risks of such losses by avoiding them or by removing their causes. For example, you may lock up your money, build fireproof buildings, maintain your good health, or save up enough money to cover possible financial losses (this is called self-insurance). The much more economical and practical approach for most people and businesses is to share the risk through insurance.

Insurance is a means by which a group of persons may share the burden of the risk of possible financial losses. Past and present events are certain -- we know what has happened and is happening now -- but we can never tell for sure what the future holds for us. Through insurance we share the risk of uncertain future events through pooling of insurance premium payments.

Acceptance of an insured risk is called underwriting. The money paid for this insurance is called the premium. An insurance contract is called a policy. The amount payable in the event of a loss is called a claim.

All of these key factors in insurance are determined on the basis of past experience and estimates of future risks. The process of underwriting risks on a scientific basis, issuing policies, calculating and collecting premiums, investing premium payments, and paying claims has become a major field of business activity in our economy.

In this chapter the business of insurance is discussed from the point of view of both the insured (you) and the insurance companies.

There are, of course, different types of insurance, covering different types of risks. Property and casualty insurance cover risks related to loss of property, damage, or liabilities. Automobile

insurance is of this type,
but also normally includes
medical insurance. Life
insurance covers the need
for financial protection
for the insured's depen-
dents, in the event of
his or her death.
Characteristics of these
and other types of
insurance are discussed
in this chapter.

In This Chapter

Insurance Info

"Considering your route and the length of time you'll be away, I'm sure you'll want to protect your loved ones with our blanket coverage that includes storms at sea, shipwreck, demons of both the land and the deep, sirens and monsters, in addition to all acts of the gods."

Drawing by Saxon, © 1971 The New Yorker Magazine Inc.

There are many different kinds of insurance -- as many as there are kinds of risks.

A common risk is fire. In 1974, over $3 billion in losses resulted from fires in the United States. These losses of property may be covered by FIRE INSURANCE.

Related to fire insurance is insurance protection against such hazards as windstorms, riots, water damage, aircraft damage, or explosion. This coverage is generally referred to as ALLIED LINES.

Insurance for fire and allied lines represents a major share of PROPERTY INSURANCE. A homeowner's insurance policy provides protection against theft, buglary, accidents, and liabilities related to home and property.

Other forms of CASUALTY INSURANCE, of which these are all examples, are automobile insurance, public liability, workmen's compensation, accident insurance and health insurance.

With rapidly rising medical and hospitalization costs, medical and health insurance is increasingly popular. Often it is provided in group policies which provide lower premiums per individual. Companies often provide this insurance as a fringe benefit.

You insure your automobile for several reasons. First, you want to be insured against the possible loss or damage to the car itself, which could be a sizable personal loss. Futher, you want some protection against law-suits that your "victims" might file against you should you have an unfortunate accident. This might protect you against liability. Finally, you might want some coverage for your own medical expenses and for your passengers.

Often these policies provide for CO-INSURANCE. That is, the insured party has to pay a share of the losses. You may have to pay losses up to a deductible amount of $100, for example, plus 20 per cent of all losses above the deductable.

If you were in the business of transporting goods, you would also want some transportation insurance, often called MARINE INSURANCE. It's called marine insurance because it was first used to insure ships and cargoes at sea. It is the oldest form of insurance.

All of these different kinds of insurance give protection when some uncertain event occurs, such as a fire or an accident. LIFE INSURANCE gives protection in the event of an individual's death.

While there is no uncertainty about death, there is uncertainty as to when it will happen. By applying the Law of Large Numbers, that is, looking at the statistics of deaths in our popula-tion over recent years, we may determine the risk of dying, or put in a positive light, our live expectancy.

It is on the basis of this statistical information, from mortality tables, that insurance companies determine the premiums that different persons should pay, according to age, to provide financial protection to their dependents.

That's what LIFE INSURANCE is all about -- sharing the risk that a person's dependents (wife, family or others specified by the insured) will be cared for financially in the event of the person's premature death. Benefits may include funeral costs, payments for the education of children, monthly income for the family, or other forms of financial payments that will allow the depen-dents to maintain a reasonable standard of living.

Life insurance comes in two basic forms: insurance that provides protection only, and insurance that provides a combination of protection and savings. The different types of life insurance will be discussed in more detail in the section on life insurance on the next page. The different types of life insurance will be discussed in more detail in the section on life insurance on the next page.

Auto pile-up: Insurers lost $3-billion in auto underwriting in the last 15 years.

Fire loss: Plant investment is so great that the present system cannot cover it.

Life Insurance

As far as Americans are concerned, life insurance is a necessity. Families rely on life insurance for financial protection when their children are young, and they continue to use it well into their retirement years.

Why rely on life insurance? What makes life insurance work? A tool that guarantees the payment of benefits 20, 30, or 50 years in the future can be quite complicated. Professional actuaries use complex computer systems and computer programs to make the necessary calculations. But you don't have to be an actuary to understand life insurance.

Life insurance protects people against many of life's risks. People pay a small portion of their incomes into a common fund to provide for the time when their incomes will become smaller or stop altogether because of retirement, poor health, or death. Life insurance is a relatively easy way for people to provide for financial security.

Life insurance offers a voluntary plan in which the individual may buy or not, as he sees fit. It is this voluntary aspect of life insurance which has made necessary certain requirements as to the health and occupation of eligible policyholders. If there were not any requirements, people in good health would tend to postpone the purchase of life insurance, while people in hazardous occupations and those in ill health would buy. This would make the cost of life insurance prohibitive.

In America, the father of a family has an obligation to provide financial support for the family, even if he should die. Accordingly, life insurance is widely used by families to fill financial needs created by the loss of the breadwinner. These needs include a) money to meet funeral expenses, b) money to live on when the family readjusts to the new conditions with the breadwinner gone, c) an income for the family while the children are growing up, and d) an income for the remaining spouse after the children have left home.

A family's life insurance needs change as the family grows. The insurance policies held should adapt to meet the changing needs at various stages of the family cycle. Privately held policies are often supplemented by group life insurance policies and retirement benefits provided through employment. Also, federal social security benefits provide a supplement to these programs.

Because of the changing needs of a family for insurance and the different sources of family financial protection, insurance companies offer the guidance and assistance of insurance agents to help policyholders plan and maintain a reasonable financial program.

MORTALITY

Life insurance is based on the natural law of human mortality -- no one lives forever. As people grow older, an increasing proportion must dies. At age 20, you may expect to live about 50 more years. At birth, your life expectancy was about 68 years. When you reach age 40, your life expectancy will be about 32 years; at age 50, 24 years; at age 60, 16 years. By the time you are 90 years old, you can still expect to live about 3 years. Each year your chances get a little better, because fewer people your age are still alive.

Mortality tables present these statistics for use by actuaries. They provide the basis for determining who should pay what in life insurance premiums, based on the probabilities of dying.

WHERE PREMIUMS GO

Part of the dollars paid in premiums are set aside to guarantee future obligations to policyholders and their families. Until needed, these funds are invested and the earnings help keep down the cost of insurance.

As a result, insurance companies represent one of the most important

LIFE INSURANCE PURCHASES IN THE UNITED STATES

	Percentage of Policies	Percentage of Amount
Sex of Insured:		
Male	70%	87%
Female	30%	13%
Income of Insured:		
Under $3000	2%	1%
$3000 - $4999	17%	7%
$5000 - $7499	37%	27%
$7500 - $9999	21%	21%
$10,000 or over	23%	44%
Age of Insured:		
Under age 15	16%	4%
15 - 24	32%	28%
25 - 34	25%	35%
35 - 44	15%	21%
45 or over	12%	12%
Size of Policy:		
Under $2000	15%	1%
$2000 - $4999	17%	4%
$5000 - $9999	21%	11%
$10,000 - $24,999	34%	38%
$25,000 or over	13%	46%

Source: Life Insurance Agency Management Association.
This data is for ordinary life insurance, also called straight or whole life insurance, on which periodic payments are paid for life, with a cumulative cash value.

sources of financial capital in our economy. About $200 billion is invested today by life insurance companies in the United States. Much of this money is invested in mortgage loans and real estate -- used to help build homes, apartments, office buildings, shopping centers, hotels, and stores. About $2 billion has been invested in a special program to provide needed housing and jobs in urban areas. Funds are also invested in plants, equipment, and working capital for business organizations. Investments include both corporate stocks and bonds. Insurance investments also include federal and local government bonds, some foreign securities, and loans to policyholders themselves.

TYPES OF POLICIES

In this chapter (on page 327), we mentioned different types of life insurance policies. In reality, there are many variations of life insur-ance, serving different needs.

Insurance that provides protection only is called TERM INSURANCE. For a specified term, say twenty years (possibly the life of a mortgage), your premiums assure benefits to your beneficiary in the event of your death. The policy must be renewed if you wish the protection to continue.

A term policy provides a form of temporary protection. A benefit is paid only if the policy-holder dies within a specified period of time.

No cash value builds up; to keep the policy alive and valid, you have to keep paying term premiums.

A term policy may be convertible; that is, it may grant theprivilege of changing into permanent insurance on either the whole life or an endowment plan.

WHOLE LIFE or ENDOWMENT POLICIES bear higher premiums because they provide lifetime insurance protection. The total cost of the policy may be paid in one single sum or as a series of premiums according to the policyholder's preference and ability to pay.

But there is more to life insurance. You don't always have to "die to win." If the insured lives to retirement, or to a specified age in the policy, he or she may receive all or part of the premiums that were paid into the policy back from the insurance company. This would be the case if the insured had a CASH-VALUE INSURANCE policy,

instead of term insurance. Cash-value insurance is thus a form of investment or savings for the individual policy-holder. Under certain conditions, you can borrow or withdraw money built up by premiums.

People buy life insurance because they may not live long enough to support their families. People buy ANNUITIES becasue they may outlive their earning years. An annuity contract complements an insurance policy.

In an annuity, an individual exchanges money with a life insurance company for a guarantee that the company will pay him a regular income as long as he lives starting at a specified age such as 55 or 65. Using mortality tables, an insurance company can calculate how much each annuity holder (annuitant) has to contribute to the pooled funds out of which benefits would be paid. Annuity payments and the cost of an annuity depend on the annuitant's sex,

age when payments begin, the mortality table used, the rate of interest guaranteed by the company, and the manner of settlement of the annuity.

To be a wise insurance and annuity purchaser, you must decide what your own needs are:
- How much money do you want to leave to your dependents? Will this change?
- When would you like to retire? How much money will you need then?
- How will you be able to pay for your overall insurance program? Will your ability to pay premiums change? Are demands on your income increasing?

Because of the complexities involved in planning your insurance program to meet your changing needs, you are well advised to talk to insurance agents. Talk to several, draw up your own idea of what you need, and then do something about it.

LIFE INSURANCE IN FORCE IN THE UNITED STATES

YEAR	NUMBER OF POLICIES (MILLIONS)	AVERAGE SIZE OF POLICY	COVERAGE PER FAMILY	TOTAL VALUE (MILLIONS)
1965	320	$4,950	$14,600	$ 900,554
1967	336	5,500	17,100	1,079,821
1968	345	5,580	18,300	1,183,354
1969	351	6,110	19,400	1,284,529
1970	355	6,620	20,700	1,402,123
1971	357	6,970	21,700	1,503,324
1972	365	7,400	22,900	1,627,985
1973	369	7,750	24,400	1,985,652
1974	380	8,400	26,500	1,985,652

Source: Institute of Life Insurance

Insurance Companies

There are two basic types of insurance companies. In one type, the policyholders are also the owners. The insured are thus also the insurors. As a MUTUAL COMPANY, this type of insurance company is a non-profit making organization, providing a pooling of the risk of financial loss.

Any excess revenue, from premiums or from investment income, is returned to the policyholders as dividends or is used to reduce their premiums. More than half of all life insurance in force is with mutual companies. Mutual companies are principally engaged in the life insurance field.

In a mutual company, policyholders elect a board of directors who are responsible for the management of the firm.

Mutual companies may limit coverage to a particular fraternal

---

25 LARGEST LIFE INSURANCE COMPANIES

(All figures in millions of dollars)

Rank	Company	Assets	Life Insurance In Force
1	Prudential*	$39,309	$236,200
2	Metropolitan*	35,138	226,288
3	Equitable Life Assurance*	19,819	119,167
4	New York Life*	13,862	76,105
5	John Hancock Mutual*	12,801	87,784
6	Aetna Life	10,415	84,555
7	Northwestern Mutual*	7,918	31,764
8	Connecticut General Life	7,682	48,207
9	Travelers	7,169	71,704
10	Massachusetts Mutual*	5,848	28,767
11	Mutual of New York*	4,812	23,169
12	New England Mutual	4,609	20,483
13	Teachers Insurance & Annuity	4,425	3,618
14	Connecticut Mutual*	3,673	15,420
15	Bankers Life*	3,420	18,660
16	Mutual Benefit*	3,387	22,888
17	Lincoln National Life	3,086	32,385
18	Penn Mutual*	2,909	12,400
19	National Life & Accident	2,420	14,020
20	Occidental of California	2,333	38,828
21	Western & Southern*	2,323	12,228
22	Continental Assurance	2,214	17,952
23	National Life*	1,846	7,897
24	Pheonix Mutual*	1,841	16,697
25	American National	1,727	13,364

* Indicates Mutual Company   Source: Fortune, July, 1976

society (as a lodge or professional society), a class of property (as lumbermills or farms), or other groups.

All other insurance companies are STOCK COMPANIES. They are profit-oriented corporations owned by stockholders who have invested financial capital in the business. Corporate income is earned in two ways: by premiums that exceed the cost of providing insurance coverage, and by investing those premiums in other businesses for profit.

Generally all profits go to the stockholders, although some stock companies offer PARTICIPATING POLICIES in which policyholders also receive dividends.

The key difference in the way the two kinds of insurance companies work is that when losses are great, policyholders bear the burden (and may be assessed for their share) in a mutual company. In a stock company, the stockholders bear the loss.

There is no clear indication that premiums are necessarily lower for one company or another. It all depends on the effectiveness of an individual company's management.

In this chapter you read about Allstate Insurance Company (Sears) and will note that their net investment income was over $175 million. This income was partially offset by a $99 million loss in insurance operations. Of the nation's 50 largest life insurance companies, the total net investment was approximately $13 billion in 1975.

LIFE INSURANCE COMPANY DOLLAR
U. S. LIFE INSURANCE COMPANIES

INCOME	
Premiums	78.2¢
Net Investment Earnings and Other Income	21.8
	100.0¢

HOW USED	
Benefit Payments and Additions to Funds for Policyholders and Beneficiaries	
Benefit Payments in Year	55.2¢
Additions to Policy Reserve Funds	20.6
Additions to Special Reserve and Surplus Funds	1.5
	77.3
Operating Expenses	
Commissions to Agents	7.1
Home and Field Office Expenses	9.9
	17.0
Taxes	4.5
Dividends to Stockholders	1.2
	100.0¢

Source: Institute of Life Insurance. Certain offsetting items such as considerations for supplementary contracts are excluded, so that the total used ($43,135 million) differs from that shown on page 57. Direct investment taxes (such as real estate) are excluded from taxes and are deducted, with other investment expenses, from investment income. Federal income taxes, however, are included in taxes.

All of these figures tell us that insurance companies, particularly life insurance companies, have a lot of money and are major investors in our economy.

There are over 1800 life insurance companies in the United States today, three times as many as in 1950. Yet the assets of the top fifty life insurance companies, over $230 billion, represents almost 85 percent of the assets of all the companies in the United States.

To go one step further, the five largest life insurance companies together have over $120 billion in assets, or almost half of all life insurance company assets in the United States. These five, for your information are Prudential, Metropolitan, Equitable life Assurance, New York Life, and John Hancock Mutual.

INVESTMENTS

How do companies invest

their assets? In 1969, life insurance assets were distributed as follows:

Bonds:
U.S. Government	2.1%
Foreign Government	.4
State & Local	2.7
Railroad	1.8
Public Utilities	9.1
Industrial & Other	25.4
Stocks	7.0
Mortgages	36.5
Real Estate	3.0
Policyholder Loans	7.0
Miscellaneous	5.0
	100.0%

Through mortgages and corporate bonds, in particular, life insurance companies make possible large-scale building projects, ventures, and other projects that require large amounts of capital funds.

Sears Merchant To Millions

Allstate Group

The Allstate Group of companies reached a new high in sales volume in 1975 but net income declined substantially, reflecting unprecedented property-liability insurance underwriting losses. Insurance premiums written and financial services revenues totaled $3.220 billion, an increase of $364 million from 1974. Total net income was $76 million, compared with $168 million for 1974. Net income represented 48 cents per Sears share, down 59 cents from $1.07 the previous year.

Property and liability insurance

Premiums written for all property and liability insurance lines rose $319 million from 1974 to a total of $2.935 billion. Allstate, a multiple-line insurance group, writes practically all kinds of insurance for individuals, businesses and other organizations and is also a major reinsurer.

The companies wrote auto premiums of $1.928 billion, an increase of $171 million from 1974. Premiums written for other property and liability lines, principally homeowners, residential fire, health and commercial, rose to $1.007 billion, up $148 million or 17.3 per cent from 1974. These other property and liability lines together with life insurance comprised 37.8 per cent of Allstate's total insurance premiums.

The combined property-liability operations resulted in an underwriting loss (before investment income) of $256.6 million before income taxes, or 9.2 per cent of premiums earned. This compared with an underwriting loss of $25.8 million, or 1.0 per cent of premiums earned for 1974. The underwriting results reflect an unprecedented combination of inflated claim costs and depressed insurance rates. Claims and claims expense rose a huge 24.3 per cent from 1974 whereas premiums earned rose 10.7 per cent. Both the number of claims and the average cost of the various classes of claims increased tremendously in 1975. Premium rate increases which previously had been resisted, were effected on the various insurance coverages and in the various states during the year. Insurance policies outstanding, however, are rerated at the new rate level when they expire and are renewed. Thus, premiums earned reflect the higher rates on a very gradual basis. During 1975, operating efficiencies were emphasized and policy acquisition costs and operating expenses rose only 4.3 per cent whereas premiums earned rose 10.7 per cent.

Allstate's net investment income from interest and dividends was $174.9 million before income taxes, up $22.2 million or 14.6 per cent from 1974. The increase arose principally from a greater amount of funds invested and higher yields on the state and municipal bond portfolio. During 1975 the amount invested in common stocks (at cost) was reduced $233 million to $762 million at year end, and the proceeds were reinvested in other categories of investments. The investment program is an important element of the com-

panies' operations. For the past ten years, net investment income has increased at a compound annual rate of 17.8 per cent.

Realized capital gains before income taxes amounted to $18.1 million compared with $14.8 million for the previous year. Valued at year end 1975 market prices, Allstate's portfolio of marketable equity securities consisting of common and preferred stocks showed a net unrealized loss of $196 million. During the early part of 1976 market prices improved generally, and from year end 1975 to March 10, 1976 the net unrealized loss on the common and preferred stock portfolio decreased $100 million to $96 million.

Total net income of the insurance group, including life insurance, was $64.5 million compared with $167.2 million the previous year. Increases in investment income, realized capital gains, and life insurance earnings were more than offset by the underwriting results of property-liability insurance.

Assets as of the close of the year were $4.7 billion, up $755 million from year end 1974. Sizeable new funds generated by the growth and operations of the companies and the rise in market values of investments in stocks both contributed to the increase in assets. Investments in bonds and stocks comprised 72.5 per cent of total assets.

Life insurance

Life insurance in force rose $1.365 billion during 1975 to a total of $19.031 billion at year end. The total included $11.460 billion of insurance on individuals and $7.571 billion of group insurance. Insurance in force on individuals increased 7.5 per cent during the year, and group insurance in force rose 8.1 per cent. A significant portion of sales during 1975 involved sales of retirement annuities which were specifically aimed at the new individual retirement account market. These annuities have no face value of insurance. Life insurance premiums totaled $166 million, an increase of 20.4 per cent from 1974.

Net income from life insurance operations, after income taxes, amounted to $30.4 million for 1975. This was an increase of $6.1 million from the previous year.

Assets of the life companies increased $108 million during 1975 to $598 million at year end. Investments in bonds, stocks and mortgages comprised 85.6 per cent of total assets.

The year ahead

A hoped for moderation in inflationary factors, plus responsible action by state insurance regulators in promptly accepting rate increases where the claims experience and rate of increase in claims costs clearly establish the need, should bring about improved underwriting results for 1976 as a whole. Nevertheless, underwriting operations for Allstate and for the property-liability industry as well are expected to produce losses (before investment income) in 1976.

Interest and dividends from investments are expected to increase as Allstate's investment portfolio grows in size. Net income from life insurance and from financial services should compare favorably with 1975.

Automobiles And Insurance

If you own or drive an automobile, you must be able to demonstrate your financial responsibility in the event of an accident. Most state laws say that you must have automobile liability insurance or else post a bond that will assure your ability to pay for losses that may result from your negligence.

Automobile liability insurance normally covers limits for each indivdiual involved in an accident, a total limit for each accident, and some allowance for medical costs for each individual (whether the automobile owner, driver, passenger, or pedestrian). Minimum coverage in many states would be 10/20 coverage -- $10,000 for each individual and $20,000 for each accident maximum. Considering what a dollar will pay for today, higher liability coverage is more common, such as 50/100 or 100/300. $5000 medical allowances would barely get injured persons in and out of a hospital.

Actually buying a car is the least of your expenditures as an owner and driver. Purchasing liability insurance is your next expenditure, and generally not a minor one. How much does this insurance cost? Like other insurance, rates depend on the risk -- determined through experience. Younger drivers, drivers of high-powered "sports" cars, and drivers in urban areas pay more.

Of course, your driving record has a big impact, too. Your insurance payments will climb rapidly if you have accidents. Many companies may even refuse to renew your policy -- which means you would have to look elsewhere for an insuror and probably end up paying premium (especially high) rates.

Another part of your automobile insurance coverage is for loss or damage to your property itself. If you have a new, expensive car you can expect to pay a lot more for protection than if you are driving an older car. It costs a lot more to fix up a new Jaguar or Mercedes than it does a 1968 Volkswagen or Ford. As your car ages, your "comprehensive" rates will fall. You may also obtain coverage on personal property that may be in your car (cameras, clothes, etc.).

You can reduce your premium payments by driving carefully, by taking special driver education courses, by reducing your coverage (raising the deductible amount on damage to your own car), by making payments annually rather than monthly, and by comparing insurance costs among different insurors. About 20% of all households in the United States don't own a car at all -- that's another alternative.

No Fault Insurance: The Only Real Reform

The multi-billion dollar U.S. auto insurance industry is a costly, unresponsive, wasteful and arbitrary system which ill serves the American consumer.

In the past six years, auto insurance premiums have increased 70 percent—but less than 42 cents of each premium dollar is returned to the consumers who have claims. And each dollar that does make it back to the accident victim costs $1.07 to deliver. Deductible levels have increased, eligibility standards are more discriminatory and the practices of arbitrarily cancelling or refusing renewal have become the rule rather than the exception.

In 1968, the growing public discontent with the crisis in auto insurance prompted Congress to commission the Department of Transportation to undertake a study of this system. Two years and 23 volumes later the study, conducted by a cross-section of government, labor, industry and consumer representatives, said this about the automobile insurance system:

"The existing system ill serves the accident victim, the insuring public and society. It is inefficient, overly costly, incomplete and slow. It allocates benefits poorly, discourages rehabilitation and overburdens the courts and the legal system. Both on the record of its performance and on the logic of its operation, it does little if anything to minimize crash losses."

That summary is damning enough, but an examination of material in the report reveals an even more grotesque picture of a self-serving system which seriously shortchanges the needs of the policyholder, the accident victim and society as a whole.

While the average motorist purchases automobile insurance to pay the losses incurred in all automobile accidents, by far the most important reason for his insurance is to protect him from catastrophic financial loss in a serious or fatal accident. He therefore buys a policy which will best protect him against such ruinous losses and expects that policy to pay all of his bills in an accident.

However, in serious accidents, 85 percent of the loss is never paid. In 1967, motorists incurred $5.1 billion in losses in accidents resulting in death or serious injury. Of that amount, automobile insurance repaid only $813 million—or 15 percent. More significantly, in the most serious cases—the 32,500 acci-

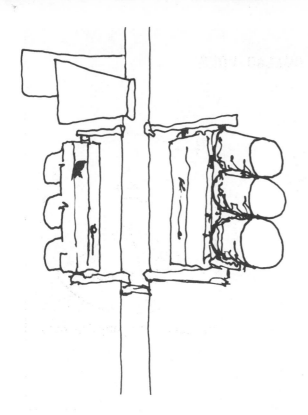

dent victims whose losses average $52,659—insurance paid only an average of $9,048, or 17 percent of the average loss after the case was settled in court. Of the 17,772 accident victims who lost over $25,000 in an accident, 93.3 percent failed to recoup the total amount to which their policies seemed to entitle them —recovering instead an average of about one-third of their losses. Overall, 42 percent of all accident victims in 1967 failed to recover their full out-of-pocket losses.

But in less serious accidents, a quite different picture emerges from the statistics. In that same year, 1967, accident victims incurring losses of less than $500 recovered an average of 4½ times their actual losses. At the next level, losses between $500 and $5,000, the victims recovered twice their total economic losses.

The principal reason for this inequity is that the big liability claims are settled in court, but the smaller ones are bargained to settlement by the insurance company. It's cheaper for the insurance company to bypass the expense of legal fees and investigations of claims. So they pay off the small ones—even claims of dubious merit. Thus rather than paying the minor accident victim the amount of loss actually incurred, some insurance companies "buy off" the claim to avoid the much greater expense of processing it.

Yet with the larger claims, enough money is at stake to make it worth the company's time to go through investigation and litigation. And the bargaining advantage is on the company's side, since it can better afford to wait for a settlement than the victim, who may be financially hard pressed by the accident.

This relationship between the size of the claim and the time it takes to settle is the most inhumane aspect of auto insurance. In 1967, almost 81 percent of the claims for $500 or less were settled within one year—and at the rate of 4½ times the actual loss. But in cases involving losses of $10,000 or more, only 19 percent were settled within the year while 37 percent remained unsettled after three years. The average delay was 19 months on all cases involving losses of $2,500 or more.

Of the 220,000 lawsuits filed in 1968 as the result of automobile accidents, over one-half remained unsettled two years later. For those involved in serious or fatal automobile accidents in 1967, the impact of the delay was devastating—45 percent had to reduce their standard of living, 14 percent had to move to cheaper housing, 29 percent missed credit payments, 30 percent had to draw on savings and in 22 percent of the cases a member of the victim's family was forced to look for work, the study shows. Thus the victims of accidents with extensive property damage, heavy medical expenses and major loss of income during rehabilitation were faced with bankruptcy, sale of homes or property or loss of savings—all because of a system built on the questionable "buy and bargain" practices of the marketplace.

The existing system is supposedly predicated on determining fault in court—tort liability—before compensation is awarded. But in fact, when the insurance company and its lawyers can see no monetary advantage in determining fault, little effort is made to do so.

But serious injury cases do end up in court to determine fault—and they have a detrimental effect on the entire legal system. Each year, automobile accidents contribute over 200,000 cases to the nation's already overcrowded court dockets—so that 17 percent of court room time is spent on auto cases.

The DOT report says insurance companies take advantage of case backlogs by using delaying tactics of their own "designed to protect the solvency of the company, to gain a stronger bargaining position with claimants or to stabilize the insurance companies' income." And of course the cost is staggering. In 1970, $9.5 billion in premiums were paid by policyholders for personal injury and property damage liability coverage, of which $2.9 billion was spent on legal expenses and related litigation fees, Department of Transportation figures show.

In short, the U.S. auto insurance system is not working. It affords more "protection" to certain vested interests than to the policyholding accident victim.

While it is a struggle for an insured driver to obtain compensation for an accident, he at least has some insurance—other consumers face a tremendous problem in getting insurance and keeping it at a rate they can afford.

The individual state insurance commissions control rates, or are supposed to. But the increase in insurance rates of some 70 percent over the past six years —twice the increase in the Consumer Price Index— shows that the states have not done their job. And cer-

337 INSURANCE

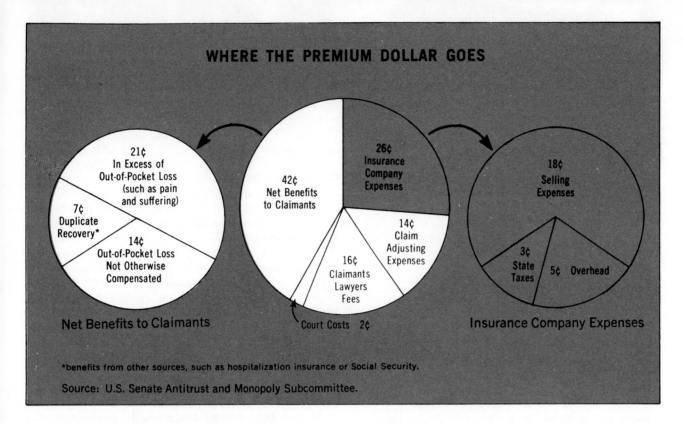

WHERE THE PREMIUM DOLLAR GOES

Net Benefits to Claimants

21¢
In Excess of
Out-of-Pocket Loss
(such as pain
and suffering)

7¢
Duplicate
Recovery*

14¢
Out-of-Pocket Loss
Not Otherwise
Compensated

42¢
Net Benefits
to Claimants

16¢
Claimants
Lawyers
Fees

26¢
Insurance
Company
Expenses

14¢
Claim
Adjusting
Expenses

Court Costs 2¢

Insurance Company Expenses

18¢
Selling
Expenses

3¢
State
Taxes

5¢ Overhead

*benefits from other sources, such as hospitalization insurance or Social Security.

Source: U.S. Senate Antitrust and Monopoly Subcommittee.

tain categories of motorists are discriminated against. For example, if you are 23 and married, even with an impeccable driving record you can expect to pay an average of $587 per year for automobile liability insurance in Los Angeles, $619 in Chicago, $706 in Philadelphia and $486 in Detroit. If you happen to earn $10,000 per year or less, as do three-fifths of the nation's families, you will pay a higher premium rate than those making over $10,000. That's because you constitute a higher risk than richer people—a risk which the insurance companies would be hard pressed to define.

Premium rates are based on risk categories, but these are often decided arbitrarily because they are derived from collective statistical data, such as age groups or income, and not on the merits of the individual's driving record. These artificial categories provide a rationale for the insurance companies to seek premium increases from the state insurance commissions. Thus many large companies seek to isolate themselves from any and all risk potential by selling policies only to the 100 percent, super-safe, low-risk applicants.

Yet even the low-risk policyholder can pay his premiums for many years, then have his policy cancelled at any time. The horror stories of abrupt cancellations are so widespread that Consumers Union, a private research organization, estimated that at least 14,000 persons were afraid to file accident claims in 1969 for fear their policy would be cancelled or their premium jacked up. One official of the National Association of Insurance Agents admits that there has undoubtedly been "too much cancellation and the problem has been quite bad for the past few years."

The practices of policy cancellation and non-renewal are everyday events in the insurance field as an increasing number of motorists are forced out of the insurance market. Once rejected or cancelled, these supposedly high-risk drivers either don't bother with insurance, creating a potential liability hazard to other motorists, or they are forced to apply to state-run insurance pools. Yet in 1969, 62 percent of the drivers assigned to the state-run pool in New York had clean driving records for the previous 36 months, as did 67 percent of those insured under the South Carolina state plan, 57 percent in North Carolina, 55 percent in Wisconsin and 50 percent in Pennsylvania. With too little help from state insurance commissions on eligibility and rates, the consumer is too often left in the hands of the insurance industry—and they are not necessarily "good" hands.

The 111 million U.S. motorists are becoming more aware that they are faced with a "legalized racket of colossal and cruel proportions," as Pennsylvania state insurance commissioner Herb Denenberg described the auto insurance industry. Public discontent is providing an ever-increasing impetus for reform.

Popular demand for change has led to a number of proposals, including the widely-discussed system of nationwide no-fault automobile insurance. Under the existing system, a person injured in an automobile accident theoretically cannot collect any compensation until fault has been determined—a procedure which has proven to be inefficient, unfairly advantageous to the insurance company and always costly and prolonged. In contrast the no-fault system would set up first-party insurance whereby those involved in automobile accidents would settle with their respective insurance companies or the company insuring the vehicle in which he or she was a passenger. An injured pedestrian would seek compensation from the company covering the vehicle.

No-fault is specifically designed to compensate the accident victim—immediately and justly—for all of his losses and, by avoiding expensive court litigation, reduce insurance costs, particularly legal fees. The amount the insurance company saves from reduced legal costs and other features of the system could be passed on to the policyholder in improved coverage and reduced premiums. Additionally those insured would be protected against many of the arbitrary methods characteristic of the present system, especially in policy cancellation, eligibility standards and cost.

While many insurance experts agree that no-fault is a responsive alternate to the present system, they have been thwarted in their efforts to enact no-fault legislation at the state level. In 1970-71, state lawyer groups and insurance lobbies succeeded in defeating reform legislation in seven states and contributed to the ineffectiveness of reforms in three other states. Only in two states—out of the 33 in which no-fault reform bills were introduced in that year—do viable no-fault programs now exist. The states' experience dictates that the only effective approach is congressional enactment of a nationwide, no-fault system of automobile insurance.

As a result of the chaos which has occurred at the state levels, advocates of reform have incorporated the no-fault concept into legislation now pending in Congress, sponsored by Senators Philip Hart (D-Mich.) and Warren Magnuson (D-Wash.) in the Senate and a slightly different version by Representatives John Moss (D-Calif.) and Bob Eckhardt (D-Tex.) in the House.

This national no-fault legislation would require that every automobile owner must have insurance to cover his personal injury losses, the losses of other drivers of his car, his passengers and pedestrians. Additionally, every insurance company must accept every applicant with a valid license at a premium based on the applicant's proper classification. Refusal, cancellation or non-renewal of the auto insurance policy would be forbidden for any reason other than revocation of driver's license or failure to pay premiums.

In general, the legislation provides for a package of comprehensive accident benefits which each insurance company is required to offer on a no-fault basis. These include:

● All medical and rehabilitation costs—plus after-tax wage losses up to $1,000 per month until return to work or appropriate gainful activity.

● Losses of future anticipated income or for impairment of earning capacity.

● All fees for any services needed during the recovery period which were normally provided by the insured party for themselves or family.

● "Stationary property" losses: all property losses other than on the motor vehicle in use or losses sustained in an accident with another moving vehicle, which would be paid to the other driver by his insurance company.

● Additional economic losses, pain and suffering losses of pedestrians or occupants not owning a motor vehicle.

● Recovery from an "assigned claims plan" of all damages caused by an uninsured vehicle, since the party insured is not responsible for the fact that the other car is uninsured. The assigned claims plan, to be established in every state, would be financed by assessing all insurance companies according to their premium volume in that state.

● Passenger-pedestrian fatality insurance would pay a death benefit over a period of time based on the decedent's monthly salary. The payment would not exceed $50,000 except in cases where a minor child is a survivor.

Concurrently, the insurance companies would also be required to make available certain optional features, such as additional coverage for those whose earnings exceed $1,000 monthly; collision insurance covering property damage to the policyholder's vehicle; coverage for tangible losses in excess of the no-fault policy; and coverage for intangible losses such as pain, suffering and inconvenience. Except in cases where a pain and suffering claim is determined by a court to be fraudulent, frivolous or excessive, the attorney's fees are to be paid by the insurance company.

To speed up payment, no-fault requires the insurance companies to compensate accident victims for their losses on at least a monthly basis. Claims unpaid after 40 days bear an interest rate of 1½ percent on the unpaid amount. The interest increases to 2 percent per month following the 61st day of non-payment and continues in effect until payment of the uncompensated amount is made. Additionally any dispute on the extent of loss can be resolved in court with the policyholder's legal fees being paid by his insurance company.

The national no-fault legislation also tackles the problem of the individual who has to pay premiums for medical benefits under both a health insurance plan and an automobile insurance policy but can only draw benefits from one or the other. Under no-fault, if a policyholder's health insurance covers medical costs in an accident, then the automobile policy premium is reduced proportionately. Additionally, the overlapping between collision insurance and property damage liability insurance would be eliminated through merger on a no-fault basis.

While the bill does not place stringent controls on premium rates, the state regulatory commissions are directed to establish a uniform classification system delineating the various risk categories of applicants. This would reverse the present discriminatory classification pattern under which companies compete for the best driving risks while other drivers are dumped into assigned risk pools—even though nothing may have changed but their age. The legislation also requires insurance groups to report to the state agencies their claims-loss data and categorical rate changes. This information would then be analyzed according to federally established guidelines for the states to use in their rate-making activities and to provide the public with information necessary for the consumer to compare price and quality of service.

As a result of these requirements, competition among insurance companies and the standardizing of premium rates, no-fault would bring about a greater degree of rate control than is now possible. Additionally, the mandatory public distribution of the insurance companies' financial and rate-making information is designed to insure that the state insurance commissions are responsive to the needs of the consumer as well as to the needs of the insurance companies.

Finally, one of the most innovative provisions of the no-fault plan is an attempt to reduce the automobile fatality rate through a pool of funds to provide better emergency service to victims. Since about 23 percent of automobile accident deaths are attributable in part to inadequate emergency medical care, the no-fault plan requires each insurance company operating within a state to invest one percent of the premiums it collects in that state in loans, grants or equity investments for new and improved emergency facilities—ranging from ambulances to helicopters.

The same arrangement would also work to improve rehabilitation facilities such as occupational or physical therapy centers. In each case the state would have the authority to raise the percentage contributions to 3 percent. Fewer fatality payments and getting the victims back on the job more quickly would save millions of dollars for the companies—savings which could then be passed on to the policyholder in the form of improved coverage and lower premiums.

In 1970 Massachusetts had the nation's highest rate of personal injury claims from automobile accidents. Ninety percent of the claims involved medical bills of less than $500. Minor rear-end accidents usually resulted in an agreement on a $500 to $600 settlement which insurance company officials said "was cheaper than investigating and contesting the claim." And the bulk of payments went to compensate questionable "pain and suffering" losses.

As a result, the claims frequency rate in Massachusetts spiraled to 1.3 claims per accident—three times the national average—but the actual amount paid per claim was well below the national standard. It was projected late in 1970 that motorists in Massachusetts would suffer a 20 to 25 percent increase in their automobile insurance premium rates in 1971.

However, on Jan. 1, 1971, a limited no-fault auto insurance system was initiated in the state. After six months of operation under this plan a comparison with the first six months of 1970 revealed:

- A 53.2 percent drop in the number of bodily injury claims cases, from 66,401 cases to 31,103.
- A 53.4 percent drop in claims paid, from 11,393 to 5,306.
- A decline in the average amount of claims paid by the insurance companies, from $343 to $160.

The reason for the decreases in all three categories was the decline in "pain and suffering" personal injury claims of the "nuisance" type. Previously, motorists had instinctively made this type of claim in comparatively minor accidents—with consequent higher insurance premiums for everyone in the state. In many instances these claims were inflated and, in most cases, overcompensated.

The Massachusetts plan has already saved motorists in the state an estimated $76 million in bodily injury insurance premiums; signficantly reduced nuisance claims; cancelled out a projected 1971 insurance rate increase of 20 to 25 percent; and reduced bodily injury insurance rates by 42.5 percent. It is also expected to bring about further rate reductions of as much as 26 to 30 percent in 1972. All this was accomplished even though the Massachusetts plan is limited in several respects in comparison with the proposed national no-fault legislation.

Puerto Rico has had a more comprehensive no-fault system in operation for about two years, with results similar to those in Massachusetts. The Puerto Rican plan—a mini-version of the no-fault bill pending in Congress—has already resulted in a number of premium rate reductions. Additionally 90 cents of every premium dollar is spent on accident loss compensation, further rate cuts are expected in the near future and the government agency administering the program is now seeking to raise the existing ceiling on benefits.

Far more importantly, however, is that despite an increase in the number of automobiles, the miles driven and accidents with injury in Puerto Rico, the total number of accident deaths has markedly decreased since the inception of no-fault 20 months ago. In 1969, Puerto Rico had 541 fatalities; in 1970, the first year of no-fault, the death rate declined to 481. In terms of registered automobiles the death rate has declined 31 percent and in terms of miles driven, it has declined 32 percent.

The Puerto Rican no-fault law pays the accident victim's medical bills quickly and fully. This provides funds which the hospitals and other medical facilities can then use for improving the emergency health care delivery system.

Although the Massachusetts and Puerto Rican plans have been successful and brought about the reforms which they were designed to accomplish, they are the only two reasonably effective no-fault reform laws in full operation. Florida has subsequently passed a no-fault law.

Other states have been unsuccessful in enacting no-fault. The few states that have enacted so-called reform plans have simply allowed drivers to buy additional medical payments and disability insurance without changing the underlying tort-liability arrangement. Under Oregon's recently enacted auto insurance reform law, for example, mandatory medical and wage benefits are to be added to each insurance policy on top of the existing tort-liability auto insurance system. The biggest contributor to inefficiency and waste—the auto accident lawsuit—has not been eliminated. Therefore, the new Oregon law will mean higher rates while the Massachusetts no-fault plan has already meant substantial savings for Massachusetts citizens.

Nationwide no-fault auto insurance has been endorsed by organized labor, a number of consumer groups, including the Consumer Federation of America, and numerous insurance companies and underwriters. But major opposition is still offered by lawyers, particularly the American Trial Lawyers Association.

The 26,000-member American Trial Lawyers Association has worked to defeat no-fault legislation wherever it appears. Working through well-financed lobbying fronts, such as LIFT (Lawyers Involved for Texas), ADOPT (Attorney's Dedicated to Ohio People Totally), FIRE (Foundation for Insurance Reform and Education in Maryland), the trial lawyers have contributed to the defeat of no-fault insurance plans—or helped to render them impotent—in over 30 states. While these state efforts are continuing, the ATLA and other lawyer groups are beginning to concentrate their resources on defeating the proposed national no-fault legislation.

A 1967 Department of Transportation study showed that over 20 percent of the fees of the legal profession in this country are derived from auto negligence cases. In the case of ATLA, over 90 percent of their members make part of their living from automobile claims and related legal action. In the past few years these fees have siphoned off about 35 percent of the total dollar amount paid to the accident victims. In 1970 these legal fees amounted to over $2.5 billion, including claims adjustment costs and court expenses, or about 60 percent as much as the accident victims received.

Among the arguments used by the ATLA in its concentrated effort to stop no-fault are several fallacies which, while easily refuted, are especially harmful because of their first-glance appeal.

No-fault insurance, they say, will encourage careless drivers by removing a deterrent to such behavior. In the first place, automobile insurance, like many other forms of insurance, is designed to afford the motorists a measure of protection from financial loss in an auto accident. It was not conceived as a deterrent to careless driving and nothing proves that the threat of a premium increase or a policy cancellation significantly influences driving behavior.

Another argument says ending the determination of fault will mean that safe drivers will be treated the same as the speeder, the drunk driver or the dragster. Again the point is that insurance is to protect, not to punish. It is the job of the courts to penalize reckless drivers; it is not the job of the insurance system. However, under no-fault, drivers with demonstrably poor driving records will be forced to pay higher premiums, as is now the case.

The victims of catastrophic accident would lose their "constitutional right to sue" for pain and suffering under no-fault, the lawyers also argue. But that "right to sue" actually means long delays in settlement; inadequate compensation for catastrophic losses; inflated payment for frequently non-existent pain and suffering; exorbitant legal fees, billions wasted in litigation and tremendous logjams in the courts. No-fault insurance, while curbing many of those abuses, would still allow the injured party to initiate a suit against his insurance company in order to recover losses for pain and suffering. Also, under no-fault, the accident victim would not have to pay the legal fees except in those cases where the court finds the claim to be fraudulent, frivolous or excessive. Thus the fraudulent "pain and suffering" claims and the "bargained" settlements would both be eliminated.

There are some exceptions to the ATLA's blind opposition to no-fault. The group's first president, Benjamin Marcus, who headed ATLA in 1946-47, has endorsed no-fault as "the only way out of a wasteful, irrelevant, burdensome and exasperating procedure now employed to compensate victims of automobile injury." Robert H. Joost, former editor of Trial, the ATLA magazine, has accused the trial lawyers of preferring "to vegetate in the pork barrel of automobile negligence work."

A canon of the legal profession's ethical code obligates lawyers to actively support legal reforms in the public interest and calls for social conscience to supersede personal financial interest, but the ATLA's stance on no-fault would be hard to square with that precept.

The lawyers' opposition to no-fault reform sets the stage for a legislative battle over what many consider the most important consumer legislation in recent years.

The crisis in auto insurance is increasingly aggravated by the growing number of automobiles and the miles driven each year in the United States. National no-fault auto insurance is the only alternative to the costly, unresponsive, wasteful and arbitrary system which the nation now has. Only under no-fault will accident victims be compensated promptly and justly, court congestion be reduced, insurance coverage and emergency medical care improved and insurance premiums lowered. National no-fault insurance will provide solutions to the problems which have plagued the accident victim, policyholder and consumer.

WHAZZIT?

INSURANCE UNDERWRITER

The company or individual that assumes a risk in return for a payment of a premium.

INSURANCE REGULATOR

A governmental agency or commission that oversees insurance activities in its area of control. Insurance is regulated at the state level.

SELF-INSUROR

A company or individual that acts as its own underwriter, accepting the risk of financial loss.

MALPRACTICE INSURANCE

Insurance protecting professional people from claims resulting from negligent performance of professional services.

POLICY

A printed document that states the terms of an insurance contract. It is issued by the company to the policyholder, generally the insured.

ANNUITY

An insurance contract that provides payment of a specific sum annually or periodically to a party called the annuitant for life or a specified number of years.

PENSION

An annuity that provides benefits to an employee who has retired becasue of age or disability. Social Security is in part a pension plan.

REINSURANCE

The sharing of a risk too large for one insurance company by transferring part of the risk to another company.

VARIABLE ANNUITY

An annuity contract in which the amount of payments of income fluctuates in relation to stock or bond market values, a cost of living index, or some other variable factor. It is thus similar in attributes to a mutual fund, a pooled investment fund.

GROUP ANNUITY

A pension plan providing annuities at retirement to a group of persons under a single master contract, with each member holding certificates stating their coverage. It is usually issued to an employer for the benefit of employees.

GROUP LIFE INSURANCE

Life insurance issued, usually without a medical examination, for a group of persons under a master policy, as for a group annuity.

CASH SURRENDER VALUE

The amount of money available in cash to the policyholder upon surrender of the life insurance policy before it becomes payable by death or maturity. Generally the policyholder may also borrow from the insuror up to this amount without surrendering the policy.

DISABILITY INCOME INSURANCE

An insurance policy that provides monthly payments for a specified period of time in event of the insured's physical disability. Many life insurance policies also provide a DISABILITY BENEFIT, a waiver of premium payments if the insured becomes permanently and totally disabled.

Careers In Insurance

Insurance is more than just selling policies. The insurance industry performs a wide variety of functions requiring personnel with highly varied areas of expertise. The sample organization chart for a large life insurance company should give you an idea of the range of jobs involved in the insurance business.

Within each of the listed operations are officers, managers, assistant managers, supervisors, and various specialists, as well as clerical and secretarial help.

About 35% of all insurance employees hold sales positions in local offices. Almost twice as many, however are therefore employed in other kinds of non-sales jobs, as underwriters, examiners, accountants, lawyers, engineers, statisticians, researchers, programmers, and investment, efficiency, and safety analysts.

More than a million persons are employed by the various insurance companies in the United States. And another quarter million people are engaged, generally independently, as brokers, agents, and in insurance-related services.

The number of people employed in the insurance industry has more than doubled since 1950. This rapid growth reflects the expanding opportunities in insurance careers.

Outlined below are some of the careers that are available in the insurance field.

SELLING CAREERS

An agent is a sales and service representative who works for one company. A broker is a sales and service representative who sells various kinds of insurance for several companies.

Together, they make up the industry's sales force -- the largest single category of professional career jobs in the industry.

Agents are paid commissions (a percentage of the premium paid on t the policies they sell) or a combination of commission and salary. Most brokers, however, are independent business-, men. Under contract with several companies, they may order policies from any of them to meet the insurance needs of various types of clients.

Selling insurance and servicing customer needs once policies are sold requires tact, patience, stability and reliability, and communications abilities. A college degree is not essential for selling insurance, but about 60% of agents today are college graduates.

NON-SALES CAREERS

Among the other jobs

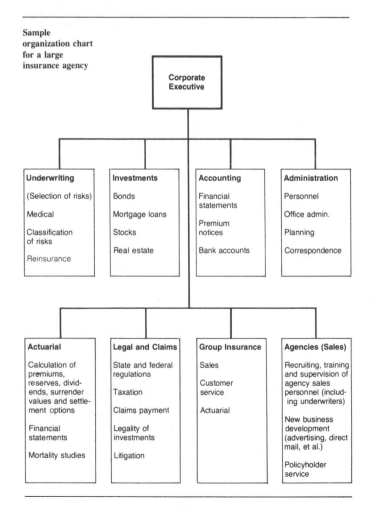

Sample organization chart for a large insurance agency

available in insurance are underwriter, actuary, investment specialist, and computer analyst. Naturally, managerial careers are available, but these usually start with one of the sales or non-sales careers.

UNDERWRITING

Someone has to make decisions on individual applications for insurance, determining the risks involved, in each request for protection. In life insurance, for example, an underwriter examines the individual's medical records and credit records and recommends his approval or rejection.

Underwriters specialize in different types of risks: life, fire, casualty, liability, automobile, and marine insurance. As a part of the work, underwriters gather information on risks by studying the company's experience, premiums paid, losses, and statistics on accidents, deaths, and the like.

CLAIMS AND MANAGEMENT

In insurance companies there is much detailed, but important and necessary work in processing payments of premiums, approval and payment of claims, direction of the activities of agents, and other business functions.

INVESTMENT SPECIALISTS

Because premiums are invested by insurors, reducing the cost of insurance, there are important opportunities

for specialists in making investments in real estate, bonds, and other revenue producing properties.

COMPUTER ANALYSTS

Becasue insurance companies are extensively using computers to determine appropriate premium rates and to handle the vast amount of paperwork involved in the business, there are wide opportunities for specialists in computer programming, operations, and systems analysis.

ACTUARIES

In life insurance, one of the most important occupations involves the collection and analysis of mortality statistics. Using mortality tables and mathematical tools, actuaries determine premium rates and help design changes in insurance policies. In addition to training and experience, actuaries must quality for membership in The Society of Actuaries by passing a series of tests.

The other side of the insurance field invovles insurance sales -- by AGENTS.

Insurance agents contact prospective policyholders and help them plan for thier financial security. It is a challenging job to convince people that they should forego other purchases in order to have protection against the "hazards of life."

Most insurance agents specialize in one or a few types of insurance, and represent only one

insurance company. Some agents share, or BROKER, their business with a number of companies.

Agents and brokers are paid by commission, a percentage of premiums paid on policies.

An agent may ear the designation of Chartered Life Underwriter (CLU) by passing examinations and other requirements set by the American College of Life Underwriters. The CLU is the insurance field's counterpart to the CPA.

MORE INFORMATION

If you would like more information about careers in insurance, there are a number of sources that you may consult.

For information on life and health insurance careers, write the Institute of Life Insurance, 277 Park Avenue, New York, NY 10017.

For information on property, homeowners' and casualty insurance, write the Insurance Information Institute, 110 William Street, New York, NY 10038.

The National Association of Life Underwriters is an organization primarily interested in selling. Its address is 1922 F Street NW, Washington, D.C. 20006..

For information on how to become an actuary, write the Society of Actuaries, 208 South LaSalle Street, Chicago, Illinois 60604.

Of course, you may know individuals who are in the insurance field. They are your best bets for helping you consider your career interests in this field.

CONSIDER

1. Why do auto insurance companies have higher rates for younger drivers?

2. Why are insurance companies interested in safer automobiles?

3. What do insurance companies do with the premiums they receive from policyholders?

4. What kinds of insurance does a small business need to have to protect it from major financial loss?

5. Why would a large corporation insure itself?

6. Why is the federal government in the insurance business, providing social security insurance?

7. Would you consider a career in insurance? Why or why not?

8. Do you see anything wrong with the concentration of assets among so few, massive life insurance companies in the United States? What risks do you see? What do you think can be done? Why?

9. Why do you think life insurance companies invest so heavily in bonds and mortgages rather than in more speculative issues such as common stock?

10. Is life insurance like savings? What are the similarities and differences?

CHALLENGES

Examine examples of current advertising for automobile insurance. What features are emphasized? Do you feel these points are important?

Find out what insurance coverage you have against injury or illness (medical and hospitalization insurance). In your evaluation, is your coverage adequate? Explain. Would expanded coverage be available to you at an increased premium? Would you add to your present coverage? Explain.

Find out what a straight life insurance policy would cost you (per $1000) today and compare the cost for the same policy proceeds (at age 65) if you were to purchase the policy ten years from now. Would there be any advantage to you to purchase the policy now instead of later? Explain.

Examine the annual report of a company that writes primarily property-casualty insurance. Does the company find all lines of insurance profitable or does it actually lose money when it writes some kinds of insurance policies? In 1975 and 1976, such companies were losing money on most kinds of policies because of inflation.

RECAP

Insurance is a means by which people may share the burden of risk of possible financial losses. Through insurance a group assumes the responsibility for losses if and when they occur.

One type of loss that we all face is the loss of life -- death. We seek insurance protection in the form of life insurance to assure some degree of financial security for our family in the event of our death. In exchange for payment of premiums, insurance companies provide this protection through insurance policies. The premiums charged are determined statistically through the use of mortality tables. The cost of a given amount of life insurance is normally greater for older persons because life expectancy declines with age.

Life insurance also offers a means for providing income -- as for retirement. Whole-life and endowment insurance are two general types of insurance that build up a cash or income value to the policyholder as well as provide life insurance protection in the event of death. Any contract that provides payments over a period of time on the basis of mortality is called an annuity. Many insurance policy contracts provide both annuity and insurance benefits.

In this chapter we have discussed the operations of insurance companies, comprising a major area of business activity in our economy. Allstate, for example, provides a wide range of services and has grown rapidly in areas of automobile and life insurance. We noted that insurance companies have an extremely large amount of capital that they must invest in order to maintain their profitability. Insurance companies are business enterprises and must be profitable if they are to survive -- even if they are mutual companies without stockholders.

Financial losses covered by insurance have soared in recent years. For example, automobile repair costs have spiralled. At the same time, premiums have had to rise and coverage limited. If insurance is to continue to serve its functions effectively, major changes may be needed. One dramatic change in automobile insurance is the move towards no-fault insurance. As we discussed, this approach removes the need for placing blame before claims are paid. Thus, legal and administrative costs are reduced and the losses reimbursed more promptly.

The field of insurance offers a variety of challenging career opportunities: underwriting, claims, management, investment, computer analysis, and actuarial science. If you want to sell insurance, you may be an agent, a broker, or have a particular specialty. You may earn the designation of Chartered Life Underwriter (CLU) by passing examinations and meeting other requirements.

WORKSHEET NO. 12

NAME_____

INSTRUCTOR'S NAME_____

DATE_____

1. What impact do you think no-fault insurance will have on the automobile insurance companies?

_____

2. What are the similarities between a mutual insurance company and a stock company? What are the differences?

3. Why are some types of life insurance policies viewed as forms of savings?

---

4. In choosing an insurance company (either for life insurance or for automobile insurance), what information would you want to help you make your decision?

CHAPTER 13

Computers And Business

The computer is a major tool used by American business. Without computers we simply would not be able to do many of the things we do. Not only would costs of processing data, conducting necessary analyses, and controlling business operations be progibitively high without computers, but it is likely that we would not be able to do many things at all.

Can you imagine our sending a man to the moon without the use of computers? Or sending monthly bills to three million different customer accounts of an oil company? Or list all of the phone calls you make each month and bill you for them on the basis of distance and how long you talked? Or calculating payrolls? Or processing checks in banks?

Without computers could Ford keep track of costs? Could Sears keep track of its inventories? Computers are part of our economic system today -- and part of our life.

The largest computer manufacturer in the world is IBM -- International Business Machines Corporation. During the past half century this firm has set the pace in the design, production, and sale of computer systems and related services. At the same time, the competition in the computer industry has stiffened, and now tough new competition is emerging in foreign countries -- markets where American-made computers have been sold.

Computers help managers solve many different kinds of problems, ranging from the fairly routine to the extremely unusual and non-recurring. Common problems include replacement and maintenance of equipment and machinery, deciding how many tellers or clerks to have (waiting line problems), how much inventory to order, allocation problems (how best to invest limited financial capital), and pricing problems. Unusual and unprogrammed types of problems include decisions about the future strategy for a business, whether to relocate a plant, whether to enter a new product line, whether to merge, whether to go bankrupt, and human problems such as who should be the next chairman of the board.

Management science techniques, and particularly operations research techniques are systematic problem solving methods that can help managers solve problems using computers.

The promise of using computers has been great; the potential continues to appear significant. Careers in computer fields offer challenges to individuals who want to help the computer users find ways to make better application of the new technologies that are emerging so rapidly.

The growth of the computer industry and the related use of computers in business have not always been with planning and control. In anticipation of the benefits promised by computerization, companies have frequently applied new data processing and communications technology without fully realizing its impact and problems.

How far we can go in using computers in managing business organizations is a tough question. Computers are not magic for management, but neither are they a menace.

The effective use of computers in business requires managers to know what computers are, what they can do, what they cannot do, and what the costs are.

Properly managed, computer systems can be a significant aid to executives. Both small business enterprises and the very largest corporations in America may benefit from this new technology. But machines -- computers -- cannot manage companies. People manage; computers help.

In This Chapter

Will Business Be Managed By Machines?

Although computers were invented for primarily scientific purposes, it soon became apparent that widespread uses were possible for business and industry.

Much of the work that has been done manually in business over the years can be done more quickly and efficiently by machine. Examples are accounting, bookkeeping, billing, inventory control, personnel record keeping, payroll, and disbursements.

The beauty of the computer is that it will do what it is told, and only what it is told. It is programmed to perform a task in a certain way, and the task may be performed over and over thousands of times and it will be done exactly the same way each time.

Further, more complex tasks may be programmed and handled with lightening speed, relative to the time it would take for people to do it manually. The size and complexity of a problem is little match for a computer.

SIMON SAYS

Accordingly management and computer expert Herbert Simon has said that the organizations of the future will be run by a higher ratio of machines to men than is characteristic of organizations today.

The people in this system will play three kinds of roles:

-- fewer "workmen" as a part of the labor force. Indeed, physical labor is less prominent as a percent of our nation's employment. -- there will be more people whose task is to keep the system operating by preventive and remedial maintenance. Machines will play an increasing role, of course, in maintenance functions, but machine powers require people powers to keep them working. -- there will be more people at professional levels, responsible for the design of products, for the design of the productive processes, and for general management.

The problems that managers at various levels face may be classified according to how structured, how routine, and how cut-and-dried they are when they come up. Managers have, on the one hand, highly programmed decisions to make: the routine buying of office supplies or the pricing of standard products sold. On the other hand are unprogrammed decisions: basic, once-in-a-lifetime decisions to introduce a new product line, relocate the business, etc. Between these two extremes are many kinds of the other decisions with blends of programmed and unprogrammed -- routine and nonroutine elements.

Why is this important? Computers affect decision making. The programmed type of decisions are more easily handled by EDP, and

are the aspects of business that can be computerized. The unprogrammed decisions may be aided by computer-provided management information, but remain largely human decisions.

DECISIONS BY COMPUTERS

Can computers make decisions on their own? If we program computers to define problems, analyze alternatives, and select optimal solutions, certainly computers are capable of decision making -- by the very definition of the process of decision making.

We are in the early stages of a significant technological revolution in decision making. It is very likely that at some future point in time we will be able to say that computers will be able to make all management decisions, programmed and unprogrammed decisions. It will be technically possible, and the key factor will be the economic cost-benefit of doing so rather than the feasibility.

MANAGEMENT SCIENCE/O.R.

On the programmed end of decision making, managers are relying increasingly on MANAGMENT SCIENCE, the systematic process of applying scientific methods to problem solving and decision making. Where problems can be defined in quantitative terms, such systematic decision making may be applied, and ultimately made a part of the computer program.

One area of management science is OPERATIONS RESEARCH, an approach for solving complex (but routine or programmed) problems using models and computer assistance. O.R. is a systematic problem solving process, often involving a team of specialists devoting in-depth attention to finding a way to handle an unusual (sticky) problem that is expected to recur.

In 1915, Thomas Edison studied antisubmarine warfare; During World I F. W. Lancaster developed models of combat superiority and victory based on relative and effective firepower; in 1915 F. Harris derived the first economic order quantity equation for planning inventory replacements. Studies starting in 1905 of telephone calls into a switchboard formed the basis of many "queueing" or waiting line problem solutions.

It was in World War II that O.R. really took hold, with teams of problem solvers formed to find solutions to important defense-related problems (such as the depth that depth charges should be fired for optimal impact). A lot of the work really involved common sense, but it's funny how hard it is to come up with that unless you follow a tough, scientific approach to defining and analyzing the problem.

Operations research involves construction of a model -- a quantitative picture (usually with computer help) -- so that

the best solution may be identified and then applied.

Today O.R. is accepted as a basic technique in the management science toolkit of businesses. Inventories, production scheduling, allocation of resources, waiting lines, teller scheduling in banks, construction sequencing, replacement of components or machinery, preventative maintenance, bidding and labor relations strategies, quality control, and many other recurring business problems are solved every day through the use of such techniques.

The unprogrammed types of decisions that managers face are less easy to solve. We're in the process of developing the kinds of problem solving techniques needed for them, but that's still boldly futuristic for common use. Simon calls the set of techniques we need "HEURISTIC PROGRAMMING". For the one-shot problems, the questions are tough to identify, let alone the answers. Computers are not yet all that helpful for these unprogrammed, or "genuine" kinds of problems. But in the future, we may expect computers to be at the center of the action.

TRENDS

There will likely be longer-range planning by businessmen as computers become used more extensively. We have already seen a boom in planning, with improved budgeting, planning, and control practices resulting from improved computer-generated reporting.

As automated systems

take over the minute-to-minute operations of the office and factory, the people in the systems will be able to spend more time planning ahead. In fact, the factories may pretty much run themselves. (Note the oil refineries that run today with nearly one-tenth as many employees as they did a decade ago before computers were so extensively applied.)

Because of computerized information systems, managers have much more extensive information available for their use, and are able to better manage on the basis of exceptions -- focusing on problems instead of the routine operations. In the factory and in the office (particularly in accounting, inventory control, purchasing, and personnel) computers and other technological aides have relieved people of many routine tasks.

Business will surely be managed with the aid of machines -- but will not be managed by them. Managers are essential to providing the judgment needed to know when to use the computer and when not to, and to help solve the unprogrammed decisions that are less amenable to available decision making tools.

What Is A Computer?

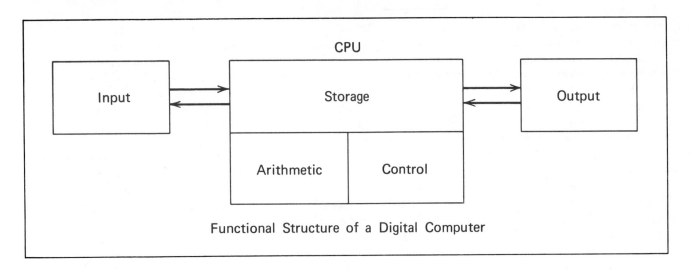

CPU

Input

Storage

Output

Arithmetic | Control

Functional Structure of a Digital Computer

A computer is basically a giant adding machine. It accepts data, processes this data, and turns out some type of useful result. It has its own language, called binary code, that it uses to translate data into a form it can understand.

The central processing unit of a computer is electronic. That is, the data are stored as electronic impulses on tapes (like recording tape), discs, or drums. This makes storage extremely compact and retrieval and analysis rapid.

There are DIGITAL computers and there are ANALOG computers. Digital computers handle and calculate data as discrete values (like 1,2,3, 5.75, words, letters, etc.). Analog computers handle continuously variable quantities and are generally used to control some physical process, such as chemical processes and petroleum refining operations.

Most computers are general purpose computers. That is, they can perform a variety of tasks well. For example, a business computer used to process payroll, customer billings, inventory reports, and other types of information needed by managment would be a general purpose computer. One designed to run an oil refinery, and nothing else, would be a specific purpose computer. Specific purpose computers are often faster, but do not have the flexibility that general purpose computers have.

Computers are used for scientific and business purposes. Business computers require more storage capacity; scientific computers emphasize analysis of complex problems. Business computers are commonly used for scientific purposes, however.

A complete computer system has both HARDWARE and SOFTWARE. Hardware are the actual pieces

of equipment, including the following:

INPUT: receives the data to be processed by reading punched cards, magnetic tape, or other form.

MEMORY: as data are received, the input places each bit into a storage unit called the memory, in such a way that it can be retrieved almost instantly when needed.

CONTROL: this unit receives the PROGRAM or directions from memory and tells the computer what to do with the data it has received and stored.

ARITHMETIC UNIT: this part of the computer performs the necessary mathematical or other processing operations on the data and sends the results back to memory or forward to output.

OUTPUT: the results of the calculations are presented in the form of printed pages,

353 COMPUTERS AND BUSINESS

punched or printed cards, or in other ways, as directed by the control unit.

As shown in the figure, these pieces of equipment comprise the structure of a digital computer. The storage or memory, the control unit, and the arithmetic unit make up the computer's CPU -- the central processing unit.

Computers are told what to do. They will do only what they are told to do and nothing more. By definition, then computers do not make mistakes -- only people do.

Each type of computer task is programmed (planned) in detail in a code language. The equipment and supplies used for this purpose and for the purpose of debugging (finding and correcting errors in the program) constitute the computer's SOFTWARE. Software makes the hardware in a computer system useful.

The languages used in programming computers are selected according to the particular purposes served and the type of hardware. Several special languages have been developed, each of which is preferable for a particular need. Fortran is basically an engineering and scientific language. The name comes from "FORmula TRANslation. Cobol is basically a business language. It's name comes from "COmmon Business Oriented Language."

The most common form of computer input is the punched card. A punched card is illustrated below. Holes punched in these cards, in various locations and combinations, can represent an endless variety of things such as names, numbers, dollars, tools, cities, products, or books.

It really works very simply. Each hole is either punched -- or it isn't. Thus, it can

represent a two-way (binary) alternative of zero or one. One is represented on a card by a hole or in a computer CPU by a clockwise flow of electricity or by a surge of electricity. A zero is represented by the opposite conditions.

Thus by combining the punched holes in a card or electrical impulses on magnetic tape, a complete set of symbols may be produced as shown on the card illustrated.

This constitutes the computer's basic alphabet. To communicate -- to receive and process data according to a program -- a computer needs this kind of input.

Inside a computer the binary code can be used directly, but it is difficult for humans to work with it. It would look like the following if it were written out:100101110001010. For example, the binary number 10111 is the

The Punched Card

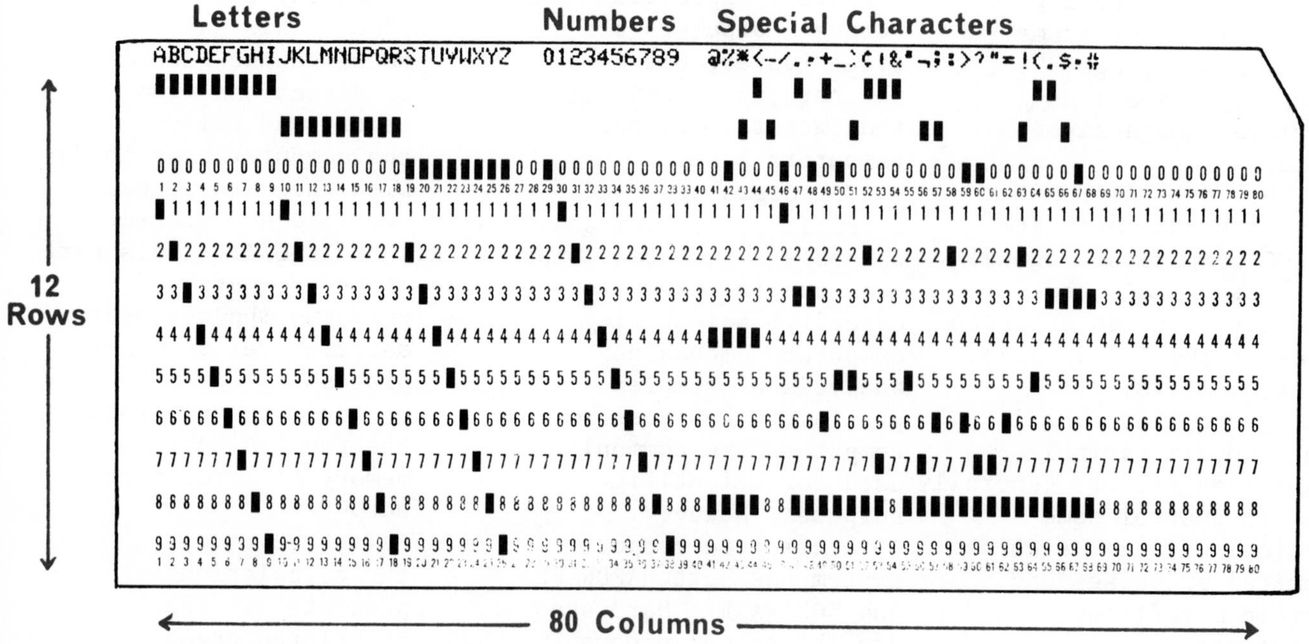

Letters   Numbers   Special Characters

12 Rows

80 Columns

equivalent of the number 23.

Punched cards may also be used as a form of computer output. The most common output form, however, is the printed page. Today's advanced computers can print as many as 2,000 lines per minute, with each line containing about 25 words. That's fast typing.

Even faster yet is a new printer that employes laser technology and is able to print at the amazing speed of 13,360 lines per minute.

Results may also be presented in the form of magnetic tape or on various types of visual display equipment. Many managers now have computer terminals with keyboards (to type in data and programmed instructions for the computer) and screens (where the results are displayed). right in their offices. It's like having a typewriter and a television hooked up to a computer.

New products are being introduced that should make the computer even more accessible to the manager. Portable computer weighing about 50 pounds are now on the market. This computer can be moved from office to office or even out into the field.

Smaller systems are being developed to provide computer power to small businesses that cannot justify the expense of a major computer system. And desk top models of computers are being introduced to put complete computer facilities in the hands of the manager who needs the infomration.

WHAZZIT?

EDP

Electronic Data Processing. The government often calls it ADP, automatic data processing. It refers to all types of information coding, storage, retrieval, analysis, and reporting, using electronic data processing equipment.

HARDWARE

The physical machinery and equipment that is used in data processing. These may be mechanical, electronic, magnetic, or electrical devices. An example is a machine that reads and punches cards.

SOFTWARE

All other components of an EDP system, such as the programs, routines and procedures which support a computer system and allow it to operate.

COMPUTER UTILITY

A service company that provides computer services to customers on a fee basis. IBM's Service Bureau Corporation, which was recently sold to Control Data Corporation is a computer utility.

TELECOMMUNICATIONS

Sending computer information over telephone lines. This allows data to be sent to a computer from a great distance away and allows two or more computers to communicate with each other.

PROGRAM

A complete plan for the solution of a problem. A program is a complete sequence of machine instructions and routines needed to solve a problem.

Pascal, Babbage, Hollerith: Or Who's Who In Computer History

Back about 1650, a French philosophy and mathematician named BLAISE PASCAL invented a mechanical machine that would add and subtract numbers. It would, he said, perform all of the operations of arithmetic without any effort. His interest stemmed, in large part, from assisting his father, a local tax collector.

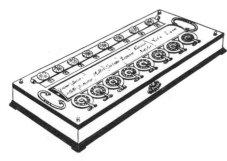

Pascal's Calculator

Not many years later, in 1671, a German mathematician named GOTTFRIED WILHELM LEIBNITZ announced his invention, a machine that would perform more complicated operations than Pascal's calculator. It could add, subtract, multiply, divide, and calculate the roots of numbers.

CHARLES BABBAGE, a British mathematician, is recognized as the father of the modern computer. With the financial support of the British government, Babbage started to build a "Different Engine," a device for calculating numbers using differences. As he progressed, he realized that he had a better idea.

He developed the concept of the digital computer, which he called the "Analytical Engine." This machine was basically the same as today's computer. It used punched cards as input, had data storage (mechanically, though), and had a stored program to control the analytic operations of the machine. The machine was designed to be steam powered.

Babbage's problem was that the machine he conceived simply could not be built. The precision tooling necessary just was not available at that time. It was not until a century later that people began to realize the importance of Babbage's idea.

At the time of the 1890 Census, the United States Government realized that existing manual means of tabulating data would be too slow because of the country's expanding population. In fact, it was estimated that such a tabulation might still be going on when it was time for the 1900 Census.

An agent of the Census Department, HERMAN HOLLERITH, set about the job of developing a machine that could be used to spped

could be used to speed up the tasks involved. He devised a punched-card machine that could count, tabulate, and sort cards faster than any existing machine.

He patented his machine in 1889, and continued to improve it over the years. His company, Tabulating Machine Company merged with another company in 1911 to form the company which was later named International Business Machines Corp.

During the 1910 Census another man invented a machine to process the voluminous census data. He patented it and organized a company to manufacture and sell the device. JAMES POWER's company, the Powers Account Machine Company, was later merged with the Remington Rand Corporation.

The first modern computers were developed by Howard Aiken of Harvard

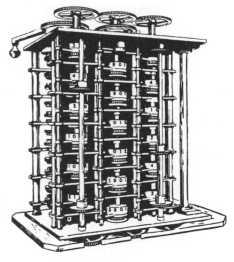

Babbage's Difference Engine

University with the technical support of IBM. The Mark 1, was an electro-mechanical calculator based on Babbage's ideas. The Mark 2, build in 1947, three years later, was a similar but faster machine, using electrical relays. These machines were termed AUTOMATIC SEQUENCE CONTROLLED CALCULATORS.

The first all-electronic computer (vacuum tubes were used instead of relays) was the ELECTRONIC NUMERICAL INTEGRATOR AND CALCULATOR, known as ENIAC. Developed at the University of Pennsylvania by John W. Mauchley (pronounced "mockley") and J. Presper Eckert in 1947, the ENIAC put calculating speeds into the milli-second range (thousanth of a second).

The company that was formed by Mauchley and Eckert to market their computer was later purchased by Remington Rand Corporation, and later became the Univac Division of the Sperry Rand Corporation. In 1951, the Universal Automatic Computer (UNIVAC 1) was produced for sale.

In the following year, the Computer Research corporation (later National Cash REgister) introduced an electronic computer. It was not until 1953 that IBM presented its first computer, the IBM-701. Although late on the scene, IBM soon emerged as the leader in the new computer industry.

WHAZZIT?

PROGRAMMER

A person who writes programs.

SYSTEM

A network of hardware and software necessary to solve a problem or serve a desired function.

SYSTEMS ANALYST

A person who determines what is being done, what can be done, and the best means of accomplishing the desired outcome with the system available.

DATA BANK

Infromation stored for a specific application.

ON-LINE SYSTEM

A computer system in which the input and output hardware are linked directly to the computer, and are at the location where the data is originated. For example, an executive may have a remote terminal (that looks like a typewriter or perhaps a TV screen) through which he may communicate readily with the computer.

CYBERNETICS

A process of communications and control using abstract mathematical models. Cybernetics implies some type of feedback which provides self-regulation, such as a thermostat provided on a home furnace.

Using Computers

A key factor in successful managment of a business is the availability of complete, timely, and accuarate information needed for management decisions and actions.

A small company may have an advantage over large, complex organizations to the extent that top managers know fully what is going on. In large organizations, managers must rely on information systems to keep informed.

Every manager has some type of information system. It may be the result of personal contacts or a more formal system. "If you know the right people you can find out what you want to know in a hurry."

It may be tied to a computer, providing current operating and financial information, personnel data, and other information and analyses. In general, a manager's information system may be improved by the use of computers. The computer aids the organization's existing communications network and the informal contacts of managers.

Of course, using computer-generated information calls for new managerial abilities -- to seek information and to use the analytic tools available to him.

For this reason, being a manager today is a particular challenge, different than it has been in past decades. You do not have to be able to write Cobol or Fortran, but you do have to be able to ask for the information you need and be able to use the output once you have it. Managers often fall down in one or both of these areas. There are many stories of managers who demand large volumes of operating reports on a weekly or even a daily basis, but rarely scan them. Even more rarely do they use the reports in making decisions or for planning future business actions.

It takes experience and skill to develop and use effectively management information systems. The capabilities of computers are barely being tapped today.

"The machine then selects the likely equations from a complicated pattern of theoretical probables. It calculates these, and the correct answer is printed on a card. Then our Miss Swenson files them God knows where, and we can never find the damn things again."

Drawing by Chon Day, © 1971 The New Yorker Magazine Inc.

EVOLVING USES OF EDP

Electronic data processing didn't just suddenly pop into the executive suite, you know. The EDP function in business started with the most basic clerical applications and evolved into broader management applications.

Naturally, the nature of applications in a business grow in parallel with the level of hardware, software, and systems expertise.

In an era of remote computer terminals, personalized data systems for executives, and integrated data bases, executives are often lost in the semantic smog of progress in EDP.

To make sense of the practical uses of computers, it is helpful to consider several generations of computer applications, representing different levels of technological development.

The five generations of computer systems described below were identified in an article by a consultant, Frederic G. Withington, of Arthur D. Little, Inc. He is an expert on computers and the data processing industry.

1. "Gee Whiz": 1953-1958

When businesses first acquired computers, the initial applications were in the financial area -- payroll, billing, accounting, because these were the most formalized systems in the company and the easiest to program.

Computers were therefore noticed by management when things went wrong --

late payrolls, mistakes on bills, etc. There were also concerns about the possible effects of EDP on employment -- displacing clerical workers, although these concerns were rarely justified.

2. The Paper Pushers 1958-1966

By the time most manufacturers had families of computers using transistors, bigger core memories, and superior logic, companies applied their fancier systems to larger tasks. Among these were airline reservation systems, stock-quote systems, on-line inventory systems, and other "big batch" tasks.

Software also came into use in a big way, with generalized programs useful in handling diverse tasks. But the emphasis still was on handling large volumes of paperwork -- Computerizing the filing cabinets of business!

3. Communicators 1966-1974

As applications expanded in many companies, computer systems functions were consolidated into centrally controlled regional or corporate centers with remote terminals. Data collection is through networks, much of the data processing is through remote terminals.

Maintaining an image of usefulness and responsiveness to managers became an important part of the EDP responsibility. And with growing demands on the function, this was a tough job -- response times were tough to shorten.

4. Information Custodians 1974-1982

Here's where we're at today, with a balanced distribution of management functions using EDP. Broader policy and longer-range decisions were put in headquarters; tactical decisions were moved out to the field. Instead of terminals, computer satellites provide operational dispatching, full transaction processing.

With large files and very large systems, companies are using EDP on a broad, integrated basis.

5. Action Aids 1982-?

In the future, computers will be based on magnetic bubble or laser-holographic technology, with private information and simulation systems for managers. Computers will be linked among companies, providing a broad network of data systems on a nation-wide, even world-wide basis.

Computers will provide semiautomatic operations decision making, with planning initiated by many individuals. The computer will serve as a medium of communication and group decision making at all levels, reducing the reliance of managers on a central EDP group. Use of the computer in business will therefore be virtually commonplace as a tool of everyday practices.

THE SHADIER USES

Then there are also the uses of computers by the crooks in the business world. With computers, modern swindles are harder to uncover than the old kinds. Computers make fraud easier to commit -- for someone who controls them or knows how to run them.

Further, a virtually unlimited amount of money can be taken without any relative increase in the danger of being detected. Once a crook has built an entry into a computer system, it's built in permanently and the dollar amounts taken don't show up.

As computer systems grow more sophisticated, and as it takes more know-how, those who can pull off a theft are going to dip in for bigger and bigger amounts.

For example, a teller in the Union Dime Savings Bank in New York was charged with stealing more than $1.5 million from the bank's deposits. He allegedly shuffled hundreds of accounts and fed false information into the bank's computers so that the accounts appeared untampered with whenever quarterly interest payments were due.

In the famous Equity Funding case, phony customers' pledges of phony mutual fund shares as collateral for phony loans to finance the purchase of many millions of dollars in phony insurance ultimately became numbers on a computer tape, which then printed out phony assets, enabling the company to report steadily increasing earnings.

Audit procedures have been changed to help track such felonious activities. Now a computer leaves a printed record of its transactions -- a printout, and special audit "trails".

Passwords, jumbled data, fictitious accounts, and rotation of programmers and other staff are all tools to keep ahead of the crooks.

In the Equity Funding case, however, it is an employee who sounded the alarm -- not the formal audit systems.

The savings bank teller was observed placing bets on horse races with a book-making operation that came under police investigation. He was betting $30,000 a day, and thus drew some suspicion.

Toward a More Productive World

The equation is timeless: our standard of living depends upon the bounty of nature, multiplied by our ability to enhance it with muscle, machines and brainpower.

Productivity is a measure of how well we do that. It is a basic yardstick of economic progress.

Worldwide, there is a gap between the desire for higher standards of living and the productivity levels that will make them possible. Productivity breakthroughs are important to any closing of that gap, to the efforts of the developing nations to solve the problems of poverty and hunger, and to the battle against inflation and recession.

Historically, increased productivity has come not just from working harder, but from working smarter–the wheel, the lever, movable type and the steam engine are landmark examples.

Modern technology has been responsible for many of our productivity increases in recent years, especially in the manufacturing of goods and in the mining and petroleum industries. In the service industries–government, finance, health, education, wholesale and retail trade and personal services–productivity increases through technology are more difficult to achieve. These areas are growing rapidly in the more advanced nations, however, and the opportunity for productivity gains is great.

The computer is one of the basic tools of our age. It can speed the answers to difficult problems, and make complex situations more manageable. The same can be said of office products which simplify the management and production of paperwork.

IBM's customers, through their creative application of such devices, are demonstrating that every day. Computers are helping design engineers test concepts without building expensive prototypes. They are helping farmers raise more abundant crops by providing information on the best land-use patterns. They are helping manufacturers increase production yields and improve product quality, while conserving raw materials and energy. They are helping hospitals improve medical care by relieving doctors and nurses of many administrative duties.

Advances in technology have made the computer itself more productive. In 1952 it cost $1.26 to do 100,000 multiplications on an IBM computer. Today they can be done for a penny on a modern large-scale computer system.

A dozen years ago even the least expensive IBM computer was beyond the financial reach of many smaller firms. Now, models with comparable capacity are available for a fraction of the cost and are proving useful for a great variety of tasks.

IBM is applying the productivity of computers and office products to its own operations, developing word processing and management information systems and applying them in areas ranging from the branch office to the production floor.

Above all, IBM is dedicated to helping its customers make their own productivity breakthroughs. Their achievements have been great, and great potential remains for further gains.

Productivity has been described as the world's biggest undeveloped resource. At IBM, our goal is to help customers develop it to its maximum.

How A Tiny Store Keeps The Books

Since May, 1970, Nassau Liquors, a tiny retailing establishment in Princeton, N.J., has been operating on a computerized management information system that far bigger companies might envy. On Monday and Thursday mornings, the store manager gets a neatly collated stack of reports current to the close of business the previous day. The stack includes complete records of sales and inventory, reorder notification for low stock, customer billing statements, aged balances, and even a sales analysis of profit and return on investment summarized by product type.

For a retailer of Nassau Liquors' size (annual gross: around $400,000), such a thorough system with such fast turnaround is something like a vision of the future in action. It is certainly an objective that many big computer·and cash register makers, including giants like International Business Machines Corp., National Cash Register Co., and the Friden Div. of Singer Co., have worked toward for years.

Surprisingly, Nassau Liquors' service comes from another tiny outfit (five employees) called Transaction Data Corp. which has developed a system that has left some veterans in the computer industry a bit wide-eyed. While the system uses an electronic cash register from one of the big manufacturers—Friden's new MDTS (for modular data transaction system)—the heart of it is a large and complex computer program put together by one remarkable young man, Thomas R. Pirelli, a 23-year-old Princeton graduate of the class of 1969.

Genesis. Pirelli began working on the system while he was a student (it was his senior engineering thesis), founded his company 18 months ago, and now has a working operation. For all this, Transaction Data has spent only $150,000. The system uses large computers—IBM System/360 Model 50s and up. But the little company has no intention of owning its own machines for a very long time, if ever. Its economics are based on buying contract time on other companies' large machines at bargain rates during night shifts and on weekends—and there is a huge surplus of such time available.

Winning aid. When he chose the formidable thesis project of designing an electronic data collection and processing system in his junior year, Pirelli was unaware of the extensive developments that cash register and computer companies already had under way. He tackled both the terminal design and the computer programming to back it up, and by the summer of 1968 the data collection terminal was emerging as a handmade prototype. Impressed with Pirelli's work, Assistant Dean Howard Menand, Jr., steered his student to Princeton Applied Research, Inc., on the chance he might get some backing to continue his project and develop a commercial product. On Sept. 5, 1968, Pirelli had what he calls his "big day." He went to Princeton Applied Research, which in turn steered him to a reliable Wall Street investment firm. There, he was told that his project was not far enough along to warrant the firm's backing, but that it might interest Morton Collins, president of Data Science Ventures, Inc., a Princeton-based venture-capital company. Collins was impressed and offered to study the project closely. After finding the financial and management help he thought he needed in only a few hours, Pirelli then logged his second big accomplishment of the day. He drove out to Princeton airport and made his first solo flight as a student pilot.

Hiring a manager. "I didn't know anything about running a business or marketing" says Pirelli, "so we had to find someone who did." He and Collins decided the ideal candidate would be someone with an engineering degree, a business school graduate degree, and management or marketing experience in some allied field. Such men were scarce in 1968 and 1969, and the search seemed almost fruitless. Pirelli himself finally turned to the Princeton master list of graduates in general engineering and went through all the names from 1950 to 1960. About four fit the profile, two in particular.

Pirelli called them up, posing as a student looking for advice. The first candidate he rejected on the basis of the phone call; the second, William Rosser, then marketing manager at nearby Electronic Associates, Inc., he talked into an appointment. He liked Rosser, so Collins and DSV went to work to recruit him. Says Rosser, now president of Transaction Data, "I took Tom on the plant tour and all that, and we talked quite a bit. I never had any idea he was interviewing me for the job of running his company."

A year ago in January, Pirelli was faced with a decision he calls the toughest in his life. At the National Retail Merchant's Assn. meeting in New York, Singer's Friden Div. introduced an electronic cash register very similar to the one Pirelli had developed. "So I had to drop the idea of manufacturing my product," he says. He flew out to San Leandro, Calif., to learn the details of the Friden machine, then came back and altered his computer program to handle its data.

Last May, one of the first Friden cash registers went into Nassau Liquors. So did Pirelli, working behind the counter and in the stockroom. "I really learned how complicated a small business is," says Pirelli. And what he learned went into the computer program: fresh approaches to product coding and correcting errors, routines for converting sales figures into gallons for tax reports, ways to automatically hold certain customers' bills at the store instead of mailing them—a frequent request in the liquor trade.

Shaping up. The program grew to some 4,000 Fortran statements, large by almost any standards. For the first few months, data was keypunched by hand from the Friden cash register's printed journal tape—an all-night job.

In December, with the program running well from keypunched data, Pirelli and Rosser installed a second cash register in the store and added Friden data collection units that record each transaction on magnetic tape. Now the computer center can call the store by phone after closing at night and read the data from the tape directly into the computer. Once read in, it takes the big computer two minutes to process three days of business and about four minutes to print out inventory and management reports. In November, the company also added its second customer, another liquor store.

Rosser thinks the company will go into the black "on a cash-flow basis" with about 50 clients, who are charged $250 to $500 a month each, But Transmission Data's eggs are not all in the local service-bureau basket. Pirelli and Rosser have landed a contract to develop a large computer program for Bond Industries, the clothing manufacturers and retailers. And they see other possibilities in the future—such as licensing their program, going national themselves, or even franchising.

I.B.M.

International Business Machines Corporation had its beginning in 1911, when three companies -- The International Time Recording Company, The Tabulating Machine Company and the Computing Scale Company -- merged to form the Computing-Tabulating-Recording Company (C-T-R). The new company came under the management of Thomas J. Watson, Sr. in 1914, when the firm had a total of 1300 employees.

Watson had been a branch manager (at age 24) and general sales manager at National Cash Register). One of his many innovations there was the "THINK" concept which became a watchword at IBM for decades.

The firm became IBM in 1924. Its line of products consisted of scales, tabulating machines, and time recording equipment. Tabulating equipment included a key punch, a hand-operated gang punch, a vertical sorter, and a non-printing tabulator

in 1928, the data capacity of punched cards was increased from 45 to 80 columns of information. This paved the way for a new series of machines and the ultimate development of today's complex electronic computers.

The company built its first education building and engineering laboratory in 1933 at Endicott, New York. During the depression of the 1930's, IBM added to its staff (rather than cutting back) and continued to develop machines and produce parts. These efforts

proved fruitful, for in 1936 IBM was in a position to provide the machines and services needed for the establishment of the massive new Social Security Program.

In World War II, all of IBM's facilities were put at the disposal of the government. IBM accounting machines were used to keep track of men and materials, including troops overseas.

After the war, new electronic computers were developed and the company's most rapid growth occurred. The revenues of the company have approximately doubled every ten years.

Rapid expansion has required broad organizational changes. In 1956, IBM created several autonomous divisions with separate administrative structures. Today, the company has 12 such divisions and two wholly owned subsidiaries.

The activities of each of these units of IBM are briefly described on page 363. The company also has a data processing group staff and a corporate staff.

The Corporate Office represents IBM's top management group. The Office includes:

Mr. Frank T. Cary, Chairman of the Board.

Mr. Thomas J. Watson, Jr., Chairman of the Executive Committee.

Mr. John R. Opel, President of the Corporation.

Mr. Gilbert E. Jones, Vice Chairman of the Board.

Mr. Jacques Maisonrouge, Chairman, IBM World Trade Europe/Middle East/Africa Corp.

Mr. Ralph Pfeiffer, Jr., Chairman, IBM World Trade Americas/Far East Corp.

WORLDWIDE COMPETITION

Both in the United States and abroad, the data processing industry is becoming increasingly competitive. Domestically, many new companies enter the industry eacy year, offering new data processing services and products. Overseas, IBM is increasingly challenged by national data processing companies supported by their governments.

In response, IBM considered moving the headquarters and staff of its overseas operations, IBM World Trade, to Europe. For various reasons, the idea was rejected, but the importance of international operations to IBM remains critical.

IBM has also taken a firm position in favor of free trade and against the trade restrictions, believing that its superior products and services will enable it to prosper internationally.

"It has been documented that multinational companies like IBM contribute substantially to the U.S. balance of payments and support thousands of jobs in the United States,"

IBM Organization

Divisions

Advanced Systems Development:
identifies and establishes worldwide market and service requirements for advanced systems; and coordinates application and services development to expand new systems capabilities.

Data Processing:
markets within the United States IBM's information-handling systems, equipment, computer programming, systems engineering, education, custom contracts and other related services to customers who require medium-sized or large systems.

Federal Systems:
concentrates on advanced technology and systems for the ground-based, seaborne, airborne and spaceborne information-handling and control needs of the U.S. Government.

Field Engineering:
provides maintenance and related services for the company's information-handling systems and equipment, and support for programming systems marketed in the United States.

General Products:
worldwide development and United States manufacturing responsibility for computer tape units, disk files and printers.

General Systems:
worldwide development and U.S. manufacturing responsibility for small information-handling systems and associated peripheral equipment, including system-related programming support; marketing and service responsibility for its products to its customers in the United States.

Information Records:
markets disk packs and data modules; manufactures and markets supplies used in information-handling systems.

Office Products:
worldwide development and U.S. manufacturing, marketing and service responsibility for electric typewriters, magnetic media typewriters, input processing equipment, direct-impression composing products, copying equipment, and related supplies.

Real Estate and Construction:
manages the selection and acquisition of sites, the design and construction of buildings, and the purchase or lease of facilities.

Research:
brings scientific understanding to bear on areas of company interest through basic research and the development of technologies of potential long-range importance.

System Development:
worldwide responsibility for systems definition, architecture and systems management of IBM's principal computer product lines and for systems programming; worldwide development and United States manufacturing responsibility for communications products, terminals and displays.

System Products:
worldwide development and United States manufacturing responsibility for IBM's principal central processor products, including main storage and logic technologies, packaging technology, channels and cables; development and implementation of advanced design and manufacturing support systems.

Subsidiaries

Science Research Associates, Inc.:
worldwide development, production and marketing responsibility for textbooks, educational kits, learning systems, guidance products and a wide range of testing materials and services for elementary and secondary schools, colleges and industry.

IBM World Trade Corporation:
IBM's business outside the United States (excluding Science Research Associates business) is conducted by two wholly owned IBM subsidiaries, IBM World Trade Europe/Middle East/Africa Corporation and IBM World Trade Americas/Far East Corporation, in more than 100 countries throughout the world.
IBM World Trade Corporation, a service company, provides support to World Trade countries in several areas, such as accounting and information systems.

stated Mr. Cary. "In IBM, we estimate that one out of every eight jobs in our Americn plants is supported by our export trade."

"Any action by the United States that would set up tax barriers, quotas, or other trade or invest-ment restrictions inevitably would cause retaliation by foreign governments against American products and companies. American jobs supported by overseas business would diminish and our balance of pay-ments problems would worsen. The results, we believe, would be to undercut the basic economy of this country and seriously damage international relationships. This is why we oppose such measures and are urging the business community to speak out on this issue."

IBM OPERATIONS

IBM characterizes its business as "problem solving." This covers the development of information-handling machines and systems to solve problems in business, science, government, education, medicine, space explora-tion, and many other areas of human activity.

Today IBM employs more that 250,000 employees in the overall process of manufacturing and selling its products around the world.

The products produced and sold by IBM number in the hundreds and include the following:
- electronic data pro-cessing systems for general purpose use,
including the System/360 and System/370 and the low-cost computer designed for small businesses, System/3.
- a broad selection of software to enable users to apply computers to many different needs.
- special purpose and advanced computer systems for commer-cial, military, and space use.
- electric typewriters, magnetic tape and card typewriters, dictation equipment, and related supplies.
- punched card accounting equipment, copying equipment, and related supplies.
- magnetic character sensing equipment and optical character readers (such as for reading checks and/or charge slips).
- industrial products, components, peripheral equipment such as printers and terminals, and products and accessories used with data processing equipment such as tapes, cards, and paper forms.
- composing equipment for typesetting.
- educational products and services.

The company has 18 product manufacturing plants in the United States plus ten others

for producing magnetic recording products and punched cards. Outside the United States, IBM has 20 plants in 13 countries, plus 50 locations in 41 countries where punched cards are made.

To market and service its products, IBM has more than 250 branch offices in the United States and 345 sales locations in 108 other countries around the world.

Research, development, and product engineering are conducted in 23 laboratories in the United States and in eight abroad.

Today, IBM's revenues exceed $14 billion. The key data on IBM's revenues and earnings for 1974 and 1975 are presented below.

Of the revenues, about 80% come from sales, services, and rentals of data processing machines and systems. About one-third of IBM's total revenues come from operations outside of the United States.

You can readily see why IBM is subject to examination and attack as the largest company in the computer industry. Whether IBM will continue to grow and to maintain its dominant position will depend in part on the actions of the government under our antitrust laws.

	1975	1974
Gross income from sales, rentals and services	$ 14,436,541,062	$ 12,675,291,832
Earnings before income taxes	$ 3,720,876,966	$ 3,434,639,361
U.S. Federal and non-U.S. income taxes	$ 1,731,000,000	$ 1,597,000,000
Net earnings	$ 1,989,876,966	$ 1,837,639,361
Per share	$ 13.35	$ 12.47
Cash dividends	$ 968,988,364	$ 819,669,017
Per share	$ 6.50	$ 5.56
Investment in plant, rental machines and other property	$ 2,438,785,856	$ 2,912,603,050

Computers: Are They Magic Or Menace?

The moment the word 'computer' is mentioned we step into a mythological world as powerful as that which surrounded Homer and his ancestors. There is meaning and power and even a sense of 'being' attributed to the technology in general, and particularly to the computer itself.

The company public relations man says: "Our company must go forward with the rest of the world and move into the computer age!" The high-powered computer salesman convinces the manager that a computer will bring him respect and power within the company.

A badly informed top management can be exposed to the grand illusions of the management information system (MIS), referred to almost invariably in terms of hardware, an illusion sustained by the best known computer advisers.

Terminal screens on the desks of the executives will be hooked up by data transmission lines to the central computer complex in real-time mode. All the information will be accessible immediately at the touch of a finger. Models can be manipulated by attached light pens right on the cathode ray screen of the terminal, so that possible courses of action can be simulated and results seen.

It would take more than a mere man to resist such temptations, especially when faced with such vague possibilities as 'future savings'.

Of course the computer is expected to bring increased savings and efficiency. It may in fact be more expensive and less efficient than the way the job is done now. No matter how sophisticated the computer hardware, it is simple arithmetic that decides whether the new system is running at a profit or a loss.

The truth is that very few computer installations are really economic propositions yet.

In the first rush of enthusiasm, however, there is no time for such thoughts. Too often the whole computer project starts at the mytho-logical level and stays there until the day of reckoning.

The first pressures arise out of the difficult and painful process of taking jobs from the tested or 'pilot run' state into the live or operating state; in other words, using real data. This is when the 'bugs' begin to show.

Then the internal pressures begin, between the insiders and the outsiders who have been brought in to help with the program; and between the technical people and the managers.

The new computer staff support the myth of the omnipotence of the new system, not only by propagating the faith, but by their very style. They can talk not only about the new hardware and software, but also about the company's operations in totally new terminology.

One of their most dangerous weapons against any one who resists is to talk about the man's job in front of his boss in such a way that they appear to know more about his work than he does. Many a reckless manager has regretted tangling with the computer staff at his first meeting.

There are constant staff problems with the independent and sought-after 'computer people'. Programmers are lured away by better offers. Your own computer man, once he is trained, will probably go to work for the computer company or set up as an independent expert.

But the first major test for the computer department comes when the other departments in the company begin to complain about the service.

"I know," the stores manager will say, "it's a very good system with great potential, but the facts are that I'm getting my figures two hours later than in the past and I can't look at my records any more. On top of this I haven't saved any staff."

That is when reality begins to replace mythology.

The truth is that job performance on the new, expensive computer is very often less than it was when operating under the manual scheme. A major reason for this is the thorny problem of *turnaround times*. Another is the lack of file accessibility.

Under the old scheme the user could look at his records any time he wished. Now he has to ask the computer department to print out the contents of certain file records from where they are sitting on tapes, inaccessible without the computer.

Even if data transmission lines are employed, he cannot get access to the records at will, unless the computer department keeps the file on-line at

"The computer is only a tool. There will always be a place for unbridled avarice."

Drawing by Lorenz, © 1971 The New Yorker Magazine Inc.

all times, which is a very expensive data retrieval solution.

Then there are the frequent program changes and the one-off jobs requested by the various computer users. Some experts will say that all these needs should be anticipated in a data base. This is science fiction dreaming. Only a fortune-teller can know what data the future researcher will probe for.

In any case, the computer manager must face the fact that all the promised goods will not be delivered by the hardware on hand. And there beside him is his friendly computer salesman, ready to sell him some more.

For a company in this fix, another computer of the same size and capacity is the best solution; especially if they can sell some of the extra computer time to others. Using a computer may not be profitable, but selling time on it certainly is.

In many companies top management has paid little or no attention to the computer project since the board signed the order for the system. Eventually, however, criticism of the computer may reach the stage where only top management can deal with it.

They can turn to the computer manufacturers, whose solution will invariably be to buy more hardware. Or they can call in outside consultants to perform a costly investigation. Or they can turn the whole system over to a facilities service organization which will run it for them, for a fee.

Does the computer user deserve what happens, and can the worst be avoided by newcomers to the field?

Sometimes he does deserve it because he didn't pay any attention to what was going on. No computer program succeeds unless top management is involved from the start.

Only they can say what *information* will be in the MIS and how it will be gathered, manipulated and analysed.

Computer people, although they have developed a sense of superiority which borders on contempt, are really uneducated. They know very little about good project planning, systems planning, methodologies of work, proper standards and security. What is worse, they know very little about management information and plain, good accounting for profit or loss.

So the first step in deciding whether or not one should use a computer is to get a policy directive, from the president or general manager, to investigate the question.

Then get outside advice. This is the best course, if the adviser is good, and obviously not trying to lure customers into a facilities service operation.

When a project leader has been appointed, the project feasibility study can take place. The most vital element in this is the cost-benefit analysis. This must be considered apart from possible future savings and non-measurable increases in efficiency.

It is a cost analysis that should be based on reasonable timings—that is, how long each computer run will take. One good way is to ask an outside expert who knows not only how long a certain job should take to run, but how long similar jobs actually take to run on other people's computers.

If it is found to be economically feasible to use a computer, a model should be chosen that allows growth in reasonable stages. One of the greatest untruths in the computer industry is that certain computer models can grow in speed and capacity by adding reasonably priced processing blocks. A good rule for small to medium computers is that the cost of the effective minimum increase is often equal to the cost of another computer.

Two very important considerations in choosing a particular computer system are the language and software to be used, and future conversions to new computers. One should aim for a language like COBOL (Common Business Oriented Language) an internationally accepted programming language developed for general commercial use, and avoid those languages and software that are tied to a specific manufacturer.

Most of the work at the proposal stage can be done by the manufacturers, as long as one doesn't become too dependent on them.

Don't buy a computer if you think there might be a new generation or model around the corner. Moving from one generation of computers to the next is painful and costly. It means taking all your programs and files off the old one and making them work on the new one. You pay for two

computers, and will continue to pay for them for some time.

The computer is the ideal hardware for an information system. The jobs that the computer is most needed for, however, are those most difficult to put onto it: the production and scheduling work, and the adaptive planning and research work. Therefore the computer, with all its fantastic technical abilities, is mostly used on the routine clerical and accounting work, on which it is often more expensive than the old manual way.

No manager should authorize a computer that will merely replace the routine accounting and clerical work, unless such a replacement promises real savings. If it does not, and no firm plans for more worthwhile projects materialize, there is a strong case for leaving certain jobs to be done on accounting machines.

What advice, then, can we give the manager who is attempting to assess the viability of a computer project? First he must ask how much of savings are based on staff savings and how much of these can be achieved within five years.

Unless most of the staff saved are being transferred, fired or retired within the five years, the staff savings figure cannot be reached; then there is a strong case for something other than a full-sized computer operation, such as a small computer with time-sharing terminal facilities.

As for the many cases where it is economically viable to use one's own computer, the decision must be to use it, by all means. But the strong warning must be repeated that in present times' staff turnover can make even the most profitable computer unprofitable.

No one is going to stop buying computers, for the simple reason that computers, like the locomotive and the jet plane, are here to stay whether one likes it or not.

However, if we want to be really mature and honest about the whole business of using computers in the commercial world, let us forget about such marginal savings as those achieved by putting jobs onto accounting machines, and let us sign for our computers using the only real justification, which is good old-fashioned progress.

Computer Careers

Careers in data processing can be grouped in three areas: those relating to the hardware of computers, those that have to do with software, and those that convert data into machine usable form. Hardware jobs have to do with the machine itself -- manufacturing, selling, operating, or maintaining it. Software is the term applied to the adapting of the machine to practical uses, through programming, program trouble-shooting, writing documentation of systems, and creating computer languages. The data handling careers involve keypunch, key entry, and other functions.

The applications of computers has a lot to do with the kind of environment you work in. Computers are found in banks, law firms, schools, government agencies, insurance companies, laboratories, factories, hospitals, weather bureaus, publishing houses, and air traffic control centers, among other places.

REQUIREMENTS

Special knowledge is required, of course, for advanced careers in data processing. But all jobs in data processing require certain basic qualities: ability to think logically, ability to think imaginatively and to create solutions to problems, patience or endurance to see a job to completion, and an appreciation for detail and accuracy.

Opportunities are growing in the computer field, so there are jobs available to those who have the proper education and abilities. This is one field, though, that specific vocational training is more important than a college degree -- and any of a number of degrees or major areas of study are acceptable as a basis for entering a computer career.

The Programmers

Programmers are exceptional individuals, and the work they do is mind bending, exhilarating and exasperating –all at the same time. Something like writing music, or winning at chess.

Programmers are known for their analytical minds, their penchant for working on complex problems in closely-knit groups, and their ability to stay cool under deadline pressure.

They also have a sense of humor–an invaluable quality when you consider the intellectual effort that goes into writing a computer program which rarely works perfectly the first time around.

A computer program can be as simple as thinking through the few hundred instructions a data processing machine needs to design a new textile pattern, or as complicated as the millions of instructions required to regulate the internal operations of a large-scale computer.

Understanding the Problem

But no matter what the size or complexity of a problem happens to be, the programmer's method of solving it is almost always the same. First, he must understand the problem, and be able to break it down into its component parts. Second, he must know the capabilities and limitations of the hardware that's going to process the data. And finally, he must know precisely what results the computer program is expected to produce.

The programmer begins work on a new assignment by spending weeks, and sometimes months, studying the problem in depth. He may need to become knowledgeable about blood pressure, respiration and pulse rates in order to write the instructions needed to create a computer system for continuously monitoring vital life functions of the critically ill. Or he may need to study a chemical company's inventory procedures in order to write a computer program that can swiftly fill individual orders for hundreds of products ranging from paper boxes to radio-active isotopes.

Finding the Solution

Once the programmer thoroughly understands the problem, he starts drawing a step-by-step flow chart that contains the significant logical steps needed to solve it from beginning to end. In preparing the program he may use standard symbols such as a diamond which stands for "decision," or a rectangle which represents a "major processing function." He'll also use plain English words such as "set distance = rate x time" to describe the decision or operation the computer must perform at that particular point.

Translating by Machine

The programmer takes his flow chart and converts it into simplified instructions which are punched into cards for entry into a computer. The machine then translates the original shorthand statements into the far more numerous and explicit machine instructions which a data processing system uses to solve a problem.

The next step consists of testing the program by actually running it on the computer to make sure there are no "bugs" or errors. Debugging is a time-consuming job, and programmers may have to test run their programs again and again before they run perfectly.

Men and women who write computer instructions to handle specific jobs such as controlling chemical production or fighting crime are called application programmers. Those who write the instructions which control aspects of the computer installation are called systems programmers.

Applications Programming

Applications programming is the writing of computer instructions to do specific jobs. As an IBM applications programmer, you'll create computer solutions to problems which run the gamut from stock market investing to ballistic missile re-entry. You may even be asked to write an applications program which will be used only once—to solve a particular equation in atomic physics, for example.

Writing an applications program requires a knowledge of both programming and the customer's business. You can't solve an insurance problem, for example, without understanding the insurance business; and you can't prepare this program for the IBM System/360 without knowing the capabilities of the machine.

You'll Get Around

As an applications programmer you'll get around. You'll talk to IBM customers, find out how things are done, what a customer's needs are, and how he can benefit from computer processing. Then you'll sit down and quietly begin thinking through a computer solution to his problems.

The applications programmer constantly moves through uncharted seas in business, government, science and education. You'll know what's happening in our society—and you'll know computers. It's a good combination. One that can help you make your contribution to those aspects of our national life which interest you the most.

Systems Programming

Systems programming is the writing of instructions that make it easier to program computers and put them to work. A systems programmer, as a result, is often called a programmer's programmer.

As an IBM systems programmer, you'll write the routines which assign incoming data to storage, dispatch messages from one memory location to another, and control peripheral units such as magnetic tape drives, high-speed printers and graphic display devices which are used to get information in and out of computers.

You'll also write program routines which applications programmers use over and over again, but which only have to be written once such as:

Utility programs employed to handle commonplace chores like moving data from punched cards to magnetic tape.

Or Sort/Merge and file maintenance routines which are heavily used in business to rearrange old data, insert new data into old files, or purge old facts from the file so they can be replaced with fresh ones.

Developing Computer Languages

As a systems programmer you may even get a chance to work on the development of high-level compilers, or computer languages such as FORTRAN (FORmula TRANslation) which was developed at IBM and is used for solving mathematical and scientific problems, or COBOL (COmmon Business Oriented Language) used in commercial applications.

And beyond that there is programming research in which you can explore the unknown reaches of the computer universe as you delve into pattern recognition, computer learning techniques, artificial intelligence and other advanced development areas.

The basic jobs are keypunch and computer operating jobs -- the areas in which the most people are employed. A technical school education followed by on-the-job training is the usual background for beginners.

Then careers can lead into programming -- first as a trainee and then later as a programmer responsible for development of computer software. Most programmers have college degrees, but this is not necessarily a requirement. Advanced degrees may be needed for some specialized or scientific programming careers.

The next level of jobs that people may seek is that of systems engineer. The title, which may mean different things to different people, generally refers to customer-liaison work, involving salesmen or representatives providing assistance to customers. Both business and technical ability is needed.

An alternative is that of systems analyst. An analyst (who may also be a programmer) has the job of planning and designing the problems for the programmer and evaluates the computer systems in the context of a proposed change. The systems analyst's job is broader, involving contacts with various people in an organization to obtain needed information and also involving broad evaluation of problems and developing solutions for them.

CONSIDER

1. Would history have been different had Babbage successfully built his Analytical Engine that he designed? Explain.

2. Why wasn't the computer invented centuries ago? What conditions were necessary?

3. Why was the census such a successful basis for developing the modern computer?

4. Why is it difficult to install a computer in a company?

5. How could the use of computers change the way schools are run -- how might your education be improved through computer applications?

6. Why is IBM in businesses other than just computers (e.g., Science Research Associates, its educational subsidiary)? Is there much potential for IBM in these areas?

7. IBM controls about 75% of all domestic sales of computer systems. Do you feel this is an unreasonable market share? Explain.

8. How can a small store justify the use of computers in management?

9. Do individuals have a right to know what data is maintained on them in computer files? Explain.

10. What would be the effects of linking all the major computer systems in the country? Explain.

CHALLENGES

Look for an application of computers that affects your life, such as a bill, a grades report, or a traffic ticket. Consider how things would be different if there were no computer involved in this application.

Identify five new ways that computers could be used in your life where they are not now used. What would be required for this application? What would be the impact?

Investigate pending legislation in your state or at the federal level regarding individual right to privacy and computerized information systems. California has a law in effect and others have laws in consideration. What would be (or is) the impact of such legislation?

You have the right to know what the federal government has on its computer files about you. The Internal Revenue Service, for example, is obliged to disclose what information it has about you and your records. Find out what is required to obtain a listing or copy of your file in this or another agency and make the request officially.

For an insight into the development of computers, read The Analytical Machine -- past, present, and future, by Jeremy Bernstein (Random House, 1963) It's an interesting book.

RECAP

A computer is basically a large adding machine that uses electronic impulses to represent numbers. By manipulating these impulses, the computer can process and analyze large amounts of information very rapidly. Computer systems include both hardware (the actual equipment) and software (the various programs and materials needed to make the system work). Because most computers are similarly constructed, the characteristics of computer systems described in this chapter generally hold true.

International Business Machines Corporation is the world's largest computer manufacturer. Founded early in this century, the company has had a record of advanced research and quality systems design. It succeeded in large part because its computer systems were efficient and were introduced in customers' organizations to serve vital needs economically. In short, IBM was at the right places at the right times with well-designed computer hardware and supporting software.

Computers serve a wide variety of purposes in business. Ford, Sears, and all other major corporations rely heavily on computer systems. Smaller businesses, took, may rely on computers to give management the information needed for profitalbe operations. Such computer appli-cations were described in this chapter.

New applications for computer capacities are rapidly being developed. One major frontier is the communications industry, where growing demands for services require more extensive, sophisticated information handling systems. New computer hardware, such as System/3, and computer service utilities are two responses to this demand.

There are potential risks in relying on computers. Computer systems are quite costly, impose demands on organizations, require new ways of providing and using infor-mation by managers, and create problems of retaining confidentiality of data. Further, many managers have seen computers as a panacea for all the ills of their organizations. They have discovered, however, that computers are neither magic nor menace. As Herbert Simon said in this chapter, machines cannot be relied upon to manage corporations. Machines are tools to be used wisely by management. When they are, the potential bene-fits are great.

WORKSHEET NO. 13

Computer are applied to a wide range of rasks in business organizations. Among the common applications are customer billing, inventory control, control of manufcaturing processes, accounting, reporting, research analysis, and forecasting. Select one of these general types of applications (or another you may think of) and answer the following questions in the context of FORD, SEARS, or CON ED.

1. Why is it more efficient to use costly computers for this task than to have it done manually by people?

2. What problems exist because computers are used in this task?

3. Does the use of computers put people out of work? What new jobs are created?

---

4. Imagine how the task may be performed in the future, say in the year 2000. Describe the role of computer as you think it might be then.

PART V

MANAGING BUSINESS

CHAPTER 14

Managing

What do Ford Motor, Sears, Pizza Hut, your local shoe repair shop, and the Department of Defense all have in common?

They are all organizations of people banded together to achieve common objectives. Their work is directed by managers -- individuals who take on the responsibility of leadership in the organizations.

No matter how large or small an organization, it is necessary for the individuals to pool their talents and to divide the work required to accomplish the objectives. It is this division of labor that is basic to managing, and to all forms of organizations.

How is this done? The job of the manager includes a number of tasks: planning, organizing, directing, coordinating, and controling. In each of these functions, the aim is to get things done through other people, as opposed to the managers

doing the work directly themselves.

Planning is the process of preparing for future business activities. It involves the setting of objectives and developing plans, policies, and programs for achieving them. Chapter 15 concentrates on how companies plan for growth and change.

Organizing is the process of putting together the physical resources and the people needed for achievement of objectives.

Directing involves guiding the activities of people as they do their jobs.

Coordinating is the process of keeping activities going smoothly by exchanging information across the organization.

Controlling is the process of making sure the activities and results are conforming to desired standards (such as the quality of goods produced or staying within budgets).

A manager is also a decision maker. Each of the above functions involves making decisions about how things will be. The manager has the authority, the discretion, and the responsibility to direct actions that will have an impact on the organization's accomplishments.

The president is the top decision maker -- "the buck stops here." But, in a sense, every employee can act like a president in the way he or she thinks and acts. This requires a broad outlook, a good understanding of the objectives, and ability to carry out actions.

In addition, there needs to be the right climate for management. Top management must be willing to delegate authority, to provide information needed by subordinates to make effective decisions and the means of coordinating and controlling the diverse managerial actions taken in the organization.

Management by objectives is a tool for achieving these conditions. It is the process of setting goals with subordinate employees so they will know what they are trying to accomplish. Individual and group performance goals represent elements of broader organizational goals (such as expanding sales, improving profitability, improving service). Individual growth and development objectives may complement performance goals by focusing on individual desires and aspirations regarding future work.

To help managers manage, some companies have developed planning models -- computer-based analysis of the factors affecting decisions. Data on finances, market conditions, and other factors are fed into the model and processed to provide answers to "what if?" questions asked by management. Such tools may be helpful to managers, but can never replace human judgment provided by the managers in charge.

In This Chapter

Organization And Management

If you wanted to make and sell leather belts, it's possible you could do so without much difficulty. You could buy your own leather, cut it into strips, dye them, tool them, put on the buckles, and sell them to your friends and others on campus. You could do all the aspects of the work yourself. You don't need any organization, any managers, or any workers.

You may have problems, for sure -- ensuring you have enough supplies, getting proper permits to sell your products, paying your taxes, and keeping your quality at least as high as your prices. But you would not have the problems of coordinating the work of other people, of dividing work among specialized tasks, of training, or other organizational matters.

In short, you would not be a manager.

ORGANIZATION

Most business activities today are more complex, and require effective organization of the talents of different specialists and managers.

The major advantage of organization is increased efficiency. Individuals perform specified duties requiring certain specialized skills instead of the whole range of duties needed to make a product.

That's how Henry Ford pulled ahead of the pack of automobile companies: by introducing division of labor and the assembly of automobiles on an assembly line.

Division of labor results in better use of talent, cost savings, efficiency through specialization, and general overall productivity improvement.

The whole idea of organization is to help people work together as individuals and groups in the achievement of the objectives of a business. Whether we consider a major business corporation, a neighborhood business, a hospital, a political party, a governmental agency, or any other kind of organization, we see certain common patterns that are essential for their survival and growth.

The first pattern that you should notice about an organization is HIERARCHY. At each level of an organization, work is coordinated by managers. Ultimate responsibility for the whole organization lies with the president as chief executive. Thus there is a chain of command that binds together the people working in an organization.

An insurance company in Dusseldorf, West Germany, built its corporate office building to represent the organization's hierarchy. Each story is occupied by a progressively higher echelon of employees, from the 360 clerks and typists on the ground floor to the president's office on the top floor.

A second aspect of organization is the logical grouping of people in their work according to the kind of activities they perform, generally according to

their specializations.

A business may base its organization on territories served (geographic), on the types of work (functions), on the kinds of customers (retail or wholesale), on the type of technology that may be involved (production method, form of transportation, etc.), on specific product lines, or on other characteristics that are often considered important. most often, a combination of factors determine the way an enterprise is organized.

Of course, each company has its own unique organization structure. There are common patterns of organization, but if you look closely, you'll see that there are differences, and usually good reasons for them. And as conditions change, management usually changes the organization to keep pace.

Bigger organizations aren't always so different from smaller ones, though. Companies like Ford or Sears are really a number of smaller companies or divisions rolled into one. In fact, the very large and diverse corporations are called CONGLOMERATES.

DECENTRALIZATION

Once management concept helps make this possible. DECENTRALIZATION means that management responsibility for decision making is pushed to the lowest possible level in an organization.

In this way, a large organization can set up a number of relatively independent divisions to operate, perhaps as PROFIT CENTERS, which are not dependent on corporate managers for decisions.

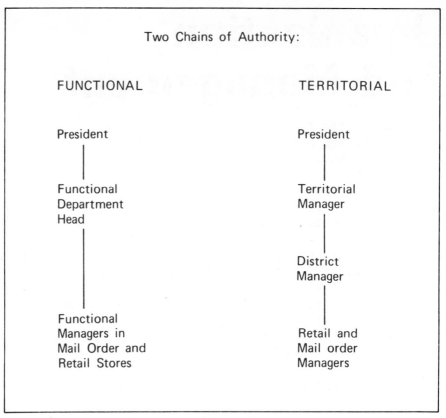

Two Chains of Authority:

FUNCTIONAL	TERRITORIAL
President	President
Functional Department Head	Territorial Manager
	District Manager
Functional Managers in Mail Order and Retail Stores	Retail and Mail order Managers

For decades Sears operated its retail business through a "decentralized multidivisional structure." The geographic territories operated autonomously, supported by a staff of officers and by close liaison with executives and staff in the Chicago headquarters. This was for help in sales promotion and merchandising advice. The territorial managers looked to Chicago only for policy guidance and a budget.

The organization continues today, although centralized staff support and controls have been expanded. Each territorial Vice President is responsible for the successful operation of the stores and mail order houses in the geographical area.

Other companies have operated under a similarly decentralized organization structure, including A & P, General Motors, Union Carbide, and du Pont.

However, there is nothing wrong with a highly centralized organization structure. Such an approach is appropriate when a high level of control is needed or in cases where the work cannot easily be divided into organizational pieces.

Usually companies go through a tug and pull process, first becoming decentralized and then pulling in the strings as necessary to keep business on the right track, and later letting responsibility back out again to the field.

Sears executives make top level decisions based on information gathered from the territories and other operating divisions. They rely on regular inspection tours in the field, a flow of reports and statistical information, and a live interchange of ideas through committees comprised of General Office and field personnel.

The forces that led to the decentralized structure in Sears were the need for effective appraisal of the individual stores and, at the same time, the need for close and constant contact with the changing markets.

The lines of authority and patterns of communication are clearly defined in this organization. It's understood that managers must have vital information if they are to make timely and meaningful decisions and they must have authority necessary if they are to see the decisions carried out.

Two ingredients are thus needed for an organization to be successful: the right kinds of people as managers and the right kind of organization structure to allow them to do their jobs. As the goals and roles of an organization change, so must the managers and the structure within which they manage.

FUNCTIONS OF MANAGING

We've talked about how organizations help get things done; we've said how important the men and women who manage organizations really are in making things happen. But exactly what does a manager do? What are the functions of managing?

While there are many different views of the manager's job, the key aspects are as follows:
-- planning
-- organizing
-- directing
-- coordinating
-- controlling.
These five functions are interrelated aspects of the job of managing in an' organization.

PLANNING involves decisions concerning how the organization intends to accomplish its goals. This includes deciding what is to be done, how it is to be done, when it is to be done, and by whom it is to be done. Planning also covers the resources needed, including capital, equipment, and raw materials. Without planning, any organization will just drift along and will probably suffer -- ultimately disappearing.

Planning may be simple and informal or it may be very complex and formal, with extensive research. Some companies have corporate models -- computer based analyses to help management consider possible alternatives in planning. Later in this chapter corporate models are discussed.

ORGANIZING involves the preparations needed to implement the plans. The managers must determine what changes, if any, are needed in the organization structure -- reporting relationships, communication paths, and assignment of individuals to positions. It may be that additional personnel will be needed to achieve the plans; these people may be recruited outside the organization. The organization is expanded to make room for them.

DIRECTING involves leading and motivating people in the organization in such a way that the overall goals may be achieved. In addition to achieving immediate goals, the manager, through his or her leadership abilities and abilities to motivate

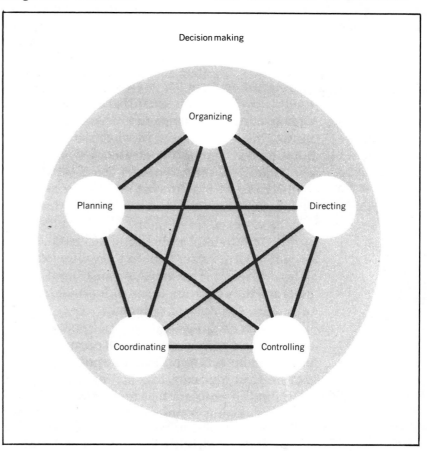

Decision making

Organizing

Planning

Directing

Coordinating — Controlling

people, to satisfy the needs of the employees. Managers recognize that individuals have personal career goals and job-related needs and desires. These must be satisfied, at least partially, if the employees are to be motivated to stay in the organization and do the work required.

In summary, directing isn't a matter of "bossing" it's a matter of leading employees as a team toward achievement of goals everyone feels are important.

COORDINATING involves insuring that the diverse but interdependent activities in the organization are directed toward the right ends -- the objectives. If the work of various units or people are not coordinated, it's tough to get anywhere. In fact sometimes people work at cross-purposes in the same organization. It's management's job to keep this from happening.

CONTROLLING involves guiding the organization in the direction that it should be going in order to achieve its goals. This involves monitoring the activities and the use of resources, in relation to the plans and budgets. If there is disagreement between what's happening and what was intended, it's the manager's job to work out an adjustment, bringing performance in line with the plans (or to change the plans, if that makes the most sense).

DECISION MAKING

You may have noticed that little has been said about making decisions. Naturally, that's a big part of the manager's job,

too. However, decision making takes place in each of the functions described above.

Decision making is the application of a manager's judgement, in light of available information, to the solution of a problem. It's a matter of making choices -- selecting between alternative courses of action. This process underlies just about everything that a manager does.

In making decisions, a manager usually goes through several logical steps in thinking:

1. Identifying and defining the problem. This first step is easy to slip by -- assuming we know what the problem is when, in fact, we have the wrong picture. A good manager takes time to dig out the facts about the real issue to be considered.

If sales of a product start to slip, for example, a manager may conclude that the price is too high, or that consumers need spurring. The real problem may be product quality, competitive advantages of some other product, or even the general economic conditions dampening consumer spending.

2. Identifying alternative solutions to the problem. Once defined, the manager identifies one or more possible courses of action that will solve the problem. The tendency is to jump on one alternative and run with it -- but the good manager considers several possiblities.

3. Evaluating the alternatives. A good manager weighs each of the possible courses of action. Which will cost least; which will take the least

time; which involves the least disruption; which will yield the most lasting benefits?

Sometimes this process can get pretty sophisticated. When companies decide to introduce a new product, obtain new financing, or build a new plant, the evaluation step is done very carefully. All the pertinent facts are weighed.

4. Choice. If the above steps are down pat, the choice is obvious to many managers. The choice, or final decision, is in favor of the preferable alternative -- the best course of action.

Sometimes the decision is so complex that a model may be needed to help pick the alternative. In other cases, managers will meet in committees and seek outside advice in making the final decision. But in every case, the responsibility for the decision rests with the managers. If the decisions turn out to be wrong, the managers carry the responsibility. In many cases, their jobs may depend on how good the decisions are.

There's a feeling that managers don't have clout in big organizations. On the contrary, large organizations, particularly those that are decentralized, put heavy responsibility on managers for effective decision making and for effective performance in the other managerial functions. This is a key feature of American enterprise, and it is getting stronger, not weaker, as organizations grow larger and more complex.

Business Says It Can Handle Bigness

Its aim is to carve up
leadership problems
into bite-size chunks

"In practically all of our activities, we seem to suffer from the inertia resulting from our great size. It seems to be hard for us to get action . . . there are so many people involved."

That introspective analysis of grappling with bigness was made by Alfred P. Sloan, Jr., in 1925. It reflected his concern as president of General Motors Corp., when the company's employment roll was little more than a shadow of today's figure of 794,000 and sales by what is now the world's biggest manufacturer were only a fraction of last year's total of $24-billion.

Concern with managing bigness obviously extends beyond GM today, into the other multibillion-dollar corporations that have proliferated across the industrial scene. There are worries that these giants will become frozen into institutionalized bureaucracies that lack the dynamism to compete effectively. The advent of the trillion-dollar economy, with its expanding markets and labor force, finds more than one chief executive officer pondering whether the single most limiting factor on his company's fortunes is simply being able to manage it.

Early stage. Alternatives to existing management structures are still in the embryonic stage, and they fly in the face of the rigid traditional way of running a company. Temporary management teams, created for specific projects and with members plucked from throughout companies if their talents mesh with the need, portend the kind of fluid management that many executives find unpalatable. Such a group approach, in which the leadership often rotates to the man with the most experience on a given aspect of the problem, exposes the shibboleth of the hard-driving man in command whose business acumen can see him through any circumstance.

GM's approach to the bigness problem, of course, was decentralization coupled with a large dose of coordinated control. It worked well enough to be copied by numerous companies wrestling with problems of size. But despite its immensity, GM is primarily in one business—making cars and trucks. For most companies, a big chunk of their growth has come with diversification. And trying to manage a burgeoning multiproduct, multimarket company such as a General Electric or a Textron, which is simultaneously expanding internationally and trying to keep pace with waves of new technology, puts management to a severe test.

Yet, it is the rare executive who will concede that growth is not a permanent part of his strategy. The "more-is-better" thesis, though more loudly challenged by business critics today than ever before, remains intact. "Business is hypnotized by size," says Peter F. Drucker, author, educator, and consultant. "The $5-billion company is still seen as a good in itself in both the public and private sector. To me, it is an affliction." Too often, says the Conference Board's Wilbur McFeely, "a large organization really lives on momentum rather than vitality."

Professional managers contend that it is simply a matter of keeping things in perspective and using the right techniques to obtain optimum results. Reflecting on his years with Royal Dutch/Shell, Monroe E. Spaght says he

---

'A large organization
really lives on momentum
rather than vitality'

---

came to the view that there is no limit to the size at which a company can be managed efficiently. "It's rather a matter of dividing it into bite-sized chunks with clear-cut lines of authority to the top," says Spaght, who retired in June as a managing director of the international oil giant.

Consultant Richard Neuschel, a McKinsey & Co. director, asserts that there "is no real significance to bigness *per se*." He says: "There may be a limit to complexity. If a company becomes too heterogeneous, the threat of unmanageability becomes greater."

"What we really need is for a company to see that one of its undermanaged, underexploited activities is really big enough to run itself, and then spin it off as an independent business," contends Drucker. "I could name 75 places where a business with volume ranging from $50-million to $300-million could be created if the big companies could divest and get out," Drucker says. "I'm convinced that we'll have to come to that."

The problems of managing increased diversity, says Ernest Dale, consultant and academician, may lead corpora-tions to follow the route taken by many individual executives who have become specialists in order to cope with bigness and complexity. The multiproduct company would winnow out unrelated activities and concentrate on a more homogeneous and manageable mix.

Local control. But for the present, decentralization will remain the primary device. And it is not limited to the biggest corporations. General Cable Corp., with 1969 sales of $366-million, is an example of a smaller company that took the step. President Donald Frey divided the company, which makes items ranging from household scouring pads to huge underground transmission cable, into five divisions when he arrived there two years ago.

Though his new environment at General Cable was dwarfed by his previous one—he had been vice-president of product development at Ford Motor Co.—Frey found decentralization was indeed applicable. While Ford's market is enormous, it does not have General Cable's variety of distribution outlets, which range from supermarket suppliers to electrical wholesalers. And in the markets it serves, General Cable is often the biggest. Decentralizing, says Frey, allows "you to match your small competitors' attention to customers. Then you apply economies of scale to research and product development. But you have to be fluid. The only constant part of this company is my desk—with me, hopefully, behind it."

Effective control of a diversified and decentralized enterprise requires a constant information flow between headquarters and operating units. And at about the time the information flow started to clog, computer technology was applied. If it has not been the panacea its proponents predicted, it has spread throughout industry to a point that not having a "management informaton system" tied to a computer puts a company in the bush league.

When the system works, says John Diebold, considered by many to be the high priest in the field, "the man half a world away can be more cognizant of what is happening in an operating unit than the man on the scene." From the initial applications of computers to payroll, billing, and accounting, Diebold and his associates see the computer becoming a routine tool in corporate decision making.

Accompanying the numbers and equations will be an "overlay of the qualitative factors" behind the formulas, to be used as another tool for operating in a volatile environment, says Cleburn E. Best of Cresap, McCormick & Paget. The consulting firm is already working with its clients on "an early-warning system for top management to see what is going into decisions rather than seeing results on financial reports at a point

Executives are using exotic new tools of management science

when it may be too late for correction," says Best.

And there is no dearth of more esoteric techniques—such as linear programming, risk analysis, or decision trees—waiting in the wings.

The majority of today's top managers are struggling to grasp the jargon used by younger managers who are attempting to apply the new techniques in their companies. In many instances, a "fear-and-sneer" syndrome arises, says the Conference Board's McFeely. But just as size and complexity will not diminish, neither will the number of young managers conversant with these techniques. As they ascend to top decision-making positions where the penalty for poor performance matches the stakes, they will call on new tools to help.

Testing solutions. When, for example, a development group comes up with ideas for three new products, company executives may choose to use risk analysis combining computer simulation with crap-shooting odds—to pick the one most likely to produce the best return Once that decision is made, the product group may use venture analysis to ride herd on the product until it reaches the marketplace.

If a new plant has to be built, managers may call on a complex mathematical tool called linear programming (LP) to help determine the best geographic location, optimum plant size and product mix, the most efficient means of distribution, and the most economic inventory size. If a company project is extremely big, complex, expensive, and involves the coordination of large numbers of skilled people, executives may want to call on PERT/CPM (program evaluation and review technique/critical path management) to determine the fastest, most efficient ways of getting the job done.

Paralleling the ventures with new techniques will be more experimentation in organizational structure. More sharing of the chief executive's responsibilities by committees of senior executives—concepts such as the office of president or corporate executive office —will logically evolve. While the concept of a high powered team at the top is well entrenched at companies such as Du Pont and Jersey Standard, it picked up momentum in the late 1960s.

Project teams and task forces will become more common in tackling complexity, contend behavioral science advocates such as John Paul Jones, senior vice-president for personnel and organization development at Federated Department Stores, Inc. A team of executives from various departments, formed to cut costs throughout a company, is not unusual. But normally the practice is limited to staff functions.

Expertise. The cutting edge of what has been tabbed "matrix management" is operating in high-technology fields such as the aerospace industry. There, the group leadership role flows to the member most qualified when the task of developing a piece of hardware reaches a point that calls for his expertise. Once this particular hurdle is

'The real job for managers is to apply the fundamentals they already know'

out of the way and another pops up calling for a different skill, leadership moves to another team member.

Matrix management will force companies to search out talent earlier. This will mean substantial upgrading of management development efforts. More companies will use computers to create employee "skills inventory" data banks to rapidly assign people with the right capabilities to a project. The resulting mobility may turn the corporate recruiting promise so often proffered—that the work will be challenging— into a reality.

Spencer Stuart, chairman of Spencer Stuart & Associates, an executive recruiting firm, sees the technique penetrating the inner circles of top management. "There will be more of what some people call 'temporary management systems' or 'project management systems,' where the men who are needed to contribute to the solution meet, make their contributions, and perhaps never become a permanent member of any fixed and permanent management group."

But top management's job will remain one of managing the totality of the enterprise and trying to identify the strategic moves to make in a changing and growing business environment. Seeking new management "secret weapons" at the expense of existing techniques, warns McKinsey's Neuschel, could make the task unnecessarily complicated. "The real job for managers," he says, "is to apply the fundamentals they already know about. Few companies are as well organized and as well managed as they could be if they were doing this."

WHAZZIT?

ORGANIZATION CHART

A picture of the organization structure at a specific point in time.

CHAIN OF COMMAND

The hierarchical relationship of managers and subordinates in an organization. Managers at each higher level are responsible for the coordination of a larger part of the organization.

CENTRALIZATION

Managers at the top of the organization make decisions that affect decisions and activities throughout the organization.

DECENTRALIZATION

Managers at all levels of the organization make the decisions that affect their own activities and the activities of their immediate subordinates.

Moving Decisions Down To Where The Action Is

Companies will decentralize along the lines of conglomerates to achieve greater flexibility

Driven by conflicting forces, Corporate America spun off in many new directions in the 1960s.

▪ Companies rushed overseas, creating multinational operations on a scale once limited to the oil majors. Today, 100 of the 500 largest companies have at least 25% of their assets, earnings, or production overseas—while another 200 are not far behind.

▪ At home, business began to redefine its relationship with society. Publicly indicted for pollution, deceptive packaging, unsafe products, or discrimination, companies started raising their sights and standards. Most dramatically, 18,500 companies—including many that had discriminated against blacks a few years earlier—joined a national alliance and found jobs for 200,000 unskilled ghetto residents.

▪ And as if to prove that old-fashioned entrepreneurial daring wasn't dead, business spawned a go-go offspring: the conglomerate.

These three main corporate trends of the past decade—the conglomerate, multinationalism, and social concern—will alter the way big business is structured and run in the 1970s and may even change the concept of the corporate role.

The growth of conglomerates will probably slow, in both number and size, as the Justice Dept. clamps down on big mergers. But in their short life so far, conglomerates have introduced highly decentralized structures that may be the harbinger of a new management style in the 1970s. Textron, Litton, and Ling-Temco-Vought, for instance, run $2-billion-a-year operations with no more than 200 people on each of their central staffs. By contrast, diversified companies like General Electric and Westinghouse, which are considered decentralized, still rely on central staffs numbering several thousand.

"The conglomerate," says Norman Berg, associate professor at the Harvard Graduate School of Business Administration, "may show us how to manage diversity more effectively."

Innovation. Conglomerates decentralized decision-making power to speed up change at the operating level. The strategy works well as a device for motivating a division president or plant manager, for it allows him to operate as though he were running his own business.

Though they forfeit some of the gestalt benefits of bigness by decentralizing, the conglomerates realize that new technology and new markets shorten product life. This means that business must keep innovating to prosper. As Ralph E. Ablon, chairman of Ogden Corp., put it in a recent speech: "The only true profit is innovation profit. The rest is making last year's profit again this year."

Increasingly, last year's profit is not enough. But the typical corporation, now largely structured to get maximum internal efficiency, is often hostile to change. The corporation needs to shift emphasis from parameters of efficiency—optimum production, cost-cutting, and the like—to a more responsive product strategy in diverse markets. "Decentralization is the only way," says management consultant John Diebold.

Manager's manager. Unlike the decentralization of the past 30 years, however, the new trend will amount to an almost total devolution of power to division managers. Just as the budget center evolved into the profit center, so will the profit center now become a decision center. Division heads will be responsible only to a single corporate overseer, what Harvard's Berg calls a "manager of managers" or a "one-man board of directors." Company headquarters in some diversified corporations, predicts Anthony J.

The conglomerate, social concern, and multinationalism will alter business structure

Wiener of the Hudson Institute, "will tend to become like central banks," supervising finance and long-range planning.

To be sure, the traditional conflict between decentralization and centralization, between autonomy and coordination, will not end. Large companies concentrated mainly in one industry will still seek—and achieve—economies from central planning and pooling. But the trend will be away from centralization.

Some management thinkers are even beginning to argue that corporations should break up such traditional central services as purchasing. What such services save in economies of scale, they contend, is lost by bureaucratic sluggishness and an inherent resistance to change.

Overseas, American companies will also devolve more power to their local companies, though for a different reason. Put simply, multinational companies, capable of moving men and material across national borders, have outraced the 19th-Century concept of the nation-state. The result is often a nationalistic fear of U. S. economic and political hegemony.

In underdeveloped countries, multinational companies will be forced into joint ventures with the government or local companies, as is now happening in Africa and Latin America. Even in Europe, U. S. corporations will increasingly set up local research labs, permit foreigners to join the board of the parent company, or share equity with local stockholders or concerns—necessary first steps toward the truly stateless or supranational company. But not until political institutions, such as the European Economic Community,

transcend national boundaries will multi-nationalism evolve into supranationalism—a development not expected soon.

Climate for change. As devolution of authority grows at home and abroad, the divisions themselves will develop a fluid structure, blurring traditional staff and line functions. Division managers will encourage competition, even conflict, in their groups. Out of it, they expect to produce a climate for continual change.

Courtney C. Brown, retired dean of the Columbia's Graduate School of Business, expects divisions to organize "constellations of task forces" that will move from problem to problem, cutting across functional lines. Others, using Defense Dept. nomenclature, label the technique "program" or "project" management, a system that frees individuals, with full authority, to work together on a project.

To keep pace with change—what Buckminster Fuller called the "acceleration of acceleration"—corporations will also evolve into educational institutions. Managers will spend as much as 10% of their

---

Companies will be able to afford to pay far more attention to the nation's social problems

---

time in campus-like executive education centers, run by companies or groups of companies. "It will be slightly subversive" predicts Kenneth Andrews, professor at the Harvard B-School, because "executives will be taught to challenge corporate policy as a way of life."

The societal role

Experts concur, to a remarkable degree, that corporations also will become major vehicles for bringing about social change. In the process, the already apparent trend away from profit maximization will accelerate, changing the corporate concept.

"Corporations will broaden the terms in which they state their goals," says Harvard's Andrews. "Management will decide what proportion of effort it should devote to public causes for what are not primarily profit-making reasons." Anthony Wiener, who is working on a Hudson Institute study of the corporation between 1975 and 1985, agrees: "The basic function of profit will become relatively less important."

New forces. In the 1960s, the main force propelling business into social involvement was undoubtedly the trauma of large-scale racial strife. Now, other forces are emerging. By 1975, the gross national product of the U. S. will be double what it was in 1960. With greater affluence, corporations will be able to afford more attention to social problems, including air and water pollution, noise, congestion, job opportunities, and housing. Narrow economic criteria will be less important as social costs are recognized.

Then, too, a new breed of managers, raised in affluent homes and educated amid the turbulence of the 1960s, will start running business. "By God, students today *are* different," says William Newman, professor of management at Columbia's B-School. "They're going to be less willing to settle for jobs whose only aim is

to increase their company's market share." Adds Wiener: "What seems economically irresponsible to today's cost-conscious executives will look very responsible to tomorrow's managers, who will consider additional values."

Problem solving. Over the next 10 years, federal revenue sharing with local government or some similar program will probably release enough money for cities and states to hire companies for civilian projects, much as companies now work for the Defense Dept. or NASA. "Business will act more and more for government," predicts Columbia's Brown. "The corporations will develop as agents, not just principals." GE, for example, might win a contract to improve garbage collection in Schenectady, or Ford might run government-sponsored vocational training centers in Detroit.

Alternatively, public development corporations could spring up in the 1970s. Like Comsat, they would profit from tackling large-scale civilian projects. Such corporations might even run schools and hospitals under proper supervision, Andrews predicts. Though many people now oppose the idea of profiting from schools or hospitals, public development corporations may be the most efficient way to service public needs now badly met in many areas.

Utopian as these ideas may sound, some should reach fruition by the end of the 1970s. Others, of course, will wither. As Benjamin Disraeli wrote in 1832: "What we anticipate seldom occurs; what we least expect generally happens."

WHAZZIT?

STAFF

Specialized personnel who assist managers in specific, usually technical aspects of their work such as engineering, accounting, legal counsel, computer science, purchasing, or personnel.

SPAN OF MANAGEMENT

The number of positions reporting directly to a manager. Generally, the span depends on the manager as a person, the qualities of the people who are his subordinates, their

activities, and other factors.

UNITY OF COMMAND

Each subordinate has only one manager. That is, an individual reports to one person for direction in his or her work. Generally this reduces confusion in an organization.

ORGANIZATION STRUCTURE

The overall pattern of the relationships of positions in an organization.

MATRIX MANAGEMENT

An organization structure with dual lines of management authority: functional responsibility and project responsibility. This means that an employee reports to two different managers -- one for his or her specialty and one for the task or type of job being done.

How To Think Like A Company President

At a recent seminar for company presidents, two executives were discussing their various presidential duties. One represented a firm with over 3,000 employees. His company was highly centralized and decisions were made at the top. The other represented a company with only 500 employees, but decision making was decentralized and decisions were made at the lowest level possible.

The president of the 3,000 employee firm complained that his job was difficult because he was directly responsible for the activities of over 3,000 people. The president with only 500 employees disagreed. "Although you are responsible for 3,000 people," he argued, "I am responsible for '500 presidents.'"

The significance of the remark should not be lost. This president was saying he had an organization of 500 who, because they were decision makers, thought like they were presidents. Although this meant he had a lot of competition, it also meant he had a lot of people who were very much concerned about the welfare of the company.

Busy throwing rocks

It's not easy to get people to think like a company president. Often they are too busy throwing rocks at the guy on top of the heap.

Throwing rocks at the guy on top does have some value. The company president is not unlike the abominable snowman to many people in his organization. Particularly in large companies, he rarely gets the opportunity to meet and talk with the people doing the work or even the people managing those who do the work. They may see him at the company picnic or the Christmas party, but for the most part he's almost mythical and legends of his abilities and failings constantly circulate through the organization.

To change the organization from one which throws rocks to one where everybody thinks they're at the top of the heap is a difficult matter. To do this requires understanding of what makes a company president tick and what pleases or displeases him. Such understanding enables executives reporting to the president to practice "anticipative management."

If you know how your president thinks, you can react in advance to what he will require even before he knows he needs it. Attempts at such understanding give an executive "presidential perspective."

Presidential perspective

Viewing the world from the president's perch can be a heady experience. From this vantage point it's amazing how quickly organizational conflicts and functional bias disappear. Responsibility and authority disputes between groups (even one in which you play a part) somehow pale in comparison to the awesome responsibility of running the company. A seemingly important decision fades to nothing in comparison to the weight of much larger decisions and their implications.

Without even knowing your company president there are some things anyone can say about him. Many are as different as from night to day. Some grew from a sales background and retain their sales orientation. Others came from production, retain their production orientation and are more at ease and familiar with the technical side of their business. Still others came from accounting and maintain the "scorekeeper" orientation with which they are most familiar. Technical specialists tend to favor their particular backgrounds.

Some presidents never successfully complete the transition. They strongly retain their old interests and bias and stubbornly refuse to grow into their new roles. Growth companies need growth presidents and perhaps the degree of company growth can be measured in some part by the degree of presidential growth.

Something else happens when a man becomes a company president. Presidents become a breed unto themselves, not unlike the early pioneers and their outward manifestations of rugged individualism. The breed tends to exhibit the characteristics of the typical business entrepreneur. This is not hard to understand for they both share the total and ultimate responsibility for risk taking.

There are other almost universal presidential characteristics, attitudes, abilities and disabilities. But the "profile" of an individual company president varies. The value in the profile is not that our president fits at all points, but what we learn from it in those areas where he does fit.

The common denominator of the presidential profile is business problems. All company presidents share them. While many of these problems appear to be different, close examination reveals that they tend to cluster or focus on specific management areas and are more common than one would suspect.

Let's examine and categorize typical problems. At the outset let's understand that a president's inability to solve particular problems doesn't necessarily mean failure for his company. Problem solving is never-ending; some will never be solved. Others are solved by diligence, hard work and sometimes sheer luck.

Success as a company president doesn't require solving all problems that arise, but an inability to solve some of the basics goes a long way toward presidential downfall. Obviously, those problems related to company profits are of utmost importance to most company presidents. Frequently, you don't know the problem is solved until some time after corrective action is taken. Sometimes problems appear to be solved but in reality they've shifted elsewhere; the company has traded one set of problems for another. Many presidents liken their own company to a piece of putty. Solving one problem is like pushing a bulge in the putty to make it fit the mold. But the putty just bulges elsewhere.

A basic problem for the typical company president is using his time—a precious commodity—effectively. Presidents have more things to do than they can possibly get to at any given work day. As a result, most presidents, contrary to popular belief, work longer and harder hours than most of their employees.

Still, he is plagued by the unfinished work and the unsolved problem, the lost production, lower morale and widespread confusion. The "pressure cooker" causes rush decisions and actions taken with inadequate evaluation of all the facts—and frequently the results show it.

Paradoxically, presidents lack time for important matters because their time is squandered on detail work that could have been accomplished easier and better by others. Too often he works on things he likes to do rather than things he should do.

At one time or another, most presidents experiment with devices that claim to save time. A would-be president should look into such things as special dictating equipment, memory joggers and files, electronic communication equipment and push button desks. Another device that claims to save time is the computer. Company presidents subconsciously identify the computer as a time-saving machine; therefore, the company should have one. Others just feel it's the thing to do. If a decision to go computer is based on such limited views then the company and the president are surely skating on thin ice.

Fact gathering and analysis may be delegated, but which facts to gather and how to analyze them? Irrelevant information frequently clouds decision making. Therefore, presidents strongly respect and reward any light shedding ability they find in their organizations. This capability is a highly desirable prerequisite for presidential assistant or anyone hoping to fill the president's shoes.

Language explosion
As business becomes more complex and specialized the president finds himself surrounded by functional technicians, each one speaking a separate language. From the president's view it's a tower of Babel. The production vice president speaks of productive capacity, production control. equipment and raw material specifications. The marketing vice president speaks about market share, product life cycles and competitors' marketing strategies. The controller speaks of ratio analysis, costs and profits and balance sheets. The R&D vice president speaks of exotic materials, new product generation and increased budgets for pure research. The data processing manager speaks of hardware, software and programing.

This "language explosion" is growing. Each functional specialist speaks, to some degree. a technical jargon understandable only to those of his own ilk. As the organization and language explosion expands a "language barrier" develops.

The language barrier creates some of the most difficult problems the president has to face. Although the specialists talk to the president (they have to), they do not talk to each other in a common language. Part of the problem is, of course, in the listening device. Too often the president is called upon as arbitrator in a dispute that has its origins in semantic misunderstanding.

Communication problems are increasing for the president because business more and more is scientifically managed.

Some presidents recognize there is a point of diminishing return for specialization within their organization. Getting too technical too fast can be just as bad, or worse, than operating by the seat of your pants. The optimum change rate for the organization has to be ascertained and carefully controlled.

A difficult problem for many company presidents is adjusting to the fact that he has to get things done through other people. Frequently, he does the work himself because he doesn't know how to get other people to do it for him. More than one company president has overcome this difficulty by saying, "Don't do yourself what you can get somebody else to do."

The company president must learn to be a tutor, planner, counselor, disciplinarian and mediator. He must learn the skills of asking effective questions and the gentle art of listening. A successful president proposes objectives. suggests alternatives, breaks bottlenecks and smooths out organizational conflict. His real job is developing people, not doing "things."

To get people to do things requires an effective organization that operates in a systematic manner. Finding, training, stimulating and motivating key executives is a never-ending presidential task. Yet many company presidents feel that all or just about all of their employees are slightly incompetent. They feel they can do every job better than any of their employees. Moreover, they're probably right.

As president, they have perspective that no other employee could possibly have. They understand the "big picture" and therefore know to what degree jobs should be completed. A clerk, for example. may do things that are unnecessary for the proper operation of the business. A president would take shortcuts that the clerk never has the option to take.

Presidents who display this impatient "know it all" attitude create an unhealthy organizational environment. Each function becomes dependent upon the president for decisions, since no one wants the responsibility of making mistakes.

Moreover. people tend to take the role we ascribe to them. If we think of them as incompetent they become incompetent. If on the other hand, we stretch them to their full potential they will develop their capabilities and do a better job. Developing their talents and encouraging their growth causes them to respond in a like manner. During a period of organizational growth and development the president has to stand on the sideline and bite his tongue when he sees mistakes being made. It's temporary, and in the long run, for the good of the company. Only in this way can the president assure the future of an organization that, at some point in time, has to continue without him.

Balancing the organization
Often you hear the statement from the sales-oriented: "If we can just sell more, everything would be fine." The company president who ascribes to that philosophy is surely in trouble. One firm that wholeheartedly believed in this selling philosophy recently went bankrupt. Their business methods and systems were so inadequate and costly that the more they sold. the more money they lost. Their's was the philosophy: "We lose a little on each sale, but we make it up in the volume."

Profit is not made by simply selling more. It results from a careful balancing of sales with the cost of those sales. Developing an organizational philosophy that properly balances each contribution is the best way to assure control and maximum profit.

Business would be better off if managers could be trained to think like company presidents.

WHAZZIT?

BUREAUCRACY

Any complex, formal organization that has defined positions, rules, hierarchy, advancement by merit, fair treatment of all employees, and impersonal relationships.

BUDGET

A plan developed for an organization or a unit of an organization that provides for costs and expenses to be incurred and revenues to be generated.

PROFIT CENTER

An organizational unit that is responsible for generation of earnings on its own, through profitable activity and the control of costs and expenses, usually through a budget.

The Management Machine, Can It Work?

When Scott Paper Co. decided to diversify its traditional one-product line several years ago, it assembled a management machine—computers, scientific formulas, staff, and the like—to help chart its growth. The result: The company's entrance into the plastic- and paper-cup business failed completely, and when its clothlike Viva paper towels proved a test-market bonanza, production facilities were found to be totally inadequate to fill demand.

Yet Scott had spent several years building a corporate model that would give it all the necessary ingredients for broad-based simulation, market analysis, financial analysis and other factors vital to growth planning. What went wrong? The same thing that is going wrong with the management machine in company after company. As one executive puts it, "You can't fault the hammer and chisel for an ugly statue, but you sure as hell can fault the sculptor."

The comparison is apt. In most companies, the efficient use of scientific tools in management decision-making is no further along than a rocket to Jupiter. What successes are reported are largely in single activities, such as inventory control, work scheduling, laboratory data-processing and sales reports. And while the components of the management machine, from computers to operations research to formulas such as PERT and CPM, are still not in their ultimate state of refinement, they are twenty years or so ahead of management's understanding of them.

This is the crisis that industry faces right now in making the $30-billion-plus it has invested in its sophisticated hardware, formulas and techniques pay off. The answers that the management machine can come up with may be infinite, but it is human judgment that must decide what questions to ask. And only human judgment can analyze the answers that the machine produces.

But judgment is the one element in the process that cannot be mechanized, and it is precisely this problem of fitting in the human being that makes many experts wonder if the management machine can ever really work. William Pharo, who as director of information systems development at Western Electric is in charge of one of the most advanced management systems in the world, describes the machine this way: "It's just a bunch of electrical components wired together, and it certainly has no inherent capability to think. In fact, all it can do is what a human being tells it to do."

When the management machine fails, then, the reasons are almost always human. To start with, there is a basic misunderstanding of what the machine is all about and what it can do. Most companies approach it in one of two ways, both of them wrong. They either practically ignore it, using it primarily to solve only isolated, routine problems. Or, with visions of a push-button world dancing in their heads, they phase it into the mainstream of the organization too quickly, before they understand its operations and potential. "When the system doesn't work," maintains Gastone Chinagri, operations research specialist at Sperry Rand's Univac division, "it's usually because it was not customized by management to fulfill its own needs. If the design is wrong, the human element simply won't respond."

More specifically, the mistakes that are most prevalent in assembling a management machine can be boiled down to four basic ones: failure to assemble the machines in the right combination of hardware, techniques and staff; failure to feed the system the right data, resulting in useless outputs; failure to tap the full potential of the machine, resulting in piecemeal outputs, costly idle time and overlong return on investment; and failure to superimpose human judgments on basically inflexible, mathematically based data.

Garbage in, garbage out

Take the corporate model, one of management's most popular scientific tools for planning. Into the computer's memory banks are fed masses of statistics, which as a whole represent a "model" of all, or part, of the corporation in mathematical terms. Then, through simulation, another space-age technique, "what if" problems are put to the model and the answers that come out tell the company how to proceed. But as the experience at Scott Paper shows, the corporate model is useless unless management knows what it wants to find out.

Basically, it is a matter of inputs and outputs. Scott's entry into the cup business failed both because the input of data into the model was inadequate and because the signs indicated by the data that came out were not read properly. It appeared to be just another example of the basic law of computers: garbage in generates garbage out. "For one thing," says Lippincott, "since we couldn't properly identify the market, our inputs were incorrect. And we didn't heed the danger signals; for example, our lack of marketing skills in seasonal goods and the relatively high price of the product versus its competitive price."

As for its experience with the Viva paper towels, Lippincott adds, "If we had developed contingency plans (mainly through simulation) to our original plan, it wouldn't have taken us two years to get started."

Another company that found out about corporate models the hard way is General Electric. About eight years ago, GE started building a long-range planning model to forecast the investment requirements and potential profits of alternate major business strategies. "About the second year," explains Sidney Schoeffler, manager of long-range plans, "after spending considerable time and energy getting it organized, we tested it in the field."

Result: "It was a catastrophe," admits Schoeffler. "It was unreliable—excellent for some of our businesses but not for others. The people in the field, presented with something new, said it wasn't worth the paper it was printed on, called it garbage, stupid and a few other choice names. They indicated that we were ignorant of their situation, said the inputs were too simple and the outputs not expressed simply enough. They accused us of using too short a span of experience, so the model couldn't possibly be representative of the future. And, finally, they told us that there wasn't enough in the model for them to make

387 MANAGING

effective judgments."

The trouble, explains Schoeffler, was that the model makers were just too ambitious and, as it turned out, created what by today's standards was a sloppy model. So after the first tests showed up every conceivable shortcoming, three tests were rigorously applied to the model: The relationships of the mathematical components in it had to strongly maximize closeness of relationships and minimize random factors; the model had to make sense to professional economists armed with the most up-to-date economic theory and concepts; and it had to make sense to businessmen who were familiar with business realities but not necessarily with the makeup and functioning of the model.

One other rule was also applied: The model makers went back to data from the previous few years to establish known values; by applying these known values, they were able to come up with more realistic projections for the future. "Now, six years later," Schoeffler says, "the model is operating effectively and in keeping with all the realities ignored when it was first tested."

Thus even the most sophisticated element in the management machine, the corporate math model, is totally dependent for its conception and use on human judgment. "Only if the user demonstrates a need for its outputs," says James I. Williams, advanced financial concepts planner at Lockheed Aircraft, "can the model be successful, because it is of value only if it plays a significant role in someone's basis for making decisions."

Management by exception?

Many attempts are being made to discover a basic science that explains the management machine, but so far none have really succeeded. Cybernetics, the intriguing study of relationships between the control and communications in machines and living organisms, comes closest. Behavioral science, the study of human behavior in an organized system, explains only the human element in the machine and disregards the rest.

Some of the newer concepts applied to the management machine actually set it back. The philosophy of management by exception, for example, places the manager in the role of an error-detecting servomechanism (a control actuated by signals from another part of the system). The manager receives information from the system, compares it with the state he wants to achieve, then issues orders that he hopes will close the gap.

The problem here, explains Myron Tribus, Assistant Secretary of Commerce for Science and Technology, is that "it is rough on the manager, for he receives nothing but bad news all day. If things are going right, he gets no signals; all he hears about are deviations from what is supposed to be happening. Servo engineers do not care about the emotional state of the controller," Tribus adds, "but humans deserve better care."

But if the human element in the management machine is hard to pin down, one thing is certain: Unless top management takes a personal and involved interest in it, the machine cannot possibly work. Middle-level executives are constantly heard to complain about their troubles in using new formulas or techniques because the company president gives the okay to go ahead with them and then shows no interest in how they are working.

In fact, some top executives even today believe that machines and formulas can play little part in managing a company. One is Chairman Sidney Friedman of National Bank of North America, who dismisses the whole idea. "People selling these machines," Friedman rasps, "are more interested in selling their hardware than in the bank." Nor is he loathe to admit, "I don't even know what PERT is."

Friedman echoes the views of many chief executives who are convinced that the management machine stops "at the teller's cage," and that the entire company is controlled and operated by humans using human judgment and rendering human decisions. These men believe that if they are not involved and on top of a situation, their own managers and the people below will not feel the need to be involved. As Friedman puts it, "Even with fancy formulas and charts, a McKinsey & Co. couldn't fire up an organization. The top executive must set the example and keep it alive."

No one would deny that such leadership is a must in running today's modern, complex corporation. But there is just as much reason to believe that technology is equally essential. Asserts Franz Edelman, director of operations research at RCA: "Experience, intuition and even the most painstaking staff support are simply not enough for those who manage in today's complex society. They need the analytic tools to help them evaluate judgment situations."

President Dick H. Brandon of Brandon Applied Systems is even more specific. "Taking today's continuing advances in communications, data-processing techniques and hardware, the new management formulas and, of course, management's understanding of them," Brandon believes, "at least three-quarters of the time-consuming routine in management will be bypassed as early as 1975."

Nevertheless, it may well be that one reason many top executives are not sold on the management machine is because they see some of the uses it is put to. One of the latest wrinkles in formalizing data-flow and decision-making, for example, is a new type of organization chart. C.I.T. Financial Corp.'s is typical. The organization is portrayed as a series of concentric circles; in the bull's-eye are listed the senior corporate officers; the lesser officers are listed in the next circle outward, and so on.

One less typical new chart is that of smallish Boyertown Auto Body Works in Boyertown, Pennsylvania. Resembling a cross between a Japanese lighting fixture and a fancy cake cutter, the chart, says Chairman Paul R. Hafer, "puts management at the center of the company in a supporting role, nòt at the top."

But what's the point? Regardless of where the chief executive is placed in the organization chart, he is still the head man. The old pyramid type of chart, more prosaic and less artistic though it might be, tells it like it is: the chief is at the top of the chart and the lesser executives are below. "You can slap together any kind of an organization chart," comments Sidney Friedman.

"Simply not workable"

Not surprisingly, one of the biggest stumbling blocks to the setting up of an effective management machine right now is the gap between the men who run the company and the men who run the machine. Many management people place a large share of the blame for costly mistakes on the technicians, who, they claim, build overly mechanized systems, communicate in scientific gobbledygook that is incomprehensible to the layman, and just do not understand enough about the problems of running a company.

At ESB Inc., for example, a battery plant was planned on paper. Computers and scientific planning formulas were used to chart everything from operating costs to return on investment. Says Robert Hadley, ESB assistant to the president for technology: "The plant was simply not workable. It was too mechanized for a business with comparatively low capital investment. The people who planned the plant were too inexperienced in the battery business. They were just too technical. Luckily," Hadley adds, "the faults were discovered before a spade of earth was turned."

Business-oriented executives generally claim that it is easier for them to relate their business experiences to technical matters. But is it? One of the biggest mistakes that management makes with the management machine is having either too much or too little faith in it—and this, of course, is simply because they do not understand what it can, and cannot, do.

ESB's Robert Hadley tells about receiving an order from a customer for 50,000 batteries. The amount had been decided by the customer's electronic ordering system, which included built-in checks on outgoing orders and was thought to be foolproof. Nevertheless, it ordered 40,000 batteries too many.

Lack of faith in the management machine is even more prevalent—and certainly just as costly. American Can Co., for example, suffered a serious jolt in earnings of 89 cents a share two years ago. Senior Vice President E. N. Funkhouser, Jr. attributes at least part of the loss to the company's refusal to pay attention to its corporate model. He explains: "We built a mathematical model of the glass business we wanted to go into, relating what we knew to be the major industry factors. In effect, the model told us to get out of the business. But we made the mistake of not believing everything it told us or following the options it pointed out. We stayed in the business five years before we got out."

"When you fall off a bike," Funkhouser adds, "you remember why. For every such mistake we've made in the past, we figure we've had twenty to thirty successes."

Nowhere is the gap between the management generalist and technical specialist more debilitating than in operations. Technologically, there is no reason why such areas as manufacturing, distribution, packaging, maintenance and material-handling cannot be worked into the management machine. Yet progress in automating operations is slower than in any other area of the company.

This can be blamed partly on company managers who are either unwilling or afraid to use the advanced systems at their disposal. But also to blame are the technicians who are building overly mechanized systems with little regard for the facts of business life.

One of the classic examples of overmechanization was Johnson & Johnson's highly touted automatic warehouse a few years back: a giant, first-of-its-kind storage-and-retrieval system, monitored and controlled by computer, set up to automatically sort and dispatch thousands of orders daily. The system was a bust, reportedly because a simple, human element in the company's operations was overlooked: A large percentage of orders were small and required hand-processing for pickup by car or small truck.

Pan American World Airways only recently solved a similar problem. Two years ago, Pan Am swung open the doors of a spanking new, 156,000-square-foot automatic cargo handling facility at Kennedy Airport. The maze of conveyers, computerized modules, automatic storage and retrieval racks looked like something out of a science-fiction movie.

And that was just the trouble. Like science fiction, the $8.5-million system was more the result of the creator's imagination than the answer to Pan Am's cargo-handling needs. It simply did not work, and the neglect of the human variables was largely to blame. Reports an insider:

"First, we built the system without enough experience; as you know, the facility was the first of its kind. Second, the system was overautomated; it didn't allow us much latitude for change. Third, and most important, it completely neglected the fact that people, especially those around the New York area, don't pick up their shipments on schedule. The system was designed for steady in-and-out handling; it did not accommodate storage."

It took a "panic survey" to straighten out the situation, adds the insider, and today the Pan Am system is operating almost to expectations. Moreover, two warehouses in the U.S. and two in Europe benefited from the lessons of Kennedy. They were built with a minimum of mechanization and are being automated only to meet demand.

What about costs?

On the other hand, one of the strangest paradoxes in industry today is the high cost of operations in the face of an endless flow of new cost-cutting tools and systems. Management, while constantly complaining about the costs of labor, rejects and the like, looks fearfully or not at all at innovations that could slash these costs considerably.

Production control, to be sure, is one of the most complicated elements in business. Yet several techniques have already been proven largely workable. One is adaptive control, which practically assures continual quality output by automatically correcting deviations in machine settings when they occur. Another is remote control of automatic processes, already proven feasible by Bunker-Ramo and others who have pioneered in the field.

If such systems were tied into the management machine, one of the main benefits would be the ability to automatically report machine system conditions, output rates, reject rates and such to management without the endless and slow-moving paperwork such factors now require. And, of course, the span of control could be markedly lessened, since few decision-makers would be needed over a greater spread of production units. Yet outside of the processing industries, where they are easily integrated, practically no company has adopted either system.

Progress in operation control will undoubtedly be made, but probably much more slowly than in other parts of a company. "Production control," notes Robert Zellmer, ESB director of manufacturing, "is one of the key strings that tie operations into the corporate management system. You need to take time to develop a good system slowly."

In fact, given the human element, it is likely that an effective management machine can be built only through a gradual step-by-step process. As GE's Sidney Schoeffler puts it, "You cannot delegate management to a machine, and executives will never be replaced by push-buttons. Nevertheless, managers will have to go through a gradual process of learning to use the new tools, adapting the system to their own needs. Management," Schoeffler concludes "can be assisted—but not formalized."

—GEORGE BERKWITT

MBO: Management By Objectives

Managers who believe that people can perform better if they know what they are trying to accomplish often follow Management By Objectives (MBO).

This is an important approach to management, even a style of managing that gets built into the minds of managers.

With MBO we assume that the organization benefits when individuals know what is expected of them and are committed to achieving results. Participation in management is built into this process -- individual involvement in setting goals and in tracking progress as they work.

MBO is a process that pulls people together as an active, satisfying, achieving organization. Through individual involvement, MBO places emphasis on ability and achievement rather than on personality or tenure. In a well-designed MBO program, goals and strategies of the company and of the individuals are established through discussions between managers and their subordinates.

Naturally, organizational goals are broader, and are refined as they are interpreted at each successive level.

Feedback is provided through follow-up discussions during the period of time set for achieving the goals. Feedback may be in the form of data on quantitative results (such as dollar sales, unit costs, number of products produced, or net profits), data on qualitative results (such as customer complaints, reductions in errors, improvement of product reputation, or development of subordinates). Person-to-person communications th through coaching from day to day are important.

Because individuals receive information on their performance results, they are able to take corrective actions when necessary.

The MBO approach assumes that people will accept responsibility for achieving goals; they will become committed when the goals are meaningful, attainable goals established through meaningful planning.

The final stage of the MBO process is the appraisal of results. At the end of the performance period, the manager and the individual check the progress in achieving the goals. This serves as a time for recognition of performance and as a time for renewed goal setting.

This process is a continuous cycle of goal setting, coaching and feedback, and appraisal of results. It is a natural behavioral process that you follow informally every day. When you go shopping, make something, or study for an exam, you have an objective in mind and are working to achieve it. It's MBO in action and you are your own manager!

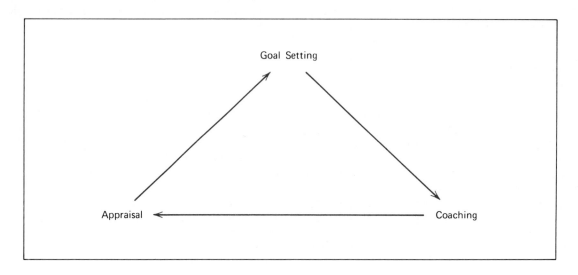

MBO: Management Strategy For The Emerging Generation

Implementation of an MBO Program

The first stage of an MBO program has been defined as the development and communication of the organization's long-range goals. The next phase is to assure top management support for the MBO program. Once the work force understands the importance placed upon the program by the chief executive, acceptance at lower levels is more probable.

Individual managers then must clarify in their own minds the job responsibilities of their subordinates. This can be facilitated by using organization charts and job descriptions. Next, the manager should ask each subordinate to write out goals he thinks he has, while in turn the manager writes out those he thinks his subordinates should have. These should be reviewed during a personal interview. After agreement has been reached, written copies of the agreed-upon goals should be prepared for both manager and subordinate. The manager should then ask how he personally can help in achieving these goals; further, he should request suggestions, and use regular follow-ups to evaluate progress.

An objective of MBO:
The merging of individual goals
with the goals
of the company

If prior results are acceptable to the organization and the individual, it is good practice to utilize them in establishing future objectives. It is important that individual responsibility be stressed and that new ideas be introduced from outside the system, as flexibility must be maintained to allow for changing environmental conditions. Of equal importance, successful achievements should be quickly reinforced through recognition of a job well done.

When asked to participate in the goal-setting process, some persons will purposely attempt to set their personal goals low in order not to make the target too difficult to achieve. This quirk of human nature demands that the superior be constantly alert and exercise sound judgment. Nor can the manager relieve himself of his responsibility for achieving results merely because goals are set in mutual consultation with subordinates.

As subordinates learn to establish objectives and to direct activities toward their achievement, the rate of control and amount of evaluation gradually can be diminished. During the initial stages of the MBO program, monthly reviews may be appropriate, and as time and experience wear on, the reviews may be extended to quarterly frequency. For maximum effectiveness, reviews probably should be performed more often than once each year.

Goals should be specific and, where possible, quantified for easier measurement. Individual goals should also be substantiated by a strategy for implementation. One of the greatest dangers in managing by objectives is that results may be stressed while there is no clearly defined program of *how* to achieve these results. Consider the production superintendent who is in the process of setting goals in the areas of inventory, quality, records, communications, development, innovation, maintenance, safety, and absenteeism. Examples of goals and substantiated strategies are as follows:

INVENTORY. Reduce out of stock items to 1 percent of total inventory items through installation of order cycling method by March 15.

QUALITY. Establish a 3 percent AOQL through installation of statistical sampling techniques; have charts posted by midsummer.

RECORDS. Have 90 percent of required reports in by due date by hiring and training an executive secretary.

COMMUNICATIONS. Hold weekly meetings with all foremen.

DEVELOPMENT. Install JIT program for new machine operators by December 1.

INNOVATION. Use program evaluation and review technique (PERT) for all new layouts.

MAINTENANCE. Reduce machine breakdowns to three per month through preventive maintenance program.

SAFETY. Reduce serious injuries to 15 per million hours worked through weekly plant tours, foreman meetings, poster campaign.

ABSENTEEISM. Reduce hours paid for but not worked to 4 percent through increased effort in human relations and participative management.

Benefits of an MBO Program

Many advantages can be derived from the effective implementation of an MBO program. Employees at all levels have a better understanding of what is expected of them and therefore they are more likely to achieve their goals. They gain satisfaction by knowing when they have reached or surpassed a goal, thus some ambiguity is eliminated from their work. Managers are more effective planners and have a better understanding of the implementation of control methods. At the same time, increased interaction between superior and subordinate tends to generate feedback that might not otherwise result.

Still another benefit is greater employee involvement. When lower level employees are forced to sit and think about their personal goals and how these relate to goals of the organization, they are more likely to link their own objectives with those of other organizational units. Thus, an additional by-product results from Management by Objectives: these same employees generally expand their general knowledge of organizational affairs and thereby increase their interest in future objectives.

It is no longer necessary to appraise employees solely on the basis of such vague and global traits as dependability, initiative, responsibility and integrity—the traits so often evaluated in traditional rating systems. Goal-oriented effort, in contrast to task-oriented effort, usually leads to greater vitality and is likely to make daily work more meaningful. A well-planned Management by Objectives program is not likely to do harm within an organization, and since the probability of its doing some good is high (with little expenditure for extra resources) should management not at least consider the approach?

A Note of Caution

Management by Objectives is far from a panacea. Those executives who have been involved very often find it difficult to apply MBO concepts to their own work habits. They find it hard to think about the results of work rather than the work itself. They tend to over-emphasize certain goals which are most easily quantified, sometimes forgetting that workers often behave almost like children at play —when the game no longer challenges them, they lose interest.

It appears that Management by Objectives does not have the same effect upon all people in all situations. H. L. Leavitt suggests that organizations be viewed as differentiated sets of subsystems rather than as unified wholes. Such a view then leads toward a "management-by-task" type of outlook. With this it is recognized that various subsystems may perform different kinds of tasks, and therefore may call for variation in managerial practices. It has been suggested also that participation in goal-setting works with certain types of followers but not with others. The extent to which an across-the-board MBO approach is applied depends on the skill and judgment of the manager. Independent personalities typically perform better when they participate; highly authoritarian personalities generally perform more effectively when they are not required to participate to a very great degree. As was pointed out earlier, most human beings want to be controlled within some limits. The manager must decide where to set these limits for each individual reporting to him. Moreover, the participative approach probably works best where there is a continuous need to change and adapt. In this light, some industries should give quick and serious consideration to adopting an MBO approach while others may wish to move slowly in the direction of participatory goal-setting. However, in today's dynamic technosocial environment, the number of industries in this latter category is rapidly diminishing.

Conclusion

In this age of dynamic change, it is fruitless to seek an ideal strategy of management since frustration would undoubtedly be the primary result of such a search. Rather, management must be concerned with "moving in the right direction," maintaining a balance between technological advancement and human need achievement. As the information revolution continues to provide greater challenge, we must seek to narrow the gap between our technology and our capability to understand and utilize it to the betterment of human dignity. Management scientists and behavioral scientists could integrate their research efforts to achieve synergistic results. At this time, very few generalizations can be made about the management of human resources. Fortunately, we are moving in a positive direction, and future generations will undoubtedly benefit from the successes and failures of our experimentation.

It is unlikely that a Management by Objectives program could harm any organization. In fact, research indicates it is probable that it will do some good with little expenditure for extra resources. As McGregor points out, "Under proper conditions, participation and consultative management provide encouragement to people to direct their creative energies toward organization objectives, gives them some voice in decisions which affect them, and provides significant opportunities for satisfaction of social and egoistic needs."

If the MBO approach is to be truly effective, executives at all levels must be able to communicate with one another, speaking the same language; those at the bottom must be willing to listen to the voice of experience, and those at the top willing to accept fresh ideas from newcomers on the lower rungs of the organizational hierarchy. Executives must keep in touch with new findings in management through practically oriented development programs. Moreover, they must stay abreast of modern ideas being introduced by recent university graduates. Objectives should be reevaluated constantly for appropriateness and direction. Imagination and creativity have brought free enterprise to the pinnacle of world prosperity. Mutual understanding and compromise through Management by Objectives may assure continued progress and even greater prosperity—in spite of the adversities of our times.

Do Profit Centers Really Work?

Last spring, President Edward B. Fitzgerald of Cutler-Hammer faced one of the chief executive's most unpleasant tasks: explaining to a group of New York security analysts why his company had suffered a precipitous 24% drop in earnings the year before. The reason for the setback, in Fitzgerald's words, was that several years of drastic organizational changes at Cutler-Hammer caused "an interim deterioration in internal operating efficiency [which] has been more severe than we anticipated and has not been corrected as quickly as we believed correction could be accomplished."

While Fitzgerald elaborated no further, one admission was glaringly implicit in his statement: the profit-center organization that he himself had adopted only four years earlier—by breaking Cutler-Hammer up into five autonomous divisions, each accountable for its own sales and profits—had developed some bugs of its own. Profit centers, Fitzgerald had discovered to his dismay, are no guarantee of either top efficiency or rising earnings.

And Fitzgerald is not alone in this respect. Ampex Corp. courted near-disaster a few years ago when it went all out for the profit-center approach and wound up wallowing in red ink. Or consider the conglomerates, the most determined practitioners of the profit-center concept. A good many of them, as every reader of the financial pages knows, have run into trouble on just this score. Thus, Chairman Ralph E. Ablon's Ogden Corp. had its eyes opened when its Avondale, Louisiana shipbuilding division suddenly went out of control with a $7-million dip in pretax earnings in the third quarter of last year. And Harry Figgie's "Automatic" Sprinkler suffered a precipitous slide in 1968 earnings—and stock price—when one of its subsidiaries ran into trouble on a military contract.

In short, profit centers, for all their advantages, are subject to a whole range of problems peculiar to themselves. The decentralized type of operation, for better or for worse, puts greatly increased pressures on the men on the firing line to perform, and thus tends to obscure their overall corporate view.

Concedes Donald A. Donahue, executive vice president of Amax Corp., a company that has been eminently successful with profit centers: "In meeting their own profit plans, they [division heads] tend to veer away from corporate objectives." Beyond that, normal interdivisional relationships can turn into a bitter rivalries that, as Donahue points out, "often end up in hellish fights."

In recent years, of course, the idea of the profit center as the most efficient form of corporate organization has spread throughout the U.S. like crabgrass through a suburban lawn. Industry has seized on the concept with growing enthusiasm ever since World War II, until today some four-fifths of all major U.S. corporations are largely or wholly decentralized. And today, with the fierce attention paid to the bottom line, executives particularly laud it as the best way to keep multi-division growth companies on the fast track.

The basic idea is simple enough. As Professor John Dearden of the Harvard Business School explains it: "The company is broken down into manageable units called profit centers, each of which is treated as an independent company. Each is controlled by a manager who is responsible for earning a satisfactory return on the investment at his disposal. Operating decisions are made by management closest to the problem. Because these people are held responsible for the effect of their decisions on profits, they are motivated to make decisions that will create the maximum profit."

Since each division manager is uniquely familiar with his own division's operations, products and markets, and with its people and their idiosyncrasies, logically he is best equipped to run the operation profitably. Too, the profit-center concept has the further value of simplicity. It takes what used to be truckloads of paperwork, huge headquarters staffs and the perpetual dialogue between divisions and front office, and boils them all down into such essentials as periodic budgeting and reviewing, occasional meetings and monthly profit-and-loss statements.

Theoretically, then, the company gets the best of both worlds. When divided into relatively small operating units, a large corporation gains all the advantages of being small: flexibility, close control, ability to make quick decisions, and so forth. At the same time, central staff coordination of the individual profit centers allows the company to retain the many obvious advantages of size.

Then what goes wrong? To begin with, disaster often strikes because of haste and lack of planning. Top management decides that profit centers are the "in" thing, and suddenly an entirely new mode of corporate life is imposed on everyone from the president down to the on-the-spot manager of each profit center. Lower-echelon men long used to certain established lines of authority discover they have new prerogatives—and new responsibilities. A company that has always been under the direct and close control of its corporate leaders overnight becomes, as Amax' Donahue puts it, "a company of little presidents."

Very often, the company fails to clearly define its profit-center concept in the first place. Says President William J. Scharffenberger of Riegel Paper Corp.: "Some managements relegate it to the position of an accounting concept; others see it as a management tool. It's just too easy to apply the term loosely so that management doesn't always have to live by it."

Chinks in the armor

Lack of clear-cut direction at the top naturally hampers the job of day-to-day management at the divisional level. Take the classic case of Litton Industries, for a dozen years the pace-setter for the new, precision-tooled look in corporate management and, with its eighty divisions, the outstanding example of the profit-center philosophy in action. Or so it seemed until early last year when the now-celebrated letter to stockholders announced that for the first time in the company's fourteen-year history, profits in the following quarter would decline.

While disappointing declines in earnings are hardly unusual, what was unusual was that Litton management felt called upon to reveal a chink in its own seemingly impregnable armor by add-

393 MANAGING

ing bluntly that much of the blame lay with "deficiencies of management personnel." And the course of corporate introspection that followed revealed a buildup of errors in everything from marketing to manufacturing, from cost estimating to pricing.

Some of the lesser-known details shed considerable light on how an apparently thriving profit center can suddenly turn sour. A notable example of Litton's left hand being completely dissociated from its right occurred at the Ingalls shipbuilding division in Pascagoula, Mississippi. While most corporations were reacting to rising operating costs in the early 1960s by clamping on tighter control systems, cost control was minimal at Ingalls because the division had no particular problems with its usual run of one-ship contracts.

But as the world's fleets became obsolete and demand for ships grew, orders mounted fast; with new production-line methods, it was cheaper for a buyer to purchase several ships at a time. As the number of ships per contract began to swell, Ingalls applied new cost controls with a vengeance. Too late. Management discovered, in fact, that its bids on multi-ship contracts were well below the market. Worse yet, a $200-million contract Ingalls had won for fourteen automated cargo vessels was discovered to be a whopping $8 million short of even covering Litton's costs.

Meanwhile, an epidemic of reverses swept other Litton profit centers. Somehow the supposedly clear lines of communication between headquarters in Beverly Hills and the widely dispersed divisions had become clogged. Most of the resulting troubles occurred in Litton's business-equipment division. In one case, a price increase, put through to offset higher costs, and then subsequent reinstatement of the original price—too late to do any good—diverted a lot of business to the competition. In another, the company announced a line of electronic calculators long after others, selling for less, were already on dealers' shelves. And so it went.

If Litton's was the classic case, plenty of other major companies of late have faced the same sort of corporate awakening. Eight years ago, $2-billion General Dynamics Corp. was rocked to its foundations when management of its Convair division at Fort Worth, Texas—maintaining a discreet distance between itself and headquarters in New York—cost the company some $200 million by contracting to produce long-range commercial jet aircraft at a price that actually involved a loss of around $2 million per plane. So freewheeling was the division (up to then, at least) that even "detailed" semiannual plans and forecasts had failed to alert top management to the impending trouble.

Comments Harvard's John Dearden: "When a division manager runs into trouble, he wants to keep top management out of his division until, hopefully, he can clean up the situation. And the more serious the situation, the stronger will be the motivation to soft-pedal it."

In many a company, the profit-center approach starts fires instead of putting them out because of intense intracompany rivalries, especially between divisions that must do business with each other. Top management, according to one executive, sometimes deliberately encourages competition between divisions to keep them on their toes—and profitable. As he adds, however, "A certain amount of competition may be a good thing, but not when it reaches the dog-eat-dog stage."

The fact is that even at this late stage of profit-center development, such highly decentralized companies as Amax, Bulova Watch, Riegel Paper and at least one giant oil producer frankly admit that they still have difficulties with pricing between divisions that buy and sell from each other. "A good executive can eliminate this type of thing," argues Amax' Donahue, "by properly supervising from a distance the internal buying and selling operation. But no matter how intelligent the competitors are or how much goodwill exists between them, transfer-pricing [pricing of transactions between divisions] can be a constant source of friction."

Such difficulties, in turn, are likely to put further strain on already weakened lines of authority. When it allows divisions to buy or sell from each other at a profit—and in the process gives up some of its other normal prerogatives—top management hopes to gain one thing: an intensified effort by every manager to improve the figures on the bottom line. Like it or not, top management then also has to expect its managers to use every weapon at their command in the drive for profit.

One division's weapon, however, may be another's red ink. And two divisions at loggerheads can cost a company a lot. Just before being acquired by a conglomerate, one of the nation's leading makers of X-ray and industrial inspection equipment was in deep trouble. The cause: a vicious battle over transfer-pricing between the autonomous marketing division in the East and the equally autonomous manufacturing division in the Midwest. The two became so uncommunicative and so uncooperative, an insider reveals, that the introduction of new products slowed down sharply. And in the aftermath, he adds, "GE grabbed half of the company's business."

An expensive mistake

Perhaps the greatest danger of all in the profit-centered company is the sacrifice of overall corporate objectives to the pursuit of short-range profitability. With constant pressure from top management to increase profits year after year, the division head must continually prove himself; this leaves him little time to devote to anything except his immediate performance. Agrees President Stephen F. Keating of Honeywell: "Many long-term opportunities have been missed because of a desire for short-term profitability."

The point, of course, is to keep the profit motive from overwhelming overall corporate goals. But how much of the decision-making process sifts down from headquarters to the divisional level is questionable. Complains one division head: "You never see corporate officers around here unless your quarterly profit falls below the goal."

With only a year to maneuver in, moreover, division heads are forced to move fast to produce the results they have targeted. Naturally, they protect themselves as best they can.

One method some division managers use is the double budget. An "official" budget is submitted to headquarters. It is purposely pitched high, but not so high that it cannot be sold nearly intact to the company's top management. Meanwhile, the division head also prepares an unofficial budget, somewhat lower and more in keeping with the division's real needs. All year he keeps peeking at the unofficial budget in his lower left-hand desk drawer, and tries to stay within it.

But the two-budget technique, warns Sarason D. Liebler, manager in the management services group for accounting firm Touche, Ross, Bailey & Smart, simply encourages more short-term thinking.' For this reason, says Liebler, the best-managed companies "look more closely at *how* profits are made, rather than just at the figures themselves."

Figures aside, the more alert executives in profit-centered organizations are gradually becoming aware of the need for greater high-level attention to the human factors in division management. Riegel Paper's Scharffenberger admits that he worries less about the tactics that some "clever" profit-center managers may resort to than about the possibility that he may inadvertently step on their toes. "We don't want to cut into their management style," he insists. "We could generate an enormous amount of frustration and destroy and possibly lose a good man."

At McNeil Corp., an Akron-based manufacturer of industrial and consumer products, President Richard A. Michelson believes in giving his profit-center managers all the authority they can handle. "We've noticed," Michelson says, "that companies that removed some of the decision-making responsi-bility from top divisional people also removed one of the strongest inducements for them to run their own show."

As a general rule, it seems to be true that the larger and more complex the corporation, the more decentralization is indicated. But that philosophy can hardly be pursued to its ultimate. "It is just one step," says John Dearden, tongue in cheek, "to the conclusion that if some decentralization will mitigate an administrative problem, a lot of decentralization will solve it."

The grave risks in the all-or-nothing approach to profit centers were demonstrated, once and for all, by the experience of Ampex Corp., the producer of commercial and industrial communications systems. Back in 1960, Ampex consisted of five wholly autonomous divisions, with even less control from above than many of today's most highly decentralized corporations. Then in 1961 the company was buffeted by several storms at once: a mini-recession in the industry and a sudden bulge in its own operating expenses, inventories and other costs. Unable to stem a tide that saw earnings plummet from $3.96 a share in 1960 to a deficit of almost identical proportions the following year, President George Long resigned.

William E. Roberts, Long's replacement as president and chief executive officer, promptly reversed gears and consolidated most of the divisions. Roberts then followed a carefully measured course back to decentralization, reconstructing the divisions one by one.

But the lesson in management was costly. Recalls Walter P. Weber, vice president of finance: "Complete autonomy almost proved disastrous for Ampex. Decentralization can be extremely beneficial. But it can also be dangerous unless it is carefully constructed and constantly monitored for the good of the company as a whole. There is simply no way to set up a company-wide, profit-centered system that will work in all situations."

Like democracy, profit centers will continue to reflect the errors and imperfections of men as well as their sound judgments. And until the concept becomes flexible enough to accommodate the foibles of its human element, its problems will continue to be at least as conspicuous as its accomplishments.

WHAZZIT?

ECONOMY OF SCALE

The greater the level of production, the lower the cost for each unit produced. Generally, there are efficiencies in larger operations.

LINEAR PROGRAMMING (LP)

A mathematical technique often used in management decision making. It shows the optimal way to allocate money or solve some other problem, given specified constraints.

PERT/CPM

Program Evaluation and Review Technique and the Critical Path Method are two planning tools used by management to keep track of the various tasks making up a project.

DECENTRALIZING

Delegating responsibility for decision making to the lowest possible level in an organization.

MANAGEMENT CONSULTANT

An independent professional, often associated with a firm of other consultants, who provides advice and specialized technical assistance to companies.

COACHING

Providing day-to-day guidance and counseling to employees as they work to achieve their objectives.

The ⬭Ford⬭ Story

In the 1920's Ford Motor Company controlled two thirds of the automobile market. Fifteen years later, by the start of World War II, the company's share had fallen to 20%. It is reputed that the company, which was privately held at that time, did not show a profit during any of these fifteen years.

The very survival of the firm seemed to be in question. In fact, there was talk about the government loaning money to Studebaker, the fourth largest automobile company, to buy out the Ford family and run its company. It was widely felt that the company might collapse without some type of intervention, endangering the ehalth of our nations's economy and our effectiveness in the war effort.

The troubles at Ford were believed to have roots in the rule of Henry Ford. As one observer said, "Fundamental to Henry Ford's misrule was a systematic, deliberate and conscious attempt to run the billion-dollar business without managers. The secret police that spied on all Ford executives served to inform Henry Ford of any attempt on the part of one of his executives to make a decision. When they seemed to acquire managerial authority or responsibility of their own, they were generally fired."

Ford, as owner, felt an extreme obligation to control all business decisions in his company. The company itself would employ only technicians. He preferred simply to hold all the reins himself, never to share management. As a result, his greatest insecurity, and the reason for the "secret police" was a fear of an uprising among his subordinates.

There was hope that Ford's only son, Edsel, would build managerial strength in the corporation. These hopes were shattered, however, when Edsel suddenly died during World War II.

HENRY FORD II

The revival of Ford Motor was led instead by Ford's grandson, who assumed responsibility for top management in 1944. With his father dead and his grandfather seriously ill, young Ford set a new course of management for the Firm. He had no business experience, but recognized the importance of bringing in capable new talent and delegating full responsibility for managment actions.

Ford was officially appointed vice president in 1943, but this was a rather empty title because his grandfather blocked his actions. The elder Ford and his hatchet men made the mistake of underestimating him. In just a few years, the reluctance of Henry Ford to surrender control was worn down and in 1945, Henry Ford II was elected President, with a free hand to manage it as he chose.

As his management team, Ford hired a group of capable senior managers and ten of his former air force officer colleagues. This group, which became known as the "Whiz Kids," provided the managerial talent needed and overhauled the company organization.

THE GENERAL MOTORS FORMULA

A book that was published in 1946 described the organization and chief management practices of General Motors Corporation. In the book, CONCEPT OF THE CORPORATION, author Peter Drucker described GM's decentralized organization as effective and harmonious with our national ideals. In general, he looked to employee participation in management, full and open communications, and identification with company objectives as elements which were important. Drucker compared this form of organization with the Prussian military organization and the Roman Catholic Church, from which he drew the concepts of staff and line.

The Whiz Kids read the book, found the ideas consistent with their thinking, and relied upon them as they proceeded to develop a new organization plan for Ford. After intensive study of the Ford organization and its needs, a systematic and comprehensive plan was adopted in January, 1947. This organization structure remains essentially unchanged today.

The plan was similar to the organization plan adopted by General Motors in 1923. Clear distinctions were made among operating divisions, as profit centers. Each division was self-contained and autonomous within the overall policy direction of the corporation. It was recognized that no one man could effectively manage a company the size and complexity of Ford Motor Company.

Under the chief executive were six vice presidents in charge of industrial relations, automotive engineering, purchasing, manufacturing, sales, and finance (all staff officials), and under them the operating departments and plants.

The concept of the manager as a personal assistant to Henry Ford had been replaced by the concept of a manager who is responsible for achievement of performance objectives. Arbitrary orders had been replaced by performance standards based on measures and goals.

The former structure had been rigidly centralized. Now power and decisions were in the hands of managers throughout the organization. Measures of results were no longer for the whole company, but were now broken down for each profit center. Instead of being closely held, all pertinent information was now readily available to all managers who needed it to take effective actions.

As shown on the organizational listing below, Ford today has three operating groups, each headed by an Executive Vice President. The three operating groups are: International Automotive, North American Automotive and Diversified Products. There is also an Executive Vice President for Finance. Within each of the three major operating units, decentralized organizational units are further recognized as profit centers. In most instances, the exeuctives of these units are corporate vice presidents or general managers. Where the divisions are subsidiary comapnies, such as Philco-Ford, the managers are presidents. These groups include:

Ford Asia-Pacific
Automotive Operations
Lincoln-Mercury Division
Technical Affiars
Ford Division
Design Center
Ford of Europe
Manufacturing Group
Ford Tractor Operations
Labor Relations Staff
Policy Board
Product Planning and
    Design
Product Development
Latin American Group
Automotive Components
Sales

Washington Staff
Marketing Staff
Public Affiars
Environmental and
    Safety Engineering
Personnel and Organization Staff
Truck and Recreation
    Products Operations
Treasurer
Governmental Affairs
    and Planning Staff
Controller
Power Train Operations

Other staff and operating executives are generally vice presidents. These specialized staff groups serve all of the operating divisions. The key corporate staff groups include:

Metal Stamping Division
Ford Motor of Canada
Ford Customer Service
General Parts Division
Scientific Research Staff
Finance and Insurance
Engine Division
Steel Division
Ford Export Corp.
Chief Car Planning
    and Research Engineer
Industrial and Chemical
    Products Division
Manufacturing Staff
General Services
Public Relations
Philco-Ford Corp.
Supply Staff
Industrial Engine
    and Turbine Div.
Assemble Division
Casting Division
Glass Division
Ford Parts Division
Chassis Division

Careers In Management

So you want to be in management? Do you know what's involved in the work? Do you know what it takes to become a manager? Do you know your own abilities and aptitudes?

MANAGEMENT CAREERS

You can't just jump into a management career. You've got to prepare for it. This usually means starting out in a functional area -- accounting, sales and marketing, finance, production, distribution, etc.

You'll work your way through a series of jobs, each with increasing levels of responsibility and wider areas of activity. If you have the ability, and if opportunities are available, you'll likely find one day that you are managing the work of others -- you are a manager.

It's the difference between being your own belt maker and salesman rolled into one and being an organizer of the talents of others for achievement of organizational objectives.

Some people set out to be a manager -- whether for the status, the higher incomes that usually go with the jobs, or for the nature of the work involved. The best way is to enter a special managerial training program. Such programs, lasting one to three years, provides college graduates (and often only graduates with M.B.A. degrees) with intensive orientation and training to prepare them for supervisory and staff management responsibilities.

While the usual route to the executive suites is through experience in one or more functions, it is possible to jump across companies into managerial assignments. Even here, however, solid experience is essential, as shown in the newspaper advertisements for managers shown on this page.

YOUR OWN ABILITIES

If you think you want to be a manager, you should look for available chances to demonstrate your skills in planning, organizing, controlling, coordinating, and directing the work of others. Volunteer for special assignments. Show how well you can organize and conduct your own work. Provide leadership to others you work with, to help them do a better job -- become an informal leader in the organization.

Naturally, specialized education is helpful. You may want to earn an MBA degree -- a Masters in Business Administration. Or you can earn a more technical degree in management sciences, operations research, or other management discipline. It may be well worth your investment of time, work, and money to get the extra education. It often accelerates the progress of individuals into responsible positions and into management training programs.

"Let us assume you are young, healthy, clear-eyed and eager, anxious to rise quickly and easily to the top of the business world.

You can!

If you have education, intelligence, and ability, so much the better. But remember that thousands have reached the top without them. You, too, can be among the lucky few.

If you have a special knack, such as drawing or writing, forget it. You may receive more at the very start for special abilities, but don't forget the Long Haul. You don't want to wind up behind a filing case drawing or writing.

It is the ability to get along, to make decisions, and to get contacts that will drive you ahead. Be an 'all-around' man of no special ability and you will rise to the top."

Such is the advice offered in "How to Succeed in Business Without Really Trying." Yet the facts are that managers become managers only through solid functional experience and training.

CONSIDER

1. Are there instances where MBO might not work? Explain.

2. Consider the objectives you are trying to achieve. Does MBO apply to your work? Explain.

3. If you were a company president, would you prefer to have centralized or decentralized organization? Why might you prefer centralization? Why might you prefer decentralization?

4. Do you think decentralization is a "fad"? Explain.

5. Can this management concept be applied to non-profit organizations such as the Army, a government agency, or a church? Explain.

6. Do computers lead to centralization of management and organization? Explain.

7. Would it be possible for a large corporation to be managed effectively today without the use of computers? Explain.

8. Can organizations grow to be too big? Explain.

9. What abilities and knowledge does a manager need to be able to use computers in the management process? Explain from your own point of view as a "manager in training."

10. Do you believe that Watson proved to be a successful executive through his own performance and capabilities or because he was the son of the most important figure in IBM's history?

CHALLENGES

List five rules that you might follow in your own work that will help you "think like a president." For a period of two weeks try to apply these rules yourself. Evaluate what effects the changes have had.

Read CONCEPT OF THE CORPORATION by Peter F. Drucker and determine whether it still applies to business today.

For some interesting cases on organization structures, read the paperback book, STRATEGY AND STRUCTURE by Alfred D. Chandler, Jr. (An Anchor book published by Doubleday & Company, Inc.).

Interview a manager and ask him or her what the work of a manager involves. Find out how decisions are made and what skills are needed to be effective as a manager.

RECAP

Management is the process of getting things done through people. In a business organization, management strives to achieve the objectives of the enterprise -- providing profits and ensuring the organization's survival.

The process of management involves planning (preparing for the future), organizing (pulling necessary resources and people together), directing (guiding the activities performed), coordinating (keeping working relationships effective), and controlling (keeping everything on the right track).

The organizing aspect of the management process can involve application of a wide range of tools -- to fit people and jobs together in the manner that is most effective for achievement of objectives. Business organization normally involves a hierarchy, or chain of command; specilization of duties; some form of departmentalizaton to divide up work by territory, product, technology, etc.; and means of coordination and control.

Can a corporation be managed by machines? The technology of computers has been applied to various management tasks. The capacities of computers for information processing are great and potential capacities that are now being developed are even greater. Properly applied, computers bring signifi-cant advantages to a business organization. Decisions affecting all aspects and levels of an organization may be made more effectively, based on more complete and current information.

But an organization functions because of human effort. Performance requires judgment, motivation, and performance from the people in a business. An approach that helps accomplish this is management by objectives. While it is not any kind of magic solution to management's problems (in fact, it requires a lot of work to be effective), it has been used by major firms such as General Motors, Ford, and Sears to gain participation of individuals in the management process. It has worked, and works today in many organization. MBO is a three-phase process: setting goals, coaching by managers as work progresses, and appraisal of results. Objectives established normally reflect both the broader objectives of the business and personal goals related to development of indivdiuals. Feedback information helps keep performance efforts on track and may be aided by a computer system as well as day-to-day contacts with managers. Really, MBO represents the core of what managers do -- the management process.

WORKSHEET NO. 14

1. What are the primary aspects of the manager's job?

2. What new management techniques are helpful in managing "bigness" in large business organizations?

3. What factors are important in making decentralized management work?

---

4. What has been the impact of computers on management planning?

CHAPTER 15

How Companies Grow

In previous chapters we have examined the basic processes of marketing, manufacturing, and financing in a business enterprise. These are the tools of capitalism.

What should these tools be used for? What should a company be trying to do? These are matters of planning -- of charting the course of an organization's future. How a company utilizes its resources through marketing, manufacturing, and financing must be planned.

Today, with increasing competition and varied pressures on profitability, companies find they need to grow in order to survive and prosper. In some industries, there is a minimum size that a firm needs to be in order to obtain the economies of scale that allow it to produce goods and provide services at a low enough price to be competitive and still make a reasonable profit.

Sears, for example, has certain advantages over other smaller and local retail chains. It can purchase or manufacture goods at lower costs and assured quality because of large volumes. It has added advantages of standardization in the way retail operations are handled. As we discussed earlier, some businesses go into franchising so as to obtain quickly these advantages of being large.

Playboy Enterprises, Inc. started as a single magazine. Sales of Playboy magazine climbed steadily over the years, to a revenue level more than $90 million. But competition has come into the magazine market, and Hefner sought to diversify the business. The company has expanded into clubs, hotels and resorts, new magazines, book publishing, motion pictures, records, and a variety of consumer products.

This strategy for growth represents a plan for diversification, however successful the record may show it has been. Some of the businesses have become contributors to the business; others are still net "takers" of investment capital. This is a natural risk in making a business grow.

Another way to grow is through mergers. Companies may join forces to obtain greater strength through unity. When a company grows large through acquisition of diverse businesses, it may be called a conglomerate. Again, the success is not guaranteed -- and some large corporations have spun off subsidiary companies as they have been shown to be unprofitable or otherwise incompatible with the overall business strategy.

There's another word -- strategy. Every company has one if it plans to grow.

In this chapter we shall examine the strategies followed by various types of enterprises including Tiffany's, National Lead, Sears, Beatrice Foods, Hershey Foods, Boise Cascade, and Textron. Each has sought to grow in a somewhat different way.

They all have, nevertheless, used the same basic tools for growth -- mergers, new products, accelerated marketing for expansion, and others. In fact, most have used a combination of these techniques, not one alone.

And as companies grow and change, their identities change. So companies change their names as they grow. Swift & Co. became Esmark; United Aircraft became United Technologies; Corn Products Co. became CPC International. What's in a name?

In This Chapter

Growth

"In the seventies, business -- and in particular, the worldwide, committed company -- will emerge as the most powerful force for peace, progress, and an improved quality of life for the people of the world. Eaton has the strength, resources, products, and people to be a leader in that effort."

This is the direction pointed out by the Chairman of the Board of Eaton Corporation, a diversified manufacturing company.

Every business needs to know where it is going if it is to survive, prosper, and grow. A firm must have a vision of the future. It must know what it wants to achieve in its environment. It must stake out its territory in the marketplace and plan steps for building in it. The more successful companies have projected an ideal concept of what and where they want to be ten, twenty, or more years in the future.

"At this moment, Eaton is a growth corporation with certain well-defined characteristics. If any one quality sets us apart from many other companies, it is our total commitment to the premise that change is our permanent business. Our goals -- to remain vital and thriving and to aggressively meet new opportunities -- are based neither on past performance, nor entirely on the expansion of our current business."

This statement of purpose spells out the general objectives that Eaton wants to achieve. Eaton wants to grow, and to grow in ways different from those of the past -- and it readily admits it does not know all the ways that the future will require change.

Eaton grew in its early years because it had literally hitched its wagon to the star of the automotive industry, providing creative support through products, technology, and research. The firm believes that new approaches are needed for continued growth and profitability in the seventies.

Some companies believe that growth is best based on past strengths, rather than bold, new directions. Sears' growth has been relatively stable, based primarily on its well-established role as our nation's largest retailer.

"Eaton is charting a course to the future by matching proven strengths to major growth markets of the 1970's. Today's management is meeting tomorrow's challenge...

-- with a diversity of products
-- born of wide ranging research
-- shaped by innovative engineering
-- manufactured with pride
-- marketed with skill and efficiency
-- and always having a concern for people
-- throughout the world."

This is Eaton's announced strategy for growth -- focusing on internal growth through product development. This is how the company will attempt to achieve its broad goals and move in the direction pointed out by its top management.

A company may grow through internal growth, through development of new products, or through mergers. It does not need to follow the same type of strategy as Eaton's.

GROWING

Being the wrong size as a company can be bad news. Too small, and competition drives the business out of business. Too large, and it's tough to keep the act together and stay profitable and alive.

Just revving up sales isn't the answer to problems of growth. Growth means more than being bigger, having more bucks roll in the door as revenues, or having more employees. It means being a stronger organization, having anchors in markets that promise continued future prosperity for the company's business.

The first task of management, as we noted in the last chapter, is planning. Now we see what this ends up meaning. There is operational, day-to-day planning -- involving budgeting, activity planning, and control. But when we consider growth planning, we are concerned with longer-range, broader strategic planning.

What's a strategic plan? It's a definition of the

direction a business is going and how it will get there. It includes defining what businesses the company will be in, how these businesses will be segmented in the organization, and how needed resources will be made available.

ALTERNATIVE STRATEGIES

In this chapter numerous cases are discussed which represent alternative business strategies. Overall, there are three basic ways for a business to plan for growth -- improved strength.

The first is to attempt to change the basic character of the business by changing its products, introducing new products, changing its image or reputation, or changing the markets it does business in.

For years, American Motors has been working to establish a character in the marketplace that would allow for growth. New car designs, most recently the Pacer, have been introduced to establish a strong image and basis for growth. Volkswagen did it with the "bug".

At one point in time a small car was the right entry to the market, at another, the wrong entry. As consumer demands shift and gas supplies wax and wane, the "right" kinds of products change. Is the Pacer the "right" car at the right time for American Motors to obtain its much desired growth? Check the record and you'll see it hasn't been all that the company had hoped.

The company had a plan -- a strategy -- to carve a bigger piece of the automobile market. In fact, American dropped most of its big car models as it concentrated on the small car models.

A second strategy, and one that is generally less risky, is to try to cure the problem with a merger or acquisition. Indeed, being the wrong size is one of the few cases where a "sudden big jump" may be desirable and possible through a merger.

Again, however, it is not quantity, but quality of growth that is desired.

Companies that have grown larger in a hurry through mergers have frequently suffered more than they benefited. Big jumps in size place heavy demands on management talents and strains on systems. It's also sometimes a combination of apples and oranges -- the product lines or types of businesses simply don't match up. As a result there may be frictions, competition for resources, and lack of managerial understanding of the diverse businesses suddenly put together.

Companies sometimes jump into unrelated businesses, without knowing very much about those businesses. As a result, there's trouble.

But on the plus side, most mergers do, in fact, work out pretty well. That's how most large American businesses got as big and as strong as they are today. General Motors is the result of the merger of a number of smaller, weak automobile manufacturers. AT&T grew through acquisition of many local telephone companies.

The third strategy for growth may very well be sale or divestment of parts of the business. Yes, getting rid of part of the company may help the business grow. For the reasons suggested above, a spinoff can allow management to concentrate on important matters. It can also free up capital that can be put to work in more fruitful areas.

Some companies have grown just for the sake of growing. It is as if size alone was seen as the answer to company success. But many companies have discovered that growth that was not well planned could have an adverse affect on the firm's ability to survive. By pruning away those portions of the firm that are drawing away more resources than they are providing, the parent company may end up smaller, but more successful. This doesn't mean that the units that are spun off are unprofitable, they just may not fit the firm to which they were attached.

ANALYZE THE STRATEGIES

As you read this chapter, analyze the strategies followed by the companies discussed. Consider whether the route followed was the best one, in your judgment. What alternate strategies could have been followed? How would the course of events have been different?

Consider also the social benefits of the strategies followed by businesses. Is growth good for society? What were the benefits resulting from the expansion or contraction described?

Tiffany's

To the eyes of most men, it was hardly the time to start a new business. It was a dull, dead time, when commerce, trade, and manufacturing were flattened by the financial hurricane of the Great Panic of 1837 (a depression).

But, then, it may be an opportune time, as many older companies had suddenly disappeared.

So reasoned Charles Tiffany and his friend and school buddy, John Young, both 25 years old, in deciding to open a retail store in New York.

Tiffany's father, Comfort Tiffany, approved of the venture and loaned the entrepreneurs $500 each. The elder Tiffany was a cotton goods manufacturer and also operated a small country store in which Charles had "discovered" the retail business.

OPENING SHOP

With this modest capital, they launched the firm of TIFFANY & YOUNG, after painfully searching for an finding a salesroom over which they could put up their own sign. They could not think of going downtown among the costlier buildings near the center of trade in Manhattan, near Trinity Church at Wall Street, and yet they were criticized as being rash in opening the shop so far up Broadway, at the Park. Tiffany was optimistic, however, and was encouraged by the fact that a dry-goods merchant, who

The Store Opposite City Hall.

had opened a shop two doors above, was doing very well.

The building was one half of a double residence (a duplex). The other half was occupied by a fashionable dressmaker. The rent was moderate and the front room, once a parlor, was large enough to display a stock of stationary and fancy goods provided by their slender capital. They were not ambitious enough to think of jewelry but offered an array of Chinese pottery and other goods, Japanese lacquer work, terra-cotta wares, umbrellas, walking sticks, cabinets, fans, leather work, bric-a-brack, stationery and other "notions."

So the place was small, unusual, and out of the normal shopping area, but had a charm reflecting good taste and judgment. Tiffany and Young could not afford

a costly grand opening with advertising, and so the start was slow. For the first three days they were open, in September, 1837, hardly any people came in and sales totaled only $4.98. One more day added $2.77.

As word of the quaint shop spread, and Christmas shopping began, sales rose. On the day before Christmas, sales totaled $236 and the day before New Years Day (the main "gift day" then as Christmas is now), sales were $675.

MISFORTUNE

On the morning of January 1, 1849, thieves broke into the shop and stole everything that could be carried away. The loss was more than $4000, four times their original capital.

The holiday sales had been made, however, and the merchants had taken the cash home with them. So they were able to restock the store immediately.

By the end of the year the business had outgrown its small quarters and a new larger, building was selected, with 45 feet of frontage on Broadway.

JEWELRY ADDED

In the new store an effort was made to present an "art effect" with Bohemian glassware, French and Dresden porcelain, cutlery and clocks.

The firm was reorganized with addition of J.L. Ellis as a partner. The firm's name was changed to Tiffany, Young, & Ellis. Each partner had his own specialty and responsibility.

A major step was taken when the firm decided to purchase stock directly from the salesrooms of manufacturers in Europe. Me Young searched Europe for goods, particularly novelties not offered by other stores in New York. Hardly any stores at that time sent purchasers abroad.

In Germany and Paris he discovered grades of inexpensive jewelry better than those sold in New York. This new jewelry became very popular. Even strangers to New York visited Tiffany's as one of "the sights". Before long, more expensive gold and silver merchandise was offered, all under the critical eye of Mr. Tiffany. It became the custom among the wealthy to ask each other if they had seen the latest novelty in precious metal at Tiffany's.

ON THE MOVE

In 1847, Tiffany's moved to larger quarters. In 1848 Tiffany's began to manufacture its own gold jewelry, reducing the proportion of its imports. Precious stones were also added to the line of merchandise, complementing the silver and gold. Silverware was also manufactured, rivalling the workmanship and quality of the silversmiths of Europe. From a small beginning, the shop of craftsmen grew to be a large plant with 500 employees.

In 1853, Young and Ellis retired and the firm became Tiffany & Co. In 1854, it moved again, to 550 Broadway.

The business expanded during the war years -- when Tiffany's pushed aside the jewelry and silverware to make room for weapons, army shoes, and supplies. The firm made badges, medals, swords of honor and flags.

After the end of the Civil War, the Tiffany name gained world-wide recognition, including the first award at the Paris Exposition and many recognitions in Europe. The firm opened a branch in London and a watch factory in Geneva. Now the firm that began as an importer was exporting large amounts of fine goods to Europe.

This is how Tiffany's began and grew.

The Store on the Corner of Broadway and Chambers Street in 1847.

Sears | Merchant To Millions
How Giant Sears Grows And Grows

Sitting down to lunch at Marshall Field & Co.'s restaurant in Woodfield Mall outside of Chicago, Arthur M. Wood, president and chairman-elect of Sears, Roebuck & Co., noticed a long line of Christmas shoppers waiting for tables. True to the Sears spirit—holiday or otherwise—the 59-year-old Wood turned to John P. Maloney, manager of the neighboring Sears store, and said: "John, why don't you make a sign saying that the Sears cafeteria is available, and then parade up and down?"

While Wood's remark was in jest, it illustrates today's one overriding fact about his company: It never misses a bet when it comes to generating business. And next week, as Sears winds up its 87th Christmas season—its biggest ever, following a record $1-billion November—the giant retailer shows no signs of letting up.

Both Wood and Chairman and Chief Executive Gordon M. Metcalf, 65, who will retire on Jan. 31, rattle off figures like $15-billion, $20-billion, and even $40-billion as realizable sales goals for their company. Sales for this year are estimated at $11-billion—up 10% from last year—and profits are projected at some $600-million, a gain of 9%. That would set records for the 18th and 12th consecutive years, respectively.

As the world's largest retailer and the country's second-largest insurer of cars and homes (through wholly owned Allstate Insurance Co.), Sears now accounts for more than 1% of the gross national product and 6% of the total general merchandise market. This Christmas, one of every three American families will buy some of its gifts at Sears' 836 stores or from the more than 16-million catalogues distributed every year. Typically, Sears' new headquarters building, scheduled for completion in 1974, will not be just another Chicago skyscraper. At 110 stories and 1,454 ft., Sears Tower will be the world's tallest building. As one store manager characterizes Sears at the local level: "Our main competition is not other retailers. It is our own stores."

More and more, the task that Arthur Wood will face when he takes over as chairman and chief executive on Feb. 1

goes far beyond meeting competition, on the outside or from within. It is the task of continually making organizational sense out of a company so colossal in size—and one with so much internal momentum. It requires, as Metcalf puts it, "real professionalism instead of seat-of-the-pants management."

For Wood, there will be the problem of a gigantic distribution system. With 23,000 suppliers, 200,000 items, and 41,800 retail merchandising departments, there is the bigness and stupefying variety of inventory. Above all, Wood must wrestle with the bigness of management itself—and the challenge of keeping communications open from top management to middle management to the store level and from there to the consumer.

Element of accountability

"When you go from $5-billion to $10-billion to $15-billion," says Metcalf, "there's just no way to keep a line of communications the same as it has been. We learned many years ago that there is only one way you can go on bigness: better communications. You must know exactly what you're doing all the time."

For Sears, that means decentralization. Driving along Chicago's Eisenhower Expressway with a reporter, Wood lauds the virtues of decentralized management, then pauses in mid-sentence to admire the massive beginnings of Sears Tower, already visible from 18 mi. away. "... Sears is a very large company," Wood continues in his thoughtful, deliberate manner. "But we're still the sum of many small units, each with its own personality, spirit, and leadership. This gives us an element of individual accountability and identity so that each store manager and his team feel that they play an important part in the total scheme of things. The field," Wood stresses, "is where the money is made in this company, and headquarters recognizes that all good ideas don't originate in Chicago. Great size can be a problem for a company like Sears if it is not willing to face up to decentralization."

Wood: "Sears is a very large company, but we're still the sum of many small units."

Sears is facing up to some other things, as well. It is restructuring its catalogue operation, which accounts for 22% of sales. It is broadening its retail marketing approach beyond its traditional middle-class audience to include more persons with low and high incomes. Through heavy advertising, it is turning many of its house brands—such as Kenmore, Coldspot, and DieHard—into major national brands. To head off a bottleneck in its merchandising and inventory control, Sears is also computerizing its whole store-level merchandising system (pages 54-55).

"This system is a key management communications tool and will help ac-

Children's clothing is one of the newer areas where Sears is leading the competition.

commodate our growth in size," says Wood. "Inventories have got to expand as we increase our outlets and our volume. This makes it all the more important that our inventories be in the right goods, that buyers' decisions are made earlier, and that facts are available earlier than ever before."

The management pyramid

In its assault on the problems of bigness, Sears' most significant move of all will be the transfer of power from Metcalf to Wood on Feb. 1. That will mark the first time in recent history that a nonmerchandiser has moved into Sears' top job.

A lawyer and 26-year veteran of the company, the bushy-browed Wood is a sophisticated, urbane intellectual with impeccable social credentials, qualities that have traditionally never counted much at Sears. His appointment reflects the changing nature of retailing and the necessity for having more than a buyer-and-seller of goods at the top. Today's merchant must have a broader grasp of government regulations and laws, finance, labor unions, real estate investment, consumerism, and the host of other complex elements that popu-

late today's retail environment. At Sears, Wood can call on what he describes as "specialists in depth" for merchandising, finance, and other areas. "We rely on them in critical decisions," says Wood. "Staff work shows the way. A lawyer may look ahead."

Backing up Wood will be merchandiser A. Dean Swift, 54, incoming president and chief operating officer. Now vice-president of Sears' Southern territory, Swift is known as a "field man" in Sears' parlance, meaning that he won his spurs during some 30-odd years of spending Saturdays in the store and nights laboring for Kiwanis and local charities.

Below Wood and Swift are five territorial vice-presidents who oversee 47 group managers in metropolitan areas and 13 zone managers in less populous sections. At the bottom of the management pyramid are the store managers.

"Every territory, group, zone, and store operates as a profit center," says Wood. "All levels of our management work against a profit-and-loss system that enables us to compare each unit with his neighbor or counterpart. This is really where you get your control. Over the years, we have developed our system of accounting to give us con-

trols not only over payroll, inventories, receivables, and physical assets, but also over profit performance. We break our expenses down into considerable detail"—including sales turnover, payroll/sales ratio, old merchandise reduction, and gross profit.

"The key is to put as much decision-making as possible on the lowest level possible," says Thomas Neal, group manager of 13 stores and 16 appliance outlets in Massachusetts. Neal makes decisions on competitive pricing for his stores and chooses which lines they will carry and promote.

"The group manager, however, is anything but a dictator," stresses Jack Freeman, manager of a new Sears store on Houston's Southwest side. "Group policy on products, pricing, and promotion is more of a democratic process. We have regular meetings of the store managers with the group manager and his staff."

On a few occasions, there are loud differences of opinion. "Some managers believe," says Freeman, "that the best way to advertise shirts is to have a special of five for $10. Others want to advertise one shirt for $2. The group manager's job is to see that the basic policies of Sears are followed by everyone and that the consensus of the group's store managers is followed." As Stew Thomas, a zone manager based in Atlanta, sums it up: "Individual managers don't think in terms of Sears but of their own markets."

A model for the industry

In attacking those markets, Sears has few equals. It was the first major retailer to move to the suburbs. It pushed credit when J. C. Penney Co. was sticking to a cash-only policy. It pioneered telephone shopping, night hours, self-service, and computerization of physical distribution. And its merchandise development and testing laboratory, set up in 1911 and employing more than 120 designers and engineers, is a model for the industry.

Now Sears is trying to break new ground by diversifying its growth and broadening its entire market. This way, the company—which is coming close to "saturating" the middle-class market that it has traditionally pursued—hopes to avoid one of the biggest pitfalls of bigness: a leveling-off in growth. To get more low-income customers, Sears recently tested "Budget Shops" for women's low-priced ready-to-wear and next year will install 80 to 100 such shops in Sears stores. For upper-incomers, Sears is adding higher-fashion apparel, along with eight-speed bicycles, electronic watches, and other luxury items.

To help widen its audience, Sears is sharply expanding its ad budget, which now runs more than $400-million a year and puts Sears among the country's top 10 national advertisers. "We are the most powerful promoters in the industry today," Wood insists.

Most of Sears' ad spending still goes into newspapers. They are used mainly to exploit markets in which Sears is strong—such as appliances and auto accessories. TV ad spending, however, is gaining fast. From nearly nothing seven years ago, broadcast spending is up to 20% of Sears' ad dollar. Of the company's 760 lines of merchandise handled by its 50 buying divisions, about 40 lines have been featured in the company's TV advertising. They include such top-priced items as DieHard batteries and steel-belted radial tires. One result of Sears' heavy TV schedule, according to tire industry sources, is that Michelin-made radials sold under the Sears name now comprise more than half of the U.S. radial market. Another result: Last month, Sears was named Advertiser of the Year by the Television Bureau of Advertising.

Researching new markets

To track its broad new markets and help anticipate more problems before they occur, Sears is also stepping up its in-house and outside market research. Many shoppers, for instance, complain that household softgoods that appear to be color-coordinated under store lighting are sometimes mismatched under the different lighting at home. So Sears came up with color and material standards that guarantee color harmony under any lighting conditions. Another complaint of shoppers: the bulkiness of window air conditioners, which interferes with the view outside. So Sears departed from the industry's standard 12-in.-high window unit and developed a 10-in.-high "Viewsaver" model.

Market research also led Sears into its higher-priced merchandise. "Research indicated a greater demand for a men's shirt at a price point between $7 and $10," says Cleveland store manager Roy Burkhart. "So we provided it. If research shows that we can sell mink coats, we sell mink." Touring his store with a visitor, Burkhart points out some delicate figurines that sell for $80. Then he stops by the homemade-wine section. "Hell, this is more expensive than buying your own," he says. "Sure, the concentrate makes more wine for the cost—2 gal. for $5. But look

at all the equipment you need. If people want it, though, we provide it."

Sears' best market research of all probably comes out of its own men in the field—at all levels. "That is one thing about this company," notes a suburban store executive in New York. "You never stop watching, listening, and reacting to the consumer—no matter how high you go in the company."

Last week on a visit to Norfolk, Va., president-elect Swift took a call from a lady in New Orleans who had tried to reach him in Atlanta. "Her furnace was on the blink, and she wanted some high-level help," he recalls. "I took the information and got in touch with the New Orleans store manager immediately, and we took care of her. To be successful in this business, you've got to look after every customer."

Around Sears' headquarters in Chicago, they tell the story of how Metcalf was touring a new store on a Sunday before its Wednesday opening when he noticed "Danger, high voltage!" signs on the backs of the electronic cash registers. Though the signs applied to repairmen, Metcalf ordered them covered. An aide immediately called the president of a metal-fabricating company and, told that he was playing golf, bundled a register into his car and raced to the golf course. Huffing and puffing from hole to hole, he finally caught up with the president and explained the problem.

The next morning the fabricator turned up personally at the store with a prototype cover, color matched to the register. While he and officials of Sears and Singer Co.—manufacturer of the register—discussed whether the shield might interfere with the register's cooling vents, the fabricator kept a line open to his plant. When the O.K. finally came, production began and 24 hours later the 150 registers were covered.

A threat to competitors

"Let's face it," says one Sears competitor in Cleveland. "Sears has a tremendous record of not making mistakes." And the bigger it gets without making mistakes, the more competitive it can get—which is one of the best antidotes of all against the problems that can beset an industry giant.

Cleveland is a prime example. Though Sears was a late arrival in the Greater Cleveland area and operates only six stores, it is No. 1 with sales of $140-million to $150-million a year. That compares with May Department Stores Co. (six stores) at $125-million, Higbee Co. (five stores) at $115-million to $120-million, and Halle Bros. (five

stores) and J. C. Penney (seven stores) at $70-million each.

Sears' six stores, of course, still trail in many categories, such as women's ready-to-wear, menswear and accessories, and "domestics," which include sheets, bath towels, and similar softgoods. However, they are gaining steadily in most major categories where they are behind and have pulled ahead in other areas. According to retail unit-sales figures compiled by the *Cleveland Press*, Sears has picked off 24.1% of the local department-store business in major appliances, four times as much as its nearest competitor. Sears similarly leads in total furniture sales (9.2%), girls' and teens' wear (15.3%), and boys' wear (17.4%).

Sears' Cleveland competitors shake their heads in wonderment. Says one, "Take 'TBA' [tires, batteries, and accessories] or their tremendous strength in appliances or basic home improvements. They just clobber us. And these are big dollars. We could sell 10,000 handbags and not make up for a week's sale of tires. Sears has also done a very good job of getting into the gut price lines of children's clothing, young people's jeans—stuff doing well. Even if we beat or match them in one area, they clobber us elsewhere. They won't beat us in men's pants or women's pants, but they'll sell a ton of them."

A consolidated operation

Sears is moving just as aggressively in its catalogue business, which has turned into a miniature publishing empire. Sears now prints two major catalogues—spring/summer and fall/winter—three other seasonal catalogues, 11 regional editions, and 18 special-interest editions offering everything from big and tall men's apparel to carpets and crafts.

To cope with its mushrooming catalogue business, up 100% in the last 10 years, Sears opened a new, fully mechanized catalogue-order facility in Columbus last spring. A prototype for streamlining the entire system, the 2.6-million-sq.-ft. plant uses computers, magnetic "fingers," and light beams to choose and route items.

At the same time, Sears is also changing its catalogue-buying operation. In the past, each of Sears' catalogue plants maintained "control buyers" and a supporting staff who bought goods just as merchandise managers do in retail stores. In a two-year experiment just before opening the new Columbus facility, Sears moved the control-buying function from Boston to Philadelphia and found that Philadelphia could successfully supply Boston by using Boston sales and inventory information data. When Sears opened the Columbus facility, its first in 25 years, the company eliminated control buyers, handling all of the merchandising from Chicago. Next February the Minneapolis buying operation will also be shifted to Chicago.

"For example," says Wood, "instead of maintaining a thin inventory, cutting machinery, and specially trained people for piece goods in three locations, we do it all from Chicago. Transportation costs are less than duplicating and triplicating facilities and personnel. This kind of mechanization is another way to cope with size."

Some unsolved problems

Sears may have solved many of the problems of bigness. But it has not cracked all of them. In regional catalogues, for instance, selections are still determined mainly in Chicago, a fact that troubles some catalogue men. As John C. Grable, general manager of Sears' gigantic 4.1-million-sq.-ft. catalogue plant in Los Angeles, notes: "The bicycle craze started out here, and we wanted more bicycles in the catalogue. Chicago thought it was just a fad and wouldn't last. They finally had to eat their words."

Sears also is saddled with a number of stores in rundown neighborhoods—though it spends $350-million annually on total capital investment and adds 35 to 40 new stores a year. One of its less-than-choice locations is a 45-year-old store in a sleazy section of downtown Hollywood, Calif. Eight years ago, the 140,000-sq.-ft. store underwent an interior facelift, and now Sears is replacing its old-style gingerbread exterior with a more modern stucco look. Yet cosmetics can only do so much. "We have a tough time getting credit approvals," says store manager Frank J. Kane. "We have a large transient population and a lot of unemployment." There is also a lot of shoplifting. "Ten years ago, we had one full-time security person and one part-time man. Now we have three full-time people and five on a part-time basis. As yet, we have no electronic surveillance, but we are seriously considering it."

Allstate considers itself a "mass merchandiser" rather than an insurance company.

One of Sears' trickiest problems of all is foreign expansion—now confined to Spain, Belgium, Latin America, and Canada. Wood admits that Sears went after the Spanish market the wrong way—as though Spain were an undeveloped country. "The competition responded very vigorously," he says. "It took us the better part of three years to get our first store open. And at the outset, we had the wrong merchandise. So we had to change our product mix and pricing and develop a whole new promotional program." Last year, the company lost $567,000 on its two stores in Spain—down from a $2.2-million deficit in 1970.

A built-in diversification

"The experience changed our thinking on any foreign market," says a chastened Metcalf. "Anything that we now go into, we will buy someone or become a partner of someone who is there." Last year, for instance, Sears bought Galeries Anspach of Belgium and operates under that name.

Earlier this month, Sears announced another new area of expansion: home-building. Allstate has teamed up with Robert J. Gale, a former executive with Levitt & Sons, Inc., and formed a new building and development company, Gale Organization, Inc. The Gale move is part of a continuing effort by Allstate to broaden its services and add to its own bigness. In fact, Allstate President Archie Boe, who calls his company a "mass merchandiser" rather than an insurance company, has set as his goal not beating out some other insurer this year—but making a bigger profit than J. C. Penney ($135.7-million vs. Allstate's $125-million last year), which happens to be Sears' chief rival in the retail and catalogue business.

Will Sears diversify further as a hedge against some of the growth limitations and problems that it might encounter as the world's largest retailer? Both Wood and Metcalf claim that Sears—like a gigantic Christmas stocking stuffed with all kinds of goodies—is already big and varied. They note that Sears even has built-in diversification with all its varied suppliers, customers, stores, markets, and customer services. "A share in Sears," Wood insists, "is a share in diversification, and a good one." It is also a very big one.

Diversification

What's diversification? It's moving into areas of activity that a business has not been in before. It's adding new products and services in entirely new areas, or in areas related to existing products and services.

How is this done? We have seen how Sears does it--Sears develops new products in its laboratories. New products start as ideas and ultimately become additions to the company's line of goods.

Also at Sears new types of business activities are added to the basic functions of the business -- the sale of insurance, a mutual fund, savings and loan association, and real estate investments.

Acquisition of ongoing businesses is another way for a company to diversify. It is also one of the quickest ways to grow. This strategy has been followed by many firms, including Sears, Hershey, and Textron.

There may come a point where a diversifying company becomes so large and so diverse in its products and services that it is a sort of conglomeration of enterprises, hence it may be called a conglomerate.

Why do businesses diversity? Mainly, businesses seek new products and areas of activity to gain stability in their revenues and to head off the potential threat of becoming obsolete like the defunct buggy-whip firms. To grow, organizations must change and develop. Diversification is at the core of this process.

Consider how Tiffany's has changed over the years since it was founded, as described in this chapter. As Sears, the whole concept of the business and its product line have undergone a lot of change.

Some businesses have a basic problem of seasonal sales -- such as a Christmas decorations manufacturer. For five or six months during the year, sales are great -- then none. The firm may be profitable, but the revenues are not exactly running smoothly. By adding other products or by merging with another firm, such as a garden supply company, the business may stabilize its operations.

Perhaps you have wondered what the fair-weather "frosty freeze" man does in the winter. If the owner of such a business does not fly south, he is often out there in the snow in December selling Christmas trees. That's diversification.

Is diversification always a good thing? That's hard to say, because sometimes it takes years for new products or new acquisitions to start paying back on the investment required.

As discussed in this chapter, Hershey Foods was traditionally the nation's leading chocolate company. For more than seventy years, Hershey had been a giant in the candy business. Three of the four top candy products in America are Hershey's, but competition is keen and growth potential is limited in such a specialized market. The candy and cocoa industry is changing and the price for cocoa (the main ingredient) has skyrocketed.

In response, Hershey belatedly moved in some fresh directions. In 1968 the company changed its name from the original Hershey Chocolate Co. and its emblem. It is diversifying into foods, tightening its distribution, strengthening its middle management and launching its first (yes, its first) mass-consumer advertising campaign in the United States.

If we look at the history of most major American business firms we will see that at some point in their growth they used a strategy of diversification. They may have bought existing firms or started new firms to take advantage of a new product or new technology. Basically it is easier to create a new business unit to handle a new product or service than to disrupt the smooth pattern of an ongoing activity to handle the new situation. Therefore we can expect to see firms continue to diversify as a way of handling new situations.

Why National Lead is changing its name to N L Industries, Inc.

On April 15th, National Lead shareholders approved a resolution to change the company name to N L Industries, Inc. From now on, that's how you'll find us listed, that's the name you'll see on our product lines.

Like many diversified companies these days, we discovered our old name no longer reflected current operations or future plans. With annual sales approaching a billion dollars, our operations have broadened to encompass a wide variety of products and services for today's essential industries.

For more information on what we're doing, write for our annual report. N L Industries, Inc., 111 Broadway, New York, New York 10006.

INDUSTRIES

Industry just wouldn't be the same without us

Our New York Stock Exchange symbol has changed from LT to NL

1970 CONSOLIDATED SALES

Metals and Bearings
(33%—$301 million in sales.)

We supply many basic metals such as zinc, tin, antimony, cadmium and primary lead. Also a wide range of finished products and components. Among them radiation shielding screws, bolts and metal fasteners, railroad and other bearings, steel containers and aluminum extrusions for aircraft. We also supply precious metals, and associated chemicals for photographic and other uses.

Titanium Pigments
(23%—$208 million in sales.)

These are the pigments that make and keep paint, paper and plastics white and bright. Employing both the sulphate and chloride manufacturing processes, we're the world's leading producer of titanium pigments.

Die Casting
(15%—$140 million in sales.)

We're the leading custom producer of die castings, working in aluminum, zinc, magnesium and brass — making parts and assemblies for appliances, business machines, aircraft, motor vehicles, lawn mowers and many other industrial and consumer needs.

Chemicals and Plastics
(11%—$104 million in sales.)

This area includes anticorrosive pigments, stabilizers, gellants, flame retardants, battery oxides, and extender pigments—for the paint, plastics, ink, electronic and adhesive industries. We also produce custom injection molded plastic products.

Oil Well Materials and Services
(10%—$90 million in sales.)

Oil is, of course, one of the most vital of today's products. We supply unique and essential drilling materials, chemicals and engineering services to the petroleum industry.

Other Products
(8%—$73 million in sales.)

Other products we make include Dutch Boy paints, electroceramic materials for electronics manufacturers and specialized high temperature refractory materials. One of our divisions provides special dies and tooling for Detroit's prototype cars. We also meet a broad range of nuclear fuel, shielding and shipping needs.

The Name Game

Umpty-ump years ago the name "Smallville Throttle & Valve Works" struck a note of quiet pride in its employees. To its shareholders it was synonymous with stability, honesty and uninterrupted dividends. The name said what it meant, and meant what it said.

Time passed. So did management: out of the hands of the old Fogey family and into the eager grip of the MBAs. After a couple of mergers, "Smallville Throttle & Valve Works"—so limiting, so backward—was changed to "Amalgamated National Controls." "The new name," said that year's annual report, "positions us squarely as a leader in this great growth area."

Now it's 1973. "Controls" has lost its magic, so the name has become a liability. A "corporate nomenclature consultant" is called in. He in turn hires a computer, which comes up with 80,000 variations on the themes of amalgamation, nations, controls and throttles. Of these, 60,000 are gibberish, 300 are obscene, 19,680 are already being used, and 20 are real possibilities.

Only one meets all the essential criteria. It has two syllables and a recognizable link with the previous name; it's easy to remember and it ends in "X." "Anthrax!" cries the consultant. "Anthrax Inc.!" bugles the board. "Doesn't anthrax have something to do with sick sheep?" a stockholder writes in. But there will always be a nit-picker in every crowd.

So far, no company has made the boo-boo of calling itself Anthrax. But Standex, Cyclops, Esmark and GAC are all considered winners by the corporations that have paid huge sums to inflict the changes on themselves.

Although the choice of names can be mysterious, the reasons for changing are often well-founded. In the case of Exxon, the change resulted from 38 years of legal complications that had Standard Oil Co. (N.J.) calling its gasoline Esso in 18 states and Enco in 28 others. (In Ohio the company had to be Humble.) The shift, which started a year ago, still isn't completed, what with 25,000 service stations, 22,000 oil wells and billions of stickers, labels and forms. And worse luck, it is already becoming known in the boondocks as the Sign of the Double Cross.

Exxon's case was unusual. More usual was National Dairy Products changing its name to Kraftco: Everybody knew the Kraft cheese brand, but who wanted stock in a milk company? Esmark was substituted for Swift & Co. last April, when the company decided it preferred the image of a forward-looking holding company to that of a staid meat-packer. Thousands of dollars in advertising and publicity made sure that the

X-Appeal. Maybe it's because X is a rare letter. Maybe, as linguists claim, it's because consonants like X and K stick in the mind as they catch in the throat. (Kodak's George Eastman was fascinated by the letter K.) Whatever the reason, X-names are highly prized—though the greatest of all, Xerox, almost didn't make it. Joseph Wilson, Xerox' late president, was afraid people would pronounce it "Ex-rox" and mistake it for a laxative.

transformation did not go unnoticed.

Whether it will make any difference is a matter of opinion. "It's just a gimmick," Donald P. Kelly told a FORBES reporter last February. At the time, he was Esmark's vice president of finance. He may think differently now that he is president.

A name change can involve more than a new set of syllables. "Disagreement over a name often indicates a power hassle," says consultant Joseph Murtha. "When that happens, we can become the shock troops for selling the young Turks' ideas." In the 11 years that Murtha and his partner Russell Sandgren have practiced the name game, they have helped to change—to what benefit no one can

say—Saturn Industries to Tyler Corp., Rex Chainbelt to Rexnord and Corn Products Co. to CPC International.

Seemingly irrelevant emotions can be a tricky hurdle for would-be name changers. General David Sarnoff, the Russian immigrant who built RCA, was fiercely proud of his adopted country. Even when his vice presidents, who had "RCA" printed on their business cards, got quicker recognition than Sarnoff did as chairman of "The Radio Corp. of America," he refused to abandon the tie with America. His son Robert finally made the familiar nickname official in 1969 after becoming president.

At one of the country's billion-dollar corporations, which has asked to remain anonymous, the proposed change never took place. The suggested name would have severed the tie with the company's original entertainment business. This now contributes less than half of corporate revenues, besides giving the company a risky, show-biz image it would prefer to forget. When the chairman heard the new name he nodded. The board approved. The president smiled. The president's wife looked him in the eye one night soon after and said: "Bill, if you're president of 'XYZ Corporation,' *nobody* will know who I am!" The company kept its original name.

If "sophisticated" name changes flounder on human sentiments, corn sometimes comes through with flying colors. Take Chessie System Inc., the railroad holding company that incorporates the Chesapeake & Ohio and Baltimore & Ohio lines. Before the new name was adopted in August, 1972 people used to refer to the company by its initials "C&O/B&O," pronounced "Ceenobeeno."

Terrible, Terrible

But no computers or creativity sessions for this company, thank you. For years employees, suppliers, stockholders and customers had lapped up Chessie calendars, neckties, pens and toys. A few people even claimed to have bought the stock because they liked the Chessie kitten. Why not (to mix a metaphor) go whole hog and name the company after her?

A year later the fan mail is still coming in. "It's more than a cat," wrote one delighted salesman. "It's a personality."

No matter how good the reception, most self-respecting name-change consultants would shudder at anything as folksy as using a kitten to symbolize a billion-dollar corporation. At Lippincott & Margulies, the New York-based firm whose $8-million-plus annual revenues probably make it the most successful name-dropper of all time, choosing the proper name is a very serious business. Some 25 to 30 L&M staffers may work on a given name change. Some of the results, like Cincinnati Milacron (Cincinnati Milling Machine), Uniroyal (U.S. Rubber) and Finast (First National Stores), are catchy if a bit obscure. Others, such as Cyclops Corp., Conwed Corp., and Amsted are just plain obscure. None, however, is cheap. A new name with accompanying trademark can run well over $100,000. Add on advertising and implementation—physically replacing the previous version—and costs can skyrocket into the millions.

Why bother? According to *Sense*, the glossy brochure Lippincott & Margulies emits several times a year, it is practically a moral duty. "A strong corporate image can not only rein-

force the positive impact of 'good information' on a company's security price, but it can also mitigate the negative impact that might result from unfavorable news or information." Translated into English, this high-sounding pomposity implies that a name change will make your stock go up and cause people to forget that your products poisoned 14 schoolchildren last year.

Perhaps because a million bucks in fees is not to be taken lightly, Walter Margulies himself is much more restrained. Take Standard Railway Equipment, which changed its name to Stanray in 1960 on L&M's suggestion. "While changing the name didn't cause changes to happen," Margulies says, "it didn't stand in their way like the old name. The company sold better and merged faster." Did it *really*? Who can tell? Pullman Inc., which scorned all suggestions to change its mossy name, has been one of 1973's hottest stocks. Why? It is finally making big money.

Will a "good" name really sell stock? It's hard to find any evidence for the idea. "Chemetron" is certainly a lot sexier than National Cylinder Gas, but a five-year earnings growth average of minus 18.9% has made for a sluggish market. Pet Inc. is too famous to tamper with, even though

to British ears it sounds like dog food, and to French ones like flatulence.

Masco isn't catchy and International Flavors & Fragrances should lose by its length. But both are institutional favorites selling at more than 35 times earnings. Nobody turns up his nose at Schlumberger because he twists his tongue on the foreign syllables. As for Fuqua Industries, the name is practically X-rated, and therefore priceless.

In fact, for memorability, originality and often appropriateness, home-grown names generally win going away over the professional products. What Park Avenue consultant would ever come up with Otter Tail Power? Or a broadcasting company that calls itself Gross Telecasting? And what computer could generate a more fitting name than Zero Manufacturing for an outfit whose stock recently sold for $3.50 a share?

"There is more force in names than most men dream of," wrote essayist James Russell Lowell as he pondered the nature of success. Unfortunately, there is also less in a name than many corporations and consultants would like to believe. As for changing anyone's mind about a stock, the name of that game is still performance. ∎

Drawing by C.E.M.; ©1973 The New Yorker Magazine, Inc.

Playboy Interview: Hugh M. Hefner

A candid conversation with Playboy's president and founder

"This has been our tenth consecutive year of record sales and profits . . . increasing profits 15 percent—going over $10,000,000 —was especially significant during what I consider to be a year of important innovations."

"Almost everyone who has seen our new Great Gorge Playboy Club-Hotel in New Jersey—including a number of people from the financial community—is impressed first by its magnificence and then by its business potential."

RICE: Mr. Hefner, Playboy has just completed its first year as a publicly held company. Were you satisfied with the over-all financial performance of the company last year?

HEFNER: While we're never really totally satisfied with our performance, we are pleased with the quite substantial growth we achieved in both sales and profits— and with the introduction of new facilities and enterprises that will assure our continued growth.

This has been our tenth consecutive year of record sales and profits. Increasing sales almost $28,000,000 to $159,000-000 is certainly gratifying. And increasing profits 15 percent—going over $10,000,000 —was especially significant during what I consider to be a year of important innovations.

GLUCK: Which innovations do you consider most significant?

HEFNER: Well, almost everyone who has seen our new Great Gorge Playboy Club-Hotel in New Jersey—including a number of people from the financial community who have made a point of visiting the property—is impressed first by its magnificence and then by its business potential. The year also encompassed a full

12 months of operations for the Playboy Plaza in Miami Beach and the Playboy Towers adjoining our Playboy Center in Chicago. The opening of our exciting new Club in the same complex was another highlight—and a major first step in improving the locations and services of our Playboy Clubs in several cities.

On the publishing side, our new Book Club became a very significant factor. We completed negotiations for publication of our first foreign-language editions and made the decision and assembled the staff to publish OUI magazine—a venture which holds great personal excitement for me. And, of course, PLAYBOY magazine continued to set really dramatic new records in circulation and advertising.

RICE: And how about next year?

HEFNER: We're looking for another good year—a continuation of the kind of over-all growth we achieved in fiscal 1972— with profits more than keeping pace. PLAYBOY's recent August issue topped 6,800,000—a new high in circulation until the very next issue—September—which set a new record of 7,012,000. Advertising revenues continue to grow—as a result of increased rates and the acquisition of new advertisers. In fact, our November 1972

issue achieved an all-time high in both pages and revenue for a single issue—topping $4,500,000—another record broken by the very next issue. Our December issue reaches new highs with 121 pages and $5,200,000 in gross revenues. Together with production economies we plan to take, PLAYBOY magazine should again establish new sales and profit levels.

We expect our program for reducing losses in our hotel division to remain on track—perhaps even run a bit ahead of schedule—further improving our profitability.

It's early, of course, but the contribution OUI might make this year could be significant. It's quite unusual for a major new magazine to be profitable within its first 12 months. But with OUI's commitment to profitable circulation, both newsstand and subscriptions—and the initial acceptance we've had from advertisers and readers—it's possible the magazine could contribute a few cents per share within its first nine months of existence. It's starting out with what we believe is the largest initial circulation of any magazine in history.

In future new ventures, we will take a conservative investment approach, striving for moderate start-up costs by normal industry standards. We have adhered to this same low-risk appoach even with a project of the magnitude of OUI—increasing the likelihood of an early pay-out.

GLUCK: Mr. Hefner, why did you decide to publish OUI?

HEFNER: In U.S. publishing history, each major successful magazine eventually has created a market in which a number two magazine could also thrive—*Life* and *Look, Time* and *Newsweek, Reader's Digest* and *Coronet,* for example. The exception has been PLAYBOY. No imitator has attained even one fourth the circulation we have. While we don't intend to create a junior copy in OUI, we do hope to lend the expertise, the knowledge of the market that PLAYBOY has acquired over 20 years, to help OUI succeed. That aside, OUI has its own character, centered on a strong appeal to youth. And it not only speaks their language—as other youth magazines do—but speaks it with a distinctive Continental accent, reflecting its European origins. There isn't another product like it on the market. Changing attitudes in society—with upwards of 20,000,000 people reading a typical issue of PLAYBOY—have created a new field of men's magazines. And we happen to be more knowledgeable about this field than any other publisher.

GLUCK: What are your plans for further expansion within the publishing field?

HEFNER: We're already active with a number of projects that were only conceptualized a year ago. One foreign-language edition, German, is a reality, and publication of an Italian edition is scheduled for Fall and will be followed by a French edition next Spring—and our expense is minimal since we have no actual investment. We have been conducting conversations with publishers in Japan and Sweden.

Our Book Division is increasing its output of hardcover, paperback and magazine-sized "flats" which sell for premium prices. Membership acquisition in our Book Club continues at a healthy rate.

We are experimenting with a number of different magazine concepts which we think will appeal to the special interests of our Playboy market. These will be introduced as one-shot publications. If they succeed on a one-time basis, we can increase their frequency as continuing periodicals.

ADLER: Has there been any unifying thread underlying your diversification beyond publishing?

HEFNER: Definitely. Essentially, our diversification tends to put into material form most of those aspects of the life style pre-sented in PLAYBOY magazine which lend themselves to commercial development—and which conform with the life style of the millions of people who read it.

The trend of other successful magazine publishers normally is to expand into other magazines, books and perhaps records. PLAYBOY's projection of "the good life"—and our reader's obvious rapport—has enabled us to expand successfully beyond publishing into products, night clubs, films, records, and hotels and resorts. Each draws heavily from its identity with the magazine—and upon the preconditioned market that identifies with PLAYBOY.

ESPOSITO: Can you elaborate on why Playboy has gone into the hotel business –and why so big?

HEFNER: We feel hotels—especially our resorts like Great Gorge—represent the ultimate in projecting this image of "the good life" I've been talking about. The Playboy Clubs achieve some of that feeling—and our hotels are the next logical step toward fulfilling some of the entertainment and leisure-time interests of our market of 1,000,000 keyholders and more than 20,000,000 magazine readers. We are still investigating the potential in singles apartments and secondary-home communities that are certainly compatible with the interests of our market; for the present, we prefer the higher cash-flow advantages of investing in hotels.

Why so big? Actually, we started quite small—by applying the experience we had gained in our Club operations to a 200-room resort in Ocho Rios, Jamaica, that we acquired in 1964. Our success there convinced us the Playboy name would hold the same magnetism for resorts in the States. Our expansion within the past couple of years to a chain of five hotels, containing about 2000 rooms, has already made us a factor in the business, but is only a beginning. Hopefully, opportunities, through management contracts primarily, will come with enough frequency to make us a major factor in the years to come, with expansion continuing in units strategically situated to cater to heavy population centers, both domestically and internationally.

RIMBERG: Why did Playboy enter the film production field?

HEFNER: We are aware of the high frequency of movie attendance of our market of millions of young adults and feel we have the talent and sources for keeping these young moviegoers entertained with fresh ideas.

We've begun with conservative, well-hedged investments with major distributors like Columbia Pictures and Universal Studios, and a reliance on professionals with proven track records in the medium. Our pattern so far has been to co-finance our first films with major studios. In the future, we expect to receive total financing in return for distribution rights.

Our role in the film industry will be essentially creative—because of our access to such a wealth of literary properties. We have no desire to tie up capital in facilities or production overhead.

RIMBERG: Last year you acquired a movie theater in New York City. Does this suggest the beginning of another "chain"?

HEFNER: Not really. The possible addition of a theater in Los Angeles to our existing movie houses in Chicago and New York will serve as our showcases for the foreseeable future and complete our involvement as an exhibitor for films.

KAPLAN: Do you have a target for Playboy's annual earnings growth?

HEFNER: While our rather consistent historic average increase of 15-20 percent a year might indicate otherwise, we don't have a specific target for annual earnings growth. We're merely attempting to take advantage of the marketing opportunities that present themselves, and doing so on a profitable basis. Therefore, we see little reason why we should not continue to grow at our traditional pace, perhaps improving as we go along.

ADLER: What is the extent of your involvement in day-to-day operations?

HEFNER: As you might suppose, my once deep involvement in routine company operations has gradually changed through the years. The change has been pretty well dictated by the expansion of our enterprises—and has been made possible by the building of an experienced management team, responsible for operating their divisions and profit centers.

While my role is concerned primarily with the determination of corporate policy, I guess you could call me the company's severest critic in evaluating new projects and analyzing operations. And I continue to draw heavily upon my editorial and creative experience in participating in the planning behind our newer enterprises.

The New Face Of Arm & Hammer

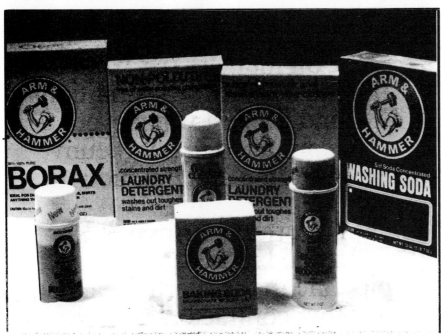

New consumer products carrying the Arm & Hammer label enliven staid Church & Dwight.

Joan Sydlow—BW

Detergent, deodorant, and oven cleaner now account for a major share of sales

Dwight Church Minton describes himself as conservative. His dark suit, crisp white shirt, spartan but comfortable office, and a slide rule on his desk attest to this philosophy. But Minton is a radical if viewed by the standards of his forefathers who ran New York's Church & Dwight Co. Inc. for 130 years.

Since Minton, 41, became president in 1969, the company, best known for its Arm & Hammer trademark, has shifted from an industrial base to consumer marketing. Revenues jumped from $22.4 million to $77 million, and earnings more than quadrupled to $3.8 million last year. The company was virtually catatonic when Minton moved into the chief executive's position, with more profits being produced from its investment portfolio than from operations.

Consumer sales now account for 60% of the company's business, a reversal of the proportion of five years ago. While the company is not frightening Procter & Gamble, Gillette, and Carter-Wallace, it is nipping at their markets.

Market share. Since its introduction in 1970, Arm & Hammer laundry detergent has captured 3.7% of the $1.4 billion market in which the leader, P&G's Tide, holds 29%. The Arm & Hammer

product is now the seventh best seller of the 25 major brands sold on grocery store shelves. Other C&D products such as Arm & Hammer deodorant and Arm & Hammer oven cleaner, coupled with the company's old standby, baking soda, have pushed earnings per share from 85¢ in 1969 to $2.80 in 1975.

Adams & Peck, a New York brokerage house, says that C&D needs only a 3% to 5% market share to be profitable. On this basis, all of the company's products are well into the black. The deodorant now has a 3.7% share of market after being on the shelves less than a year. The oven cleaner claims a 21% share, and baking soda 100%. Borax, although a money-maker, is the weakest

When Minton took over, more profits came from the portfolio than from sales

line and is destined to be phased out completely.

A change in style. Minton is uneasy when quizzed about the changes he made, since comments could be interpreted as a reflection on the decisions made by relatives. More than 80% of the company's stock is controlled by descendants of the company's founders, Austin Church and John Dwight. With extreme diplomacy, Minton explains the company as he found it when he took control from his father.

"The old company operated in the traditional method," he says. "There was an advertising department, and

there was a sales department, and they did their things. They got along well if one didn't interfere with the other."

One of the first moves Minton made was to create a marketing department, merging the sales and advertising units under it. In reality the merger was simply a paper exercise. Since Church & Dwight holds a virtual monopoly in the sodium bicarbonate business, salesmen did little more than take orders from industrial clients, and advertising was limited to a few trade periodicals.

Recruited to fill the job of vice-president of marketing was Robert A. Davies III, an alumnus of Procter & Gamble and American Home Products, who arrived on the scene to find an office and nothing more. He did receive an assignment from Minton to develop a string of consumer products, ones that would exploit the only two strengths the company had: bicarbonate of soda and a trade name that was recognized by an estimated 90% of U.S. households.

New products. Davies' first new product was the detergent, an unlikely start when the competition is surveyed. But the company looked for an opening, spotted the ecology issue, and launched a product that was nonpolluting. Although P&G, Lever Bros., Colgate-Palmolive, and others later entered the market with phosphate-free, nonpolluting detergents, it soon became clear that C&D had already found a niche in the marketplace.

"We're very proud of the fact that we know of no one else who has cracked the Big Three," says Davies. "We're bent on changing the Big Three to the Big Four." Davies has since added a phosphate detergent to the product line.

Ambitions. Davies has no illusions that C&D will overtake any of its competitors, but he thinks the company will eventually dominate what he calls the "subcategories" of the markets. One example is a deodorant that is soda-based and contains no additives, appealing to people who want only natural ingredients.

Minton says the company is now intent on expanding its base of operations. He states that new products will continue to be introduced and that acquisitions are now being considered, particularly in the industrial segment.

Minton concedes he is under no pressure to keep Church & Dwight growing at a 20% to 25% rate, but he leaves no doubt that he would be disappointed if the company were to rest on its laurels again. "A well-managed company can achieve 10% to 15%," he says. "To get any more, it has to be both well-managed and lucky. I wouldn't be embarrassed if we operated at somewhat less than 20%." ∎

Mergers

Many owners of small businesses become sellers for the same basic reasons. If they have only a single line of products they may find it difficult to meet competition. Many small firms cannot afford the cost of acquiring other firms or of building new capacity for growth internally. Thus, they sell out.

Also, business is becoming increasingly complex, and also large-scale production and marketing are becoming essential for profitable operations. Small firms do not have the specialized staff or the scale of operations that permits them to compete effectively in this modern business arena. Selling or merging may be the most practical solution.

A successful business may sell simply because of tax advantages. Where businesses were started with a small investment but which have increased in value, the owner can usually receive an amount equal to many times his annual after-tax income from the business, and he can probably remain in the business at a high salary if he chooses. Thus, the owner saves tax money by merging.

If a small business, particularly a privately held company, were sold, the owners also gain the advantage of having readily marketable stock. In the event of the owner's death, the company would have an established value, and would facilitate the payment of estate taxes. Federal estate taxes,

ranging from 3 to 77 percent of assets, must be paid in cash.

There are additional advantages in mergers that we will not discuss here, such as tax loss carryovers. The laws affecting mergers and tax law effects are detailed and complex.

Business enterprises join forces to gain greater strength through size and diversification. Through a merger, two different business organizations may gain greater stability, an improved image in the market and, of course, larger size. As a means of growing, mergers are a relatively easy way to move into new activities.

When a manufacturer expands his producing capacity in order to increase earnings, his first decision must be whether to build new capacity or to acquire capacity already in existence. If a company builds, it creates additional capacity and, therefore, competition. When a company buys, it reaps the advantages of increasing its capacity and acquiring some or all of the market previously served by a competitor. The decision of whether to build or buy, then, involves the weighing of economic advantages and disadvantages.

The ultimate reason for mergers is to improve economic strength of a firm -- and in many cases this is necessary for survival. A successful concern cannot afford to stand still.

Some of the more important reasons for mergers are:

--To broaden markets
--To insure sources of supplies
--To diversify
--To minimize cycles of sales
--To acquire talented managerial or research personnel
--To get nearer a major market
--To enter new markets quickly
--To gain additional facilities
--To gain cash resources
--To gain tax advantages

TYPES OF MERGERS

Mergers, as a form of corporate reorganization, are subject to the regulations of the Internal Revenue Code and the laws of the state where the companies are incorporated. In general, there are three ways to achieve a merger.

First, there is a statutory merger or combination. In this type of merger the stockholders of both companies vote and approve the merger, usually with a two-thirds majority required. This process is time consuming because it requires preparation of proxy materials, scheduling of stockholder meetings, etc.

Second, there is the simple acquisition. In this type of merger, one corporation gains control of the stock, generally at least 80% of the total voting stock, of another. It does not require the approval of stockholders except from companies listed on the New York and American Stock Exchanges.

Control may be gained by exchanging stock for stock or a combination of stock, cash and other securities for stock. The method is often used by large corporations acquiring ownership of smaller and often privately owned companies.

Third, there is purchase of assets. In this type of merger, the assets or properties of one company are purchased outright by another for stock, cash, notes, or any combination of these. In many states, a favorable vote by a majority of the stockholders of the selling corporation is required. This type of merger is commonly used to acquire smaller, private companies where the owners wish to get cash gains immediately. In purchasing assets, the acquiring corporation need not assume the liabilities of the company. The acquisition is of property only; the company is still alive and must clear up its own affairs.

Mergers of companies are not always cases of sunshine and flowers. When the hard realities of corporate finances and the results of business operations are examined, many mergers do not look wonderful anymore.

Sometimes the problems are tax problems. Sometimes they are problems in accounting for mergers. Sometimes the managers who are brought together in one company do not get along, and bring down the whole house together.

Sometimes the companies that are acquired are not as healthy as they once looked. After a merger, the sales levels, effi-ciency, and profits may drop. It takes careful study to determine how much potential a firm has to offer, and a lot of good management to make an acquisition an effective one.

Thus, for a dozen mergers in our economy, there may be several un-mergers, and several more unhappy "marriages" that are simply tolerated. Un-mergers are discussed later on in this chapter.

Beatrice Moves Into Money

Beatrice Foods Co., one of the top 10 U. S. acquisition makers for four straight years, was at it again this week. The Chicago-based giant, with 1972 sales of $2.7-billion and earnings of $90-million-plus, signed an agreement under which Southwestern Investment Co., a financial services operation, would become a wholly owned subsidiary. Then it announced an agreement to absorb Samsonite Corp., the Denver-based maker of luggage and specialty furniture, in a stock swap valued at about $100-million.

Both deals are still subject to ap-

Samsonite luggage joins other acquisitions keyed to recreation

Beatrice's Karnes: "The real strength and reason for our success is balance."

proval by stockholders and the appropriate regulatory agencies. Samsonite totted up sales of $106.5-million in fiscal 1972, excluding the operations of a toy division discontinued during the year. Net income was $5.8-million before adjustment for losses and extraordinary charges attributed to the toy business, which reduced the figure to $3.6-million. Southwestern, headquartered in Amarillo, owns a savings and loan association, one life and one casualty insurance company, and has 131 consumer finance offices as well as commercial finance operations. It had revenues of $47-million and earnings of $3.7-million in fiscal 1972.

The latest moves by 75-year-old Beatrice are part of the program of William G. Karnes, 62, chairman and chief executive, to continue the records he has set for sales, net earnings, and per-share earnings every year since becoming boss in 1952.

Despite having made at least 20 acquisitions last year, Karnes bridles at questions about the importance of acquisitions and his strategy for avoiding problems with federal antitrusters. A normally warm but intense man, Karnes asserts, "You get a warped picture of Beatrice if you talk only about acquisitions." Internal growth accounted for 70% of last year's sales gain of $320-million, he says. "The real strength and reason for our success is balance," he adds. "We never go too heavily into a geographical area, we avoid jumping in where competition fails, and we stick with branded products in both foods and nonfoods, keeping away from commodities."

That is also Karnes' formula for avoiding antitrust troubles.

Food and meat. The major recent deals include the 1968 acquisition of John Sexton (institutional foods) with sales

of $91-million, and last year's landing of Peter Eckrich (specialty meats) with sales of $243-million. The Federal Trade Commission dropped its challenge to the Sexton deal last year, but Beatrice accepted a consent decree in 1967 forbidding acquisition of bottled milk or ice cream plants for 10 years without FTC approval.

To diversify sales, only $229-million when Karnes took over, he bought companies like Sexton and Eckrich and then moved into fields including recreational products, picking up Airstream travel trailers, Hart skis and Striker aluminum yachts, Holiday and Jacobsen mobile homes, and Charmglow barbecue grills and gas lamps. He also moved Beatrice into soft drinks, baked goods, agricultural products, and home, auto, and garden accessories. And an 11-year-old international division accounts for 15% of sales.

WHAZZIT?

HORIZONTAL INTEGRATION

Expansion, often through merger, to increase the firm's share of a particular market. For example, a major supermarket chain may buy out a smaller chain.

VERTICAL INTEGRATION

Expansion, often through merger, either backward to supply sources or forward into markets. For example, a steel manufacturer may vertically integrate by buying a coal mine, on the one hand, or a

finished products company on the other.

CONGLOMERATE

A group of firms, usually in unrelated industries that are now merged together. The hope is that the whole is greater than the sum of the parts.

Hershey

At the age of 19, in 1876, Milton Hershey opened a shop in Philadelphia to make and sell candy to the crowds at the Independence Centennial. Without money and with strong competition, it failed.

A few years later he tried again with a shop in New York City. It also failed.

He finally got started by making caramels, with the help of his Aunt Mattie, and then chocolate confections were added. His first big order was for milk caramels from an English importer. He decided to specialize in just two items: the plain milk chocolate and the almond milk chocolate bars.

Sales steadily grew. In 1901 annual sales were just $600,000. In 1920 they were $20 million. In 1950, $150. And in 1965 they had grown to $211 million.

But the rate of sales growth has leveled off in the last decade. To try to grow, Hershey turned to the Canadian market, where it had only 1% of potential sales. It built a plant and also bought the local H.B. Reese Candy Co., makers of Reese Peanut Butter Cups. This marked Hershey's first excursion beyond "solid" chocolate and the first of numerous diversification steps.

In 1966, Hershey decided it needed and even broader base -- so it bought San Giorgio Macaroni, Inc. and Delmonico Foods, Inc., both regional manufacturers of macaroni, spaghetti, and other pasta products. Then, Hershey bought Chicago-based Cory Corporation, a maker of coffee-cart and coffee-brewing equipment, applicances and utensils. Later additional acquisitions included Portion Control industries and a cookie manufacturer, David & Frere, Ltd., since dropped.

There has been little attempt to tie these varied businesses together, but they provide the foundation for the company's planned future growth and profit expansion.

We Are Pleased To Answer Questions Asked Most Frequently About Our Operations

Q.

Since 1966, Hershey Foods has acquired a number of companies in the food business and in such related fields as food equipment and service. Why were these acquisitions made?

A.

We felt that diversification would lessen to some extent the impact of cocoa bean costs on our overall operations and would increase total corporate profitability. However, we are convinced that our chocolate and confectionery business also has considerable growth potential.

Q.

Is the company continuing to seek acquisitions; if so, in what fields?

A.

Yes. We will continue to seek lines or companies to complement existing businesses, specifically convenience items for the food service field. We are interested in other food and food related products.

Q.

What can you do about the effect of cocoa bean price fluctuations on your earnings?

A.

Cocoa bean costs can materially affect earnings. We can lessen the impact of price fluctuations in several ways. One method is through diversification mentioned before. Price changes can be made within certain limits to offset or partially offset changes in cost. Another is to promote products with a lower cocoa content, such as Reese's Peanut Butter Cups and Rally bars. We can also try to minimize the effect of price fluctuations by forward buying.

Q.

Comment on the international cocoa agreement.

A.

The agreement intended to control the price of cocoa beans within stipulated limits was signed on January 15, 1973 by all of the major producing and consuming countries with the exception of the United States. We concur in our government's position that the agreement, as written, will be unworkable, as it is much too complex. Time alone will tell whether we are correct in our contention but it should be pointed out that since there is no surplus of cocoa in the world there is presently no way of enforcing the maximum price established by this agreement.

Q.

What is your plan for the corporation's growth?

A.

We believe the most profitable expansion of the company can be achieved by a combination of four objectives: 1) Steady growth in our current line of products, 2) Introduction of new products, 3) Entering new markets and 4) Acquiring well-managed companies which have above average growth and earnings potential.

Q.

Which part of the company, chocolate or other foods, will provide the greatest growth over the next 5 years?

A.

We would expect our Chocolate and Confectionery Division to continue to provide the largest share of our sales and profits. However, on a percentage basis we would expect to see a greater improvement in both sales and earnings from the other areas of our business.

Q.

Why did you sell David & Frere?

A.

This Canadian producer of cookies and biscuits had annual sales of about $14,000,000 and was profitable. However, it did not lend itself to combination with our other Canadian operations because of differences in marketing and channels of distribution. A small, not significant, profit was realized from the sale.

Q.

Would you comment on your plans for capital expenditures?

A.

Capital expenditures have been increasing in recent years due to capacity needs and replacement or modernization of facilities. It is anticipated that capital expenditures will approximate $20,000,000 to $25,000,000 in 1973 compared with $25,000,000 in 1972.

Q.

How important to the company is the plant tour program?

A.

We believe our visitor program enables us to build a lasting friendship with large numbers of consumers (966,863 people visited our Hershey, Oakdale, and Smiths Falls plants in 1972) because it educates and entertains at the same time. Since 1927, more than 10,000,000 people have visited the Hershey plant, and we are convinced that most of them left with very positive feelings about the company. New plans for the program are noted on the back page of this report.

Q.

What is the corporate philosophy with regard to government relations?

A.

Government relations is an ever increasing aspect of importance to Hershey. Our approach, which we believe to be the best course of action, is to analyze trends as they evolve and ensure that government decision makers are aware of our views. This objective requires continuous analysis of the legislative and regulatory aspects of government, the thinking of the academic community, and a knowledge of consumer attitudes and expectations.

Q.

What are your observations about the food industry?

A.

The food industry in the USA continues to supply the requirements of its consumers without eroding the consumers' disposable income. In 1972, the average consumer spent a lower percent of income for food than in 1962. The industry, however, is not without its problems. Profitability at the retail level is one of great concern. Hopefully, it will be resolved without any great upheavals in the industry.

A Bullish View of the Conglomerates by G. William Miller, President of Textron

G. William Miller has degrees in marine engineering from the U.S. Coast Guard Academy and law from the University of California at Berkeley. After practicing law for four years in New York with Cravath, Swaine & Moore, he joined Textron in 1956 as a vice-president. He has been a close observer—and practitioner—of conglomerate tactics ever since.

Q. *What's the basic advantage of the conglomerate or, as you prefer it, the multimarket approach to business?*
Miller—Its flexibility and responsiveness to change. I see nothing to suggest that the rate of change is slowing in technology, markets, social institutions, international business—and all of these changing conditions are best met by a flexible form of enterprise. As a multimarket company, we're not wedded to a classic textbook sort of organization designed for a single product or market. We have a lot of interplay among our people, and it adds up to a vitality that helps us to respond to new needs and markets.

Compared with many conglomerates, you sailed through the recession in good shape. What sets Textron apart?
We've been operationally oriented for a long time. We've put a big emphasis on developing our people, and we've spent a lot of money in making our facilities cost-effective. We spend more than most companies on new product development. We've managed our assets conservatively, put realistic values on our inventory. During the big years when everything was going straight up, we kept reminding ourselves that there would be a rainy day, so when the rains came, we were ready. In the enthusiasm of the mid-60s, some companies patterned after us felt that good times would be here forever, that you could come up with winners by throwing darts at a board.

Why have conglomerates had so much grief?
I'm not sure they've had more

trouble than others. Don't just look at conglomerates. Many of the recent write-offs have been in old-line companies. Look at Penn Central, Lockheed, American Can. The problem with conglomerates is that they made many of their misjudgments in mergers and acquisitions, and these are highly visible mistakes.

Do you object when Textron is called a conglomerate?
Yes, but only because the word has taken on an unsavory meaning associated with "arithmetic mergers," aggressive accounting, and so on. If it's applied to mean diversified companies such as General Electric, or AMF, or RCA—that's all right.

What's the future of the conglomerate?
Excellent We see new imitators popping up all the time. But you'll see a change to this extent: Smaller companies, like we were in 1953 when we started the "new Textron," will be making most of the acquisitions. Take the classic example of the young, aggressive manager running a single-product company. He should be encouraged to look for acquisitions.

When can you do to stimulate internal growth that an independent company can't do alone?
We can provide an umbrella for a period of product development and market introduction that's just too costly for an independent company to tackle alone. Where an independent might be reluctant to invest in new plant, we're more willing to do it.

But it sounds like the glamour days of the huge conglomerates are over.
No, there's lots of glamour ahead, but I hope the merger-mania days are over. While there would be no restrictions in a perfect world, I think the restraints and cautions the government has imposed since the merger-mania days of 1968-1969 are justified. We never felt they constrained us, anyway, because we weren't raiding people or

Bill Miller: "You don't see big black cars here, no executive dining rooms."

trading on fictitious values.

A lot of conglomerates are "mixed bags" of companies compared with your emphasis on manufacturing. Is that a weakness?
Not necessarily, but a mixture of manufacturing, insurance, real estate, etc. is harder to manage. We've been cautious, wanting to build professionalism in manufacturing, but we're looking some at other fields. Acquiring ARD, our new venture capital company, does mean a change, because that puts us in the business of evaluating people, markets, and ideas, and not always in manufacturing.

If conglomerates are here to stay, what are the biggest dangers?
Lack of quality of management. A lot of operators have felt their strategies were perfect, but have been found to have feet of clay. The idea of the multimarket company is sound—it works or does not work depending on the people, which is why we have spent so much time on people development.

Is Textron Ready To Take Off?

Earnings are up after dip.
Next thrusts: Expansion at
home, acquisitions abroad

ITT has had its scandals, LTV and Litton have had financial miseries, and sundry other flashy conglomerates have suffered their own bitter tribulations. One company that has emerged relatively unscathed from the tumultuous shakeout of the conglomerates is Textron, Inc., the onetime textile manufacturer from Providence, R. I., that pioneered the conglomerate concept two decades ago by branching out into the aerospace, industrial hardware, and consumer goods markets.

Of 15 major conglomerate corporations listed in BUSINESS WEEK's latest Survey of Quarterly Corporate Performance, Textron showed the highest return on stockholders equity, 19.7%, for the 12 months ending June 30, 1972. Moreover, while the other conglomerates were taking their lumps, Textron sailed through the economic recession with only minor distress. Earnings dipped in 1970, rebounded last year, and may.reach a record this year.

"We showed we could cope," boasts G. William Miller, the 47-year-old Texan-turned-New Englander, who has been Textron's president since 1960. "We proved the Textron concept works."

The heart of that concept is the now familiar idea that a quick way to fast corporate growth and superior return on investment is to acquire a large number of unrelated companies and put them under a single corporate roof. The parent company functions largely as a portfolio manager, putting its investment chips on the most alluring ventures and providing the motivation and direction for them to grow.

Textron's founder, Royal Little, put a conservative twist on the conglomerate strategy, and Miller has assiduously adhered to it. Many conglomerates went on helter-skelter acquisition binges, taking on staggering debt loads, getting into industries they knew nothing about, and buying at inflated prices ailing companies whose maladies they did not recognize. Their objective was simple: to buy earnings, push up their stock's price/earnings multiples, and then go on to buy still

more companies and earnings. In many of these conglomerates, of course, the bubble eventually burst. Operating problems of the acquired companies became insurmountable, profits were drained off, interest charges became intolerable, and corporate swingers were converted into disaster situations. To Bill Miller, such companies are "our shallow imitators."

Textron's stance has been the most cautious of the conglomerates. It has devoted more attention to operating than to financial wheeling and dealing. Its debt load has been light, and it has concentrated on acquiring manufacturing companies with proprietary products and leading positions in medium-sized industries. To be sure, Textron has made some acquisition mistakes, weeding out over the years an ocean cruise ship (sold at a $6-million loss) and a chicken-producing business. But it has never been forced to make the kind of wholesale divestitures that have become commonplace for conglomerates desperate for cash or eager to dump losers.

Textron has also practiced the managerial philosophy it preaches. All conglomerates are decentralized, but Textron has an obsession about placing operating decision-making at the divisional level. Says William B. Gisel, president of the Bell Aerospace division: "Our real happiness with Textron is the way Providence manages, which is to say without interference. We submit our plans and list our financial needs. Other than that, we're left alone. It is a helluva lot different from Litton and others I've bumped into."

Now, with the economy humming and record earnings expected this year, Bill Miller has set his sights on a lofty goal: $3-billion annual sales by the end of the decade.

Seeking the excitement of growth

For Textron, the challenge is formidable. For the past five years its sales have been essentially flat, and last year's earnings were just about the same as in 1967. At one time, Textron was an exciting growth company, boosting per-share earnings at an average annual rate of 14.5% during 1961-71. More recently, its strength has simply been stability at a time when so many other conglomerates have been

coming apart. Now Miller wants to make Textron a growth company once again.

Much of Textron's sales growth—from $71-million in 1952 to a peak of $1.7-billion in 1968—was achieved through 60 acquisitions. But the acquisition climate has changed. Textron's size now inhibits big purchases. Acquisitions are also more expensive, and Textron is renowned for its unwillingness to pay premium prices. In recent years, for instance, it has been outbid by AMK Corp. for United Fruit Co. and by Colgate-Palmolive Co. in a planned takeover of Kendall Co.

Miller knows that "it will continue to be difficult to make major acquisitions in the U.S.," though he hopes to pick up a few smaller companies "for the sake of balance." And, he adds: "We never rule out opportunities to take new directions." He says that the $3-billion sales goal can be reached without major domestic acquisitions.

More than ever, Textron will now have to generate growth through internal expansion. The company has always prided itself for increasing sales and earnings in its acquired divisions. The company claims to have tripled pre-tax earnings of 14 divisions during 1960-70, and that in the late 1960s, more than half its annual sales increase stemmed from internal growth.

But its most dazzling internal increases have come from Bell Helicopter, the largest division, which rang up 23% of total sales in 1971 and once accounted for at least one-third of Textron's volume. The division's stimulus: Vietnam war orders. Military helicopter procurement has tapered off, however, and the division was defeated a few weeks ago by Boeing and United Aircraft in competition for an Army contract to develop and later build a successor to Bell's famous UH-1 "Huey" helicopter, the workhorse of the Vietnam war.

'Little Textrons' overseas

To make Textron a growth company again, Miller is cooking up new tactics. One major thrust will be a new emphasis on foreign acquisitions. Miller sees a fertile market for what he calls "Little Textrons" in Europe and Asia.

A European counterpart of Providence headquarters, called Textron At-

Textron's products: from Fafnir bearings and Gorham silverware and glassware to Bell's air cushion amphibious vehicle and coil-fed nailing machines developed by Bostitch.

lantic, Inc., has been established in Brussels with nine divisions under its wing. These include foreign production operations of such Textron divisions as Bostich (stapling equipment), Talon (zippers) and Sheaffer (pens and pencils), and recent acquisitions such as Adcock-Shipley, Ltd., a British maker of milling machines.

Textron Atlantic's role is largely to finance acquisitions and expansion with Eurodollars and to offer legal and accounting help, as well as to provide liaison with Providence. Its scouts are on the prowl for European family-owned manufacturing companies that gross $5-million to $25-million, make proprietary products, and show a good return on investment. As in the U. S., Textron Atlantic will consider only friendly takeovers on a wholly owned basis. Miller is sure that family estate situations throughout Western Europe will yield a flow of good companies.

Textron Atlantic sales this year will be about $80-million. By the time Textron's total sales reach $3-billion, Miller expects Textron Atlantic and other foreign manufacturing operations to yield sales of $500-million. Last year, foreign sales accounted for 13% of Textron's volume, roughly half of it in goods exported abroad. In 1967, foreign sales accounted for only 7% of corporate volume.

Bowing to custom and law, Textron will not insist on wholly owned acquisitions in most of Asia, but will seek joint ventures. The company already has a 30% interest in a Tokyo manufacturer. Using this as a base for a new company called Textron Pacific, Inc., it

is trying to help Textron divisions move into Asia. Its Homelite division, which makes chain saws, may work through Textron Pacific to find a production partner for a light, inexpensive saw suited to Asian woodlands. Homelite now exports American-made saws to Europe, but its president, Robert Straetz, thinks that cracking the Asian market requires overseas production facilities, plus a lot of on-the-scene help with financing, marketing, and dealing with government officials.

In parts of the world closed to American ownership by ideology, Miller is mounting a major export drive. He has been to Eastern Europe himself this year, and visited Moscow twice before. He expects significant trade in these countries, and eventually with China, where he once served as a naval officer.

Indeed, his zeal for trade with the Soviet bloc and China has affected his personal politics. A onetime Democrat who was a delegate to the party's 1968 convention, Miller is supporting President Nixon this year, largely because of the President's success in establishing friendlier relations with the two Communist nations.

Textron's new thrust abroad began only after Miller became disillusioned with plans to expand in service industries, whose growth potential has attracted scores of diversification-minded industrial companies. "We decided that it is easier to extrapolate our conglomerate management skills to manufacturing overseas than to service industries in the U. S.," he says. "I understand how to control manufacturing costs, but I'd be at a loss to con-

trol some of these services outfits that have 347 locations and no 'things.'"

The stepped-up pace at home

Despite all the hoopla about going abroad, the challenge of becoming an aggressive growth company again will probably be settled essentially at home, where Textron is grappling for new directions and new ways to use its vast capital resources. For example, the $57-million acquisition this spring of a Boston venture capital company, American Research & Development Corp., brings Textron indirectly into such glamour industries as data processing and pollution control.

At first blush, Textron's acquisition of ARD conflicts with Miller's hesitancy about moving outside manufacturing industries. Georges F. Doriot, ARD's founder and long-time Textron director, wanted to sell his company to Textron upon his retirement because he thinks that Textron provides the proper industrial environment for the 40-odd companies in the ARD portfolio—most of them small and struggling. Doriot thinks that under Textron's aegis these companies will be safe from encroachment by financial operators.

For Textron, true to its cautious image, the ARD deal offers a sort of backdoor opportunity to move into new growth markets via minority ownership of a flock of new companies. "American Research & Development adds a whole new Textron to our company," says Miller, eying the likes of Ionics, Inc. (pollution control), Documation, Inc. (data processing), and Wolper

Organization, Inc. (TV, movies). Textron hopes that some of these affiliates will get over their growing pains, that the prices of their stocks will jump far above ARD buy-in levels, and that Textron will reap fat capital gains when it sells off its investments.

A question of patience

Some critics charge that Textron will not have the patience to nurture its ARD investments. Robert S. Ames, ARD's president and a former executive at the Bell Aerospace division, retorts that "patience is our style at Textron." He adds that ARD under Textron will continue the Doriot policy of taking only minority positions in companies it backs with seed money. There will be no Textron takeovers. But the investment pace will be stepped up as Ames dips into Textron's cash reserves of $104-million. "We think," says Ames, "that Textron's reputation as a sound manufacturing company will help us attract some good entrepreneurs who realize that we can help them with more than money."

One ARD affiliate is a large conglomerate itself, Teledyne, Inc., which Doriot spotted as a comer years ago when he acquired about 230,000 shares worth $581,339. In January, 1972, the stock was worth $5,449,818. Holdings of "mature" companies such as Teledyne probably will be sold before too long, Ames says, as ARD goes after small companies that hopefully have the payoff potential of Doriot's all-time best buy, Digital Equipment Corp. A $461,400 investment in DEC was worth about $400-million when it was sold just before the Textron takeover. "Just give us one more DEC," sighs Bill Miller.

The key to Textron's ability to return to anything close to prerecession growth levels, however, lies in the success of its existing divisions to come up with salable new products. Textron claims that it spends more than 2% of its sales on research and development, a high figure for a company that is not largely defense or science oriented. More than 20% of Textron sales last year were products that were introduced in the past five years.

Among the most promising new products is a twin-engine, executive-style helicopter that the Bell Helicopter division is now showing off around the world. Others include various air cushion vehicle (ACV) projects that Bell Aerospace is working on. Bell's Gisel predicts that ACV production will "blossom to volumes as high as helicopters" by the late 1970s or 1980s. He pins spe-

cial hopes on a high-speed ACV called a surface-effect ship (SES). Admiral Elmo R. Zumwalt, Chief of Naval Operations, has said it "represents a technological breakthrough that offers the potential for revolutionizing naval warfare." The ships, which travel on a stream of air rather than in the water, have potential speeds of 100 knots.

Right now, the Navy is testing a 100-ton Bell SES in waters off Louisiana. And Bell is competing for a Navy contract to develop a 2,200-ton prototype that would be ready for testing in 1976.

Gisel sees big commercial applications for ACVs, both the fast SES-type ships and the slower but amphibious ACVs of the type that have carried thousands of passengers across San Francisco Harbor and at Montreal's Expo 67. Earlier this year Bell sold a 25-ton ACV for $1.1-million to the Canadian government, which plans to use the vehicle in the Arctic over water, ice, and tundra.

Meanwhile, the two Bell divisions and the other 28 Textron divisions must develop and sell a lot of goods on a here-and-now basis to keep growth alive. The economic turnaround is helping the 14 companies bunched in the two Textron product groups that sell capital goods, but it is neither a fast nor dramatic upsurge, admits Miller. Companies such as Bostitch, Fafnir (ball bearings), and Bridgeport (machine tools) were hard hit by the recession, but have rebounded well. But some smaller, less profitable divisions in the industrial and metal products groups may be weeded out.

Miller would like to see the divisions make more equitable contributions to corporate profits. Ten of the company's 30 divisions produced 65% of sales and 84% of pretax income last year: Bell Aerospace, Bell Helicopter, Bostitch, Camcar (metal fasteners), Dalmo Victor (aerospace), Fafnir, Homelight, Shuron Continental (optical products), Speidel (watchbands), and Talon. "And everybody else is No. 11," Miller complains.

The move into consumer goods

Textron's major emphasis in the past six years has been to move into proprietary consumer areas. Talon, a 1968 acquisition, is Textron's biggest consumer group company, accounting for 11% of total sales in 1971. In all, consumer products produced just under 50% of Textron's pretax profits last year on only 31% of total corporate sales.

Erskine N. White, Jr., Textron's executive vice-president for operations,

and former president of the Gorham silverware division, makes a special effort to keep the company's best performing divisions from growing fat and satisfied. A lot of management tightening has occurred in consumer divisions in recent years. A few ace troubleshooters have been transferred, including John Keenan, who turned around Sheaffer pen after Textron acquired the company. Keenan moved from Iowa to Rhode Island to take over Speidel at a critical time for that company, as patents on its flexible watchbands expired.

"There's no way I can coast or sit back," says Homelite's Straetz. "That friendly vice-president from Providence is always saying 'that's nice but what's next?'" So Homelite, which sits one-two atop the chain saw market with McCulloch Corp., is now moving into the home gardening market in the U.S., and thinking about expanding to Asia—the sort of marketing movement that gladdens the heart of a boss with Miller's compulsion for corporate growth.

Miller is a lawyer who became president of Textron at the age of 35. He comes across as a combination supersalesman, business philosopher, and moralist.

A Puritan austerity

Men who have sat across the table from him during acquisition negotiations are likely to add such descriptions as tough, shrewd, and easily irritated. His Puritan streak flares when he talks of corporations that are "more show than substance." "You don't see big black cars here, no executive dining rooms," he says, while ticking off the advantages of working in a small city such as Providence, where executives do not waste a lot of time getting to and from their jobs.

Miller, who was born in Sapulpa, Okla., and raised in Texas, notes that most of Textron's divisions are located in small cities or towns, with a special concentration in New England. He likes to shock jet-wise visitors by saying he always takes the bus when he goes to Boston, 44 mi. to the north.

Miller's personal style blends well with Textron's corporate personality. "I think," says a Boston management consultant, "that Textron comes closer to motivating its people through respect for each other and challenge than through just money. Its people are loyal, and they are not deal-oriented. When you come down to it, this is the sort of thing that Harvard Business School really teaches."

The Age of Un-merger

James Shaver is a mobile executive as seen through a kind of Alice-in-Wonderland looking glass. In the past year-and-a-half, he has worked for three corporations—and yet he has not changed jobs once. What has happened is that his whole company, Polan Industries, has been mobile. In January 1969, the manufacturer of infrared instruments and electro-optical systems was bought by Republic Corp. The new letterheads hardly had time to dry when the division was divested—this time with top management bailing out—to Wollensak, Inc.

For Shaver, who hung on as director of finance while his company went through the revolving door, the changes have caused him to sweat out two separate independent audits. "We didn't have time to get totally straightened away the first time," he says, "and we haven't gotten straightened away yet." Jim Shaver's experience is being duplicated increasingly around the nation. For he is one of the early victims of the age of un-merger.

"By 1975," says Richard M. Hexter, executive vice president of Donaldson, Lufkin & Jenrette, "any corporate president who has not sold off a division will be as much behind the times as if he had not bought a company or two by 1965."

Is this financial analyst and "un-merger" maker predicting a new era of selling? Yes. And he is not alone. John Silver, vice president at City Investing, expects a "great wave" of divestitures during the next few years. "And not only by conglomerates," adds Bangor Punta President David W. Wallace. "Other corporations, too."

In fact, a reaction to the acquisitions binge of the late 1960s is already taking place. There were 43% more divisions sold in 1969 than in 1968, according to W. T. Grimm & Co., the Chicago consultant that keeps a talley on acquisitions and divestments. Moreover, the pace is quickening. In the first quarter of 1970, 58% more divisions were lopped off than in that same period last year.

The "supermanager"

For many companies, the principal spur to divestiture is the need for cash. In a year of narrowing profit margins, high interest rates and tight money, the sale of assets is often the most direct and painless route to raising capital. Elsewhere, however, the rash of selling is providing an insight into two of the most significant management themes of the 1960s: The "supermanager" and assets management.

For the supermanager, the age of un-merger marks the end of an illusion. This generalist was the 1960s man of all businesses. He grew up under the theory that a manager was a problem-solver who, through the use of financial controls and systems management, could effectively mold profits from any enterprise that came under his purview. Today, at least in some corporate circles, that theory is suspect. "A few years ago," says a spokesman for Union Carbide Corp., which has been divesting itself of some substantial properties, "we thought we could run anything as long as it was profitable. Not any more." Adds DLJ's Hexter, "We are disenchanted with the idea that any one management can run anything."

On the other hand, the concept of assets management is only now getting its first major test with the age of un-merger. Assets management carries maximizing return on investment to the extreme. It holds that a division, a product group, a subsidiary are all subject to the same financial scrutiny and the same buy-or-sell decision-making that governs the formation of an investment portfolio. "Most of us think there is a logical parallel," says Arthur R. Cahill, financial vice president of Brunswick Corp. "Obviously, there is a difference in flexibility," he adds. "We cannot necessarily walk away from a business that is not doing well." Adds Richard Hexter: "There is a world of difference between liquidation and a positive program of divestiture. Companies have been selling losers for years; now they are selling potential winners."

Kindling the internal dynamics of de-conglomeration have been some external pressures and incentives. Most notable among the pressures has been the year-long stock market slide, with its particularly drastic devaluation of conglomerate companies. Add to this the continuing pressure being applied by the Federal Trade Commission (note its current proceedings against the AMK-United Fruit combination) and the Securities and Exchange Commission challenge to pooling of interest accounting principles and its proposal that corporations report sales and earnings by product categories.

And now the government is also providing an incentive to divest—through the Tax Reform Act of 1969. Among the benefits tailored to divestiture is a brand-new tax-loss carryback, which allows a corporation to apply losses on the sale of a division to its capital gains from three previous years. An added kicker: The government promises the tax rebate within ninety days of a company's filing for it.

Un-merger is being accomplished either through the outright sale of a division or subsidiary to another company or by the sale of some of its stock to the public. In either case, most of today's moves are defensive—motivated by the pressing need for cash or the desire to lop off an unprofitable operation. Seilon Corp., Whale Co., Levin Townsend, Commonwealth United Corp. and Saturday Evening Post Co. are on the long list of companies that have gone onto the defensive with recent divestitures. And at Ling-Temco-Vought, partial spinoffs of a number of properties have been motivated, at least in part, by a debt service bill that amounts to about $1 million a week.

A classic about-face

For a classic about-face from offense to defense, consider the case of Dolly Madison Industries. The company began by acquiring the Northeastern Division of Foremost Dairies in 1963. From then on, Dolly Madison expanded its food line while moving into the manufacture of furniture. In 1968, when the expansion program spurted ahead with the acquisition of seventeen properties of various sizes, Dolly Madison reported earnings of $4 million on revenues of $70.9 million, which prompted Chairman Robert Rittmaster to point out in his annual letter to stockholders that "a considered strategy of growth has been [one of] the integral ingredients in the Dolly Madison story."

Using pooling of interest accounting, Dolly Madison saw sales jump to $140.9 million last year. But the new businesses also multiplied the company's problems, and it posted an earnings deficit of $3.2 million.

This spring, Dolly's fortunes still looked bleak. A bank loan was arranged for $5 million with terms that called for 14½% interest and a pledge of $6 million in accounts receivable collateral.

Management had already begun jettisoning acquisitions to save the ship. First its Sea Pass frozen food processing business was sold to Brown & Williamson Tobacco Co. for an undisclosed amount of cash. Now, the company is seeking stockholder approval to complete the sale of the ice-cream and furniture manufacturing businesses. In brief, the operations either sold or in the process of sale contributed almost two-thirds of Dolly Madison's 1969 sales. Once a prominent food processor, the company has cut back to furniture retailing and leasing, manufacture of office furniture, the operation of a chain of 23 Grab-It food stores in Illinois and Indiana and other miscellaneous activities including pretzel baking.

Small companies are not the only ones taking a defensive posture these days. Companies that in more bullish times were willing to absorb the losses from smaller divisions now are paring them away. For instance: blue-chip tiremaker Uniroyal Inc. "We are considering selling some of our smaller operations that aren't paying their way," says Chairman George Vila. Uniroyal profits, it should be noted, dipped 24% in the first quarter of 1970. "When you keep a scorecard on yourself and find one or two losers in your stable," adds Avco Corp. President James Kerr, "you wake up fast."

In other companies, the concept of "fit" is coming back into vogue, with its concurrent discrediting of the "we-can-manage-anything" theory. Apparel-maker Hanes Corp., for example, recently sold an athletic apparel line to Southern Athletic. Southern has a viable distribution network to schools and athletic clubs where such apparel is sold; Hanes does not.

At Brunswick Corp., a lack of fit has resulted in a 15% spinoff of its Sherwood Medical Division. The move was aimed at establishing independent identity—"Medical men were leery of buying supplies from a bowling equipment company," explains a company officer. Budd Co.'s mica products line has been sold to New England Mica Co. (Budd is also "streamlining" its corporate profile with the sale of its paper-products division to Household Finance and a major part of its railway division to General Electric.)

Standard International Corp., whose products range from frying pans to surgical instruments, has given up on its Lestoil, the household cleaner. After a five-year struggle with the giants of the soap business, Standard threw in the

towel and dealt Lestoil to Noxell Corp.

Even profitable divisions are being sold when the returns are inadequate. "When money costs at least 8%," observes investment banker Hexter, "and when one division is earning 20% an other 6%, selling the 6% division is often the cheapest source of working capital." To President F. Perry Wilson of Union Carbide, this process is simply one of "identifying strong and weak businesses." "We can," he adds, "either strengthen the weaker ones or phase them out." At Carbide, which has begun to emphasize consumer markets, divestiture not only has weeded out subperformers but also units that lacked sufficient fit. During the last two years, Carbide has sold a semiconductor division, Neisler Laboratories and the Stellite Division, thereby garnering extraordinary revenues of $71 million and capital gains on the sales of some $6.5 million.

The carbide strategy

The Neisler Laboratories sale illustrates Carbides' strategy. The company bought the closely held pharmaceutical firm for a little more than $3.8 million in 1965 with the intent of using its marketing capability to develop a consumer market for some biologically-active compounds developed in-house. The idea did not work out. Instead, Carbide found the compounds did not have the potential, the consumer pharmaceutical business was time-consuming and development costs high. So Neisler was sold to Mallinckrodt Chemical Works for $11.5 million, resulting in a 9-cents-a-share capital gain to Carbide.

The Stellite division had come into the company as part of Haynes-Stellite back in the early 1920s. The high performance metals division is engaged essentially in the manufacture of turbine blades for aircraft engines. Though there are some exciting prospects for a ground-vehicle market, a company officer suggests that they are at least five years away. A willing buyer, President Robert A. Charpie of Cabot Corp., a former Carbide executive very familiar with the operation, agreed to pay in excess of $55 million for Stellite, a compromise between the book and tax value. Carbide registered a slight capital gain of some 2 cents a share on the sale. Carbide, in other words, has demonstrated a willingness to sell profitable divisions when an eager buyer was available.

Another company with a divestment program aimed at long-term improvement of profit margins is W. R. Grace.

"Our divestments, with a few exceptions, are planned to get out of low-return businesses and increase our return on capital employed," says President J. Peter Grace. Few companies have more actively pursued such a goal.

Though Grace has yet to prove that its strategy will improve return on equity (in 1969 the return was a low 7.4% on equity on $635 million), the company has toted up some $200 million from its divestitures, which is now available for new, high-return investments. "If the highest return you can get from a business is 3% to 5%," says Grace, "you are better off with cash in gilt-edged securities until another investment opportunity comes along."

Carried a step further, this strategy leads to the use of divestiture not as a defensive ploy but as a part of an aggressive program of "asset management." "The present economic climate is inviting partial spin-offs and selling or closing less profitable operations at a faster clip," says Chairman Fred R. Sullivan of Walter Kidde & Co. But this does not represent a change in philosophy in acquisitions-minded companies, says Sullivan. "They are still taking the assets at their command," he argues, "and using them in a way that will get the most out of them."

While the acquisitions side of the strategy has received widespread public attention, the disposition phase has gained little notice—perhaps intentionally. Chairman James E. Robison, for instance, has not permitted the disposition section of an Indian Head Inc. case study to be circulated outside of the business-school classroom.

The head of another company admitted to DUN's he had been trying to sell a major division for years, "but don't report it," he pleaded, "or my distributors will head for the hills." Adds Arthur Cahill of Brunswick, which has divested a number of properties in recent years: "We have no expectations of selling any more, but even if we did, I would not tell you because it disturbs distributors, it disturbs customers and it disturbs employees."

James Shaver, now with Wollensak, would agree with that, and the chances are a good many others will, too, as the age of un-merger unfolds. The time is coming, says Wesley Marple Jr., a professor at Northeastern University's School of Finance who has studied divestiture for many years, when "the chief executive will be making a buy, sell or hold decision for each division every year."

Boise Cuts Itself To Manageable Size

Boise Cascade Corp., the debt-ridden conglomerate, keeps lopping off appendages as it returns to its business of the 1950s: forest products. The largest, and perhaps most surprising, divestiture of all occurred this week when the company agreed to sell its Fort Bragg (Calif.) redwood operations to Georgia-Pacific Corp.

Boise is getting $120-million for the property, which is the former Union Lumber Co. that it had acquired in 1969 for $55.1-million in stock. Taken together, Boise's divestments have now raised about $350-million, most of it used to pay down the company's long-term and realty debt, which peaked at $916-million in 1971.

But in selling Union, Boise raised some eyebrows because for the first time it is getting rid of one of its basic forest products operations. Union earned a respectable $8-million before taxes on sales of $29-million last year, and its holdings include 225,000 acres of timber, two mills, and a particleboard plant. One analyst wonders if Boise is "murdering its earnings power" by selling the company that generated 15% of the parent's lumber and 7% of its plywood. In the first nine months of last year, Boise lost $185.2-million on sales of $1.1-billion.

Sour Investments. A Boise executive insists that the Fort Bragg operation was "the most expendable" of the company's timber ventures, mostly because it was impractical to feed the redwood chips from it to other Boise pulp mills. Ironically, Georgia-Pacific just recently spun off all of its redwood operation as part of an antitrust settlement with the Federal Trade Commission. With this acquisition, G-P goes back into redwood. Says G-P's president, Robert B. Pamplin: "We are pleased with this transaction which repositions us as a factor in northern California."

Boise will use the Union money to reduce its debt and help pay for expansions at the company's building materials and paper businesses.

Debt woes have plagued Boise since its land development programs and its $237-million of Latin American investments soured two years ago. That led to a $78-million extraordinary writeoff in 1971 and a $200-million writeoff last July after the company liquidated most of its realty group.

What started in May, 1971, as a program to raise $100-million by divestment jumped to $200-million two months later, and has now crossed the $300-million mark. But as Boise has paid down its debt, the company's debt/equity ratio has dropped from near 60%, and Boise aims to bring it down to 33% by the end of the year.

Divestments. Boise has shed most of the nonforest businesses it acquired during the past decade and dropped out of two joint ventures, including an Argentine petrochemical operation. Most have been sold, some liquidated, and one, American Buildings Co., became an independent company. Virtually all of Boise's construction and engineering group, which generated sales of $378-million in 1970, is now gone. Of 26 land sales projects, only two remain. Those two minor operations, and a single factory-built home operation, are all that are left of the housing and realty ventures that plunged Boise into financial straits.

Except for the Union divestment, Boise's mainstay—the timber, building materials, and paper-packaging groups—remains intact. The company still has some 7-million acres of timberlands. To demonstrate the company's return to its traditional mold, a Boise executive says he expects "almost zero" revenues from nonforest product sources this year. In 1971, nearly $800-million, or 44% of the company's $1.8-billion sales, came from such sources.

So Boise executives are now feeling bullish. One says that last year the company's timber operations were the best ever and that paper had a very good year. But some experts are predicting a falloff in housing later this year. If so, that could hurt Boise just when it is trying to recapture some of its old-time momentum.

How Boise Cascade has slimmed down

May, 1972, to February, 1973

Sold	Buyer	Amount realized
Guatemalan electric utility	Guatemala	$18-million
American Buildings	American Buildings	Undisclosed
Detroit Automotive	Aspro	Undisclosed
Detroit Tullar Envelope	Seaman-Patrick Paper	Undisclosed
Mobile home and recreational vehicle operations	Bendix	$61.3 million
Ebasco Services and Vernon Graphics	Halliburton	$65-million
Kansas City container plant	Hoerner-Waldorf	Undisclosed
Guatemalan, Brazilian, and Colombian bonds	Various buyers	$30.2-million
Panama Power & Light	Panama	$18.1-million
Chemical Construction	Aerojet-General	$20-million
Union Lumber	Georgia-Pacific	$120-million

Liquidated

Walter Kidde Constructors, Power Line Erectors, Tyee Construction

Putting A Company Back On The Growth Curve

Two young executives learn the lessons of building a business enterprise

A dozen years ago Merle H. Banta and Stephen F. Hinchliffe, Jr., bought a small sprinkler manufacturer in Los Angeles, using only $8,000 of their own money and borrowing $550,000. With that heavily mortgaged base, the two partners set about showing the business world how a couple of bright young Harvard Business School graduates could achieve fame and fortune while constructing a classic business enterprise around the concept of leisure.

Banta and Hinchliffe (above) must sort out troubles at Leisure Group that they never saw while riding to success in the 1960s on such products as Flexible Flyers.

They almost made it. By 1970 an acquisitions binge, which led Leisure Group into everything from sleds to rifle ammunition, had made the company a high-flyer with sales of $66-million. But by 1971 the "leisure-time conglomerate" was falling apart even more rapidly than it had been assembled. It ran up an incredible $31-million loss on sales of $57-million. And with $38-million in debt that cost $5-million a year just to service, the company teetered on the brink of bankruptcy.

But Leisure Group is still around, and even more miraculously, Banta and Hinchliffe, older (both are 42) and wiser, are still at the helm. Now,

though, their management style has become so conservative that they worry about taking too few—rather than too many—risks.

For four years Hinchliffe, who is chairman, and Banta, president, have been playing it close to the vest just to stay alive, and it has paid off. Leisure Group divested half its business to pay its debts and has been slowly tidying up what was left. Now it looks for sales of $31-million in the current fiscal year, up from $26.9-million last year. Losses of $7.7-million in 1972 were whittled down so that 1973 was a break-even year, and last year the company showed a $1-million profit. This year the company may double that. Meanwhile, the debt has been pared to $7.7-million, a hefty load for a company the size of Leisure Group to bear but at least manageable.

No credit. The two executives agree that the most meaningful lesson they have learned is to have contingency sources of financing. "We're going to have plenty of options when we make an acquisition," says a chastened Hinchliffe.

The company's troubles began when it bought Lawn Man, a lawn mower maker with $25-million in sales, intending to bolster its operating capital with a sale of Leisure Group common stock. But when the stock fell from $30 to $17, the company turned to its banks for $10-million in credit, instead. Then two bad years in the lawn mower business left Leisure Group with big inventories but no money to pay off the loans, and the banks cut off its credit.

The second lesson the managers have learned is to push authority down to their division heads, who used to channel most of the decisions up to Hinchliffe and Banta. The conversion from a functional to a divisional structure seems logical for a company with such diverse operations. These include High Standard, a producer of hand guns and shotguns; Dodge Trophies, which produces such awards as the Oscars and Emmys; and a lawn care division, which makes such products as spray guns and planting mixes. An important bonus was a cut in corporate overhead from $4.6-million a year to $1-million.

The new system also allows the chairman and president to sort out fi-

nancial problems. "Before, we focused on profit and loss controls," Hinchliffe says, "but the problem wasn't cash flow, it was leverage."

Looking to expand. The third lesson, seemingly the most simple of all, was simply to pay attention to the bottom line. With an eye to growth, Leisure Group acquired a string of 19 plants with more than 3,000 employees. But it was done, says Hinchliffe, without thought as to whether the companies were well-financed or profitable. "If the products were good and well-recognized, we thought we could figure out how to finance them and make them profitable ourselves," he says.

Now that the company is back on its feet, Hinchliffe and Banta once again have expansion on their minds, but this

Hinchliffe: 'We're going to have plenty of options when we make an acquisition'

time they think they can avoid a messy aftermath.

Hinchliffe says growth will be more cautious. "We'll look for a history of profitability and we'll ask how much capital has to be invested and whether return on capital is adequate. We'll let the earnings per share take care of itself," he says.

Acquiring companies will not be as easy as before simply because Leisure Group, with its stock now selling at a little over $1 a share instead of $30, has less to trade. Before their stock can again become an attractive acquisitions vehicle, Hinchliffe and Banta will have to restore their credibility with investors as painstakingly as they have with their lenders.

"I think they've done a manful job of seeing this thing through," says Robert Stillman, vice-president of American European Associates, an investment group that owns more than 1-million shares of Leisure Group's convertible preferred stock. "It's rare that bright young men stick with a company in a situation like this. More typically the hot shots abandon ship."

Hinchliffe and Banta think the ship was worth saving. Although their own Leisure Group stock, once worth $10-million, has fallen to the point where neither man now has a net worth of more than $100,000, their entrepreneurial spirit is still burning bright. "The easiest course would be not to expose ourselves," says Hinchliffe. "It's so comfortable right now. But that would be the biggest risk of all." ∎

CONSIDER CHALLENGES

1. Do you agree with Sears' strategy for diversification? Explain.

2. Would you say that Sears' goals have changed over the years? Explain.

3. What was the "key" to Tiffany's business growth?

4. What kind of financial reports do you think Tiffany needed to manage his firm effectively?

5. How much "luck" and how much "good" management are involved in the success of a small business? Of a merger?

6. Would Tiffany and Hershey be a good "marriage?" Explain your answer.

7. Is it necessarily good for a company to be a "growth" company? Explain.

8. Is large size, whether gained by internal growth or by mergers, always advantageous? Explain.

9. Are conglomerates or highly diversified businesses generally more profitable than others? Explain.

10. What do you think will be the trends in business mergers? Explain.

In a corporation's annual report, examine the kinds of companies owned as subsidiaries and what percentage ownership is indicated. From your analysis, would you consider the corporation to be a "conglomerate?" In general, what approaches have the company used in its mergers?

Look for the manufacturer's name on the package of a TV dinner and trace the company's line of ownership. A useful reference is a book called WHO OWNS WHOM. If you don't like TV dinners, try a can of Chung King chow mein.

Examine the financial statements, the annual report, or POOR'S RECORDS for Hershey Foods Corporation. From an analysis of this information, where do you see the company's principal strengths? What issues do you see? Does Hershey have an unusually large amount of retained earnings? What affect does this have on earnings?

Using the information in this chapter and any additional current data you can find, decide whether or not you would be willing to invest in Boise Cascade common stock. Explain your answer.

Read and analyze the WRECK OF THE PENN CENTRAL by Joseph Daughen and Peter Binzen. Now, what do you think about diversification?

RECAP

A successful company needs to know where it is going. It needs to have an idea or concept of what it should be like ten or twenty years in the future. A company also needs to have a plan or strategy for achieving specific objectives that will move the firm from where it is now to where it wants to be.

Strategies for growth may include internal growth (expansion on the present base of activities), development of new products or markets (such as expanding world wide), and merger or acquisition of other business organization.

A company that broadens the range of its products and activities is practicing a strategy of diversification. It is becoming more diverse. Diversification has a number of advantages -- you do not have all your eggs in one basket, you can reduce the effect of economic cycles, you improve your chances of being in potentially profitable markets, and you may enhance your overall company image.

Most companies attempt to expand through internal growth and through the introduction of new products. Playboy successfully built up the circulation and revenues of its original publication to become a major corporation. The company has also added many new products at the same time.

At the same time, Playboy and many other businesses have added new activities through merger or acquisition. This strategy for growth tends to attract a lot of attention because it involves the combination of different enterprises and yields immediate visible growth.

Companies merge to improve their economic positions, broadening their markets and expanding their facilities. Merging is another way of diversifying a business. There are many advantages to companies found through mergers -- a larger, stronger organization, reduction of duplication, and the advantages of a broader business base. From our brief look at Hershey, we see that a plan for growth through acquisition may be effectively developed and followed.

In some instances, mergers do not work out as well as anticipated. The reasons are varied and were discussed in this chapter. A larger, conglomerated business is not necessarily more profitable. Growth may actually be impeded, rather than facilitated, by mergers or too rapid diversification.

An important strategy for the growth in the 1970's and 1980's is expansion of business activities internationally. The "multinational" corporation is an ideal held high by many businesses today. Achieving the objectives implicit in becoming a world-wide organization, however, is a difficult process. It is examined in depth in chapter 17.

WORKSHEET NO. 15

NAME_____

INSTRUCTOR'S NAME_____

DATE_____

1. Why might a company change its name when it becomes more diversified?

_____

2. Why do companies in the food industry seem to be diversifying into other industries?

3. Why did Boise Cascade spin off some of its operations?

4. Why do you think Sears has not merged with any other firms?

CHAPTER 16

Manufacturing

In this book we have given a lot of attention to products -- how they are created, priced, advertised, marketed, and distributed. This chapter considers where these products come from. To many people, making goods for sale is the heart of business enterprise.

Manufacturing is the process of making raw materials into useful goods. There are different kinds of manufacturing, based on the nature of the products made. Steel, for example, is made night and day, on a continuous basis. Building a large office building or making custom designed furniture is an intermittent process. It's more like a series of projects or jobs.

There has been a trend in manufacturing toward automation -- the making of products with a minimum of human participation. This is possible through mechanization and the use of computers. The results are increased efficiency, less fatigue, greater control, and overall lower costs in relation to the amount produced.

Yet automation creates new pressures for manufacturing managers and for workers on the production lines. We are adapting to new technological systems, but it is a tough process to do so. New skills are required of manufacturing managers and specialists today. New attitudes toward work are necessary as the nature of the work shifts to the technical and specialized.

To date, advancing technology in manufacturing has resulted in more jobs in technical, engineering, administrative, and other support areas. The mix of employees has shifted to a higher skill level, but the number of jobs has continued to grow. In the future, however, the coming of increasingly automated factories may result in even more loss of factory jobs. Included may be computerization of many routine tasks now performed by engineers and other technical specialists.

There's little doubt, though that American technology will further change manufacturing processes as we know them today and that these changes will further reduce costs of goods. That translates into a benefit for consumers, stockholders, managers, and all concerned.

Within the plant, another concern has come to management's attention. While safety of workers has long been an important concern, a new federal law requires more extensive actions than ever before to assure employee occupational safety and health. The Occupational Safety and Health Act, known as OSHA, has compelled industry to review and improve working conditions. The costs of improvements have been great in many cases, but there have been gains, as well. The Act has burdened many firms, and even forced some to close manufacturing operations. Despite the problems in implementing the law, the net effect has been beneficial.

Finally, pollution is a major problem that must be solved in manufacturing. The problem stems, of course, from the fact that making products often has a built in "byproduct" of affecting the physical environment. Bethlehem Steel represents one of the oldest and biggest polluting industries. Yet the company has taken major steps forward in reducing pollution, with major costs to the company, but measurable results. In many cases, new approaches in manufacturing have to be devised.

In This Chapter

The Manufacturing Process

Manufacturing is the process of transforming raw materials into finished products. It happens every day and we take manufactured goods for granted.

But it hasn't always been this way. The advanced processes of applying systems, technology, and mechanization in the making of goods is a relatively new idea.

Until about 200 years ago, when the industrial revolution changed everything, goods were made primarily by hand and in the craftsmen's own homes. One person was responsible for making a product, from start to finish, much like a high-quality cabinet maker works today.

From the time man first shaped natural material into spear tips and mud into pottery, he has been manufacturing.

THE FACTORY

Craft manufacturing still exists today, but the bulk of our goods are produced on an organized basis, in factories. Through automation and large-scale operations, America's industrial companies are able to produce a much higher quantity of goods, often with higher quality at a lower cost than would be possible by the craft method.

The "revolution" took place in England in the late 1700s with the substitution of machinery for human labor. Back then it was a matter of using animal power or water power

to run grain mills and textile mills. It led to development of machinery which could use the new power sources and it established the factory system -- putting workers together in a central location with assigned duties in the process of making goods.

Productivity is a lot greater in factories than in small craft shops. A group of workers can turn out many times more shoes, for example, in a factory than they could if they worked individually making shoes by hand.

Again, the key benefit is the substitution of machinery for human labor. An average of $30,000 is invested in machinery for each worker in American manufacturing industry. The actual figure is higher in some industries ($60,000 in petroleum and chemicals, $50,000 in automobile manufacturing).

And when you think that nearly a quarter of all workers in American business are employed in manufacturing, you realize we are talking about a big chunk of the action.

The investment, the talent, and the technology applied to industry are reasons for America's long leadership position in world industry.

TRENDS

As industries have developed, several trends have developed -- which continue today.

The number of firms engaged in manufacturing has declined. There are fewer, but larger firms sharing each market. We see this in the automobile industry, petroleum, chemicals, food products, aircraft, publishing, and other industries.

Mass markets have been developed, largely as a result of lower prices and ready availability of goods made possible through large-scale manufacturing. Look what happended in the calculator business, or in home videotape recording. At first the product was high-priced and virtually unavailable. When mass production is established, the mass markets emerged.

And, of course, the techniques used in manufacturing have advanced significantly over the years. More money, research, use of computers, and other technical advances continue to refine manufacturing processes. There is no end in sight.

SPECIALIZATION

A key principle in manufacturing is the division of labor into its simplest form. Henry Ford's early assembly line had each individual performing one or more highly specialized and simple tasks on each car. This allows each individual to concentrate on a specific task without wasted effort or time.

Also, the use of specialized machines and tools is more efficient than using general purpose tools. Of course, plants themselves are specialized, producing only a given product or family of products.

As a result, an automobile is actually an assembled package of parts manufactured not by one, but by literally thousands of companies supplying them.

The inherent risk in specialization among manufacturers is the interdependence created. Without one key part, you can't assemble the automobile. If the person with a needed special skill calls in sick, the production may halt.

STANDARDIZATION

One of the keys in manufacturing is having each unit produced identical to all other units produced. Standardized parts are interchangeable, making repairs possible. Products may vary in style, color, or accessories, but the basic goods are the same.

Further, management practices and systems are standardized. This includes work flow, inventory ordering and handling, records, and technical activities.

The 100,000th Ford Granada that comes off the line should be the same as the 1000th.

AUTOMATION

When we say automation we think of robots. And this may very well be reality in manufacturing. Already many production systems are highly mechanized and controlled by computer systems

The objective of automation is to reduce to a minimum the need for human labor to be involved in manufacturing.

Mechanization means substituting mechanical effort for human effort, but humans are still

involved in operating
and controlling the
machines.

In automation, computer
systems start and stop
equipment, adjust settings,
check on quality, maintain
timing, and keep records
on the results.

Futuristic? Not at all.
Oil refineries, for
example, now require fewer
than several hundred
technical employees where
thousands were needed
decades ago before
advanced systems were
developed and applied.

The space programs have
introduced many forms of
automated functions making
possible successful
the landings on the Moon,
Venus, and Mars. The
technology has had spinoff
for varied manufacturing
processes in industry.

Is automation bad?
Not at all, because it
increases productivity,
thereby improving the
economic competitiveness
of the products. Don't
think that people are
thrown out of work by
automation. More jobs
are actually created by
advancing technology,
although higher-skilled
jobs, in management,
professional and technical
areas.

TYPES OF MANUFACTURING

For the most part
today, manufacturing is
either continuous or
intermittent. In
continuous manufacturing,
the production of goods
flows at a steady,
predetermined rate,
generally without any
storage of partially
finished goods. An
example of this type of
manufacture is an oil
refinery, where crude oil
is transformed into
gasoline, fuel oil, motor
oil, and other products.

Current trends toward
automation and mechaniza-
tion point toward more
and more use of continuous
manufacturing. The use of
loading, unloading, and
assembly devices result in
mechanized production
lines. As a result,
increased control over
production is possible,
and goods can flow through
the factory like "oil".
The efficiency gained is
usually great.

When continuous
manufacturing is not
feasible or efficient,
either for large or small
quantities of a product,
intermittent manufacturing
is uesd. Here the product
is made in "job lots,"
such as parts made in
a machine shop. The
manufacture of special

space hardware, such as
satellites or the space
shuttle, is also inter-
mittent, since only a few
are made under a contract.

MANUFACTURING FUNCTIONS

The process of building
and producing a line of
products, as you would find
in an automobile company,
requires intricate
planning and coordination
between four operations:
Design, which must create
a product acceptable to
product engineers and to
the market; Product
Engineering, which must
develop specifications from
which the product can be
constructed at a previously
established cost; Manu-
facturing, which must make
the product according to
these specifications; and
Sales, which must market
the product.

At the division and
plant level, coordination
among other technical and
operating functions become
important. These include,
in an automobile company,
manufacturing engineering,
quality control, plant
engineering, production
planning and control,
and production supervision.

These manufacturing
functions represent career
opportunities which are
discussed later in this
chapter.

The New Men In Manufacturing

Gathered at the rustic Ozark Mountain resort near Jefferson City, Missouri several weeks ago were seventy executives from the International Harvester Co. On the surface, it looked no different than any other three-day, fun-and-business company conference. But to Dan Chimenti, there was nothing ordinary about it at all. As vice president for manufacturing of the giant farm machinery and truck producer, Chimenti was in charge of a singular event in International Harvester history: the first meeting ever of all its production managers from around the world.

The purpose of the conference was nothing less than to shake the company out of one of the longest sleeps in recent corporate history. Since the mid-1960s, International Harvester's sales have inched up at a listless 3.1% a year, its return on sales have remained stuck below the 4% industry average, and its profits have actually declined at the rate of roughly 15% a year.

Finally, late last year, President Brooks McCormick singled out the major reason for IH's poor showing: waste in manufacturing. For the immediate future, ruled McCormick, improved productivity would be the company's top priority. "It was a battle cry," acknowledges Chimenti today, "and there was no doubt at whom it was directed—me! So while the conference might not seem like much to an outsider, we in manufacturing have never gone to such trouble before."

Brooks McCormick is by no means the only chief executive to recently—and belatedly—discover the inefficiency of his company's manufacturing operation. After years of being beguiled by the dazzling successes of their marketing forces and the wizardry of their financial experts, hundreds of companies are now paying the price for neglecting that once dull and prosaic function.

The recession, of course, made it clear that an unhealthy proportion of U.S. industry's production facilities and equipment is outmoded and inefficient, particularly in the face of the newer, more highly productive machinery of Japan and much of Western Europe. On top of that, in just a few short years some new and powerful forces from within and without the corporation have begun to question the entire manufacturing process. Almost simultaneously, it seems, companies are being besieged by the increasing job dissatisfaction of their employees, the rising power of consumer groups, effective antipollution pressures and tough, new federal safety regulations.

The pressure point

As a result, as manufacturing consultant Eugene C. Moore of Lester B. Knight Associates puts it, "Manufacturing has become the most critical pressure point in the corporation." And that pressure, needless to say, is falling most heavily on one man: the head of manufacturing.

But he is not the manufacturing manager of old. No longer the up-from-the-ranks foreman who knows his way around a machine and little else, he is a true "management" type with strong

profit orientation and exposure to many corporate disciplines. President Frank Tobin of U.S. Industries' Great Lakes Screw Co. division describes him this way: "We are looking for a vice president of operations with manufacturing experience, a good profit-and-loss background, cost-price experience (and I don't mean a three-hour AMA course), and the ability to plan, spend and coordinate capital expenditures wisely."

The manufacturing man's most pressing concern right now is the productivity lag. And here, the federal government is a major goad. For not only must industry cope with the government's price freeze, the Nixon Administration has also made it clear that it wants the national level of output per man-hour raised. The U.S. has seen its yearly growth in output per man-hour slip from a postwar average of 2.6% to 1.7% currently—while Japan now boasts an incredible 10.6% growth.

Even Xerox, one of the best-managed companies around, has had to face up to poor productivity. It is well-known that Xerox' Data Systems computer-making operation in California has been draining profits from its parent ever since it was acquired in the late 1960s. Indeed, with sales shrinking, much of the division's production capacity has been lying idle.

Early this year, Xerox for the first time in its history brought manufacturing up to the top-management level. It created the post of corporate vice president for manufacturing, and reached across the sea to Britain for the man for the slot: Frederick Wickstead, the managing director of Rank Xerox. Wickstead, who calls himself a "general management type with emphasis on manufacturing," was first given the task of switching a sizable portion of the company's copier and duplicator parts production to the West Coast to make full use of Data Systems' facilities. Beyond that, he is expected to play a key role in Xerox' recently announced plans to marry the computer to the copier.

But how do you increase productivity when worker disgruntlement on the job seems to be fast reaching the proportions of a national malaise? Absenteeism and turnover throughout industry are generally running three to five times the rate of a few years ago. Workers are becoming more militant, too. At Ford Motor this summer, a combination of extreme heat and a demand by management for overtime led workers to walk off and cause the shutdown of an assembly line in Mahwah, New Jersey. The earlier General Motors' walkout in Lordstown, Ohio is, of course, well known.

Moreover, there is no doubt that the potential for this kind of trouble exists at many another company. John Royan, vice president of operations at the semiconductor division of International Rectifier, for one, says his division is suffering from a high rate of turnover of unskilled workers bored by repetitive chores. International Paper Co., says Albert Oetken, vice president of manufacturing, is having its troubles over the issue of seniority and the lengthy time required for advancement. And at International Harvester, says Dan Chimenti, employees are reacting strongly to the impersonal nature of their work. "There's a new kind of employee out there who is of enormous concern to us," explains Robert W. Newson Jr., vice president for operations at Lorillard Co. "He's looking for more than money. He wants a more interesting job. But how to make jobs more interesting is a question we haven't been able to answer yet. Only one thing is sure," Newson adds wryly: "We used to be able to turn that problem over to the industrial relations guy. No more. Now it's our problem."

In addition to the people problem, the manufacturing manager today must also grapple with the increasing complexity and cost of the operation he controls. Including labor, plant and machinery, says Eugene Moore, close to 70 cents of every sales dollar is absorbed by manufacturing. In order to achieve the kind of cost savings that top management is demanding, then, the manufacturing man must be able to deal with the much more sophisticated elements that go into determining his profitability —for one, the hidden costs of such things as material handling and inventory control; for another, the greater mechanization and automation of the manufacturing process. He must also, Moore says, "thoroughly understand financial and accounting techniques."

Take the situation at industrial-machinery maker Koehring Corp. Faced with several years of slumping profits, President Orville O. Mertz decided the company was not allocating its capital funds properly. To solve the problem, Mertz consolidated all the responsibility for operations—from planning and production to quality assurance and engineering—in one corporate-level position, and named Erwin Brekelbaum as vice president of operations. Brekelbaum, who had been the group director at the company's largest division, has a wide-ranging background in engineering, manufacturing and finance.

Consumerism and pollution

The bulk of industry's outside problems are also getting right down to the manufacturing level, making the head man's job even more hectic. "In a very real sense," notes Robert Hendrickson, vice president for operations at Merck, Sharp & Dohme, "the changes in the job are a reflection of the changes in the country generally."

For one thing, he must deal with the newfound power of the consumer. Organized consumer groups, backed up by a rapidly growing number of official ombudsmen-type agencies, are rejecting and returning a variety of products—ranging from cars and tires to drugs and toys—that they consider inferior or unsafe. Added to that, of course, is the new, tough posture of the Food and Drug Administration and the Federal Trade Commission, which have been forcing the recall of more products than ever before.

The effect that the consumer movement is having on manufacturing can be seen in just one small example. Lou-Ana Industries is a $30-million-a-year producer of edible oils and animal feeds in Louisiana. A few months ago, relates Donald Van Sickle, its new vice president of production, the company turned out a large shipment of salad oils that "looked inferior." In the past, says Van Sickle, the company would probably have tried to sell them at a discount. This time, he ordered the entire shipment recalled and dumped.

But to many companies, the Number One manufacturing headache they see ahead—in terms of both money and time—is the fight against pollution. Just one company, International Paper, is pouring $125 million into upgrading eleven mills to comply with new antipollution standards. And Boise Cascade, on top of all its well-publicized troubles, had barely opened a new $6.5-million pulp mill in Salem, Oregon early this year when it was forced to close it down temporarily for failing to comply with new state regulations. Overall, predicts Chase Manhattan Bank's Chase Econometrics Associates, manufacturing men can expect to see some 200-300 plants permanently closed by 1976 because of new antipollution regulations.

For the manufacturing man, the implications are obvious. On the one hand he has the demands of government officials and ecology groups to contend with; on the other, the exhortations of top management to do the job as economically as possible. "Manufacturing men," snaps Walter Scott, manufacturing vice president of Motorola, "are sick of hearing about pollution—it's coming out of their ears."

The manufacturing man also has the major responsibility for implementing the government's new safety standards, which are expected to cost industry billions of dollars, plus contending with a plethora of state and local laws. The time-consuming job of complying with all these laws is pointed out by George Hoff, vice president of the industrial division at food products company CPC International Corp.: "In order to operate a multidivision corporation like ours, there are thousands of permits that must be filed each year. Consequently, I have one full-time man at each plant doing nothing but taking care of permits. And I have another man in Chicago who spends all his time going to meetings to keep up with all the regulations we have to observe."

Beyond all the above problems, the manufacturing chief is sure to be saddled with a few more. For one, with the U.S. now committed to adoption of the metric system of weights and measurement, production operations—from product design to the manufacturing process itself—face massive changes in the decades ahead. For another, as more U.S. companies expand their operations abroad, the problem of coordinating manufacturing operations from headquarters will become more difficult. Then, too, he can expect to be responsible for more plant start-ups as the economy improves and for the introduction of still more complex production tools.

In short, what is happening in manufacturing is nothing less than a renaissance of both the function and the man in charge. Indeed, as the head of manufacturing becomes more visible to top management and rises in the corporate hierarchy, his own chances for the top spot are fast improving. "It's a much tougher, more demanding, more professional job," sums up Merck, Sharp & Dohme's Robert Hendrickson. "That's why we like it."

The Production Line, Men Or Robots?

Robots have been few and far between in American industry because of their newness, cost, reliability problems, and fear of labor reaction. But there are signs that use of robots is increasing both in the United States and abroad.

General Motors' plant at Norwood, Ohio, has a robot line at work welding body panels of Chevrolet Camaros and Pontiac Firebirds. Workmen fix the panels in place the usual way (by tack welding). Then a floor conveyor moves the car down the line of 14 robot welders, seven on each side. The car stops at each welding station and two robot arms, one from each side and each holding a welding gun, move out and go to work. The robots follow instructions programmed into their magnetic memories. The robots even have wrists to permit them to do complex welding tasks. When the arms have done their job, the conveyor moves one place forward and the process is repeated. The line can handle 57 cars an hour.

A similar line, but twice as big has been in operation at Lordstown, Ohio, where GM's Vega is built. There are 26 robots, 13 on a side who can weld car bodies at a rate of 120 per hour.

Robots cannot do anything that people could not do with semi-automated tools. But they often can do the work more cheaply, require less start-up and model change-over time (because they are programmed), and do not fatigue.

GM has robots throughout its fabricating operations -- a few in each plant -- to find out what kinds of jobs they can do well. Some industry experts think that the auto industry could be a big user of robots.

It was back in 1962 that the first robot was put to work in American industry -- at Ford Motor Company. Today hundreds of such robots are at work, in a wide variety of industrial situations.

Robots are going international also. The Russians put robots to work in the automobile assembly line at the Togliattigrad plant Fiat built. The Japanese are not only using robots in production, but are making them and exporting them all over the world.

Generally, robots do jobs that people do not want to do. In the United States, the most common job is unloading

An artist's conception of robots at work welding auto bodies on the General Motors' assembly line at Norwood, Ohio

hot parts from automatic diecasting machines. Robots work in forging and glass making, and are taking over jobs where the parts or hand tools are heavy and cause fatigue.

At a transmission and axle plant in Kentucky, a robot helps make ring gears for truck drivers. A robot picks up a rough rink of metal weighing 50 to 75 pounds and hands it to a vertical lathe. After the outside diameter has been machined to proper size, the robot hands the ring to another machine, which cuts the inside diameter. Next the robot moves the ring to a drill that makes a number of holes in the metal. After a total elapsed time of 90 seconds, the robot turns to pick up its next ring.

In the future, robots will become more flexible. For one thing, more robots will be linked to computers -- and thus have "brains". Most robots up until now have been rather simple-minded, programmed to perform a single series of routine tasks. Robots may become able to "see" what they are doing, avoid mistakes, identify and correct problems, and communicate with people responsible for the production line.

PEOPLE AND ROBOTS

How do people fit into such automated production systems? If you have heard anything about the Norwood or Lordstown plants in the news in recent years, you will know that people do not fit in easily.

While robots may push cars down a line at the rate of 100 or 120 an hour, the workers report that they feel the pace is too rapid, the work too de-humanized, and the pressure of the work too great.

The employees walked off the job at Lordstown and Norwood as a reaction to these feelings. The workers were young, generally in their twenties. The fast pace, the routinization, and the impersonalized work on the production lines did not make sense to them. It was not that they wanted more money, they wanted to get off the line or to change it.

Yet, General Motors designed the line to be efficient -- and that meant high speed and routines. According to company sources, the lines never had run up to the pace they were supposed to. To build quality small cars at attractive retail prices requires efficient production -- production on lines manned by robots and people.

You can program the robots but you cannot program the people. A production line is a production line -- it has requirements that are not all that flexible. So what gives -- the line or the people?

What happens is that the production lines do not run as conceived on the drawing boards. GM has to make its Vegas, and has a significant investment in the plants at Norwood and Lordstown. So the human element is given a little more attention and production efficiency takes a little

setback from what was thought to be possible by the designers and engineers.

The production lines are running today. Sure, there are some problems -- technical, human, economic -- but the plants are operating and GM is achieving its business objectives.

While automobile plants provide classic examples of production lines, there are a multitude of other types of operations that involve the same type of manu-facturing process -- and the use of automation.

For example, a paper company in the United States has built a new plant for manufacturing rolls of a new paper towel product. Housed in a long, narrow building is a highly automated production line. Into one end of the building is received raw pulp and synthetic fibers. This material is fed into hoppers and are chewed up and formed into a web. A complex series of rollers, sprays, and heat and air treat-ments forms this crude matting into a thin, resilient paper and rolls it into massive tubes, ten feet long. Then the paper is rolled onto small paper tubes, decorated, and cut and packaged.

The line is virtually automatic, and turns out paper at the rate of 100 feet per minute or more. The machinery cost millions of dollars to build and is expensive to operate. Yet only seven workers are required to run the line -- from start to finish. Efficient? Yes. Human? Yes.

Are We Ready For The Automatic Factory?

One machine can handle 15 different parts, all requiring complex machining, in Cincinnati Milacron's "Variable Mission" manufacturing center.

THE AUTOMATIC FACTORY is our ace and our key to survival in an international war that's heating up.

This superfactory will be fantastic by today's standards and so expensive that it may take a consortium of companies and even government assistance to handle the financing.

It will include the fruition of today's Space Age technology: machines that can "think" for themselves and respond to spoken commands; "smart" robots capable of modifying their own behavior in order to take care of emergencies; and, overall, a novel system of nearly paperless planning and managing, computer-based and imaginatively created from the roots up by engineers, scientists, and experienced management people.

Sound exaggerated? Not at all, say a growing number of authorities who reluctantly agree that our world competitive posture is threatened and who are concerned about the potential social impact of this supertechnology we're being forced to develop. Already we are seeing some of the forerunners of the types of hardware we'll need:
• A Sundstrand Corp. unit at Ingersoll-Rand Co.'s plant at Roanoke, Va., automatically machines 500 different parts in 16 different designs.
• Both Ford Motor Co., Dearborn, Mich., and Cincinnati Milacron Inc., Cincinnati, have invested heavily in a concept called *variable mission man-ufacturing*. The experimental unit demonstrated that it could make in any sequence three Ford parts and two Cincinnati parts. Ford did get the prototype working, says Norman W. Hopwood, manager of manufacturing component systems. But Cincinnati Milacron determined that completion of a full-sized unit would require a $100 million investment and decided not to continue the project. It is, however, going ahead with a modification of the idea, producing five-axis machining centers which allow several operations to be done automatically and at the same time.
• Kearney & Trecker Corp., Milwaukee, has Systems Gemini, which handles a large variety of short-run parts quickly and efficiently.
• Bendix Corp., Southfield, Mich., hints it will introduce a new product for this field this year.
• Existing robots are already rugged and reliable, but new ones under development at Stanford Research Institute, Menlo Park, Calif., respond to simple voice commands and can modify their own behavior via "eyes" and "feeling" in their "hands."
• The advent of microprocessors and microcomputers (those in our hand-held calculators are small examples) is already revolutionizing various phases of process control needed for automatic factories. Robert D. Carlson, manager-numerical equipment engineering and computer-aided manufacturing (CAM), McDonnell Douglas Corp.'s McDonnell Aircraft Co., St. Louis, predicts that machining centers in tomorrow's automatic factories will get their instructions via broadcasts from satellite computers transmitting to microcomputers and microprocessors. He has coined a new phrase for it: smart numerical control (SNC).
• At the Government Accounting Office (GAO), Washington, Elmer B. Staats, controller general, says, "We seem to be moving in the direction of the automatic factory. Some of our foreign competitors are already investing hundreds of millions of dollars in research to further that technology." In a report to Congress, GAO will deal with the alternatives.

For example, the Japanese are investing $100 million in a joint industry-government effort called the National Big Plan. Its goal is an automatic factory module (MUM) that can be used universally. Ten operators per module will do what formerly required 700 operators working with individual machines.

Giacomini SAS, Novora, Italy, manufactures a

wide variety of valves (1.5 million to 2 million per month) completely automatically on standard machinery linked with automatic material handling devices, says Howard H. Deem, president, Conval-International, Cincinnati, who has been there. It manages with perhaps 10% of the people normally used in a comparable U.S. plant. And its product costs *in this country* 50% of what it can be made for here.

In West Germany, Heidelberg Press has a highly automatic factory south of Heidelberg which GAO observers say is advanced beyond anything we are currently doing.

Via unspecified channels, government investigators have details on a hitherto unpublicized plant at Karl Marxstadt, East Germany. Operated by Fritz Heckert Machine Tool Co., "It is the most sophisticated automatic factory we have ever seen," says one expert.

Technology can do it. *"Machine units will respond to information as we do to our five senses. [We] propose an entirely different view of machine design, one that combines both the machine itself and the functions of a workman who might operate it . . . each new machine will be made of many small machines plugged together, capable of doing all the operations required to build a given part. The complete machine will be highly adaptable, with easily detached components designed to be shuffled and rearranged at any time to build an entirely different product."*

Those amazingly accurate predictions were written some 30 years ago (*Fortune, The Automatic Factory*) by a couple of Canadian radarmen, Eric W. Leaver and J. J. Brown.

Many experts today regard Mr. Leaver as one of the "fathers" of automation. Now living in Toronto, he predictably agrees that the automatic factory is inevitable. "We have only two alternatives: to keep on muddling the way we are and be priced out of our own marketplaces, or get really serious and down to cases about introducing these changes," he advises.

He sees standardization and cooperation as two sure routes to technological success in this area. "Developments in computer programs involving large numbers [mainly for computer-aided design] might be expanded to aid the attack on practical computer-controlled manufacturing," he says. Hardware and software, he believes, could be examined for common denominators that could be agreed upon by both suppliers and customers.

Shape of things to come. The predictions of experts polled by IW fall generally into three categories: those who see the development of huge superfactories that will largely displace the small-batch manufacturer; those who envision an evolutionary development utilizing present-day machine tools and equipment; and those who think that our advancing technology will be adopted even by the small manufacturer, enabling him to keep pace on his own level.

Robert E. Esch, group executive, Factory Automation Section, Bendix Corp.'s Industrial Group, Detroit, firmly believes that the ultimate kind of automation will filter down from large shops.

Why? "Simply because of the capital needed. Only the large companies can afford this," he notes. What will happen, he firmly expects, is that machine tools will be designed to make small batches of a wide variety of products automatically and economically. They will be programmed via small computers.

"I suspect mammoth central computers either won't be needed or may be used much later. Earlier planners simply had no way of knowing that the cost of small computers would drop so fast, nor did they anticipate the fantastic costs of telemetering," he concludes.

"We made an evaluation of this market [leading to the automatic factory] some two years ago," relates Thomas Shifo, manager-marketing services, Sundstrand Corp.'s Sunstrand Machine Tool Div., Belvidere, Ill.

"Since the current systems we have been selling cost $5 million or $6 million, you find that most companies aren't willing to invest that kind of capital. As a result, I'm convinced that much of the direction toward the automatic factory will come from the larger companies," he concludes.

Still, Sundstrand has what it calls incremental implementation. This usually takes the form of "five-year plans" which allow a company to buy machines one at a time until they have the whole system. He thinks there is enough private capital to handle this kind of investment.

Mr. Leaver suggests that the large, nationally funded program, a la Japan's MUM project, isn't necessarily the best approach. "In Canada or the U.S., the results of such a program would probably be obsolete before it was completed," he believes.

Also, he smells the dry rot of technological rigidity and further industrial concentration. "Automatic factories don't have to be extremely large and complex. We'd be better off focusing the mainstream of our efforts towards a multiplicity of small factories, some doing quite different things, others doing the same thing," he exclaims.

He thinks the smaller approach offers more economic and social advantages than large agglomerations. "Only great increases in throughput quality and consistency on a shutdown-for-maintenance-only basis can possibly pay the freight for the large plants," he insists.

Conval International's Mr. Deem leans more toward the utilization of standard machines upgraded and adapted to the needs of automatic factories. Having seen what Giacomini has done with this approach, he's convinced that robots, or even super-robots, will have a major role.

"I'm enthusiastic about what I see at Giacomini. You buy standard machines, add some old machines you already have, and build material handling into the system. You can completely automate a plant that way at much lower cost. And you can still have the great flexibility."

Bendix Corp.'s Mr. Esch doesn't agree entirely with this viewpoint. "I do see a growth in different kinds of machines, particularly those which can make a batch of parts too large for a numerical control tool and too small for a hard tool transfer line," he explains. Robots and artificial intelligence seem to fit into this concept.

GAO's Mr. Staats' studies suggest that, especially in small-batch manufacturing, existing technologies — computers and numerical control tools — are not sufficiently diffused throughout manufacturing. He thinks we ought to push more in these areas.

There are prerequisites. C. H. Link, executive secretary and general manager, Computer Aided Mfg. International Inc. (CAM-I), Arlington, Tex., is the focal point of a multicorporate effort to automate the planning work of today's manufacturing engineer. He notes that 85% of what this engineer does is simply repetitive paperwork — some of it costly and a surprisingly high percentage of it undependable. He sees the transfer of this know-how to a computer possibly saving 50%.

CAM-I's roster of a hundred or so large corporations, plus dozens of the world's advanced institutions of technical learning, is working on the means to standardize the terminology and software needed to bring this plan to reality.

Why the manufacturing engineer? Once a new product has been designed, his functions are the key to successful manufacturing. He decides how long it will be before the product can be made, whether it is suitable for the plant scheduled to make it (e.g., a casting can't be made in a machine tool plant), how much it will cost to make it, how much capital will be needed, and so on.

"Unfortunately, even an experienced engineer has trouble retrieving consistent answers to such questions. If we transfer his know-how to a data base, in effect automating his paperwork, we can eliminate the many problems we currently experience with this function," explains Mr. Link.

But more importantly, all of that data are easily expanded into a viable, practical manufacturing information system, something that has been elusive to many managements and quite expensive to the few who have been successful.

He sees the rest of the technology for the automatic factory coming from modular tools — extensions of the Variable Missions, the System Gemini, and the Sundstrand concepts in current use. "You start with one piece you can manage. You use microprocessors for sensors, then a minicomputer to switch miniature factories within a factory," he points out. "With that data base, we can create the kind of monitoring function so essential to advanced management planning and even to what's called 'adaptive scheduling.'

"The majority of our equipment is less than 10 years old, so we're going to work with that. Any idea that we are going to build huge demonstration factories is simply academic, unrealistic." He believes that once this data base is computerized it will define the destiny of hardware.

Fewer factory jobs. "Long before ten years are up, we're going to see some major changes that will affect people working in factories. I think those who see the automatic factory as some kind of Tinkertoy will be shocked," predicts Mr. Link.

GAO is also concerned about this kind of impact. Its reports to Congress will point out that the continuing adoption of automatic methods will accelerate the trend toward fewer factory jobs. The report notes that 35.4% of our population in 1947 was employed in factory jobs. By 1985, that figure will drop to 24%, GAO says, although in actual numbers there will be 7 million more employed.

Some experts regard that estimate as too conservative if we build only a few superfactories that will be able to turn out what hundreds of smaller factories produce today. Costs will be so low that they will put small operators out of business. Census figures show that of more than 300,000 manufacturing plants, 80% employ fewer than 50 people. Further analysis shows that perhaps 80,000 plants that specialize in making small batches of parts might be affected.

"The small-batch manufacturer of discrete parts one day will go the way of the mom and pop grocery store," says one expert. And it's conceivable that the giant superfactories might rent out their production lines to others.

Mr. Link sees this as part of an international productivity war, with the winner staying stable as a result. He is convinced we may have to share our know-how to avoid a shooting war.

Ted Stewart, corporate chief industrial engineer for Motorola Inc., Chicago, agrees.

"Ten years from now, we'll see the first batch of automatic factories, but I firmly believe they'll be imports." The reasons, he says, is that in the U.S. labor fights management, which in turn fights government. "To get things done we ought to do what the Germans do: coordinate and finance what is good for everyone," he maintains.

Tony Connole, assistant to the president, United Auto Workers (UAW), Detroit, feels quite alone in his concern about the potential impact on workers. "Not enough is being done to take care of displacement," he mourns.

"When most companies move upper-level people around they pay moving expenses, pick up the tab for seminars, and generally encourage adult education. Not for hourly people. I feel that it ought to be automatic when someone is laid off by technological innovation to have his expenses and retraining paid for.

"When technology like the automatic factory comes along the effects aren't the same as replacing a casting with a plastic part. Some companies will fold and you create structural unemployment; you have people who need jobs but have no marketable skills."

Mr. Connole likes the idea of a national, tax-supported program to retrain people. "They need bread and coffee while they're studying. Foreign countries already do this, but here we run into budgets when we bring it up," he insists.

Something's astir. There is some fresh evidence that some things are being done to address these problems. A new law (No. 94136, from the Percy-Nunn Bill which President Ford signed in December) establishes the National Center for Productivity & Quality of Working Life.

Its acting director, George Kuper, says the center will deal with problems that arise from technological advances and their impact on people. Conceivably, it could encourage legislation aimed at solving some of these troubles. Among other things, he is looking for more data on the impact of automation, because in the past people displaced by such events tended to disappear into the industrial environment.

Mr. Staats, the controller general, thinks the center will provide an excellent umbrella on the federal level for coordinating government efforts. And he believes that it may foster the creation of other solutions in the private sector.

CAM-I's Mr. Link also suggests that education will be needed for the people who work with the automatic factory. "You can't create an environment like an automatic factory and just dump people into it," he notes.

Not everyone sees the automatic factory as a bogyman. Mr. Leaver says that if an automatic factory is properly designed and executed — with people as well as product in mind — it will be attractive enough to hold skilled people.

He believes we need not worry about a "people

impact" unless and until we put into operation an automatic factory that is self-reproducing, self-adapting to its environment, self-mutating, and self-maintaining. "Needless to say, this isn't in the foreseeable future," he concludes.

"The totally automatic factory requires too much overhead," adds James Wearn, who heads the office of technology specialties at Westinghouse Electric Corp., Pittsburgh. "And I think that the little guy will still survive, finding some niche where he can make something cheaper." Westinghouse, he says, has had great success in this area.

At the rainbow's end. There's not much argument among experts that the automatic factory can cut costs, and that this in turn could improve our export posture.

In both this country and Canada, for instance, we are exporting jobs faster than we can make new ones. Mr. Leaver estimates that 13% of Canada's exports and 40% of its imports represent manufacturing jobs. He notes that, although automation is less labor-intensive, we ought to consider the fact that imports' labor content — for the country receiving the imports — is zero.

Is the automatic factory inevitable? Or merely a possibility? Much depends on how well we put together the complex parts of a giant puzzle — parts that seem to be basic management problems that we can solve. Getting managers to accept and understand that position may give us the route to that pot of gold. □

Manufacturing And Pollution

In the process of transforming materials into useful goods, manufacturing creates pollution.

In the article that follows, Bethelem Steel explains how it is attempting to control pollution resulting from the company's extraction, analytic, synthetic, and fabrication processes.

Bethelem extracts raw materials from the earth (limestone, iron ore, and coal) to use in the stell-making process. In this minig process wastes are generated and must be disposed of without injuring the environment.

As a manufacturer, Bethlehem must either do this extraction itself or buy from another firm. In either case, the potential pollution of water, land and air must be minimized.

In the analytic process, in which raw materials are broken into component parts, pollution is also created. The use of electricity, water, heat, or pressure necessarily involves the use of natural resources and the discharge of pollutants. Often the problem is one of converting toxic discharges into safe substances, or possible useful goods. Conversion of coal into coke creates coal tars that are now converted into useful chemicals, dyes, and other materials.

In the synthetic process Bethlehem puts

limestone together to make steel. The process creates huge amounts of heat, smoke, and energy --which we have seen is a real pollution problem at Con Edison. Tools such as electrostatic precipitators and high energy wet scrubbers have been put to work to help reduce this pollution problem.

In the fabricating process, basic materials are put together to form new products. At Bethlehem basic steel is converted into products such as ships, bridges, and buildings, In the process, solid wastes such as scrap are created. Disposal of solid wastes is a big problem. Some scrap can be recycled -- such as scrap metal into new steel.

Any step taken by a manufacturer to reduce pollution involves a direct expenditure of money. Sometimes there is a return on this

investment through the creation of marketable goods using waste material. Normally, however, the pollution controls add to the cost of the products. If consumers want reduced pollution, they have to be willing to pay more.

The problem is that the average consumer doesn't know whether the product he or she is buying came from a factory that was clean or one that was a polluter. Since the consumer is expected to make a rational choice, that is purchase the less expensive product if these is no difference between several products, the consumer could end up "rewarding" the manufacturer who was polluting. Because this can happen, our government has developed a set of anti-pollution laws that make all producers operate at the same level of pollution control, and no company can get a competitive advantage by polluting.

Pollution Is A Dirty Word At Bethlehem Steel

Whether we use the term pollution to describe air or water contamination, or even land devastation, the condition is just as distasteful to Bethlehem Steel's management as it is to the staunchest conservationist. The fact is that we at Bethlehem have been working for decades to eliminate or control environmental contamination throughout our plants, mines, quarries, and shipyards.

Our efforts in this regard are not merely attempts to stay ahead of the law. Nor is our pollution control program merely a public relations campaign. We want to be good neighbors wherever we have operations. And since the vast majority of our employees live in the communities surrounding our operations, any contamination we permit to go unchecked is literally "fouling our own nest." _We_ are our own neighbors. Our plant managers and their employees drink the same water and breathe the same air. So do their friends and families.

Further, we believe that the needs of modern industry can be met without seriously affecting the balance of nature, and that the interests of technology and ecology need not conflict.

In its simplest form, coping with the many facets of pollution abatement is merely a matter of looking realistically at our social and economic responsibilities and doing everything feasible to eliminate pollution where it can be eliminated, and to control it where its prevention is not possible.

Each a special problem

But there's nothing simple about pollution control. The diversity of our organization is such that we must deal with nearly every kind of potential pollutant in a wide variety of environments. We must cope with gases, waste water, ammonia, coal tar, iron oxide dust and fumes, mill scale, acid, oil, sediment, slag, trash, garbage, and sewage, to mention only the most obvious ones.

All these wastes are generated in enormous quantities and preventing them from polluting air and water requires specialized and extensive equipment.

To further complicate the picture, pollution problems often require different solutions even though the pollutants may be similar. The age and design of the furnaces or steelmaking equipment, the location of the equipment relative to other facilities, the geography and topography of the location with respect to prevailing winds and natural drainage—these and many others are factors which affect, and sometimes limit, our efforts.

These factors mean that solutions must be developed on a case-by-case basis. We cannot go out and purchase off-the-shelf control equipment with any assurance that it will satisfactorily solve our every problem. Each case must be developed and engineered for each specific situation. And even then, we cannot be sure the control devices will function as planned.

And then there's the cost

Currently we are spending many millions of dollars each year on pollution control and related equipment. We estimate that in the next few years about 11 per cent of Bethlehem's capital investment in property, plant, and equipment will be spent for pollution control.

Our spending in this area has increased substantially during a period when Bethlehem and the steel industry have been subjected to the keenest competition in their history, both at home and from abroad — during a time when a severe profit squeeze has us hustling for dollars, for new markets, for modernized facilities, for new and improved products.

Unfortunately, unlike production equipment, pollution-control equipment does not increase earnings, improve competitive position, expand production, or cut expenses. And, it is costly to maintain and operate.

But, we are spending these funds on pollution control because we believe in it.

Bethlehem has been working hard for many years to eliminate pollution, and we feel we have been making great progress. Much time-consuming research and engineering development remain to be done. More millions of dollars will be spent. More progress will be made as we build on what we have learned.

Americans throw about 200 million tons of contaminants into the air each year. This fouling of the air causes an estimated $13 billion worth of property damage annu-

ally, in addition to creating health hazards under certain adverse meteorological conditions.

The uncontrolled discharges from smokestacks, the pollutants rising from streets and highways, the eye-burning smoke from municipal dumps and incinerators . . . can add up to a lot of smog.

Who's to blame?

In the search for a villain, an aroused public often points an accusing finger at industrial smoke-

Smoke is released during the short time it takes to load electric steelmaking furnaces. Baghouse dust collectors efficiently gather in and clean the dust-laden air before it is discharged into the atmosphere.

stacks. They are much more easily noticed than the exhaust pipe of your own car, a household chimney, or an outdoor barbecue grill. However, manufacturing industries account for only about 16.5 per cent of air pollutants, according to the U. S. Public Health Service.

PROGRESS BRINGS PROBLEMS . . .

Basic oxygen furnaces (BOFs) are the newest, fastest, most efficient steelmaking facilities in the world. BOFs are a major advance in technology and they produce high-quality steel ten times faster than

conventional open hearth furnaces. Bethlehem operates nine such furnaces, and we pour more tons of BOF steel than any other producer in the nation.

But BOFs generate tremendous quantities of dust-laden gas.

Our first three basic oxygen furnaces were installed at our Lackawanna, New York, plant. The pollution controls at this facility are three high-energy wet scrubbers, each designed to spray water through a system of 385 throats and nozzles, and wash the contaminated air. The furnaces have also been provided with improvements which include modifications to the furnace hoods and additional fans for the gas cleaning system.

As a result of these controls, we are now collecting 190 tons of dust _daily_ at this installation which would otherwise be discharged into the air.

Additional controls assist in the area where hot metal is poured at the BOFs. There, closely fitting hoods, with associated ductwork, direct fumes to a newly installed baghouse dust collector where the solids are removed from the gas stream.

When two BOFs were installed at our plant in Sparrows Point, Maryland, on Chesapeake Bay, similar wet scrubbers were installed to gather the iron oxide dust. At this location, another design was selected which uses one large throat and associated sprays rather than 385 small throats as in the earlier installation. This change reduced maintenance and increased the unit's reliability.

In addition to the scrubbers, a gas spinning device (cyclone) slings droplets of polluted water to the periphery of the device, removing the particles in the form of a slurry. The cleaned gases then pass out through a discharge stack.

This combination of scrubbers and cyclones collects better than 99 per cent of the fine fume particles discharged from the BOFs.

But a system designed for one plant may not solve the problem of a similar operation at a different location.

Over the years, municipalities and industries have poured so much raw sewage, acid waste water, chemical and bacteriological slop into the streams and lakes of this country that their ecological balance has been disrupted. Their natural ability to cleanse themselves no longer can keep pace with the amount of pollution being added.

Through federal and state legislation, and through the cooperation of industry, many streams and other bodies of water are being cleansed; water pollution abatement practices are bringing the problem under control.

A great industrial thirst

In a typical year, Bethlehem steel-making operations require over 550 billion gallons of water, or about 27,300 gallons for each ton of steel we produce. We use the water to cool our furnaces, provide steam for our turbines, wash furnace gases, quench coke, and remove scale from rolling mill products.

But we don't consume this water in the sense that there's nothing left when we're finished with it. Most of the water is used for cooling purposes and does not become contaminated. We run the water through our plant, use it an average of 1.5 times, treat that water which comes into contact with pollutants, and discharge it with an actual loss by evaporation of only 8 per cent. Of every 20,000 gallons we take in, 18,400 gallons are returned to rivers, lakes, or bays.

Only a small portion of the water we use comes from city mains. For example, our steel plant at Bethlehem, Pennsylvania, uses four different sources for its water requirements: the Lehigh River, inplant wells, a nearby creek, and city

Photograph (at top) shows how fumes would pour from the stack if the control system had not been installed at the Lackawanna Plant. Photograph (bottom) indicates successful control with the precipitators at work.

mains. Water is returned to the river and the creek in good condition.

Expenditures by Bethlehem Steel for water pollution control have been monumental because our problems are varied and our control techniques must be efficient.

Mining and quarrying operations necessarily change their surroundings adversely. Unless proper steps are taken, they create unattractive coal refuse disposal piles, steep hillsides prone to erosion, and other wasteland areas.

Over the years, Bethlehem foresters have developed planting programs to reclaim wasted areas and to restore the natural ecological balance. For example, after we closed our old iron-ore concen-

trator near Lebanon, Pennsylvania, the abandoned tailings pond dried up, leaving a 300-acre wasteland of powdered rock.

There was no soil and not a trace of nitrogen. The refuse was highly alkaline. The native vegetation wouldn't take hold, and dust clouds rose high when wind whipped the surface. Our foresters carefully selected a variety of trees, shrubs, and grasses, including nitrogen-fixing black locust, European alder, and legumes. Nearly a quarter of a million tree and shrub seedlings and cuttings were hand-planted.

This planting was followed by the seeding of ten varieties of grass in a fertilized paper-pulp mulch.

Today the former wasteland is a forest of locust, aspen, birch, poplar, spruce, and pine, along with alder, coralberry, privet, and honeysuckle. It's thick with grasses, and small game and wild birds abound.

Restoring the beauty to the land

Coal refuse piles provide another kind of challenge, but surprisingly there are often more plant nutrients in these piles than in many top-soils. The nutrient minerals, however, are imprisoned in small pieces of rock so that the plants cannot reach them. Heavy fertilization during the first year helps the plants develop their initial root systems which soon begin secreting enzymes, dissolving the rocky material, and providing the plant with natural nutrition.

To provide a quick cover of grass to halt erosion, we've experimented with planting a wild millet grass mixture which contains a variety of weed seeds. Weeds will grow where conventional grass won't. Although some yucca from the dry southwest is being planted, most of the plantings are more conventional—pine trees and varieties of soil conservation grasses.

Bethlehem's Mine No. 44 near Idamay, West Virginia, is another example of our extensive planting program. There's a lush, ankle-high cover of bluegrass, fescue, lespedeza, and rye grass growing on a former coal tailings basin.

POLLUTION IN THE PLANT...

Our attention in the preceding pages has been directed to air and In an effort to present Bethlehem's programs to combat pollution, there is a risk of losing the reader's attention by trying to touch upon too many aspects of those efforts. After citing dollar expenditures, the mind glazes and figures become meaningless.

But we are a large corporation, with diverse operations, employing more than 130,000 people. Although the amounts are so large that they may be difficult to grasp or comprehend, our expenditures are real. They represent a necessary commitment to the future of our firm, our industry, our environment, and to generations yet to come.

Many jobs in our steel plants, shipyards, mines, and quarries must be performed in surroundings containing potential hazards. We have gone to great lengths to protect the employees with appropriate safety equipment, safeguards on machines, and with in-depth safety educational programs to help them protect themselves.

In certain operations, dust, fumes, mists, gases, and vapors may contaminate working environments. Noise, ionizing radiation, heat, pressure, vibration, and illumination also contribute to environmental stresses.

Bethlehem has worked just as aggressively to reduce, eliminate, and control these on-the-job stresses and contaminations as we have tried to combat the broader effects of pollution in the community environment.

Much has been accomplished.
More remains to be done.

Pollution control is a monumental job which will require more research, more engineering, more time, and more millions of dollars. Bethlehem's plan of action was formalized more than 20 years ago. At that time only a few states had laws on water pollution control, and none had laws on air pollution or solid waste disposal. Motivated by the desire to be a good neighbor, Bethlehem established an Environmental Quality Control Division to coordinate and guide a program of pollution control at all operations.

The Environmental Quality Control staff of more than 20 engineers, scientists, and technicians carries out these major activities:

☐ measuring and inventorying effluents
☐ monitoring community air pollutants

☐ keeping abreast of pollution control legislation at all levels of government
☐ participating in boards and commissions advisory to various governmental pollution control agencies
☐ designing and evaluating environmental control systems
☐ investigating employee exposures to air contaminants, as well as to noise, heat, and ionizing radiation.

This Division coordinates all environmental quality control programs by serving as consultant through other corporate departments to all Bethlehem plants, mines, quarries, shipyards, and fabricating works. The ultimate aim is to achieve, with maximum efficiency, these objectives:

1) equip all plants and all new installations with pollution control systems that will equal or exceed community or state requirements for disposal of wastes;
2) engage in research and development which seeks to provide techniques and equipment for those steelmaking processes where an effective means of controlling pollution has not yet been found;
3) cooperate with all levels of government to provide a comprehensive pollution-control program.

The challenge is immense, but our commitment is clear. Bethlehem's chairman and chief executive officer has commented: "To ignore the problem of pollution, or to make only token compliance, would be to forfeit our position as a responsible member of society."

BETHLEHEM STEEL

BETHLEHEM STEEL CORPORATION, BETHLEHEM, PA. 18016

Occupational Safety

"We were warned over and over that if something wasn't done the federal government would step in with really tough laws to force us to act in the area of safety. Now we've got what we deserve and we've got no grounds for complaint."

Few labor laws passed by congress have created as much controversy in business as the one whose acronym sounds like a Japanese import -- OSHA. The Occupational Safety and Health Act, passed in 1970, has had a stormy effect, although no one involved-- industry, labor, and government -- has any serious quarrel with the noble objectives of the legislation.

Basically, the law requires American industry to eliminate all conditions in plants and warehouses that could possible contribute to disabling injury of either immediate or cumulative nature. (The cumulative category covers partial deafness from continual high noise or lung ailments from constant breathing of air-borne chemicals).

The overall goal of the nation's first all-embracing safety and health law is "to assure as far as possible to every working man and woman in the nation safe and healthful working conditions and a right to a workplace free from recognized hazards that are causing or likely to cause death or serious physical harm."

To enforce the law and its detailed regulations developed to spell it out in practical applications, the Labor Department has a small army of special inspectors who visit businesses and thoroughly inspect facilities. These inspectors look at virtually everything imaginable that could affect the safety and health of employees -- from the cleanliness of rest rooms to the solidity of building supports, from aisle clearance to potentially dangerous parts on machines, from electrical wiring to the visibility of exit signs.

Inspectors have the power to issue citations for violations they find. Companies cited are subject to fines for each violation and are visited again to see that things have been corrected. If an infraction is deemed serious enough, the inspector has the power to close the plant. There is not any advantage is simply paying fines and ignoring the infractions, etiher. Continual disregard can result in a closed plant and a jailed chief executive. The government is cracking down with a vengeance.

As a result, there is widespread concern that the new law, however morally desirable, may be injuring business enterprise. In fact, the John Birch Society has launched a "Put OSHA Out of Business" campaign with an appeal to businessmen for funds to lobby for the act's demise. The society argues that "OSHAcrats" are using health and safety as a camouflage to nationalize industry.

Businessmen have never been very gracious hosts to uninvited outsiders, be they union organizaers, Internal Revenue Service agents, or others not particularly interested in a casual tour of the plant. The inspectors from OSHA receive particularly cold greetings.

In 1972, when OSHA enforcement was just getting started, 14,200 American workers died as a result of work-related accidents. Another 2.3 million were injured seriously enough to lose some time away from work. OSHA aims to reduce these figures. Ironically, one of the provisions of the law will probably result in a rise in the number of disabling injuries reported, because companies are now required to keep detailed records of deaths and injuries.

Where The Safety Law Goes Haywire

"It was a red-letter day for us," says Robert J. Starr, president, Safety and Industrial Net Co., Colebrook, Conn.

His firm makes a patented heavy-duty net used on bridge and high-rise building construction.

Mr. Starr, 67, founded his company about nine years ago, and it prospered.

But it was after April 28, 1971, that sales really took off.

That was when the federal Occupational Safety and Health Act went into effect. It spells out a whole raft of regulations affecting every business and industry.

Its greatest impact, perhaps, has been on the construction industry. It specifies, in minute detail, how a construction job must be run—from dispensing of paper drinking cups to operation of laser beams.

One requirement is for safety nets on high-rise, skeleton steel construction, where planking or scaffolding isn't practical.

"Since then," Mr. Starr says, "our safety net sales have shot up 50 per cent."

His firm's heavy-duty, small-mesh net costs 40 cents a square foot. On a big job, that runs into money.

"Our nets are being used on the Gold Star Bridge at New London, Conn.," he says. "The bridge is about 3,000 feet long. They're using about 250,000 square feet of nets."

Or, $100,000 worth.

"His sales will go up a lot more," says Keith Nystrom, assistant safety director, Brown & Root, Inc., a big Houston, Texas, construction firm.

"Many builders still don't know that, in many cases, they must use nets.

"The nets' use on high-rise steel erection—like boiler structures for power plants—may hike costs 100 per cent or more for that part of the operation. They're expensive to buy and install. And they make it much more difficult, and costly, to hoist up building materials."

Brown & Root, he points out, is all for safety and health. So are other members of the Associated General Contractors, a group which acts as an industry spokesman.

Says AGC President James D. McClary, who is senior vice president, Morrison-Knudson Co., Inc., Boise, Idaho:

"We can't buck the objectives of the safety law. We're for one."

The record is good

But how badly does the building industry need the eagle-eyed surveillance of the new Occupational Safety and Health Administration?

Well, its safety record is pretty good.

National Safety Council statistics show it is less dangerous than these industries—coal mining, other mining, meat packing, air transport, transit, lumbering, leather, quarrying, wood products and marine transport. Its accident rate, per million man-hours of exposure, is 13.48.

Mr. McClary says a prime irritant in the many OSHA standards is that they do not fit a construction site, but are more appropriate for industrial plants.

Another prime irritant is what the Act does to costs.

"I've heard estimates that the law will boost construction costs anywhere from 10 to 35 per cent," Mr. McClary says. "Personally, I don't think it will be as high as 35 per cent.

"But if the standards are applied as they are now, and as the OSHA agency plans to apply them, they could hike building costs 10 to 20 per cent."

Construction is a $100-billion-a-year industry.

A 10 per cent hike would add $10 billion to the price Americans pay for homes, highways, subways, office buildings, high-rise apartments and other construction.

Waterloo, Iowa, the county seat of Black Hawk County (pop. 76,000) recently discovered what that means.

"We took bids last December on a lift station," says Mayor Lloyd Turner. "It was part of a $3.8 million sewer project. HUD paid half the cost; we paid the rest.

"Our engineer's estimate for the job was $270,000.

"It was made before OSHA became the law of the land.

"When the bids came in, they were staggering—the lowest was $485,000. We held them up several weeks for evaluation. It turned out that the lowest bid was realistic, even though far higher than we expected.

"There were other factors, but about 15 per cent of the cost was attributed to OSHA by all the contractors.

"We had to sell another $100,000 worth of bonds this April to pay for the added costs."

How's that again?

Vernie Lindstrom Jr., executive vice president, Kitchell Contractors, Inc., Phoenix, Ariz., explains why OSHA increases construction costs. "Some standards are impractical, costly and complex," he says.

As examples, contractors cite rules like these:

• "A fire extinguisher, rated not less than 2A, shall be provided for each 3,000 square feet . . . or major fraction thereof"—even on a steel skyscraper with poured concrete floors. And "travel distance from any point of the protected area to the nearest fire extinguisher shall not exceed 100 feet."

What's a 2A fire extinguisher?

Is a 1A better—or worse? How about a 3A or a 2B?

The 70-page rule book, "Safety and Health Regulations for Construction," doesn't say.

That's spelled out in National Fire Protection Association manuals.

"To understand the ratings, you really should have two NFPA booklets," an NFPA spokesman says: "They're 'Standards for the Installation of Portable Fire Extinguishers,' 36 pages, price $1. And 'Standard on Recommended Good Practices for the Maintenance and Use of Portable Fire Extinguishers,' 33 pages, also $1."

If a builder writes NFPA, gets the booklets and reads them, he'll learn that a fire extinguisher tagged Class 1A isn't as good as one with a Class 2A rating.

But a 3A is better.

And a 2B is for a different kind of fire altogether—one involving flammable liquids and greases.

That 2A extinguisher, required even on a steel and concrete skyscraper, is for wood, paper and cloth fires. Or, OSHA says, you can substitute for it a 55-gallon drum of water with two fire pails.

• "Wall openings, from which there is a drop of more than four feet, and the bottom of the opening is less than three feet above the working surface" shall be protected with a guard rail.

What does this mean in plain English? It means, contractors say, that a window with a sill less than three feet off the floor must have a railing or other barrier across it. Apparently even after glass has been installed, including thermopane glass that's hard to fall through.

And many modern office buildings have sills lower than three feet.

No detail is too minute for OSHA's attention.

Take drinking water, for example. You can't put ice in it. It's not sanitary.

"That means," a contractor says, "that to give workmen a cool drink of water, you must have a jacketed water cooler. One that plugs into an electrical socket.

"But you don't always find those utilities everywhere on a half-built building."

A lot of reading matter

To comply with the law, a builder really needs more than the 70-page "Safety and Health Regulations for Construction," which is issued by the Labor Department. For starters, he needs the Department's 248-page "Occupational Safety and Health Standards," plus the two NFPA pamphlets cited above—and hundreds of other pamphlets.

When OSHA became the law of the land, it blanketed into its code a long list of guidelines drawn up earlier by private organizations like NFPA and the American National Standards Institute, and by some government agencies. For example, the list includes:

• "Standards for Protection Against Radiation (10 CFR Part 20)," published by the Atomic Energy Commission.

• "Threshold Limit Values of Airborne Radiation Contaminants for 1970" of the American Conference of Governmental Industrial Hygienists.

• Z89.1-1969, Safety Requirements for Industrial Head Protection," drawn up by the American National Standards Institute.

The list could go on and on.

Sen. Carl T. Curtis (R.-Neb.) is sharply critical of the blanketing. He says:

"The Act Congress passed, in effect, made these rules the law of the land without a prior specific review ... to see what they do, how they should be applied, or whether or not they are adequate."

Sen. Curtis has introduced one of a number of bills now on Capitol Hill to modify OSHA. Among other things, his would exempt businesses with 25 or fewer employees from the Act.

A similar bill has been introduced in the House by Rep. Joe Skubitz (R.-Kans.).

The Associated General Contractors gives some idea of the size of the thicket of guidelines, standards and cross-references.

"To get all he needs to be fully informed," an AGC spokesman says, "a building contractor would have to spend about $6,000. And he'd wind up with a stack of documents 17 feet high."

Obviously, few if any builders are familiar with all these binding regulations.

"I think it's true to say they are so complicated and lengthy," says the safety director of a large Eastern construction firm, "that you can find a violation of them on almost any job."

The Occupational Safety and Health Administration's own statistics bear him out. In the first nine months of this fiscal year, its inspectors visited 20,688 places of business.

Nearly eight out of 10 were found in violation of the safety law.

Battle of the boatyard

The inspector's word is final—unless the alleged lawbreaker requests a formal hearing. Few win the appeal. One who did was a West Coast boatyard owner.

Arsene (Blackie) Gadarian has been in the business, at Newport Beach, Calif., a dozen years.

He says his firm, Blackie's Boat Yard, Inc., is "a mom and pop operation."

Actually, it's a little bigger than that—he and his wife have a half-dozen employees. But it's pint-sized, as boatyards go—the smallest of six in Newport Beach.

Mostly, it overhauls yachts owned by wealthy residents of the seaside spa.

So the proprietor was quite surprised last fall when a federal inspector drove up, put on a hard hat and began to tour the yard.

Blackie felt he hardly rated this personal attention from Washington.

The inspector strolled down the pier to a small boat under repair not far from shore. He pointed to a worker crouched in the cramped bilge and asked. "Why doesn't he have a life jacket on?"

"Because," Blackie replied, "he couldn't move if he did."

"What would he do," the inspector persisted, "if he fell into the water?"

"He'd stand up," Blackie said. "The water's only two or three feet deep there."

The inspector went on inspecting.

A $1,000 fine?

A few weeks later, the Gadarians were notified they had violated OSHA regulations—Section 1501 84. (c)(4). Offenders are subject to fines of up to $1,000.

"They said the rules were that we had to have a ladder nailed to that dock," Mrs. Gadarian says, "so an employee could climb out of the water if he fell into it.

"We wanted to comply with safety standards, and we always have. We have a good safety record. Our workmen's compensation inspector has testified to it.

"But we didn't know what the OSHA regulations were.

"We asked the OSHA inspector for a copy. He said he didn't have one on him. We asked the local area office. The director said he didn't have one for us—but was working night and day to get some out.

"So we denied the violation, and asked for a hearing, partly in hope of getting a copy of the law we were accused of breaking."

After the Gadarians said they'd fight, the occupation safety agency proposed a penalty of $16—eventually reduced to $15.

Two weeks later, a 248-page document arrived covering—among other things—safety regulations for ship repairing, shipbuilding, breaking up of ships and longshoring.

"We read practically everything in it," Mrs. Gadarian says. "But it said nothing about ladders on the dock."

The Gadarians again asked the OSHA agency office for a copy of the regulation they allegedly had violated.

"About a month after we were cited," Blackie says, "it arrived." It was a 48-page booklet, a supplement to the 248-page publication they received earlier.

"We found the part about ladders in that," Mrs. Gadarian says. "But it said nothing about one being nailed to the dock. Only that you had to have one near the boat under repair."

The full majesty of OSHA

Last November, the OSHA hearing was held.

"They rented a meeting room at the Newporter Inn," says Mrs. Gadarian, "a very posh hotel."

President Nixon often uses it for press conferences and other meetings. It's about 20 miles from the West Coast White House at San Clemente. Japan's Premier Sato stayed there when he met with the President before Mr. Nixon went to Peking.

Seven federal officials were on hand for the hearing, which took four hours. As the Gadarians pointed out, all the OSHA regulation stipulated was that:

"In the vicinity of each vessel afloat in which work is being performed there shall be at least one portable or permanent ladder of sufficient length to assist employees to reach safety in the event they fall into the water."

The Gadarians said they had a ladder "in the vicinity" of the boat being repaired, and produced witnesses.

The OSHA inspector contradicted them. The closest ladder, he said, was 400 feet away.

The Gadarians showed that the boat yard was only 200 feet long, including their 66-foot dock. The Occupational Safety and Health Review Commission ruled for the Gadarians.

So they didn't have to pay the $15.

Why did the Gadarians fight a fine the size of a parking penalty?

"That's what a lot of people ask," Blackie says.

"They figure, if all it takes is 15 bucks to get them off your back, let's pay it. But I don't feel that way, if I'm not in the wrong.

"Besides, what about the next time?"

Mrs. Gadarian has carefully hoarded all the citations, summonses and reports, including the 19-page decision that dismissed the charges.

"Some day," she says, "I have to show them to my grandchildren so they can see how 1984 came early to our country."

WHAZZIT?

MANUFACTURING ENGINEERING

Manufacturing Engineering is the process of determining how to manufacture a product in the needed quantities at the lowest possible costs while still meeting quality standards.

OSHA

The Occupational Safety and Health Act. This law, passed by Congress in 1970, is designed to eliminate all unsafe and unhealthy conditions in the work environment.

JOB SHOP

A type of manufac-turing which is inter-mittent. The work is organized around particular jobs rather than around the finished products (e.g., a machine shop).

INTERMITTENT MANUFACTURING

"On again, off again manufacturing." Different products are made at different times on the same production line.

CONTINUOUS MANUFACTURING

A type of manufacturing in which a product is worked on from start to finish before it is stored. The process is designed around the product. Oil refining and automobile manufac-turing are examples of continuous manufacturing.

AUTOMATION

The use of highly specialized equipment for the automatic handling of materials and the control of production.

STANDARDIZATION

The use of uniform production methods and patterns for equipment, products, parts, etc. It brings about cost reduction because adaptation of equipment and procedures becomes unnecessary.

Careers In Manufacturing

There are many different types of careers possible in manufacturing. Not only are there many different types of jbos, but there are many different types of industries, providing varied challenges.

No other area of business offers the wide range of work available in manufacturing. The type of work depends to a large extent on the type of product manufactured and on the types of technologies involved.

You might get directly involved in line (supervisory) management, responsible for direct operations. Upon graduation you might, for example, join a management training program in a steel company. You would start out as a trainee, learning about supervision and the jobs of managers in a given plant. After your training, you would become a production foreman, responsible for the work of a group of employees. After the experience of being a foreman, your career could include advancement to department foreman, plant superintendent, and on into company management.

Another possibility for you would be staff work -- specialized positions that provide technical support to line management.

You might, for example, do work in production control, quality control,

inspection, production planning, manufacturing engineering or inventory control. Each of these plays an important role in keeping the production process moving effectively.

Furthermore, with automation and increasingly complex manufacturing processes, new specialties are becoming necessary. Computer programmers and operators, systems analysts, laboratory technicians, and many other jobs are now common in manufacturing. They can represent interesting technical work in themselves, or may be stepping stones to other staff jobs or to line management.

Naturally, many careers in manufacturing are technical. The skills and knowledge required may require education in engineering, perhaps at the graduate level. It depends on the level of technology involved in the manufacturing process.

Engineering careers in manufacturing can be clas-

sifed under the general term of Manufacturing Engineering. Within this general category are found three engineering specialties: new product planning, manufacturing planning, and process planning.

New product planning involves the basic decisions concerning what types of products consumers will see on the market in the future.

Manufacturing planning decides what parts and assemblies the firm will make itself and which ones it will purchase from the outside.

Process planning is the step in which the best way fo producing a given product is determined. The type of manufacturing process to be used is chosen at this time.

All engineering careers may be life-long, or they may lead into other areas of work, such as management.

CONSIDER

1. What would happen if the major polluters in the nation were closed down?

2. Given the problems faced by Bethlehem Steel, do you think the company is doing enough to combat pollution? Explain.

3. How much would an automobile cost today if we did not have the assembly line process? Explain.

4. Is is possible to make working 100% safe?

5. What management skills are needed in an automated factory?

6. Will hand crafted goods ever be obsolete? Explain.

7. Is OSHA necessary? Explain.

8. Can the federal government legislate safety in a steel plant? Explain.

9. What might manufacturing be like in the year 2000?

10. Would it be possible to build a fully automated automobile assembly line? Explain.

CHALLENGES

Examine a common product you use every day and try to determine how it was manufactured.

If you have a job, look for hazards to your safety or health. Suggest steps to eliminate these hazards, if any exist.

Describe how this textbook might be produced using an assembly line process.

Find a book that describes the early days of the automobile industry and compare how cars were made then with how they are made today.

Read Charles Babbage's book ON THE ECONOMY OF MACHINERY AND MANUFACTURE published in 1835 and see if Babbage's ideas about manufacturing a still valid today.

RECAP

Manufacturing, always a critical aspect of business, is becoming a tougher process because of new pressures: pollution control, imports, and automation. While we are concerned with producing goods at reasonable prices, managers must also be concerned today with the impact of production upon the physical environment, upon worker safety and health, and upon the marketability of the goods.

The problem of pollution control is a major task facing the manufacturing manager. It is a truism that the process of transforming raw materials into finished goods brings about some degree of pollution. There is a basic question whether pollution can ever be fully controlled with our available technology and, secondly, whether we can afford the high costs involved. In this chapter we have seen how Bethlehem Steel has tackled the difficult tasks of pollution control.

We will also see a significant trend towards greater use of automated manufacturing processes in industry to improve efficiency and reduce costs. Automation may result also in higher quality and more reliable products and closer control of manufacturing processes. Technical skills, such as in manufacturing, engineering, production planning, inventory control, and quality control are all needed to support automated manufacturing.

The Occupational Safety and Health Act has placed additional responsibilities on manufacturing management. Not only must management do its best to provide safe and healthful working conditions, but it must comply with federal regulations in this area. In some cases, compliance with the law is tough because of expenses and conflicts with the economics of manufacturing.

To meet all these challenges, a new breed of manufacturing manager is appearing on the scene. Broad-gauge businessmen are needed to balance the different pressures and needs.

WORKSHEET NO. 16

NAME_____

INSTRUCTOR'S NAME_____

DATE_____

1. Why is manufacturing engineering necessary?

---

2. Will manufacturing be different with "automated factories?"

3. How does pollution control affect the manufacturing process?

4. What are the good and bad points about OSHA for business?

CHAPTER 17
International Business

American enterprise thrives on serving needs and wants in markets throughout the world.

Most of America's largest corporations are today what we call "multinational corporations." They produce goods and services for sale throughout the world, purchase materials, obtain money as capital, and actually operate plants and offices in many different countries.

As companies expand their international operations they run into a wide range of unusual problems and challenges. The task of selling and shipping goods into foreign countries brings management into direct confrontation with national trade barriers. Furthermore, the competition for international markets makes the going extremely rough for companies arriving late on the scene.

When American business organizations sell goods and services in other nations (we call these exports) and buy goods and services in other countries (imports) they are engaging in international trade. International consumers, governments, and other organizations also engage in international trade through the exchange of money, goods, and services.

Trade barriers have both advantages and disadvantages for an economy. On the one hand, they protect local industries, but on the other hand, they limit the flow of ideas and products. Today, there is a strong feeling favoring barriers.

Lesser Developed Countries (LDCs) would probably benefit from increased free trade by supporting their local enterprises and pro-

viding an exchange of goods produced for other goods needed. Trade barriers impede this open international exchange.

The United States is reluctant to lower barriers, in part, because we are now importing more goods than we are exporting. Our balance of trade is therefore unfavorable to us and the financial relationship with other nations -- the balance of payments -- is also unfavorable.

Certain groups of countries have set more favorable terms for trade. The best known, the European Economic Community (EEC), has opened up trade between countries on the continent by lowering trade barriers. It makes it more difficult for the United States to export goods to the member nations because of their greater self-sufficiency as a group.

Another organization of nations that is worthy of note is OPEC. This is the Organization of Petroleum Exporting Countries. Created in 1960, the organization has shown its muscle in influencing the price of crude oil shipped from the twelve nations that are members. The aims of the group are to raise revenues -- taxes and royalties -- earned and to assume control over production of oil from the major international oil companies.

Unfortunately, the U.S. has not had the same kind of economic power in its exports. Discussed in this chapter are IBM, the Colonel's Kentucky Fried Chicken, McDonald's, Nabisco, Ford, General Motors, Dow Cehmicals, and others.

Will business continue to grow multinationally? Most likely, it will, but business practices will change as demands on multinational managers evolve.

In This Chapter

Balance of Trade

Our nation does not and cannot provide all of the resources, goods, and services that our economy needs and desires.

Thus, we import a variety of goods, including diamonds, rubber, oil, spices, cacao, coffee, bananas, tin, precious metals, lapidary work, jute, cobalt, copper, tea and a variety of products too numerous to mention.

At the same time, we export such goods as computers, airplanes, automobiles, lumber, tobacco and tobacco products, soft coal, oil drilling equipment, machine tools, agricultural equipment, earth-moving equipment and a variety of agricultural products including wheat, corn, soybeans, chickens, cotton, and produce.

As consumers, Americans also buy a wide range of products that are imported form other countries, including automobiles, clothing, shoes, radios, televisions, electronic gear, books, movies, beer, scotch whiskey, and a wide variety of food-stuffs.

Overall, we tend to import more than we export. This is a recent development, as historically, the United States was a major source of natural resources and manufactured goods.

Our exports over the decades have effected the development of the economies of many nations, to the extent that today they are strong and are now competing directly with us for markets. The rebuilding of the economies in Japan and European nations, and trade with developing

UNITED STATES BALANCE OF TRADE

(Millions of Dollars)

YEAR	EXPORTS	IMPORTS	BALANCE
1960	$19,650	$14,744	$4,906
1961	20,107	14,519	5,588
1962	20,779	16,218	4,561
1963	22,252	17,011	5,241
1964	25,438	18,647	6,831
1965	26,438	21,496	4,942
1966	29,287	25,463	3,824
1967	30,638	26,821	3,817
1968	33,576	32,964	612
1969	36,417	35,796	621
1970	41,963	39,799	2,164
1971	42,770	45,459	-2,689
1972	47,391	54,355	-6,964
1973	71,379	70,424	955
1974	98,309	105,586	-5,964
1975	106,981	95,410	11,571

Source: Economic Report of the President

nations have been major factors in the ultimate reversal in our patterns of imports versus exports. We refer to this pattern as our balance of trade. Trading patterns comprising our current balance of trade are depicted in the figure below.

The United States, the United Kingdom (Great Britain), West Germany, and Japan are the dominant nations in world trade today. About half of the free world's exports are accounted for by these few countries, and about 40% of its imports.

The United States has only 6% of the population of the world, yet consumes about one-third of the world's goods and services. Since World War II, the United States has increased the amount of goods imported by three-fold. Exports

during this period have doubled. Hence, our balance of trade has been shifting toward a negative balance.

COMPARATIVE ADVANTAGE

What determines what goods are to be imported or exported?

It makes sense for a country to produce goods it can produce more cheaply than other countries can. This principle is known as the Law of Comparative Advantage. By specializing in the goods it can make best and selling these abroad while buying other goods abroad, a country benefits.

Everyone should do those things that they can do best. Yet, the law is broken more than it is followed. The Italians are able to manufacture shoes more cheaply than we are able

to in the United States. Yet, we insist on making and buying our own here at home. Granted, imports of shoes from Italy have increased greatly in recent years, but manufacturers in the United States have resisted this and sought protection from these imports.

A camera manufacturer has announced that it welcomes competition from imports, believing that this spurs efforts to improve our own efficiency and the quality of our products. As our labor costs climb in the United States, other countries are gaining greater advantages in labor-intensive manufacturing.

If trends continue, we may be importing a whole lot more of our goods than we even are now.

WHAZZIT?

GATT

The General Agreement on Tariff and Trade. This is an agreement, signed in 1948, which formed an orgnaization of nations, including the United States, to establish a system of rules for controlling tariffs and reducing trade barriers.

TEA

The Trade Expansion Act of 1962. Signed by President Kennedy, this amendment to the old (1934) Reciprocal Trade Act gave the President the power to cut tariffs by 50%

in negotiating new trade pacts during the five years following its inception.

TARIFF NEGOTIATIONS

The most sweeping reductions in tariffs in history were the result of negotiations involving more than fifty member nations of GATT. Under the power of the TEA, during his tenure as president, Kennedy reduced duties on more than 60,000 items.

Tariff reductions are believed to be a significant factor in the growth of international trade and economic prosperity. Reductions

directly aid lesser-developed nations, while strengthening industrialized nations, making them better able to help the lesser-developed nations.

EFTA

The European Free Trade Association. This was an agreement among eight nations for free trade among themselves. It was a competitor of the EEC, and was composed of the European countries not involved in the EEC. The withdrawal of Britain and Denmark to join the EEC has effectively destroyed the EFTA.

Who Are The Economic Powers?

THE UNITED STATES

At the end of World War II, the United States was the only real economic superpower. Western Europe was war-ravaged, Japan's economy had been destroyed, and the Russian economy was on the verge of collapse. Of the major combatants, the United States alone, had not felt the sting of bombs and shells falling on its cities and industries.

With the start of the war, the economy of the United States, stagnant during the Great Depression of the 1930's was thrown into high gear. The United States became the "Arsenal of Democracy" as hugh amounts of war material was supplied to the American and other Allied armies.

At the end of the war, the Gross National Product of the United States was $211 billion. In 1973, the GNP was in excess of $1200 billion. This is almost a six-fold increase in 28 years. Even considering that some of the increase was caused by inflation, this is a very healthy increase.

As the world's biggest producer and the world's biggest consumer (the United States accounts for approximately one third of the world's Gross National Product), what the United States does on the world economic front affects all of the world members. The United States has seen the dollar devalued in 1971 and again in 1972, and there is some question whether the dollar can withstand the pressure and remain the standard of the international monetary system.

There is little question that, today, the United States is the most affluent country in the world, with the highest Gross National Product, and the highest per capital income. The United States is the largest exporter in the world, and we are the largest importers as well (see the sections of the Balance of Trade and the Balance of Payments). On the international trade front, the United States is a major exporter of computers, jet aircraft, space technology, equipment for automation,

WORLD'S GREAT ECONOMIC POWERS

	Six-Nation E.E.C.	Nine-Nation E.E.C.	U.S.A.	U.S.S.R	Japan
Area (sq. km.)	1,167,500	1,524,900	9,363,400	22,402,200	369,700
Population (millions)	189	253	205	243	104
G.N.P. ($ billions)	$485	$626	$991	$288	$196
Exports ($ billions)	$88.5	$112.2	$43.2	$12.8	$19.3
Auto Production	8,029,600	9,670,600	6,550,200	348,000	3,178,700

Source European Economic Community Commission

and other high technology products. Paradoxically, along with all of this high technology equipment, the United States is also a major exporter of basic agricultural products like corn, soybeans, and other kinds of cereals.

JAPAN

The rebirth of the economies of Japan and West Germany following their complete destruction during World War II, is an amazing story. Suffice to say that our two major enemies during the war are now our two most vigorous competitors on the trade front today.

Under the occupation of Japan at the conclusion of the war, the rebirth of Japanese industry was begun. Under the guidance of General MacArthur, Japan was started on the road to economic recovery.

Today, Japan with a population about one half of the United States, has a Gross National Product which is about one fifth that of the United States. Starting with the competitive advantage of low labor costs, Japanese industry has developed to the point where now, in some industries (like the steel industry) the average Japanese worker is more productive than his American counterpart.

It is for this reason that Japan is now one of the economic superpowers. By combining the traditional Japanese loyalty to the group,

with modern manufacturing techniques, Japanese industry has prospered and grown. Today, Japan has one of the strongest Balance of Payments in the world. In 1972, for example, the Japanese exported over $19 billion. As you can see from the trade map on page 484, over $4 billion of Japan's $6 billion trade surplus was achieved in the United States.

The Japanese are now beginning to make economic inroads into the People's Republic of China, in hopes of opening that vast potential market to goods manufactured in Japan.

If there is any weak spot in the Japanese economic picture, it is that Japan must import almost all of the raw materials used to produce goods for export.

RUSSIA

The Union of Soviet Socialist Republics is the only economic superpower that has a centrally controlled economy. By that, we mean that the traditional market forces of supply and demand are not allowed to function, and all decisions concerning production and consumption are made by central economic planning groups.

A planned economy is not the most efficient way to allocate economic resources, but still the Soviet economy is able to boast a Gross National Product about one third that of the United States.

One of the victorious Allies during the Second

World War, the Soviet Union took that opportunity to place under its control vast areas of Eastern Europe. From these countries the Russian economy has drawn raw materials and a market for Russian made goods not needed at home. Most of this trading was done with prices and other conditions of trade dictated by the Soviets. It has not been until recently that Soviet industry has really been active on the international trade scene.

The Soviet Union is blessed with abundant deposits of many raw materials like coal, iron ore, oil and gas, and the industrial capability to convert those materials into products that can compete in the international marketplace. To date, the problem has been that the quality of consumer goods produced in the Soviet Union has not been up to the standards of the United States and Western Eurpoe.

The Soviet Union has one overriding economic weakness -- the country is unable to produce enough food to bring the level of nutrition up to that of the Western nations. As a result, new trade agreements between the United States and the Soviet Union are being made where the United States will provide agricultural products in return for Soviet oil and gas.

THE COMMON MARKET

The European Economic Community (EEC) was formed in 1958 in an attempt to integrate the economies of the member nations into a unified economic entity. The ultimate goal of the EEC is the political unity of Europe. The original EEC, also called the "Common Market," was composed of six member countries: Belgium, France, Germany, Italy, Luxembourg and the Netherlands. Recently, three new members, Britain, Ireland and Denmark were admitted.

The nine nation EEC, taken as a whole, is indeed an economic superpower. With a population about 25 percent greater that the United States, the EEC has a Gross National Product that is about two thirds that of the United States. In terms of international trade,

the EEC has exports three times those of the United States. That figure is somewhat misleading, though, because a large part of those exports were to other member nations of the EEC. Nonetheless, the nine nation EEC is a formidable competitor on the economic front.

The complete elimination of customs charges on goods shipped from one EEC member nation to another has facilitated the flow of goods throughout the nine nations, and has made economic cooperation more likely, even though the old habits of nationalism are hard to break.

If there is one weakness in the EEC, it is that the member nations

must import a significant portion of the raw materials used in production. This is particularly true in the case of oil and other petroleum products. Apart from that, there is no reason to expect that the EEC will not continue to exert a growing influence on the world's economy.

THE OTHERS

In a real sense, there are other nations with significant clout. Twelve of them are members of OPEC, the Organization of Petroleum Exporting Countries. These nations and their economic clout are discussed in depth in the following article.

What about others? Countries with large populations include India,

The Expanded Common Market—An Economic Profile

	GNP $ billions	Population millions	Annual Growth Rate % '60-'70	Exports $ Billions	% of GNP	Current Balance 1972 millions	Consumer Prices % Change 3rd Qtr '71-'72	Cereals Production Million tons	Crude Steel Output Million tons	Autos Per 1,000 Pop.
West Germany	$186.4	60.8	4.8	$34.2	18.3	+$300	8.7	18.4	45.0	234
France	147.6	50.8	5.8	17.7	12.0	+ 700	9.0	32.5	23.8	245
Britain	121.4	55.7	2.8	19.4	16.2	+ 250	10.5	13.3	28.3	213
Italy	93.2	54.5	5.7	13.2	14.3	+2,800	8.7	14.9	17.2	187
Netherlands	31.3	13.0	5.1	11.8	37.7	+1,000	5.5	1.5	5.0	200
Belgium	25.7	9.7	4.9	11.6	43.8	+1,200	7.6	1.7	12.6	215
Denmark	15.6	4.9	4.8	3.3	21.1	−50	4.1	6.6	.5	219
Ireland	3.9	2.9	3.9	1.0	27.6	−50	13.7	1.4	.1	122
Luxembourg	1.0	.3	3.4	*	*	*	*	.1	5.5	267
United States	991.1	205.4	4.0	43.2	4.4	− 8,400	3.4	193.0	122.1	432
Japan	196.1	103.5	11.0	19.3	9.8	+ 6,300	6.1	1.7	93.3	85

All figures are for 1970 except where otherwise specified. "Current balance" comprises trade in goods and services.
✳ Included with Belgium.
Source: European Economic Community, except O.E.C.D. for Current Balance estimate and Consumer Prices

The People's Republic of
China, and Indonesia.
Canada, Sweden, Brazil, and
Venezuela are also noteworthy.

These nations and all
of the others not listed
here account for about
one third of the world's
gross nationall product,
but support nearly four
fifths of the world's
population. Certainly
many of these countries
will be of economic
importance to the super-
powers both as sources of
raw material and labor
and as markets for goods.

As trade between
nations increases, there
is hope that the nations
will realize they are
interdependent. This
will help preserve peace.

WHAZZIT?

COUNTERVAILING DUTY

A duty is a tariff. It
is a countervailing tariff
if it works both ways --
we tax their goods as they
come into our country and
they tax our goods as
they go into theirs.

PREFERENTIAL TRADING

Application of tariffs
on a discriminatory
basis. For example,
granting lower rates of
duty on goods imported
from certain "preferred"
countries than on the
same goods from other
countries, such as members
of the British Commonwealth
(Canada, Britain, New
Zealand, Australia, and
others).

INTERNATIONAL MONETARY FUND

An agency of the United
Nations, this fund pro-
motes and aids international
monetary cooperation,
stability in international
exchange, and avoidance of
competitive depreciation
of money.

EXPORT-IMPORT BANK

A United States federal
bank which makes loans
to foreign governments
and commercial enterprises
for the purpose of buying
goods produced in the
United States.

DEPRECIATION OF MONEY

A decrease in the
exchange value of money.
For example, if the
dollar is depreciated
10% compared to the
German mark, German goods
become 10% higher in
the United States and
American goods become
10% less in Germany.

EXPORT TAX

A self-imposed trade
tariff. By placing
an export tax on coffee
exported, Brazil avoids
having us place a tariff
on it as an import.
Further, Brazil gets to
keep the tax money!

OPEC: The Economics Of The Oil Cartel

The 12-nation club is powerful today—but may have to lower prices later

In the past 13 months, the oil cartel has succeeded in doing what it could not do in the previous 13 years of its existence: fundamentally alter the structure of world economic power. Since its creation in 1960, the Organization of Petroleum Exporting Countries (OPEC) has had two main goals: to raise the taxes and royalties earned by member governments from crude oil production and to assume control over production and exploration from the major international oil companies. With government revenue now well above $10 a bbl.—a ninefold increase over the last four years—and Saudi Arabia moving to complete 100% acquisition of the companies' producing properties, these goals are close to achievement.

The OPEC cartel now holds unprecedented power over a commodity vital to the health of the world's economies, and there is little reason to expect that power to disappear quickly. Reversing previous Administration optimism, Assistant Treasury Secretary Gerald Parsky now says, "I believe the cartel can and will be maintained on economic grounds for about three years no matter what we do economically."

And Shell Oil Co.'s President Harry Bridges is impressed by the deeper strengths of the cartel. "I just don't see any weakness in OPEC," he says. "Tell me of another organization that has two nations like Iran and Iraq, which are at war with each other and yet sit together in OPEC and show no signs of breaking the cartel up or quarreling over oil prices. That indicates to me that these countries have found the mechanism they need to achieve their goals, and their loyalty to it transcends traditional political enmities."

However, looking beyond the next two or three years, OPEC's continued cohesion will depend on how well it handles the changing supply and demand trends that its own success in increasing prices has unleashed. OPEC will have to find and enforce a price structure that maximizes revenue without generating such huge new sources of petroleum and other forms of energy that its control over the market is destroyed. At the same time, that price structure will have to reconcile the often conflicting economic and political requirements of the member nations.

Most oil industry authorities think these requirements will be more and more difficult to achieve, the longer the present real price of oil persists. They,

The oil ministers of OPEC countries showed their solidarity at their Dec. 12 meeting in Vienna.

therefore, question whether the current high price level can be maintained indefinitely.

The growth of cartels

OPEC may now look like the most successful cartel in world history, but it is certainly not the first. Cartels are just one species of the broader category that economists call "oligopolistic market structures," in which a few large sellers dominate the market for a product. What distinguishes a cartel from looser forms of oligopoly is the presence of a formal, explicit, and detailed plan for market sharing and coordination of production levels and prices.

Cartels flourished in the period between the two world wars, especially in countries such as Germany where the legal system condoned and often enforced market-sharing agreements. Such industries as chemicals, explosives, glass, steel, and pharmaceuticals were prone to cartel organization because of the large scale of operations required and the strong tendency to vertical integration from raw materials to distribution of the product. Sometimes the cartel became virtually a single company—a trust—as in the German dyestuffs cartel, I. G. Farben.

Because competition from uncontrolled sources is death to an oligopoly, cartels had good reason to extend themselves internationally and attempt to divide up the whole world. In the 1930s, international cartels emerged in steel, chemicals, matches, aluminum, and a whole range of raw materials. Many of the industrial cartels retained a significant amount of strength until the war broke them up.

After World War II, industrial cartels virtually disappeared, partly because of the influence of U. S. antitrust regulations but mainly because of the rapid growth of world demand. But producers of primary commodities, buffeted by sharp fluctuations in price and output, attempted to set up so-called "international commodity agreements" in such areas as tea, coffee, sugar, tin, copper, cocoa, copra, and bauxite. Most of these were only marginally successful. They were generally undone by the availability of substitutes or by the impossibility of preventing cheating by countries whose economic welfare was crucially dependent on sale of a single commodity.

OPEC superficially resembles those ill-fated international commodity agreements that have come and gone during the last three decades. But it has far more staying power because it has many of the strong points of an industrial cartel:

■ A relatively small group of countries controls a large part of world oil reserves. The top six OPEC countries have well over 50% of total world reserves of 620-billion bbl., and all 12 countries together have more than two-thirds.

■ While some major producers such as the U. S. and the Soviet Union can use virtually all of their own production, the OPEC countries can use only a small fraction. Thus, they provide more than 85% of world trade in oil and can control the world market. Europe and Japan are totally dependent on OPEC oil, and the U. S. is now importing one-third of its oil from OPEC sources.

■ The solidarity of the member nations has been strongly reinforced by the group's success in 1973 and 1974 in increasing its revenues, moving toward government ownership, and using oil as a political weapon.

International oil companies have functioned like a cartel since the 1930s for the purpose of regulating Middle Eastern production and European refining. They became the subject of a major Federal Trade Commission investigation in 1952 because U. S. companies were deeply involved. But throughout the 1950s and 1960s, the market power of the "majors" diminished. Smaller independent companies and state oil units—such as the Italian Enrico Mattei's ENI—opened up new concessions and gave governments a better deal. Nevertheless, the basic formal structure of a cartel was maintained: the concession agreements under which a few companies divided up the available producing areas and held options on unexplored territories.

In his massive study, *The World Petroleum Market*, published in 1972, MIT economist M. A. Adelman explains: "The history of the industry since World War II is that of a gradual loosening: less concentration in crude production, less also in refining, due largely to market enlargement and unification of the Western European economy; and less vertical integration."

Nonetheless, Adelman notes that the major companies still possessed considerable market control, which the OPEC countries were able to exploit once they had effectively displaced the companies' cartel with their own. "The

huge resources of the original Persian Gulf concessions were effectively locked up," he says, "and only by the late 1960s was there a comparable rival, in Libya. In Venezuela, concessions were granted only once in the entire postwar period, in 1956. Although some good discoveries were made, no great volume of oil was available to compete with the Persian Gulf producers, whose overlapping joint ventures allowed the coordination of output and hampered individualistic sales and production policies."

Even a little loosening of market control, however, was enough to pull

Venezuela's Juan Pablo Perez Alfonzo

The OPEC oil cartel was born nearly 15 years ago, and the man who knows as much as anybody about how it took shape is Juan Pablo Perez Alfonzo, Venezuela's former Minister of Mines & Hydrocarbons, long-time nemesis of the oil companies, and now a 70-year-old éminence grise whom government officials still consult at his home in Caracas. Here is the story, as Perez Alfonzo and other knowledgeable oil experts tell it:

Shortly after World War II, oil-producing countries from Iran to Venezuela began trying to exert more control over the operations of major oil companies in their countries. In 1948, Venezuela forced companies to accept a 50-50 split of oil profits, a pattern that quickly spread to other countries. Three years later, Iran's fiery Premier

market prices down, and in 1960 the companies cut the posted prices that government taxes were based on. In self-defense, Venezuela's Minister of Mines, Juan Pablo Perez Alfonzo, joined with Middle Eastern leaders to initiate OPEC (box, page 78.)

By any other name

Nothing makes OPEC ministers unhappier than applying the "cartel" label to their organization. According to Interior Minister Jamshid Amouzegar of Iran, OPEC is not a cartel because "if we were a cartel, we could have increased our prices in the 1960s." He says, "Of course, we did not, because we had no control over the supply-and-demand situation." Abderrahman Khene, OPEC's outgoing secretary-general, prefers to call OPEC a "trade union" in which disparate parties band together to fight a common enemy—in this case the international majors.

Whatever OPEC may have been until 1973—and Khene's description fits pretty well—there is no question in the rest of the world that OPEC is now acting as a cartel and will have to do so even more in the future. Several countries, including Kuwait and Libya, have indeed cut output as world consumption of crude oil in 1974 dropped 4% from the 1973 level. Shell's Bridges says: "I would not be surprised if in 1975 OPEC adopts a prorationing scheme to formally assign each producing country a rate of production that is a certain percentage of capacity. The scheme would relate population and infrastructural needs of each producing country to its available crude supplies. Venezuela has been suggesting such a mechanism for 10 years."

The purpose of any cartel is to maximize the earnings of its members. It does so when the cartel ignores its in-

The birth of OPEC, and how it grew

Mossadegh nationalized oil operations. Though he was subsequently overthrown in a coup engineered by the U.S. Central Intelligence Agency—abetted by Iran's difficulty in finding Western marketing outlets for its oil—the Teheran government retained ownership of the oil industry. The majors worked the oil fields under contract.

By the late 1950s, the Arab world was stirring with a new sense of power. "The Arab League," as Perez Alfonzo points out, "already existed, and the Suez nationalization had taken place, lifting the spirit of the Arabs and inspiring confidence in themselves." The Suez shutdown had demonstrated the potential bargaining power of the oil-producing countries as suppliers of energy to Europe.

Some oilmen were worried even then that a price confrontation between the oil companies and the host countries could push the latter into an exporters' bloc. One oilman who is now a director of a major U.S. oil company recalls that he cautioned top executives as early as 1958 that any price cut would trigger the formation of an OPEC-type cartel. But his warning was ignored.

The beginnings. Meeting in Cairo in 1959, the first Arab Oil Congress agreed that oil companies should consult with governments of the exporting countries on proposed price changes. Iran and Venezuela attended as observers, and Iranian delegate Manucher Farmanfarmaian, now his country's ambassador to Caracas, recalls that sessions were held in a James Bond-like atmosphere of secrecy "because of oil company spies."

In 1960, as Perez Alfonzo describes it, the political climate in Venezuela was ripe for OPEC because the country's militant left-of-center *Acción Democrática* party had just returned to power. At the time, both Perez Alfonzo and his friend Sheik Abdullah Tariki, Saudi Arabia's firebrand oil minister, were searching for ways to create a common front of oil exporters.

Their opportunity came in August of that year when Standard Oil Co. (New Jersey)—now Exxon Corp.—led a wave of posted price reductions by oil companies, ranging from 4¢ to 14¢ per bbl., on Middle East crudes. Even such cautious governments as Iran, still wary after the political upheaval accompanying oil nationalization, and Kuwait were angry enough to join in establishing the new OPEC cartel at a meeting in Baghdad on Sept. 14, 1960. The companies quickly rescinded most of the price cuts.

Building up power. In the early 1960s, though, a worldwide oil glut limited the new cartel's bargaining power. Perez Alfonzo says that oil companies tried to divide OPEC members by offering incentives to some and putting pressure on others, such as Iraq, through cutbacks in investments. In Saudi Arabia, Tariki was ousted as oil minister. Had he stayed on, Perez Alfonzo believes, OPEC would have acted much earlier to raise prices and limit oil production.

Surprisingly, OPEC encountered hostility at the outset not only from oilmen and Western governments but also, Perez Alfonzo says, from the Soviet Union. The reason: Moscow suspected the cartel of being a front for the international oil companies. In a little-known move to end Soviet opposition, Perez flew to Mexico City to talk with the Soviet Union's top official for Latin American affairs and later went to Moscow to explain OPEC's goals.

Despite OPEC's slow beginning, coordinated actions by the group and by individual members gradually strengthened the hand of the oil exporters. In 1965, for example, members agreed to tax oil companies on the full posted price of oil even if it was sold at substantial discounts. Venezuela halted all grants of new oil concessions and hit the companies with higher taxes. Libya exploited its position as a nearby source of oil for Europe to hike prices unilaterally after the second closure of Suez in 1967. That, and the world's growing thirst for oil, set the stage for the steep price runup of the past few years.

OPEC was slow to realize its current power, Perez Alfonzo maintains, because of "fear of the companies, and the countries most affected by this fear were two of the largest, Iran and Saudi Arabia." If OPEC had been able to forge a stronger organization and limit the growth of oil production in the 1960s, Perez Alfonzo argues, the world would have been spared 1974's jolting rise in energy costs. Such a program, he maintains, "would have led to a slow increase in prices and this, in turn, would have allowed for better management of the crisis that had to come."

ternal differences and sets the same price that a monopolist would in the same circumstances. If consumers are unable to substitute readily for a given commodity or do without it, the price can be raised quite high without—in the short run—a great loss in volume of sales, so total revenue will increase.

Edward Hudson of Data Resources, Inc., and Dale Jorgenson of Harvard University have calculated in an oft-cited study of U.S. energy demand, that, in the short run, a 100% increase in the price of crude oil leads to only a 15% reduction in consumption—what economists call a price elasticity of -0.15. So OPEC price hikes are very profitable.

But over a longer period, such as 5 to 10 years, consumers have a better opportunity to substitute other forms of energy, and the price elasticity of petroleum will be higher, perhaps even approaching -1.0, where higher price is completely offset by loss of sales volume. In a longer time perspective, a still greater threat to OPEC comes from the supply side of the equation: High prices and profits induce a worldwide expansion of exploration and production of crude oil, perhaps creating alternative supply sources that undercut OPEC's control of the market.

The forces of a surplus

Several recent studies see these demand and supply adjustments coming strongly together in the early 1980s to force OPEC either to allow prices to fall (in real terms) in a managed way or else risk a breakup of its group. Hollis Chenery, former economics professor at Harvard and now vice-president for development policy at the World Bank, writes in *Foreign Affairs* that if OPEC holds to the present real price until 1980, in that year it will have 16-million bbl. a day of idle productive capacity out of total capacity of 49-million bbl. and will have great difficulty in allocating that much shut-in capacity among its members.

MIT's Energy Laboratory Policy Study Group, relying chiefly on Adelman for guidance on the world oil market, calculates that OPEC will face a

Who's who in OPEC

	Reserves (billions bbl.)	Production in 1973 (millions bbl./day)	Years of reserves (at 1973 production rate)	Population (millions)
Saudi Arabia	140.8	7.7	51	8.1
Kuwait	72.7	3.1	66	0.9
Iran	60.2	5.9	28	31.9
Iraq	31.2	2.0	44	10.4
Libya	25.6	2.2	32	2.1
United Arab Emirates (Abu Dhabi, Dubai, 5 others)	25.5	1.5	45	0.1
Nigeria	19.9	2.0	27	73.4
Venezuela	14.2	3.5	11	11.3
Indonesia	10.8	1.3	22	125.0
Algeria	7.4	1.0	20	14.7
Qatar	6.5	0.5	31	0.2
Ecuador	5.7	0.2	78	6.7

surplus of 10.6-million bbl. a day of producing capacity by 1980. It argues that "the price could fall, due to the Persian Gulf countries' perceptions of their own long-run interest or to a succession of price shadings and a failure of understanding, powerfully aided by attempts of buyers to obtain long-run contracts at lower prices."

Secretary of State Henry Kissinger's oil price strategy is based on the idea that the OPEC countries will have trouble reducing oil production (page 66). He believes countries such as Iran, Iraq, and Venezuela cannot reduce production very much without damaging their own economic development.

Richard Gonzalez, a Houston oil economist and consultant, says: "You can almost bet that OPEC has overshot the mark on the price of oil for the long term. They'll find out that the real equilibrium price of oil in the 1980s will be less than it is today. It is possible that OPEC will see the development of alternatives coming and will ease off on the price of oil to keep it from getting out of hand. They can afford some overbidding at this point because they will have plenty of notice on what alternative energy sources will be developed, and at what cost."

Gonzalez is presenting the possibility that OPEC is following a very sophisticated strategy of price discrimination. Economists generally call it price discrimination when a monopoly seller charges different prices to consumers who have different reactions to price changes. What OPEC is doing, Gonzalez

and others claim, is discriminating through time, charging a very high price now when alternative supplies are held back by the need for massive investments and long lead times, and then planning to lower prices slowly and just enough to discourage development of those alternatives by creating uncertainty about where the price of oil is going to end up.

Such a strategy would reconcile the two major groups of countries in OPEC whose interests diverge on price and production policy. On one side are such countries as Iran, Venezuela, Iraq, and Algeria, with large populations and ambitious development plans. These countries want maximum revenues now and are not overly concerned about the erosion of OPEC's market by high prices in the very long term. They have many fewer years of production left in the ground anyway than the second group. That second group, which includes Saudi Arabia, Kuwait, and the Persian Gulf sheikdoms, now has much more money coming in than it can possibly use, and it is more concerned about maintaining the long-run viability of the OPEC export market.

All this is speculation since OPEC authorities have never explicitly explained their pricing criteria. But Iran's Amouzegar, interviewed at OPEC's Dec. 12 meeting in Vienna, said that OPEC has been using as its pricing peg the lowest-cost alternative to a barrel of oil. This is a barrel of oil made from coal, and its price ranges from $7 to $11 a bbl.

Equilibrium by 1980?

That still leaves a wide range within which to set the price, and OPEC has commissioned several studies to help it to determine the profit-maximizing price level and price sequence. The most important of these reports will be coming from the Geneva office of Battelle Institute in 12 to 18 months, examining the long-term effects of oil prices on investment in alternative energy sources. A dozen major research institutes and think tanks in Europe are reported working on related problems, under contract to OPEC countries, along with several in the U.S.

While OPEC awaits the result of its own research, Western experts are busy with major studies to determine the strains that the cartel would experience if the oil price stayed at its current level. Generally, they use a four-step analysis:

■ First, world demand for oil must be predicted for the reference year, usually 1980 but sometimes 1985.

■ Next, it is necessary to estimate how much oil will be added from non-OPEC sources by the reference year. This can include increased production within consuming nations, such as oil from offshore U.S. and the North Sea, as well as supplies from new or expanding exporters that stay outside OPEC.

■ Subtracting estimated non-OPEC supply from estimated world demand gives a figure for the world market open to the OPEC countries. This in turn can be compared with the total productive capacity that OPEC nations will have in place by the reference year. The comparison gives an indication of how great a problem OPEC will face in allocating output among its members.

■ Not to be overlooked are the internal differences within OPEC in terms of oil reserves, population, revenue needs, and military ambitions. These will determine whether the members can achieve a mutually acceptable scheme

of prorating production or will break up, with each country paring the price to reach its desired market share.

Estimating future worldwide oil consumption is especially chancy now that prices have skyrocketed far outside the range of previous experience, but a number of experts have made the attempt. The World Bank's Chenery suggests that total energy demand for the major non-Communist industrial countries will grow at 3.8% a year, on the average, for the rest of the decade. That is well below the 5% annual rate of the past few years. Gulf Oil's director of energy economics, Warren Davis, expects demand to grow at only 2% to 3% a year in the period.

If consuming countries themselves can step up their own oil production to match a 2% to 4% rate of growth in consumption, OPEC's export market will obviously be frozen at its present level. In 1973, OPEC produced an average of 30.2-million bbl. a day, almost all for export. Chenery figures that if oil stays at about $9.60 a bbl. in 1974 dollars, OPEC's 1980 production will be 33-million bbl. a day. The MIT group puts OPEC's 1980 output at 32.2-million bbl. a day—a remarkable coincidence for two completely independent studies.

Much worse prospects for OPEC can be foreseen if non-OPEC production, such as the North Sea fields, increases

as some experts feel it will. Rotterdam University economist Peter Odell thinks that by 1990, North Sea oil and gas will satisfy 75% of Western Europe's total demand. Other experts tend to be less ebullient.

The stresses of cutting back

Estimates of OPEC's excess productive capacity in 1980 cluster around 25% to 33%. Gulf Oil's Davis notes that most of the world's 6-million bbl. a day of shut-in oil capacity already is in Saudi Arabia, Libya, Kuwait, and the United Arab Emirates. He predicts that OPEC in 1980 will be holding 25% of the world's oil-production capacity off the market. How OPEC could handle a surplus of this magnitude involves the question of internal politics as well as the international situation.

OPEC spokesmen express confidence that the group could retain its cohesion. Valentin Hernandez Acosta, Venezuela's Minister of Mines & Hydrocarbons, told BUSINESS WEEK: "We are already producing too much oil—oil in excess of our financial needs. We think it is good that the world is cutting back its consumption, and the cutback will not hurt us. It will only allow us to conserve the oil that we have longer. Right now, if the OPEC countries cut back production by 33%, we would all be able to handle our financial needs. As for my country, I could cut back production by 50% without hurting our investment program."

As excess capacity develops, Saudi Arabia clearly will have to shut down the most on production. Engineers say that Kuwait, for example, cannot reduce production much without harming the related gas output on which most local industry depends. And Iraq, Algeria, Nigeria, and Indonesia can be expected to resist any hold-back orders. Iraq, in fact, recently announced projects to raise its productive capacity to 3.5-million bbl. a day by yearend and 6-million bbl. a day by 1981.

While shutdowns of excess capacity in Saudi Arabia would not seriously disturb that nation's economy, limits are set by the political rivalries in the region. The Saudis and the Shah of Iran have long been rivals for influence in the Persian Gulf and are building big military forces. There has been no slowdown in Saudi Arabia's exploration activity in the oil fields, and the gap between capacity and production could be huge by 1980.

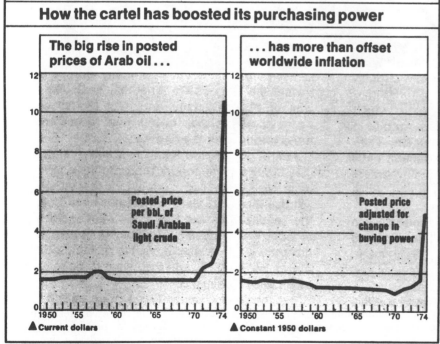

How the cartel has boosted its purchasing power

The big rise in posted prices of Arab oil . . .

Posted price per bbl. of Saudi Arabian light crude

▲ Current dollars

. . . has more than offset worldwide inflation

Posted price adjusted for change in buying power

▲ Constant 1950 dollars

Mario DeVincentis—BW

Data: Platt's Oilgram Price Service, Commerce Dept.

European Computer Makers Gang Up On IBM

Europe's computer makers share certain common miseries: a desperate market situation in which IBM towers over everyone, heavy financial losses that seem to have no end, and future development costs that none of the companies can face alone. In something of a last-ditch tactic, they are banding together in hope of eliminating cost duplications and, in the long run, capturing perhaps 40% of the world computer market.

Three of Europe's four major home-grown manufacturers are taking part in working out the fine points of a pooling arrangement: Compagnie Internationale Pour l'Informatique (CII) of France, Siemens of West Germany, and Philips of Holland. They will announce their long-range plan in the next few weeks. Only business computers are involved, but combined sales of

The French, Germans, Dutch form a combine aimed at selling a joint product line

■ Start planning an entirely new line of computers aimed at bucking IBM's nearly 50% share of the European market. A "plans and programs committee" will decide which maker will build each component, but the new line will be sold under a single trademark. The combine expects to announce the first machine in 1975, with initial deliveries within a year or two later.

The pooling arrangement, unlike a merger, leaves each company free to produce items other than business computers, retaining its own identity in such items as military computers and industrial process control machines. "This wouldn't work in any other in-

panies, even though Siemens and Philips can offset their computers' drain on resources by major sales of telephone and telecommunications equipment. In fiscal 1972, Siemens sold $1.1-billion of such equipment, 23% of its total revenues. Philips sold $430-million worth—nearly three times its computer sales.

IBM has also entered the telecommunications market in Europe with its 3750 system, an electronic telephone switchboard for both data and voice. It does not offer the product in the U. S. If André George, vice-president of Diebold Europe, is right, IBM may need the diversification in Europe. He sees IBM as likely to be the first U. S. computer maker to feel the squeeze as national European markets favor the new combine more firmly.

Honeywell, Univac, National Cash Register, and Burroughs, together

West European computer combine

Britain's computer makers resist being dragged into the combine set up by the Dutch, French, and Germans.

Richard Pryor

these items at the outset amount to an annual $625-million. And if Britain's International Computers, Ltd. (ICL) yields to urging and joins, another $400-million in annual sales would be added. Eventually, too, a U. S. partner—Control Data Corp. is most often mentioned—may be invited to join.

Once the three charter members have signed a general agreement, they will:
■ Create a joint worldwide marketing subsidiary. So far, they have agreed only on home market arrangements, in which each company will reign in its own country and the other two will have minority roles in sales of medium and large systems. In minicomputers, Philips will be the major seller in all three national markets.

dustry," says Pierre Audoin, deputy director of the French government agency that hands CII some $25-million a year in R&D aid. "But we believe that with IBM's peculiar strength in the market, we have to make it work. Otherwise we will disappear. We are determined to regain our right to survive." CII President Michel Barré sounds a more upbeat note. "We are at the beginning of something big," he says. "We are open to a fourth partner, and even a fifth."

Pinch on U. S. makers. The first phase of the alliance became operational last month when CII took over Siemens' 300-man sales and service subsidiary in France and Siemens absorbed CII's staff of 60 in Germany. Cost savings cannot come too soon for all three com-

holding about 30% of the European market, will also have to take the new combine into account. But Control Data, whether or not it joins the group as the fifth partner (after ICL), may profit; it already has a dormant agreement with CII to develop a medium-large computer. U. S. antitrust laws would complicate and limit any U. S. company's role in the group, however.

Right now, the three charter members of the European combine account for only 8% of the installed value of business computers in Europe, compared with Diebold Europe's estimate of nearly 50% for IBM. The three-company group aims at boosting its market share in Europe to 15% to 20% by 1980 or, if ICL comes in, to 25% to 30%.

British reticence. ICL's entry into the

group could well be the key to success. The British market is now virtually untouched by the three Continental companies. It would open up overnight. The British company's chairman, Thomas Hudson, said as recently as two weeks ago that he is "very doubtful" about the benefits to be gained by joining the group.

Governments of Britain, France, and Germany are pushing for ICL participation. Britain's Industrial Minister Christopher Chataway explained a few weeks ago that his government feels that Europe is destined to have only one or two computer makers by 1980. "I think this obviously implies that there should be mergers," he said, "and it certainly is our policy to encourage co-operation in Europe and to initiate early studies on merger possibilities." However, Hudson and his new managing director, Geoffrey Cross, a former Univac executive, are more intent on expanding their penetration of the Continent's market, where they now sell a meager 12% of their production.

The Continental group, meanwhile, is miffed at what it regards as ICL's superiority complex. "Now that it has waited this long," says a German who is close to the negotiations, "ICL is in a much weaker position to impose anything on the group."

However, Pierre Audoin says that ICL "will have no choice but to join." Diebold Europe notes that ICL's deliveries have been running some 20% below the combined figure of CII-Siemens-Philips, foreboding a drop to a distant fourth place in Europe by the end of next year, behind IBM, Honeywell-Bull, and the new combine. This trend, says Diebold, will be a big persuader for ICL participation.

Audoin goes even further to foresee a linkup between the European group and IBM's major surviving competitors by 1980 "to form a real counter-force."

Why IBM is the target

In these countries...	the national computer maker...	has this much of the market...	and IBM holds this much
Germany	Siemens	16.0%	53.0%
France	CII	8.5	51.0
Holland	Philips	12.0	50.0
Britain	ICL	40.0	40.0

Data: Diebold-Europe

He says that France favors such a transatlantic combine because no computer company can support itself with 15% to 20% of the world market while another company has more than 50%. "The level we are reaching for is somewhere around 40%," he says.

A long road. Officials of CII, Siemens, and Philips have no illusions about obstacles to full integration of manufacturing. Indeed, they needed 18 months of formal talks to get where they are. It took RCA's withdrawal from computers in the fall of 1971 to break the ice, after companies in Europe had been talking privately and desultorily for a couple of years. Audoin says that Siemens, which makes RCA's Spectra series under license, was badly shaken by RCA's bombshell.

"They quickly saw that we had been right in urging a European grouping," he says. "Serious talks got under way in short order." In four months of negotiations, Siemens and CII reached agreement in principle on joint marketing and product rationalization. But literally on the eve of their announcement last February, Philips informed them privately of its willingness to take part, too. Tripartite talks then dragged on for more than a year.

"In a cooperative arrangement, one plus one must always equal at least two point two," says Siemens' Chairman Bernhard Plettner. Philips

enlarged the group's potential with its highly successful line of office mini-computers and a customer base of some 15,000 users to go with it. "But Philips' entry complicated things enormously," says Barré. "They are so different in so many ways, notably in their absence of government financial support."

The group may already have harmed its image by its poky start. Some competitors refuse even to take the combine seriously. "When I see that CII and Siemens have needed all this time to agree on the French and German market situations, I wonder how they are ever going to make a larger agreement," says Maxime Bonnet, marketing director of Honeywell-Bull.

Product line. Still, the three companies are so confident that they could make the alliance work that they secretly detached teams of engineers six months ago to evaluate each other's equipment and decide on a new product line that will eliminate the overlapping of machines. The technicians have already agreed on some basics. Each of the "X" series of medium and large machines will correspond to an IBM 370 series.

"We will probably end up alternating with Siemens up the line from X-1 to X-6," says a CII official. "Neither will get stuck with only the big machines." The flaw in the plan is that Philips has no intention of being relegated exclusively to the bottom of the line.

Although complete integration of manufacturing may be as much as five years away, the three partners seem psychologically ready to merge their interests. Asked if there is an escape clause in their agreement, one participant in the talks says: "Of course, the lawyers will write one in, but there is no real escape. We need each other."

Not For Export?

WITH ALL THE FERVOR of the Pilgrims returned, McDonald's set out to introduce Europe to the joys of the *real* American hamburger. Most people assumed that golden arches, like blue jeans and Coke, would sprout up overnight across the Continent. A few years back McDonald's set a goal of 300 European stores by 1977. So far, there are 38. After four years, the company has lost none of its zeal. But it has learned the hard way about doing business with the natives.

"It's corny," says smiling, silver-haired Steve Barnes, head of McDonald's international operations, "but I feel like a missionary over here." Barnes, based at McDonald's Oak Brook, Ill. headquarters, and his 37-year-old European manager, Tony Klaus, talk enthusiastically about providing a place where the French are not embarrassed to bring their children and where the Germans can taste "a better bun." Says Dutch-born Klaus: "We're bringing one of the purest American things to good old Europe." Reflecting this, McDonald's starred-and-striped sales campaign in Britain features "The United Tastes of America."

But Barnes and Klaus would rather talk mission than money. Understandably. European sales are probably no more than $18 million out of $2 billion worldwide. Financial chief Richard Boylan says for the first time non-North American operations are making enough to cover operating and expansion costs this year. But that includes Japan and Australia; he won't say whether this is true of Europe.

Carl DeBiase of Fourteen Research Corp., who is very bullish on the company domestically, thinks it may take a decade before McDonald's makes real money in Europe. Analyst Al Simon of Sanford C. Bernstein estimates that, with a few notable exceptions like the record-breaking Stockholm store, European stores average $480,000 in yearly sales against $740,000 worldwide. For company stores, Simon puts average unit profit margins in European and Australian stores at 11%, though this is up from 6% last year, compared with 19% for American and Canadian stores.

Some of the qualities that made McDonald's so successful in North America may be nibbling at its margins abroad. Fast service for one thing, which gives McDonald's much higher labor costs than Kentucky Fried Chicken or Britain's Wimpy International. It takes four people per shift to sell take-out chicken; McDonald's averages up to 30 in its London stores. McDonald's is fanatical about quality. A Big Mac tastes the same in Des Moines as in London or in Amsterdam. The company adheres to strict specifications for meat, buns, apple pies and most everything else, specifications that may differ from those of European suppliers. So it must either import long distance (french fries from Canada, pies from Tulsa) or place special and more costly orders locally. When McDonald's has blanketed an area with stores, it can promise big orders and get discounts. Until that day arrives, the company will have to pay for being finicky.

Wimpy hamburger bars, by contrast, don't worry so much about consistency, and most franchisees solve their supply problems by buying from Wimpy's giant parent food company, J. Lyons ($1.4-billion sales). Wimpy's quality may suffer, but profits don't.

It takes under $25,000 to open a Wimpy or KFC store in Britain. A McDonald's costs over $200,000. This big capital requirement—and the fact that there are fewer entrepreneurs in Europe than in the U.S.—will make it hard for the company to find franchisees abroad, especially in capital-scarce Britain. Ten of the European stores are franchised, compared with 73% of the U.S. stores. Klaus concedes European development would come much faster if franchising could be pushed.

In Europe, the competitors who ostensibly thought small—either with low per-store capital costs like Wimpy and KFC or with limited expansion plans like Switzerland's Mövenpick—have already made big strides in European fast foods, where McDonald's is just getting going. KFC, in the U.K. since 1965, has 254 stores there and 40 on the Continent, while Wimpy has 950 outlets all over Europe. Both have mostly franchise stores. Mövenpick has 16 Swiss quick-service restaurants with varied menus that have the advantage of being identified with the company's 49 dining-room-type restaurants thoughout Switzerland and Germany.

Barnes concedes that McDonald's made mistakes. It thought it should put its first European store—Amsterdam—in the suburbs, just as it had started up in suburban Chicago. But as Barnes soon learned, the suburbs are not where it's at in Europe. Most people still live in cities, and they are less mobile than Americans. The out-of-town shopping centers that sprang up all over the U.S. and provided good sites for fast-fooders have not caught on in much of Europe. The original Amsterdam store was moved into town. "We learned our lesson," Barnes recalls. "Now we are choosing shop-front sites in the cities." But rents in those areas are often astronomical, and all four of the new London stores are more or less suburban.

McDonald's says that, as in the States, it is aiming to get the whole family in. McDonald's contrasts its relaxed approach to the more refined European restaurant, where the waiter may look askance at messy, noisy children. But Vice President Mario Wang of Mövenpick has his doubts, at least about Germany where McDonald's has made its biggest European commitment with 22 stores. "The Germans and Swiss are still quite traditional, and we are more gastronomically minded. Even if the wife works, dinner means a home-cooked meal. And once the family is home at the end of the day, it is not likely to go out again." So the real promise seems to lie with the lunchtime and Saturday shopping crowds.

From Hamburgers To Beer

McDonald's has made a few changes in its menu to accommodate European tastes: tea in Britain, beer and—to head off Kentucky Fried-chicken on the Continent. As for expansion in Europe, "We don't really make projections," said Barnes when FORBES first talked with him. "We work on a one-by-one basis with our stores." Financial Chief Richard Boylan ventured that there are 13 European stores under construction, but wouldn't say how many more are planned. Surprisingly, Barnes talked more recently of 40 new stores by the end of 1976. Time will tell.

New York Times columnist Tom Wicker recently lamented that McDonald's was luring Swedes away from their good old smoked herring. His worry may prove to have been a bit premature. Even missionaries have to adapt.

At War
once again
over brandy and birds

The Atlantic community's oldest continuing trade dispute, the so-called "chicken war," is flaring up again. And if U. S. and European Community negotiators meeting in Brussels this week fail to work out a settlement, it could touch off new retaliation and threaten trade negotiations.

"It may be senseless, but we are still fighting, and if there is no back-off by Washington now, there will be grave repercussions," warns a senior EC official.

The latest shots in the transatlantic "chicken war" could lead to broader retaliation.

Roy Doty

cial. With equal vehemence, a high-level U. S. trade source predicts that "either a settlement flies, which means substantial give on the EC side in the Brussels meeting, or we hit back."

At stake is some $55 million in two-way trade, mainly European brandy and American poultry, but the "chicken war" could spread to other products. When it all started 13 years ago, brandy was singled out for retaliation to compensate for $26 million worth of exports—mainly chicken—that the U. S. had lost during the formative years of the EC's common agricultural policy.

Now Washington is threatening to raise duties on European brandies once again. This would be accomplished by reinstating the $5 per gal. duty on brandy valued at $9 per gal.—calculated

to hit French cognac hardest. For the past two years the threshold has been $17 per gal., in effect placing most brandies beyond reach of the duty.

The object of the July, 1974, rollback was "our unilateral effort to give the Europeans a chance to facilitate entry of our turkeys into the EC," explains a U. S. trade official. But between July 1, 1974, and last July 1, the EC raised total import levies on turkey parts 397% for breasts and 966% for drumsticks.

Tough policies. Pushing hardest for new retaliation against the EC are U. S. poultry growers, who last year exported some $30 million to Europe, mainly turkey parts, a business they are eager to expand.

Retaliating now, however, would have disastrous effects on the $25 million-a-year imported brandy business. "It will

cost us 30% of the U. S. market the first year and as much as 50% of the market in the second year," laments Gerald de Goffre, chairman of the French Cognac Producers Assn. Moreover, declares William Street, chairman of Jos. Garneau Co., the cognac-importing division of Brown-Forman Distillers Corp., "the presently proposed duty increase would have a ripple effect on the U. S. [brandy] distribution system. Prices would increase, sales would decline, advertising would be reduced, the price increases would cause distributors to lose interest in the product, and consumers would switch to other products."

At midweek neither side was hinting at its negotiating position. But some well informed sources were giving the meeting only a 50-50 chance of succeeding. ∎

WHAZZIT?

OECD

The Organization for Economic Cooperation and Development. Founded in 1948 as the Organization for Economic Cooperation, this international organization, to which the United States adheres by Senate ratification, promotes free trade practices.

AID

Agency for International Development. This federal agency was set up by the United States after World War II to assist the recovery of war-ravaged countries. Today, it guarantees American investment abroad against political and economic risks.

EMBARGO

An order forbidding the export of some particular commodity, either to all countries or to selected countries.

LABOR INTENSIVE INDUSTRIES

Industries which require a high mix of labor to capital. For example, the garment industry.

CAPITAL INTENSIVE INDUSTRIES

Industries which require a high mix of capital to labor. For example, the oil industry.

Trade Barriers

The Law of Comparative Advantage says that it is to the economic advantage of a country to produce those goods that it can produce cheaper than other countries. This means that nations should refrain from producing goods and services that others can produce more cheaply elsewhere. As we have noted, however, countries are reluctant to follow this rule. They want to keep on making what they have been making and selling, regardless of the comparative advantage. In the United States, there are firms that do not want to quit producing a product. To protect their enterprise and their investment in the equipment and technology involved in producing the product, they seek special protection from the federal government.

Thus, a wide range of barriers have been established by the government at the urging of business, to protect American enterprise from the "threat of foreign competition." These trade barriers hinder the free movement of goods and services between nations.

Labor unions have joined in the cry for protection from foreign competition. They argue that increased imports takes away jobs that Americans would otherwise hold.

Trade quotas and trade restrictions are limits imposed by the government upon the actual volume of certain goods that may be brought into this country.

Tariffs are taxes imposed on goods as they enter (or leave) a country. Tariffs may be specific, that is, imposed on he number or bulk of goods, or general, that is, imposed on the dollar value of the goods.

Tariffs and trade quotas, argue proponents, improve our country's balance of trade by giving encouragement to the exporting of goods and discouraging the importing of goods.

This promotes expanded employment and production in our economy and stability in our needs for specialized talents, such as in the textile industry. It also ensures a stable supply of the goods, avoiding the risk of cutoffs in time of war or restrictions placed on exports by the supplying nations.

Other arguments for trade barriers are that we need to protect our "infant" industries and particular industries deemed to be "essential for our national defence."

Others argue that, on the contrary, we should put our resources to the best possible use. Free trade among nations promotes this, they believe.

"The better to protect us from intruders, my dear."

L.D.C.

Since World War II, the "developed" countries of the world have provided substantial contributions of capital funds, manpower, and technical knowledge to lesser developed countries (LDCs). This has not been becasue of a sudden discovery that there is poverty in the world, but rather to an increased sense of responsibility toward these countries and the perceived long-range advantage of increased trade. It was after World War II that most colonial territories had gained political independence and, as emerging nations, sought higher living standards and economic growth.

Economic growth is important in LDCs because it permits achievement of major social, political, and economical goals. An expanding economy provides employment, strengthens social welfare programs, stimulates business expansion, and promotes education and individual initiative.

Further, growth eases military obligations, international economic commitements, and doemstic tensions. Because LDCs purchase goods from one another and capital goods from developed nations, internatonal trade is strengthened by economic growth.

Under a United Nations classification, countries are "developed market economies," "Centrally planned economies," and "developing market economies." The first group includes Canada, the United States, Western European nations, the Rupublic of South Africa, Japan, New Zealand, and Australia.

The centrally planned economies are the U.S.S.R., Eastern European nations, the People's Republic of China, North Korea, and Mongolia. The remaining areas of the world comprise the developing market economies.

LDCs are exporting more today than ever before. This represents a third wave of economic relationships between developing countries and foreign capital. International businesses originally put money into mines, plantations, and other resource-based investments, aimed at supplying raw material for needs at home. This was helpful to the balance of payments and trade of the LDC, but put foreign companies in control of basic national natural resources. We have seen nation after nation throw such foreign control out, often resulting in the nationalization of the property.

Then there was a period (the 1960's primarily) when the LDCs put up high trade barriers to keep imports out. The idea is to encourage production at home of the goods previously imported. When foreign firms could not export goods over the barriers, they moved right on inside and set up plants for making automobiles, chemicals, pharmaceuticals, paper, farm machinery, and other goods. These were small operations, though, and not generally very efficient. Prices for the protected goods ended up being higher than original imports.

To overcome these problems, the LDCs are now pushing to open the doors for increased trade. They have an advantage of lower labor costs, and often an advantage of available natural resources. If they can export more goods, they will gain economic strength at home and will have the money to import other goods that are needed, including capital goods.

But as we have discussed, the developed nations have strong protectionist sentiments. If trade tariffs were dropped, trade quotas or other restrictions would likely take their place. The strong feeling of self interest in international trade will persist and will continue to be an obstacle in developing the LDCs.

Balance Of Payments

Every nation has a balance sheet, similar in concept to a corporate balance sheet. This balance sheet, however, reports the nation's balance of payments.

This is a statement of all of the nation's external financial transactions. It reports balances for exports and imports of goods, tourist spending, shipping and transportation services, business investments in other countries, government expenditures and foreign assistance programs.

There is an important difference between balance of payments and balance of trade, which we discussed earlier in this chapter. Balance of trade has to do with exports and imports of goods. Balance of payments

includes not only the exchange of goods, but also tourist expenditures in other countries and military expenditures abroad.

Balance of payments indicates the difference between what our country spent abroad and what it received from other countries, in total account amounts.

Thus, a country may actually have a favorable trade balance and at the same time, have an unfavorable balance of payments, a deficit in total spending versus receipts in international transactions.

As a "financial report" the B.O.P. gives us an overall picture of our international economic and trade positions. The report is therefore useful

to government agencies, central banks, and others who are concerned with maintaining our international trade and economic policies. Trade quotas, tariffs, foreign aid, flow of capital abroad, and other policies depend on our international balance of payments.

If a deficit in our balance of payments should persist, the debts must be settled. It used to be that debts were settled by the payment of gold. We "bought back the dollars sent overseas" with real gold. Gold was accepted as the international monetary exchange among the nations of the world.

Today, however, we no longer pay our debts with gold. Instead, foreign governments hold

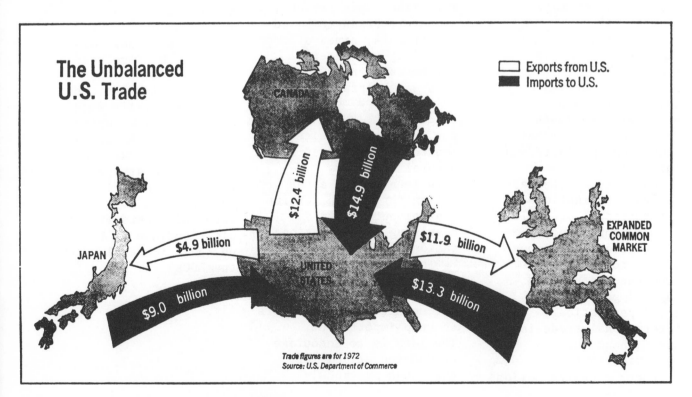

The Unbalanced U.S. Trade

☐ Exports from U.S.
■ Imports to U.S.

$12.4 billion
$14.9 billion
$4.9 billion
$9.0 billion
$11.9 billion
$13.3 billion

JAPAN
CANADA
UNITED STATES
EXPANDED COMMON MARKET

Trade figures are for 1972
Source: U.S. Department of Commerce

dollars or short-term government securities used to buy back dollars.

Accordingly, the value of the dollar fluctuates today ("floats") in response to the willingness of financial communities in various countries to accept dollars or securities.

The net effect of our floating dollar value (generally downward) has been to make imported goods more costly in the United States and the exporting of goods easier. This encourages exports and usually makes imports more costly. But demand for our goods is not a sure thing, especially at higher costs. So we face a continuing problem of a payments deficit -- we pay out more money for goods than is paid in.

Growing world demand for U.S. agricultural products may significantly improve exports in the future. But concurrently, increased imports of oil and other basic fuels may more than offset the export improvement. Perhaps, the only certainty at present is the United States foreign trade is going to loom significantly larger in the future of the United States economy than it has in the past.

"Don't be childish, man! Kicking Toyotas is no answer to our balance-of-trade gap."

Drawing by Donald Reilly: © 1971: The New Yorker Magazine, Inc.

The Law Everyone Is Breaking

**The law of
comparative cost
can make both
parties to a deal
better off, even
if the terms
look lopsided**

Two of the most durable figures in economic literature are the lawyer who types well and his secretary who types badly. They have come down through the years with all their smudges and erasures as an illustration of the principles that determine trade patterns between nations.

Here, for instance, is how they appear in Richard T. Ely's *Outlines of Economics*, a text that introduced two generations of students to the dismal science in the days before Keynes and Samuelson: "A good lawyer may be able to operate a typewriter better than his typist. But it will still pay the lawyer to specialize in law and buy the stenographic services he needs. . . . Each country manufactures the products in which it has a *comparative* advantage and buys with these products other goods which it needs. It specializes in the production of those things in which the comparative cost is lowest. This is the *law of comparative costs.*"

In other words, if two nations want to trade, they can always find a way to split up production so that each has something to sell the other. And, theoretically at least, each will be better off than it would be if it tried to make everything for itself. This is true even when the terms of the trade appear very lopsided. Early fur traders swapped a musket for a stack of pelts that matched its height, stood on end. On the face of it, this looks like another swindle of the Indians, but at the time, both parties were satisfied. The traders made enormous profits, and from the standpoint of the Indians, it was no great trick to catch beaver, whereas it was impossible to make a musket.

New market forces. In the modern world, however, the law of comparative costs is only one of the forces at work in international trade. National pride, national economic policies, and national defense requirements conflict with it. Cost relationships change. And losers in the competitive scramble for world markets seek political help to strengthen their trading positions. Much of the confusion and uncertainty in international trade and finance today arise because comparative costs pull one way and national policies pull another.

For a quarter of a century after the end of World War II, the U. S. thought it was selling muskets and the rest of the world was selling it beaver pelts. U. S. businessmen and government officials took it for granted that each year would produce a comfortable surplus in the merchandise balance of trade.

Toward the end of the 1960s, the U. S. realized with pained surprise that other nations were not just customers but also competitors. Italian shoes moved in on the American market with high style and low prices. Japanese textiles began to take business away from manufacturers in the Carolinas and Georgia. Volkswagens, once a curiosity in the Detroit-dominated auto

market, made a permanent place for the subcompact car, and Japanese Datsuns and Toyotas promptly moved in to share it.

What happened?

One thing was that Europe and Japan rebuilt their war-ravaged industries and changed the whole structure of comparative costs. As capacity and efficiency in its industries increased, West Germany no longer had to depend on cuckoo clocks from the Black Forest to build its export markets. It could match prices and quality with the U. S. or anyone else in machinery, autos, and other sophisticated, high-value items.

The pattern of postwar rebuilding and expansion was dictated more by national pride and the universal fear of unemployment than by comparative costs. Every nation wanted an airline and a steel mill. As a result, every country but the U. S. is picking up the deficits of its national airline. And, according to one U. S. executive, only the American and West German steel industries operate at a profit.

Nationalistic tactics. In a clean competitive situation, U. S. industry would have been chased out of some markets, but in others, it would have driven uneconomic overseas suppliers out of business. In the past decade, however, the situation has been anything but clean. There have been tariffs and quotas, special tax tricks, and subsidies for industries that could not show a profit on their own.

In addition, there has been an international currency system loaded in favor of the nations making a bid for the markets of U. S. producers. Instead of changing to reflect the increasing strength of Europe and Japan, the fixed rates provided by the Bretton Woods apparatus helped overseas competitors undercut U. S. industry by offering bargain prices.

With the dollar floating, the way is now open to design a new payments system with flexible rates. This should go a long way toward solving the financial problems generated by the huge balance-of-payments deficits that the U. S. has been running. But a new monetary agreement will not by itself keep nations from subsidizing unprofitable industries and protecting home markets with tariffs and quotas.

The U. S. faces two tough jobs in the upcoming trade talks with other nations. One is to persuade foreign governments to pull down trade barriers, trim subsidies, and let the law of comparative costs dictate new patterns of world trade. The other is to persuade U. S. producers to accept the verdict of the world market when fair competition demonstrates that they cannot match their overseas competitors.

Neither task will be easy. Too many secretaries like the idea of practicing law. And even though it clearly is costing the world billions in lost production, they do not want to go back to typing.

Multinational Corporations

By this definition there are no more than 200 truly multinational companies in the world. Three quarters of these are American.

There are many other companies that do business internationally -- selling goods and services in other countries and buying materials or hiring labor in other countries. but these are international firms, not multinational firms by the currently accepted deifnitions.

Doing business multinationally requires a company to provide benefits for both the host countries and ours. You may be able to barge in and do business for a time, even winning support of local governments, but you will run into trouble in the end unless the relationship is of mutual benefit and advantage. This is recognized by the major multinatioanl firms.

there are several important trends that are influencing multinational business today.

First, there is a strong and growing sense of nationalism. Governments andpeople are seeking to control their own resources and economies and resent or even reject the activities of multinational companies. It is still true that most multinationals today have an overwhelming national identity. Most of the investment

decisions come from the headquarters nation; top management, stockholders, and directors are largely from one nation. The trend, however, is toward broader participation in the ownership and management of the firms. There is also a trend toward more cautious and carefully planned growth multinationally by companies.

A third trend is toward greater interaction between government and business, particularly in various countries. Companies may become extensions of the nation's foreign policy or economic development plans.

There's nothing particularly new about business on a worldwide basis. Britain's East India Companies were a multinational concern before the Pilgrims landed at Plymouth Rock.

Many companies in the United States and Europe have been operating on a multinational scale for many years. A great many American consumers are probably unaware of the multinational nature of the products they buy from Unilever, Shell, Nestle's and Massey-Ferguson -- products of companies with headquarters and management in other nations.

By the same token, people in other lands often view products there as their own -- Heinz, Ford, or Singer. The low ebb in understanding what multinational business is all about may have been the "Buy American" bumper

sticker placed by a college student on his Volkswagen.

What is a multinational corporation? One concept holds that it is any firm that operates in at least six countries and that has foreign operations accounting for at least 20% of total assets, sales, or employment.

Obviously, size is a key factor in looking at the importance of multinational corporations. No company with sales of less than $100 million can be seriously considered to be a multinational firm, especially in terms of political clout in various nations.

Multinational companies typically have above-average growth and profits. They deal in high-technology industries and rely on trading, mining, and oil as major activities.

Critics of multinational firms see them as "shadowy private states putting their own interests ahead of those of any one country." Proponents see them as "efficient, profitable tools for the development of world-wide economic strength."

Since it is obvious that the multinational corporation does aid in the development of LDC's by transferring capital, technology and managerial expertize it will be important to answer the critics. Currently attempts are being made to develop inter-international agreements to control the power of the multinational corporation without destroying its usefulness.

The (Ford) Story

Common Marketing For The Common Market

THE U.S.-BASED multinational company, source of so much corporate growth and profitability, is at a dangerous crossroads. Abroad, it is attacked as an American Trojan horse. At home it is accused of exporting both jobs and the capital needed to produce jobs. The foreigners say, "Ami, go home." The Americans are saying, "Brother, *come* home," and are talking about laws that would virtually compel the multinationals to do so.

Few big U.S. multinational corporations have more at stake than Dearborn Mich.'s Ford Motor Co. In Europe the companies coordinated by its Ford of Europe subsidiary comprise a giant in its own right, with 113,000 employees, 1971 sales of about $3.4 billion. In Europe alone Ford has twice General Motors' dollar sales, and hopes to oust Volkswagen from second place after Fiat in the automobile industry. Significantly, this year Ford has been gaining ground on VW and Fiat. Ford manufactures and assembles throughout western Europe and sells its output there and in the Middle East, parts of Africa and even the Far East.

And Ford of Europe is only the largest segment of Ford U.S.' multinational empire; it is a kind of multinational company within a multinational company. Other subsidiaries sell Ford automotive products elsewere in the world, while the tractor division is a multinational in its own right, with plants in Belgium, the U.S. and Britain.

At Ford, multinational does not mean a mere holding company. Most of the decisions in the Ford empire are made locally, but they can be and are overruled from time to time; the very big decisions are still reviewed in Detroit. "The closer you get to the top," complains one former Ford of Britain executive, "the more you realize you never make the real decisions. Detroit does." For example, when Semon Knudsen was president of Ford, he ordered two inches pared from the height of the 1970 Cortina.

It is not only its size that makes Ford of Europe important these days. Ford in Europe is not just a collection of national subsidiaries; it is very much a truly multinational operation that spreads across national boundaries as though they were of little more importance than state boundaries are within the U.S. It manufactures in Belgium as well as in Britain and Germany, and has assembly plants in Holland, Portugal and Ireland. This is a deliberate long-term policy that looks toward the day—around 1980—when the European Common Market could encompass 400 million people and an automobile market at least as large as that of the U.S.

Ford has been in Britain since 1913 and in Germany since 1926, but its operations in these two countries were originally geared to serve a limited national market: British cars for the British market, German cars for the German market and export cars for any other countries that would have them. As the Common Market loomed larger and tariff barriers began to fall, Ford found itself producing two lines of cars for what had become basically a single market, and wisely decided to switch emphasis. In the mid-Sixties, the late John S. Andrews, for seven years managing director of Ford's German subsidiary and later Ford U.S.' European vice president, sold Henry Ford II on the idea of creating a new management body to coordinate Ford's German and British companies. "And now," says Paul F. Lorenz, for the past three years Ford of Europe's chairman or president and now a newly appointed executive vice president of Ford U.S., "everybody is trying to copy us."

Andrews recognized that the European auto market was going to become a single market as it was in the U.S., informed with a broad common taste and consumer appetite. It also was apparent that the biggest growth in prospect lay on the Continent where Ford of Germany was entrenched, while the real manufacturing and product-engineering knowhow was behind the tariff and corporate barrier in Britain. Ford of Europe offered a way of bringing the strengths of the two companies together.

"With the market growing the way

Biggest Benefit? *Britain's entry into the Common Market won't do much for sales of Ford cars like the Cortina (above) or the Taunus (left). But in opening up the Continent to Ford's British truck production (right), it could provide a major opportunity—providing Ford can set up supporting service and distribution facilities fast enough and keep its perennially disruptive labor problems under control.*

it was," Paul Lorenz says, "the question was: How do you expand? And the answer was: Not just by expanding the existing structures, but by consolidating functions and assigning responsibility where the skill is greatest in order to get a more efficient operation." In short, by obliterating the national boundaries that separate Germany, Britain and the rest of Europe, and organizing on a truly multinational basis.

Under what Lorenz calls "John Andrews' 40-year concept," a new management organization was created to make all the critical decisions for both the British and German companies. There were obvious operating economies in the arrangement—the duplicate dealer organizations in third markets could be eliminated, and responsibility went where the skill was: Body development work was concentrated in Germany, power train development concentrated in Britain. "The pooling of the two companies," says Ford-Werke's managing director, Hans-Adolph Barthelmeh, "cut the engineering bill in half for each company, provided economies of scale, with double the volume in terms of purchase—commonization of purchase, common components—provided the financial resources for a good product program at a really good price that we could still make money on."

Three years or more are involved in developing a new car and the six-year product cycle is traditional at Ford. Thus change was bound to come slowly, but come it did. At the time Ford of Europe was formed, Britain was preparing to introduce a smallish, VW-sized car, the Escort, into the British market as a replacement for its Anglia. Ford of Germany lacked any small car to pit against Volkswagen, and Ford of Europe urged it to take on the Escort. Ford-Werke executives were cool to the idea, but Ford of Europe persisted. "We kept saying to them," one Ford of Europe executive recalls, "'Are you sure there's no market for it? It's going to be cheap. You don't have to pay for the tooling, it's already been tooled.'" Somewhat unwillingly, Ford of Germany bowed to the perhaps inevitable and began making the Escort at Genk, Belgium for the continental market. Introduced in 1968, the Escort was a resounding success in Britain—it is still Britain's second-best-selling car—and after a bad start it seized a small but respectable portion of the German market and did even better in France and Italy.

The Escort was frankly a British car. The next model to emerge from Ford of Europe—a somewhat larger, medium-priced vehicle—was more nearly a joint effort of the British and German companies. The Germans and British could not agree on the external styling, and so the British Cortina and the German Taunus, as they continued to be called, emerged different in appearance, but identical under the skin. The next step will be a new car, alike both inside and out, which will bow around 1976.

In spite of some resistance at the national level, Ford of Europe was dedicated to the proposition that there was a common European taste, just as there was a Common Market. The embodiment of that notion is the Capri, introduced in 1969 and designed specifically for Europe and European tastes. As such it proved a stunning success, particularly in Germany and in the U.S., where it unexpectedly proved to be Ford of Europe's first success in the U.S. market. "Neither the British nor German company," says William B. Batty, managing director of Ford of Britain, "could have come up with the Capri separately, tooled it separately. Only with the whole volume of Europe in prospect did the Capri become a viable product development program."

A Ferrari for $2,900?

More recently, Ford introduced the Consul/Granada as a replacement for its generally unsuccessful range of upper-medium-priced British and German cars. A large car by European standards, with innovations like independent rear suspension, and selling for between $4,000 and $5,000, the Consul/Granada may win Ford an important position in that segment of the market. Says one Ford executive: "It's a BMW at half the price."

Multinational with a vengeance, Ford does not hesitate to take successes from one country and apply them to another. Just as it aimed for the BMW market in the upper range, so it applied the Mustang philosophy from the U.S. to Europe: the poor man's sports car. Ford reasoned that what Europeans wanted was a low-priced four-passenger sports car—a fair imitation of what Lamborghini, Porsche or Ferrari sold for $10,000. "The question was," Paul Lorenz says, "could we produce a Ferrari for $2,900?" The answer was the highly successful Capri, no Ferrari but a slim, sleek beauty of a car that provided Ford with the base for an advance into the French and Italian markets. In the past decade, Ford has gone from 1.1% to 5.7% of the Italian market, from 0.4% to 4.8% of the French market.

To Americans and even to Europeans, Ford's new product line looks strikingly familar. The Escort recalls the Maverick as the Capri does the Mustang, but that, Ford executives insist, stems not from any deliberate policy but from the pervasiveness of the Ford mentality. And unquestionably it's there. In the early Sixties, when U.S. Ford launched a subcompact project named the Cardinal in honor of the American redbird, the story goes that British Ford undertook a similar venture and understandably dubbed it the Archbishop.

A common product range for a common market is only half of Ford's multinationality. The other is what Ford executives call commonization—using the same components in as many vehicles as possible, the same engines, the same axles, the same transmissions. It puts the same 1.5-liter engine in both the Escort and the Cortina, for instance, and the same Essex engine in both the Capri and the Consul/Granada. Ford, in short, hasn't gone multinational just for the sake of sales, but for the sake of big operating economies as well.

When you make over a million cars a year, as Ford does in Europe, you can manage diversity even amidst such uniformity. Ford uses only three engine blocks, for instance, on which it builds eight or nine basic engines, and one of these, the fabulously successful Kent engine used in the Pinto, can be produced in 180 different variants. This means, of course, that Ford's cars tend to be pretty conventional mechanically, and that the differences between them are often slighter than they seem. But it also means lower costs to sustain Ford's long-term policy of providing basically inexpensive but relatively high-quality cars. It's what enabled Ford to sell the Capri for $2,900 and yet dare to claim that it was competing with the $10,000 Ferrari. "Though the Capri was a completely unique motor car, for example, with a completely unique body," one Ford executive concedes, "it still had a lot of carry-over mechanicals, simply because carry-over mechanicals have always been our theory and policy."

So now, five years after its formation, Ford of Europe has established a powerful position for Ford in the emerging European auto market. It now has a single product line just as its major competitors do, and it has a marketing and distribution system throughout Europe that none of its competitors can match. British Leyland, Fiat and Volkswagen still rank first in their home markets, but it is Ford that ranks second in Britain and Italy, third in Germany, even first among imports into France. Perfectly true, Ford's total share of the European market has slipped from 14.5% in 1965 to 12.6% in 1970, but in part this is due to the stagnation of Ford's important British market and in part to the efforts of the continental producers to establish themselves in Britain and elsewhere in Europe in anticipation of an enlarged Common Market. In the Common Market countries, Ford's market share has remained virtually unchanged.

Unavailing Powers

Ford of Europe's basic production capacity is now concentrated at Halewood and Dagenham in Britain, Cologne and Saarlouis in Germany, Genk in Belgium. Each model in the Ford line, in fact, is now produced at two locations; the Escort at Halewood and Saarlouis, the Cortina/Taunus at Dagenham and Genk, the Capri at Halewood and Cologne, the Consul/Granada at Dagenham and Cologne. There is considerable flexibility to this multinational pattern. "Once you tool up," says one Ford executive, "it's just a question of moving the tools."

This very flexibility is one of the elements that so alarms both government and labor about Ford's multinational structure these days. "This produces many fears in the people working on the shop floor," says Transport & General Workers' Union's B. Passingham, "because it means the company can automatically switch from one plant to the other with no loss of production. We are now getting the line, especially with the dual models, of management saying, 'The Germans are getting on with theirs. If you don't watch out, you'll be out of work.'"

Ford executives deny that dual production provides any special protection against labor unrest, except in very special circumstances. "We can't plow around labor unrest," says Bill Batty. "If you're near capacity, as we are now in both Britain and Germany, you can't step up production quickly to deal with a sudden storm." "When you've got a volume requirement and a line on both sides, that gives you some protection," Paul Lorenz admits, "and during the strike last year we kept stealing engines out of Genk to keep Saarlouis going. But you can't dual source and protect everything and get the advantages we're after. Duplication is too expensive, so you minimize it and take a few risks."

As Ford executives explain it, purely economic considerations rather than protectionism are the determining factors in investment decision. Ford built at Genk and later Saarlouis rather than at Cologne because cheap land and local labor were readily available.

For the Consul/Granada, it produced the engines in England and the sheet metal in Germany because it could get the economies of volume production by manufacturing each component at a single location.

Such multinational sourcing has made Ford's multinational plants inordinately interdependent, so that, far from protecting it against labor problems, Ford's multinational structure is as likely to make the effects contagious. The Escort uses the Kent engine, for instance, just as the Pinto does, and the British strike shut down Saarlouis just as it did some Pinto production in the U.S. Ford is chary with figures, but a month-long British strike in 1969 cost Ford of Europe about $117 million in lost production, over $26 million of it on the Continent.

"In calculating an investment," Lorenz says, "what we do is go through an economic and financial evaluation that says: Here is the best and most economical place to produce such and such a component. We went through that exercise when we selected Bordeaux for the automatic transmission plant we're now building. People said that was politically motivated, but it wasn't. You sat down and considered the alternatives, and everything finally said that Bordeaux was the best place to go. We were already in Belgium, heavily concentrated in Germany and Britain, we had nothing in France, a significant market, so it was a natural place to look." Bordeaux had local labor, a local university, a tidewater location.

The unions, however, do not buy this argument. "We know their alternative supplies can only be boosted for a short period," says David Lea, secretary of the Economics Department of Britain's powerful Trades Union Congress. "The problem is that capital is more mobile than labor. It's freer to move in response to cost fac-

tors and market factors. So it is in the area of investment decisions rather than sheer wage pressure where the impact of the multinational corporation is really seen."

Indeed, during last year's strike, Henry Ford threatened British labor with the mobility of Ford's capital. He crossed Britain off his list of possible sites for a $72-million engine plant. He warned that Ford's directors would have to consider carefully the suitability of Britain for further investment. Finally, he announced plans to pull Pinto engine production out of Britain and build the new engine plant in Lima, Ohio.

Yet Ford's response was not quite so brutal as it seems. Ever since the mid-Sixties, the emphasis of Ford of Europe's capital investment has been shifting away from Britain and onto the Continent. So Ford's threat simply confirmed an existing trend. And once the Pinto production is withdrawn, Dagenham's engine plants will hardly stand empty: Ford already needs the capacity to meet European demand.

Nothing Doing

In Europe, where labor still has a strong socialist tradition, this shifting of capital may one day lead to threats of nationalization. But that is easier said than done: No single national unit of Ford of Europe is really self-sustaining, so that if any government should attempt to take one over, it would get a business dependent upon Ford subsidiaries in other countries—for components, for markets and for management. The new automatic transmission plant Ford is building at Bordeaux, for example, will supply Ford's U.S. and European operations. If the French should ever decide to take it over, unless they develop alternative markets for their output, they would very probably get something of very little long-term value. Ford would unquestionably be hurt, but its loss might not constitute any appreciable gain for anyone else. A transmission plant in this respect is not like a copper mine or an oil well.

Clearly Ford's position is no casually considered one. Until a decade or so ago there was substantial minority interest in both the British and German companies. Ford deliberately bought them in order to be free to allocate without fear of conflict of interest their financial resources as it chose, to manufacture, market, plan on a multinational and mutually dependent basis. Ford is clearly betting that governments will have more to gain by leaving it alone than by interfering in its affairs.

Countervailing Interests

"The demand for local ownership," Lorenz says, "is almost inversely related to the stage of development of the country. You move into a more sophisticated economic and financial environment like the Common Market, and they say, 'You want to spend $100 million on a plant employing 5,000 people? Let's talk business.' So I'm not greatly worried. You can't insist on local ownership on the one hand and solicit major investment on the other."

Ford executives concede that, when the day comes when it is possible to incorporate within the Common Market, it might be possible to sell shares in Ford of Europe without impairing the effectiveness of what it has built, though how this would be preferable to selling shares in Ford Motor Co. is difficult to see. Christopher Tugendhat, Conservative Member of Parliament and author of *The Multinationals*, probably the best and most detached of a whole spate of recent books on the subject, questions whether individual share ownership would accomplish much for anybody. "The interests of the small group of people who hold shares in a company are not necessarily those of the country as a whole. Their interest in terms of dividends, for example, is not the employees' interest in terms of jobs. If the British government ever forced Ford to make such a sale, I think we would lose more than we would gain."

Tugendhat makes an important point. By and large, the excitement of what Servan-Schreiber once called "The American Challenge" seems largely to have subsided in Europe. Ford, after all, employs 68,000 people in Britain, so that anyone who damages Ford of Britain damages the British economy. And not simply through the loss of jobs: through the loss of exports. For Ford is Britain's second largest exporter—to the tune of $750 million last year—and without its network of dealers in Europe and the U.S., Ford would be exporting only a fraction of what it does now.

Tugendhat, in short, is looking at multinationals from a broader point of view than the narrow one of national prestige or the interest of a few people. In defending the multinationals, he is looking at basic economics.

Left to themselves, most democratic governments probably would accept this point of view: that the border-hopping multinationals contribute more to their economies than they take out; because they are efficient, multinationals produce more and better jobs, and people without jobs have

a way of voting politicians out.

Labor, however, is another matter. In Europe there is much talk though little action of international trade unions confronting multinationals with a common front, thus inhibiting management's ability to shift production from high-cost labor areas to lower-cost areas. But so far the most anyone hopes for is simultaneous bargaining on an industrywide basis.

Within the U.S. itself there is the Burke-Hartke bill and all it represents: the mythology that Ford has sent to Europe capital that it *could* have used to provide jobs in Detroit. That, of course, is a fallacy on two points. Point one is that, without Ford in Europe, the business would have gone to Fiat or VW or Renault or British Leyland; Ford's hope of *exporting* cars to Europe today is virtually zero. Point two is this: There was *no* capital export. Ford's equity in its European holdings, better than $1 billion, represents almost entirely the reinvested earnings of some 60 years of doing business in Europe. In a good year, however, dividends from Europe bring perhaps $110 million into the U.S. and onto the credit side of the U.S. balance of payments.

Ford is betting heavily that the multinational corporation will prevail. "We've got," a Ford executive says, "a rhythm of not thinking short term." He means by this that Ford expects to see the boundaries continue to come down for business. That Ford thinks the consumer's insistence on quality at a price will eventually overwhelm national prejudices and trade union truculence. Henry Ford was talking about a slightly different subject to stockholders last month, but he very nicely summed up the case for multinational corporations:

"I believe that the social responsibility of corporations is fundamentally what it always has been. To earn profits for shareholders by serving consumer wants with maximum efficiency. That is not the whole of the matter, but it is the heart of the matter." It is very much the heart of the matter for the multinationals.

Col. Sanders' Tokyo Fried Chicken

TOKYO—It's just past dawn when the Shinto priest, dressed in ceremonial robes, enters the red-and-white-striped pagoda-shaped tent. Chanting a few brief prayers, he picks up a shovel and scoops out a spadeful of dirt.

Ground has been broken for still another Kentucky Fried Chicken outlet.

Later, on the other side of the world's largest city, a yellow truck, trimmed in red and with "NABISCO" lettered in blue on its side, weaves skillfully through rush-hour traffic. Its cargo: thousands of freshly baked Ritz crackers which are being moved to supermarkets and other outlets.

Both scenes are evidence of why two companies, KFC (a division of Heublein, Inc.) and Nabisco, Inc., have become something of an American legend in Japan. In two short years of operations here, each firm managed to muscle its way through a maze of government restrictions and tough local competition, successfu ly bridge the East-West cultural gap, and make its products Japanese household words.

Today, Nabisco's Ritz is Japan's biggest selling cracker, while KFC is the nation's largest fast-food franchiser.

To be sure, there have been many American success stories in Japan over the years. Coca-Cola and Pepsi, for example, currently hold more than 50 per cent of the Japanese soft drink market. Kellogg's corn flakes is the top-selling breakfast cereal. NCR cash registers are found everywhere from offices and shops to Ginza bars and *sushi* (raw fish) restaurants. A wholly owned subsidiary of IBM has some two thirds of the local market for large-capacity computers.

But in most cases, these and other U.S. firms owe their success to such things as proprietary technology (as in the case of IBM) or seniority (NCR has been in Japan in one form or fashion since before 1900) or to the fact that they have introduced a new product to the Japanese and, hence, created a market which had

East meets West—with pleasure—when a KFC restaurant opens. Col. Sanders' product, it seems, tastes something like Japan's popular yakitori—broiled chicken on a stick.

John P. Wiggin, head of Yamazaki-Nabisco, Ltd., feels Nabisco's success in Japan stems from a good choice of Japanese partners and from "working closely" with them.

not existed before (such as in the case of breakfast cereals).

Unlike Japanese firms, which have blitzed existing markets world-wide with their autos, cameras and electronics products, few American companies have gone to Japan, taken on an established product or industry, and done well. That is, until Nabisco and KFC came along.

Plenty to chew on

When Nabisco set up a joint venture company with Yamazaki Baking Co.—Yamazaki-Nabisco Co., Ltd. —it was the first foreign firm to enter the well-developed and highly competitive biscuit market in Japan.

A variety of rice- and wheat-based crackers and biscuits were already being offered—the top seller was a butter-sprayed cracker, similar to Ritz, called Nice, made by Morinaga Confectionary Co. Ltd. (Even Yamazaki made a similar cracker, called Gold, which it dropped after linking up with Nabisco.)

Nevertheless, the time seemed ripe for Nabisco to make its appearance. For one, snack foods were rising in popularity in Japan. Industry volume, believed running around $150 million, was growing between 10 per cent and 15 per cent yearly.

In addition, Ritz, Nabisco's biggest seller world-wide, had established something of a name for itself in Japan as an imported cracker sold through specialty food shops. "Most sales were to *gaijin* (foreigners)," admits John P. Wiggin, head of the Nabisco affiliate. "But the Japanese obviously were big cracker-eaters. So, we decided the market had great potential."

Only cost and freshness had held Ritz back in the past.

A 40 per cent tariff, export charges, and freight and packaging expense had boosted its price in Japan to $1.10 a box (compared with about 35 cents in the U.S.)—far beyond the pocketbooks of most housewives.

There was the added headache of shipping to a market 8,000 miles away. By the time the merchandise reached Japanese markets, much of it was stale.

Making crackers in Japan was the obvious answer to both problems. Yamazaki-Nabisco currently operates a plant which last year churned out some $21 million worth of cookies, crackers and candies—with Ritz accounting for around 80 per cent of volume. This year, sales are expected to total $26 million, and they're targeted at more than $30 million by the end of 1974.

One promising note: Less than a year after the first Ritz cracker came from a Japanese oven, Yamazaki-Nabisco ran out of capacity. The oven at its plant in Chiba had to be extended to 330 feet, making it the biggest Ritz oven in the world. Plans for another plant are on the drawing board.

Big chicken-eaters

KFC also benefited from the food tastes of the Japanese. The restaurant business, though highly competitive, was booming. Some 320,000 restaurants, big and small, serviced more than 100 million persons. Moreover, the growing appetite of Japanese for Western-style foods had sparked a rush to Japan by fast-food franchisers, including McDonald's, Dunkin' Donuts and Wimpy.

KFC, however, had one particular asset: The Japanese were big chicken-eaters. Until about 100 years ago, chicken was the only meat eaten in Japan, except for seafood, notes Loy Weston, executive vice president of KFC's Japanese operations. "Religious laws," he says, "prohibited eating anything that didn't walk around on two feet. So it wasn't like we were introducing a new food."

Also, KFC had a couple of other things in its favor: Its chickens were cooked similarly to *tempura* (deep fried shrimp) and tasted something like *yakitori* (broiled chicken on a stick), both popular foods in Japan.

The company set up two test outlets—one at Expo '70 in Osaka and the other at a Tokyo department store. The Expo '70 store broke company records, with sales peaking at $100,000 a month.

A few months later, a joint venture company—Kentucky Fried Chicken Japan, Ltd.—was formed with Mitsubishi Corp., Japan's biggest trading company. Currently, it has 60 outlets in 12 cities, including Tokyo. It is expected to have 300 to 400 stores, some company-owned, some franchised, in five years. Of the present stores, 29 are company-owned. Their annual volume is about $5 million.

In the soup

Of course, not everything has gone according to schedule for Nabisco and KFC. Indeed, both companies ran into some initial start-up problems that for a while threatened to sabotage their plans.

For example, when it was first announced that Nabisco, the world's largest biscuit and cracker producer, was planning to team up with Yamazaki, Japan's biggest baker, the Japanese confectionary industry rose up in opposition. "There was quite a hue and holler," recalls Mr. Wiggin, "and

people kept throwing banana peels in our way, hoping we would slip up before government approval came through. We were characterized as the 'bad guys' and accused of disrupting national markets around the world. It was pretty tough trying to get our side across."

Finally, a team of Japanese officials visited Nabisco plants in France and Britain. "They found that we weren't such bad guys after all, that we employed nationals in key positions and were good corporate citizens," Mr. Wiggin notes. "Things quieted down after that."

Originally, Nabisco wanted a 50-50 venture with Yamazaki, but under industry pressure the government "persuaded" the biscuit maker to agree to a 45-45 venture (with the remaining 10 per cent held by Nichimen Co., a trading firm) by threatening to disapprove use of such Nabisco brand names as Ritz, Oreo and Premium. There also were other conditions, including government approval of future plant expansions, limits on advertising, and restrictions on the company's market share, at least temporarily.

In KFC's case, the pressures were more subtle. For its initial Expo '70 store, KFC imported most of its chickens from the U.S. and Europe, but it soon ran afoul—no pun intended—of Japanese customs inspector who claimed the frozen birds had skin diseases. Also, the implication was, with so many plump Japanese chickens available for Col. Sanders' ovens, why did KFC need to import in the first place?

The company got the message and switched to Japanese chickens. Besides, KFC's partner, Mitsubishi, was in the chicken and chicken feed business, which was one reason KFC teamed up with it in the first place.

"The lucky company"

KFC's success has earned it the nickname of *tsuiteru kaisha*—"the lucky company." Indeed, Mr. Weston credits a combination of "lucky coincidences" and superstition with KFC's rapid acceptance in Japan.

"KFC's buildings are shaped like pagodas and our company colors are red and white—Japan's national colors, which stand for happiness," he says. "We usually try to open our new stores on one of the 12 lucky days in the Japanese calendar. Once. because three is a lucky number, we opened three stores on March 3—the third day of the third month."

Mr. Weston recalls that another time, when arriving for the opening of a new outlet, he discovered the door had been built in a different place than he had originally planned it. "It turned out," he says, "that a Chinese astrologer had told the owner's mother that unless we put the door where he suggested, the store would be unlucky. He may have been right, because it quickly became the highest volume unit in Japan."

Nabisco, on the other hand, attributes much of its good fortune to a savvy choice of partners. Distribution is a complicated business for any retail operation in Japan, but selection of Yamazaki gave the company access to some 35,000 "mom and pop" stores while Nichimen opened the way to supermarkets and other retail outlets.

Summarizes Mr. Wiggin: "As a joint venture, our early success can be attributed to working closely with our partners. We have used each others' know-how and experience to the benefit of all."

WHAZZIT?

GATT

The General Agreement on Tariff and Trade. This is an agreement signed in 1948 forming an organization of nations to establish a system of rules for controlling tariffs and reducing trade barriers.

TEA

The Trade Expansion Act of 1962. It was signed by President Kennedy and gave the President power to cut tariffs by 50% in negotiating new trade pacts during the five years after its inception.

KENNEDY ROUND OF TARIFF NEGOTIATIONS

The most sweeping reductions in tariffs were the result of negotiations involving more than fifty member nations of GATT. Under the power of the TEA, duties were cut on more than 60,000 items.

Careers In International Business

Many students think that a career in multinational business would be great. Travelling, living in Paris, meeting all sorts of interesting people -- these are attractions.

Is that what careers in multinational companies are like?

In some instances, yes. As in any organization, there are assignments that are attractive. But, then, to some people living overseas isn't all roses. There are language and cultural differences. Schools for children, inflation, taxes, and housing are all problems. And travelling can get old, too, after the bloom is off.

There are indeed multinational careerists who don't see their work as glamorous at all. Some, in fact, are stuck in another country without a "return ticket" and would like very much to land a comparable level job back in the United States.

The careers we are describing are those of U.S. Expatriates -- Americans representing American businesses in other countries. Such careers are rare and are becoming more rare as companies staff operations with local nationals or third country nationals. It is costly to maintain expatriates at an American standard of living. And in some countries their presence may be detrimental to the company's aims, regardless of expertise.

So what careers are open in multinational business? Overseas assignments are available. Below is described the opportunities offered by Bank of America in its World Banking Group.

Also, many stateside assignments can have international aspects -- whether in marketing, auditing, purchasing, manufacturing, advertising, personnel or other areas of business.

International business means an added dimension to your career. You may prepare yourself to take on international duties by learning necessary languages, by studying business conditions and concerns in other nations, and by expanding your personal understanding of international affairs through travel and contacts with persons in other countries.

Once equipped, you may make your interests known and a career may click. But you have to have a specialization: marketing, finance, etc. as well as being a well-rounded businessman.

WORLD BANKING

With more than 1,100 domestic and international offices, Bank of America offers multinational careers. Clients are served on a decentralized basis to assure responsiveness to their needs. So staff are placed in offices close to the clients they serve. This provides direct and simplified communications, a knowledge of the local environment, and an edge for Bank of America.

There are four major geographic divisions: Asia; Europe, Middle East and Africa; Latin America; and North America. Each is headquartered in its geographic area and includes a number of regional and branch offices, along with subsidiaries and affiliates, which serve local markets.

When you begin in world banking, you are assigned to the division into which you are hired. In practice, this means that those hired for the Latin America Division start in Latin America.

Beyond your first assignment, geographic mobility is basic to your career. Your development will be as a broad-based global banker will depend on a variety of experiences, probably in several different locations.

In addition to the career implications, travel can be immensely rewarding, culturally expanding, personal experience.

Your career will probably involve movement and more responsibility within the geographic division which you initially join.

Multinational Managers

The General Motors Overseas Operations division employs 180,000 people outside the United States. Only 300 of them are Americans.

The Dow Chemical Company, with 18,000 employes overseas, has 200 American "expatriates" in that force.

The Bendix Corporation, with 28,000 people working in its behalf outside the United States, has an average of 500 Americans who may be called upon to cover assignments abroad—often of short duration. Among the 500 persons, 46 are career executives who catch foreign assignments.

What these companies have in common is that they are prominent among American corporations whose business is increasingly multinational.

Furthermore, in expanding their activities abroad, they met their executive staff needs by hiring non-American managers.

Statistics on the number of Americans serving their companies overseas are hard to obtain. Consulting firms that make money by helping corporations find executives may tend to be generous in their estimates.

Thus, James A. Skidmore Jr., president of Handy Associates, recently placed the number of multinational managers abroad at 40,000-to-50,000.

John Farley, of Organization Resources Counselors, consulting firm, said that a survey of 176 multinational companies conducted in 1969 showed that they employed 20,600 American "expatriates," 9,800 third-country nationals and 1,353,000 host-country nationals.

Mr. Farley said that the changes in recent years did not show so much in the number of American expatriates serving multinational companies (a fact that seems to be borne out in part by the experiences of General Motors, Bendix and Dow), but in the different mix between expatriates and third-country nationals.

Citing his firm's findings, Mr. Farley said that in 1965 there were three United States expatriates for every third-country national at the management level of multinational companies. In 1967 the ratio dropped to 2.5 to one, and in 1969 to two to one.

Mr. Farley attributed the change to the high cost of posting Americans overseas. In addition, he said, increasingly third-country nationals have been given training for higher management functions.

Mr. Skidmore based his company's much higher estimates of United States managers abroad on the continued rapid growth of direct foreign investments by multinational concerns.

In this context he cited projections by the United States Department of Commerce, predicting that during 1971, these investments would have reached $15.3-billion. This would have represented an increase of 16 per cent over the 1970 total.

The investment had been pushed ahead, he said, because of the need for new markets, tougher competition and the slowdown in the United States economy from late 1969 through most of 1970.

Mr. Skidmore said that his company had found that American multinational companies tended to rely heavily on American managers in cases where a host country was beset by political instability. These companies also pay more to the managers of their foreign affiliates if the affiliates experience business difficulties, he continued.

There seems little difference of opinion between consulting firms and multinational corporations that a foreign assignment is not a deadend street.

Most managers going abroad are given specific time periods for their assignments, and a chance for advancement on their return.

"We consider a foreign assignment as part of a man's grooming period," one corporate executive said.

R. E. Lenon, the president and chief executive of the International Minerals and Chemical Corporation, acknowledged that the company had been using its Paris office as a training ground for top executives.

He said that the company's foreign sales manager, domestic sale chief and head of its industrial group spent various periods of time, but a minimum of 18 months, at the I.M.C. Paris office.

A spokesman for Dow Chemical commented: "The preponderance of men who have completed overseas assignments for Dow now hold jobs in the United States, which are substantially more responsible than the jobs they held in the United States before going overseas."

He said that there would always be some Americans abroad for Dow. However, the company believed that more and more foreigners would be competing for and winning top jobs in corporate management in the United States.

CONSIDER

CHALLENGES

1. Do you favor further reductions of trade barriers? Explain.

2. If you were a senator, how would you explain the law of comparative advantage to voters who are unemployed because of foreign competition?

3. How has Ford sought to expand its share of the international market? Is there a better way?

4. When does a country stop being an L.D.C.?

5. The U.S. imports vast quantities of rubber, oil, metals, lumber, and other material from LDCs. Does this mean the U.S. has an obligation to help these nations develop? Explain.

6. Does our nation's Balance of Payments proglem matter to you? Explain how it affects your life.

7. Why does a company become multinational?

8. Would it be best for an American company to hire Dutch or American personnel to run its operation in Amsterdam?

9. Can OPEC push its prices higher and higher? What are the limits?

10. What are the languages of multinational business? Should managers be fluent in languages other than English?

Some people deposit money in numbered bank accounts in Swiss banks. What impact does this have on our balance of payments? Why is this practice discouraged by our government?

You may have read that some LDCs have, on occasion, expropriated (taken over by government dictate) foreign-owned industries in their lands. Why do they do this? What impact does it have? Analyze a case of this type.

Look at your possessions and list those that are made in other countries. Analyze why you bought them rather than American-made goods.

Read a copy of the Economist, published in London and available in your library. Identify any areas in which business or economic attitudes are markedly different from your own. Are these due to cultural, economic, or other differences?

Obtain a one-pound note at a currency exchange. Try to spend it at local stores ($1.80 won't go far). Then explain why the stores are reluctant to accept valid foreign currency.

RECAP

International trade is a significant aspect of American business activity. It has, further, provided major impetus to our own economic growth in past decades.

The controversy that continues to rage is whether our enterprise system is better off operating in a free trade system, where supply and demand determine the fate of American and foreign goods, or in a protective trade environment, where government imposes trade restrictions such as trade quotas and tariffs on goods produced by competing companies in different countries. In this chapter we have examined the issues in this signficant controversy and the nature of trade and barriers that impede it.

Business has, of course, expanded significantly among the major countries of the world. Lesser developed countries have also shared in this growth, but not as much as they would generally like. We have seen how the challenges of international trade have fostered growth of participating economies.

One group of countries, the petroleum exporting countries, formed an organization to control the prices of their primary asset -- oil -- and to further their mutual interests. The result has been that this bloc is now a major force in our worldwide economic system.

A type of business firm has emerged that is truly international in its operations, management, and perspective. Today about 200 major corporations may be classified as multinational corporations. Of these, three fourths are American corporations. Multinational firms not only sell goods and services in other nations, but they may conduct all business functions -- manufacturing, financing, marketing, etc. -- in a number of nations. We expect to see more new multinational firms developing in the years ahead.

The United States used to be a leading supplier of natural resources and of high technology know-how. We used to export far more goods than we imported. Today, however, the tables are turned. We are importing more goods, both manufactured and raw material, than ever before. And the quantity exceeds our total exports. Thus our balance of trade with other nations is no longer favorable to us.

The balance of trade situation creates a particular problem for our economy because we end up owing money to other nations. Our balance of payments deficit is due, in large part, to the government's major expenditures for foreign aid and defense assistance. Tourist expenditures overseas also contribute to the problem. To bring our exchange into balance, we send dollars and government securities abroad. The large flow of these dollars and securities has caused the value or purchasing power of the dollar to decline abroad.

Ford Motor Company is one of our leading multinational corporations. As discussed in this chapter, it is successfully competing in Europe with automobiles produced there. The competition remains stiff, both at home and abroad, but international trade continues to be a large growth area for Ford.

1. What factors make OPEC strong as a cartel?

_____

2. Why don't we just close our borders and not import or export anything?

3. Why do American firms enter joint ventures with firms abroad, such as in Japan?

4. If you were "King", what actions would you take to bring about a more favorable balance of payments?

PART VI

PEOPLE IN BUSINESS

CHAPTER 18

Human Resources In Business

To manage an organization effectively, you must satisfy both the needs of the organization and of the individuals in it. You have to have motivated people to bring an organization to life. You have to manage people in such a way that they will be able to achieve their personal and organizational objectives simultaneously.

Too often, managers underestimate the abilities of individuals to manage their own work. Through management by objectives, organization development, the design of jobs, and other processes, management can provide a climate that supports and promotes individual motivation, while, at the same time, increases the organization's effectiveness.

Young men and women today are looking for freedom, responsibility, and recognition in their work. They insist on this sort of management philosophy and on work that tackles, in some way, our environmental and social ills.

The process of managing people -- managing human resources -- includes four key action areas: manpower planning, manpower development, organization development, and compensation.

Manpower planning ensures that the organization will have the talent it needs to achieve its objectives in the future. It involves forecasting the number and kinds of people it will need, and subsequently, the planning of action steps to be taken to meet those needs.

Manpower development assures opportunities for individual growth through work experiences and developmental activities. It also plays a vital role in assuring that the organization will have the types of people it needs to meet its objectives for the future. Manpower development includes both on-the-job development, training programs and tuition reimbursement plans. Companies in the United States spend billions of dollars each year on training for employees.

Organization development assures that the organization will respond effectively to changing conditions that affect working relationships of individuals and groups in the organization. It may involve changes in organization structure, job design, or the way people work together.

Compensation includes the various incentives and rewards for work given by a company -- wages or salaries, fringe benefits, and psychological benefits. Money is not everything, but it is what we think of when we mention compensation.

Attitudes towards work have changed in the last decade. Corporations have been forced to recognize the need for better management of their human resources. Major corporations do recognize that people are an important asset. In this chapter, we will discuss the four key action areas of human resource management as well as examples of how some corporations have responded to the changing needs of the organization and desires of their employees. Ford, for example, has extensive programs and a deep commitment to motivation, organizational change, and the key elements of human resource managment.

In This Chapter

Managing Human Resources

FOUR KEY AREAS

There are four key areas of management action in human resource management: manpower planning, manpower development, organization development, and compensation.

First, manpower planning refers to the rather difficult and often complex task of forecasting and planning for the right numbers and kinds of people to be at the right places at the right times to perform activities that will benefit both the organization and the individuals.

You might say that it has two basic elements: forecasting manpower needs in the organization and programming -- or planning of actions to satisfy these forecasted needs. Managers forecast future talent require- ments through analysis of operating budgets and plans and by looking ahead at career patterns of people already in the organization. How far in the future forecasts go depends on the type of business and the characteristics of the organization.

Manpower planning is important to a business

because talent is critical in building a business. It is important to individuals because it defines what opportunities will be available within a company.

The information gained from manpower planning is used to plan for recruitment and selection of new talent, assignment and promotion of individuals already in the company, and termination of others -- through retirement or dismissal. Thus, the result is a flow of talent in, up, over, and out of the organization. Conditions change and management helps them change in the best manner.

Human resource manage- ment concerns the respon- sibilities of managers for dealing effectively with individuals at all levels of an organization. Our overall aim in managing human resources is to utilize effectively talent on jobs appropriate to individual interests, abilities, aspirations, and the organization's needs.

That's the name of a pretty tough ball game. We have entered an age when human resources are the greatest investment of corporations. Yet competent, productive, and loyal individuals are felt to be rare. There are many pressures on management to utilize human talent more efficiently and effectively, but putting ideas and techniques into action is a difficult challenge.

In one sense, management of talent is up to indivi-

duals themselves. If you are to achieve your personal objectives, to get onto jobs you think you would like, and fully develop and tap your "hidden" talents, you have to carry the ball. No manager can run your career.

In this Chapter, we are examining what managers can do for you. At most, management can provide opportunities -- a climate in which you can "do your thing," develop your potential, and at the same time, make a contribution to the organiza- tion's objectives -- and profitability.

Manpower development is concerned with the improvement of individual skills and knowledge and changing individual attitudes related to work. People develop primarily through work itself -- growing through experience and through striving to achieve challenging objectives.

The core of manpower development, then, is really day-to-day management. described in the last chapter as management by objectives. It involves goal setting, coaching,

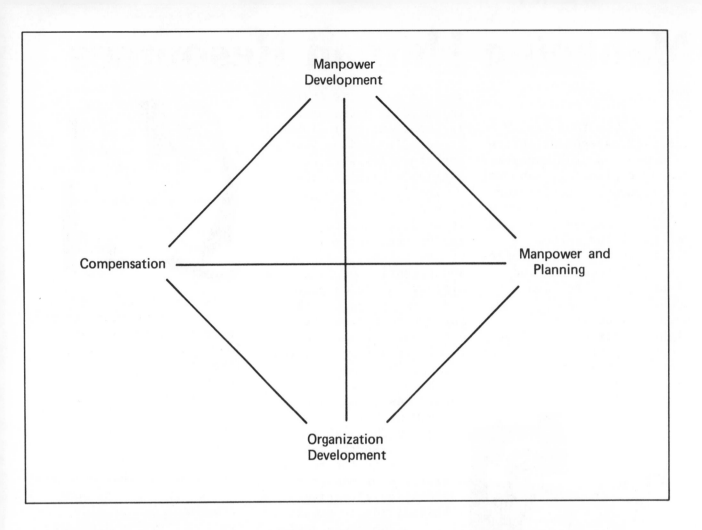

Manpower
Development

Compensation

Manpower and
Planning

Organization
Development

supplemental training and development activities, and appraisal of results. It can be extremely informal, or set up as a formal management system.

Where managers do not consciously or formally follow a management-by-objectives process, or where it is ingrained in the way managers manage, manpower development is viewed largely in terms of supplemntal developmental and training activities. Companies commonly provide specialized skills training programs and courses, supervisory and management training and development programs, cooperative education programs with schools and colleges, special

university programs, individual study and reading programs, temporary job assignments, task-force assignments, apprenticeships, internships and other means of building skills and knowledge and changing attitudes.

Normally, "training" refers to programs aimed at improving your present capabilities and performance; "development" refers to programs aimed at building capabilities for future responsibilities.

Would you believe that American business organizations spend more money on education of employees than is spent by all of the colleges and universities in the nation put together? It is true.

In fact, some companies actually have their own "universities", some complete with their own campuses. General Electric, IBM, and General Motors, for example, operate large facilities for training and development of their employees. In Chapter 19, a program sponsored by Bethlehem Steel will be described.

While manpower development (or management development when it is for managers) deals with individuals, companies are also concerned with development of entire organizations. Organization development includes all management efforts aimed at improving the working relationships of people in an organization. OD, as it is often called, is the process of bringing about change in the ways people work together. It includes personal change efforts, such as counseling and special types of training, and non-personal change efforts such as redesigning jobs or changing the organization structure.

Often, the term organization planning is used to refer to aspects of organization development that affect the structure of jobs and the organization itself. Traditionally, organization planning was concerned with keeping the organization charts up to date. Today, this task is considered minor compared with the task of modi-fying patterns of communications, work, and other behavior in organizations.

To be effective, of course, organization development efforts need to be linked with manpower development and manpower planning efforts.

The final element of human resource management is COMPENSATION. This is the process of recognizing individuals for performance and development. The key form of compensation is money -- particularly wages and salaries. But today we have a wide range of benefits, "fringe benefits," that supplement direct compensation. These may include paid medical and life insurance, retirement and pension plans, paid vacations and holidays, savings or thrift plans (in which the company kicks into your savings account), and even discounts on company products. Some companies offer stock options, bonuses, profit sharing, and other special compen-sation -- particularly for executives. Payments for fees and tuition for university courses may also be considered to be a form of compensation.

In a broader sense, job titles, office furnishings, cute secre-taries (or bosses), job freedom, and special privileges are all forms of compensation.

Motivation: Can Work Be Fun?

That may sound like a stupid question. Work and fun, we are led to believe, are incompatible. We work during the week in order to make a living so on weekends we can enjoy life. For many people, work brings only only tension, frustration, pressure, and weary bones.

It is not necessary that jobs be dull, boring, and routine in order to have a productive organization. Technology is not all that constraining in most cases.

Work can be fun -- and when it is fun, people often work harder to achieve objectives that are mutual. That is, work can be fun when it is aimed at personal and organizational goals that a person feels are important and meaningful.

Much of our evidence of business life today suggests that deeply and continually satisfying jobs are rare. Most of our business practices and jobs are designed to suit technology rather than the human needs of people who bring them to life.

Work can be fun when the manager tries to make personal and organizational goals compatible, narrowing the all-to-common gap between work and satisfaction. Total involvement on the job and maximum satisfaction from this productive involvement make work fun. Of course, it takes a heck of a manager to be able to pull this off. Motivating people is the toughest part -- and really the most important part -- of a manager's job.

To do the job, managers must provide for effective organization, career opportunities, performance and development goals and plans, and total compensation. All of this is based on a solid understanding of what makes people tick.

Ask yourself why you are willing to work for an organization (assuming you have had that opportunity) and you will probably think first of the pay check. If you are lucky, you may think about the work (which you enjoyed), the friends you have at work, or even the impact you made through your diligent efforts on the job.

Behavioral scientists generally agree that the factors that are most satisfying to people are freedom, responsibility, and recognition.

Regardless of how good the pay may be in an organization -- or the vacations, benefits, retirement plans, or the pastel paints that are supposed to make the place "homey," people simply will not be excited and enthusiastic about working there.

People want to do things that are meaningful -- to achieve something that they feel is important. By letting people manage their own work, we give them a chance to stretch their capacities and accomplish something -- and know it.

FREEDOM on the job means giving the individual enough elbow-room so that he/she can make decisions affecting his/her own work. It may mean fewer supervisors or less direct management of work activities. It may mean fewer rules and policy constraints, paperwork forms, approvals, and other controls. Simply, it is giving the person a chance to do what he can on his/her own.

RESPONSIBILITY on the job means holding the individual accountable for achieving mutually expected results. Notice the catch phrase here -- "mutually expected" -- this goes back to the MBO idea of setting objectives that an individual and his/her manager can agree are attainable and relevant. In large organizations, individual work becomes so lost in the morass of what everyone else is soing that no one can ever really identify what he is personally trying to accomplish. Even if he has freedom to act (authority, really), he also needs to know what he is trying to do and to be held accountable for doing it.

RECOGNITION for this performance may include any form of reward or satisfaction that is related to the work. Traditionally, the pay check has served as our primary form of work recognition. Perhaps this is because managers have not built satisfaction into the work itself or encouraged the social form of recognition -- rapid advancement and expansion of responsibility (and related status symbols) -- at the same rate as individuals have performed and developed.

Nude jobs are a particular motivation problem. They simply do not make for a great deal of commitment and enthusiasm. Over the years, companies have denuded jobs, stripping them of FREEDOM, RESPONSIBILITY, AND RECOGNITION. For maximum technical efficiency, industrial engineers have broken up jobs, reducing tasks to their simplest, most basic elements.

Henry Ford's early assembly line is an example of this "scientific" engineering of work. Through this extreme specialization, work became less interesting, meaningful, intellectually challenging, and -- in short -- LESS FUN.

Today, jobs are not always fantastic. In fact, many are downright dull. But many companies are rebuilding jobs, trying to make them more attractive to people.

At American Telephone and Telegraph (AT&T), for example, women employees in one department were plainly NOT having fun in their jobs. These persons, most of them college graduates, were hounded by supervisors and second-guessed in every step of the way in their handling of correspondence with stockholders. Management lifted the tight reins and let

the women write and sign
their own letters,
develop and use expertise
in problems that interested
them personally, and
assume responsibility for
their own work. The
result? Productivity
rose, turnover among the
employees dropped, and
satisfaction with their
jobs soared, all within
six months -- and
without any pay increases.

Similar results have
been experienced in
companies around the
world -- in Sears, TRW,
Texas Instruments,
Delta Airlines, Volvo
(in Sweden), and many
others. This is not
all a bunch of idealistic
puffery, either, It
can work -- in a practical,
down-to-earth business
context.

In managing people,
the idea is to stop
being "bosses" and "gate-
keepers" and "controllers."
People are not sheep.
Experience in applying
our behavioral science
knowledge has shown
that people can and will
manage their own work
if given the chance.
To "boss" people really
works against the
purposes of management --
to motivate individual
performance and growth
for the achievement of
personal and organiza-
tional objectives.

The whole idea of
decentralization in an
organization is to build
into management the
philosophy that behavioral
science suggests.
By delegating managerial
authority in an organiza-
tion we automatically
build freedom, respon-
sibility, and recognition
into jobs. It is often

essential, in fact,
that an organization
reflect this philosophy
if the desired results
are to be achieved.
An open, participative
climate is necessary
for managers to deal
effectively with their
subordinates.

CAREERS AND MOTIVATION

We have said we want
to utilize talents in
achieving objectives
in accordance with indi-
vidual interests, abilities,
aspirations, and the
organization's needs.
This means we have to
find out what people
really want and can
do. And that means we
have to have a good
deal of communications
-- about careers.

Individuals see their
jobs as steps in a
series of jobs which
comprise careers. When
you take your next job,
it is unlikely that you
will view it as the job
to end all jobs. Rather,
you will probably take
it because it appears
to meet your immediate
needs and also fits
your overall career
plan.

BASICS ABOUT MOTIVATION

In sum, we think we
understand what turns
us on in work, and thus,
what turns on other
people. Work is not
always fun, but with
effective management,

the chances are that it would be fun, or at least satisfying.

Managers must approach their responsibilities with the following basic assumptions well in mind:

1. Work is as natural as play or rest. Most people do not really dislike work. Depending on the conditions of work, including physical conditions, friends, supervision, and rewards, work may itself be a source of satisfaction. People may voluntarily perform work, just as they do for a club, charity, or around the house.

2. Control and punishment are not the only means of achieving objectives. Most people will work to achieve objectives with self-direction and self-control when these objectives are considered important and meaningful.

3. If achieving objectives leads to rewards, people will be committed to them. Satisfaction of personal needs may be achieved through work -- the achievement of organizational goals that people see as meaningful and relevant.

4. People learn not only to accept, but to seek responsibility. Avoidance of responsibility, lack of ambition, and emphasis on security are generally results of experience, not inherent human qualities.

5. Imagination, ingenuity, and creativity are widespread in an organization. These capacities are not held by an elite few. If given the opportunity, many people would show latent talents.

That's what motivation is all about. Believe it? Do it.

Job Monotony

"The trouble with kids today is they just don't want to work!"

Right on! Especially on dumb jobs.

Workers today are better educated, more sophisticated, and more capable of taking on bigger responsibilities. As a 31-year old assembly line worker said, "A revolution is starting now -- it has to come. Workers should have the right to decide who's going to do the job and how they're going to do it. The supervisor can tell them what to do, but not how to do it."

Past generations of workers have fought the speedup of work and hated dirty, menial, boring, or routine jobs. But they have accepted these conditions in their work, in part in fear of dreaded unemployment. The memory of the depression sticks.

But the new generation has different ideas. Job monotony is a critical issue in many companies, particularly where assembly lines and other "machinery oriented" work are the basis of jobs.

A United Auto Workers official commented, "Management has solved other problems. It can solve this one. It has a hell of a lot to lose if it doesn't."

Companies are taking the question of job monotony seriously. A variety of experiments have been conducted, exploring the idea that the way to get production is to stimulate the worker's interest rather than to expand the paycheck or to further simplify the job.

The following article describes several of these noteworthy attempts to upgrade undesirable jobs and to make work generally more attractive and satisfying.

"Frankly, I feel we can learn much from China: For example, restoring dignity to the concept of menial labor."

Wanted: Ways To Make Jobs Less Dull

Against a backdrop of dollar devaluation, soaring costs, and sluggish productivity, worker discontent in the factory and office has suddenly become something of a national issue. A decline in the will to work has been blamed for dulling the nation's competitive edge in world markets and frustrating consumers with products that are shoddily made and services that are arrogantly offered and grudgingly performed.

Worker discontent is basically nothing new. It has been around as long as work. Laborers who built the Pyramids staged a short-lived revolt—perhaps the first strike—over working conditions. Why should job dissatisfaction be so critical a problem now? Workers have the shortest week and the highest pay ever. Technology has eased or even eliminated much of the old manual work. Conditions of work, jealously supervised by unions, are the best ever. Yet increasing numbers of workers seem dissatisfied with their jobs—frustrated, alienated, apathetic, and poorly motivated. Pollsters find evidence of it; corporate managers say they see it in poor productivity, deteriorating quality of work, rebelliousness, growing use of drugs, even sabotage. Unions concede that it exists, though most labor leaders think it is exaggerated as a work factor. They see it as a mere symptom of society today.

Real or trumped up? Social scientists and politicians tend to feel that today's work dissatisfaction is genuine, brand-new, and an urgent problem. Along with labor chiefs, some top executives question its uniqueness to our times.

The academics see a parallel between the surge of worker dissatisfaction and the spread of dissension on college campuses, in the church, in the armed services, and elsewhere. Discontent, they say, has intensified as a reflection of contemporary society's mood.

The social scientists are getting support in Washington to try to do something about it. The National Commission on Productivity wants to launch experiments on ways to humanize work—a "Quality of Work Program." Senator Edward M. Kennedy (D-Mass.) has introduced a bill to authorize the Health, Education & Welfare Dept. and the Labor Dept. to study the real extent of worker discontent. Among other things, the two departments would be expected to measure the costs of absenteeism, turnover, sabotage, and productivity losses. Last year, a HEW report on "Work in America, prepared under the auspices of the W. E. Upjohn Institute for Employment Research, fueled vigorous debate over worker alienation. It bluntly called for redesign of jobs to increase productivity and improve the quality of life for "millions of Americans at all occupational levels."

Labor historian Thomas R. Brooks delivered one of the sharpest criticisms of the HEW report and of "radical-chic academics and pop sociologists." Says Brooks: "I detect an underlying contempt for working people and a scorn for their unions, as well as the creation of a new myth and a new conventional wisdom."

Businessmen, too, weighed in with denial of HEW's thesis. James D. Hodgson, former Labor Secretary and now a vice-president at Lockheed Aircraft Corp., scoffs at efforts to make job discontent "a contemporary phenomenon." Malcolm L. Denise, Ford Motor Co.'s vice-president for labor relations, calls the issue "a creation of the pundits."

Chairman Richard C. Gerstenberg of General Motors Corp. takes a more pragmatic view of the job enrichment movement. The "plight" of the worker in the auto industry, and other industries, has been "magnified by political leaders, union officials, and social critics," he says. But he adds that it would be "unwise of us to rationalize inaction merely because the case has been overstated." GM signaled its awareness of the problem when it hired Stephen H. Fuller,

Sal Barracca

a Harvard Business School professor of organizational behavior, a year ago last November to find answers in worker motivation (page 140).

With its high rate of absenteeism and its frequent callbacks of defective cars, the auto industry has become a focal point of debate over worker alienation. The auto assembly line epitomizes the idea of reducing work to simple, repetitive tasks, performed under rigorous, continuous supervision. Such an approach, says the HEW report, can lead only to alienation of human labor.

Thus, last year's strike at GM's Lordstown (Ohio) plant became a *cause célèbre*. The plant, built to produce GM's Vega at a rate of 100 per hour, is a showcase of assembly line efficiency. Young labor leaders said Lordstown was struck because workers felt that their jobs were inhumanly dull and the pressure too high.

Ammunition for both sides. Behavioral scientists seized on this explanation as support for the point they were making: that breaking work down into simple, repetitive tasks is anachronistic. The technique worked when it was introduced at the turn of the century, because the work force then was largely immigrants with only a grade school education. Now workers are mostly second- or third-generation Americans who average better than a high school education. They will not settle for the way things used to be.

GM officials deny the widespread impression that Lordstown represented a revolt by a new breed of younger, more sophisticated worker against the monotony and pressure of the assembly line. They contend that the strike really was over work standards stemming from the consolidation of two GM arms, Fisher Body Div. and the GM Assembly Div., and the subsequent merging of two union locals.

In Detroit, United Auto Workers officials say that the real issue was the layoff of 700 workers—GM says 400—with no significant drop in assembly-line speed. That amounted to more work at the same pay, they say, and when GM agreed to slow the assembly line, workers returned.

Whatever triggered the trouble at Lordstown, it gave the 30-year-old president of the UAW local there a chance to have his say. "The attitude of young people," he said, "is going to compel management to make jobs more desirable in the workplace and to fulfill the needs of man."

Schools of thought. In an attempt to carry out this purpose, several companies have turned to the behavioral scientists for help through such techniques as job enrichment and organizational development. The concepts are broad and flexible, yet entrenched attitudes of both managers and workers make them difficult to apply to the work situation.

Psychologist Frederick Herzberg, now a professor of management at the University of Utah, advanced the job enrichment theory in the late 1950s. His idea: Satisfaction and motivation of the worker can be provided by systematically giving him greater responsibility, autonomy, and feedback on his performance.

Organizational development takes a slightly different tack. It is a structured way of fostering communication between worker and supervisor. Groups of employees informally hash over problems, propose solutions, and set mutual objectives with their supervisors. As the theory goes, each will see the other's side more clearly.

In the phone system. One of the first big companies to redesign jobs was AT&T, which began in 1964. Robert Ford, personnel director for manpower utilization, says: "We had to start by finding out what was wrong with existing jobs. The second step was to organize new jobs. The third step, which we started within the last year, is to design new equipment and the jobs required to operate it."

Ford's department is working wth Bell Labs in design of equipment to be used in the 1980s. The goal is to tailor jobs to the new equipment so the workers feel that they are giving a service and are "in charge." Says Ford: "With the more technologically advanced equipment, we have to avoid making the worker feel he is only a machine tender. If we don't, I can guarantee we will have unhappy people. We'll have another of those dumb-dumb jobs."

AT&T may be deeper into job redesign than any other company so far, but an increasing number of companies are experimenting with the idea, including A. B. Dick, Bankers Trust, Corning Glass, General Foods, IBM, Motorola, Polaroid, Prudential, TRW, and Western Union.

Some skepticism. Not all behavioral scientists are convinced that these experiments are the whole answer, despite their evidence of improved morale. Dr. David Sirota, an associate professor of management at the University of Pennsylvania's Wharton School, for example, thinks management will have to probe deeper into the meaning of work to individuals before basic answers to alienation are found. He does not doubt that redesigning jobs has value—he spent 12 years supervising job enrichment programs at IBM—but he is disturbed when managers seize upon it as a panacea for productivity problems. And he is very annoyed that consultants prescribe it indiscriminately. "Selling job enrichment like soap is bound to create a high failure rate," states Sirota.

Industrial engineer Mitchell Fein is more skeptical. "If job redesign is so wonderful, why have no major unions asked for it?" he asks. "Workers are not stupid. They're not bashful. They'll strike for more money—why not for job enrichment? And if bosses saw any mileage in job enrichment, they'd all be doing it."

Fein does not doubt that many workers are "turned off" by highly routinized jobs. But, he asks, "To what extent is dissatisfaction caused by the work or by insufficient pay? Is it possible they might have a greater interest in the work if their living standards were raised and they could see their jobs as contributing to a good life?"

In the long run. Social scientists argue that more pay might produce a brief spurt in job satisfaction but is no long-term answer to the problem. Employees at all levels are saying that they will not accept management's manipulative tactics, says Harry Levinson, president of the Levinson Institute in Cambridge, Mass., and a former visiting professor at the Harvard B-school. "People are willing to put up with a lot when they have no other choice, or a very limited one," he says. Today, when that is not the case, techniques such as job enrichment, worker teams, and participative management will only provide temporary relief, Levinson says.

"The real issue is whether you paste these new techniques on questionable assumptions about people, or do you step back and ask what's really going on?" he says.

As the Labor Dept.'s Neal Herrick, a key member of the task force that wrote the HEW report, sees it, managers must look dispassionately for the key to effective productivity. Says Herrick: "What we have to look at, despite the people who say worker discontent is the creation of pop sociologists, is the gap between what satisfaction from the job is and what it might be. How much could people benefit if changes were made in the way work is structured? How much would productivity improve?"

The 'Humanistic' Way of Managing People

Saga finds it pays off in improved employee morale and productivity

The 17-acre headquarters site of Saga Administrative Corp. resembles a country club more than an office complex. Oak trees rise through redwood decks, halls are lined with oriental carpets and modern art, and badminton courts and barbecue pits abound. Explains Saga Chairman W. Price Laughlin: "The feeling of belonging to a good organization is important."

At Saga, a Menlo Park (Calif.) institutional feeding contractor, that feeling of belonging is carried far enough to make it a most unorthodox company. It pays employees to attend special meetings where they meet their bosses, its board members and clerks call each other by their first names, and Laughlin sends cartoon books and philosophical tracts to employees.

This offbeat corporate behavior reflects Saga's application of "organization development"—one of the latest buzzwords in management science. The OD concept holds that organizational change can be made simply by improving the way people work together. In essence, this means allowing employees a larger voice in how they do their jobs and assuring that management does not treat employees as impersonal and interchangeable cogs in a machine.

But the application of this seemingly obvious and simple principle is fraught with complications. It frequently involves the sensitive task of changing basic attitudes of both supervisor and subordinates. It requires a delicate balance to maintain the supervisor's authority without stifling the subordinate's incentives.

Saga is not unique in trying OD. Other OD practitioners include TRW Systems, Polaroid, Union Carbide, and the U.S. Navy. Nor is the interest confined to the U.S. Executives from Royal Dutch/Shell Group and J. Lyons & Co., Ltd., of England have visited Saga to study its ways.

Team building. The theory at Saga, explains William Crockett, a former Under Secretary of State who joined the company in 1968 as vice-president for human relations, is that employees will do a better job for the company and its customers if they are enthusiastic about their work. The byproducts should be increased productivity and greater security for employees, permitting them to disagree with their boss without fear of reprisal.

Saga has stressed a facet of OD theory called "team building." This involves grouping a supervisor at any level with his subordinates into a team, usually 6 to 12 people. At Saga, for example, a food service manager at a campus and his staff make up a team.

"Every person is involved in two teams," says Crockett, "one with his boss and one with his subordinates. In most organizations you get feedback only from your boss. In our groups, it works both ways. The concept of boss is to find the needs of one's subordinates and serve them." Laughlin calls the approach "humanistic management," and contends that it "must ultimately be the total way of corporate life."

Identity crisis. Saga was founded in 1947 when Laughlin and two Hobart College classmates took over the failing campus cafeteria. The company now has 23,000 employees serving 238-million meals a year. It is a major factor in the college contract feeding business with contracts at 270 colleges in 48 states. It also manages food programs for 164 hospital and industrial clients. Since 1969, Saga has diversified and now runs two restaurant chains and 140 pizza parlors.

In the past 12 years, Saga's revenues have increased 15 times to $180-million, its earnings 25 times to $5-million. But this rapid growth has been accompanied by problems. Says Sherman A. Moore, a divisional president: "When we were a small company with 22 employees, it was easier to convey our spirit and management style."

By 1967, says Moore, the company was plagued by high employee turnover. Visiting Saga's operations, he encountered "grousing" from employees who said that Saga had become a bureaucracy clogged with red tape.

Moore and Laughlin, who were familiar with behavioral science techniques in management, decided that the team-building facet of OD might recapture the informality of a small business characteristic of Saga's early days. The technique started at the vice-president level and was gradually expanded to include the college cafeteria

'The concept of boss is to find the subordinate's needs and serve them'

managers and salad tossers. It is an ongoing process in which management fosters an open expression of attitudes. It winds up each year in a one-day, team-building session away from the work location to thrash out problems.

How it works. In the past year, Crockett, who was once director of executive resources at IBM World Trade Corp., and his six full-time "facilitators" (group leaders) have held 225 such sessions. One was held last month at a hotel a few miles from Saga's headquarters. Attending the 10-hour session—the

Moore and Laughlin: Headquarters resembles a country club more than an office complex.

Robert A. Isaacs

group's second—were nine female clerks and supervisors, their department manager, and a group leader.

The group leader asked the participants to give their objectives for the session. After an OD film was shown, a clerk said she needed "to be accepted by the group." The manager responded, "I've got a need to belong, too. I try to make people feel they are working with me rather than for me."

Rating sheets on how the group functioned as a team were filled out, and "feeling charts" were prepared on which members drew their relationships with colleagues. One clerk drew a tree topped by three coconuts labeled with the supervisors' names. "I think you are like coconuts—set high up and hard to get at," she said. A secretary told the manager she disliked his reading letters on her desk. "Seriously," he answered, "the next time it happens, slap my hand."

Although the costs and benefits of Saga's OD program are not measurable, Laughlin claims that the economics are very sound. "Profitability is borne out by increased productivity," he says.

Saga's open management style goes beyond team building. There is an element of participative management, too. Laughlin bombards the staff with appropriate memos. He has sent out a piece on Jefferson's concept of man, 1,500 Peanuts books, and John Gardner's *Self-Renewal*.

The results. One major objective of Saga's effort is to encourage innovation at all levels. Laughlin was pleased, for example, when a campus food service manager veered away from Saga's 75 prescribed meals and served hamburgers and hot dogs. This solved two problems: overcrowding at the full-service counter and excessive costs.

Notes Laughlin: "Remember, we are primarily businessmen. We believe in

management by objectives. We take a systems-result-oriented approach, and OD is just another tool in our box. Business can't work on sensitivity alone."

Saga's employee turnover rate has been reduced to 19%, compared with 34% for its industry. Saga executives are also delighted to see employees who have quit the company return. One who did so is Chuck David, who left his manager's post at the University of Pittsburgh. After working for two other food service companies, he rejoined Saga with a $2,500 cut in pay. "I wanted to be with a company I could respect," says David.

A crucial question is whether Saga's brand of OD can be applied to other companies and other industries. Says Harold J. Leavitt, a Stanford B-school professor: "Lots of organizations could benefit, but it's not the panacea. Bringing in team building is not like bringing in a new computer."

(AN ACTUAL COMPANY MEMO)

```
To:        All Employees

Subject:   Use of Vending Machines

Vending machines are located near work areas for the convenience of our
employees.  However, because it is necessary to reduce non-productive
time to a minimum, I am asking for the cooperation of all employees in
voluntarily refraining from using these machines at the following times:

    For one hour after the beginning of their shift and for
    one hour prior to the end of their shift.

    For thirty minutes prior to and following lunch period
    and rest breaks, as applicable.

Employees must not abuse the use of vending machines.  They should, for
example, return to their work area immediately after making their pur-
chases and not loiter or gather in vending machine areas.

Supervision in each department should call any abuse of this privilege to
the attention of the individual for correction.
```

Changing Organizations

It takes a changing organization to deal with a changing environment. As markets shift, technology advances, social attitudes and values take new directions, and other economic, social, and political conditions change, organizations have to change, too. In large part, the prosperity of a business organization is dependent on management's ability to keep the company in tune with the times.

Within an organization, people often resist changes in job relationships, job responsibilities, policies, and other aspects of work. We all tend to develop patterns in our work and our organizational relationships to which we become accustomed. A changing organization encourages individual receptiveness to change -- and overcomes resistance to change through the free and open exchange of information and through individual involvement in management planning for the changes themselves.

Remeber the story of Tiffany's? This small business prospered largely because it seized opportunities to change and grow, making it a large, profitable enterprise. It changed locations, its staffing, its basic organizatiion structure, and its product line in response to changing customer needs. At the same time, the firm's basic goals and philosophy (quality goods and service) remained constant -- and proved to be relevant over the years.

Similarly, Sears succeeded in large measure because the company seized its opportunities to expand. It changed its organization, its facilities, and its marketing approaches after World War II, while its competitors did not. This capacity to change propelled Sears to the forefront of its field.

An organization may follow two general strategies in managing change: GROWTH and DEVELOPMENT. Through growth, a company may expand the scale of its activities, diversity its lines of products and services, and otherwise nurture the company's evolution. Through development, a company adapts the ways that employees and managers work together in achieving objecitves. Interpersonal, intergroup, and inter-organizational communications and cooperation are strengthened through organization development.

ORGANIZATIONS GROW

Like people, organizations grow, changing as they mature and develop. They may go through different stages, or phases of life cycles, much like economic cycles, as follows:

ESTABLISHMENT -- a period of cautious, generally personal management aimed at assuring the organization's survival.

GROWTH -- a period of rapid expansion in sales, assets, employment, market share, or other important qualities of the firm that mark achievement.

MATURITY -- a period of rational, institutional management of the organization, which by now is generally large and complex.

When we talk about changing organizations we often like to think in terms of the growth phase of an organization's life. Of course, that's okay because we also like to prolong this phase as long as we can -- just as we emphasize youth throughout human lives.

When an organization is growing, changing conditions compel attention to the needs of people. Managers have to help people to changing conditions of work. Organizational relationships, individual responsibilities, managerial styles, the objectives that are seen as important, and just about everything else seems to go topsy turvy when a company is growing rapidly.

Growing pains may be severe if managers are not responsive to these needs. Even in young, generally small (Stage I) and mature (Stage III) business organizations, the need for sensitive, responsive management is very important.

WHAT CAN MANAGERS DO

First of all, managers throughout an organization may look for signs of growing pains or indications of conditions that call for management action. They may change the organization structure, drawing new lines around jobs and among jobs and departments as they see fit. They may reshape jobs to ease tensions in work and increase individual motivation. They may change the policies that influence work -- changing past decisions that do not seem to work anymore.

When a manager looks for opportunities to improve the functioning of his organization, he is acting as a CHANGE AGENT. Every manager should be a change agent as a basic part of his or her job.

In some instances, individual managers become so involved in the ways that the firm is organized and managed that they do not want to change anything. The seven most dangerous words in management are often said to be "We've always done it this way before." Founders of companies are notorious for holding back major changes in managerial style or strategy (such as Henry Ford).

In such cases, one way to get the organization moving is to bring in new top managers (such as Henry Ford II and his Whiz Kids). The new managers act as change agents. Changes in governmental administrations after an election are another example of the major organizational changes that may result from new leadership.

New managers are generally free to make major organizational changes, changes in organizational objectives and strategy, and leadership at lower levels. New leadership often is enough to swing a "mature" organization back into a period of dynamic growth.

TRAINING

Another way of changing an organization is through training -- changing the attitudes and interpersonal relationships of individuals in the organization. Any kind of training may have such an effect, such as a secretary who goes back to school or a training course and becomes a stenographic whiz. Other secretaries then either admire her and follow her fine example -- or they hate her and disrupt the organization. The impact of training depends on how it is handled.

There are special kinds of training aimed directly at organization develop. Through group discussions, sometimes called T-groups (training groups), individuals from an organization or a number of different organizations may increase their sensitivity to each other, to their own behavior, and to key types of organizational problems.

All too often, there is simply no effect of training upon the organization. People may be "all fired up" while at the training program, but "cool off" when they get back to work -- and the realities of normal routines.

Changing organizations is not easy.

What does it take for effective organization development?

1. Pressure from changing conditions -- from within the organization or from its environment.

2. Sensitivity to these changing conditions and the need for adaptation to them.

3. In-depth diagnosis of organizational ills and needs for change.

4. Leadership of change by some "rascal" or change agent, a manager or a consultant.

5. Participation by individuals from all parts of the organization affected, including close collaboration among managers and staff specialists.

6. A willingness among the people involved to try something new -- an openness to change.

7. A willingness to face the facts of the situation and to invest the time and resources needed to bring about effective organizational change.

8. Meaningful recognition of individual efforts in the process of bringing about change, including rewarding individuals for short-term results.

On The Usefulness of Organizational Rascals

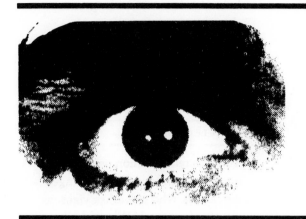

Are rascals — the "kooks", the unusual, even the dangerous — important additions to the ranks of modern organizations?

It is common place and true that we live in a world of change. Organizations, particularly economic ones, are the major vehicle for initiating and supporting most of the significant changes in our society. Yet, paradoxically, organizations as we know them today are among the most conservative and stable of society's elements. As the bureaucratic form has become widespread and coupled with a corps of "professional" managers, organizations themselves have become one of the most resistant of structures. Yet society's dependence, even need for change, is tied to the capacity of organizations to change themselves. Now it is apparent that organizations will change given some minimal capacity when some stimulus for change exists. Such stimuli are either external, as in a competitive market, altered legislation, or the person of a consultant, and so on, or "internal". To date, internal sources of stimuli have been relatively neglected, with the result that those that are designed into an organization·tend to be well controlled or simply lack much punch. Needed, I am arguing, are members whose personality and role set them apart from others and who furnish a source of constant stimulation for organizational development and change.

THE PARADOX OF CHANGE FOR ORGANIZATIONS

Most of the key issues for today's executives revolve around the intelligent promotion and management of change. Scientific, technological, and social advances are legion, yet the means to efficiently, economically, and justly utilize them continue to obstruct progress. The major means for utilization is the organization, that crucible of multiple resources that orders and patterns individual as well as societal existence. I suggest that a lot of the difficulty in living with change today is simply that organizations themselves have become dysfunctionally resistant to internal adaption; that is, they do not operate as effectively as they might in the initiation, transmission, or enhancement of change because they themselves are relatively unchangeable. Organizations are caught in a dilemma: to achieve efficiencies and economies with large scale and complex components requires stable, standardized structures and quite a lot of internal controls, yet to foster innovation, acquire growth, diversity, or renewal requires structural adaptiveness and flexibility of organization.

The internal environments of modern, large organizations (the prevalent type, to be sure) are rampant with mechanisms which result in an overriding conformity and acquiescence on the part of their staffs. I refer to mechanisms such as policies, procedures and rules, budgets, appraisal systems, supervisory practices — the host of control devices referred to as "channels and red tape." Management itself is becoming more and more highly trained, to the point where we have idealized the professional manager as someone well adapted, "cool," with technical competence — an "organization man" no less. What this means of course is that management is becoming relatively obedient, passive, and reactive. While these trends occur, we, perhaps subconsciously knowing better, decry the disappearance of risk takers, power and achievement-driven men. To recapitulate: training, formal and informal, operates to constrict freedom of thought and action, to reduce the variety of persons, and to reduce individual autonomy. Hence organizations are peopled more and more with "commissars," whose mission is to insure conormity to existing ways, to the image that is current.

OF IMAGES AND CHANGE STRATEGIES

The emphasis on internal conformity and the dilemma that puts organizations in vis-a-vis the management of change has alarmed thoughtful practitioners and observers for some time. Efforts at offsetting or otherwise altering the situation have been fostered; they are roughly of two types: altering the executive's image of himself (and hopefully altering his practice) and devising and incorporating into organizations a variety of non-personal change strategies.

Several new images of the executive are being promulgated to counteract the comissar one. Worthy of note are the efforts at bringing formerly secondary aspects of the executive role to the front and of highlighting them as the major functions for the future. One line of reasoning is as follows: human resources are the critical organizational resources, especially those loosely referred to as leadership. The development of executive leadership, therefore, is crucial and one of the primary responsibilities of incumbent executives. Thus an image of the executive as teacher follows. A somewhat complementary image is promoted by C. West Churchman:

. . . in the future management will have to become research minded. Good management of the future will have to rely on a sound research base. We are beginning to realize that we shall not be able to solve all the problems of organizational planning for at least several centuries, if ever. The problems are too big for a blueprint theory. This means

that the successful manager will have to view his job as not only to earn money, i.e., to maximize profit, but also to learn more about how his organization and the environment function. The successful manager will have to consider himself a researcher . . .

Paralleling the reorientation of the executive's image of himself have been numerous advancements in implementing change in organizations through strategies other than affecting the personnel. Here efforts at altering the nature or combination of tasks, (e.g., job enlargement) the revamping of technology, (e.g., computerization), and the modification of structure (e.g., project and matrix organizations, have been focused upon. These strategies of course exploit our preferences for dealing with ideas or things rather than with

people (which would mean ourselves).

Let me be clear that new images and new change strategies are useful and no doubt needed. My argument is that they may be necessary but not sufficient for the production of viable internal organizational changes. It appears as if these developments function best to support and develop change, not to continuously prompt it.

A CYCLE OF RENEWAL

To focus our attention once again on the stimuli for internal change, we can ask who unleashes vigorous efforts of renewal? Where do the sparks inciting change come from?

If we examine social units over time, whether persons, groups, or organizations, we can discern them moving through a cycle of renewal. Typically the first phase of the cycle represents some sort of relative equilibrium, a time when habits have taken over. Organizational members then are prone to experience staleness and various sorts of impasses. After a while a second phase begins, this one characterized by spreading monotony and boredom. Sometimes it slips unretrievably, deepening for some members into frustration or even despair. This second phase, if interrupted in time, then becomes a fertile ground for the third phase —the insemination of a new focus, usually in the form of an invitation or challenge. This focus sparks the ambitious, talented, or progressive organization members, provoking a fascination, calling forth their energies and competencies. When a sufficient fascination exists, the fourth phase occurs. Here the whole organization's resources are tapped, mobilized, and channeled in a wide-spread change program, one that produces programs, structures, and practices that transcend previous ones. The concrete manifestation of these phases are familiar enough. However, we have tended to see the first and second phases, as well as the focus of the third, most often as "problems", not viewing them as natural events. Also we tend to perceive mostly external or formally instigated problems. Assured that these will go on occurring, our attention returns to the issue of internal stimuli.

BEYOND COMMISSARS TOWARD CATALYSTS

I propose that large, complex, modern organizations badly need to make a deliberate, calculated investment in a form of human resource that can offset or counteract the complacency and conservatism of trained professional managers and the multiple formal and informal forces which pressure for conformity. If we, in the natural cycle of renewal, require from time to time foci which stimulate, fascinate, "turn us on", why not intentionally spice our organizations with persons capable of this? Let me put this melodramatically: we need "specialists" who, when the organizational doldrums set in, would create dissatisfaction, shatter our rigidities, even foster subversion. Useful, I argue, are persons known to be rogues, gurus, authenticators, and entrepreneurs Mark II! Perhaps it would be useful to briefly indicate what each of these roles is.

A ROGUE is a free-roving adventurer, often manifesting a streak of lawlessness. He tends to operate outside of contemporary structures, violating on occasion the old boundaries of time, place,

conscience, and probability. The rogue, as one of his advocates has noted, is "the man of many devices, constantly exploring, probing the environment — learning". Little appreciated is the rogue's frequent use of the frontiers of technology and other innovation in his struggles against being swept up in the establishment.

AN AUTHENTICATOR is the person who values candidness and truth, who is unafraid to "say it like it is". He relishes being "connected or engaged" with others, but doesn't hold back his feelings toward or reactions to these others. He often is embarrassing to ordinary folk, for he is self-disclosing, often very much in tune to the pattern and flow of sentiment, and passionately seeking greater awareness. The authenticator in a word is transparent.

THE ENTREPRENEUR MARK II is Professor H. J. Leavitt's label for a white-hatted entrepreneur, not the shady, corrupt kind, rather a promoter, operator, developer, man with connections. He is, to be sure, usually self-centered and biased toward expediencey. His specialty is getting people to swallow things — anything, searching relentlessly for new angles, new openings, new opportunities, for new "marriages". While his activities are often looked down upon, they are often surprisingly socially functional, for the entrepreneur Mark II is primarily the archetype of a bridge builder or mediator, whether between society and technology or science or knowledge. He is the out-and-out highly charged promoter.

GURUS are persons who live with vividness and serenity, un-

fettered by the "games people play". The guru experiences more and more fully than normal individuals. He is in touch with himself in all dimensions; enlightenment from himself and liberation from himself and his culture exemplify him. Gurus invite others to full experiencing of self and worldly things without becoming captive of either.

Each one of these rascals has the quality to provide fascination for the rest of us. When we, or our organizations need, in the cycle of renewal, stimulation, encountering or confronting these roles can "turn us on". Clearly they pose invitation or challenge by just being there. When stale, bored, or frustrated, encountering a rogue, authenticator, entrepreneur Mark II, or a guru charges us to either be different from or like them in some way. Often their very presence is encouraging; we feel that becoming more than we are, or different than we are, is once again possible. They, by example or directly, encourage us to stretch our imaginations and create discontent with the status quo in ourselves and our situations. They sometimes simply confirm our humanness, rekindling aspirations and fostering independence. At minimum these anti-commissars spark curiousity or produce wonder in us. In short when we most need it, they provide the stimulus to "get with it" or at least to re-examine.

Traditionally, of course, society as well as organizations isolate, negatively sanction, disenfranchise, damn, and otherwise attempt to drive out these roles. They are potentially potent foes of the familiar, and we so far have unquestionably feared they might corrupt, breed dissent, tempt us from the status quo. This is all so, but to put it positively, these four roles can help free us from the pressures of social conformity, strengthen our individual autonomies, and promote engagement with the normally unthinkable, unlovable, unfeelingable.

The existence of rascals will have many consequences, only some of which can be hinted at here. The patterns of sponsorship and the practices of personnel counseling will have to be altered as well as to take seriously the notions of organizational and professional allegiance as opposed to only organizational loyalty. Re-warding rascals will be tricky, perhaps management will be prompted to become more conscious of non-formal rewards. Consciously counter-balancing rascals with conservatives will be another consequence. Protecting rascals will probably require the wider use of mechanisms not widespread today, such as appraisal by top management in addition to immediate supervision and more extensive motivational practices. Clearly the various team approaches to management would less likely suppress the existence of rascals.

CONCLUDING COMMENT

In this paper I have suggested that the roles of guru, rogue, entre-preneur Mark II, and authenticator be incorporated, protected, and rewarded. The argument has been that vital, self-renewing organizations require internal as well as external sources of stimulus in the cycle of renewal, that the four roles elaborated are functional as internal stimulus sources, and hence their existence should not be left to chance. While the impact of these four roles can be thwarted or nullified, recent developments in the executive image, in organization forms, and above all in the personal and interpersonal change mechanisms such as sensitivity training, suggest organizations are now ready to tolerate and even exploit these organizationally uncommon persons.

The Ford Story

PEOPLE—THE KEY

Organization Planning

Organization planning is concerned with providing a corporate organizational structure which facilitates the attainment of Company objectives on a world-wide basis. This involves identifying and grouping the work to be performed, assigning responsibility and delegating authority for performing this work, as well as establishing relationships that assist people in working together effectively.

In Ford's line-and-staff structure, line management is assigned responsibility and authority for operating matters wherever practicable, although staffs are responsible for performing certain centralized functions in the interests of economy or efficiency. Staffs also provide advice and assistance to line management, particularly with respect to long-range plans and major Company policies and programs.

Organization planning is a continuous process. If the Company is to adapt to new technology, product diversification and the changing environment, as well as to continue to grow and improve its performance, the organizational structure cannot remain static. It must respond to new situations and constantly strive to obtain maximum utilization of management strengths and abilities. This evolution is the key to continued progress.

Management Personnel Planning

The essence of management personnel planning is to provide enough properly trained people at the time they are required to fill key positions in the Company. The term "management personnel" has many interpretations. At Ford Motor Company it means salaried employes — supervisory and professional — who make the day-to-day decisions required for the successful operation of the business.

Although the development of these people is fundamentally the individual responsibility of each supervisor, the management personnel planning department is responsible for coordinating the Company's over-all management development effort. This department develops, recommends and administers policies and procedures affecting placement and utilization of people in key positions throughout the Company. It assists in developing an environment in which individuals with promising talent can be recognized early and given appropriate opportunities for development. It also provides supervisory personnel with a set of common ground rules for assessing the progress of their employes. Each staff and division, however, retains responsibility for ensuring that its local management personnel needs are met.

Manpower planning consists of analyzing and projecting the size and composition of the workforce. It provides a basis for the development of programs to meet projected hiring requirements and changes in workforce composition and for improving the utilization of present employes. Many of these studies are used in developing placement policies and practices. Two examples of recent studies are a three-year, computerized manpower forecast and a study of production supervision.

Education and Training

Education and training activities are designed to enable employes to develop their abilities throughout their careers with Ford. Two approaches are utilized to achieve this goal: assigning primary responsibility to supervisory personnel for the development of their subordinates; making available formal Company training programs through individual plant and division training components.

Since it is natural for an employe to learn and grow in the course of job performance, the supervisor who assigns the work is in a unique position to encourage this growth. To do his job well, the supervisor must maintain an atmosphere conducive to development. He accomplishes this by assigning work that will enable his employes both to reinforce previous learning experiences and to gain additional knowledge in new areas. The supervisor also encourages participation in appropriate formal education and training programs.

Consistent with the policy of decentralization, each division and staff is responsible for determining its own education and training needs, developing or obtaining necessary materials, administering programs and for evaluating results.

The Staff education and training department, however, is responsible for total corporate training. This department assists management in developing education and training policies and programs. It provides advice and assistance to all Company components involved in training. It has continuing responsibility for evaluating the effectiveness of new training materials, programs and techniques. In addition, it develops and evaluates experimental training programs.

Equal Employment Opportunity

The Company has long had a policy of nondiscrimination in employment. The function of the equal employment opportunity activity is to ensure continued affirmative action toward meeting the Company's objectives in this area and to assist management in providing governmental agencies with statistical information regarding the employment of minority group members.

Personnel Research

Personnel research is broadly defined as the systematic investigation of practices and problems arising from the employment of human resources, using the knowledge and techniques of the social sciences. Its principal objective at Ford is to assist management in improving the effectiveness of the Company's employes. Personnel research projects may be initiated either in response to a corporate or divisional request for assistance in dealing with a particular problem, or by the staff itself. The personnel research group monitors the research of outside consultants brought in for special projects, consults with internal components on day to day personnel practices and problems and conducts research. Research activities include attitude and opinion surveys, test development and validation, organizational analyses, training evaluation, as well as studies of turnover and absenteeism.

College Recruiting

This department develops policies and practices for the recruitment of college graduates. Recruiting and placement personnel at divisions and plants implement certain of these staff programs and assist in carrying out others.

Under the direction of the Staff's professional recruiters, more than 400 specially trained management representatives from components throughout the Company recruit at more than 200 college and university campuses. They interview as many as 12,000 graduates annually, of which approximately 1,400 were hired in 1967. Qualified college graduates are referred to divisions and plants, as well as to other staffs for further screening, interviewing, selection and initial placement.

College Graduate Program—College students selected for employment are placed on the College Graduate Program, which provides them with an opportunity to develop the skills, background and judgment necessary to qualify for advancement and greater responsibility in the Company. The key feature of the program is that each graduate receives several work assignments in his first two years of employment. During this time his immediate superiors assist him in every possible way. This includes orienting him to the Company, its products, policies and objectives; providing him with a variety of work assignments to develop his abilities; and counseling him to aid in his development and progress. This program helps both the Company and the trainee determine the type of employment for which he is best suited.

College Cooperative Program — Another important phase of the college recruiting effort is the College Cooperative Program. Students from some 52 colleges and universities are currently employed at Ford, making the Company one of the largest employers of cooperative students.

The 750 students now enrolled in the Ford Co-op Program alternate between campus classrooms and appropriate work assignments on a quarterly or trimester basis. Assignments normally start with the junior year and frequently continue through graduate school. Co-ops are currently employed in most functional areas of the Company. The theory which the co-op student learns in the classroom is given practical application during his work period. The program also helps outstanding students finance their education and provides

them with an opportunity to evaluate Ford employment opportunities and their ability to perform them.

Compensation Planning Functions

The Compensation Planning Office is responsible for salary administration, personnel benefits and foreign service administration. The latter responsibility refers to personnel policies affecting United States citizens working for the Company overseas, as well as for foreign personnel employed by Ford in this country.

Salary Administration

The primary objectives of Ford's compensation system are to provide remuneration for salaried employes that reflects the skills and responsibilities required at various job levels, and to provide salaries equal to or better than those paid elsewhere for similar work.

Policies and procedures governing the compensation system are developed and interpreted by the salary administration department. This staff department also advises divisions and plants in the administration of these policies and procedures.

The Ford compensation system has a salary structure containing a series of grades, each with an assigned salary range. The dollar value of the range increases as skill requirements and position responsibilities increase. The spread within each grade permits pay increases for employes who show improvement in their performance. This system not only provides for uniform administration of salaries throughout the Company, but also gives management the opportunity to reward meritorious performance.

Salaries of all employes are reviewed regularly. Merit increases are given as earned through performance. Promotional increases are usually granted when employes move to positions with additional duties and responsibilities. In this way the uniform system encourages self improvement by rewarding individual performance.

Personnel Benefits

Ford has a liberal personnel benefits program for employes and their families. The Company has consistently been a leader in the development of personnel benefits in order to attract and retain competent employes and to build high morale and sound employe-employer relationships.

These programs for all employes are conceived, developed and administered by the personnel benefits department on Staff. Analysts continually research and review benefits to evaluate their effectiveness and to recommend appropriate changes. Administration of these programs includes interpretation of the intent of specific provisions to ensure consistent application. The staff department develops operating manuals and informational materials. It also provides assistance to divisions on unusually difficult administrative problems.

Compensation

Total compensation is what you get. It includes all forms of pay and benefits provided to individuals for work performed in an organization. We may describe various forms of compensation as direct pay, benefits, and non-monetary (non-financial) benefits.

DIRECT PAY

The most significant aspect of compensation is direct wages and salaries. You get a paycheck and that's what you think of first as your compensation. It's what you can spend, or save, as you wish.

The following are elements of direct pay:

WAGES: pay based on hours of work or on specific units of work completed. Commissions, such as paid to salespeople, are an example of pay for specific results achieved. In a factory, you might be paid on a piecework basis -- for the number of products or pieces of work you turn out.

SALARIES: pay based on time at work, but generally weeks, months, or years rather than by the hour. Individuals on managerial, professional, and technical positions are normally paid on a salaried basis. Frequently, clerical, office, and plant personnel are also paid on a salaried basis.

MINIMUM WAGE: under the federal Fair Labor Standards Act of 1938, as amended in 1966, employees engaged in commerce or in the production of goods for commerce must be paid at least a minimum level, set by law.

GUARANTEED ANNUAL WAGE: through negotiation, a labor agreement may provide for a set annual wage to employees. Actually, "GAW" provides for guaranteed employment, not wages, as most plans guarantee a number of hours or days of work per year.

OVERTIME: pay, specified by law, at one and a half times the regular hourly rate of pay, for any work in excess of 40 hours a week. Exempt from the law are executives, administrative, professional, and outside sales employees. Employees in agriculture, food processing, and forestry are also excluded. Frequently, labor agreements provide for premium pay at double or even triple rate for overtime, Sunday or holiday work.

INCENTIVE PAY: any form of compensation aimed at increasing motivation of employees to work toward organizational objectives. Piecework, commissions, group incentive plans, and profit sharing, as well as periodic pay reviews are examples of incentive pay.

BENEFITS

Benefits represent a second element of total compensation. Today, the cost of benefits represents as much as 35% of total compensation cost. Since World War II, the variety of benefits provided to employees in the United States has grown.

Principal types of benefits provided by companies today are the following:

PROFIT SHARING: a formal plan whereby employees participate in the profits of the company. In some companies this is actually an important incentive and is really considered to be direct pay -- a part of expected salary.

STOCK OPTIONS: an opportunity given employees to purchase at a specified price, shares of the company's stock. When exercised, the price is below the stock's market price. This is a benefit normally provided to executives to help them identify with the overall prosperity of the company.

STOCK PURCHASE PLAN: a formal program through which employees may purchase the company's stock at the prevailing market price. The company often contributes to the cost of the stock and normally pays the costs of handling the transactions (there is no cost to the employee as there would be if he went directly to a stock broker and bought the stock on the market).

THRIFT or SAVINGS PLAN: a formal program whereby employees may set aside part of their pay for saving or investment. The company normally provides the management of the fund and may match or contribute to the payments made by employees.

INSURANCE: life insurance, health insurance, and disability income insurance are often provided to employees on a fully paid or on a shared cost basis. Unemployment insurance and workman's compensation insurance (for injury on the job) are provided by law.

RETIREMENT PLAN: companies normally provide a pension for retirement income, based on an individual's length of service and pay level during working years. It may be fully paid by the company or the employee may pay part of the cost and get his part back if he ever leaves the firm. When this benefit is owed to an individual even after he or she quits, the pension is said to be vested. If the benefit may be transferred to a plan provided by another employer it is said to be portable.

PAID VACATIONS AND HOLIDAYS: you may take these for granted, but paying you for time off costs a company money -- you are not on the job working and producing. The number of paid vacation days, sick days, and holidays allowed with pay is an important benefit to be considered.

NON-FINANCIAL REWARDS

   In addition to all of these elements of total compensation, you may receive discounts on com-

pany products, free use of company recreational facilities, special gifts such as turkeys at Christmas, or leaves of absence for military service. Virtually any aspect of you job may be a benefit -- if you view it as a reward for your performance and development.

Pensions

Retirement is either the golden age of life or the scrapheap of life, depending on your point of view. But the "last third" of your life can be a challenge for you to plan and live.

Most employees these days decide to retire at age 65 or before. Many people are retiring at age 60, 55, and even age 50.

RETIREMENT INCOME

The key factor, it seems, in retirement satisfaction, is income. And there are three sources of retirement income: social security (provided by the federal government through the payments made by you and your employers over the years), your personal savings and investments, and your pension.

All three legs of this "stool" need to be strong or your retirement income may not be all you would like it to be.

Social security income is set by law (and increases in benefits have been made available through new laws). There is some concern whether the present way of funding social security programs is adequate -- because the number of people receiving benefits will grow very large in the decades ahead. But we can expect, nevertheless, social security income to be a strong leg on the stool. It is a vital social program that will always be alive -- and likely will grow stronger.

Your own savings is a sore subject, in all likelihood. It's tough to put money away, when inflation makes the prices go up on all the things we want and need to buy to enjoy the first two thirds of our lives. Nevertheless it's important to put money away for the years when you'll be less able to earn money. Insurance can be one form of savings. A company-sponsored savings plan or a profit-sharing plan can also help you put money away.

WHAT'S A PENSION?

A pension, simply, is a payment to an individual as income after retirement. In most cases, employees and employers share the costs of building up a pension fund over the working lives of the employees. Then the company pays out the income to the retired employees for as long as they live, and to a surviving spouse thereafter as long as he or she lives.

Employers are picking up a tab of more than $15 billion a year to build up the pension kitty. Employees add $1.5 billion as deductions from their pay checks. The total reserves built up in private pension plans are more than $200 billion and growing, expected to hit $250 billion by 1980. This money is, of course, invested in stocks, bonds, real estate, and other income-producing property. Banks and insurance companies are usually responsible for managing pension funds.

Some pension funds are administered by labor unions. There is no real difference in the nature of the pension provided.

An amazing fact is that the whole private pension system is purely voluntary. No law forces a company to set up a pension plan. Not even the recent well-publicized pension law requires any company to have a pension plan. Rather, pensions have grown to be an integral part of our compensation system, adding the essential third leg to the retirement income stool.

Given the lack of regulation, the private pension system has performed remarkably well. Most companies have steadily improved vesting, funding, and benefit levels in their plans ever since the plans were introduced decades ago. A recent government study indicates that 90% of all employees covered by private plans today are entitled to vested rights or early retirement benefits by age 55 if they have worked 15 years or more under a plan. Pensions cost companies a lot of money, up to 30% of base compensation or more. And liberal benefits are being paid to millions of retirees.

Of course, there are a few cases where companies have not been fully responsible in their actions, and have not had adequate money set aside for benefits due (funding). In some, employees never gained a permanent guarantee of a pension (vesting), so when they were terminated or the plant closed, they were without any accrued pension. These plans are the target of legislation, and of public attention.

How IBM Avoids Layoffs Through Retraining

Its program provides job security and a loyal, stable work force

Until six months ago Karyl Nichols worked a routine eight-hour day as a secretary in an office of International Business Machines Corp. in Westchester County, N. Y. Then she went through a "career bend," as IBM calls it, and became a sales representative in New York City. Today, instead of pounding a typewriter, she sells IBM typewriters and other office equipment. Eager to advance—and to make her sales quota—she voluntarily puts in 10-hour days, or "whatever it takes," and loves it.

The 24-year-old Nichols does not go so far as to sing company songs at lunchtime, but her loyalty and hard work are typical of benefits that IBM gets for offering near-total job security to its employees.

In more than 35 years, IBM claims, the company has never laid off a worker for economic reasons. Instead, it retrains workers unneeded in one job and assigns them to another. Since 1970 it has retrained and physically relocated 5,000 employees as part of the most extensive corporate education program in the U. S.

The philosophy. Job security has been a cornerstone of the "enlightened paternalism"—as a former executive terms it—with which IBM has dealt with employees for decades at a cost that most companies would consider prohibitive. Yet this policy "was not motivated by altruism," former IBM Chairman Thomas J. Watson Jr. once wrote, "but by the simple belief that if we respected our people and helped them to respect themselves the company would make the most profit."

Retraining to avoid layoffs, for example, pays off in intangible but real benefits for a rapidly growing business. "If people are not worried about being laid off, they are flexible in making the changes we ask of them," says present IBM Chairman Frank T. Cary. "We get a high degree of cooperation from the work force in making changes that are beneficial to the corporation. This is very important to us in a high-technology business."

IBM is not immune to recessions, but it has been able to maintain its tradition of "full employment" because, unlike many companies, some part of its business is always growing. So far this year, IBM has retrained and transferred about 1,000 of its 159,000 employees in the U. S. About 500 were transferred from offices and plants that produce computer components and related products to divisions that handle office equipment and smaller information systems. The other 500 were reassigned within several divisions.

It does this through a sophisticated "manpower balancing" program, which is coordinated at the corporate level and supervised by Cary himself. From monthly projections of the work load in 13 divisions, the Corporate Resource Group is able to match units that need people with those that have an excess. The receiving division bears the cost of retraining, and while IBM divisions operate fairly autonomously, this cost factor sometimes breeds a reluctance to accept transfers that must be overruled by corporate officers.

"Sometimes we have to exercise corporate discretion," Cary admits. "Left to their own preferences, division managers might decide to hire from the immediate locality instead of going through a hiring process at other plants."

Job openings are posted on bulletin boards and outlined at employee meetings. Although her job was not being cut, Karyl Nichols simply wanted more challenging work. Last March a representative of IBM's Office Products Div. (electric typewriters, dictation equipment, copiers, etc.) visited her office as part of a company "road show," soliciting applications for transfer. Nichols was interested in sales job openings and after an interview was accepted as a trainee.

Like all trainees, she received her previous salary during 13 weeks of full-

Frank Cary: IBM's job security makes employees flexible in accepting change.

Pictures: Joan Sydlow—BW

Karyl Nichols, from secretary to sales: "For me at this time, this is the best."

Arthur Bauer, from warehouse to field service: "I couldn't ask any more."

time training in New York City and Dallas, where the company has a special training facility. IBM is paying her relocation expenses and gave her a "substantial" raise when she began work last August as a sales representative in Manhattan. Peppery and ambitious—as IBM wants its sales people to be—she views this job as "a steppingstone." She says: "If you're going to work, you may as well work for the best—the best job, the best money, and the best company. For me at this time, this is the best."

The big stick. IBM's instructors try to inculcate this gung-ho attitude, but the spirit also arises from good feelings about the new opportunities and job security that the company offers. Yet IBM has been known to deal harshly with people it thinks are nonproducers, particularly salesmen and managers. And it does fire and demote people for disciplinary and other causes. "We're not running a home for unproductive people," Cary says. "But our business has always recognized the effect that job security can have on the morale of the work force. Very frequently you make a fellow very happy when you move him to a new job, and when you can fill the old job you also make someone else happy."

While IBM has avoided layoffs and dislikes use of the phrase "force reduction," it does shrink the work force, like most companies, by offering incentives to older employees to leave. Some 1,900 workers have opted out this year under a "special opportunities program," a IBM euphemism for beefed-up early retirement. The company insists that it does not force people out, and the benefits are liberal. A worker with 25 years' service can retire and collect half of his annual salary for four years, or until he becomes 65. In addition, he receives a pension, if eligible—and reduced pensions start at age 55.

IBM's liberal employee policies began taking shape under its founder, Thomas J. Watson Sr., who ran the company from 1914 to 1956. Instead of resorting to mass factory layoffs during the Depression, Watson kept people on the payroll by producing for inventory. He eliminated piecework in 1934, believing that it resulted in an inequitable wage system.

Watson's son, Thomas Jr., who headed IBM from 1956 to 1971, carried on the same philosophy. In 1958 he wiped out the hourly wage and put all employees on straight salary, eliminating the distinction between blue- and white-collar workers. And IBM's employee benefits rank among the best.

Not surprisingly, IBM has never been the target of a major union organizing drive in the U.S., though many of its 100,000 foreign workers are organized. "I don't know what a union at IBM would do," says one salesman incredulously, when asked if he would join a union.

The open door. IBM's "open door" policy, under which a worker can protest his manager's decision on work-related issues, appears to work as well as the grievance procedure in union plants. Started by Watson Sr., the policy enables an employee to appeal to the chairman himself. "You couldn't take a bum complaint up that high," admits a low-echelon employee, "but the possibility is there." Though complaints have to go through successive levels of managers, some do get to Cary—about a dozen last year. IBM makes the procedure work by appraising how fairly its managers treat "open door" gripes.

The company began formal education programs in 1916. More than 5,000 full-time and part-time instructors in 200 domestic education centers now give three major types of courses: management development, technical updating, and job retraining. Some 10 million student hours are logged each year—the equivalent of nearly 40,000 full-time students receiving 15 hours a week in a 32-week college.

Since 1970 IBM has retrained and relocated 5,000 of its employees

The impetus for such large-scale programs came largely from the need to update customers and employees in fast-changing computer technology. "As a side benefit," says Charles R. DeCarlo, one-time director of IBM education and now president of Sarah Lawrence College, "IBM has ended up with a work force that believes in change."

Since the early 1950s, computer technology has gone through three generations, with components dramatically decreasing in size. Not only has miniaturization demanded several retraining cycles for production workers, but it also has drastically shrunk the number of people needed in manufacturing. For several years IBM has been moving people out of manufacturing—and out of administrative forces when overhead had to be cut—and into such jobs as programmers, computer operators, facilities engineers, and sales and service specialists.

The costs. Cary points out that such wholesale retraining and relocation would have been much more difficult if IBM's sales volume had not grown so rapidly—at a 14.6% average yearly rate from 1964 to 1974. For this reason, Cary claims that IBM's retraining programs have not been "all that expensive." He adds: "When other people say that retraining must be tremendously expensive, they're thinking about training people for jobs in which you don't need them. But we're growing. In 1970 and 1975, when we had an excess of people in manufacturing, we had a need elsewhere. If we hadn't found them in the business, we'd have had to bring them in from the outside."

Because each division handles its own education program—and calculates the cost differently—IBM says it has no accurate estimate of the over-all cost. DeCarlo estimates a total education expenditure of $80 million to $90 million a year during the mid-1960s when he headed the program. Another former IBM manager in education estimates that the cost had risen to about $100 million in 1970, and informed sources believe the figure now exceeds that.

IBM's way of dealing with its employees does not produce a regimented work force. While protective job security can produce stagnation, IBM insists that it enables employees to be more individualistic and willing to try new ideas. "If you operate in high job security without demanding performance," Cary says, "there'd be a problem. But we demand performance."

A former IBM executive says a fundamental "attitudinal difference" between IBM and other companies helps explain IBM's success. He says: "IBM knows that you don't keep workers happy by puffing the work force up and down as though it didn't matter what happened to the people."

Employee response. If the several employees that BUSINESS WEEK interviewed privately are typical, IBM must indeed have a relatively happy work force—at least among young, retrained employees. Arthur R. Bauer, 27, was retrained to become a "customer engineer" (an office equipment repairman) after starting with the company as a forklift operator. He says, with some astonishment: "From loading and unloading trucks to this. I couldn't ask any more."

Robert C. Alexander, 24, recently switched from customer engineer to office products salesman. "I was a problem-solver before, but not in a human sense," he says. "Now I'm dealing with customers and running my own little show. I'm looking forward to management."

Dr. Alan A. McLean, IBM's Eastern Area medical director and a noted industrial psychiatrist, says in assessing the benefits of corporate retraining: "When the company pays attention to the individual in a highly individualized way, it fosters a real, honest increase in self-worth and self-esteem."

There are few who fault IBM's education programs. "The only thing that ever worried me," DeCarlo says, "is that IBM professionals and managers were so intensely directed toward the job. This lovely quality of paternalism may make the worker suffer in his outside life." ∎

Careers In Personnel

Recruiting employees with the right combination of talent and experience used to be the only function of personnel managers or directors. Today, the field involves a number of functions ranging from employment and recruiting to compensation, training, and organization development.

What should a company do about equal employment? About labor relations? How about changes in the pension plan? Should we have a shorter work week? Job enrichment perhaps, or organizational changes? These are questions that personnel professionals help answer.

Coping with change in the workplace is a key role. The effects of technology, of company growth, or union activities, of external compensation or labor market changes, of employee attitudes toward work, and legal requirements are all important aspects of human resource management. These are the bread and butter of personnel people.

Human resources is a crucial term, for the field has evolved into a more direct business support function than it was, say, thirty years ago. It used to be that personnel staff were primarily administrative in function. They got employees on and off the payroll, saw that each got the right paycheck and benefits. They provided employment interviewing and subsequent counseling and maybe some basic training. Often the personnel staff assumed charge of the cafe-

teria, recreational programs, and other administrative tasks. Safety and public relations were often included.

Further, it used to be people got interested in personnel work because they said they "liked people." That has to be the world's worst possible reason to go into this career area. Yes, a human resource specialist works with people, but so does every other manager and most employees. If anything, the personnel career requires better "knowledge about people" because so many of the decisions and programs relate to this basis.

THE JOBS

About 160,000 people work in the personnel area in the United States today. And it is a growing field because of the expanding nature of the functions required.

Of course the functions vary with the size of the firm. You are likely to be more specialized if you join a staff in a large company. In a small business, you may be responsible for the full gamut of personnel programs.

The requirements are the same as in other business careers -- you need to know your specialization. You can't administer employee benefits unless you know the facts and systems that are involved. You can't be a training and development specialist just because you are interested in it.

CAREER STEPS

The best way to get ahead in this field is to move through a series of solid job experiences. A sound education is helpful, not necessarily in personnel subjects, but general business administration and humanities. Writing skills, ability to read and comprehend, oral communications skills, skills of persuasion, and understanding of human behavior are all essential for success.

On your first job you're bound to get involved in a specific task area. It may be in employment: recruiting on campuses, interviewing job applicants, testing potential employees, or counseling employees regarding other jobs and transfers.

Or you may write job descriptions and evaluate jobs in terms of pay level. You may survey other companies to set scales for pay, or you may be involved in setting up a new salary system.

In labor relations you may help in preparation for negotiations or in settling grievances. But this area requires more specialized training and experience. Also, of course, there have to be unions around.

You may look after the administration of benefits and other personnel programs and policies such as vacations, employee records, medical benefits, pension administration, and employee communications (newsletters and magazines).

CONSIDER

1. As an employee, what would be your reactions to the memo on page 516? Please explain.

2. How could management achieve the desired results of this memo in a more humanistic manner? Explain.

3. Will organizations change by themselves, without any special organization development by managers? Explain.

4. Are all people motivated by freedom, responsibility, and recognition? Explain.

5. How does money fit into the scheme of motivating people?

6. Is work in a governmental agency or in the military affected by the same motives as work in business? Explain.

7. What motivates individuals to work in a commune?

8. What would be the role of staff specialists in the human resource management process in a corporation?

9. What impact do you think the increased use of computers has on the need for organization development? Explain.

10. How would you describe the ideal organization to work in?

CHALLENGES

Make a list of the things you feel are important to you on a job. Explain why each is important to you.

Analyze the faults you saw in your manager on your last job. What might he or she have done to correct these problems?

On your last job, did any significant changes occur in the organization you were working in? How were they put into action? Was the change managed effectively? What were the results, if any?

In the annual report of your "favorite" corporation, look for indications of the organization's human resource management. does it appear that the company is effectively responding to the needs for change?

Read ORGANIZATION DEVELOPMENT: ITS NATURE, ORIGINS, AND PROSPECTS by Warren G. Bennis (Reading, Massachusetts, Addison-Wesley, 1969). This is a paperback book.

Also read one or more sections of the ASPA HANDBOOK OF PERSONNEL AND INDUSTRIAL RELATIONS (Washington, D.C.: Bureau of national Affirs, Inc., 1977). This is a series of paperback books.

RECAP

Managing is the process of getting things done through people. So human resource management -- managing people -- is a basic part of every manager's job. Human resource management has four basic aspects: manpower planning, manpower development, organization development, and compensation.

Manpower planning is the process of preparing for the organization's future talent requirements. It involves having the right numbers and kinds of people at the right places at the right times to perform activities that will benefit both the organization and the individuals. The two basic elements of manpower planning are forecasting of manpower needs and the planning of actions that will satisfy these needs. Typical actions include recruitment of people, assigning people to jobs, development of people, promotion, and retiring and terminating people as employees.

Manpower development is the process of increasing individual skills and knowledge and changing individual attitudes related to work. Companies provide a wide range of training and development programs for this purpose, but the process of goal setting and coaching with managers is the core of this process.

Developing the relationships between individuals and groups is the process of organization development.

Organizations must change if they are to survive and prosper in a changing environment. There are several ways to change an organization, including counseling, training, changing the structure of the organization, or changing the design of jobs.

Recognition of individual performance and development is usually thought to be in the form of a paycheck. But there are many forms of compensation -- including non-financial and financial rewards. Even the satisfaction gained from work itself may be viewed as an element of total compensation.

Because attitudes are changing in our society, employee motivation presents a significant challenge to management. Generally, employees will contribute to the achievement of objectives they believe to be meaningful and relevant. Of course, these objectives should be attainable and should be established through mutual discussions by managers and individuals.

Individuals may be motivated to learn, to grow, and to perform if they are given freedom, responsibility, and recognition on the job. Further, a view of a job as a step in a career promotes individual performance and growth. We'll talk about careers in some depth in Chapter 19.

WORKSHEET NO. 18

NAME_____

INSTRUCTOR'S NAME_____

DATE_____

1. What are the basic elements of human resource management and how do they relate?

_____

2. What makes a good job?

3. How can an organization be changed?

---

4. Why is organizational change and effective human resource management necessary?

CHAPTER 19

Labor Relations And Employment

In a year, there are thousands of work stoppages, affecting millions of workers in the United States. Fifty million or more man days may be lost, at significaqnt financial loss both to workers and businesses.

Why do we put up with this loss? Why are workers willing to be idle and go without their wages? Why does the public permit labor unions to strike business organizations and halt productive activity?

Labor unions provide a means for employees to negotiate -- to bargain collectively with management -- and administer the terms and conditions of their working relationships. Strikes are one of the tools, and the strongest tool available, used by unions to win the terms considered favorable to the workers.

From their beginning in the late nineteenth century, labor organizations have developed as a significant factor in management-employee relationships, particularly among operating-level employees.

Today, more than twenty million workers belong to unions associated with the AFL-CIO. More than 15% of them are white-collar workers. Even public sector employees have joined the union ranks. In fact, unions currently represent more than a quarter of the entire working force in the United States.

The government has assumed an ever-increasing role in labor-management relations, and now frequently sits as a third party in collective bargaining. The federal government provides a wide range of services to labor and industry affecting labor relations and overall patterns of employment.

Labor relations has become a highly specialized field. To work in this area requires considerable education and experience; a law degree is highly desirable. You may specialize in labor relations of "industrial relations" at many universities and may pursue graduate degrees in this area as well.

Accordingly, the field has its own set of terms -- a language that you really have to understand to know what is going on in labor relations activities today.

Government, business,

and labor all strive to maintain full employment of the talent in our work force. We do not particularly want to have labor strikes, and avoid them when possible. We want automation, but without creating hardships for people. We want to be sensible about jobs and people, using talents in the most effective and economical manner, but we also want full employment so that everyone who wants a job can have one.

These are big challenges, ones that are difficult to meet. In this chapter we will discuss each of these, presenting a variety of viewpoints as well as the basic facts. For example, the history and role of unions are told from the union perspective, and future trends in labor relations are discussed from the industry point of view. You will have the opportunity to think through the issues and develop your own views.

In This Chapter

Unions, Freedom, And Democracy

Our system for labor relations in America is widely considered to be an important democratic process in our economy. Through collective bargaining, representatives of labor and management "meet and confer in good faith regarding wages, hours, and other terms and conditions of employment."

By means of the labor agreement reached and ratified through negotiation by union and management representatives and ratified by union members, labor and management have a basis for administering policies governing work and for resolving any disputes that may arise at work.

Underlying the whole idea of collective bargaining is the concept of self-determination. By bargaining collectively, individuals gain a powerful, direct voice in decisions governing their working conditions. Managers frequently

argue that unions are not needed -- that they come between them and the individual workers. Yet unions came into being, unions respond, because management failed to provide adequate working conditions and a voice for workers in determining their working conditions.

With the Wagner Act, our nation took a position of encouraging labor organizations and collective bargaining. Over the years, further legislation and court decisions, interpreting detailed applications of the law, have modified labor relations practices. Our public policy continues to support the free collective bargaining process, with due protection of both labor and management against undue use of power or coercion by either side.

The National Labor Relations Board helps maintain this process in two ways. The five-man board, established by the Wagner Act, cer-

tifies union representatives for collective bargaining (this is determined through supervised elections) The board also reviews alleged unfair labor practices, as defined by law. The federal courts may enforce the NLRB's decisions, compelling labor or management to cease and desist any practices found to be unfair.

There has been a controversy whether individuals should be required to join a union as a condition of employment. Certainly unions would like to represent all employees in order to have maximum bargaining strength. Employers and individuals, however, often feel that the individual should have the privilege of choosing to be a union member or not. He has, they argue, a "right to work" without having to join a union. The Taft-Hartley Act permits states to pass

laws prohibiting closed and union shops, hence affirming the "right to work". There is pressure on Congress to repeal this provision of the Act, thus wiping out such laws now in effect.

Unions may claim that employers have too much economic power today. Big corporations hold all the cards in the game: diversity, size, market, physical resources, financial capital, and often the alliance of the public. Their large size and vast economic resources make collective bargaining difficult, unions frequently contend.

Companies may argue that unions have far too much power today, with large strike funds, government favor, and the power to shut down whole industries. Unions, they say, can drive an employer right out of business.

Unions and employers both say that the government is becoming way too large, too powerful, and far too deeply involved in various aspects of labor-management relations. Expanding government intervention, they say, will destroy free enterprise. As our federal government takes on more and more functions in our economy, we are creeping more toward "socialism."

So who's right?

The truth is that all three major sectors of our economic society are becoming more and more powerful. Our concern is that their powers be kept in balance. Government has expanded its role largely to help balance labor and management. By this "countervailing power" the interests of stockholders, labor, and the public will all be safeguarded.

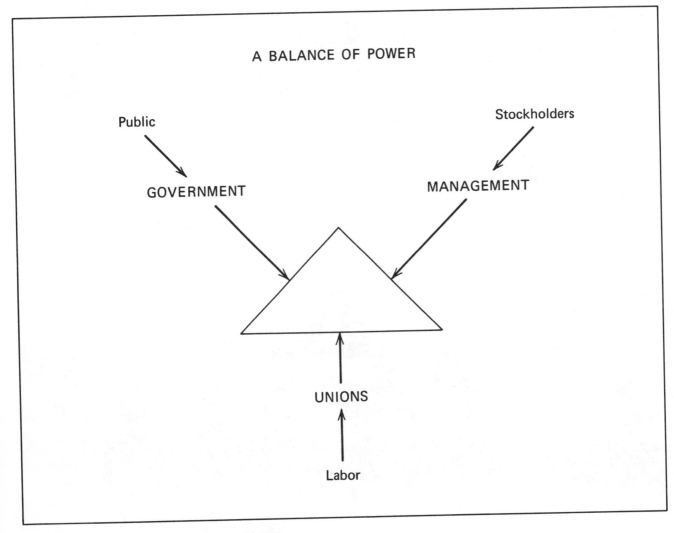

A BALANCE OF POWER

Public → GOVERNMENT

Stockholders → MANAGEMENT

UNIONS

Labor

"What Makes America Work? Responsible and Free Collective Bargaining."

by George Meany

President, American Federation of Labor and Congress of Industrial Organizations

Those who read only headlines probably believe labor and management are constantly at each other's throat and can't agree on anything. That, of course, is the nature of news—conflict is newsier than peace.

So a strike—which occurs in less than 2 per cent of all negotiations—is news; the 98 per cent settled without a strike are not.

That is my point: Labor and management do agree that responsible and free collective bargaining is the way to settle disputes.

Of course, collective bargaining is not perfect. Labor and management are constantly striving to improve it. For example, in the steel industry, labor and management have agreed on an alternative to the strike—binding arbitration.

It has been successful, but only because both sides <u>agreed</u>. Nobody forced either the union or the companies to agree.

Some editorialists contend the answer to strikes or lockouts is to have the government compel all unions and all companies to settle their disputes through arbitration. But compulsion would be the death knell for collective bargaining, a free trade-union movement and the free enterprise system. It would undermine a basic American freedom.

Only a dictatorship can compel workers to work against their will or force management to sign a contract it does not want. No free American wants any form of totalitarianism.

While strikes sometimes cause public inconvenience, they are an inherent part of the liberties we all enjoy—free speech, freedom of association, the right of contract. The exercise of liberties in a democratic society is not only healthy, it is vital.

As President Dwight D. Eisenhower put it: "The right of men to leave their jobs is a test of freedom. Hitler suppressed strikes. Stalin suppressed strikes.... Each also suppressed freedom. There are some things worse, much worse, than strikes. One of them is the loss of freedom."

So labor and management support free collective bargaining, which has brought to American workers the highest standard of living in the world, strengthened the economy by increasing consumer buying power, and provided a common sense mechanism for resolving problems.

Collective bargaining is not perfect, but it works. And responsible labor and responsible management must and do work to make it better.

Technological Change: How Fares the Worker

The pace of technological change in the 1950's and early 1960's touched off widespread predictions that considerable unemployment and worker displacement would result. To date, the forebodings have proved unfounded. That does not mean, however, that technological change has not had a substantial impact on workers and their jobs. It has. And, according to a nationwide survey made for the U.S. Department of Labor's Manpower Administration, the overwhelming majority of workers affected by technological change benefited.

Conducted by the University of Michigan Survey Research Center, the study covered 2,662 persons representative of a cross section of the labor force. Information was collected on how changes in machinery affected their jobs and working conditions over the 1962-67 period.

The survey indicated that a very large segment of the work force is directly or indirectly affected by machinery and equipment. Although affecting a relatively small number of persons in a given year, changes in machinery were substantial in their cumulative effect. Hypothetically, machine change can mean everything from the acquisition of new pencil sharpeners in an office to the complete overhaul of an industry's production equipment; from change that affects the job of one worker, to change that requires the adjustment of thousands of workers in direct and indirect contact with the machinery. The study considered only those changes which the respondent indicated had a significant impact on his job.

Of workers undergoing machine change, the large majority said they benefited as a result. Finding persons who had experienced "serious hardship" as a direct result of changes in machinery was almost impossible, the study says. And it suggests that failure to introduce machine changes may, in fact, have adverse effects on the worker.

Approximately 2 of every 3 persons responding to the survey operated machinery or equipment on the job. When applied to the total work force, this would mean that in 1969 about 56 million persons were employed in jobs requiring the operation of machinery as an important aspect of their duties. Forty-two percent of the survey sample said they operated machinery almost constantly. One-third of the sample felt that machinery which they did not operate was important to their work. For example, although installation of a computer in a chain of banks creates only a small number of new jobs, it also affects other bank employees who will not need more than a superficial knowledge of the computer operation and who may even operate other kinds of equipment.

The study estimates that during 1962-67 changes in machine technology had a significant impact on 7.5 to 10 million jobs. Twenty-two percent of the sample reported changes that altered their work to some appreciable extent, including 13 percent who experienced a machine change in connection with either a transfer within the same company or with a change of employers. But very few workers said technological change caused them to switch jobs. On the whole, workers having a machine change, regardless of whether they changed jobs, were better off than those who worked with the same technology throughout the study period (or had no contact at all with machines).

Regardless of machine use or machine change, the income of approximately 75 percent of the workers surveyed increased between 1962-67. But as a group, workers whose jobs had no significant connection with machines fared the worst. Fewer of them—69 percent—reported increased incomes, and more of them—31 percent—had no increase or a decline in income during the period studied. Workers who were affected by equipment but did not operate it fared best; 80 percent of them reported income increases. Next in line were workers who both operated equipment and were indirectly affected by equipment operated by others; 78 percent of them had increases.

The extent of income increase rose with the technical level of equipment used. For example, 66 percent of those operating computers and other logically controlled hardware reported promotions in the 5-year period as compared with 32 percent of those operating fixed mechanically controlled equipment—the next highest category of machine operators receiving promotions.

Machines Spur Hiring

Workers in firms which were expanding production and employment were more apt to undergo machine change than those in declining companies, leading the study to conclude that "in a majority of cases, reductions in employment due to automation of equipment are more than offset over a period of time by the growth of the firm's market." Production growth resulting from machine change may, in fact, be the basis for increased hiring.

The study points out that a firm that falls behind technologically usually is put at a competitive disadvantage and may be forced to cut hours, reduce pay, and lay off workers. This not only supports the conclusion that changes in machine technology in an expanding economy do not usually lead to adverse employment experiences, but have important implications for activities directed at combating unemployment. With the identification of technological lag as a cause of unemployment, training and upgrading re-

"Most workers . . . used the term 'friend' in describing their machines . . ."

sources could be better organized and directed.

Overall, 20 percent of all workers surveyed reported being out of work sometime during the 5 years. Those only indirectly affected by machines experienced the least unemployment, while those not working with any machines—directly or indirectly—had the highest rates of joblessness. Of workers who experienced machine change but stayed in the same job over the 5 years, 8 percent reported some unemployment, as contrasted with 11 percent of those who stayed in the same job and were not involved in machine changes. This would tend to show that even over a long period of time machine change does not increase unemployment.

In addition, most workers said they believed they were better off as a result of machine change with or without a job change, with respect to promotions, income, unemployment, and their workweek. Workers who switched jobs because of a machine change, however, said they saw less chance of advancement and security in their work, even though they fared about as well as other job changers. The study maintains that by practically all measures, including employment experience, income, promotions, job challenge, and satisfaction, technological advance in an expanding economy usually has positive effects for the individual and the economy.

Not to be overlooked in this optimistic picture are the study's conclusions about those instances where adverse consequences do result:

. . . the impact of advances in machine technology on employ-

ment is largely indirect. . . . Much of the unemployment resulting from labor-saving machinery "trickles down" to the most marginal groups in the labor force. Workers who might have been hired in the absence of technological change are not needed. The last to be hired are the people with the weakest labor market qualifications for reasons of age, experience, education, health, location, race, previous employment record, and other possible handicaps. These people, together with those employed by technologically backward firms, seem to bear the bulk of technological unemployment.

In a technologically changing situation, the worker who is at all initially inadequate to the job naturally suffers most from the introduction of machine changes which demand different and more difficult skills from him.

The two primary cushions for adverse effects of technological change on these workers, the study points out, are the economy's ability to absorb technological unemployment through increased labor demand, and retraining and other special programs to ease the impact of technological unemployment for the marginal segments of the labor force—in effect, the two prongs of current manpower policy.

The 5-year period covered by the study was one of unusually rapid economic growth and declining unemployment. Study findings, particularly those relating to adverse effects of technological change, must be viewed in that context. Approximately 4 percent of the workers affected by changes in machinery reported some unemployment during the transition period, and another 2 percent reported a shorter workweek. This 6 percent does not take into account any unemployment occurring as an indirect consequence of machine change.

The study shows that the more education a person has the more likely he is to work closely with complex and highly automated equipment. And younger workers more often operate equipment on the job than do older workers.

Most workers expressed a favorable attitude toward the machinery they operated. In fact, 73 percent of the respondents used the term "friend" in describing their machines, and workers operating automated equipment more often reported that they enjoyed their work than those working with more traditional equipment.

Young persons reported increased job satisfaction as a result of machine change more often than older workers, blue-collar workers more often than white-collar workers, and men more often than women. Overall, of all those involved in some kind of machine change, about two-thirds reported increased job satisfaction over the 5-year period. About 1 in 10 of the workers reporting machine changes, or job changes related to technological considerations, were less satisfied with their jobs. One of the chief causes of decreased job satisfaction was prolonged or intermittent periods of unemployment.

Higher income, of course, was the most important factor in producing greater job satisfaction. Other important considerations reported by workers were the chance to learn new skills, more interesting work, and opportunity for advancement. Opportunity for more skilled work and greater responsibilities for planning and judgment also were important to a worker's job satisfaction. Challenge and responsibility were far more important than job security.

New Technology by 1980

The concern for challenging work was well nigh universal, extending to young and old, more and less well educated, and blue- and white-collar workers. For example, the 59-year-old manager of a glass factory where production was increased by mechanization, reported that his greater responsibilities for planning and coordination of the cutting operation and the demand for more initiative on his part added to the interest and personal challenge of his job.

If the economic growth rate of recent years continues with a parallel pace of technological change, a complete technological turnover in the major industrial segments of the economy can occur by 1980. This would not only demand increased efforts to upgrade the skills of the work force, but also would require totally new views of work, education, technology, and leisure. Concepts such as multiple careers for the individual, interspersed with education and training throughout life, may be the rule of the future. Changing technology may be the most significant impetus for broader, more diverse, and more frequent educational and training experiences for all workers. Monotony and estrangement could be displaced by continuous challenge and learning.

WHAZZIT?

GRIEVANCE

A demand by an employee that the employer honor a recognized working condition provided by law or by a labor agreement. The labor agreement usually provides for a grievance procedure, or series of steps for resolving the grievance, frequently culminating in arbitration.

CLOSED SHOP

All employees in the organization must be union members.

UNION SHOP

After a specified period of time, all employees in the organization must become members of the representing union.

OPEN SHOP

Employees may or may not join the union, as they wish.

RIGHT TO WORK LAWS

Many states have enacted laws that prohibit closed shops and union shops. In the absence of such laws, union membership may be required for employment.

WAGNER ACT

The National Labor Relations Act of 1935, which established the right of workers to organize unions and bargain collectively.

MEDIATION

A procedure in which a neutral third party attempts to persuade the parties to resolve a labor dispute. Unlike arbitration, mediation does not give the third party authority to make a binding decision.

LOCKOUTS

Locking workers out of the plant as a management strategy to promote bargaining.

TAFT-HARTLEY ACT

The Labor-Management Relations Act of 1947, amending the Wagner Act. It balances the rights and privileges of labor and management by limiting some of the advantages held by labor.

What Can We Do About Unemployment?

UNEMPLOYMENT AND JOBS

Unemployment represents a loss of potential production of goods and services available to the market as well as a loss of potential income to purchase items in the market. The hardship imposed on society by a period of joblessness does not fall evenly on all.

In some households there are two or more wageearners who can cushion the blow of unemployment. Some households have other sources of income, such as income from trusts or inheritances. This also helps cushion the economic effect of being without a job.

Financial obligations taken on during good times sometimes become burdens later during times of unemployment. It's tough to keep making payments on a color television when you don't have a paycheck coming in regularly.

Those who find themselves without jobs for a long period of time are of course the hardest hit. It seems harder and harder to find employment, available financial cushions disappear, and personal feelings of self worth and ability to get a job get pretty tender.

THE FACTS

We're not talking about just a few people who are without jobs. The average number of persons out of work and looking for a job during any month in 1975 was about six million, or about 4% of our total working age population.

In addition, some persons already employed were looking for new positions elsewhere. Granted, these persons are not unemployed, but may be under-employed, in the sense that they could be performing other more productive work, given their skills, abilities and training.

Unemployed males account for 54% of the job seekers and females in this group accounted for 46%. Job holders were 60% men and 40% women. Women have become increasingly inclined to enter the labor market. Many women are re-entering the market, having been employed years before, and now are coming back for jobs now that their children are grown or because they are encouraged to work by changing social attitudes. In fact the participation by women has steadily increased in the work force in recent years, swelling the available pool of talent for American business and industry.

"There are plenty of jobs around. People just don't want to work."

Drawing by Drucker, © 1972 The New Yorker Magazine Inc.

543 LABOR RELATIONS

Unemployed males tend to be individuals who lost their jobs due to layoffs from production cutbacks or other reasons. The amount of time unemployed is a key factor in evaluating who is unemployed. The government keeps track of unemployed job seekers, through sampling, various survey reports (e.g., through unemployment compensation payments), and special interview studies.

It's very important to know who's unemployed so that the government can take actions to spur job creation in the right areas of our economy.

The overall rate of unemployment reached 9.2% in 1975, a high level by historical standards. Since then, major efforts have been taken to bring down the rate of unemployment across the nation.

The 1975 rate was higher than in 1958, 1961, and 1962 -- all recession years, and only exceeded during the depression. Unemployment tends to be worse when the economy turns down. The rate was as low as 3.5% in 1968, a year regarded as strong economically, and a year of near "full" employment.

Nearly a third of those experiencing unemployment during a given year are out of work for more than one period. About five million people were unemployed for a time during 1974, returned to work, then experienced unemployment again later.

THE UNEMPLOYED

Unemployed people are of four basic types. One group is made up of the job losers -- the people who were laid off or otherwise lost their jobs.

Another group is the job leavers type -- the people who left their jobs voluntarily for one reason or another. This is a far smaller group, but points up the fact that jobs aren't always easy to find, so don't leave one until you have another.

Reentrants to the work force is a third group. This includes women coming back for jobs, but also includes military service personnel coming back to the civilian sector and graduating students looking for full time jobs.

Finally, there are the new entrants. When you first looked for a job you were a new entrant. Everyone is a a new entrant once! And with an expanding work force, related in part to the large number of younger people looking for full time jobs, the competition for jobs among new entrants is keen.

Naturally, the patterns of unemployment also vary by age group. The unemployed tend to be <u>younger</u>, because they have less work experience to rely upon in seeking jobs. They tend to be <u>male</u>, in part because there are far more men than women in the workforce. Further, <u>minorities</u> tend to be counted among the unemployed far more frequently, again in part because of the experience and skills requirements of many jobs.

As individuals there is very little we can do to improve the level of employment. As a nation, however, there is a great deal that we can do.

Our actions are subject, of course, to our general economic conditions. As we have discussed, employment policy actions have little effect when our economy is sluggish and the GNP is lagging. What is needed then, is strong economic stimulation -- through fiscal and monetary actions.

For common ills in unemployment, the following are some remedial actions:

LABOR IMMOBILITY

Unemployment is generally high among groups for which job mobility is low. So we may relieve unemployment by providing programs to improve mobility of labor, provide information on job opportunities in a given area and in other geographic areas, to pay for travel and moving costs for investigating and taking job opportunities, require vesting of pensions to encourage mobility, and expand area economic expansion to stimulate employment. The federal government has developed a complex computer-based job-matching system that provides immediate information on jobs across the nation that fit a person's interests and qualifications.

AUTOMATION AND TECHNICAL CHANGE

To respond effectively to changing employment requirements in our society, we need to provide continuing education and job retraining. Under various federal acts, the government has conducted or sponsored a wide range of training programs.

DISCRIMINATION

Unemployment among non-whites is well above the overall rate. Among the actions we may take to increase employment among non-whites (and among youth and women, too) include affirmative hiring programs and programs to educate individuals for jobs that are available.

PRODUCTIVITY AND WAGES

When unions push wage rates above market rates or restrict the output of workers (as 400 bricks laid per day instead of 1200), the effect is reduced employment. Only improved understanding by unions and improved labor-management cooperation can help.

OVERTIME WORK

When some workers work more than their normal hours, others are being deprived or work. At least the idea of overtime pay is that -- to encourage employers to spread the work around, and increase overall employment.

WHAZZIT?

LABOR AGREEMENT

A contract between a labor union and management covering the terms and conditions of working relationships.

COLLECTIVE BARGAINING

The negotiation of a labor agreement by representatives of labor and management.

COOLING-OFF PERIOD

By law, the President may order a suspension (eighty days) of a strike that is deemed to threaten the public interest. The hope is that an agreement will be reached during this time.

ARBITRATION

A procedure for resolving a dispute (such as an interpretation of an item in a labor agreement) in which a third party or a board hears both sides of a controversy and issues an award, usually accompanies by a decision, ordinarily binding on both parties.

NLRB

The National Labor Relations Board, established by the Wagner Act. This board, with regional offices throughout the country, provides a means of administering our labor laws.

S.U.B.

Supplemental Unemployment Benefits are payments made by an employer, usually under a labor agreement, above and beyond unemployment benefits paid by the government under the law.

E.P.P.

Earnings Protection Plans provide payments for a temporary period of time to sustain the incomes of individuals affected by technological change.

BOYCOTT

A strategy used by unions to stop the purchase of the employer's products in order to promote bargaining and win concessions.

Unions In America

Around the beginning of the Nineteenth Century, workers in many trades began to form local unions to engage in collective bargaining with their employers over such matters as wages and hours. Shoemakers, tailors, carpenters, and printers were among the earliest workers to engage in collective bargaining.

In 1806 a group of Philadelphia shoemakers who had formed a union were indicted upon charges of unlawful conspiracy. Trial Judge Levy, in his charge to the jury, characterized the shoemakers' union as "pregnant with public mischief and private injury." He declared that under common law wherever two or more persons conspire to do something jointly, even though they are individually entitled to take such action, the public interest is endangered. The shoemakers were found guilty of conspiring to raise wages.

Similar cases were brought before the courts in Pittsburgh, New York, Connecticut, Maryland, and Massachusetts and always the decisions were the same; efforts to organize unions were conspiracies to raise wages, a crime against society.

Workers nevertheless persevered in their efforts to form unions and to engage in collective bargaining with their employers. When the Erie Canal was opened in 1825, twenty unions joined in the parade celebrating the occasion. Bakers, cabinet makers, and dock workers were among those to join the growing list of crafts to form unions. In 1827, unions in Philadelphia had become well enough established to form the first city-wide labor federation, a delegate body consisting of the representatives of fifteen different unions in the city. Other workers established unions in Baltimore, Boston, and even as far west as Ohio.

The first purpose of these early unions was collective bargaining, an effort to win a voice for the workers in determining wages and hours. In addition, however, these early unions demonstrated a lively interest in the general improvement of American society.

As an illustration of how differently employers were treated by these early courts, workers in Pennsylvania in 1821 sought to apply the doctrine of criminal conspiracy against their employers who combined to reduce the workers' wages. In this case the court held that where "the object to be attained is meritorious, combination is not conspiracy."

It was not until 1842 that the legality of trade unionism was first established by an American court of law in the case of the Commonwealth of Massachusetts vs. Hunt. It was again a group of shoemakers, this time from Boston, who provided the occasion. The charge against the union was again criminal conspiracy, but in this case it was a conspiracy to refuse to work alongside a worker who would not join the union.

The attorney for the shoemakers, Robert Rantoul, Jr., endeavored to show that a combination of men for improvement of economic conditions was not a crime, but that it was actually in the best interests of society. Rantoul asked how these shoemakers differed from professional men who formed organizations. The Medical Association, he noted, was a combination for the improvement of its members. It had regulations concerning dues and fees and it refused to permit non-members to practice medicine in the community. The Boston Bar of which the presiding judge was a member, Rantoul noted, had rules fixing minimum fees and forbidding members "to advise or consult or be in any manner associated with any non-member attorney."

The jury nevertheless found the Boston shoemakers guilty of criminal conspiracy. The union appealed the verdict to the Appellate Court of Massachusetts and in 1842 Chief Justice Lemuel Shaw rendered a decision directing that the indictment against the defendants be dismissed. "We cannot perceive," Justice Shaw declared, "that it is criminal for men to agree together to exercise their own acknowledged rights in such a manner as best to subserve their own interests."

For the first time, a court had held that workers could legally form a union to engage in collective bargaining as long as they pursued "virtuous ends by virtuous means." During the years that followed, unionism and collective bargaining spread to almost every craft and to a majority of American cities. In many of these cities the local unions had formed city-wide central bodies.

Growth of Modern Unions

By the time of the Civil War, several national unions had come into existence, including national organizations of printers, molders, stone cutters, machinists and locomotive engineers.

Important economic considerations led to the

development of these national unions. Workers in one city might form a union, engage in collective bargaining, and win good working conditions and then be frustrated by one of two things. In some industries, it was relatively easy to send the work to other cities where working conditions were not as good and where the work might therefore be done cheaper. On the other hand there were industries like house construction in which the work itself could not be moved to another city, but in these industries the good working conditions negotiated by unions frequently attracted workers from other cities, thus resulting in a surplus of labor that made it impossible for the local union to maintain the standards which it had won.

Local unions therefore discovered that if they were to maintain good working conditions in their own cities, it was essential that similarly good working conditions prevail in other cities. National unions were born out of the realization that

real collective bargaining cannot take place in any industry if a substantial part of that industry is non-union.

The development of railroads, welding the country together into a more unified whole, speeded up this process and made the development of national unions more urgent. By 1869 there were twenty-four national unions in the nation. In that year there was established the first truly national organization of workers. It was the Knights of Labor, an organization which eventually reached a membership of 700,000.

The Knights, however, never succeeded in developing an organizational structure that could permit effective collective bargaining, and it was this very failure which led to the formation of the American Federation of Labor. The Federation, established in 1881 as the Federation of Organized Trades and Labor Unions and renamed the American Federation of Labor in 1886, was an organization of national unions including the

Major Agreements Expiring Next Month

Company and location	Industry	Union [1]	Number of workers
Admiral Corp. (Illinois)	Electrical products	Electrical Workers (IBEW)	6,500
American Standard, Inc. (Swissvale, Pa.)	Electrical products	Electrical Workers (UE) (Ind.)	1,000
American Standard, Inc. (Wilmerding, Pa.)	Transportation equipment	Electrical Workers (UE) (Ind.)	3,500
American Stores Co., Acme Markets, Inc. Division No. 7 (Northern New Jersey).	Retail trade	Retail Clerks	1,400
Associated Men's Wear Retailers of New York, Inc. (New York, N.Y.)	Retail trade	Retail, Wholesale, and Department Store Union.	1,400
Atlas Chemical Industries, Inc., Volunteer Army Ammunition Plant (Chattanooga, Tenn.).	Chemicals	District #50, Mine Workers	1,800
Avco Corp., Ordnance Division (Richmond, Ind.)	Ordnance	Electrical Workers (IBEW)	2,000
Baltimore Transit Co. (Baltimore, Md.)	Transit	Amalgamated Transit Union	1,650
Borg-Warner Corp. Morse Chain Division (Ithaca, N.Y.)	Machinery	Machinists	1,050
Building Managers Assn., Elevator Operators (Chicago, Ill.)	Finance, insurance, and real estate	Service Employees	1,050
Building Managers Assn., Janitors (Chicago, Ill.)	Finance, insurance, and real estate	Service Employees	4,000
California Bakery Employers Assn. (California)	Food products	Teamsters (Ind.)	3,500
Chicago Luggage and Leather Goods Manufacturers Assn. (Chicago, Ill.)	Leather	Meat Cutters	1,000
Columbia Broadcasting Systems, Inc. (Interstate)	Communication	Electrical Workers (IBEW)	1,100
Consolidated Gas Supply Co. (Clarksburg, W. Va.)	Utilities	Allegheny Mountain Gas Workers' Union (Ind.).	1,500
E. I. du Pont de Nemours and Co., Spruance Plant, Film Department (Ampthill, Chesterfield County, Va.).	Chemicals	Transparent Film Workers, Inc. (Ind.)	1,150
Field Construction Work [2] (Ohio, Kentucky, and West Virginia)	Construction	Boilermakers	1,000
Florida Power & Light Co. (Florida)	Utilities	Electrical Workers (IBEW)	3,000
Food Fair Stores, Inc. (New York, and New Jersey)	Retail trade	Retail Clerks	1,450
Hotels and Motels [2] (Washington, D.C.)	Hotels	Hotel and Restaurant Employees	5,500
Maremont Corp., New England Division (Saco, Maine)	Machinery	Textile Workers Union	1,000
Mason & Hanger-Silas Mason Co. Inc., Iowa Army Ammunition Plant and Burlington AEC Plant (Burlington, Iowa).	Ordnance	Machinists	1,850
National Electrical Contractors Assn. (Southern Florida)	Construction	Electrical Workers (IBEW)	2,500
National Lead Co. (Fernald, Ohio)	Primary metals	Fernald AFL–CIO Atomic Trades and Labor Council.	1,000
Northeast Airlines, Inc., clerical employees [3] (Interstate)	Airline	Transport Workers	1,500
Northwest Airlines, Inc., clerical, office, fleet, and passenger service employees.[3] (Interstate).	Airline	Railway Clerks	2,000
Pari-Mutual Department of Southern California Race Tracks [2] (California)	Amusements	Service Employees	1,000
Pet, Inc., Dairy Division (Interstate)	Food products	Teamsters (Ind.)	2,000
Prudential Insurance Co. of America (Interstate)	Finance, insurance, and real estate	Insurance Workers	17,700

[1] Union affiliated with AFL–CIO except where noted as independent (Ind.).
[2] Industry area (group of companies signing same contract).
[3] Information is from newspaper account of settlement.

carpenters, the printers, the iron and steel workers, and the molders. It concentrated its attention upon developing a structure and a program fitted to the necessities of collective bargaining. There was at last a national organization of unions, each capable of bargaining with employers on a basis approximating equality.

Perhaps the most deceptive weapon of all against collective bargaining was the "company union." Recognizing the strong desire of workers to form a union, many employers responded by organizing unions which they themselves controlled. Thus the employers were able to create the illusion of collective bargaining, even though it was a collective bargaining in which the employer sat on both sides of the bargaining table. The first employer-dominated union on record was organized in Boston in 1898. The device became increasingly popular among employers, especially in the years following the first World War. In 1928, the peak year of company unionism, more than one and a half million workers were "represented" by company unions.

Yet despite this determined opposition, unionism grew and collective bargaining spread throughout industry. It spread because it fulfilled a critical need on the part of workers.

The development of orderly and democratic ways of settling industrial disputes was a matter of national interest as much as a matter of interest to the workers immediately involved. Yet it was not until the enactment of the National Industrial Recovery Act and the Wagner Act in the early New Deal days that the acceptance of collective bargaining became a matter of public policy. Previous court decisions and legislative victories had been hailed by union leaders as providing a legal sanction for collective bargaining, but the actual results always proved disappointing. Although the court decision in the Commonwealth vs. Hunt case in 1842 had upheld the legality of unionism, the effects of the decision were soon nullified by court injuctions. AFL leaders believed that the Clayton Act of 1914 was "Labor's Magna Carta." The Clayton Act, declaring that "the labor of a human being is not a commodity," exempted unions from the provisions of the Sherman Anti-Trust Law. But the Clayton Act did not stop court injunctions, industrial spies, and company-dominated unions. The Norris-LaGuardia Act of 1932, regulating court injunctions against unions, was an outstanding legislative victory for labor. Employers responded, however, by stepping up their hiring of labor spies and professional strike breakers.

The National Industrial Recovery Act and the Wagner Act finally declared, as a matter of public policy, "that employees shall have the right to organize and bargain collectively through representatives of their own choosing." The impact was beyond all expectations. In the five years between 1933 and 1938, union membership in the United States jumped from slightly over two million members to more than seven and a half million members.

How Collective Bargaining Works

A union becomes the bargaining agent for a group of workers when the employer agrees that it represents the majority of them. Most commonly this is determined by a secret vote, conducted by the National Labor Relations Board under exacting conditions of fair play. If a clear majority of the workers involved indicate a desire to be represented by the union, then that union is "certified" as the collective bargaining agent for the employees.

Representatives of the union and representatives of management then meet together at the bargaining table and they try to get together on a collective agreement or contract. Rarely are the two sides in agreement when they begin their meetings, and rarely is the final product of their deliberations precisely what either side wanted when they began. Collective bargaining is a matter of give and take, with labor and management gradually moving closer together. When the union representatives and the management representatives have finally agreed on a contract, the union representatives take the contract back to their members. If it does not satisfy them, they will send their union representatives back to continue the bargaining process or they may decide to reinforce their demands by going on strike.

Once the contract has been ratified by the union and by the management, it becomes the guiding principle of labor-management relations for the duration of the agreement. No longer are workers subject to the arbitrary whims of the employer or his representative. Industrial relations have been established on an orderly basis.

There are approximately 150,000 of these collective agreements in force in the United States today. Of these, 147,000 were successfully negotiated without any work-stoppage taking place. This is an important fact, often overlooked in discussions about collective bargaining. There is an element of excitement about a strike that draws public attention, but there is much less attention given to the thousands of union-management agreements that are regularly negotiated without any work stoppage taking place. An average of 300 collective bargaining agreements are concluded every day without strikes. This triumph of free democratic labor-management relations is so commonplace that it is not newsworthy and it is therefore usually overlooked.

To say that most collective bargaining agreements are effected without strikes is not to deny the importance of those strikes which do take place or which might take place. In the final analysis, labor's power at the bargaining table is closely related to its potential ability to strike.

The employer has many weapons that he can use to force the union to move closer to his position. Greatest of these is the threat that he will shut down his operation either temporarily or permanently or the similar threat that he will move his operation to another state where he may get more concessions from labor. The principal strength of the workers at the bargaining table comes from the fact that if the employer does not sufficiently heed their demands, they will withhold their work. Because both sides know what the other can do, it is rarely necessary for either side to use its ultimate economic strength. Moreover, it must be remembered that it is a major decision for a group of workers to call a strike. A strike, especially if it is of long duration, costs workers a great deal in lost wages and it places heavy drains upon the resources of their union. Union members therefore do not lightly reach a decision to go on strike. But without their ultimate strength, they could not engage in realistic collective bargaining.

Bargaining: A Variety of Patterns

The precise forms of collective bargaining vary considerably from industry to industry, depending largely upon the nature of the particular industry involved. Inevitably a union engaged in collective bargaining with industrial giants such as the automobile manufacturers will operate differently than a union engaged in bargaining in an industry of relatively small producers such as the garment industry. Within the general framework of democratic collective bargaining, therefore, each union and each industry has developed its own unique patterns of bargaining.

One kind of bargaining situation is that involving the building construction industry. Building contractors operate essentially in a local market. The work must be done where it is needed, unlike some kinds of manufacturing which can easily be moved from one city to another. Since their product is not transportable, building contractors are competitive only in the local market area.

Local market bargaining is therefore characteristic of the building trades. Collective bargaining takes place between various local unions of construction workers and the local trade association of contractors. These local unions have a great deal of autonomy in bargaining, and no attempts are made by their international unions to impose a uniform pattern of wages or working conditions.

Construction unions are among the oldest in America, so well established in their industry that most contractors have long accepted the practice of collective bargaining. An important fact which has shaped collective bargaining in the construction industry is that workers are usually employed at a job site for a period of short duration. When disputes arise between the union and the employer, they must be settled quickly. The time consuming process of arbitration would in most cases only result in settling the issue long after the job was finished. Settlement of grievances is

therefore largely the responsibility of the local union's business agent and the employer.

Recent years have seen the rise of national building construction contractors, employers who go from city to city doing construction work. This development has introduced new problems and led to national agreements in the construction industry, but even under these national agreements, the employers are required in each city where they operate to observe local wages and working conditions. Even the national agreements therefore follow the pattern of local market bargaining.

This method of collective bargaining works well for a union which is dealing with employers who are not nationally competitive. Retail food stores and newspaper publishers are similarly competitive on a local market and here too collective bargaining is ordinarily conducted locally.

On the other hand these patterns of bargaining would not work at all in such an industry as the women's apparel industry. Manufacturers of apparel are fiercely competitive over a nation-wide market. Most of the employers are small scale producers. The industry requires relatively little capital investment and labor cost accounts for a considerable part of the cost of the finished product. A difference of a few cents in labor costs may well make the difference between financial success and bankruptcy for an employer.

The local market bargaining which is logical for the carpenters' union would be meaningless for a union dealing with General Motors whose assets are spread across the nation and whose financial control may be located far away from its major centers of production.

The automobile workers have therefore developed their own unique patterns of collective bargaining. Workers in each General Motors plant belong to their own local union of the United Automobile Workers. Each of these locals is part of the UAW's General Motors Council and it is this Council which negotiates a collective bargaining agreement with General Motors. Purely local issues are left to be settled in separate negotiations between the local unions and the local plant managers, but the basic structure of collective bargaining is determined nationally, and it must be so. What is more, having reached agreement with General Motors, the union must then press for similar benefits from Ford and Chrysler. Otherwise General Motors would be at a competitive disadvantage because of the benefits to which it had agreed in collective bargaining with the union.

The local union of the Carpenters' Union is a logical unit to negotiate a collective agreement with building contractors, but for a local union of General Motors workers to attempt to negotiate an agreement with General Motors Corporation would be futile.

In short, there is no single pattern of collective bargaining which can meet all of the varied conditions under which labor-management relationships must take place. It is a major achievement of America's free democratic unions and of its responsible employers that we have been able to evolve an infinite variety of patterns of collective bargaining to meet an infinite variety of industrial situations.

Labor Relations Today and Tomorrow

The general climate of labor relations today raises some serious questions in many quarters as to where it is headed, and what shape it will take in the future. Recent confrontations between labor and management, for example, have been dramatic and in many cases costly in terms of both strikes and settlements. Relations between unions and within unions, in addition, have been showing signs of stress and distress. At the same time, labor unions have been making gains in the unionization of white collar personnel.

How do businessmen react to these developments? Responses of 143 senior executives of U.S. manufacturing corporations participating in the Board's latest Survey of Business Opinion and Experience give the following general indications:

• There is general agreement among the executives that union wage demands and negotiated settlements are too high—and decidedly inflationary, at least to the extent that they exceed increases in productivity.

• There's a wide range of opinion, however, as to what can or should be done to break—or brake—the present pattern. Many see the answer resting with government (fiscal reforms, wage and price guidelines or controls, legislation to reduce the power of unions), while others look to business to hold the line. Still others believe that probably nothing can be done.

• General displeasure is also voiced over the recent record of strike activity; the respondents are uniform in their indictment of strikes as being very costly—often to the public as well as the parties involved.

• As with the wage pattern, participating executives are far from unanimous as to what should be done about strikes. Many maintain that strikes must be tolerated in a free enterprise economy. Others propose a variety of legislative and non-legislative schemes to either eliminate strikes or to reduce their impact, scope, or frequency.

• Beyond the pressing problems of the present wage pattern and strike record, about as many executives on the panel think that union leaders accurately reflect the will of the members as do not. As to white collar unionization, over two-thirds predict that recent increases in such unionization will be a continuing trend.

• Looking further ahead into the future of labor relations and collective bargaining, almost half the responding executives expect a substantial increase in government intervention or control by 1984. The rest either envision changes that will not entail government intervention or foresee no marked changes at all.

WAGES AND INFLATION

Perhaps the single largest concern among businessmen today in the area of labor relations is the present level of union wage demands and negotiated wage settlements. The opinions of the 143 survey participants about these demands and settlements amount to a uniform indictment of the present pattern as too high. In characterizing the present level of demands and settlements these businessmen frequently use such words as "excessive," "exorbitant," "unreasonable," and "unrealistic," and some add "preposterous," "ridiculous," "shocking" and "out of sight."

There is also general agreement that current settlements are inflationary, and that they have been for some time. A few executives point out that this inflationary pattern started with the airline settlement in late 1966 and has continued—or "snowballed"—up to the present time. The common view is that present wage settlements are inflationary because they exceed increases in productivity. As an aircraft executive states, increases are inflationary "to the extent that they exceed increases in productivity—and in recent years this has been anywhere from 50 to 66⅔% of the wage increases." Many other respondents cite a figure of 3% as the annual average increase in productivity and a figure of between 5 and 7% as the general pattern of current wage settlements.

It is the opinion of a few companies, however, that while the pattern of demand and settlement is inflationary, in certain cases the unions have exercised restraint in the face of competition from non-union companies and from abroad.

Some participants emphasize that negotiated settlements are only one part of the inflationary picture. A general industrial machine executive says, for instance, that "the causes of inflation are very complex, and it would be inappropriate to focus on negotiated wage increases as the major cause of inflation."

A few executives, in fact, see present negotiated settlements as being more of a response to rising prices than a cause. "With prices rising about 4% a year, which is greater than productivity increases, you can't blame labor for its adamant stand," asserts the head of an electrical appliance firm.

In terms of what sustains the present pattern of union demands and settlements, a number of factors are suggested in addition to rising prices. These include an anticipation of future inflationary price movements, an effort to make up take-home pay losses occasioned by increases in taxes and social security contributions, strong inter-union competition at the bargaining table, increases in the starting salaries of college graduates, a tight labor market with shortages in skilled labor, the rising costs of medical care (typically a substantial part of the fringe benefit package), and even a reflection of the rebellion which, to some respondents, appears to be endemic in today's society. A substantial number of executives specifically cite settlements in the construction industry as contributing a great deal to the present inflationary pattern.

But whatever the causes of such demands and settlements, and whatever the effects, the one word that appears over and over in the comments of the cooperating executives is "spiral," and a significant number of them see this spiral as a serious threat to the economy.

STRIKES AND ALTERNATIVES TO STRIKES

The displeasure expressed by survey participants over the present wage pattern is paralleled by their views on the recent record of strike activity; they are unanimous in their belief that strikes are very costly to the parties involved and often to the general public as well.

Yet, a large number of them say that the right to strike is a price that probably must be paid lest some form of government intervention or control be instituted. As an auto company executive states, "I don't think we can classify the right to strike as outmoded until we are prepared to consider free collective bargaining outmoded; when and if we come to this point we shall have decided to give up a substantial area of individual freedom." The president of a chemical company makes a similar comment: "As costly as are strikes and the threat of strikes, I can conceive of no alternatives to collective bargaining which would not pose threats to important institutions of our free society." An oil company president is concerned primarily with the abandonment of labor and management's prerogatives. "Both labor and the business community should be very reluctant to push for alternatives which would eliminate the responsibility of labor and management jointly to resolve their differences."

Among those who do see alternatives to strikes as necessary, compulsory arbitration is frequently mentioned—in some cases on a blanket basis, but in most cases limited to those strikes that have an adverse affect on the general public. (All executives commenting on the point agree that the right to strike has no place in government employment). Advocacy of compulsory arbitration tends to be conditional, though, as a comment from the chairman of an iron and steel foundry illustrates:

"It would be a great thing if we could eliminate strikes by making use of compulsory arbitration provided that it would be done in a non-political, non-biased atmosphere. Compulsory arbitration is only as good as the arbitrators are earnest, sincere, and unbiased."

Quite a few executives, however, denounce compulsory arbitration, expressing either a general aversion to government intervention or a fear that a pro-labor bias would tend to develop. But these prospects are not the only factors arguing against compulsory arbitration. According to some executives, there would be practical problems as well. A diversified consumer products company executive believes that "compulsory arbitration is an alternative, but probably not very effective since neither management nor the union could reach a settlement. The majority of settlements would go to arbitration, and this would be a very time-consuming process with resulting employee discontent." But regardless of the reasons, there appear to be a substantial number of executives who go along with the view of a metalworking machinery company chairman that "compulsory arbitration would be a long step backwards."

Other legislative suggestions made by responding executives to eliminate strikes or reduce their impact, scope, or frequency include:

• Limiting the power of unions by subjecting them to antitrust laws.

• Modifying existing labor laws to restore the balance of power between management and labor.

• Restricting negotiations to single plants.

• Limiting the allowable duration of strikes in important industries.

• Establishing a mandatory cooling off period in all disputes such as the one used at present in national-emergency disputes.

• Requiring a secret ballot vote for employees on whether to accept or reject the company proposal for settlement.

"Gentlemen, instead of trying to mediate this thing, why don't you just slug it out?"

Reprinted by permission from *Management Review*

© 1967 by American Management Association

- Providing more extensive non-binding mediation.

Three other proposals are advanced by respondents which would not involve legislative enactments. One is that earlier negotiations might help to ease the race against time that so often bedevils contract negotiations. Several companies, one executive observes, have adopted this practice.

The second non-legislative alternative to strikes consists of variations on a scheme that received some attention four years ago—a strike-work agreement entered into between a local of the Upholsters Union and the Dunbar Furniture Corporation in Berne, Indiana. The agreement calls for a continuation of work after the termination date of the agreement, with half of the employees' pay and a matching amount from the employer being put into escrow. If the parties settle within six weeks, the money is returned to each party; if no settlement is reached in six weeks, the percentage recoverable by the parties is progressively reduced, with the balance going to local public service projects; and if no settlement is reached by the twelfth week, all the money in escrow is given to such projects. Only then can a strike or lockout take place.

UNION LEADERSHIP AND MEMBERSHIP

A question which arises frequently in the labor relations area today, particularly in light of the high level of strike activity, is how responsive union leaders are to the rank and file. About two-fifths of the respondents offering opinions feel that union leaders do not accurately reflect the will of the members. The most frequent observation by this group of executives is that the leadership of today tends to be somewhat more reasonable and conservative than its membership, as evidenced by the substantial number of rejections of negotiated settlements by union members. As the president of an industrial machinery company phrases it, "the union leadership has lost control of the rank and file."

Other explanations advanced for the failure of union leaders to reflect the will of the membership are:

- Union security clauses and laws such as those providing for dues check-off and compulsory union membership remove the necessity for leaders to reflect the will of the membership.

- Union leaders very often merely reflect the will of a militant minority rather than the majority of members.

- Trends in the structure of collective bargaining towards company-wide, industry-wide and coordinated bargaining make leaders less responsive to the will of the members.

A very few respondents say that union leaders, far from reflecting the will of their members, direct or create the members' will. According to a nonferrous metals company, "More often than not, the membership

---

White Collar Individualism

Recognizing the individuality of the white collar worker is frequently mentioned as important in preventing white collar unionism. This view finds expression in the statement of a textile company executive:

"White collar unionism will continue to increase unless business begins to treat its white collar and professional people with respect to their needs and desires, and less with respect to what the hourly workers have negotiated. We must accept the fact that as our population increases the trend will continue for less identification as individuals and more as members of a group or profession. As this group identification increases, the tendency to vent grievances as a group will grow.

"Unless we as businessmen are perceptive and receptive to the needs of the individuals within these groups, we will be dealing with a situation where we will have highly organized groups in every area of our companies. The strategy with respect to our own companies must be to listen attentively to the concerns and desires of our white collar and professional people and, in our personal relations, to develop opportunities for emphasizing the individual and to deal with him more as an individual and less as a member of the salaried group.

"I believe that a person will respond well to this emphasis on him and on his job contribution. Giving employees an opportunity for recognition as individuals with respect to their jobs will offset, to a large degree, the de-emphasis of individual contributions in a highly populated society."

---

has reflected the will of the union leaders. It is interesting to note that as the members have become increasingly vocal in their opposition, the government has counter-moved to strengthen the power of union leaders over their members."

Of the two-fifths of the survey participants who see union leaders as being responsive to the will of the membership, several indicate that this may be unwise and not always in the best interests of the members.

WHITE COLLAR UNIONIZATION

Over two-thirds of the executives commenting on the point express the belief that recent increases in white collar unionization[1] will be a continuing trend in industry. In addition, several who hold the opposite view think that there will be a growth in white collar unionization among *government* employees. The reasons given include:

- Unions will expend more effort in organizing office, sales, and professional employees since the blue collar sector offers diminishing organizing potential.

- Unionism today appears more profitable to the white collar worker, particularly in light of recently negotiated settlements.

- Unionism is becoming more respectable due to the increased unionization of government employees, professionals, and teachers.
- Computers have created more routine and depersonalized white collar occupations which tend to be compatible with unionization.
- The sociological bridge between white collar and blue collar workers is narrowing.
- Unions are becoming more sophisticated in appeals to white collar groups.
- White collar workers have less job security due to mergers.
- There is a general trend to group identification, less to individual achievement.
- The present labor laws and NLRB decisions are conducive to unionization.
- White collar workers feel increasingly less able to influence their work environment and, like other groups in society, feel the need for more power.
- Supervisors continue to make mistakes that lead to employee discontent.
- The vast size of many companies has led to a loss of identity among white collar workers.

The list of reasons offered by survey participants who do not expect white collar unionization to be a growing or continuing trend in the private sector is shorter:

- Management is doing a better job.

- Unions do not understand the needs of the white collar employee.
- White collar employees are independent and do not want unions.
- The opportunity for and expectations of promotion to managerial positions make the case for unionism weaker.
- Unions do not have enough organizers to unionize the growing white collar sector.
- White collar workers are too intelligent to want union representation.

One respondent gives an "it depends" answer to the question of further unionization of white-collar workers: "White collar unionization indicates a failure on the part of management to communicate with their white-collar employees and whether it increases or not depends upon the extent to which management develops proper communications programs with its white-collar employees and listens to the needs and wants of this employment group."

Asked to indicate what their companies do, if anything, to prevent the unionization of their white collar personnel, a good number of respondents point out that the policies and procedures they adopt are not specifically designed to thwart unionization, but rather reflect good management practice. The most commonly cited in this connection are paying competitive salaries and offering fringe benefits in line with area practice, and matching or bettering bargaining unit compensation; fostering close personal relationships; making regular salary reviews, including cost-of-living reviews in some cases; offering stock options, profit sharing plans, and incentive compensation systems; maintaining good communications; treating employees as individuals; making employees feel that they are part of management; attempting to achieve stable employment; establishing grievance procedures; training supervisors to be responsive to employee needs and complaints; and, in a few cases, using employee representation committees. A few companies report that they openly communicate to their white collar employees that a union would be undesirable and not in their best interests.

LABOR RELATIONS IN 1984

What will labor relations and collective bargaining be like in 1984? The participants' answers to this possibly leading question vary widely, but certain general observations can be made:

- The largest group of executives—53 in all—see collective bargaining and labor relations coming under greater governmental intervention, control or regulation. The expected variety of forms it will take include compulsory arbitration, labor courts, tri-partite bargaining, statutory regulation of fringe benefits and pension plans, and socialism.
- Another 21 executives, on the other hand, foresee no marked changes in collective bargaining in the future, or at most forecast relatively mild variations.
- Other executives predict significant changes that will not entail government intervention: more enlightened bargaining relationships, more scientific bargaining, more centralized and coordinated bargaining, a restoration of the balance of power between the parties, and an expansion in the subject matter of collective bargaining to include such items as tuition aid, auto insurance and extra vacation pay.

Thus the forecasts run the gamut from pessimism to optimism. Representative of those who see a significant increase in government intervention and control are the statements of the presidents of a paper company and an industrial machinery company:

"As to what labor relations and collective bargaining may be like in 1984, I can only say that I shall be happy to have long since retired before that date comes around. My feeling is, however, that if the present trends continue, with increasing governmental regulation of industry and commerce, management will have lost its right to manage, and we will no longer have a free society. The present socialistic trends will bring about an impossible situation that will in turn lead to the establishment of authoritative government either of the right or the left, and those who are responsible for operating production units will be doing so as instruments of the state."

"Perhaps not by 1984 but certainly sometime before 1990 I expect that labor relations will follow much the same pattern as Sweden. It is my understanding (although in conversation it is frequently denied) that actually wage negotiations in Sweden are conducted and wage levels set by a tri-partite negotiating group—the unions, management, and the government. In essence, the government representatives must bring the negotiations into patterns which satisfy labor so far as the cost of living is concerned and still not be inflationary so far as the economy is concerned. This technique, combined with compulsory arbitration for the industries providing utility services, will, I think, become the pattern for America too. It isn't necessarily good, but I think it will happen."

Typical of those who foresee no drastic changes in labor relations and collective bargaining, an oil company executive submits this analysis:

"In most respects the labor relations and collective bargaining of 1984 will probably not be dramatically different from today's. This conclusion is based on two premises: (1) both unionism and collective bargaining are relatively mature institutions which are not likely to undergo any self-generated changes, and (2) the collective bargaining system is working well enough that major changes will not be imposed from without. This second premise seems somewhat more questionable than the first.

"If we look backwards 16 years to 1952 we observe (1) little change in the size and structure of the labor movement, despite the AFL-CIO merger; (2) a moderately increased role played by government relating largely to the conduct of the two parties; (3) increased emphasis upon benefit plans, particularly in the area of job security; and

(4) a decline in the importance of the role played by unions and collective bargaining in the political, social and economic affairs of the country. It seems likely that these trends will continue for the next 16 years, leaving unions and the collective bargaining process diminished in importance but essentially unchanged in character. If more basic changes do take place, they are likely to be the introduction of incomes policy or some related form of wage-price controls. However, the limited success of such techniques in Europe suggests that indirect approaches to the control of wage and price movements, such as fiscal and manpower policies, will receive the main attention."

At the brighter end of the spectrum are those executives who are optimistic about the future of labor relations and collective bargaining. One of these is the chief executive of a steel company who prognosticates:

"Hopefully by 1984 we may have found practical and effective alternatives to strikes, but I am not at all certain this will be the case. I think by 1984 we will see a more mature and practical relationship between labor and management, one that has been developing over the past 20 years and will continue to develop. Perhaps this in itself will be the main factor in reducing costly strikes. This relationship will be improved over the years ahead through the development of greater confidence on the part of labor and management in each other. I also think that both parties will play a more active role in facing up to their responsibilities for contributing to a stable and healthy economy. By this I mean that labor leaders will recognize the importance of the relationship of productivity improvements to wage and benefit improvements, and a more responsible attitude on the part of management in sharing a fair portion of the productivity improvement with the labor force."

National Airlines Finally Finds Labor Peace

In the 14 years that L. B. Maytag Jr. has exerted his one-man rule over National Airlines, it has been shut down a total of 397 days by strikes. This record, the worst in the industry, reflects Maytag's willingness to take strikes rather than "give the unions everything they want."

This policy has kept labor costs down, but the constant strife it has created has severely undercut worker morale, traffic volume, and profits. Last week Maytag took an unprecedented step to change that picture, and he may well have charted a new labor relations course for the airline industry.

After months of secret talks, National signed the industry's first no-strike agreement with its largest union, the Air Line Employees Assn. (ALEA), which represents 3,300 ticket, reservation, and station agents. The pact prohibits strikes or lockouts and calls for binding arbitration of unresolved economic issues when ALEA's contract comes up for renewal in May, 1977. ALEA is guaranteed wage increases of at least 5% a year—it can try to negotiate more—and though work rules are not arbitrable because of their complexity, the union agreed not to strike over them.

This agreement, along with last week's ratification of a three-year wage contract by the International Assn. of Machinists (IAM), guarantees labor peace at the nation's most strike-prone airline until 1978. The period of stability would be much longer if National's six other unions also accept a no-strike pact.

"It's a great step even if only one union goes along," says Maytag, who is chairman and president of National. "It could put pressure on the other unions, and I hope it will."

The IAM and unions representing pilots, flight engineers, and flight attendants have all talked favorably of the concept and are now negotiating separately with National. Further agreements could be announced soon. Negotiations are also under way at some of the other airlines. Captain J. J. O'Donnell, president of the pilots' union, says that he has discussed "no-strike" with three carriers and that he

hopes to reach the first agreement by May.

Profit tailspin. Airline profits went into a tailspin last year, and the companies are anxious to avoid crippling strikes. It takes months to regain traffic volume after a prolonged walkout. But few of the larger carriers have major union contracts coming up this year, and none—with the notable exception of Northwest—have been as plagued with labor troubles as National. Thus, most lack National's compelling reason for letting an outside arbitrator make costly decisions on wages and benefits.

However, the basic steel industry and the United Steelworkers used a no-strike procedure in 1974 negotiations without having to rely on arbitration. Their fear of submitting issues to an arbitrator—at best, the results are unpredictable—forced the union and 10 major companies to settle all issues by themselves. Without a strike threat, the industry avoided customer hedge-buying and the consequent boom-bust cycle, layoffs, and loss of profits.

National Airlines' strike record

Union	Year	Length
ALEA (Air Line Employees Assn.)	1964	1 day
Machinists	1966	43 days
Machinists	1969	wildcat*
ALEA	1970	118 days
ALEA	1973	6 hours
Machinists	1974	108 days
Flight Attendants	1975	127 days

*Operations were not shut down

Data: National Airlines

David H. Stowe, chairman of the National Mediation Board, which oversees airline bargaining under the National Railway Labor Act, is pushing the no-strike concept and feels that it could spread. A further impetus comes from the fact that some union and airline executives—Maytag, for one—dislike the NRLA's lengthy mediation procedures, which can drag out contract negotiations for a year or more.

Mort B. Wigderson, an ALEA vice-president who negotiated the new procedure with National, says its main virtue is that it speeds up wage bargaining. In 1977, if ALEA and National fail to reach agreement on new contract terms during 120 days of negotiations and mediation by the NMB, they

will select an arbitrator who must rule within 45 days. The procedure is designed, Wigderson says, "to cut away unnecessary time and, most important, to cut away the emotionalism that develops on both sides as negotiations drag out and that is destructive to intelligently arriving at an agreement."

Question of survival. Since 1970, National's employees have lost nearly a year of work because of strikes, including a 118-day ALEA strike in 1970, a machinists' walkout of 108 days in 1974, and last fall's 127-day strike by the Assn. of Flight Attendants. National has yet to recover from the last strike; it lost $3.4 million in January

> **'It's a great step even if only one union goes along. It could put pressure on the others'**
>
> L. B. Maytag Jr., National Airlines chairman

because of post-strike start-up costs, and its January traffic plunged 38% from the previous year.

Only a few months ago, with National shut down by the flight attendants and the IAM in negotiations, Maytag was questioning whether the airline would survive. He then called the union leaders to his Miami office and broached the no-strike idea. As it turned out, the IAM was not eager to strike. Six weeks after the flight attendants returned to work, the IAM settled for a 25% wage increase for 1,350 mechanics over three years.

Far from going out of business, National will now probably resume its money-making ways. Since Maytag, now 48, became chief executive in 1962, National has reported a loss in only one year—1970, when the ALEA struck for four months. Along with Delta and Northwest, it is the most consistently profitable of the nation's 11 trunk carriers. Despite last year's strike, National reported a $10.5 million profit in calendar 1975, largely because it received $52 million from other airlines under the industry's Mutual Aid Pact (MAP). This provides for a strike-bound airline to receive a portion of extra revenues generated for competitors by the strike.

National's consistent profitability is attributable partly to a good route structure. It has relatively few of the puddle-jumping hops that characterize the routes of its larger competitor, Eastern Airlines. But Maytag, like Northwest's Donald W. Nyrop (BW—

> **'To me, the whole purpose of the agreement is to not use the arbitration proceeding'**
>
> Jack Donlan, National vice-president

Feb. 16), also runs a very tight ship. He operates with only 11 subordinate officers, the smallest number of any trunk carrier. And through tough bargaining on work rules, the productivity of his 7,000-person work force exceeds that of most airlines.

Blunt criticism. Says A. A. McKesson, president of the flight engineers' local union at National: "They [Maytag and his staff] operate close to the chest, and that's why they make money. They're astute, smart, cost-conscious operators, and I see nothing wrong with it."

Maytag, who is exceedingly blunt in his assessment of other airlines, contends that many are "on the brink of bankruptcy" because they give in to the demands of unions. He is particularly disdainful of Eastern. "I think Eastern let the work rules eat them up," Maytag says. "They have all kinds of restrictive rules that hurt productivity, while lots of others, like us, don't. We're willing to strike rather than give in. If we weren't willing, we'd be dead."

Frank Borman, Eastern's new president, concedes that in the past Eastern often surrendered too much to the unions. But a few months ago he persuaded the IAM to agree to a one-year wage freeze. "We didn't give up anything in the work rules," he adds. "The business of giving up on the work rules is over as far as I'm concerned."

The work rule provisions in National's union contracts allow the airline greater flexibility in scheduling work than some other carriers. The IAM contract, for example, permits National to switch mechanics between on-line maintenance and engine overhaul as needed; other airlines cannot "cross-utilize" crews in this way. National's 825 pilots fly about 60 to 62 hours a month, compared with only 48 at Eastern, and National gets more work out of its pilots in a variety of ways. "If National were flying Eastern's schedules," says Captain Charles Caudle, president of the Air Line Pilots Assn. local at National, "we'd do it with 1,000 fewer pilots because we fly more hours."

In addition to the ALEA, National must also negotiate new wage terms next year with the flight attendants. Their contract becomes renewable in May, 1977. But even if that union rejects a no-strike pact, the NMB would probably keep negotiations under way well into 1978.

None of National's other unions will bargain before then, assuring the airline of at least two and possibly three years of labor stability. And the other unions could well follow the ALEA's lead in pledging not to strike.

Growing process. John Burch, head of National's IAM local, says he is not opposed to such an agreement "with certain guarantees," including the recall of 91 furloughed mechanics. Although the national leadership of the IAM disapproves of no-strike agreements in principle, Burch's local has the autonomy necessary to make its own decisions. A major obstacle, however, may be the insistence of Burch—and of the pilots' leaders—that National withdraw from the industry's Mutual Aid Pact.

Maytag had indicated that he would consider this demand in return for "five years of labor peace." But the ALEA pact guarantees only two years, and a further barrier to withdrawal is that MAP contains a retroactive clause: If National pulls out and then decides to return, it would have to reimburse other airlines that are struck in the meantime.

The ALEA no-strike agreement, however, has a feature that is attractive to both sides. If any issues go to arbitration in 1977, the binding award will prevent the ALEA from striking for two years. But because one or both sides might feel that arbitration is unworkable, it could not be used again unless both sides agree.

"To me, the whole purpose of the agreement is to not use the arbitration provision," says Jack Donlan, National's industrial relations vice-president. "Every time we don't use it, the parties will become more familiar with settling on their own. It will be a growing process for both of us."

UAW's Bluestone Sees Unions In 'Managing The Enterprise'

MANAGERS—already fretting over what they call the erosion of management rights to the swelling tide of unionism—have seen only the beginning if observations of Irving Bluestone, director, General Motors Dept., United Auto Workers, prove accurate.

"Workers organized in unions have drastically modified the traditional, unadulterated, autocratic managerial control over the worker and the workplace. In the 35 years of industrial unionism's growth, the concept of workers' rights has taken root and has flowered. The time is now ripe for the second stage [of the drive for industrial democracy]: the worker's direct participation in the decision-making process," the union leader told the Conference Board during its two-day session in New York devoted to exploring "American Competitiveness in the World Marketplace."

In a calm and unheated presentation, he asserted it is "too early" to tell "what forms new inroads toward the fulfillment of industrial democracy will take." But he indicated "it will evidence itself initially in the area of 'managing the worker's job' and then will spread to aspects of 'managing the enterprise.'"

System paramount—Attacking what he called the "profits before people" system, Mr. Bluestone charged that "management has concluded that in order to achieve these objectives [maximally advanced technology with maximum production at lowest

BLUESTONE — *Time is ripe for worker's direct participation in the decision-making process.*

possible unit cost, and maximum profitability], it is necessary to break down the worker's job into the smallest divisions of work consistent with productive efficiency. The worker is then positioned into this rigid work system; it is the system that is paramount, and not the human being."

He dismissed human engineering concepts which "may make for more comfortable employer-employee relationships" by charging that even in those concepts "managerial administration of the workplace remains fundamentally unchanged."

"Humanizing the workplace . . . must move to a higher plateau and relate to job satisfaction, a closing of the widening gap between the ever-increasing mechanization of pro-

duction by scientific management and the participation which the worker can enjoy in the productive and decision-making process," he added.

He pointed out that "workers young and old continue to aspire toward a better life — to be won at the bargaining table and in legislation."

Mr. Bluestone conceded that technological progress is inevitable and desirable, that a better living standard depends on increased productivity, and that the purpose of business is to make and maximize profits. But at the same time he felt it was "a sad commentary on our society that it has not embraced with equal enthusiasm the concept of full employment."

No thaw—And he left little hope that the current economic and trade situation might bring a general thaw in union-management relations. He prophesied:

"New challenges are in the offing as workers question traditional authoritarian managerial prerogatives and seek more meaningful ways and means to participate in the decision-making process that directly or indirectly affects their welfare."

And those managers who feel that industrial democracy is already here probably took little heart in Mr. Bluestone's definition: "Industrial democracy is a broader concept than is currently incorporated in the provisions of the usual labor contract; it is essentially the extension of workers' rights and responsibilities in the management of his work and in the decisions of the enterprise."

CONSIDER

CHALLENGES

1. Do you feel that it is fair for unions to have the power to strike and perhaps close down an entire industry on a national basis, such as the railroads or trucking? Explain.

2. Do you support state legislation that provides for the "right to work?" Explain.

3. Would there be no unemployment if there were no technological change? If there were no economic downturns? Explain.

4. Consider what your grandfather did for a living. How did technology affect his occupation? Will it exist in 1985?

5. There is trend towards a shorter work week -- 35, 30, even 20 hours a week. What will be the likely impact on employment?

6. Do you feel that an earnings protection plan is fair? to the workers? to the stockholders? to the consumers? Explain.

7. Do you agree with union demands for annual pay increases to meet inflation? Explain. What is the impact on our economy?

8. Do you think management would be any different if companies had no unions? Explain.

9. Should the federal government ban strikes altogether? Explain what the impact would be.

10. Have the purposes of labor unions changed over the past century?

Outline a plan for creating 1000 new jobs in your community. Indicate what resources you would need and whose support would be required.

Find out the rate of unemployment in your community during each of the past twelve months. Explain why the rate is what it is and why fluctuations occurred.

Interview a friend or relative who is a member of a union. Ask him why he joined and what the benefits of being a member are.

Find out if the faculty at your college or university are represented by a labor organization. Trace the history of the organization or of attempts to establish representation.

Identify in the newspaper, a strike that is going on. What are the issues? What is your opinion on the dispute?

RECAP

Collective bargaining provides a means for free, competitive determination of the terms and conditions of employment by workers (represented by labor unions) and management. The process of collective bargaining varies with the specific character and history of the industry involved, but it is generally regarded as an important and viable part of our democratic system. As a matter of public policy, we support union organization, collective bargaining, and fair administration of labor agreement terms.

The federal government acts as an impartial thrid party in labor-management relations, representing the general public welfare. Through the courts, the NLRB, and various agencies, the government acts to maintain fair labor practices. At a broader plane, the government also acts to maintain a high level of employment in our nation. In this chapter, we have examined some of the causes of unemployment and some of the actions that are taken to combat it.

Downturns in economic activity are major contributors to unemployment. Lack of mobility of workers -- access to jobs that are available is also a major factor. Technological change and automation are often blamed for unemployment, but their impact is generally exaggerated. In time, people learn new skills required by new, upgraded jobs that are created by the change and by automation. We must learn to accept and adapt to changes that new technology and economic shifts create.

In the future, we may anticipate a continued strong impact by unions on management and on our society. Unions see their future as depending on their ability to attract white-collar professional and technical talent and their ability to broaden the base of historical union roles and demands on management.

We may expect government to play a larger role than it has in the past, to facilitate the democratic collective bargaining process and protect the public interest. The government may become involved in the activities and management of unions, as it has in business organizations. Unions, as Bluestone notes, may become involved in the management of business organizations. Thus, the three may be more closely linked in the future.

WORKSHEET NO. 19

NAME_____

INSTRUCTOR'S NAME_____

DATE_____

1. What are the key trends in labor-management relations?

_____

2. Why is the role of government increasing in labor relations?

3. What impact does changing technology have on employemnt in the
   United States? Unemployment? Different Occupations?

---

4. Who are the unemployed?

CHAPTER 20

Minorities And Women In Business

Blacks, Chicanos, Orientals, Indians, and other racial minorities are demanding their fair share of the action in business today.

Women, too, expect equal treatment regarding employ- ment, promotions, assing- ments, compensation, and work responsibilities.

Young people and older people are seeking equal opportunity to work, to perform, and to develop their capabilities.

The stimulus for increased management attention to the interests of these groups in business organizations came with the Civil Rights Act of 1964.

Through this act, it became unlawful for any employer to discriminate against individuals in hiring or in treatment after employment on the basis of race, color, sex,

religion, or national origin. Age has also been added as an unlawful basis for discrimination.

Since 1964, additional laws have been enacted, and interpretations of the law have been made by the administration and by the courts. Today the specific requirements for employment practices are varied and complex, but the basic intent remains clear: to remove barriers to employ- ment opportunities that are based on wholly un- justifiable discrimination.

The laws cover not only business firms, but labor unions, employment agencies, educational institutions, and state and local govern- ments. The federal law covers such organizations with 15 or more employees or members.

In addition, the federal government has required

all contractors or sub- contractors to ensure equal employment opportunity. Under this executive order (by the president) a written plan for affirmative action must be prepared if the contractor has 50 or more employees. This has had a major impact on employment of minorities and women because most large corpor- ations are suppliers of goods or services to the government.

The government itself has attempted to help the cause by providing various training and development programs, new tools for matching people with avail- able jobs, and by conduct- ing pertinent research on employment, testing, and training.

Government programs, government-business pro- grams, and government-union programs are all contributing to the advancement of minority employment opportunities. Some efforts to encourage minority business enterprises have also been successful. Further work in all of these and additional areas are needed, however, to meet the demands of the disadvantaged.

Of all the changes that have occurred in business in recent decades, the turn toward employment on an equal opportunity basis is among the most significant. The people who make up business organizations are bringing in new ideas, new attitudes, and new challenges for management.

In This Chapter

Equal Employment Opportunity

Blacks have always been in business -- as employees and as entreprenuers. The problem is that their "share of the action" has not been in proportion to their numbers. The employment statistics show that minorities (generally the non-white sector of our workforce) suffer greatly from unemployment and lesser employment status than whites.

For decades, Americans have tolerated the plight of blacks in business. Only recently have we become sensitive to the importance of bringing minorities more closely into the mainstream of our economic activity. The stability and welfare of our buisness system depends in part on racial peace and our capacity to tap the potential of these human resources.

Our attention often goes to blacks (Negroes or Afro-Americans) because their numbers are so great in our population. We are equally concerned, however, with the utilization and development of other minorities such as Indians and Chicanos.

We're concerned about discrimination against women in business, too, because their opportunities have also been limited in past decades. But women are not a minority; they constitute an actual majority in our population. In the workforce there are more men than women, but this is due in part to the lack of employment opportunities for women.

The responsibilities of business in the area of equal employment opportunity have been stated clearly by Henry Ford II as follows:

"It is clearly in the self-interest of business both to enlarge its markets and to improve its work force by helping disadvantaged people to develop and employ their potential. Good employees are any company's most valuable resource. Good employees are also hard to find. Any company that limits its access to good employees by imposing such irrelevant criteria as race or color is also limiting its profit potential."

Ford further explains why business has been slow to open doors to the disadvantaged:

"I will readily admit that business did not move soon enough and has not moved far enough to provide full equality of opportunity. But we have not lagged because of the profit motive. We have lagged in spite of the profit motive and in opposition to our own best interests."

"Businessmen have lagged because they are people who share the prejudices and preconceptions of the society around them. Like other people, businessmen are reluctant to change the way things have always been done. In a community where Negroes have never been hired except as janitors or sweepers, it takes an exceptional man to break the pattern."

Of course, Ford Motor Company has been a leader in giving minorities access to both entry-level jobs and to higher-level advancement opportunities.

Since Ford's comments, made in 1969, the company has established far-reaching programs on several fronts. Dealerships were put into the hands of minority-group members as managers. Special hard-core programs were established, involving extensive training and development activities. Changes were made in the structure of the organization, operating procedures, and the design of jobs. Priorities, targets, timetables and reporting procedures, make up budgets, incentives, and all of the other tools for achieving objectives were applied. Diverse equal employment efforts were integrated and coordinated for greater impact.

Basically, Ford notes, the results depend on hard work and good management, not on good intentions and good-will.

Equal employment opportunity has been a high priority objective in our nation's overall manpower plans. A statement of our aim, for the Manpower Report of the President published in 1973, reflects

his continuing concern:
    "This isn't a simple
matter. Change and results
cannot occur overnight.
It requires an overhaul
of our whole view of
individuals as employees --
affecting the way we
recruit, assign, test,
develop, appraise, and
compensate employees.
Business, with the help of
government, is making
progress, but it will be
a long haul."

    On the pages that follow
are described some of the
programs, both federal and
corporate, that aim to
improve the employment
opportunities of minorities,
women, and other economically disadvanteged groups
in our labor amrket.

    As discussed in the
column on this page (from
the Manpower Report of
the President) and the
section following, the
federal government has
mounted a campaign on
several fronts to combat
discrimination in employ-
ment. The impact has been
noticeable in business
employment practices, if
not in the overall proportions of minorities and
women employed.

Achieving Equal Opportunity Employment

One reason for the disproportionate number of minority group members among the low-income population is the corrosive impact of prejudice, which interferes with their access to the more desirable, better paid jobs. But the problem of employment discrimination goes beyond those in poverty, affecting members of racial and ethnic minorities in all income groups as well as women, teenagers, and older workers.

A much broadened Federal initiative—legislative, executive, and judicial—to reduce and eliminate discrimination in employment has been achieved in recent years. And considerable progress has been made, through private as well as Government action, in lowering the discriminatory barriers in hiring, training, and promotion. Besides attacking the multiple inequities confronting minorities, the Federal Government has recently taken the lead in reducing the special handicaps that women encounter in the labor market—including lower average earnings than men receive for comparable work—and in removing the arbitrary age restrictions which limit opportunities for older workers.

A number of Federal agencies share responsibility for eliminating employment discrimination, including the Equal Employment Opportunity Commission, which has, in the last several years, handled a rapidly increasing number of employment discrimination complaints; the Office of Federal Contract Compliance, which enforces the Executive orders prohibiting discrimination by Federal contractors; and the Civil Service Commission, which promotes and enforces equal opportunity in Federal Government employment. Much more effort will have to be expended, however, before equal employment opportunity will be a reality for all Americans.

Human Resources Programs

There is hardly any aspect of government policy or programs that does not have manpower implications -- and often very far-reaching ones.

In the 1960's, the federal government gave heavy emphasis to activities aimed at removing discrimination in employment. Three agencies were responsible for the equal employment opportunity effort: The EEOC, the OEEO, and the OFCC. These are described briefly below.

THE EQUAL EMPLOYMENT OPPORTUNITY COMMISSION (EEOC) was established by the Civil Rights Act of 1964. It strives to end discrimination in hiring and firing -- and also in wages, working conditions, promotional opportunities, and training -- by employers, unions, employment agencies, and training sponsors. The Commission works through investigation, conciliation, persuasion, and through the courts -- for the benefit of Negroes, Indians, Spanish Americans, and other ethnic minority groups, as well as for women.

Until 1972 the EEOC could only investigate, persuade, and bring information to the attention of the Justice Department for possible suits. Under the Equal Employment Act of 1972, however, the EEOC gained the power to institute civil actions in response to violations of Civil Rights laws. Important aspects of the law, as amended, are:

--coverage is extended to state and local government, employees of educational institutions, and employers and labor organizations with 15 or more employees or members.

--the time limit for filing a charge of employment discrimination is increased to 180 days; any time after 30 days from filing, the EEOC may institute a lawsuit.

--the EEOC may now file charges "by or on behalf of" aggrieved persons.

--the EEOC may also seek temporary or preliminary relief by way of an injunction before final disposition of a charge.

THE OFFICE OF EQUAL EMPLOYMENT OPPORTUNITY in the Department of Labor is responsible for assuring that the national policy of equal opportunity is observed and promoted in all manpower activities under the Department's responsibility. Its field of concern extends to the Federal-State employment service programs administered by the Department, to apprenticeship programs, and to research and demonstration projects.

THE OFFICE OF FEDERAL CONTRACT COMPLIANCE (OFCC), also in the Department of Labor, is charged with enforcement of the Executive orders that prohibit discrimination on the basis or race, creed, sex, color, or national origin by any firm with a contract for $10,000 or more from the federal government. These contractors and subcontractors include most large companies and account for about a third of all employment in the country.

According to OFCC rules, contractors must develop plans of affirmative action for arriving at nondiscriminatory employment patterns. Early in 1970 these rules were strengthened by a new requirement that specific goals and timetables must be part of the action plan whenever there is underutilization of minority workers.

Despite these government programs to promote equal employment opportunity, the most likely successful and the more desirable solution remains voluntary agreement. Since the enactment of the Civil Rights Act of 1964, company employment of minorities and women has accelerated; in large measure as a result of recognized management responsibilities.

From 1965 to 1974 the percentage of women and minorities in the workforce increased from 40.7% to 44.6%. While this percentage increase may not seem impressive it accounts for over 10 million jobs. In 1965 there were 31.4 million women and minority members in the workforce, by 1974 this number had increased to 41.9 million.

Many of these new jobs were entry level positions, but some were also technical, professional and managerial jobs. Women and minorities have not only achieved more jobs, but also better jobs, and there is nothing to indicate that the trend is changing.

Company Programs

There isn't a major company in the nation that isn't committed to equal employment opportunity.

Under the eye of the EEOC and the OFCC, business organizations have moved ahead quickly in the past decade to remove obstacles to the employment of minorities and women, where any existed, and to aggressively pursue the employment and advancement of minorities and women.

In most instances, the commitment is a natural, voluntary one, prompted by our widespread social concern for equal employment, but not forced by it.

The problem has been, and continues to be, an economic one -- whether to hire a white male with the necessary experience and education or a black woman with aptitude and potential but with no direct experience or normal educational credentials. To hire the black woman means an additional investment may be needed to train and develop her to fulfill the required job.

Now this doesn't mean that all women and minorities don't have what it takes to start with -- on the contrary, many are in high demand for their skills and abilities. As a result they are actively recruited.

The problem of special training, recruitment, and orientation costs have been largely alleviated by special programs sponsored by the government, including direct payments for partial costs incurred. Often, companies have simply accepted the costs as among those of doing business -- to meet the desired standards of equal employment.

And all of this isn't just for good public relations, either. In fact, it's hard to find companies talking about their employment programs or affirmative action plans. They're accepted as part of normal routine today.

The  Story

Equal Opportunity at Ford

The Company is firmly committed to equal opportunity and nondiscriminatory practices in every aspect of its personnel relations, beginning with the recruitment of new employes and extending throughout their careers with Ford.

In an effort to ensure equality of opportunity in this connection, Ford's affirmative action plans focus special attention on members of minority groups and women.

At year-end 1975, members of the minority groups as defined by the U.S. government made up 18.1% of Ford's U.S. work force. These include blacks, Orientals, American Indians and Spanish-surnamed Americans. The 18.1% representation compared with 19% at the end of 1974, and with the 19.6% achieved at the end of 1973 after several years of expanding employment.

Women accounted for 8.8% of Ford's U.S. employment at the end of 1975, down from 9.3% at the end of 1974 and 9.6% at year-end 1973.

The Company's efforts toward equal opportunity progress continued during 1974 and 1975, although seriously hampered by sizable reductions in Ford's U.S. employment. With hiring of new employes virtually at a standstill, Ford's principal concern was the proper consideration of women and minority-group employes for the limited number of promotional opportunities that were available.

Both women and minority employes received more of the promotions available during 1975 than was accounted for by their proportion in the work force. Women comprised 14.7% of the salaried work force at year-end, and received 17.1% of the salaried promotions made during the year. Among hourly employes, 6.1% of whom were women at year-end, 8.2% of promotions went to women.

Minority-group salaried employes received 8.8% of salaried promotions during 1975, compared with 6.8% representation among salaried workers at year-end. Minority-group members received 26.8% of promotions within the hourly work force in 1975, compared with their 23.3% representation in the hourly work force.

Table A on page 17 shows that minority-group representation among Ford's U.S. salaried employes was 6.8% at year-end 1975. Women made up 14.7% of Ford's U.S. salaried work force. During the 1974-75 period, Ford's U.S. salaried employment was reduced by 11,200.

Among hourly employes, unavoidable layoffs conducted in accordance with long-standing seniority procedures reduced Ford U.S. employment by 29,500 from year-end

1973 to the end of 1975. At year-end 1975, women made up 6.1% of Ford's U.S. hourly work force, down from 6.9% at the end of 1974 and 7.2% at the end of 1973. Minority-group employes formed 23.3% of hourly employment at the end of 1975, a decrease from 24.4% at the end of 1974 and 25.2% at the end of 1973.

As shown in Table B below, both women and minority-group personnel made up a slightly larger percentage of Ford officials and managers at the end of 1975 than at year-end 1973. Minority-group employes made up 6% of Ford officials and managers at the end of 1975, compared with 5.6% at the end of 1973. Women held 1.2% of such positions, compared with 0.9% at the end of 1973. Women also increased their representation among employes defined

by the Federal government as professionals during 1974 and again in 1975.

Ford's concern for nondiscriminatory practices in every phase of its operations extends to its business relationships and participation in community efforts to ensure equal opportunity.

At 1975 year-end, 57 Ford and Lincoln-Mercury new-car and Ford Tractor dealerships in the United States were owned in whole or in part by members of minority groups. Among these were 20 dealerships in which blacks had ownership. In addition, 78 dealerships were owned in whole or in part by women active in operating the business.

In 1975, Ford advertising in minority-group media totaled $690,000; purchases from minority-group suppliers amounted to $4.6 million; and Ford made tax deposits at an annual level of $81 million with 64 banks owned by minority groups.

Table A—Employment of Minority-Group Personnel and Women at Year-End

	1975			1974			1973		
	Company*	Minority	Women	Company*	Minority	Women	Company*	Minority	Women
Hourly Employes	155,900	23.3%	6.1%	166,200	24.4%	6.9%	185,400	25.2%	7.2%
Salaried Employes	70,700	6.8	14.7	73,300	6.6	14.8	81,900	6.8	14.8
Combined	226,600	18.1%	8.8%	239,500	19.0%	9.3%	267,300	19.6%	9.6%

*Includes Ford U.S. and its domestic subsidiaries.

Table B—Representation of Minority-Group Members and Women in EEO-1 Job Categories at Year-End

	1975		1974		1973	
Job Categories*	Minority	Women	Minority	Women	Minority	Women
Officials and Managers	6.0%	1.2%	5.6%	1.0%	5.6%	0.9%
Professionals	5.3	5.7	5.4	5.6	5.7	5.0
Technicians	10.5	7.5	9.2	6.5	9.1	5.5
Office and Clerical	14.1	42.7	13.7	43.3	14.0	45.3
Craftsmen (Skilled)	7.7	0.1	7.9	0.3	7.7	0.3
Operatives (Semiskilled)	27.4	8.3	28.5	8.9	29.6	9.7
Laborers (Unskilled)	30.3	2.4	28.4	4.3	29.5	3.2
Service Workers	26.8	8.3	31.1	7.3	31.7	6.6
Total	18.1%	8.8%	19.0%	9.3%	19.6%	9.6%

*Excludes Sales Workers, a category that is not applicable to Ford.

Unions And Manpower: A Natural Partnership

The story of the growth of the labor movement and its struggle to gain recognition as the legitimate bargaining representative of American working men and women is widely known. By law and by custom, unions are universally accepted in their bread-and-butter role of seeking better pay and improved working conditions for their members.

What is not so widely known is the part labor unions have assumed in contributing to the growing strength and confidence of the Nation's manpower training effort. As Howard D. Samuel, vice president of the Amalgamated Clothing Workers of America, pointed out in a recent speech, labor union manpower efforts embrace "Job Corps camps, the Apprenticeship Outreach Program, on-the-job training, the Job Opportunities in the Business Sector Program, Public Service Careers, and many more. Telephone workers have been trained in Kentucky; hospital workers upgraded in Maryland; operating engineers trained in Tennessee; laborer trainees placed on jobs in Massachusetts; ironworkers trained in Birmingham, plumbers in Oklahoma City, retail employees in Pittsburgh. And so it goes, in virtually every trade and skill, in almost every area of the country."

Samuel did not overstate the case. Union involvement in manpower programs spans the Nation and encompasses every level of organized labor—the national AFL-CIO; individual national and international unions; regional, State, and local councils; and individual locals. More than 70 individual union organizations now have training contracts with the Manpower Administration.

The greatest growth in union participation in and sponsorship of manpower training programs has come in the last 4

Mr. Fasser is Deputy Assistant Secretary of Labor for Manpower and Manpower Administrator.

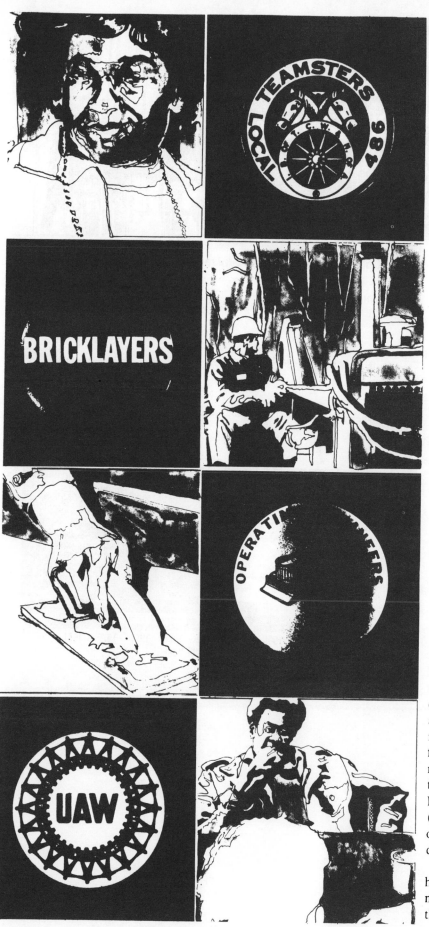

years. While the Labor Department has provided $104 million in manpower training funds to labor unions over the last 9 years, the bulk of it—$72 million—was provided in the past few years (see chart on page 4).

But these figures by no means tell the whole story. Unions play an integral role in many manpower programs which they do not sponsor and for which they receive no funds. For example, if an employer who has a bargaining agreement with a union signs a manpower training contract under the Job Opportunities in the Business Sector (JOBS) Program, union cooperation is essential to the success of the effort. The union may have to agree to hiring procedures that go outside the stipulations of the bargaining agreement. Or other changes in the union contract or in traditional labor-management practices may be required. The success of the JOBS Program attests to the fact that unions have been willing to go the extra mile.

Labor Had Own Program

Labor's interest in seeking solutions to manpower problems through a concerted national effort goes back to 1962, when the mounting concern for persons whose livelihoods seemed threatened by automation and technological change prompted enactment of Federal manpower training and retraining legislation. But although a representative of the AFL-CIO was the first witness to urge the Senate Subcommittee on Employment and Manpower to take favorable action on the proposed Manpower Development and Training Act (MDTA), extensive participation by labor organizations in the program that resulted did not come about immediately.

Organized labor long had had its own highly developed program with management to produce skilled workers through the apprenticeship system. MDTA was aimed at persons with no skills or those whose skills were becoming obsolescent. Furthermore, MDTA could not provide funds for on-going training programs—so apprenticeship programs were not eligible for Federal financial aid.

At about the same time MDTA was going through its birth pains, the country's minority community began building up pressure on industry and government to do something about the lack of equal employment opportunity. The generally poor educational preparation of minorities seeking work in the skilled construction trades proved to be the door for labor and government cooperation on job training.

Bricklayers Broke the Ice

A major construction union, the International Union of Bricklayers, Masons, and Plasterers, broke the ice on union participation in federally funded manpower training with the first of a series of MDTA contracts to prepare minority and other disadvantaged youth to qualify for entry into apprenticeship programs. This was in 1963, and by the end of the fiscal year the Labor Department's Bureau of Apprenticeship and Training had written on-the-job training contracts with a variety of labor organizations for a total of $488,200.

The successful record of cooperation between the Bricklayers Union (which to date has trained and placed more than 4,000 people) and the Government prompted the Operating Engineers Union to follow suit with an ambitious program that resulted in additional hundreds of unemployed persons being trained by that organization. The United Brotherhood of Carpenters and Joiners also contributed to this training and development effort with multimillion dollar contracts that have resulted in more than 15,000 trainees being accepted into apprenticeship or upgraded to journeyman status. Similar programs with other unions in the construction industry were carried forward with excellent results.

This cooperation assumed a broader dimension when, in 1968, the Manpower Administration began to reach out to bring greater numbers of minorities into apprenticeship. Through the Apprenticeship Outreach Program, the AFL-CIO Building and Construction Trades Councils in more

Obligations to Labor Organizations for Manpower Training — by Fiscal Year

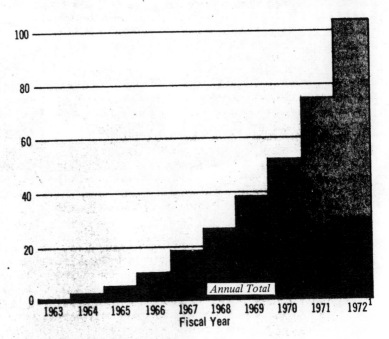

[1] Covers contracts executed through May 19

than 20 cities joined with the Labor Department in recruiting and preparing youth, mainly blacks, Puerto Ricans, and Mexican Americans, for apprenticeship examinations. As a result, hundreds of young men were placed in apprenticeship programs in most construction trades available in those cities. Outreach techniques and similar efforts were instrumental in boosting the proportion of minority apprentices in programs registered with the U.S. Department of Labor from 6.6 percent in January 1969 to 9.8 percent in July 1971.

Meanwhile, unions outside the construction trades also have been making significant and lasting contributions to the training and placement of the Nation's unskilled work force. The International Union of Electrical, Radio, and Machine Workers (IUE) has helped thousands the past several years and recently signed its fourth on-the-job training contract with the Manpower Administration, this time to train and upgrade 1,250 workers by February 1974.

Twenty-two locals of the United Steelworkers are aiding the AFL-CIO's Human Resources Development Institute in a "buddy" system for upgrading workers. The union also has cooperated in a project through which union members have upgraded their skills and acquired high school diplomas in remedial education and training courses funded by the Manpower Administration.

The American Federation of State, County, and Municipal Employees (AFSCME) has been using manpower programs to develop career ladders in hospital occupations and to train low-ranking employees. Through a series of Manpower Administration contracts, AFSCME has helped some 2,000 nurse aides, and kitchen, laundry, custodial, and similar workers in public hospitals qualify for and get better jobs.

Independents Also Active

In Appalachia, a regional organization known as the AFL-CIO Appalachian Council is training and placing jobless and underemployed people in 12 States. The Council, composed of the AFL-CIO State directors in the region, represents hundreds of locals and thousands of organized workers. Council activities in the manpower field have included educating union leaders on the Government's antipoverty programs, recruiting youngsters for the Job Corps, and—its newest venture—preparing 75 Choctaw Indians for construction jobs.

Independent unions also are supporting and taking part in manpower programs. For more than 5 years, the Teamsters Union, with Manpower Administration funding, has been training and placing blacks, Spanish Americans, and other minorities in southern California in highly paid truck driving jobs and related trades. And the United Auto Workers Union recently completed two contracts to train 2,600 workers and is in the midst of two others to train and upgrade 2,500 more.

Probably the most diversified and geographically far-reaching union manpower operation is that of the AFL-CIO Human Resources Development Institute (HRDI). Through some $5 million in Manpower Administration contracts, HRDI, under the chairmanship of AFL-CIO President George Meany, is developing approximately 800 JOBS projects; promoting Neighborhood Youth Corps summer programs with employers and unions; assisting in the posttraining placement of Job Corps graduates and in locating qualified instructors for Job Corps installations; helping returning veterans find work; and working with the so-called "hometown solutions" minority group hiring plans in the construction industry by providing technical assistance to building trades councils.

Labor's ability and willingness to help the poor and disadvantaged obtain and keep productive jobs should come as no surprise to anyone familiar with the history of unions in America. Throughout its existence, the labor movement has fought to give meaning to the phrase "the dignity of work." It has sought for its members both the material and psychological benefits that flow from a useful job—a job that affords a worker and his family a decent standard of living. Manpower programs have the same goals. Thus the continuing and expanding involvement of unions in manpower programs is simply the realization of a natural partnership.

The Hard Core Unemployed

What has business learned about efforts to bring the hard-core unemployed into the mainstream of American economic life?

The many different activities that are commonly conducted by business may be described as RECRUITING the hard-core, TESTING and HIRING the hard core and coaching their supervisors, and ON-THE-JOB counseling and supportive services to facilitate integration of the hard-core unemployed into the world of work.

Recruitment is difficult because business must develop means of communicating with the hard-core in the ghetto and through their own media (television and radio, for example). General Electric, as one case, set up a mobile trailer for recruiting. Ford Motor Company set up employment offices in the ghetto. Various associations and agencies also work with companies to place hard-core unemployed into training programs provided by employers.

When it comes to testing and selection, a Ford executive said, "Throw the hiring manual out the window." The hard-core require different treatment than usual applicants -- interviewing must create a receptive atmosphere; testing must be fair and unbiased. New approaches for testing and selection of talent, as a result, have been developed and put to use in business.

Training? Hard-core training generally includes fundamental education to bring the trainee up to minimum school level (usually grade six or eight) associated with successful job performance. Social skills training is needed to help the hard-core unemployed adapt to the customs of behavior at work -- that we may often take for granted. Job skills development is at the heart of the hard-core training effort, giving the trainee essential work skills, usually in the plant where the workers will be employed.

Because the hard-core recruits have special needs as they adjust to the world of work, supervisors and foremen need to have a good understanding of their needs and attitudes. Training of supervisors is often provided, followed by on-the-job counseling and supportive services.

To be effective, programs to hire the hard-core must have the total support and commitment of top management. One top executive said, "Unless top management lays it on the line, lower-echelon people won't do it. Even then, they may not do it without follow-up."

Lessons learned? "They won't come knocking at your door -- recruiting may call for special efforts. You may have to relax your hiring standards and change your hiring practices," said one study. You may have to hire people with police records and consider applicants in a different light.

Some jobs have to be redesigned to make them easier to handle. Often, though, training to handle existing jobs is more satisfying to workers in the long run.

In general, training is the key to bringing hard-core unemployed individuals into the workforce, and a job at the end of training is the payoff for management and for the individuals.

Turnover is often high in hard-core programs, but for those individuals who do adjust and perform successfully, the reward to business and society in general is great. When you deal with badly under-skilled people, you need big money. That's why the government often lends a hand to the task of hiring and training.

Building from a rather modest level of expenditure of $22 million in 1965, the federal government's efforts in comprehensive manpower assistance has grown to over $2.4 billion in 1975. This money has been used to train individuals to fill entry level positions, supported state manpower programs, and assisted in basic education for the "hard core" unemployed.

But clearly, money is not enough. For the problems of the "hard core" unemployed to be eliminated will require major efforts at all levels and using all of the resources that are available. Money, education, family assistance, vocational training, assistance in finding jobs, and counseling on the job will all be required to solve this problem.

A Piece Of The Action

One American in six is either black, Indian, Eskimo, Puerto Rican, or Mexican-American; yet the figures show that members of these minorities own only 3 per cent of all business enterprises. The capital worth of minority business is an even smaller share of our national total -- less than one-half of one per cent. Little wonder, then, that many members of the minority 16 per cent have come to feel they have little stake in our enterprise system.

The path to full participation in our enterprise system has been blocked -- or at least full of frustrating detours -- for a large number of disadvantaged minorities.

There are considerable differences between one minority group and another, plus different combinations of problems that may affect individuals within each group, but successful business ownership inevitably has four ingredients: the entrepreneur, the business idea or opportunity, the money or capital, and business know-how. To bring minorities into the ownership of business enterprises, these factors must be provided.

Why minority enterprises? At least three basic reasons may be given. First, we can't afford to waste the potential contribution to economic progress that may be possible by those now excluded from our system. Instead of sapping demand, as some fear, new enterprises will

Jim Clancy (right), supervisor of procurement planning for Supply Staff, and Bob Renfroe, president of Renmuth, Inc., examine one of the stampings Ford purchases from the Detroit firm. Under its Minority Group Supplier Program initiated in 1968, Ford materially assisted in the founding of the black-owned firm.

heighten competition and strengthen our enterprise system.

Second, excluding so many people from the upper levels of productive society can be dangerous -- by encouraging criticism instead of support. Those who know that they may participate in building our enterprise system will be less disposed to join those who would destroy it.

Third, the doors of ownership should be open to all because it is the right thing to do. It's basic to our whole philosophy of democracy and free enterprise.

The program to build minority business enterprise initially was labeled

"Black Capitalism." Certainly that's part of it, but not all of it. It's not limited to blacks, not to urban ghettos. It's a broad program for bringing all disadvantaged minorities into ownership of business as well as employment in business.

WHAT'S REQUIRED? The development of markets for products of minority enterprises is one key. The government has met this need by contracting with fledgling enterprises or by specifying use of minority enterprise products by contractors. This preferential treatment does ensure a fully developed market for enterprises, but it has several problems.

First, it puts the government or contractors on the spot for the quantity and quality of goods and services needed to satisfy government requirements. A minority enterprise, as a small business generally, may not be able to meet the standards. Further, the market may not last, thus dropping the ball on an enterprise that demonstrated long-range potential. An enterprise needs a permanent, balanced market to survive and grow.

A business cannot survive on an economic basis just from ethnic appeal or a social commitment to give it support. It needs to be established on good footings and produce products for an integrated market on a cost/quality basis.

Financial backing for a minority enterprise is relatively easy to obtain. The Small Business Administration (SBA) provides loans with liberal requirements through banks. Money is also available from industries interested in investing in such enterprises and from the communities directly.

Investment corporations such as the Chase Manhatten Capital Corporation have been formed specifically to invest in minority enterprises.

Direct grants from large and profitable white businesses are also common. Support provided by Eastman Kodak, Xerox, IBM, and others has been noteworthy.

Training and upgrading unskilled workers on a large scale requires an effort that is both costly and arduous. Small businesses have neither the resources to train the underemployed nor the facilities to employ them. Programs involving assistance by larger firms, by the SBA, and the Department of Labor have helped to meet this critical need.

Ford Motor Company, for example, alone hired 21,700 hard-core unemployed during a single eight-month period. Can a small business absorb and train such a group?

It's particularly tough for a minority business to attract talented young managers. Large corporations are more attractive in terms of opportunities, income, and responsibilities.

Franchising is one means for getting a minority business off the ground. As we discussed earlier in this book, a franchisor provides the know-how, the training, the idea, and the opportunity. If financial capital is available, a potentially strong, profitable business may be started and operated by anyone.

Minority business enterprises, particularly if they start out as franchises, may never become a major part of our enterprise system. The obstacles will continue to exist, as they are the same obstacles as face any small business.

But, combined with equal employment activities in large organizations, this attempt to foster minority-owned businesses is significant. In spirit and in fact, it is important that blacks and other minorities have a direct hand in competition -- a piece of the action.

Women In Business

Womanpower is one of our important assets. Women have been responsible for the major share of the growth in our labor force, actually 60% of the total increase since 1940. Women now represent one-third of all workers in the United States. The increase in the number of women in the labor force is one of the major indicators of economic, social, and political change in our society.

Today women are better educated and trained and there are more and more jobs available to them. There are fewer and fewer "men only" occupations left in the world today -- since bona fide sex requirements for jobs are rare. In fact, in many occupations, women outnumber men -- and in the future this may be true of many more occupations.

Most women say that they work because they want the money. They want to improve the standard of living for themselves or their families. They want to help send their children to college, or they want to help buy a house. And it is true that in most cases the additional income of the wife has helped to raise the family's standard of living. Employed married women now earn more than one-fifth of their family's total income.

Other women simply want to have the same career opportunities as men. Women may work because they want financial independence and freedom. Many women, faced with increasing leisure time, want to make constructive and creative use of their talents. In the future we may expect this motive to become even more compelling than the economic one.

Other reasons women are getting into business?

-- Automation, converting many jobs to mere meter-watching and button-pushing, gives women opportunities in work once necessarily reserved for men because of the strength required to perform the work, such as in foundries.

-- New industries produce new kinds of jobs women can fill without getting men in an uproar. More

In 1888 Frank Leslie's Illustrated Newspaper inveighed against the exploitation of women workers, many of them newly arrived immigrants, with these engravings made from sketches by a staff artist. The layout was entitled "The Female Slaves of New York—'Sweaters' and Their Victims," and the three panels were described as "1. Scene in a Sweater's Factory; 2. The End; 3. Scene at the Grand Street Ferry."

and more jobs are in service industries, and many are in entirely new areas. Health care, in which women already predominate, will be the single largest area of employment by 1985.
-- More employers see advantages in hiring older women, who will likely live longer than their male counterparts, and will have less turnover.
-- Attitudes toward having wives work are changing. It used to be that men always wanted their wives at home; now many want them to work.
-- Women find home life less demanding than in the past and want to use their leisure profitably.
-- Women are getting better educations and are anxious to cash in on them. Enrollment of women in colleges has steadily climbed over the years.
-- Increased use of birth control methods and devices will reduce the time that the average woman will spend away from the labor force caring for children.
-- Feminist groups are getting more militant in demands for "women's rights" and aren't likely to quiet down.

One of the errors of business has been the underutilization of women's skills. This may be the result of a number of factors. Myths still persist about a woman's intelligence and performance, although business is becoming aware of the often hidden talents that women may bring to managerial and technical jobs. Recent legislation and government efforts may also help to open doors to jobs and advancement opportunities for women.

At I.B.M., for example, women have always been treated with "courtly gentility," putting them on pedestals but not on high-level jobs. Now women are demanding more, and I.B.M. has promoted one woman to vice president and put another on the board of directors. The director, by the way, is former Ambassador Patricia R. Harris, who is black, a woman, and a partner in a Washington, D.C. law firm. She may soon be on more corporate boards than anyone since financier J.P. Morgan.

According to company figures, women hold 8 per cent of the professional jobs at I.B.M. and about 3 per cent of the managerial jobs. The company expects these percentages to climb as women advance in the organization with development and experience.

While "Women's Lib" isn't a big issue in I.B.M., it has been in other firms, and is bringing significant pressure to bear on management in many companies, on the government, and other sectors of our society. The inferiority of the female sex is a myth that is slow to dispel, for it demands a basic change in attitudes and job qualifications in many instances.

It's ironic, but in many states there are laws on the books that actually work against the employment and equal treatment of women on jobs. They aim to protect the welfare of women, limiting their hours of work and the kinds of jobs they may fill. These laws are being struck down in the courts or changed in legislatures to conform with federal civil rights laws.

EQUAL PAY

In many organizations, women have been put on equal jobs, to perform on the same basis as men, but at lower rates of pay. This practice violates the Equal Pay Act of 1963. This federal law prohibits paying different wages or providing different fringe benefits to men and women who do the same work under similar working conditions in covered positions when equal skill, effort, and responsibility are required.

This law was recently interpreted to mean that medical benefits covering pregnancies, leaves of absence, and pensions all must be on an equal basis. This means that the payroll costs of employers go up, adding to total labor costs when women are employed.

What is a woman's work? What is a woman's place in the world of business? It's an open marketplace today.

Saleswomen On The Go . . . Go . . . Go!

With an on-the-go routine, Mary Ellen Brinker has become a perpetual time-watcher.

At one time or another, we've all heard about the traveling salesman. Or was it the saleswoman?

At Baxter it could have been either, for the number of women entering the sales field for medical products is definitely on the rise.

For many women, the traditional role of the "woman in the home" has long worn out. Now they are skipping coffee to make appointments, driving station wagons filled with product samples rather than groceries, and kissing their husbands goodbye as they dash to make a 7 a.m. meeting.

Beyond any doubt, the commitments are many, and—man or woman—not everyone can meet the test of a successful salesperson. According to many of Baxter's saleswomen, the profession requires an appreciation of people in general, the ability to listen well and be sensitive to people's needs, as well as keep a positive attitude.

Waiting in a hospital lobby for her next appointment, Anita Goddard takes time to jot down some thoughts about an earlier meeting.

"A salesperson really has to be involved with what she is doing," explains Anita Goddard, sales representative for the Baxter/Travenol Division. "Since I'm the only rep that my customers meet, the entire company is judged on what they think of me."

Anita's territory, which covers northern W. Virginia and parts of Maryland, requires a fair amount of traveling. Besides keeping her car in good repair so she can meet all appointments promptly, she must be energetic, dedicated to her customers and, she says, willing to make personal sacrifices to accommodate a customer.

"No day is typical," Anita comments, and other saleswomen agree. "I set up my own schedule, according to a certain route, but I'm always speaking to different people, and presenting new ideas and products."

The young woman embarked on her sales career in 1970 after receiving a bachelor's degree in sociology. The field

Mary Ellen's territory includes Chicago, as well as suburban and rural areas.

attracted her, she notes, because it promised challenge.

And challenging it is. In addition to enthusiasm, a salesperson is also required to attend a series of training sessions, and must pass a battery of tests. Although the type and amount of training vary with Baxter's divisions, each salesperson must learn all aspects of the division's products as well as the advantages and disadvantages of competitors' products. Sales skills training is also part of the education.

"It's also necessary to be geared up all the time," Anita comments. "When I wake up in the morning, I'm ready to sell. Anyone who really likes what she is doing will find it's not difficult to be enthusiastic all the time."

Like Anita, most saleswomen find it difficult to describe a typical workday. Usually, the morning begins at about 7 a.m. when they begin calling on pharmacists, purchasing agents, nurses, operating room supervisors or "anyone connected with a hospital." Once they leave home, their schedules adapt to their customers' needs.

With a degree in home economics from the University of Wisconsin, Mary Ellen Brinker, Flint Division, began her sales career with the Patricia Stevens School of Modeling. With two years of experience behind her, she then moved into pharmaceuticals—a field which she describes as "bigger and better things."

Mary Ellen's territory is large and varied, and thus affords the opportunity to work with many different people. A great deal of auto travel is required to meet the demands of customers from Chicago north to the Wisconsin border.

Mary Ellen claims that one key to her success is that she enjoys going to work. Being a woman in a field traditionally reserved for men, she claims, has not created any difficulty for her.

"I find that if people are good at their jobs, they're going to be accepted by those they work with—whether they're men or women," she says. In a field in which moderation does not generate success, Mary Ellen claims, there would never be room for a "token" woman.

WHAZZIT?

MINORITY BUSINESS ENTERPRISE

A business organization that is owned (at least predominantly) and operated by members of minority racial groups.

BLACK CAPITALISM

The ownership of business enterprises by blacks.

SMALL BUSINESS ADMINISTRATION

An agency of the federal government which lends money and provides training and counseling to qualifying business enterprises.

INVESTMENT CORPORATION

A business organization established for the purpose of supplying money as capital for other businesses, particularly fledgling enterprises.

Don't Lose That "Bunny Image"

Don't lose that "bunny image" . . .

"Bunny image" in a place like the Playboy International in Detroit is a great asset one does not trifle with. It means pride as well as job; lose it, and both are gone. Even the union contract in the present case listed the "loss of bunny image" as a just cause for discharge.

The plaintiff here must have been a rather articulate and popular bunny; she was a union steward and, for a while, an acting "bunny mother" (a supervisor) —not that she was that old; she wasn't, because there were other bunnies who were years older. She liked to circulate among her fellow workers, explaining the union contract, and so on.

And everything was fine, until a new manager was hired and the regular bunny mother came back and took over. Then things began to happen. The manager called the plaintiff in and told her she had been "reevaluated"—twice—by the regular bunny mother, each time with disastrous results. She would have to go for the "loss of bunny image"—a "just" cause for discharge under the union contract. Even a panel of bunnies, convened under the contract, upheld the discharge. (The union was Local 705, Hotel and Restaurant Employees.)

Because of a complicated contractual procedure, the plaintiff had difficulty bringing her dispute before an arbitrator, but finally managed. Again the Playboy International explained now the new manager and the regular bunny mother evaluated the plaintiff, and how they met with her and counseled her on what to do—with regard to such things as makeup, costuming, scheduling, etc., etc.—but it was no use, they said. Although she did what they suggested— changed the color of her hair, her makeup, and so on—she was deemed hopelessly "unsalvageable," they said.

But the arbitrator could not absorb all these protestations of the management. "The accuser speaketh too much," he said. He just could not believe that one who was good enough to be an acting bunny mother was the only one among the 30 bunnies in the place who was not good enough to be just a plain bunny. "Suddenly, she is discharged," he said. "The cause is alleged loss of bunny image. The accusation is that this was gone while she was at the peak of her advancement and recognition by the employer. The contention is advanced that she didn't even have sufficient image to be hired in the first place. All this just does not make sense or ring true. . . . It just has to be accepted that she had image . . . or else how to explain her advancement? That these physical attributes withered overnight so as to mark her apart from the other 29 as the only one to be scrutinized is equally unbelievable."

The only conclusion the arbitrator could reach was that the Playboy's charge was "out of whole cloth." He ordered the grievant reinstated immediately, with compensation for losses sustained "by reason of being denied work opportunity." The discharge was rescinded and removed from her record. (*Playboy Club International, Inc.*[10])

The Young And The Old

Discrimination in employment on the basis of age (40 to 65 years) is prohibited by the Age Discrimination Act of 1967. Administrative responsibility for protecting more than 45 million middle-aged and older workers from the same discriminatory patterns that face ethnic minorities and women is lodged with the Wage and Hour Division of the Department of Labor.

The Division relies mainly on informal conciliation, conference, and persuasion in accomplishing the purposes of the Act and has therefore expended much effort in educating and obtaining pledges to eliminate age discrimination.

Age discrimination has also been made part of the coverage of the Civil Rights Act, so that the EEOC also has responsibility for assuring equal employment opportunities for these people. This area has not yet had the degree of thrust given to women and minorities.

Younger workers also suffer discrimination in employment, but they are not protected by law. And the discrimination they face is not as much a concern as the lack of qualifications to perform available work.

For decades we have had an increasingly serious youth unemployment problem. In 1930 the youth unemployment rate was 1½ times the national average unemployment rate. By 1975 it had climbed to three times the national rate, with approximately 20% of the teenage workforce unemployed.

Another dimension to the problem is the still rising stream of black teenagers entering the labor force. Their rate of increase during the seventies will be five times as large as that for whites. Here again we will be looking to private industry to provide most of the job opportunities that these young people seek and need.

If we can't provide training and work for young people and older people, not only will our unemployment be high, but the costs of unemployment benefits and, for some, social security benefits, will rise. We must support in some way these people if not through employment.

Because the young and the old (or middle-aged, as 40 or 50 isn't exactly over the hill) have a great deal of capability to provide to our economy, we really should develop means of keeping them productively occupied.

This means that again business must adapt employment practices to look out for unwarrented obstacles to hiring, training, assigning, and promoting individuals on the basis of age. It also means that the government must help out in footing the cost of basic training for youth and retraining of older workers.

A wide variety of government programs were developed and provided in the 1960's and early 1970's to foster full employment of older citizens who wanted to work and who were able to work.

CONSIDER

1. Does the government have the right to tell you who you may or may not hire? Explain.

2. Do you think that black capitalism helps solve the problems causing minority unemployment? Explain.

3. Should government subsidize minority business enterprises? Explain.

4. Should government subsidize business enterprises run by women? Why or why not?

5. If you were a white businessman competing with a minority enterprise, would you think it fair that the money you paid in taxes is used to subsidize your competitor? Explain.

6. As a stockholder, would you be willing to accept lesser dividends so that the company can provide special training and management for hard core unemployed? Explain.

7. Over the years we have counted more and more people (younger people, women, and temporarily unemployed persons) among the unemployed. Would this tend to distort the extent of our employment problems for women and youth? Explain.

8. Government contracts may cost the public more when they are given to firms employing minorities. Is this fair to the taxpayers? Explain.

CHALLENGES

Read the help wanted ad below and discuss the question, "Can a man apply?"

Read BLACK AMERICANS AND WHITE BUSINESS by Edwin M. Epstein and David R. Hampton (Encino, Calif.: Dickenson Publishing Co., 1971), a paperback book.

Read BUSINESS LEADERSHIP AND THE NEGRO CRISIS by Eli Ginzberg (New York: McGraw-Hill Book Co., 1969).

Read BEYOND THE MELTING POT by Nathan Glazer and Daniel P. Moynihan (Cambridge: M.I.T. Press, 1963).

Read BEYOND RACISM by Whitney Young (New York: McGraw-Hill Book Co., 1969.)

Read BLACK CAPITALISM by T.L. Cross (New York: Antheneum, 1969).

RECAP

Providing equal employment opportunity to all individuals in our society is a concern that we give high priority. But it is a very tough challenge, particularly as the rates of unemployment are greatest among the groups of people with the least education and applicable job skills.

Racial minorities, younger workers, older workers, and women all face particular difficulty finding suitable, satisfying jobs and career opportunities in our society because they often lack the experience and training necessary for successful performance.

Also, there remains the problem of discrimination, intentional or not, in the recruitment, selection, assignment, and advancement of talent. The Civil Rights Act of 1964, as amended in 1972 and other legislation provided a significant foundation for building work capabilities through a variety of training programs and for opening doors to jobs that may not have been available to minorities and women.

A variety of programs, some run by the government alone, others with the government and other sectors of our society have contributed to the advancement of employment opportunities for minority group members and women. Government efforts to foster minority business ownership have been successful. But as far as we have progressed, we must do more to meet the needs of the disadvantaged.

For youth and women, special programs are needed, because many of their needs are quite different from those of racial minorities. These will become more and more important as their numbers increase in the workforce.

To bring blacks and other racial minorities into the mainstream of American economic life is important not only for humane reasons, but because their contributions stimulate our whole economy's growth and development. When people work they not only add their own productivity, but they also become consumers of the goods and services our economy produces. This generates work for others, and thus makes us all better off.

There is much valuable talent in our society that lies untapped -- idle because of lack of training and work opportunities. The challenge will continue to be a great one in the years ahead.

1. What can be done to increase minority employment in the higher-skilled occupations?

_____

2. What can be done to improve job opportunities for youth?

3. Can employers give preference to women in hiring? What does the law require?

_____

4. What kinds of actions may the federal government take to assure equal
    employment opportunity in industry?

PART VII

THE FUTURE OF BUSINESS

CHAPTER 21

Business In The Future

Is the past a prologue of the future? Or is our only certainty uncertainty? What can we expect as we pursue our careers? What can we do to keep abreast of the times and avoid obsolescence?

The future of business in America is dependent on the changes that will occur in our society and our economy. We may believe that business enterprise is an enduring institution, providing employment and creating real value for our society, yet the very fabric of business may become different in the next decade.

If we are to prepare ourselves effectively for the future and plan careers in business and government, we will need to take a close look at the trends in social change.

The future of business will not be a wholly different world than it

is today. If it were to be, there would be little point in telling it like it is today in this book. There will be some threads of continuity from past to future, but there will be some discontinuities, too.

What will be new and different? In this chapter we will examine the basic areas of change in our society and consider their implications for our future and the future of business enterprise.

We'll consider trends regarding attitudes toward work and leisure, shifts in our population and work-force, changes in business structure and the relationships of business with government and unions.

You may agree with some of the projections presented here and you may disagree with others. That's okay because there's one thing we can all be sure of -- no one knows what the future will hold for us.

Our economy may have its ups and downs, there may be energy shortages or we may develop new energy sources, and our relationship with other countries may change. But nonetheless, we see continuing affluence, continued business growth, continued expansion in the use of computers, and continued increase in services as a base of our economic activity

We see more innovation in non-business organizations, more non-profit types of organizations, more interest and activity in education, more attention to social and environmental needs, and more attention to leisure activities.

Business organizations will operate on a global activity basis, will work closely with government, will be much larger than the largest even are today, and will be responsive to social needs as well as needs for profit and survival.

Stake your career on your view of the future. You can help shape business organizations in our enterprise system.

In This Chapter

Looking Ahead

During most of the 17th, 18th, and 19th centuries, our country existed largely as an agricultural society. For the next century, from about 1870 to 1970, it was an industrialized society.

In the future, we may expect it to be a POST-INDUSTRIAL society -- a form of society and economy that we have never known before and that will affect most aspects of our lives.

Trends in the future are difficult to project because, as Peter Drucker has noted, this is an age of DISCONTINUITY. We aren't going to have "more of the same" right down the line. We'll have to have deep roots in the past, and have a strong grasp of today's career building tools, but we'll also need to be sensitive to innovations and to the significant changes that will likely occur in our social, economic, political, and technological environments.

One of the basic qualities of the post-industrial society will be a decline in the relative importance of business and industry, as the prime mover in our society, at least. As in agriculture, fewer people will be required to produce the goods and services required by our growing nation. While half of our workforce was active in agriculture a century ago, only about 5% are in the field today, providing foods and fibers for a much larger population.

In the future, services (such as finance, maintenance, communications, and transportation), education, government, and the professions (such as law and medicine) will become greater contributors to our GNP. More activity will thus be outside of our traditional private, market-oriented enterprise system. That doesn't mean that business will start to dry up. Rather, business will expand at a slower rate than these other areas of activity. Business will continue to be important.

These shifts in our basic economic structure will be accompanied by shifts in our human values and attitudes. Profit motives will become less important and other, socially oriented motives will become more important. Learning will become more important as a life-long process. In the long-term leisure, too, will become predominant in the lives of most people, and work as we know it today will be less common.

In the decades ahead, the dominant roles now assumed by business organizations and government will be taken over by universities and other educational institutions because they will best serve the needs of people.

The principal determinants of the major changes that we may anticipate in the decades ahead are advances in technology, affluence, education, and the internationalization of our economic and political activity.

The changes themselves may prove to be very unsettling for many people in our society. Those who do adapt to them, however,

DOONESBURY

by Garry Trudeau

will be the most satisfied and the most prosperous.

Many people resist the changes that will come with the post-industrial society in an effort to keep the values that they knew in our industrialized society. Already we see serious social tensions arising from conflicts which have roots in struggles over these changes and the values that relate to them. Call it the "generation gap" if you wish -- it's the problem of people changing at different paces and having different expectations and values.

Yet the very pace of change will be stepping up. In the seventies we are moving deeply into this new type of society. By the 1980's it will be largely the pattern of life in America. This is a very short period of time for such a major adaptation.

To bring about changes in our society there will be greater emphasis on the individual and his personal initiative. We see this in the trend toward MBO and decentralization in organizations. We see it, too, in strengthening local and metropolitan governments. These efforts may allow greater responsiveness to changes as they develop and greater involvement of people in the very process of changing our society in a direction we feel we want it to move.

As our voices become heard within the organizations we belong to, the organizations will work more closely together. There will be greater interrelatedness of our institutions -- unions, government agencies, businesses, and other organizations.

POST-INDUSTRIAL SOCIETY

If you want to know more about what we may expect the future to be like, you may read a book written by Herman Kahn and Anthony Wiener, THE YEAR 2000: A FRAMEWORK FOR SPECULATION ON THE NEXT THIRTY YEARS (New York: Macmillan, 1967).

In the book, the following conditions are viewed to be characteristic of our society in the year 2000.

1. Average individual income will be about fifty times what it is today.

2. Most "economic" activities will be in the areas of services rather than in manufacturing.

3. Business firms won't be the major source of innovation any more.

4. There will be more non-profit types of enterprises in research, education, health, welfare, and the arts.

5. A minimum income and welfare level for all will be provided in our society.

6. "Efficiency" will not be emphasized as much as it is today.

7. Social needs will be more important than consumer needs.

8. There will be a widespread use of computers and more "cybernetics."

9. It will be a "small world" because of rapid communication and transportation.

10. Out total body of knowledge will double every thirty years or less.

11. Ours will be a "learning" society, with lifelong education well accepted.

12. Educational institutions and techniques will improve rapidly.

13. Work, achievement, and advancement will erode as motives.

14. There will be less "nationalistic" loyalty and more international relations.

15. Human, sensate, and self-indulgent factors will become more central to life. People will live more for the fun of it.

The future belongs to you. Do you want it?

"Mother" Taps Hippie Vein In Conventional Folk

On January 1, 1970 a young couple in Ohio scraped together $1,500 and published the first slim (64-page) issue of a magazine devoted to giving people back their lives. John and Jane Shuttleworth plunged deep with that first issue . . . they had exactly 147 subscribers lined up and their $1,500 barely covered the printing bill for an optimistic 10,600 copies. "We figured we'd already had it," Shuttleworth recalls now. "We were tired, we had no money left, no up-front advertisers, no distribution contacts, no staff, and no place to work other than our tiny cottage . . . which was so full of magazines we had to move all the furniture into the yard except for the bed. And during the day we used that for a desk."

But now, just three short years later, their publication, *The Mother Earth News,* has become the cornerstone of a two-million-dollar-a-year corporate entity. *"Mother",* as she is affectionately referred to by her readers, has blossomed into a bi-monthly 132-page periodical that is inspiring and helping tens of thousands of people start their own businesses, garden organically, build low-cost homes, develop alternative power systems and — in general — find their ways to richer, more satisfying lives.

A second "sister" publication, *Lifestyle!,* successfully launched last fall is establishing an impressive growth rate of its own . . . *Mother's* syndicated radio programs are being aired daily on over 80 stations from coast to coast, and in Canada, Australia and Alaska . . . more than four thousand names a week are pouring in from readers of a syndicated three-times-a-week column appearing in 81 leading newspapers . . . the third edition of a 100-page country mail-order catalogue, offering everything from straight razors to windmills, has

been nearly depleted just 60 days after a 100,000-copy press run . . . and *Mother's Bookshelf Catalog,* a separate mail-order operation, has grown into the leading (if not the only) central clearinghouse for back-to-the-land and how-to-do-it books.

The Mother Earth News, called by *The National Observer* as "a magazine for a gentle revolution", has clearly found a unique market . . . one that just happens to be right smack in the mainstream of an ecology-conscious society reaching for alternatives to the present so-called "system".

"I suppose *Mother's* basic message," says editor-publisher John Shuttleworth, "is consume less and enjoy it more. Almost every article hammers away again and again on the do-it-yourself use-it-up wear-it-out make-it-work grow-your-own start-a-home-business theme. We're not saying that everyone should go 'back' . . . but we're pretty certain that we're all going to have to start going forward in a slightly different direction than we have in the past."

Mother's editorial slant is relentlessly ecological. "We're not angry at anyone," explained the Shuttleworths in a recent interview. "Most counter-culture publications advocate forcing the steel companies to stop making steel . . . closing down the automobile manufacturers . . . all negative things. We're not trying to put anyone down. We're not trying to overthrow the system . . . we're trying to *underwhelm* it. Saving this earth and giving people a chance to live is something we really care about.

"We're trying to build something productive out of a deep discontent that has been simmering on our earth for years. Most people, I believe, want nothing so much as to be left alone to live their lives as they see fit. We just want to help individuals do that. Our whole mes-

sage is 'yes, you can take life in both hands and make it give you what you want'."

The world, it seems, is ready for that message. Readers in every one of the 50 states and in 48 foreign countries range from teen-agers to folks over 90. *Mother's* mailing list, a growing roster of over 107,000 names, includes left-wingers (who love *Mother* because she "shows how to get out of the corrupt system") and right-wingers (who love *Mother* because she "stands for traditional American values"). The retired chairman of the board of a "Fortune 500" company has bought gift subscriptions for Mike Mansfield, Abe Ribicoff, George Romney and other prominent friends. Fan letters (over 25,000 pieces of mail a month) come from doctors, lawyers, teachers, students, scientists, legislators, prison inmates, ministers, longhair freaks and librarians . . . but most are from just "plain folks", somewhere in the middle of the social-economic-political spectrum.

Potential space advertisers are politely given the brushoff unless they measure up to *Mother's* standards. (No more than 15 percent of the book is ever devoted to ads.) *The Mother Earth News* bans both cigarette and liquor advertisers. It turns thumbs down on sex and truss offerings, get-rich-quick schemes, devitalized "plastic" foods, planned obsolescence consumer items and contributors to high pollution. *"Mother* might let you place an ad or two in her magazine," promises the rate card, "but don't count on it. Don't count on it, that is, unless your company or your client is clean, reverent, kind, brave, trustworthy, loyal and thoughtful. Because *Mother* is just a little bit particular about what goes into her publication."

Taking an equally unorthodox (but highly successful) approach to magazine distribution, *The Mother Earth News* turned down offers of immediate national exposure from the big distributors. The Shuttleworths instead decided to establish their own distribution channels. "After that first issue got around we had letters from hundreds of small health food stores, head shops and book dealers," explains Shuttleworth. "They trust us and they believe in what we're trying to do. If we had put *Mother* into an established distributorship we would have been just one more step removed from the people we want to reach."

Mother's army of dealers is multiplying rapidly. Small stores like The Egg And The Eye, Mole Hole, Incredible Edibles, Magic Twanger, and Harper's Chicken River Trading now find themselves in the company of Walden's, Carson Pirie Scott, The Pickwick Stores and other prestigious firms. Over one million copies of *The Mother Earth News* have been sold; roughly half to paid subscribers, the other half through *Mother's* house-controlled network. Plans are underway to use this captive outlet for retail distribution of other magazines, posters, special interest catalogs, books, reprints, periodicals and *Mother*-related items. (Two versions of *The Mother Earth News Almanac* have already been completed and are scheduled for release later this year.)

Back-issue sales testify to the almost insatiable demand for *Mother's* timely — and timeless — "live with less and love it more" information. With an unlimited shelf life (the covers carry no date), there is no real "current issue" of *The Mother Earth News.* Although a new number is published bi-monthly, the book is sold more as a paperback than a magazine. Back issues are continuously reprinted and supplied to dealers, who invari-

Jane Shuttleworth, who now manages MOTHER's highly profitable mail-order arm, thumbs through a recent catalogue offering everything from windmills to butter churns.

ably stock as many *Mothers* as shelf space allows . . . and to subscribers, who, having sampled *Mother's* messages of ecological concern, workable alternatives and homespun philosophy, clamor for everything she's ever printed.

Keeping pace with this phenomenal growth has expanded *Mother's* operations into every available office, storefront and basement in her present home base at Madison, Ohio. First priority has been given to a move, scheduled for this summer, which will transport the entire *Mother Earth News* complex to a several-hundred-acre tract of land in the Smoky Mountains.

Following the move, work will begin immediately on a number of projects including the formation of a non-profit research center (more detailed information will be released shortly) to conduct experiments on wind, water, solar and other alternative power sources. Construction techniques utilizing ram-

med earth, stone, domes, yurts, etc., will be explored, as well as natural farming and gardening, aquaculture, alternative transportation and recycling projects. A separate publishing arm will be set up to produce a series of back-to-the-land, do-it-yourself books, manuals and newsletters . . . several new periodicals will be tested (including a citified version of *Mother,* edited for ecology-conscious urban cliff dwellers) . . . and a major expansion and streamlining of all mail-order operations will employ some highly innovative "non-marketing" techniques to reach *Mother's* "non-consumers".

Long-range plans include an extensive manufacturing operation . . . a studio for producing films, records and video-cassettes . . . a second research center (possibly on the south island of New Zealand) . . . and a massive all-out effort to further tip the scales in favor of the real Mother Earth.

People Tomorrow

In the decade of the seventies, we expect 15 million persons to join our workforce in the United States, as many people as presently live in the state of Pennsylvania. This will bring the workforce up to slightly over 100 million people by 1980. About half of all this growth will be accounted for by young adults, 25 to 34 years old.

Young adults in the workforce will not only be a bigger group, it will also be a different kind of group. Tommorow's workers will be better educated, less patient, and more creative. They will want more opportunity for expression and meaningful experiences. They will want to share in making the important decisions.

Along with the growth in this age group, there will be a decline in growth among those in their teens and early twenties. The growth rate will fall from 53% in the sixties to 19% in the seventies. This will alleviate some of the problem of youth unemployment -- among perosns 16 to 24 years old.

The upswing in the proportion of women in our workforce will accelerate in the latter portion of the seventies. Married women, in particular, including married women with young children, are streaming to work. The changing roles of women at work are related to the broader shifts in attitudes and values in our society. Women's liberation further reflects the pressures for

rapid changes in the direction of the post-industrial society.

As we more toward the eighties we anticipate shifts away from the lesser-skilled occupations and jobs and toward the higher-skilled occupations. White-collar and service occupations will grow at a faster rate than these. Government employment will grow faster than all other fields and will surpass manufacturing as our largest employment group.

By 1980, for the first time, there will be as many professional and technical workers as blue-collar workers. Yet there will be many good jobs in the economy for which a high school education is sufficient; there will be more than 15 million operative jobs and 17 million clerical jobs -- more jobs than in any other occupational group. Of course, a lot of these jobs will

be with the government, as noted above.

People will still be work-oriented in the future, but for somewhat different reasons than they are today. They will still work for money, but more important will be the satisfactions that come from achievement. We see this to be the case today in many of our professions.

Jobs will become more flexible and more challenging, taking advantage of increased capabilities of higher-educated talent. Jobs will have built-in opportunities for continuing education -- through flexible work schedules, work-study programs, and sabbaticals (periods of time away from work for study, rest, or social action).

In our post-industrial society, jobs will reflect changed goals of business organizations. Social and political concerns will be among corporate functions -- and so many jobs will reach beyond the traditional boundaries of business enterprise. This will, of course, make work more interesting and stimulating to many individuals. Work will definitely be less physical, routine, and repititous in the future and more personal, technical, and theoretical.

The whole concept of work as an unpleasant duty will be less common, as work and leisure become equally valid types of activity. They will, in fact, blend together as satisfying activities.

The Stormy 70's—
Big Changes Still To Come

Now at the quarter mark, see how the decade is shaping up.
It's been full of surprises so far . . . and the rest of it
promises to be pretty exciting as well.

FASTER GROWTH . . . GOOD JOBS . . . MORE LEISURE . . . NEW TECHNOLOGIES . . .
MEDICAL ADVANCES . . . MORE AND BIGGER PROBLEMS, BUT BETTER SOLUTIONS, TOO.

Even as America bustled through the "soaring sixties," it looked ahead to a still more promising time. Next would come "the surge of the seventies." Technological advances, population growth, economic growth—all these illuminated the approaching decade as an era that would bring spectacular achievements.

But when the nation finally crossed into the 70's, there wasn't much to cheer about. Fear seemed to be the mood of the land. There had been rioting in the streets, protests had flared up on the nation's campuses. Inflation undermined the dollar and unemployment was on the rise. The word "revolution" bounced around as it had not since the birth of the Republic nearly 200 years before.

Change ripped at the very fabric of family and community. Personal and social values were challenged. Traditional institutions were frontally attacked. The youth rebellion, the drug culture, "emancipation" from respected sexual mores, and abandonment of long-established criteria in schools and colleges all compounded to widen the gap between baffled elders and their children. Minorities spoke out in emotional protests, the poor organized themselves into pressure groups, women's lib became something more than a gag. New spokesmen, new leaders emerged.

Today, only four years short of the nation's bicentennial, citizens find themselves looking inward and outward—questioning their own values and convictions, appraising the extent and nature of change swirling over the land. Contradictions and paradoxes can be read as indexes to the country's confusion and pessimism. Among them:

► An economy that produces in excess of a trillion dollars' worth of goods and services annually, but has only about 5% of its national income going to the 20% of its families at the lowest end of the economic ladder.

► An outpouring of material goods of every type and design, intended to provide higher living standards for everyone but also provoking questions about the need for such material wealth and its consequences for the nation's natural resources and environment.

► A society that points with pride to new towns, fabulous shopping centers and superhighways while struggling with the ills of slum housing that scars its cities.

► A nation equipped with excellent medical resources, but with an infant mortality rate in excess of that of ten other advanced countries.

Now that we've traveled a quarter of the way down the road through the 70's, it is reasonable to wonder whether as a nation we can resolve some of these contradictions that trouble our society. Can we solve the new problems that must be faced up to in the rest of this decade?

It begins to seem clear that economic vigor and resilience will help the country cope successfully with the problems of the 70's. A new thrust forward in technology may rival even the accomplishments of the years after World War II. And dramatic growth in public awareness of our difficulties will be accompanied not by a wringing of the hands but by a readiness to face up to their solutions.

Any solution to immediate problems, though, may have within it the ingredients of future crises. For example, does "more" really mean "better"? Should each generation live better than the preceding generation? Yes is no longer the automatic answer to both questions.

At the heart of the new concern is mounting evidence that this country's natural wealth cannot last indefinitely. Gas, minerals, timber and other products of nature's bounty are in some instances already in jeopardy. In the next ten or twenty years shortages will become significantly worse. So pressure will continue to build to control growth or even to throttle it.

As an issue, this question of curtailed growth is more critical for the 80's and 90's than for the 70's. It is then that the major impact of uncontrolled growth would be felt.

Dollars are a symbol

IMAGINE, IF YOU CAN, two trillion dollars. In figures it looks like this: $2,000,000,000,000. Picture a billion dollars all in a heap. It would take 2,000 heaps to make two trillion dollars.

Look at it another way. Last year for the first time in recorded history this nation produced one trillion dollars' worth of goods and services in a single year. All over the world economists and statesmen, of whatever political persuasion, regarded it as an achievement of monumental proportions. It took this country almost two centuries to reach that one-trillion-dollar milestone. It is expected to take less than ten years more to reach two trillion, given the current rate of inflation.

An outpouring of goods and services in such fantastic amounts will require an annual growth rate slightly in excess of the average 3.4% of the last 15 years. This should not be too difficult to achieve. The economy has demonstrated that it can sometimes far exceed the 3.4% rate if conditions are favorable. From 1961 to 1968, for instance, the growth was at a rate of 5.1% a year—a figure that generated that phrase "the soaring sixties."

The two-trillion-dollar figure does not represent just gadgets and gimmicks. It includes the value of what we need to supply better health care, more education, new kinds of transportation and better communications, the materials to ease such social problems as housing and poverty and such physical problems as pollution. The dollars are the symbol of what the nation has to work with to better the life of its people, the functioning of its government and the conservation of its environment.

Incomes and jobs

MOST PEOPLE will be better off at the end of the decade than they were at the start. In 1970 here is how families fared—total annual incomes in 1971 dollars:

income	percentage of families
$25,000 and over	5%
$15,000 to $25,000	19%
$10,000 to $15,000	28%
$7,000 to $10,000	19%
$5,000 to $7,000	11%
$3,000 to $5,000	10%
under $3,000	8%

About one out of four families had an income exceeding $15,000. About six out of ten had between $5,000 and $15,000 a year. And almost one out of five American families in 1970 had to live on $5,000 a year or less.

Now look at the projection for 1980, as estimated by the Conference Board:

income	percentage of families
$25,000 and over	13%
$15,000 to $25,000	33%
$10,000 to $15,000	23%
$7,000 to $10,000	12%
$5,000 to $7,000	8%
$3,000 to $5,000	6%
under $3,000	5%

By 1980 almost one of two families can expect an income of $15,000 or better, figured in 1971 dollars. About 43% of all families will fall in the $5,000 to $15,000 bracket. Those with less than $5,000 a year to live on will be about 11% of the total.

Earning this income will bring far-reaching changes in the way people work and the kinds of work they do. These are some of the changes coming:

More people at work. Approximately 100,000,000 people will be at work or looking for work by the end of the decade, meaning about 1,500,000 additional jobs must be created every year through the 70's. (On the average, unemployment during the decade will probably hover be-between the 4% and 6% levels.)

Who will these new workers be? The biggest increase in people at work will be in the 25 to 34 age bracket—the young adults who made up the postwar baby boom, then inundated the schools. They'll be well-educated and thus eager to move up the ladder. Black workers are expected to make rapid gains in job status. (In the last decade the number of nonwhites who got college degrees tripled, and in this decade the number is expected to double again.) Working women will number about 37,000,000, twice as many women as 30 years earlier.

More meaningful jobs. The young, in particular, think it's futile to spend one's working lifetime at a job that produces a paycheck and little else. Industry is responding to this by moving toward greater recognition of individual effort and responsibility—employers are more aware of the demoralizing impact of vocational boredom. This decade may well produce a minor revolution in the whole approach to job and career.

Fewer manufacturing jobs. Currently, only about four out of ten jobs involve production of goods. The rest are in the so-called service industries, from accounting to zipper repairing. Dr. Carl H. Madden, chief economist of the U.S. Chamber of Commerce, anticipates that the manufacturing segment will get even smaller. Fewer people will be making goods,

more will be distributing, selling and servicing them. Automated machines and computerized plants will displace millions at the workbench. But they will turn out far more goods.

Farming? At the turn of the century close to 40% of the working population was engaged in it. Today 4% of the employed population produce food and fiber for themselves and the rest of the country. That 4% figure will be cut back even further as the mechanization of great corporate farms transforms agriculture into "agribusiness."

More government workers. Today about 13,000,-000 people work for federal, state and local governments. By 1980 that figure will be approaching 16,000,000 or 17,000,000—about one out of six in the labor force.

More time to play. The workweek has been declining for several generations. As recently as 1930 it averaged over 46 hours; now it is close to 37 hours. By 1980 it will be around 36 hours. Remember, those are averages. Millions of people will be working less time, many of them on four-day-week schedules. Vacations and holidays will be longer, retirement will come earlier.

To reiterate, then: The U.S. will have the most highly trained and educated work force in history as it enters the 1980's. And its technology will be unsurpassed. These two pluses—work force and technology—could be important ingredients for successfully confronting the agonies that beset us. From these resources, say the experts, can come solutions for such problems as poverty, poor housing, pollution, environmental degradation and all the other social and economic needs of our times.

How living will change

AMERICANS WILL HAVE almost twice as much to spend on themselves by the end of the decade as they did at the beginning. Much of that will go for the usual things (or the 1980 version of the usual things)—houses, cars, appliances, clothing, food, education, travel, medical care, grooming, the maintenance and upkeep of

Fastest-growing cities and regions

The American dream may be the house at the side of a country lane, but the American reality is a gregarious crowding together in cities and suburbs. Seven out of ten people will live in or around major cities by 1980, according to projections of the National Planning Association. They will gravitate toward the outer rings of suburbia rather than to the central city. The notion that there may be a reverse flow back to the city itself gets little support from the demographers.

Biggest population increase in the decade will be in the South and the West. The fastest-growing states will be Nevada, Florida, Arizona, California, New Mexico and Colorado.

Which of the largest metropolitan complexes will grow the fastest? San Jose, Anaheim, Phoenix, Dallas, Miami, Atlanta, San Bernardino, Sacramento, Houston, Denver, Fort Lauderdale and Tampa-St. Petersburg. All will add at least 25% to their population in this decade.

In which will incomes rise the most? Anaheim, San Jose, Dallas, Miami, Tampa-St. Petersburg, Houston, Atlanta, San Bernardino.

As has been true for a long time, the great waves of migration will carry people toward the sun and the sea. More than half the population already lives within a few hours' driving distance of a coastline (including the Great Lakes). And that proportion will increase.

one's home. But a basic shift is ahead: People will spend a greater proportion of income on such things as health and education and recreation and a smaller proportion on things like food and clothing. Some predict this will come about in part because of a new antimaterialistic attitude among young families who feel there should be less emphasis on the accumulation of things and more on the happiness of people.

In any event, the ways we handle our spending will change. One possibility is a universal credit card, good for everything from the purchase of groceries to payment of taxes. Another likely development is billing to a central source —probably the local bank—that will pay the bills and debit depositors' accounts.

Shopping itself may see some radical innovations. A basic one will be shopping from home via computer and TV. Two very real possibilities emerged from a recent session of the Electronics Industries Association on the subject of the 1980's:

► Video tapes used in place of ads and catalogs. You would receive them in the mail for playback on your TV set. You would see and hear what's available, then make your choice accordingly.

► Computer-assisted shopping. This would involve a computer terminal in the home that would give instant responses to a shopper's queries about availability of desired products shown on TV. To buy, you would simply punch your order on the computer keyboard.

An allied development—not just for shopping—is the coming breakthrough in CATV (community antenna television). In a very few years systems will be installed in most cities offering 15 to 20 different channels of information and entertainment, with a much larger potential. Enthusiasts foresee the day when people will be able to use their TV sets not only for shopping but for hobby instruction, professional training, education and an almost endless variety of other purposes. Together with the video cassette, this innovation will produce a fantastic communications revolution, eclipsing by far the consequences of the arrival of TV only a quarter century ago.

Other changes coming involve far greater use of synthetic materials in everything from housing to foods, and new appliances for the kitchen and laundry using the latest developments in microelectronics and automated controls. For instance, expect to see such innovations (by Westinghouse) as "air speed" infrared cooking, in which infrared energy is used to cook food while air heated to 350° is blown across it.

One intriguing speculation: Shopping from home, being entertained at home, having education home-based will bring people back to the hearth. Might that cure one of the basic ills of the 50's and the 60's—the great breach in family cohesion and intimacy?

Shifting patterns in education

THE SCHOOLING of Americans is coming into a period of vast change: On the one hand, the number of students in the elementary grades will decline. On the other, the number of people seeking post-high-school education will take an enormous jump. The Office of Education draws the picture this way:

Elementary enrolment: down 2,000,000 by 1980
Secondary enrolment: about the same in 1980 as now—20,000,000
College enrolment: up 55% by 1980 to a total student body of 13,300,000

Very simply, the drop in the birthrate in the past decade has lessened the load on elementary schools significantly and by the mid-80's will similarly reduce the number of students in high schools.

But look what's going to happen in higher education. America's infatuation with degrees and college credentials is propelling millions more students toward public and private institutions, seeking skills, training and, above all, that magic diploma. Only about 10% of college students are expected to be nondegree students.

Two-year community colleges, whose enrolment more than quadrupled in the 60's, will double their student bodies within this decade. They are the big new wave in American education.

Eli Ginzberg, a professor at Columbia, observes: "While the labor force as a whole will increase 20% between 1968 and 1980, the number with bachelor's degrees will increase just under 50%, those with master's degrees about 100%, and those with doctorates over 115%.... the proportion of educated persons seeking employment will be far higher than in any previous decade."

The cost of all this? Over 100 billion dollars a year, predicts the National Center for Educational Statistics—up more than 15 billion from current figures.

Most of it will be for public schools and colleges, but the private educational bill will also escalate. For parents of students who will be going to college in 1980, the word is that they will pay an average $3,908 a year for tuition, room and board at a private university, $1,681 at a public one (both figures are in 1970-71 dollars).

Private colleges will have a tough go. Many will have closed their doors by 1980. Increasingly, public-financed universities and colleges will carry the higher-education load of this country.

A question that remains unanswered: Are the kinds and types of education students seek necessarily the routes to personal fulfillment and happiness? Says Education Commissioner Sidney P. Marland Jr.: "While post-secondary education is certainly both desirable and necessary, degree 'fixation'—or the misguided notion that respectability must be equated with a bachelor's degree—is at the heart of the career dilemma in America." For educators and students alike, this will probably be the real question of the future—not "whether education," but "what kind of education."

The nation's health

WHAT ARE THE HEALTH NEEDS of the 70's? Primarily, to bring medical care to the millions of Americans now denied it. A study by Lincoln First Banks Inc., of Rochester, N.Y., finds that "50% of the poor have not had adequate immunization; 64% have never seen a dentist; 45% of all women who have babies in public hospitals have not had prenatal care. And Negro infant mortality is twice, often three times, that of whites in some sections."

It is not only the poor who suffer. Millions of other Americans, for one reason or another, 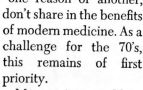 don't share in the benefits of modern medicine. As a challenge for the 70's, this remains of first priority.

More training and better placement of medical personnel will help. Already, new paramedical technicians are being trained to help shoulder doctors' loads. Several medical schools are shortening the time needed for a medical education. Young doctors are being encouraged to set up practice in the inner city as well as in poorly served rural areas, and to become family doctors rather than specialists.

The high cost of medical care remains a major obstacle. Most experts agree that by the end of the decade, some form of government health insurance will be in force, covering everyone,

and involving profound changes in the practice of medicine in this country.

The science of medicine will move forward dramatically. Among the predictions: Perfection of an artificial heart, probably atomic-powered; a kidney machine of miniaturized design; an increase in organ transplants (heart, kidney, liver and—maybe—lungs); significant progress in diagnosis and treatment of cancer and heart disease; better understanding of the cause and cure of mental illness; impressive progress in eliminating tooth decay; a better understanding of basic cell structure and function that may lead to prevention of genetic diseases. But a conquest of the common cold? Not likely.

Cars, cars and still more cars

THERE'S A NEW KIND of automobile coming down the highway, reflecting major changes in

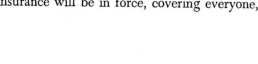

design and operation. It will be safer and practically pollution-free.

Today's motor vehicles cause 60% of all air pollution. By the late 70's the extent and the cost (12 billion dollars a year) of such pollution will have been cut substantially, largely as a result of government requirements.

New power units will be developed. The most promising designs are those using rotary combustion (the Wankel), turbines, electricity, steam or combinations of some of these. Not only will they be cleaner but they promise to be quieter as well.

Safety will continue to be a major ingredient of new-car design (though the designs themselves won't change with as much frequency as in the past). That means heavier bumpers, stronger body panels, improved restraint systems. Among the more exotic ideas being considered are radar controls that could actually prevent collisions.

Cars will cost more, and probably be more expensive to operate, but that won't stop people from buying them. The two- and three-car family will become commonplace.

How many automobiles on the road? Between 120,000,000 and 130,000,000, compared with about 93,000,000 now. Add to these about 28,000,000 trucks and buses barreling down the highways.

Parking and servicing this traffic will test the ingenuity of city planners. Already, for example, about two-thirds of the downtown area of Los Angeles is, in one way or another, used for driving, parking and servicing cars. One likely development is the barring of automobiles from midcity areas, reserving these areas for pedestrians and public transit. "People movers"—small vehicles run by computers—will pick up and drop passengers at office buildings, apartment houses, shopping centers, etc.

Mass transit (subways, interurban trains and buses) will become increasingly important. After all, say the advocates, one ordinary highway lane 12 feet wide can carry only 3,600 car passengers an hour. That same lane used for mass transit can carry 60,000 passengers an hour by bus, 42,000 an hour by train.

Even so, these will be used only for short hauls. Long-haul passenger transportation in this country will be largely by automobile or by air. Air travel is expected to more than double in volume by the 1980's.

Postscript

THERE IS MUCH MORE that could be written about tomorrow's technology: the great potential of the laser, a new generation of appliances derived from microelectronics, fusion power, data communications, holography, solar energy and a dozen other advances whose time will be more of the 80's than the 70's.

And more could be said about social and economic problems: the huge cost of environmental protection (estimated currently by General Electric at 288.5 billion dollars over the next ten years), the increased pressure for more revenue sharing by the states, increased social benefits for the poor, better transportation for cities, better housing, more recreational areas, more attention for the aged.

Methods and costs of problem solving will create the political issues of the decade ahead. Whatever decisions are made, the country's human, technological and economic resources will be adequate for the task. And most forecasters believe that America, having seen how a lack of awareness and preparedness in the 50's and 60's delayed and distorted the early promise of the 70's, will learn from its errors.

Avoiding Obsolescence In The Age Of Aquarius

by Ernest C. Arbuckle, Chairman of the Board of Wells Fargo Bank

First of all, you are off to a good start—you have a fine education. But it's only a start. The ultimate goal of a university must be to have its graduates take over the responsibility for continuing their own education for the rest of their lives. No one can any longer expect to go to college just once and be educated for life. As Sir Eric Ashby, Master of Clare College at Cambridge, has said:

> The present generation of students will still be employed in the year 2000. But long before then their degrees and diplomas, at any rate in science technology and the social sciences, will have become obsolete. The only students who can be sure of escaping obsolescence are those very few who will themselves become innovators. Our investment in the rest, the great majority of our human resources, will inevitably be devalued by technological and social change.

Measures to combat obsolescence, therefore, become of prime importance.

Experience can be a great teacher, but in a world of rapid change it can also be a millstone around your neck. Everything depends upon what kind of experience you have. It can be a constructive, causative force, which provides the solid background and confidence needed if management is to move into new areas, or it can be the experience that consists of doing the same thing over and over again until the rut has been dug so deep that you cannot see up and out. Experience deserves our respect, but it also can be deceptive if the circumstances of today's decisions have changed since the experience was gained. The phrase, "We tried that once and it didn't work," will often prevent your making the same mistake twice. It may also inhibit innovation and destroy initiative, thus committing an organization to slow dègeneration and decay. This is especially true in today's competitive market place.

The best kind of experience is that which you gain by accepting responsibility, taking calculated risks, trying new ways of doing things, making mistakes but profiting from them. So let us validate our experience against all the conditions that exist at the time the decision must be made. And let us not accept any decision as final merely because it is the easiest way to get an answer to a tough problem.

You want a job which will test you, one that will give you a chance to apply what you have learned and one that offers an opportunity for development as well as for advancement. You want your job to make you feel you are doing something worthwhile, participating in important activities, and carrying out significant responsibility. You would like to work for people whom you will respect and from whom you can learn. You are hoping for a job which will provide you with the opportunity to be creative and original so that you can try out some of your own ideas. You want to count—and to be counted. You are not afraid to be judged fairly on performance.

It is interesting now to wonder what some of your employers think about you as they add your name to their payroll, because we never see ourselves as others see us. In the first place, they recognize the value of your education. Otherwise they wouldn't be hiring you or paying you at the current salary levels, since they have to get a return on the investment. So they start out by thinking you are pretty good, but they also have some criticisms about you.

They think that many of you are overambitious and unrealistic in your expectations, that you are often too theoretical and too idealistic. Very frequently they regard you as immature, inexperienced, and sometimes egotistical. Many of them claim that you don't know the difference between having a good idea and selling it. They say that you've got to learn the hard way and must be broken in before you are any good.

I have perhaps exaggerated these criticisms somewhat, but they are more widespread than you might imagine. What do we do about them?

Give more consideration to the quality of humility than you have ever done before; as an M.B.A. you are suspect. The support of your colleagues is absolutely essential to your success on the job, but you will never get it by reminding a fellow worker that *you* have an M.B.A., particularly if he doesn't have one, or if he has one but started at a lower salary, which sometimes happens these days. I have never had a job that I could do by myself, that I could not do better with the full support and cooperation of my peers. There is no surer way to alienate such support than to create the impression that you think you're just a little better than the other fellow. I do not imply that you should not have confidence in your ability and have the courage to take a stand. I am referring to what Benjamin Franklin had in mind when he said, "He that falls in love with himself will have no rivals."

Merchandise your ideas. You may have good ideas, but they are not going to be accepted merely because they are yours or because you graduated from Michigan. Ideas, like products, must be developed. They have to be carefully designed to meet customers' needs, in this case the needs of your boss. They have to be market-researched with other people who will be using them. And they have to be effectively sold. You all know that to be an effective salesman you have to know a lot about your customer. Don't forget that possibly your most important customer is your boss.

Don't give primary consideration to geography as the basis for selecting your first job. In the first place, you may move many times, especially if you're the man they want to train for bigger things. Secondly, the kind of a community that appeals to you now may not give you the outlet you need for your energies and interests ten years hence. Finally, and most importantly, the satisfactions and the stimulus derived from your work, the excitement of steadily increasing responsibility and of meaningful endeavor will have much more to do with your development than the place of the initial job or the location of headquarters. At least while you're young, treat yourself to the education that comes from living in different parts of our country and understanding its different cultures, its diverse values and points of view.

Insist upon periodic self-renewal. Most of us have more ability and greater capacity than we ever use. Utilize your environment for your full self-development. Today, talent is mobile. I am not implying that if you find your first job boring and unfulfilling you should immediately shift to another. Self-renewal requires conviction, commitment, and self-discipline.

Discontent is never a sound basis for trying something else until you have first attempted to broaden the opportunities that exist where you are. But, having done that, if you see new opportunities in our changing society that rekindle a waning enthusiasm, have the courage to exchange certainty for uncertainty.

I hope you will always feel your responsibility both as a citizen and as a businessman. Far from being conflicting, the two roles are complementary. Each is self-supporting, but in their essentials they are inseparable. Ten to fifteen years ago the separation of private business and public affairs was a valid and workable premise; today it is no longer tenable. If free enterprise is to remain in the hands of men who lead society, the corporation will have to involve itself in more of the central concerns of society. Business today is exercising greater leadership than ever before in helping to solve major economic and social problems, but it will have to do even more in the future. This statement is not a response to the do-gooders; it is made because in business management are found resources, special skills and abilities, and above all the kind of leadership which must be brought to bear on these problems if we are to make significant headway toward their solution. Most young people in our colleges and universities have a high degree of social consciousness, and they have responded to social needs with energy and initiative. I hope this consciousness, as well as the initiative and energy that goes with it, will not be lost as you assume the responsibilities of families and careers.

A school can fill your cognitive bank with large deposits of knowledge: facts and ideas of all kinds. The bank can be well stocked with experience and with administrative skills. But how these resources will be applied when they are withdrawn from the bank depends to a large extent on your attitudes and personal values. Never forget that the ethics and moral values of the business community of tomorrow will be determined by you young men and women who are graduating from universities today. If the private enterprise system is to survive, there must have been instilled in you a belief that integrity, rooted in the bedrock of principle, is more important than operational competence.

Educators cannot indoctrinate a student with a fixed set of beliefs and expect him to adapt to a world in revolution. This would be the surest way to ensure the obsolescence of both the individual and the education. The school's job is to equip the student with the inner resources that will enable him to meet unforeseen challenges and help him to develop as an intellectually versatile person in an unpredictable world. Business in turn must do everything it can to create an environment in which the graduate can not only retain, but develop further, his idealism and a flexible, innovative, receptive attitude, one that accepts controversy and different points of view, one that permits him to learn from all events and circumstances—no matter how adverse or unpalatable.

In the age of Aquarius, tradition and convention are suspect. Scientific research is "in," and so is respect for the individual. There is no room in business for the man who blindly follows the traditions and conventions of yesterday. For no institution hoping to survive is so dependent upon its adaptation to change as American business enterprise.

I invite you to join us in this environment—to bring to our revolution your idealism, your skills, and your determination to make this a better society in which to live. Good luck to all of you.

Future Organizations

In the future organizations will respond to changing conditions. Thus organizations will not only be different from those we know today, they will be continually changing.

Because of their greater involvement in social and political concerns, the organizations of tomorrow will evaluate performance in a different way. More emphasis will be placed on education and development of employees, care for product quality, concern for the quality of the environment and the community, and less concern for strict profits and efficiency. Economics will become social economics, balancing the needs and demands of all the "stakeholders" of the organization -- owners, customers, employees, managers, suppliers and the public.

Already we are seeing SOCIAL AUDITS becoming part of corporate practice. Under such labels as "social measurement," or "social performance assessment," companies are attempting to examine and report to the public the costs and impact of their various activities. Training, pollution, product quality, safety, and use of natural resources are among the factors normally considered.

To manage effectively the higher-educated talent in tomorrow's organizations, management will become more flexible and less structured. Communications will become more open, fluid, and flexible.

More and more use will be made of the project or task-force form of organization. This project management style allows management to shift personnel assignments from one task or project to another, according to changing needs. Today we see it used principally in aerospace and other advanced-technology industries.

Bureaucratic organization, with rigid organizational relationships, established policies and procedures, and specific job duties will give way to flexible organizations. As work needs to be done, people will be assigned to the tasks, given training if needed, and the responsibility to carry them out with minimum supervision.

The decisions that managers make in the future will be more important ones, because of increased use of computers. Today's repetitive, routine, day-to-day decisions will be replaced by more critical strategic and policy decisions. Tomorrow's managers will thus have to have much more flexibility and freedom of action to keep their organizations moving ahead.

In business organizations there will also likely be a corporate "techno-structure," a body od specialists who are equipped to advise and educate the key decision-making managers in a company. Today's staff groups suggest this increasingly important function.

These changing patterns of organization and management will apply to both large and small organizations. Both are subject to the increasing pressures of technology, attitudes, and consumer demands. Those organizations, large or small, that do adapt effectively will survive and prosper.

Can Small Business Survive?

What is the status of small business today? Is it as strong as it was a decade or more ago? What will it be like in the future? Will small business "go by the boards" in the face of competition, new technology, and other pressures?

It would be an understatement to say we would feel badly if small business enterprises were to wane in our economic society. It's part of our democratic heritage. Small businesses represent one of the basic freedoms of American life -- to enter or leave business at will, to start and grow big, to expand, contract, or even to fail.

Actually, in many markets, notably in local services and providing products made to particular specifications, small business is able to do a better job than big business.

The ingenious small enterpriser often is a source of new materials, new ideas, new services, new processes, and other innovations that older, larger, better established firms cannot or will not offer. Ventures start out

as small businesses, and are often adopted when tested and proven to have merit. The whole business system is given new life and blood by the zeal of small business.

Because of this spirit of adventure, innovation, entrepreneurship, and participation in democracy, many young people start their careers in small businesses. They feel their talents will be better used, and sooner, than in a larger, impersonal corporation.

PAST AND FUTURE GROWTH

The numbers show that the small business segment of our economy is in fact growing -- at about a 2% rate per year. Approximately 100,000 new enterprises are added each year. Of course, more new businesses are formed during good economic times than during recessions. From the record of small business growth during the past few decades, there appears to be no immenent threat of losing this important part of our enterprise system.

But the facts do show that the growth of small

business in our economy isn't all roses. The 100,000 net increase is just that -- net. In recent years about 450,000-500,000 new business concerns have been started annually and about 350,000-400,000 have been discontinued annually.

This means there is a tremendous rate of failure among new small businesses. The risk of failure has a significant personal impact on the entrepreneurs, but it's easy to overlook in the total statistics.

Once the number of failures climbs, the total number of small businesses will start to tumble. We must be sure that small businesses are as strong as they can be. We want to give them the help they need to get started, to compete effectively, and to grow strong.

Government assistance is one tool. But money from the Small Business Administration isn't enough. As one SBA official noted, "Money isn't the main problem any more; it's management assistance that is needed." Without basic skills, small firms are run marginally and the results are often fatal.

Relations: Government, Unions, And Business

In this decade, labor unions are finding their growth coming from white-collar membership, including technical, clerical, and public employees. In the past few years we have seen the growth and militancy of unions representing public employees: police, firemen, teachers, as well as clerical and other municipal employees have formed unions and have used the strike to obtain the economic benefits that their membership demands. Since these public employee unions strike the public, their actions are very visible and attract public attention.

In the longer-term, however, labor unions will diminish in economic influence. With increased automation, greater attention to the needs of people in organizations, and expanded education and government services, the benefits of union membership will become considered less important.

Within unions, there is emerging a militancy among younger workers. This is resulting in changes in the structure and management of union organizations, similar to the changes occuring in business organizations: decentralization, greater individualization, more flexibility in policies, and greater openness of communications. Unions will also open their membership doors to minority workers who have often been excluded in the past through traditional

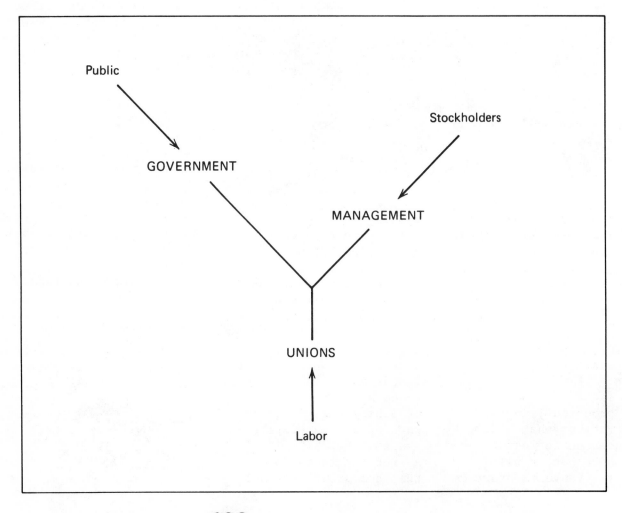

membership rules. This will have a further impact in inducing changes in union practices.

In fact, there is apparent a rising sentiment among local unions against the domination in policy-making and bargaining by the national or international leadership. Younger union members often question the need to pay union dues and then turn over their "voice" as well. In response the union leadership has attempted to improve communications and overall understanding of the benefits provided by union membership and active participation.

In an effort to make up for their declining share of the American Labor force, some unions are becoming more actively involved in political and community efforts, such as the development of inner cities. Unions may be expected to move to the front of popular causes: welfare reform, health insurance, pension reform, pollution control, safety, etc.

Labor-management relations, including collective bargaining, are pretty well established as an institution in our society and will survive in the future. Competent and imaginative management will be needed, though, to keep established practices working and attuned to changing conditions.

The need for flexibility in management will force significant changes in collective bargaining and union-management relations. Union resistance to changes in job design and work processes will likely give way to greater union-management cooperation. The challenges posed by younger workers must be met. Equal employment opportunities must be provided. Unions must be able to handle diverse groups of talent -- skills, ages, attitudes, and occupations. If they don't, we may see some new unions forming and some new union associations splitting off from the AFL-CIO.

Enlightened collective bargaining in the future will involve greater use of continuous bargaining, joint study teams, longer-term contracts, and greater participation by governmental representatives -- representing the public interest.

Some people project that we will never have nationwide strikes such as in trucking or on the railroads. The toll on the public welfare is simply too great to tolerate.

We will see less use of raw economic power -- such as the use of strikes and lockouts in collective bargaining, and increased willingness to cooperate in the solution of critical social, economic, and technological problems.

The extent and frequency of government involvement will depend on the extent that unions and businesses recognize their key roles in our economic society, as illustrated on the previous page. Government employment will also bring greater public involvement into employment relationships -- in the setting of pay, benefits, and conditions of work. When public employees get certain benefits, private industry takes not.

Unions and government will have greater voice in decisions that have traditionally been solely the responsibility of management. In addition to human resources policies, they will share in the setting of prices, production planning, quality control, safety, and many basic business management functions.

At the same time, business will expand its involvement in public affairs, and will provide services to the public and the government that have not been its concern in the past.

Rather than seeing a diminishing of the power of one sector -- unions, management, or government, we will see an increase in all three. But we will see a continuing balance among them as their roles in our changing society expand.

Our World Economy

In the future, ours will be a global economy. The American economy is becoming an integral part of a larger, complex economic system. Marshall McLuhan has noted that our "global village" will be drawn together by instantaneous, world-wide communications.

The internationalization of economic activity will break down our national political boundaries. Economic realities will take precedence over nationalistic loyalties.

Problems that we will be facing in future dacades will be worldwide, not national problems. These include critical problems of trade, pollution, energy supplies, nuclear power, the population explosion, progress of lesser developed countries, and the conservation of limited natural resources.

As a result, it will be more difficult for the United States or any other nation to assume that what is best for the nation is necessarily the best policy for the world.

In the decades ahead we may expect our economy to grow, as shown in the table below. Our economy will likely become more stable than we have known it to be in past decades.

Our effective use of fiscal and monetary policy, together with sensible approaches to international trade, cpaital investment, and resource allocation will help maintain our steady rate of economic growth. Employment and productivity will continue to rise, with advancing technology and growth in our work force

By 1980 we may expect our GNP to swell to $2.0 trillion, up 50% from today's level. Our GNP in the year 2000 is anybody's guess.

GROWTH AND PROSPECTS FOR THE UNITED STATES

	1900	1974	2000
Population, millions of people	76	212	250
Value of the dollar, 1967 prices	$3.96	$.68	$.30
Wages per hour	$.17	$3.86	$7.50
GNP, current prices in billions	$19	$1,397	$5,100
GNP per family, real 1967 dollars	$4,950	$17,300	$27,000

Based on U.S. Chamber of Commerce and U.S. Census data.

How "Free" Is Free Enterprise?

Memorial Day orators and campus recruiters who harangue undergraduates on the glories of the corporate life are likely to tell you:

Free enterprise built America. It enabled our forefathers to conquer wildernesses, expand our frontiers, create cities, factories, industries and win wars. Free enterprise made us the world's richest, most powerful and envied nation.

Who doubts that? Free enterprise is a noble concept—so typically and uniquely American. But whatever became of it?

Free enterprise is dead, says Douglas Grymes, president, Koppers Company, Pittsburgh. He recently told steelmen gathered at a Steel City meeting that, "Our economy is neither 'free' nor 'enterprising' and the time has come for us to recognize that fact."

Its demise has not been recent or sudden. Free enterprise began disappearing "slowly but relentlessly" around the middle of the 19th Century. The Great Depression of the '30s, the New Deal and World War II killed whatever was left of it, he said. "By 1950 America was living under a form of planned economy which, obviously, has continued to be more and more planned by our government."

Government regulates public utilities, sets rail rates, monitors securities markets, licenses television and radio, censors advertising, establishes import and export quotas, enacts laws to control mergers and acquisitions, pollution, protect consumers and husband our national resources. And the Internal Revenue Service extracts 48 percent of a corporation's profit to help pay for this Niagara of regulation.

In the 1890s such harsh strictures would have had the tycoons of that era chewing the gilt from their watered securities. Business today, however, "had better learn to accept government as an important, indispensable, yes, and even welcome partner."

Strange talk from a modern, topflight executive. But that partnership, Grymes believes, need not be as inimical to the interests of business as old-line industrialists would have us believe.

On the contrary, the governments of two of our most formidable competitors—West Germany and Japan—have long worked hand in hand and harmoniously with their industries. "These countries," Grymes observes, "certainly didn't labor under the misconception that free enterprise would conquer all. Instead, they decided that the strongest possible alliance for competing in world markets was one forged between government, industry and labor."

Late in the '60s American government, business and labor "finally began to realize that such foreign coalitions posed a serious threat to both our balance of trade and the jobs and profits of American industry. Typically, however, our pride in our industrial technology blinded us to the increased competence of foreign competition."

When West Germany and Japan began to undersell America both domestically and abroad, American business attributed their competitive edge to their lower wages. This convenient cop out is no longer good enough. Most American economists now believe that foreign industry could live with our labor costs and still undersell us. Grymes finds this "an alarming fact yet I must think it is true."

The new type of enterprise West Germany and Japan have developed within the last 25 years "squarely aligns government participation with business. The result is, indeed, a planned economy but I don't think any of us can deny that these countries are prospering under this unique setup. Nor am I at all sure that their economies are more planned than ours. I think they're just *better* planned."

If American free enterprise is dead—or at least on its death bed—"thus far we have come up with no adequate substitute for it." Our new laws and regulations "are enacted with no real understanding of our new industrial climate."

American business, Grymes believes, can no longer afford to close its eyes to the achievements of planned economies, nor comfort itself in the rationalization that, after all, foreign industry is nationalized and subsidized. Nor is this entirely true. "Foreign industries are shareholder-owned just as ours. They have the same profit motive."

Moreover it is "possible" that these motives are even stronger than ours. In foreign economies weak and nonprofitable companies "are stripped away and the available money and energy are guided into the better planned and profitable companies."

In contrast, weak companies in America are "protected" through antitrust laws enacted in the 1890s. Our original laws were written to break up large trusts that strangled competition—and they did exactly that. "But that era is long gone."

Nevertheless, these "blue laws of business are still on our books." Still handicapping and hamstringing business with the philosophy that all bigness and monopolies are bad. And that unlimited competition is good for both producer and consumer. "This," he maintains, "is

another anachronism. Make no mistake, unlimited competition leads directly to marginal operations, lower efficiency and higher prices."

What facts must business recognize if it is to live and prosper in its new soil of planned economy? Grymes offers seven suggestions:

1. We must foster growth and competition in industry under government guidelines "that encourage rather than frustrate."

2. Government and business must accept the "concept of economy of scale and wipe out the last vestiges of the curse of bigness."

3. Business and labor should invite the government to "create a friend of society, authority to monitor so-called monopolies in big business and labor."

4. The Federal government should provide for quicker capital recovery through faster write-offs of capital equipment.

5. Government, business and labor must cooperate to combat wage/price inflation "with little hope of eliminating it entirely but with a great effort to control it better."

6. Business, government and labor must understand that "we cannot responsibly bring on an international trade war to protect a troubled American industry."

7. The government must establish Federal national resource and power policies to supervise our use of coal, oil, gas, timber and other resources. We must, in short, "make sure that there are not brown-outs on the East Coast, coal shortages in Pennsylvania and gas prices out of sight."

Admittedly, each of these suggestions acknowledges and "invites" greater governmental regulation. On the other hand, they do not mean "abdication of business responsibility but the realization that in the 1970s this country must update its attitudes toward the regulation of our economy or surely the economic tide from both oceans will inundate us. The economic facts are overwhelming."

What is the alternative if we fail to improve the spirit of cooperation among business, government and labor? "The same economic deterioration we are witnessing in Great Britain." With West Germany and Japan pressing hard on our economic tail "we have no other choice," Grymes concludes.

Keep Informed

It's going to be a lot tougher to be well informed in the future because there is going to be a lot more to know about.

Already today we see the explosion of information confronting managers, professionals, and technical people. You have to know what's going on all around the world, not just at home. You have to know what's new -- right up to the minute, practically. And there's more information being created to know about, too.

It used to be that an engineer, for example, could expect to be fully equipped upon college graduation to perform ably during his entire career. Today an engineer may find his education out-of-date within ten years after graduating. Obsolescence can catch up with you quickly today, and will catch up even more quickly in the future.

As a result, the process of learning will not end at the university door. It will, by necessity, continue through a person's career. It will be aided by new programs and new educational relationships between business, government, unions, schools, and universities. The very nature of education will shift, too, from transmission of knowledge towards preparation for change. You will be learning what you'll need to know before you actually need it.

The technology of education is changing, too. Educational television,

programmed instruction, self studies, and multi-media courses (using printed material, exercises, and television or tape recordings) will be commonplace. One of our big hopes is that with increased leisure time, the general public will take an interest in continuing education.

Current business publications are important to keep businessmen informed on conditions, trends, and practices that may affect their enterprises. Today numerous business publications are widely read and recognized as important sources of information.

Most of the articles in this book are from the following prominent business publications. If you go into business, you are well advised to consider them part of your own continuing education.

THE WALL STREET JOURNAL

Published since 1880 by Dow Jones & Company, the Journal is read by businessmen around the world who want the current news about business finance, our economy, and general national and international developments. Over a million copies are sold each day. Three regional editions are published, but differences are mainly in advertising.

BUSINESS WEEK

With one-sixth the circulation of PLAYBOY, this is the most widely read business magazine. Pub-

lished weekly, it features in-depth reports on current business issues and practices.

FORTUNE

Next in popularity, but published monthly, is FORTUNE. This fine journal features extensively researched studies of issues and in-depth case studies of particular enterprises and industries.

FORBES

Twice monthly, FORBES features news about companies and issues regarding their management. It's a more personal journal, edited by Messrs. Forbes.

DUN'S REVIEW

DUN'S offers stimulating reading about current business and social issues and management responses to them. Published monthly, it also offers some fine case studies and biographies of executives.

THE ECONOMIST

Published in Great Britain, THE ECONOMIST presents one of the finest in-depth analyses of the international economic situation.

CONSIDER

1. Do business executives really plan effectively for the long-term future? What evidence do you see for your answer?

2. Do you disagree with any of the projections given in this chapter? Explain.

3. Would you consider working for a small business as a career? Explain.

4. Do you really think it is worth the time and expense to earn a graduate degree? What impact might it have on your career plans?

5. What will come after the post-industrial society?

6. Do we really have a "free enterprise system" in the United States? What are the implications of your answer for careers in business?

7. If the post-industrial society comes into reality, what are the implications for business as we know it today?

8. How do you reconcile the need for profit to keep an enterprise above with the demands of the public and consumers for social action?

9. Who has more power to influence the way a company does business: the public, the customers, the managers, or the stockholders? Explain.

10. What kinds of business enterprises do you feel offer the greatest potential opportunity for profits in the future? for career advancement? for impact on our society? Explain.

CHALLENGES

Interview a local retailer or other small business owner-manager and get his or her views regarding the long-term prospects for that type of business and his or her advice for your possible career in that type of business.

On a sheet of paper, list the major factors you think will influence your personal success when you are 40-45 years old: education, abilities, experience, personality, etc. How do you plan to develop these characteristics?

Interview a friend to find out how he or she views the future. How does this concept differ from yours? Do you think you are far-sighted or short-sighted? Why?

Write a job description for a job that you imagine you would like to have in 2025, but that doesn't exist today. What will you do? Will the job be important then? What will be the job qualifications required?

RECAP

What are the basic trends for the future in our economic society? Among those discussed in this chapter are the following:

--Increasing affluence
--Economic stability with a rising GNP
--More young people and older people in our workforce
--New attitudes toward work and leisure
--Expanding education in response to more rapid obsolescence
--Growing interdependence among our social institutions, including unions, business, government, and educational organizations
--Greater consideration of social concerns such as employment opportunities for minorities, pollution abatement, and conservation of natural resources
--Increased international interaction, and global business enterprise
--A shift from blue-collar to white-collar employment
--A shift from manufacturing to services as our economic base
--Expanding government, including greater employment by the government.

But the future is not foreseeable. Projections are uncertain -- and are changed as each tomorrow draws closer. Our short-term vision, as a result, is far clearer than our long-term vision. Yet when we plan our careers, we must look far down the road, even into the 21st century. If we draw an unlikely picture of what the world will be like, we may find ourselves on the wrong track.

In this emerging POST-INDUSTRIAL SOCIETY, the best we can do is try to keep informed, to think, to plan, and to be responsive to changes as we become aware of them. We can't accept things as they are, because if we do, we'll find ourselves passed by. This is the dilemma of business; this is the clear challenge for our careers.

YOUR CAREER PLANNING WORKSHEET

Career planning, in its broadest sense, is your looking ahead toward the work you'll be doing during the rest of your life. Of course there's more to a career than a job -- there is your personal development through education and self development, there's sports and hobbies, and community activities. These may also be part of your career plans.

Life style is an important part of living. How do you want to spend your career? Are you concerned more with achievement or leisure? with money or other forms of rewards and satisfaction? Are you a loner or is being with other people important to you?

Have you really thought through who you are, what you want to be, and what you want to do? This worksheet provides a broad format to help guide your own self analysis and career planning.

In ISSUES IN BUSINESS you've seen a whole range of possible career paths, in all areas of business enterprise. Maybe one is right for you. Maybe none is your suit. But the fact is that it's up to you to make that decision.

And you can make the right decision only by thinking through the questions listed on the following pages -- your personal career planning worksheet.

I. YOUR FANTASIES

Pretend you have a year to do virtually anything you would like. You have no financial or family constraints. What would you like to do with this year?

Why have you selected what you did? Analyze the activities you say you'd like to have. What are the reasons for your fantasy?

How do these reasons relate to your career? What types of work activities do they indicate you would enjoy? What types of careers would you like to have?

II. YOUR CAPABILITIES

What things have you done
of which you are proud? Think
back to one or two special
accomplishments in each of
the categories listed below.

A.   In school

B.   On jobs (paid or unpaid)

C.   Personal (hobbies, travel, social, etc.)

What are your outstanding
skills or abilities? What
are your strengths, as
reflected in the accomplishments
listed above?

How can these skills and
abilities be put to work in
your career? What kind of
career opportunities would
best utilize your capabilities?

III. YOUR CAREER GOALS

The world is full of
alternative opportunities.
The question is what do you
want? Think about your
fantasies and your personal
capabilities, and describe
your long-range career goals?

What are you looking for?
Rank the five most important
values in your career planning.

Salary	Improving society	Responsibility
Prestige	Achieving a goal	Scenery
Doing something worthwhile	Discovering new things	Location
Having friends at work	Seeing the world	Cultural activities
Climbing the ladder	Climate	Size of company
Opportunity to learn	Vacations	Type of industry
Enjoying yourself	Being with family	
Security	Hours of work	

1.

2.

3.

4.

5.

Looking ahead five years,
what will you be doing?
Describe briefly a typical
day in your life five years
from now.

IV. CAREER ACTION PLANS

But, of course, you have
to make some decisions and
take some actions if your
career goals are to be achieved.
Outline below the key needs you
face for development of skills
and knowledge in order to
achieve your career goals.

___

If your career plans are
in one of the areas of business
enterprise discussed in ISSUES
IN BUSINESS, what steps do you
need to take to prepare yourself
for a successful career?

___

What actions will you take
during the next six months
to help you prepare for your
career? List specific actions
and set target dates for
you to review your results.

SUPERWHAZZIT

ADVERTISING
Any form of communication through the various media used to present information about goods and services to the public and to induce the public to buy.

AICPA
The American Institute of Certified Public Accountants, a professional organization of accountants.

AID
Agency for International Development. This federal agency was set up by the United States after World War II to assist the recovery of war-ravaged countries. Today, it guarantees American investment abroad against political and economic risks.

ANNUITY
An insurance contract that provides payment of a specific sum annually or periodically to a party called the annuitant for life or a specified number of years.

APB
The Accounting Principles Board of the AICPA, which makes rules to guide accounting practices.

ARBITRATION
A procedure for resolving a dispute (such as an interpretation of an item in a labor agreement) in which a third party or a board hears both sides of a controversy and issues an award, usually accompanied by a decision, ordinarily binding on both parties.

ASSETS
Anything of value that is owned, including cash, securities, inventories, prepaid charges, property, receivables, land, equipment, buildings, and patents.

AUTOMATION
The use of highly specialized equipment for the automatic handling of materials and the control of production.

BAIT-AND-SWITCH
Offering an item for sale, but intending to sell the buyer another, more expensive item.

BANKRUPTCY
The condition of an individual or a corporation unable to pay debts to creditors as they come due.

BIG EIGHT
The largest eight public accounting firms in the United States.

BLACK CAPITALISM
The ownership of business enterprises by blacks.

BOYCOTT
A strategy used by unions to stop the purchase of the employer's products in order to promote bargaining and win concessions.

BUDGET
A plan developed for an organization or a unit of an organization that provides for costs and expenses to be incurred and revenues to be generated.

BUREAUCRACY
Any complex, formal organization that has defined positions, rules, hierarchy, advancement by merit, fair treatment of all employees, and impersonal relationships.

BUSINESS CYCLES
Changes in business conditions over time.

CAPITAL INTENSIVE INDUSTRIES
Industries which require a high mix of capital to labor. For example, the oil industry.

CAREER PATH
A perceived course of progress in jobs or responsibilities.

CARTEL
An international agreement among businessmen to split up and control markets and the production of goods.

CASH SURRENDER VALUE
The amount of money available in cash to the policyholder upon surrender of the life insurance policy before it becomes payable by death or maturity. Generally the policyholder may also borrow from the insuror up to this amount without surrendering the policy.

CATALOG
A listing of articles that a company is offering for sale (often illustrated) including descriptions of the articles and the prices. The catalog is usually used in mail-order sales operations.

CENTRALIZATION
Managers at the top of the organization make decisions that affect decisions and activities throughout the organization.

CHAIN OF COMMAND
The hierarchical relationship of managers and subordinates in an organization. Managers at each higher level are responsible for the coordination of a larger part of the organization.

CLASS ACTION SUIT
A legal suit by one or more individuals on behalf of all individuals affected.

CLAYTON ACT
This act (1914) was designed to close loopholes in the Sherman Act.

CLOSED SHOP
All employees in the organization must be union members.

COACHING
Providing day-to-day guidance and counseling to employees as they work to achieve their objectives.

COLLECTIVE BARGAINING
The negotiation of a labor agreement by representatives of labor and management.

COMMERCIAL BANK
A bank that accepts deposits and creates credit by making loans, primarily to businesses.

COMPETITIVE MARKET
Many buyers and sellers in a market where prices and quantities are subject to negotiation and bargaining.

COMPUTER UTILITY
A service company that provides computer services to customers on a fee basis. IBM's Service Bureau Corporation, which was recently sold to Control Data Corporation is a computer utility.

CONGLOMERATE
A group of firms, usually in unrelated industries that are now merged together. The hope is that the whole is greater than the sum of the parts.

CONTINUOUS MANUFACTURING
A type of manufacturing in which a product is worked on from start to finish before it is stored. The process is designed around the product. Oil refining and automobile manufacturing are examples of continuous manufacturing.

CONTRACT
An agreement between two parties for exchange of goods or services for money or other forms of consideration.

CONVERTIBLE
Generally, a bond that may be exchanged for shares of stock.

COOLING-OFF PERIOD
By law, the President may order a suspension (eighty days) of a strike that is deemed to threaten the public interest. The hope is that an agreement will be reached during this time.

CORPORATION
". . . an artificial being, invisible, intangible, and existing in the contemplation of the law. Being the mere creature of law, it possesses only those properties which the charter of its creation confers upon it, either expressly or as incidental to its existence." — Chief Justice John Marshall, 1819.

As an "it" a corporation outlives its owners because the stock, representing the ownership interest, may be transferred or sold. Unlike the other forms of businesses, the liability of the owners (stockholders) is limited to their investment in the stock of the corporation.

COUNTERVAILING DUTY
A duty is a tariff. It is a countervailing tariff if it works both ways — we tax their goods as they come into our country and they tax our goods as they go into theirs.

CPA
A Certified Public Accountant. In Great Britain and Canada, the equivalent designation of an accounting professional working independently of any one company is a Chartered Accountant (CA).

CREDIT
The ability of an individual or a business to obtain money, goods, or services in return for a promise to pay for them in the future.

CREDIT UNION
An association (not a bank) whose members usually belong to the same occupational group or are employees of the same company, organized to pool savings (deposits) from members and make loans to members. Originated in Germany in the 1800s.

CURRENCY
Money which by law must be accepted when offered in payment for goods and services.

CYBERNETICS
A process of communications and control using abstract mathematical models. Cybernetics implies some type of feedback which provides self-regulation, such as a thermostat provided on a home furnace.

DATA BANK
Information stored for a specific application.

DECENTRALIZATION
Managers at all levels of the organization make the decisions that affect their own activities and the activities of their immediate subordinates.

DECENTRALIZING
Delegating responsibility for decision making to the lowest possible level in an organization.

DECEPTIVE PACKAGING
Presenting the product in a way that it appears to be something that it isn't.

DEPRECIATION OF MONEY
A decrease in the exchange value of money. For example, if the dollar is depreciated 10% compared to the German mark, German goods become 10% higher in the United States and American goods become 10% less in Germany.

DEPRESSION
The period of a business cycle when business is poorest — production is lowest, prices are highest, unemployment is highest, and people are pessimistic.

DISABILITY INCOME INSURANCE
An insurance policy that provides monthly payments for a specified period of time in event of the insured's physical disability. Many life insurance policies also provide a DISABILITY BENEFIT, a waiver of premium payments if the insured becomes permanently and totally disabled.

DIVERSIFICATION
An attempt by a company to achieve stability in sales and profits by expanding the number and variety of its products and services.

DIVIDEND
Earnings or profits that a corporation pays its stockholders. It may be cash, stock, or other property.

ECONOMY OF SCALE
The greater the level of production, the lower the cost for each unit produced. Generally, there are efficiencies in larger operations.

EDP
Electronic Data Processing. The government often calls it ADP, automatic data processing. It refers to all types of information coding, storage, retrieval, analysis, and reporting, using electronic data processing equipment.

EFTA
The European Free Trade Association. This was an agreement among eight nations for free trade among themselves. It was a competitor of the EEC, and was composed of the European countries not involved in the EEC. The withdrawal of Britain and Denmark to join the EEC has effectively destroyed the EFTA.

EMBARGO
An order forbidding the export of some particular commodity, either to all countries or to selected countries.

E.P.P.
Earnings Protection Plans provide payments for a temporary period of time to sustain the incomes of individuals affected by technological change.

ESTATE TAX
A tax on the total value of property left by a deceased person.

EXCISE TAX
A tax levied on the sale of certain goods such as jewelry, luggage, or furs. It may be levied on a wholesaler, retailer or consumer.

EXPORT-IMPORT BANK
A United States federal bank which makes loans to foreign governments and commercial enterprises for the purpose of buying goods produced in the United States.

EXPORT TAX
A self-imposed trade tariff. By placing an export tax on coffee exported, Brazil avoids having us place a tariff on it as an import. Further, Brazil gets to keep the tax money!

FRANCHISE
An agreement between a manufacturer or other type of company and a private distributor allowing the franchisee to sell the franchisor's product or service in a specific geographic area or market segment.

F.T.C.

The Federal Trade Commission. A five-member board charged with investigating any illegal activities involving interstate commerce. Fraudulent advertising falls in this category, and the agency can force the offender to stop what he is doing or impose other penalties.

GATT

The General Agreement on Tariff and Trade. This is an agreement, signed in 1948, which formed an organization of nations, including the United States, to establish a system of rules for controlling tariffs and reducing trade barriers.

GNP

Gross National Product, the money value of the total output of goods and services in our country during a year.

GOODWILL

In accounting, this is an intangible asset representing the value of good relations with customers and the public, the firm's trademarks, and the firm's future earning power generated by past operations.

GRIEVANCE

A demand by an employee that the employer honor a recognized working condition provided by law or by a labor agreement. The labor agreement usually provides for a grievance procedure, or series of steps for resolving the grievance, frequently culminating in arbitration.

GROUP ANNUITY

A pension plan providing annuities at retirement to a group of persons under a single master contract, with each member holding certificates stating their coverage. It is usually issued to an employer for the benefit of employees.

GROUP LIFE INSURANCE

Life insurance issued, usually without a medical examination, for a group of persons under a master policy, as for a group annuity.

HARDWARE

The physical machinery and equipment that is used in data processing. These may be mechanical, electronic, magnetic, or electrical devices. An example is a machine that reads and punches cards.

HORIZONTAL INTEGRATION

Expansion, often through merger, to increase the firm's share of a particular market. For example, a major supermarket chain may buy out a smaller chain.

HOLDING COMPANY

A business firm that holds the stock (part or all of the ownership) of one or more other companies.

IMPACT REPORT

A written report of a project's potential effects on its surrounding environment, such as the proposed construction of a building or a dam.

INCOME TAX

A tax based on the income of an individual, a corporation, or other business. It is a direct tax that is based on your "ability to pay." Income taxes may be federal, state, or local.

INFLATION

A period when a given amount of money will purchase fewer goods and services than in the past.

INSURANCE REGULATOR

A governmental agency or commission that oversees insurance activities in its area of control. Insurance is regulated at the state level.

INSURANCE UNDERWRITER

The company or individual that assumes a risk in return for a payment of a premium.

INTEREST

Payment to a lender for use of money. A corporation pays interest on its bonds to its bondholders.

INTERMITTENT MANUFACTURING

"On again, off again manufacturing." Different products are made at different times on the same production line.

INTERNATIONAL MONETARY FUND

An agency of the United Nations, this fund promotes and aids international monetary cooperation, stability in international exchange, and avoidance of competitive depreciation of money.

INVESTMENT CORPORATION

A business organization established for the purpose of supplying money as capital for other businesses, particularly fledgling enterprises.

JOB SHOP

A type of manufacturing which is intermittent. The work is organized around particular jobs rather than around the finished products (e.g., a machine shop).

KENNEDY ROUND OF TARIFF NEGOTIATIONS

The most sweeping reductions in tariffs were the result of negotiations involving more than fifty member nations of GATT. Under the power of the TEA, duties were cut on more than 60,000 items.

LABOR AGREEMENT

A contract between a labor union and management covering the terms and conditions of working relationships.

LABOR INTENSIVE INDUSTRIES

Industries which require a high mix of labor to capital. For example, the garment industry.

LINEAR PROGRAMMING (LP)

A mathematical technique often used in management decision making. It shows the optimal way to allocate money or solve some other problem, given specified constraints.

LOCKOUTS

Locking workers out of the plant as a management strategy to promote bargaining.

LOOPHOLE

Any perfectly legal maneuver that a taxpayer uses to reduce his or her tax liability.

MALPRACTICE INSURANCE

Insurance protecting professional people from claims resulting from negligent performance of professional services.

MANAGEMENT CONSULTANT

An independent professional, often associated with a firm of other consultants, who provides advice and specialized technical assistance to companies.

MANUFACTURING ENGINEERING

Manufacturing Engineering is the process of determining how to manufacture a product in the needed quantities at the lowest possible costs while still meeting quality standards.

MARKET SEGMENT

A portion of the market which has specific characteristics which makes that segment different from others.

MATRIX MANAGEMENT

An organization structure with dual lines of management authority: functional responsibility and project responsibility. This means that an employee reports to two different managers — one for his or her specialty and one for the task or type of job being done.

MEDIA
The instrument used to get the advertising message to the consumers. For examples, newspapers and television are media.

MEDIATION
A procedure in which a neutral third party attempts to persuade the parties to resolve a labor dispute. Unlike arbitration, mediation does not give the third party authority to make a binding decision.

MINORITY BUSINESS ENTERPRISE
A business organization that is owned (at least predominantly) and operated by members of minority racial groups.

MOBILITY
An individual's ability to move from one company to another, one job to another, or one occupation to another.

MONEY
Any medium of exchange for buying or selling goods and services.

MONOPOLY
Only one seller in a market, who can control both the price and the quantities of goods.

MUTUAL SAVINGS BANK
A bank in which the depositors are the owners and share in the earnings.

NLRB
The National Labor Relations Board, established by the Wagner Act. This board, with regional offices throughout the country, provides a means of administering our labor laws.

NO-FAULT INSURANCE
Auto insurance that provides immediate payment to a policyholder who has been involved in an accident, regardless of who was to blame.

OCCUPATION
An individual's primary type of work or trade.

OECD
The Organization for Economic Cooperation and Development. Founded in 1948 as the Organization for Economic Cooperation, this international organization, to which the United States adheres by Senate ratification, promotes free trade practices.

OLIGOPOLY
Only a few powerful sellers in a market; they can influence both the prices and the quantities of goods and services.

ON-LINE SYSTEM
A computer system in which the input and output hardware are linked directly to the computer, and are at the location where the data is originated. For example, an executive may have a remote terminal (that looks like a typewriter or perhaps a TV screen) through which he may communicate readily with the computer.

OPEN SHOP
Employees may or may not join the union, as they wish.

ORGANIZATION CHART
A picture of the organization structure at a specific point in time.

ORGANIZATION STRUCTURE
The overall pattern of the relationships of positions in an organization.

OSHA
The Occupational Safety and Health Act. This law, passed by Congress in 1970, is designed to eliminate all unsafe and unhealthy conditions in the work environment.

PAR VALUE
The value printed on the face of a stock or bond certificate. It may be any amount and may have no relation to market value.

PARTNERSHIP
A business owned and operated by two or more individuals, but not necessarily equally is a partnership. As in a sole proprietorship, all partners are personally liable for the firm's debts, including the actions of the other partners. This provides more managerial talent and often more financial resources, but requires a good working relationship. Law firms and other professional firms are often partnerships.

In addition to registering the name, a partnership requires a formal agreement between the partners. If the composition of the partnership changes (one of the partners dies or a new partner is added to the firm) the old partnership is dissolved and a new one must be formed.

P/E RATIO
The ratio of price (current market price) to earnings for a company's stock.

PENSION
An annuity that provides benefits to an employee who has retired because of age or disability. Social Security is in part a pension plan.

PERT/CPM
Program Evaluation and Review Technique and the Critical Path Method are two planning tools used by management to keep track of the various tasks making up a project.

POLICY
A printed document that states the terms of an insurance contract. It is issued by the company to the policyholder, generally the insured.

PREFERENTIAL TRAINING
Application of tariffs on a discriminatory basis. For example, granting lower rates of duty on goods imported from certain "preferred" countries than on the same goods from other countries, such as members of the British Commonwealth (Canada, Britain, New Zealand, Australia, and others).

PRICE
The price to be charged for the product. This is a function of the costs of production, legal restrictions, and competition.

PRICE DISCRIMINATION
Offering identical goods and services to different buyers at different prices.

PRODUCT
The good or service provided by the firm to the buying public.

PROFITS
The income of a firm after all costs and expenses are paid, but before taxes or the payment of dividends. If profits are "after tax," they are so indicated.

PROFIT CENTER
An organizational unit that is responsible for generation of earnings on its own, through profitable activity and the control of costs and expenses, usually through a budget.

PROGRAM
A complete plan for the solution of a problem. A program is a complete sequence of machine instructions and routines needed to solve a problem.

PROGRAMMER
A person who writes programs.

PROMOTION
Communicating to the market about the product offered for sale.

PROPERTY TAX
A tax paid periodically on property that you own, such as real estate, your automobile, or personal property such

as home furnishings or a boat. Property taxes are state or local levies.

PROPRIETORSHIP

A business owned by one individual who gets all the profits (if there are any after taxes) and assumes all of the liabilities as personal debts. (If his business goes broke, he may lose his shirt.)

You can start a proprietorship simply by hanging out your sign (your "shingle") saying you are in business and registering your business name with the County recorder's office so the public will know that your company name is really you. The sole proprietorship may use the name "Company" but "Inc." means the business is a corporation.

PROSPECTUS

A brochure that describes securities being offered for sale to the public by a company.

PROXY

A statement signed by a stockholder allowing some other person (usually the company management) to vote for the stockholder at the annual meeting.

RECESSION

A mild form of depression.

REINSURANCE

The sharing of a risk too large for one insurance company by transferring part of the risk to another company.

REVENUES

Total cash or other property (such as securities or goods taken in trade) received as a result of business activities; including investments and the sales of goods and services.

REVENUE SHARING

Transfer of federal taxes to state and local governments.

RIGHT TO WORK LAWS

Many states have enacted laws that prohibit closed shops and union shops. In the absence of such laws, union membership may be required for employment.

ROBINSON-PATMAN ACT

This Act (1936) amended the Clayton Act and specifically aimed to make price discrimination illegal.

SALES TAX

A percentage paid on the price of goods and, in some states, services.

SAVINGS AND LOAN ASSOCIATION

An institution that finances through mortgage loans the building and purchase of homes with money invested by stockholders.

SEC

The Securities and Exchange Commission.

SELF-INSUROR

A company or individual that acts as its own underwriter, accepting the risk of financial loss.

SHERMAN ANTITRUST ACT

This Act (1890) was passed to combat restraint of trade by businesses. It was aimed at breaking up monopolies.

SMALL BUSINESS

An enterprise is considered to be small if in manufacturing it employs fewer than 250 people. In wholesaling yearly sales should not exceed $5 million or $1 million in retailing. Another rule of thumb that is used is any business with sales below $25 million.

SMALL BUSINESS ADMINISTRATION

An agency of the federal government which lends money and provides training and counseling to qualifying business enterprises.

SMALL CLAIMS COURT

Under state laws, a type of court permitting settlement of disputes between buyers and sellers regarding terms of contracts.

SOCIAL AUDIT

An evaluation of the social performance of the business. Its aim is to point out areas for future improvement that will serve the needs of society.

SOCIAL SECURITY TAX

A tax paid by an employer and an employee to provide old age and survivor benefits under provisions of the federal Social Security Act.

SOFTWARE

All other components of an EDP system, such as the programs, routines and procedures which support a computer system and allow it to operate.

SPAN OF MANAGEMENT

The number of positions reporting directly to a manager. Generally, the span depends on the manager as a person, the qualities of the people who are his subordinates, their activities, and other factors.

STAFF

Specialized personnel who assist managers in specific, usually technical aspects of their work such as engineering, accounting, legal counsel, computer science, purchasing, or personnel.

STANDARDIZATION

The use of uniform production methods and patterns for equipment, products, parts, etc. It brings about cost reduction because adaptation of equipment and procedures becomes unnecessary.

S.U.B.

Supplemental Unemployment Benefits are payments made by an employer, usually under a labor agreement, above and beyond unemployment benefits paid by the government under the law.

SYSTEM

A network of hardware and software necessary to solve a problem or serve a desired function.

SYSTEMS ANALYST

A person who determines what is being done, what can be done, and the best means of accomplishing the desired outcome with the system available.

SUBSIDY

Aid provided by the government to private firms, usually to spur economic growth or to support vital but unprofitable operations.

SURTAX

A special tax over and above the normal tax, imposed on the amount due in taxes or on income level.

TAFT-HARTLEY ACT

The Labor-Management Relations Act of 1947, amending the Wagner Act. It balances the rights and privileges of labor and management by limiting some of the advantages held by labor.

TARIFF NEGOTIATIONS

The most sweeping reductions in tariffs in history were the result of negotiations involving more than fifty member nations of GATT. Under the power of the TEA, during his tenure as president, Kennedy reduced duties on more than 60,000 items.

Tariff reductions are believed to be a significant factor in the growth of international trade and economic prosperity. Reductions directly aid lesser-developed nations, while strengthening industrialized nations, making them better able to help the lesser-developed nations.

TAX
A compulsory payment to the government to defray the costs of public services.

TEA
The Trade Expansion Act of 1962. Signed by President Kennedy, this amendment to the old (1934) Reciprocal Trade Act gave the President the power to cut tariffs by 50% in negotiating new trade pacts during the five years following its inception.

TELECOMMUNICATIONS
Sending computer information over telephone lines. This allows data to be sent to a computer from a great distance away and allows two or more computers to communicate with each other.

TRIPLE DAMAGES
Three times normal payment for damages in a legal suit.

TRUST
A legal device that puts title and control of property in the hands of one party (called the trustee) for the benefit of another party (called the beneficiary).

TRUSTEE
An individual assigned by the court to control the operations of a bankrupt company while it is attempting to reorganize.

UNEMPLOYMENT COMPENSATION
Benefits paid to workers laid off, funded by taxes paid by employers.

UNION SHOP
After a specified period of time, all employees in the organization must become members of the representing union.

UNITY OF COMMAND
Each subordinate has only one manager. That is, an individual reports to one person for direction in his or her work. Generally this reduces confusion in an organization.

VALUE ADDED TAX (VAT)
A tax based on the value added to a product at each step of the production process.

VARIABLE ANNUITY
An annuity contract in which the amount of payments of income fluctuates in relation to stock or bond market values, a cost of living index, or some other variable factor. It is thus similar in attributes to a mutual fund, a pooled investment fund.

VERTICAL INTEGRATION
Expansion, often through merger, either backward to supply sources or forward into markets. For example, a steel manufacturer may vertically integrate by buying a coal mine, on the one hand, or a finished products company on the other.

WAGNER ACT
The National Labor Relations Act of 1935, which established the rights of workers to organize unions and bargain collectively.

WARRANT
The right to buy a stock at a given price.

WARRANTY
An assurance, whether expressed directly or implied, that the goods are as described — of reasonable quality, proper quantity, and consistent throughout.

CREDITS

CHAPTER 1

Drawing by Erdoes, copyright © 1972 by the New York Times Company, reprinted by permission; "A Portrait of the Chief Executive," reprinted from the May, 1970 issue of *Fortune Magazine* by special permission, copyright © 1970, Time, Inc.; "Soap Opera" (cartoon) *San Diego Evening Tribune* (November 16, 1970); Excerpts from *Merchant to the Millions*, Sears, Roebuck & Co., 1970; The definition of "Entrepreneur" is used by permission from Webster's *Third New International Dictionary*, copyright © 1971 by G. & C. Merriam, Co., publishers of the Merriam-Webster Dictionaries; Richard Gerstenberg, "Corporate Responsiveness and Profitability," *The Conference Board Record* (November 1972); "A Steel Boss Looks at His Industry," *The Wall Street Journal*, copyright © 1973 Dow Jones & Company, Inc., all rights reserved; "Bich the Ballpoint King," reprinted from the August 1969 issue of *Fortune Magazine* by special permission, copyright © 1969, Time, Inc.; "The Giants of '29 Revisited," reprinted from the May 1970 issue of *Fortune Magazine* by special permission, copyright © 1970, Time, Inc.; "Profits with Honor: Some Thoughts Thereon," Koppers Corp.; "The Competitive Enterprise System," advertisement by the Pennwalt Corporation, Three Parkway, Philadelphia, Pa., 19102.

CHAPTER 2

"Trade-offs for a Better Environment," *Business Week,* April 11, 1960, copyright © 1970 by McGraw-Hill, Inc.; Johnny Hart, "B.C.," copyright © 1970, reprinted by permission; "The War Business Must Win," *Business Week*, November 1, 1969, copyright © by McGraw-Hill, Inc.; David Rockefeller, "A 'Social' Audit," copyright © 1972 by the New York Times Company, reprinted by permission; "How Companies React to the Ethics Crisis," *Business Week*, February 9, 1976, copyright © 1976 by McGraw-Hill, Inc.

CHAPTER 3

Brant Parker and Johnny Hart, "The Wizard of Id," copyright © 1970, Field Enterprises, Inc.; "American Business Activity," Cleveland Trust Company; "Prices Rising 5¢ on Some Chocolate Bars," copyright © 1976 by the New York Times Company, reprinted by permission; "Argentine June Inflation 2.8%," *American Banker*, June 6, 1976; "Small Business: The Maddening Struggle to Survive," *Business Week*, June 30, 1975, copyright © 1975 by McGraw-Hill, Inc.; "This is No Fairy Tale," (cartoon) *San Diego Evening Tribune* (November 19, 1970); "How Inflation Works," is excerpted from "Mechanics of Inflation," Chamber of Commerce of the United States (1964).

CHAPTER 4

"When Companies Get Too Big to Fail," *Business Week,* January 27, 1975, copyright © 1975 by McGraw-Hill, Inc.; "A Tentative Start for the ConRail Plan," *Business Week*, November 24, 1975, copyright © 1975 by McGraw-Hill, Inc.; "A Landmark Law That Boxes in the Banks," *Business Week*, April 19, 1976, copyright © 1976 by McGraw-Hill, Inc.; "Is John Sherman's Antitrust Obsolete?" *Business Week*, March 23, 1974, copyright © 1974 by McGraw-Hill, Inc.; "Anti Monopoly Takes on Parker Bros." *Business Week*, June 28, 1976, copyright © 1976 by McGraw-Hill, Inc.

CHAPTER 5

"The Mobiocentric Generation, A Conversation with Dr. Eugene Jennings," reprinted from *Careers Today* Magazine, January 1968, copyright © Ziff-Davis Publishing Company; "A Young Liberal Meets a Payroll," copyright © 1976 by the New York Times Company, reprinted by permission; "Total Commitment — Starting a Business as a Way of Life," *The Graduate*, copyright © 1975 by Approach 13-30 Corporation, reprinted by permission; "Job Hunter's Survival Kit," *The Graduate*, copyright © 1975 by Approach 13-30 Corporation, reprinted by permission.

CHAPTER 6

"How to Introduce a New Product," advertisement by Ogilvy & Mather, 2 East 48th Street, New York, New York, 10017, published in *The Wall Street Journal*; Norbert Enrick, "Market Experimentation," from 'Employing the Test Market' chapter in N. Enrick, *Market and Sales Forecasting*, copyright © 1969, Chandler Publishing Co., (A Division of Intext, Scranton, Pa. 18515), adapted from the author's article "Market Experimentation," in *Industrial Canada*, Vol. 68, No. 12, pp. 34–39, (April 1968); "Is the Soap Leader Getting Soft?" *Business Week*, July 19, 1969, copyright © 1969 by McGraw-Hill, Inc.; "The Bad News in Babyland," reprinted by special permission from *Dun's*, December 1972, copyright © 1972, Dun & Bradstreet Publications Corporation; "The ReHoning of Gillette," reprinted by permission of *Forbes* Magazines (December 1, 1972); "Bill Bailey, Where Are My Groceries?" *San Diego* Magazine (August 1971); "Kellogg: Target for Today," reprinted by permission of *Forbes* Magazine (June 1, 1973); "Horatio Hamburger and the Golden Arches," *Business Week*, April 12, 1976, copyright © 1976 by McGraw-Hill, Inc.; "J. C. Penney: Getting More From the Same Space," *Business Week*, August 18, 1975, copyright © 1975 by McGraw-Hill, Inc.; "Cereal Fighting For Shelf Space," copyright © 1976 by the New York Times Company, reprinted by permission; "Becoming a Product Manager," reprinted from the August 1975 issue of *Money* Magazine by special permission, copyright © 1975, Time, Inc.

CHAPTER 7

"How to Make a Brand Popular," *Business Week*, September 9, 1972, copyright © 1972 by McGraw-Hill, Inc.; " 'Positioning' Ads: Why Is Schaefer Beer the One to Have When Having More . . .? Secret is in Ads, Not Brew, and it's Part of Latest Trend on Madison Avenue; A New Name for an Old Idea?" *The Wall Street Journal* (December 13, 1972), reprinted with permission of *The Wall Street Journal*, copyright © 1972, Dow Jones & Company, Inc., all rights reserved; "Coke's Formula — Keep the Image Fresh," *Business Week*, April 25, 1970, copyright © 1970 by McGraw-Hill, Inc.; "A Splash of Whimsy . . . is Adding a Barrel of Profits to Seven-Up Co.," reprinted by permission of *Forbes* Magazine (August 15, 1972); Herbert G. Lawson, "Chevron's F-310 Gas: A Lesson in How Not to Promote a Product — Controversy Over Ads Irks Some and Confuses Others; But Firm Defends Additive," (Excerpts) *The Wall Street Journal* (January 7, 1971), reprinted with permission of *The Wall Street Journal*, copyright © 1971 Dow Jones & Company, Inc., all rights reserved; "The Corporate Image and NBC's 'N'," copyright © 1976 by the New York Times Company, reprinted by permission.

CHAPTER 8

"Disgruntled Customers Finally Get a Hearing," *Business Week*, April 21, 1975, copyright © 1975 by McGraw-Hill, Inc.; Rose DeWolfe, "Consumers Aren't All Angels Either," reprinted from issue No. 1/1973, *Du Pont Context*, published by the Du Pont Company; "The Pressure is on for Safer Products," *Business Week*, July 4, 1970, copyright © 1970 by McGraw-Hill, Inc.; "Do We Need All That in the Bread?" copyright © 1972 by The New York Times Company, reprinted by permission; "Iowa Money-Maker: Maytag Co. Prospers by Stressing Quality, Selling at High Price. Washers Once Were Sideline; But is the Company Dull or a Really Shrewd Place?" *The Wall Street Journal* (July 12, 1972), reprinted with permission of *The Wall Street Journal*, copyright © 1972, Dow Jones & Company, Inc., all rights reserved; Excerpts from *Merchant to the Millions*, Sears, Roebuck & Co., 1970.

CHAPTER 9

"Getting Accountants 'Involved'," *Business Week*, November 24, 1973, copyright © 1973 by McGraw-Hill, Inc.; "More Meat in Annual Reports," *Business Week*, April 26, 1976, copyright © 1976 by McGraw-Hill, Inc.; "Behind the Scenes at the Annual Meeting," reprinted from the June 1975 issue of *Baxter World*; "How to Read a Balance Sheet," reprinted from the October 1970 issue of *Business Management* Magazine with permission of the publisher, copyright © 1970 by CCM Professional Magazines, Inc., all rights reserved.

CHAPTER 10

"Doonesbury," by Gary Trudeau, copyright © 1971 by G. B. Trudeau, distributed by Universal Press Syndicate; "Why Bulls Shun Bunnies," reprinted by permission of *Forbes* Magazine (March 1, 1973); "New York Stock Exchange Listing," (excerpt) *The Wall Street Journal* (March 14, 1973), reprinted with permission of *The Wall Street Journal*, copyright © 1973, Dow Jones & Company, Inc., all rights reserved; "The Dow Jones Averages," (excerpts) *The Wall Street Journal* (July 13, 1976), reprinted with permission of *The Wall Street Journal*, copyright © 1976, Dow Jones & Company, Inc., all rights reserved; "Cash Prices," *The Wall Street Journal*, (July 13, 1976), reprinted with permission of *The Wall Street Journal*, copyright © 1976, Dow Jones & Company, Inc., all rights reserved; "Futures Prices," (excerpts) *The Wall Street Journal*, (July 13, 1976), reprinted with permission of *The Wall Street Journal*, copyright © 1976, Dow Jones & Company, Inc., all rights reserved; "An Unacademic Course in Stocks," Reprinted from the October, 1973 issue of *Money* Magazine by special permission, copyright © 1973, Time, Inc.; "Why Coors Finally Had to Take Public Money," *Business Week*, September 22, 1975, copyright © 1975 by McGraw-Hill, Inc.

CHAPTER 11

"Flow of Money," reprinted from *American Capitalism* (Washington, D.C.: Council for the Advancement of Secondary Education, 1958), p. 51; "Getting Along Without Money," copyright © 1973, *Nation's Business* — the Chamber of Commerce of the United States, reprinted by permission; "The Trick is Managing Money," *Business Week* June 6, 1970, copyright © 1970 by McGraw-Hill, Inc.; "Dangling Less Bait for Savers," *Business Week*, September 22, 1975, copyright © 1975 by McGraw-Hill, Inc.; "Toy Giveaway Unbearable for Bank," copyright © 1976 by the New York Times Company, reprinted by permission; "Digging Out the Dirt in Your Credit Report," reprinted from the August 1976 issue of *Consumer Reports* Magazine, copyright © 1976 by the Consumer Union of the United States, Inc., all rights reserved.

CHAPTER 12

Michael Gildea, "No Fault Insurance: The Only Real Reform," *The American Federationist* (May, 1972).

CHAPTER 13

Illustrations from *Principles of Automatic Data Processing* (Park Ridge, Illinois: Data Processing Management Association, 1965); "How a Tiny Store Keeps the Books," *Business Week*, January 9, 1971, copyright © 1971 by McGraw-Hill, Inc.; "Computers: Are They Magic or Menace?" *International Management*, July 1971, copyright © 1971 by McGraw-Hill, Inc.

CHAPTER 14

Excerpts from *Merchant to the Millions,* Sears, Roebuck & Co., 1970; "Business Says it Can Handle Bigness," *Business Week,* October 17, 1970, copyright © 1970 by McGraw-Hill, Inc.; "Moving Decisions Down to Where the Action is," *Business Week*, December 6, 1969, copyright © 1969 by McGraw-Hill, Inc.; "How to Think Like a Company President," reprinted from the October 1970 issue of *Business Management* Magazine with permission of the publishers, copyright © 1970 by CCM Professional Magazines, Inc., all rights reserved; "The Management Machine, Can it Work?", reprinted by special permission from *Dun's Review,*

December 1969, copyright © 1969, Dun & Bradstreet Publications Corporation; Robert D. Smith, "M.B.O.: A Management Strategy for the Emerging Generation" (excerpts) *ASTME Vectors*, Vol. 4, No. 6 (November-December 1969); George Berkwitt, "Do Profit Centers Really Work?" reprinted by special permission from *Dun's Review*, May, 1969, copyright © 1969, Dun & Bradstreet Publications Corporation.

CHAPTER 15

"The New Face of Arm and Hammer," *Business Week,* April 12, 1976, copyright © 1976 by McGraw-Hill, Inc.; "Putting a Company Back on the Growth Curve," *Busines Week*, July 21, 1975, copyright © 1975 by McGraw-Hill, Inc.; "The Name Game," reprinted by permission of *Forbes* Magazine November 15, 1975); "How Giant Sears Grows and Grows," *Business Week*, December 16, 1972, copyright © 1972 by McGraw-Hill, Inc.; "Playboy Interview: Hugh M. Hefner," *Playboy 1972 Annual Report;* "Beatrice Moves Into Money," *Business Week,* April 14, 1973, copyright © 1973 by McGraw-Hill, Inc.; "Is Textron Ready to Take Off?" *Business Week*, October 7, 1972, copyright © 1972 by McGraw-Hill, Inc.; "The Age of Un-Merger," reprinted by special permission from *Dun's*, June 1970, copyright © 1970, Dun & Bradstreet Publications Corporation; "Boise Cuts Itself to Manageable Size," *Business Week*, February 10, 1973, copyright © 1973 by McGraw-Hill, Inc.

CHAPTER 16

"Are We Ready for the Automatic Factory?" *Industry Week* (February 23, 1976), copyright © 1976, The Penton Publishing Co.; "The New Men in Manufacturing," reprinted by special permission from *Dun's* October 1972, copyright © 1972, Dun & Bradstreet Publications Corporation; "Where the Safety Law Goes Haywire," copyright © 1972, *Nation's Business* — the Chamber of Commerce of the United States, reprinted by permission.

CHAPTER 17

"OPEC: The Economics of the Oil Cartel," *Business Week,* January 13, 1975, copyright © 1975 by McGraw-Hill, Inc.; "At War Once Again Over Brandy and Birds," *Business Week*, November 8, 1976, copyright © 1976 by McGraw-Hill, Inc.; "Not for Export?" reprinted by permission of *Forbes* Magazine (October 15, 1975); "Common Marketing for the Common Market," reprinted by permission of *Forbes* Magazine (July 1, 1972); "Col. Sanders' Tokyo Fried Chicken," copyright © 1973, *Nation's Business* — the Chamber of Commerce of the United States, reprinted with permission; "The Unbalanced U.S. Trade" (chart), copyright © 1973 by The New York Times Company, reprinted by permission; two charts from "The Powerful Nine," copyright © 1972 by The New York Times Company, reprinted by permission; "European Computer Makers Gang Up on IBM," *Business Week*, February 24, 1973, copyright © 1973 by McGraw-Hill, Inc.; "Multinational Managers," copyright © 1972 by The New York Times Company, reprinted by permission.

CHAPTER 18

"How IBM Avoids Layoffs Through Retraining," *Business Week,* November 10, 1975, copyright © 1975 by McGraw-Hill, Inc.; Illustrations by James Saxon, reprinted by permission; "Wanted: Ways to Make the Job Less Dull," *Business Week*, May 12, 1973, copyright © 1973 by McGraw-Hill, Inc.; "The 'Humanistic' Way of Managing People," *Business Week*, July 22, 1972, copyright © 1972 by McGraw-Hill, Inc.; Craig Lundberg, "On the Usefulness of Organizational Rascals," *The Business Quarterly* (Winter 1969), pp. 7–12; Lillian C. Harris, "Great Expectations: The Work Ethic on Campus," (excerpts) *Manpower* (August 1973).

CHAPTER 19

"National Airlines Finally Finds Labor Peace," *Business Week,* March 8, 1976, copyright © 1976 by McGraw-Hill, Inc.; "What Makes America Work," advertisement by United States Steel Corporation; "Technological Change: How Fares the Worker?" *Manpower* (September 1970); "Labor Relations Today and Tomorrow," (excerpts) *The Conference Board Record* (August 1968); "UAW's Bluestone Sees Unions in 'Managing the Enterprise,' " *Industry Week* (January 31, 1972), copyright © 1972 The Penton Publishing Co.

CHAPTER 20

"Saleswomen on the Go . . . Go . . . Go," reprinted from the November 1975 issue of *Baxter World;* Paul J. Fasser, Jr. "Unions and Manpower: A Natural Partnership," *Manpower* (August 1972); Eugene Skotzko, "Don't Lose That 'Bunny Image.' " *Monthly Labor Review* (January 1973); photo of Hugh Hefner reprinted by permission of *Forbes* magazine.

CHAPTER 21

"Doonesbury," by Gary Trudeau, copyright © 1972 by G. B. Trudeau, distributed by Universal Press Syndicate; "The Stormy 70's — Big Changes Still to Come," reprinted by permission from *Changing Times*, the Kiplinger Magazine (August 1972 issue), copyright © 1972 by The Kiplinger Washington Editors, Inc., 1729 H. Street, N.W., Washington, D.C. 20006; Ernest C. Arbuckle, "Avoiding Obsolescence in the Age of Aquarius," University of Michigan, Graduate School of Business Administration, 1969, excerpted from the 1969 Annual Business Leadership Lecture; "How Free is 'Free' Enterprise," reprinted from the May 1971 issue of *Business Management* Magazine with permission of the publisher, copyright © 1971 by CCM Professional Magazines, Inc., all rights reserved; " 'Mothers' Taps Hippie Vein in Conventional Folk," *Air California* Magazine (1973).

INDEX

Abbreviations and Acronyms Commonly Used in Business and Accounting

AAA	American Accounting Association
ABC	Activity-based costing
AICPA	American Institute of Certified Public Accountants
CIA	Certified Internal Auditor
CIM	Computer-integrated manufacturing
CMA	Certified Management Accountant
CPA	Certified Public Accountant
Cr.	Credit
Dr.	Debit
EFT	Electronic funds transfer
EPS	Earnings per share
FAF	Financial Accounting Foundation
FASB	Financial Accounting Standards Board
FEI	Financial Executives International
FICA tax	Federal Insurance Contributions Act tax
FIFO	First-in, first-out
FOB	Free on board
GAAP	Generally accepted accounting principles
GASB	Governmental Accounting Standards Board
GNP	Gross National Product
IMA	Institute of Management Accountants
IRC	Internal Revenue Code
IRS	Internal Revenue Service
JIT	Just-in-time
LIFO	Last-in, first-out
Lower of C or M	Lower of cost or market
MACRS	Modified Accelerated Cost Recovery System
n/30	Net 30
n/eom	Net, end-of-month
P/E Ratio	Price-earnings ratio
POS	Point of sale
ROI	Return on investment
SEC	Securities and Exchange Commission
TQC	Total quality control

Classification of Accounts

Account Title	Account Classification	Normal Balance	Financial Statement
Accounts Payable	Current liability	Credit	Balance sheet
Accounts Receivable	Current asset	Debit	Balance sheet
Accumulated Depreciation	Contra fixed asset	Credit	Balance sheet
Accumulated Depletion	Contra fixed asset	Credit	Balance sheet
Advertising Expense	Operating expense	Debit	Income statement
Allowance for Doubtful Accounts	Contra current asset	Credit	Balance sheet
Amortization Expense	Operating expense	Debit	Income statement
Bonds Payable	ZLong-term liability	Credit	Balance sheet
Building	Fixed asset	Debit	Balance sheet
_____ Capital	Owner's equity	Credit	Statement of owner's equity/ Balance sheet
Capital Stock	Stockholders' equity	Credit	Balance sheet
Cash	Current asset	Debit	Balance sheet
Cash Dividends	Stockholders' equity	Debit	Retained earnings statement
Cash Dividends Payable	Current liability	Credit	Balance sheet
Common Stock	Stockholders' equity	Credit	Balance sheet
Cost of Merchandise (Goods) Sold	Cost of merchandise (goods sold)	Debit	Income statement
Deferred Income Tax Payable	Current liability/Long-term liability	Credit	Balance sheet
Delivery Expense	Operating expense	Debit	Income Statement
Depletion Expense	Operating expense	Debit	Income statement
Discount on Bonds Payable	Long-term liability	Debit	Balance sheet
Dividend Revenue	Other income	Credit	Income statement
Dividends	Stockholders' equity	Debit	Retained earnings statement
_____ Drawing	Owner's equity	Debit	Statement of owner's equity
Employees Federal Income Tax Payable	Current liability	Credit	Balance sheet
Equipment	Fixed asset	Debit	Balance sheet
Exchange Gain	Other income	Credit	Income statement
Exchange Loss	Other expense	Debit	Income statement
Factory Overhead (Overapplied)	Deferred credit	Credit	Balance sheet (interim)
Factory Overhead (Underapplied)	Deferred debit	Debit	Balance sheet (interim)
Federal Income Tax Payable	Current liability	Credit	Balance sheet
Federal Unemployment Tax Payable	Current liability	Credit	Balance sheet
Finished Goods	Current asset	Debit	Balance sheet
Freight In	Cost of merchandise sold	Debit	Income statement
Freight Out	Operating expense	Debit	Income statement
Gain on Disposal of Fixed Assets	Other income	Credit	Income statement
Gain on Redemption of Bonds	Other income	Credit	Income statement
Gain on Sale of Investments	Other income	Credit	Income statement
Goodwill	Intangible asset	Debit	Balance sheet
Income Tax Expense	Income tax	Debit	Income statement
Income Tax Payable	Current liability	Credit	Balance sheet
Insurance Expense	Operating expense	Debit	Income statement
Interest Expense	Other expense	Debit	Income statement
Interest Receivable	Current asset	Debit	Balance sheet
Interest Revenue	Other income	Credit	Income statement
Investment in Bonds	Investment	Debit	Balance sheet
Investment in Stocks	Investment	Debit	Balance sheet
Investment in Subsidiary	Investment	Debit	Balance sheet
Land	Fixed asset	Debit	Balance sheet
Loss on Disposal of Fixed Assets	Other expense	Debit	Income statement
Loss on Redemption of Bonds	Other expense	Debit	Income statement